T0190345

Communications in Computer and Information Science 1745

Editorial Board Members

Joaquim Filipe
Polytechnic Institute of Setúbal, Setúbal, Portugal

Ashish Ghosh
Indian Statistical Institute, Kolkata, India

Raquel Oliveira Prates
Federal University of Minas Gerais (UFMG), Belo Horizonte, Brazil

Lizhu Zhou
Tsinghua University, Beijing, China

More information about this series at https://link.springer.com/bookseries/7899

Ying Tan · Yuhui Shi (Eds.)

Data Mining and Big Data

7th International Conference, DMBD 2022
Beijing, China, November 21–24, 2022
Proceedings, Part II

 Springer

Editors
Ying Tan ⓘ
Peking University
Beijing, China

Yuhui Shi
Southern University of Science
and Technology
Shenzhen, China

ISSN 1865-0929   ISSN 1865-0937 (electronic)
Communications in Computer and Information Science
ISBN 978-981-19-8990-2   ISBN 978-981-19-8991-9 (eBook)
https://doi.org/10.1007/978-981-19-8991-9

© The Editor(s) (if applicable) and The Author(s), under exclusive license
to Springer Nature Singapore Pte Ltd. 2022
This work is subject to copyright. All rights are reserved by the Publisher, whether the whole or part of the material is concerned, specifically the rights of translation, reprinting, reuse of illustrations, recitation, broadcasting, reproduction on microfilms or in any other physical way, and transmission or information storage and retrieval, electronic adaptation, computer software, or by similar or dissimilar methodology now known or hereafter developed.
The use of general descriptive names, registered names, trademarks, service marks, etc. in this publication does not imply, even in the absence of a specific statement, that such names are exempt from the relevant protective laws and regulations and therefore free for general use.
The publisher, the authors, and the editors are safe to assume that the advice and information in this book are believed to be true and accurate at the date of publication. Neither the publisher nor the authors or the editors give a warranty, expressed or implied, with respect to the material contained herein or for any errors or omissions that may have been made. The publisher remains neutral with regard to jurisdictional claims in published maps and institutional affiliations.

This Springer imprint is published by the registered company Springer Nature Singapore Pte Ltd.
The registered company address is: 152 Beach Road, #21-01/04 Gateway East, Singapore 189721, Singapore

Preface

The Seventh International Conference on Data Mining and Big Data (DMBD 2022) was held in Beijing, China, during November 21–24, 2022. DMBD serves as an international forum for researchers to exchange latest advantages in theories, models, and applications of data mining and big data as well as artificial intelligence techniques. DMBD 2022 was the seventh event after the successful first event (DMBD 2016) on Bali Island, Indonesia, the second event (DMBD 2017) in Fukuoka, Japan, the third event (DMBD 2018) in Shanghai, China, the fourth event (DMBD 2019) in Chiang Mai, Thailand, the fifth event (DMBD 2020) in Belgrade, Serbia, and the sixth event (DMBD 2021) in Guangzhou, China.

These two volumes (CCIS vol. 1744 and CCIS vol. 1745) contain the papers presented at DMBD 2022 covering some major topics of data mining and big data. The conference received 135 submissions. The Program Committee accepted 62 regular papers to be included in the conference program with an acceptance rate of 45.92%. Each submission received at least 3 reviews in an double-blind process. The proceedings contain revised versions of the accepted papers. While revisions are expected to take the referees comments into account, this was not enforced and the authors bear full responsibility for the content of their papers.

DMBD 2022 was organized by the International Association of Swarm and Evolutionary Intelligence (IASEI). It was co-organized by the Computational Intelligence Laboratory at Peking University, the Advanced Institute of Big Data, Beijing, the Key Laboratory of Information System Requirement, the Science and Technology on Information Systems Engineering Laboratory, and the Southern University of Science and Technology and technically co-sponsored by Research Reports on Computer Science (RRCS), the City Brain Technical Committee of the Chinese Institute of Command and Control (CICC), the International Neural Network Society, the Nanjing Kangbo Intelligent Health Academy, Springer, Entropy, MDPI Electronics, and the Beijing Xinghui High-Tech Co. The conference would not have been such a success without the support of these organizations, and we sincerely thank them for their continued assistance and sponsorship.

We would also like to thank the authors who submitted their papers to DMBD 2022, and the conference attendees for their interest and support. We thank the Organizing Committee for their time and effort dedicated to arranging the conference. This allowed us to focus on the paper selection and deal with the scientific program. We thank the Program Committee members and the external reviewers for their hard work in reviewing the submissions; the conference would not have been possible without their expert reviews. Furthermore, this work is partially supported by the National Natural Science Foundation of China (Grant No. 62076010 and 62276008), and also partially supported by the Science and Technology Innovation 2030 - New Generation Artificial Intelligence Major Project (Grant Nos.: 2018AAA0102301 and 2018AAA0100302).

Finally, we thank the EasyChair system and its operators, for making the entire process of managing the conference convenient.

November 2022

Ying Tan
Yuhui Shi

Organization

General Chair

Ying Tan — Peking University, China

Program Committee Chair

Yuhui Shi — Southern University of Science and Technology, China

Advisory Committee Chairs

Xingui He — Peking University, China
Gary G. Yen — Oklahoma State University, USA

Technical Committee Co-chairs

Benjamin W. Wah — The Chinese University of Hong Kong, Hong Kong, China
Guoying Wang — Chongqing University of Posts and Telecommunications, China
Enhong Chen — University of Science and Technology of China, China
Fernando Buarque — University of Pernambuco, Brazil
Haibo He — University of Rhode Island, USA
Jihong Zhu — Tsinghua University, China
Jin Li — Guangzhou University, China
Kay Chen Tan — The Hong Kong Polytechnic University, Hong Kong, China
Nikola Kasabov — Auckland University of Technology, New Zealand
Qirong Tang — Tongji University, China
Yew-Soon Ong — Nanyang Technological University, Singapore
Yi Zhang — Sichuan University, China

Invited Speakers Session Co-chairs

Andres Iglesias — University of Cantabria and Santander, Spain
Shaoqiu Zheng — The 28th Research Institute of China Electronics Technology Group Corporation, Nanjing, China

Special Session Co-chairs

Ben Niu   Shenzhen University, Shenzhen, China
Kun Liu   Advanced Institute of Big Data, China

Publications Co-chairs

Radu-Emil Precup   Politehnica University of Timisoara, Romania
Weiwei Hu   Tencent Corporation, China

Publicity Co-chairs

Eugene Semenkin   Siberian Aerospace University, Russia
Junqi Zhang   Tongji University, China

Finance and Registration Chairs

Andreas Janecek   University of Vienna, Austria
Suicheng Gu   Google Corporation, USA

Conference Secretariat

Maiyue Chen   Peking University, Beijing, China

Program Committee

Muhammad Abulaish   South Asian University, India
Abdelmalek Amine   Tahar Moulay University of Saida, Algeria
Sabri Arik   Istanbul University, Turkey
Nebojsa Bacanin   Singidunum University, Serbia
Carmelo J. A. Bastos Filho   University of Pernambuco, Brazil
Mohamed Ben Aouicha   University of Sfax, Tunisia
Chenyang Bu   Hefei University of Technology, China
Walter Chen   National Taipei University of Technology, Taiwan
Shi Cheng   Shannxi Normal University, China
Zelei Cheng   Purdue University, USA
Khaldoon Dhou   Texas A&M University–Central Texas, USA
Yuxin Ding   Harbin Institute of Technology, Shenzhen, China
Philippe Fournier-Viger   Shenzhen University, China
Hongyuan Gao   Harbin Engineering University, China
Shangce Gao   University of Toyama, Japan
Weifeng Gao   Xidian University, China
Xizhan Gao   University of Jinan, China

Ke Gu	Changsha University of Science and Technology, China
Salekul Islam	United International University, Bangladesh
Roshni Iyer	University of California, Los Angeles, USA
Ziyu Jia	Beijing Jiaotong University, China
Mingyan Jiang	Shandong University, China
Lov Kumar	BITS Pilani, India
Vivek Kumar	Università degli Studi di Cagliari, Italy
Germano Lambert-Torres	PS Solutions, USA
Bin Li	University of Science and Technology of China, China
Xianghong Lin	Northwest Normal University, China
Jian-Wei Liu	China University of Petroleum, Beijing, China
Ju Liu	Shandong University, China
Kun Liu	Advanced Institute of Big Data, China
Qunfeng Liu	Dongguan University of Technology, China
Yi Liu	PLA University of Science and Technology, China
Wenjian Luo	Harbin Institute of Technology, Shenzhen, China
Haoyang Ma	National University of Defense Technology, China
Lianbo Ma	Northeast University, China
Chengying Mao	Jiangxi University of Finance and Economics, China
Seyedfakhredin Musavishavazi	University of Applied Sciences Mittweida, Germany
Sreeja N. K.	PSG College of Technology, India
Qingjian Ni	Southeast University, China
Neelamadhab Padhy	GIET University, India
Mario Pavone	University of Catania, Spain
Yan Pei	University of Aizu, Japan
Xin Peng	Hainan University, China
Mukesh Prasad	University of Technology Sydney, Australia
Radu-Emil Precup	Politehnica University of Timisoara, Romania
Fezan Rasool	LUMS, Pakistan
Jiten Sidhpura	Sardar Patel Institute of Technology, India
Vrijendra Singh	Indian Institute of Information Technology, India
Ying Tan	Peking University, China
Daniel Tang	Institute of Computing Technology, CAS, China
Eva Tuba	University of Belgrade, Serbia
Dujuan Wang	Sichuan University, China
Guoyin Wang	Chongqing University of Posts and Telecommunications, China

Hong Wang	Shenzhen University, China
Hui Wang	Nanchang Institute of Technology, China
Lukun Wang	Shandong University of Science and Technology, China
Jiang Wenchao	Guangdong University of Technology, China
Ka-Chun Wong	City University of Hong Kong, Hong Kong, China
Shunren Xia	Zhejiang University, China
Shuyin Xia	Chongqing University of Posts and Telecommunications, China
Fuyuan Xiao	Chongqing University, China
Ning Xiong	Mälardalen University, Sweden
Jianhua Xu	Nanjing Normal University, China
Yu Xue	Nanjing University of Information Science and Technology, China
Yingjie Yang	De Montfort University, UK
Guo Yi-Nan	China University of Mining and Technology, China
Jianhua Yin	Shandong University, China
Peng-Yeng Yin	National Chi Nan University, Taiwan
Xiaomei Yu	Shandong Normal University, China
Hui Zhang	Southwest University of Science and Technology, China
Jie Zhang	Newcastle University, UK
Jiwei Zhang	Beijing University of Posts and Telecommunications, China
Wenbin Zhang	Michigan Technological University, USA
Xiaosong Zhang	Tangshan University, China
Xingyi Zhang	Huazhong University of Science and Technology, China
Yuchen Zhang	Shaanxi Normal University, China
Xinchao Zhao	Beijing University of Posts and Telecommunications, China
Shaoqiu Zheng	The 28th Research Institute of China Electronics Technology Group Corporation, China
Yujun Zheng	Zhejiang University of Technology, China
Jiang Zhou	Texas Tech University, USA
Miodrag Zivkovic	Singidunum University, Serbia

Additional Reviewers

Chafekar, Talha
Chen, Changchuan
Deng, Yang
Elbakri, Idris
Han, Yanyang
Huang, Ziheng
Li, Linguo
Li, Zeyu
Liang, Mengnan
Liu, Li
Shengyao, Sun

Wang, Chunyang
Wang, Ruobin
Wang, Wenjun
Wang, Zichong
Xing, Tongtong
Xue, Yu
Yang, Zheng
Zhang, Shiyan
Zhang, Shuai
Zhu, Haifeng

Contents – Part II

Identification and Recognition Methods

Optimization Methods

Big Data Analysis

Big-Model Methods

Generating Adversarial Examples and Other Applications

Contents – Part I

Deep Neural Networks

Clustering Methods

Prediction Methods

Classification Methods

Identification and Recognition Methods

Complementary Convolutional Restricted Boltzmann Machine and Its Applications in Image Recognition

Jian Zhang[✉]

School of Computer Science and Technology, China University of Mining and Technology, Xuzhou 221116, China
zhangjian10231209@cumt.edu.cn

Abstract. Restricted Boltzmann Machines (RBMs) are widely applied in Image Classification and Image Reconstruction. However, although highly expressive conditional distributions of RBMs commonly produce effective features for the two tasks, building these expressive conditional distributions and sampling from the distributions are difficult for conventional RBMs. In this paper, a Complementary Convolutional Restricted Boltzmann Machine (CCRBM) is proposed. The CCRBM designs complementary factors in its visible layer and uses the factors to produce highly expressive conditional Gaussian distributions under low sampling cost. To further extract hierarchical image features, a Complementary Convolutional Deep Belief Net (CCDBN) is proposed for Image Processing based on CCRBM. Experiments verify that the proposed CCRBM and CCDBN perform better than other commonly used RBMs and probabilistic graphic models with the help of the designed complementary factors.

Keywords: Restricted Boltzmann Machine · Deep Belief Net · Convolutional Neural Net

1 Introduction

In the research of Image Processing, Probabilistic Graphic Models and Convolutional Neural Nets (CNNs) have become two commonly used models [1, 2]. As undirected probabilistic graphs, RBMs can extract statistically interpretable image features explicitly and build effective probabilistic inference between their units. RBMs can be stacked for building Deep Belief Net (DBN) and Deep Boltzmann Machine (DBM), and they are widely used in Image Classification and Image Reconstruction [3–5]. Meanwhile, CNNs introduce convolution operation in their structures to extract invariant features for Image Processing [6–8]. As an effective combination, Convolutional RBMs (CRBMs) can extract invariant features and explicitly model them in probabilistic forms. CRBMs are widely used for visual images and other images, but the limited feature expression ability of conventional RBMs hinders the applied range of CRBMs.

The conventional RBM uses a binary visible layer to model input data as explicit distributions, and it uses a binary hidden layer to extract probabilistic features from input

© The Author(s), under exclusive license to Springer Nature Singapore Pte Ltd. 2022
Y. Tan and Y. Shi (Eds.): DMBD 2022, CCIS 1745, pp. 3–17, 2022.
https://doi.org/10.1007/978-981-19-8991-9_1

data. For many applications, images are real-valued and binary units cannot accurately model real-valued images. To solve this question, Gaussian-binary Restricted Boltzmann Machine (mRBM) [9], spike-and-slab Restricted Boltzmann Machine (ssRBM) [10, 11], and other undirected probabilistic graphs are proposed to build real-valued distributions for visible units to fit real-valued images [12–14]. The mRBM, mcRBM [15], and multi-view RBM use Gaussian distribution as the activate probabilities of visible units [16], while the Truncated Gaussian RBM (TGRBM) uses truncated Gaussian distribution to build its visible layer [12]. Based on Gaussian distribution or truncated Gaussian distribution, the real-valued distributions of hidden units can be built, and some improved Gaussian Graphic Models are proposed. However, although Gaussian Graphic Models build highly expressive distributions, they are not suitable for Image Processing tasks because of their high computational complexity. For the TGRBM, the gradients of its energy function cannot be directly calculated based on the integral of the Truncated Gaussian distribution. As an effective unsupervised learning method, the ssRBM [10], s4RBM [11], and mcRBM [15] introduce additional units into their hidden layer and build expressive real-valued distributions for their hidden units and visible units. However, these real-valued RBMs are proposed for 1-dimensional real-valued vector data rather than 2-dimensional real-valued images. Moreover, although the CRBM and its improved real-valued CRBMs introduce convolutional layers to model 2-dimensional real-valued images, they do not build a highly expressive visible layers to extract the correlation between 2-dimensional pixels [17, 18]. There are also other Probabilistic Graphic Models and CNNs used for image processing, such as Variational AutoEncoders [19], Generative Adversarial Networks [20]. These models focus on modeling data distribution of images with neural networks in implicit forms. However, we hope to build effective explicit expressive expression for images.

For building highly expressive distributions to effectively model 2-dimensional real-valued images, this paper suggests that both expectation and covariance in the conditional Gaussian distribution of visible units should be parameterized, and the correlation between 2-dimensional pixels can be modeled as the distribution's covariance. Therefore, this paper proposes a Complementary Convolutional Restricted Boltzmann Machine (CCRBM). The proposed CCRBM introduce convolutional operation between its visible layer and hidden layer to extract structural features, and then designs complementary factors in its visible layer to model expectation and covariance in the conditional Gaussian distribution of the visible units. Based on complementary factors, the highly expressive Gaussian distribution with non-diagonal covariance matrix can be decompose into two Gaussian distributions with diagonal covariance matrix, and the CCRBM can be effectively trained by using Gibbs sampling based on the two diagonal Gaussian distributions. In experiments, this paper illustrates the effectiveness of our methods in Image Reconstruction and Image Classification.

The remainder of this paper is organized as follows: Sect. 2 gives a brief introduction to the foundations of deep learning. Section 3 gives an introduction to the proposed CCRBM. Section 4 is the experiments. Section 5 is conclusion.

2 Theory of Foundations

2.1 Restricted Boltzmann Machine

A Restricted Boltzmann Machine is an undirected probabilistic graph model based on energy functions, it contains a visible layer v and a hidden layer h. The energy function of RBM come from physics background, and the diagram of RBM is shown in Fig. 1,

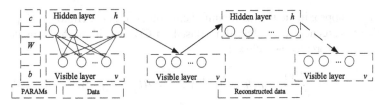

Fig. 1. The diagram of RBM.

where, c, b are the biases, and W is the weight matrix between the visible units and the hidden units. If the visible units and hidden units are binary, the energy function can be defined as follow:

$$E(v, h) = - \sum_{i=1}^{n_v} a_i v_i - \sum_{j=1}^{n_h} b_j h_j - \sum_{i=1}^{n_v} \sum_{j=1}^{n_h} h_j \times W_{ji} \times v_i \tag{1}$$

where, n_v is the number of visible units, n_h is the number of hidden units. Based on $E(v, h)$, the probability distribution can be expressed as Formula (2):

$$P(v, h) = \frac{1}{Z} e^{-E(v,h)} \tag{2}$$

where, Z is a partition function: $Z = \sum_{v,h} e^{-E(v,h)}$

The RBM aims to maximize the marginal distribution $P(v)$. The object function of RBM is expressed as the logarithmic form of $P(v)$

$$L_s = \ln(P(v)) = \ln\left(\sum_h P(v, h)\right) = \ln\left(\sum_h e^{-E(v,h)}\right) - \ln(Z) \tag{3}$$

The Stochastic Gradient Descent algorithm (SGD) can be used to maximize the likelihood function. Let $\theta = (a, b, W)$, the derivative of L_s is shown as formula (4):

$$\frac{\partial L_s}{\partial \theta} = - \sum_h P(h|v^{(0)}) \frac{\partial E(v^{(0)}, h)}{\partial \theta} + \sum_{v,h} P(v, h) \frac{\partial E(v, h)}{\partial \theta} \tag{4}$$

where, $v^{(0)}$ is the original data. The activate probabilities can be expressed as follows:

$$P(h_k = 1|v) = sigmoid\left(b_k + \sum_{i=1}^{n_v} W_{ki}v_i\right) \tag{5}$$

$$P(v_k = 1|h) = sigmoid\left(a_k + \sum_{j=1}^{n_v} h_j W_{kj}\right) \tag{6}$$

In order to approximate the maximum likelihood estimation, Hinton et al. proposed Contrastive Divergence (CD) algorithm. Based on CD algorithm, the estimate of the gradient can be expressed as follows:

$$\frac{\partial \ln P(v)}{\partial W_{ij}} \approx P(h_i = 1|v^{(0)})v^{(0)} - P(h_i = 1|v^{(k)})v^{(k)} \tag{7}$$

$$\frac{\partial \ln P(v)}{\partial a_i} \approx v_i^{(0)} - v_i^{(k)} \tag{8}$$

$$\frac{\partial \ln P(v)}{\partial b_i} \approx P(h_i = 1|v^{(0)}) - P(h_i = 1|v^{(k)}) \tag{9}$$

where, k is the number of steps in K-steps Contrastive Divergence algorithm (CD-K). Weights between visible units and hidden units are updated with the following formulas:

$$\triangle W_{ij} \approx \eta_w(P(h_i = 1|v^{(0)})v^{(0)} - P(h_i = 1|v^{(k)})v^{(k)}) \tag{10}$$

$$\triangle a_i \approx \eta_a(v_i^{(0)} - v_i^{(k)}) \tag{11}$$

$$\Delta b_i \approx \eta_b\left(P(h_i = 1|v^{(0)}) - P(h_i = 1|v^{(k)})\right) \tag{12}$$

where, η is the learning rate.

2.2 Deep Belief Nets

DBN is a hybrid graph, and it is proposed by Hinton [21]. In a DBN, the top 2 layers constitute an associative memory with undirected connections, and the layers below have directed, top-down generative connections. In training process of DBN, the net is initialized layer by layer based on RBM algorithm. The topology of DBN is shown as Fig. 2:

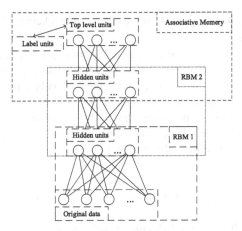

Fig. 2. The diagram of RBM.

The DBN model is widely used in Image Processing tasks, and it provides an effective pre-training method in neural nets. By changing the topology of neural nets, DBN can be realized as the Convolutional Deep Belief Nets (CDBNs).

2.3 Convolutional Neural Nets

The Convolutional Neural Net is a multilayer neural net inspired by the natural visual perception mechanism, and the topology of a CNN is shown as Fig. 3:

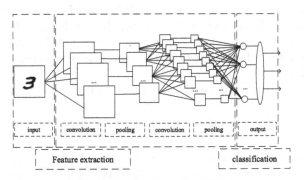

Fig. 3. The topology of a CNN.

As shown in Fig. 3, a typical CNN has two operations in the feature extraction phase: convolution aims to extract translation-invariant features, and pooling aims to extract scaling-invariant features. For the convolution operation, the feature value $y^l_{(i,j),k}$ at location (i, j) in the k-th feature map of l-th layer can be expressed as the following formula:

$$y^l_{(i,j),k} = f(W^l_k * x^l_{(i,j)} + b^l_k) \tag{13}$$

where, $f(.)$ is the activate function, W_k^l is the convolutional kernel, '*' is the convolution operation, b_k^l is the bias.

The pooling operations can be categorized as max-pooling, average-pooling and stochastic-pooling, etc. [22], which aim to achieve shift-invariance and scaling-invariance by reducing the resolution of the features. Usually, a pooling layer is placed between two convolutional layers. Each feature map is connected to its corresponding map of the preceding convolutional layer. By stacking several convolutional layers and pooling layers, more abstract features can be extracted.

The pooling operation is denoted as $P(.)$. For each feature map, we have the following formula:

$$y_{(m,n),k}^l = P\left(y_{(i,j),k}^{l-1}\right), \forall (i,j) \in R_{(m,n)} \tag{14}$$

where, $R_{(m, n)}$ is a neighborhood around the location (m, n).

Usually, one or more fully-connected layers are used after the feature extraction layers. For classification task, outputs of the last fully-connected layer will be fed to a classification layer.

3 Complementary Convolutional Deep Belief Nets

3.1 Complementary Restricted Boltzmann Machine

In conventional RBMs, the binary visible units are conditionally independent based on hidden units. When input data are binary, conventional RBMs perform well in pattern recognition tasks. However, when input data are real-valued, the activation of the visible units is not fit for input data. In most improved RBM models, auxiliary units are introduced to their hidden layer or visible layer to get effective features. In this paper, the proposed Complementary Restricted Boltzmann Machine (CRBM) introduces complementary factors to its visible layer to build a highly expressive distribution for modeling real-valued images.

The energy function of proposed CRBM can be written as follow:

$$E(v, c, h) = -\sum_{i=1}^{M} (v_i c_i) W_i h + \frac{1}{2} v \Lambda v^T + \frac{1}{2} c \alpha c^T - hb^T - \sum_{i=1}^{M} u_i \alpha_i v_i \tag{15}$$

where, u is treated as the expectation of complementary factors c, α and Λ are diagonal matrixes. M is the dimension of the visible units. Every visible unit consists of a complementary factor c and an input unit v. The complementary factors are used to calculate conditional distribution of v, and the activate functions are shown as the following formulas:

$$P(h_i = 1|v) = sigmoid\left(\frac{1}{2} v^T W_i \alpha_i^{-1} W_i^T v - b_i\right) \tag{16}$$

$$P(v|h) = N\left(\frac{\alpha \mu}{\Lambda - \sum_{i=1}^{N} W_i h_i \alpha_i^{-1} W_i^T h_i}, 2\left(\Lambda - \sum_{i=1}^{N} W_i h_i \alpha_i^{-1} W_i^T h_i\right)^{-1}\right) \tag{17}$$

In formula (17), the correlations between 2-dimensional pixels are modeled as the distribution's covariance, and this covariance is a non-diagonal complex matrix. Although this distribution contains enough information of 2-dimensional images, the Block Gibbs Sampling cannot be used to sampling the states of v because of the non-diagonal covariance. For Gaussian distribution with a non-diagonal covariance matrix, the hybrid Monte Carlo sampling can be used. However, the hybrid Monte Carlo sampling runs much slower than Block Gibbs sampling. To model the correlation and run the training algorithm with low sampling cost, the CRBM uses complementary factor to construct a distribution with a diagonal covariance. Based on the energy function, the activation of complementary factors can be calculated as formula (18),

$$P(c|v, h) = N\left(\alpha^{-1} \sum_{i=1}^{M} v_i W_i h, \ \alpha^{-1}\right) \tag{18}$$

Based on the complementary factors, the activation of v can be written as follow:

$$P(v|c, h) = N\left(\mu + \Lambda^{-1} \sum_{i=1}^{M} c_i W_i h, \ \Lambda^{-1}\right) \tag{19}$$

In $P(v|c, h)$, the covariance is diagonal, and this distribution can be sampled by using Gibbs Sampling. By minimizing the contrastive divergence, the CRBM can be trained. The Contrastive Divergence (CD) method and Persistent Contrastive Divergence (PCD) algorithm, which are based on the blocked Gibbs sampling, are widely used in training RBM. In this paper, PCD algorithm is used for training the log likelihood function, which is expressed as formula (20),

$$\frac{\partial \log(P(v))}{\partial \theta} = E_{P(h,c|v)}\left[\frac{\partial(-E(v, c, h))}{\partial \theta}\right] - E_{P(v,c,h)}\left[\frac{\partial(-E(v, c, h))}{\partial \theta}\right] \tag{20}$$

where, θ denotes the parameters in CRBM, and the Gibbs Sampling is used for calculating the expectation of $P(v, c, h)$ in formula (20).

3.2 Analysis for Complementary Restricted Boltzmann Machine

In the CRBM, we introduce square items in the energy function (Formula (15)) and use factor α to build a relation among each units of its visible layer. Moreover, we introduce complementary factors c to the visible layer to build an explicit distribution for modeling the correlation of the visible units based on the covariance in this explicit distribution, and this distribution can be expressed as Formula (17). As Formula (17) shows, the activation of features h is expressed as a parameterized Gaussian distribution, and the covariance shows the correlation of image pixels. Therefore, highly expressive features are built based on Formula (17). However, as its covariance matrix is non-diagonal, sampling from this Gaussian distribution is difficult. To draw effective samples efficiently, we introduce 3-step Gibbs sampling based on the complementary factors c to build diagonal covariance in Formula (18) and Formula (19). Unlike Truncated Gaussian distribution, the expectation of the gradient in this proposed CRBM can be easily calculated.

3.3 Complementary Convolutional Restricted Boltzmann Machine

To extract translation-invariant features and reduce computational complexity, this paper introduces convolution operation to the structure of CRBM and builds a two-dimensional graphical model: Convolutional Restricted Boltzmann Machine with complementary factors (CCRBM). The topology of the CCRBM is shown as Fig. 4:

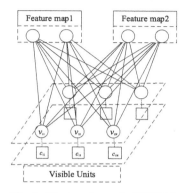

Fig. 4. The topology of a CCRBM.

The small rectangles in Fig. 4 denote the complementary factors. As Fig. 4 shows, the hidden layer has one kind of units h, and the visible layer includes the input pixels v and the complementary factors c. In the training process of CCRBM, the complementary factors are only used in generating the activation of the visible units v, the activation of the hidden units can be obtained from the visible units. According to this topology of CCRBM, the energy function can be expressed as follow:

$$E(v, c, h) = - \sum_{k=1}^{K} h_k \cdot \left(\tilde{W}_k * (v \cdot c) \right) - \sum_{k=1}^{K} b_k \sum_{(i,j)} h_{(i,j),k} + \frac{1}{2} \alpha \cdot \left(v^2 + c^2 \right) - \alpha \cdot v \cdot \mu \quad (21)$$

where, a is the bias matrix, μ is used to construct the Gaussian distribution of complementary factors. Like CRBM, the Gaussian distribution $P(v|h)$ has a parameterized expectation and covariance based on the parameter μ and complementary factors c. The activation probabilities are shown as follow:

$$P(v|c, h) \sim N \left(\mu + \frac{1}{\alpha} \sum_{k=1}^{K} h_k \cdot \left(\tilde{W}_k * c \right), \alpha^{-1} \right) \quad (22)$$

$$P(c|v, h) \sim N \left(\alpha^{-1} v \cdot \sum_{k=1}^{K} W_k * h_k, \alpha^{-1} \right) \quad (23)$$

$$P\left(h_{(i,j),k} = 1|v \right) = sigmoid \left(\frac{1}{2} \left(\tilde{W} * v \alpha^{-1} v * \tilde{W} \right)_{(i,j)} + b_k \right) \quad (24)$$

In CCRBM, the complementary factors are used in the visible layer, and each hidden unit is independent when visible units are given. The activate function of complementary factors can be obtained after calculating the activation of hidden units. Based on the complementary factors, the blocked Gibbs sampling can be used.

In order to alleviate the over-fitting and build a deep model, stochastic pooling layers can be used. The pooling operations can be categorized as max-pooling, average-pooling, and stochastic-pooling etc., which aim to achieve shift-invariance and scaling-invariance by reducing the resolution of features. According to the probabilistic max-pooling in Convolutional RBM, the probabilistic stochastic pooling method is designed in the CCRBM, and the energy function and activation functions can be expressed as follows:

$$E(v, c, h) = -\sum_k \sum_{(i,j)} \left(h_{(i,j),k} \left(\tilde{W}_k * (v \cdot c) \right)_{(i,j)} + b_k h_{(i,j),k} \right) - \alpha \sum_{(i,j)} v_{(i,j)} \mu_{(i,j)} + \frac{1}{2}\alpha \cdot \left(v^2 + c^2 \right)$$

$$subj.to \sum_{(i,j) \in B_a} h_{(i,j),k} \leq 1, \forall k, a. \tag{25}$$

$$P\left(h_{(i,j),k} = 1 | v\right) = \frac{\exp\left(\frac{1}{2}\left(\tilde{W} * v\alpha^{-1} v * \tilde{W} \right)_{(i,j)} + b_k \right)}{1 + \sum_{(i',j') \in B_a} \exp\left(\frac{1}{2}\left(\tilde{W} * v\alpha^{-1} v * \tilde{W} \right)_{(i',j')} + b_k \right)} \tag{26}$$

$$P\left(p_{\alpha,k} = 0 | v\right) = \frac{1}{1 + \sum_{(i',j') \in B_a} \exp\left(\frac{1}{2}\left(\tilde{W} * v\alpha^{-1} v * \tilde{W} \right)_{(i',j')} + b_k \right)} \tag{27}$$

The probabilistic stochastic pooling method is similar to probabilistic max pooling in pre-training and training process of Convolutional RBMs, the difference lies in the pooling units are selected randomly in the training process. The topology of the CCRBM with pooling layer is shown as follow (Fig. 5):

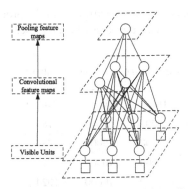

Fig. 5. The topology of the CRBM with pooling layer.

In the CRBM model, the hidden units and the pooling units are still binary, the visible units are real-valued.

3.4 Complementary Convolutional Deep Belief Nets

The Convolutional DBN model is a deep neural net, which includes several RBM models. Based on the convolution operation, the Convolutional DBN performs better in image recognition and image reconstruction than the conventional CNN and DBN. Therefore, this paper proposes a Complementary Convolutional Deep Belief Net based on the proposed CCRBM, the topology of CCDBN can be expressed as follow (Fig. 6):

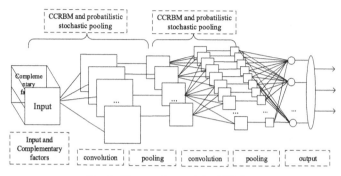

Fig. 6. The topology of the CCDBN.

The CCDBN model we used in this paper has a topology of 3 convolutional layers, 2 pooling layers, a fully connected layer and an output layer. As a DBN, this CCDBN model could be used in both in image recognition and image reconstruction. In the experiments, we verify the effectiveness of the proposed model.

4   Experiments

In this paper, in order to illustrate the effectiveness of the proposed models, 5 data sets are introduced to experiments. The attributes of the data sets are shown as Table 1:

Table 1. The attributes of data sets.

Data sets	Train	Test	Attributes	Labels
MNIST-Basic	10000	50000	784	10
Rectangles	1000	50000	784	2
MNIST	60000	10000	784	10
CIFAR-10	50000	10000	1024	10
NORB	24300	24300	1024	5

The MNIST dataset comes from the National Institute of standards and technology. The training set consists of handwritten figures from 250 different people, 50% of whom are senior high school students, and the other come from the Census Bureau. The test set is the same amount as well. NORB is a synthetic 3D object recognition dataset that contains five classes of toys (humans, animals, cars, planes, trucks) imaged by a stereo-pair camera system from different viewpoints under different lighting conditions. The stereo-pair images are subsampled from their original resolution of $108 \times 108 \times 2$ to $32 \times 32 \times 2$ to speed up experiments. The CIFAR-10 dataset consists of $60000\ 32 \times 32$ images in 10 classes, with 6000 images per class. There are 50000 training images and 10000 test images. In this experiment, the CIFAR-10 images are transformed into gray images. The experiments run on the PC, which has the following configuration: CPU 12700, GPU RTX 3070Ti and 32 g Memory.

In this section, firstly, we test the image reconstruction ability of CRBM based on MNIST, Rectangle, NORB and CIFAR-10, the reconstructed images are shown as Fig. 7:

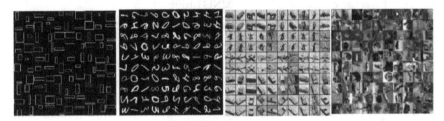

Fig. 7. The reconstructed images.

As we can see, the binary images are reconstructed well based on CRBM, however, generating the real-valued images is hard, the pictures with background are not clear. Although RBMs can be treated as generative models, it is difficult to get clear high-dimensional images, we guess the reason may be that the number of hyper parameters is large, and the assumed Gaussian distribution may not well match the real input data.

Secondly, we test the classification ability of CRBM. In this section, the CDBN model is built based on the CRBM for ease of comparison between the other RBM models. The CDBN models have two hidden layers (4000 units in the first, 2000 in the second) and an output layer, the classification accuracies are shown as follows:

Table 2. The classification accuracies.

Data sets	MNIST-Basic	Rectangles	MNIST	NORB
DBN	96.9%	97.1%	98.5%	86.3%
ReLu-DBN	97.6%	97.8%	98.7%	87.1%
Exp-DBN	97.9%	97.4%	98.8%	86.6%
ssDBN	97.6%	97.5%	98.3%	89.9%
CDBN	97.9%	97.6%	98.7%	90.7%

The error rate of CIFAR-10 is high, so we don't list it. ReLu-DBNs were stacked by ReLu-RBMs, and Exp-DBNs are based on the Exp-RBMs, in which the activation function is softplus unit and the Gaussian approximation is $N\left(f(\eta), \left(1 + e^{-\eta}\right)^{-1}\right)$ [18]. As shown in Table 2, the pre-training process is effective compared with the conventional DBN model, and the complementary factors are useful in modeling the conditional Gaussian distribution. The classification accuracies of binary images are high. The CRBM performs better than ReLu-RBMs. However, the model did not perform well in the real-valued data sets. In order to model the real-valued images, this paper proposes CCDBN based on CRBMs. The topology of CNNs is shown as Table 3:

Table 3. The topology of CCDBN.

Layer name	MNIST-basic
Convolution_1	Pretrained by the CCRBM
pool_1	
batch normalization_1	Batch normalization
Convolution_2	Pretrained by the CCRBM
batch normalization_2	Batch normalization
Pool_2	Max-pooling
full connected layer_1	Pretrained by the CRBM
full connected layer_2	Pretrained by the RBM
Output layer	

Based on the CCDBN, the classification accuracies are much better than the conventional full connected nets in CIFAR-10. The parameters of CDBN and CCDBN are shown as Table 4:

Table 4. Parameters of CCDBN and CDBN.

Model	Hidden units	Learning rate	Kernels	Method	Initial
CCDBN	-	1e-3 (1e-5)	256(128)	Adam	Normal
CDBN	2000, 1000	1e-3 (1e-5)	-	Adam	Normal

As Table 4 shows, the CDBN and CCDBN use 1e-3 initial learning rate for MNIST, Rectangles, and MNIST-Basic datasets, meanwhile, they use 1e-5 initial learning rate for CIFAR-10. The CCDBN has 256 convolutional kernels in the first hidden layer and 128 kernels in its second hidden layer. The weights are initialized using Gaussian distribution. The classification accuracies are shown as Table 5:

Table 5. The classification accuracies of CCDBN.

Data	MNIST-Basic	Rectangles	MNIST	NORB	CIFAR-10
CNN	98.6%	98. 4%	98.9%	92.3%	85.9%
VAECNN	98.5%	98. 5%	98.9%	92.7%	86.5%
CCDBN	98.8%	98.7%	98.9%	94.6%	89.1%

As we can see from Table 5, VAECNN is a CNN which uses trained VAE encoder as its pre-training method, and the proposed model obtains better classification results.

The effectiveness of convolution operation is verified in above experiments. We also do ablation experiments to verify the effectiveness of the complementary factors. The experimental results are shown as Table 6.

Table 6. The classification accuracies of ablation experiments.

Model	MNIST-basic	Rectangles	MNIST	NORB
realDBN	97.6%	97.8%	98.7%	87.1%
meanDBN	97.5%	97. 5%	98.5%	88.7%
CDBN	97.9%	97.6%	98.7%	90.7%

As we can see from Table 6, realDBN is a real-valued DBN model without complementary factors, and meanDBN is a real-valued DBN which uses additional units to model diagonal covariance. As the results show, the proposed CDBN obtains better classification results.

The CCRBM is a kind of probabilistic graph model, which provide a feasible pre-training process for neural nets, and the probabilistic graph model can be viewed as the theoretical basis of neural nets. However, there are still some problems in this paper, the reconstructed real-valued images are not clear, the hyper-parameters are hard to tune, and the deeper CNN models are hard to pre-train, such as ResNet [23]. What we are going to do is reducing computational complexity and the number of hyper parameters and improving image reconstruction ability of probabilistic graph models.

5   Conclusion

This paper proposes CCRBM and CCDBN which introduce complementary factors to visible units to model real-valued images, and the CCRBM model is verified in Image Processing tasks. The experiments show that the CCRBM performs better than conventional RBM models. However, there are still some problems about the proposed models. The gradient descent process is easy to merge into local optimal solutions, the learning rates and covariance coefficients are hard to select, the high-dimensional real-valued images are difficult to be reconstructed, and the CCRBM is not easy to be applied in nets with special structures, such as ResNet. In our future research, we will try to reduce the computational complexity and the number of hyper-parameters for applying the CCRBM to deeper neural nets.

Acknowledgement. This work is supported by "the Fundamental Research Funds for the Central Universities" (No. 2021QN1073).

References

1. Sainath, T., Kingsbury, B., Saon, G., et al.: Deep convolutional neural networks for large-scale speech tasks. Neural Netw. **64**, 39–48 (2015)
2. Huang, G., Lee, H., Learned-Miller, E.: Learning hierarchical representations for face verification with convolutional deep belief network. IEEE ICVPR **157**(10), 2518–2525 (2012)
3. Zhang, N., Sun, S.: Multiview graph restricted Boltzmann machines. IEEE Trans. Cybern. **52**, 1–15 (2021)
4. Taherkhani, A., Cosma, G., McGinnity, T.: Deep-FS: a feature selection algorithm for deep Boltzmann machines. Neurocomputing **322**, 22–37 (2018)
5. Zhang, N., Ding, S., Zhang, J., Zhao, X.: Robust spike-and-slab deep Boltzmann machines for face denoising. Neural Comput. Appl. **32**(7), 2815–2827 (2018). https://doi.org/10.1007/s00521-018-3866-6
6. Li, Z., Liu, F., Yang, W., et al.: A survey of convolutional neural networks: analysis, applications, and prospects. IEEE Trans. Neural Netw. Learn. Syst. **33**, 1–21 (2021)
7. Kim, J., Salamon, J., Li, P., et al: Crepe: a convolutional representation for pitch estimation. In: Processing of 2018 IEEE International Conference on Acoustics, Speech and Signal, pp. 161–165 (2018)
8. Solanki, A., Pandey, S.: Music instrument recognition using deep convolutional neural networks. Int. J. Inf. Technol. **14**, 1 (2019). https://doi.org/10.1007/s41870-019-00285-y
9. Gu, L., Yang, L., Zhou, F.: Approximation properties of Gaussian-binary restricted Boltzmann machines and Gaussian-binary deep belief networks. Neural Netw. **153**, 49–63 (2022)
10. Courville, A., Desjardins, G., Bergstra, J., et al.: The Spike-and-Slab RBM and extensions to discrete and sparse data distributions. IEEE Trans. Pattern Anal. Mach. Intell. **36**(9), 1874–1887 (2014)
11. Courville A, Bergstra J, Bengio Y.: Unsupervised models of images by Spike-and-Slab RBMs. In: Processing of International Conference on International Conference on Machine Learning (2011)
12. Su, Q., Liao, X., Chen, C., et al.: Nonlinear statistical learning with truncated gaussian graphical models. In: Processing of International Conference of Machine Learning (2016)
13. Kingma, D., Dhariwal, P.: Glow: generative flow with invertible 1x1 convolutions. Process. Adv. Neural Inf. Process. Syst. **31**, 1–15 (2018)
14. Tang, K., Wan, X., Liao, Q.: Deep density estimation via invertible block-triangular mapping. Theor. Appl. Mech. Lett. **10**(3), 143–148 (2020)
15. Ranzato M, Hinton G.: Modeling pixel means and covariances using factorized third-order boltzmann machines. In: Processing of IEEE Conference on Computer Vision and Pattern Recognition (2010)
16. Zhang, N., Ding, S., Sun, T., et al.: Multi-view RBM with posterior consistency and domain adaptation. Inf. Sci. **516**, 142–157 (2020)
17. Jiang, Y., Zhuo, J., Zhang, J., et al.: The optimization of parallel convolutional RBM based on Spark. Process. Int. J. Wavel. Multiresolut. Inf. Process. **17**(02), 1940011 (2019)

18. Bi, X., Wang, H.: Contractive slab and spike convolutional deep Boltzmann machine. Neurocomputing **290**, 208–228 (2018)
19. Zhao, W., Kong, S., Bai, J., et al.: HOT-VAE: learning high-order label correlation for multi-label classification via attention-based variational autoencoders. In: Proceedings of National Conference on Artificial Intelligence (2021)
20. Hoang, Q., Nguyen, T.D., Le, T., et al.: MGAN: training generative adversarial nets with multiple generators. In: Proceedings of International Conference on Learning Representations(2018)
21. Hinton, G.E.: A practical guide to training restricted Boltzmann machines. In: Montavon, G., Orr, G.B., Müller, K.-R. (eds.) Neural networks: Tricks of the trade. LNCS, vol. 7700, pp. 599–619. Springer, Heidelberg (2012). https://doi.org/10.1007/978-3-642-35289-8_32
22. Norouzi, M., Ranjbar, M., Mori, G.: Stacks of convolutional restricted Boltzmann machines for shift-invariant feature learning. In: Processing of IEEE Conference on Computer Vision and Pattern Recognition, pp. 2735–2742 (2009)
23. He, K., Zhang, X., Ren, S., et al.: Deep residual learning for image recognition. In: Proceedings of the IEEE Conference on Computer Vision and Pattern Recognition, pp. 770–778 (2016)

Text-Independent Speaker Identification Using a Single-Scale SincNet-DCGAN Model

Yanna Zhang, Guangcun Wei$^{(\boxtimes)}$, Hang Min, and Yunfei Xu

College of Intelligent Equipment, Shandong University of Science and Technology,
Taian 271019, Shandong, China
weigc@sdust.edu.cn

Abstract. The state-of-the-art x-vector technique has been successful in text-independent speaker recognition tasks. However, neural networks are susceptible to overfitting issues in small sample settings, which impairs network performance. Recent studies have attempted to improve the regularization of speaker recognition networks using generative adversarial networks and have shown competitive results. In this paper, we propose a novel deep convolutional generative adversarial network-based speaker identification technique, which adds single-scale SincNet to the DCGAN network and performs text-independent speaker recognition directly using discriminators in the DCGAN network. Also, the loss function in the original model is replaced by the Wasserstein distance. Additionally, by jointly optimizing the "true/false" and classification objective functions, the discriminator enhances the speaker recognition system's capacity for generalization. On the LibriSpeech corpus, our technique outperformed the baseline model x-vector utilizing the dropout method and L2 regularization by a margin of 55.11% and 67.08%, respectively.

Keywords: Speaker identification · SincNet · Deep convolutional generative adversarial network · Text-independent

1 Introduction

Speaker recognition [1] is one of the key research directions in voice recognition technology [2], aiming to emphasize the individual differences between different people. Speech recognition, on the other hand, extracts common information about the words in a speech signal and does not focus on the differences between different speakers. Speaker identification is a subtask of speaker recognition and corresponds to the one-to-many retrieval problem, i.e., indicating which of a few speakers speaks a given speech segment. Based on the features of the speech that will be evaluated, speaker recognition may be separated into two primary categories: open-set recognition and closed-set recognition [3], where the key is whether the speech that will be tested can be matched to the speaker model in the set. Then the answer to closed set identification is yes, i.e., the speaker is required to belong to a known set of speakers. In addition, according to the recognition content can be divided into text-independent and text-related speaker recognition.

© The Author(s), under exclusive license to Springer Nature Singapore Pte Ltd. 2022
Y. Tan and Y. Shi (Eds.): DMBD 2022, CCIS 1745, pp. 18–28, 2022.
https://doi.org/10.1007/978-981-19-8991-9_2

The former is text content that does not indicate the speaker's pronunciation, making it more challenging to extract vocal features and develop models, but it is also more extensively used, does not require user assistance, and is a hotbed for study. Contrarily, the latter requires that the user pronounce the text exactly as it is provided during both training and recognition, which generally produces good recognition results but is not frequently applied in application contexts. In this research, we investigate closed-set text-independent speaker identification.

From statistical modelling to neural networks, the research and development of speaker identification has been carried out for decades with significant progress and results but remains a challenging task. Classical speaker recognition algorithms include Gaussian Mixture Model-Universal Background Model [4], Gaussian Mixture Model-Support Vector Machine [5], Joint Factor Analysis [6], and i-vector [7]. Their different characteristics in terms of speaker modelling representation and scoring judgement make the channel robustness of each method also vary greatly between them. With the enhancement of computational power, there has been a gradual increase in the emphasis on using deep learning methods to solve problems in the speech domain, such as speech recognition [2] and speaker recognition [1]. The key to performance improvement in speaker recognition tasks lies in obtaining features that are both rich in speaker information and less in extraneous information such as channel or noise. With the rapid development of science and technology, artificial intelligence techniques are widely used in various fields, such as target detection [8, 9], speech recognition, and voice recognition. And in vocal recognition, using deep learning based DNN to capture speaker features is a common method used by researchers nowadays. One way to identify speakers is by combining DNNs with established frameworks. For instance, Prince et al. 2007 [10] coupled DNNs with i-vectors to estimate posterior probabilities using DNNs rather than UBM. The other side of the coin is to use DNNs exclusively to explore a range of embedding features such as d-vector [11], x-vector [12], j-vector [13] and so on. However, most past attempts have used hand-crafted features such as FBANK and MFCC coefficients. These engineered features were originally designed based on perceptual evidence and there is no guarantee that these representations will be optimal for all speech-related tasks. Standard features may, for instance, flatten the speech spectrum, making it difficult to extract important narrowband speaker characteristics like fundamental tones and resonant peaks. To address this issue, some recent work has suggested using a sound spectrum box [14] or even the original waveform [15] to enter data directly into the network.

In recent years, GANs have been heavily studied and applied to domain transformation and data generation in the speech domain, such as speech enhancement [16], speech transformation [17] and speech synthesis [18]. The literature [19] proposes categorical GAN for unsupervised and semi-supervised learning using categorical generative adversarial networks. By requiring discriminators to output category labels, odena [20] extends GANs to semi-supervised contexts. The process produces higher-quality samples while also producing an effective classifier. The literature [21] proposed unsupervised adaptive using CycleGAN with outstanding results under low resource domain limitations. Additionally, the literature [22] developed a novel speaker identification system called SpeakerGAN using an enhanced conditional generative adversarial network, outperforming state-of-the-art DNN-based techniques in terms of recognition performance. In summary, deeper network layers and more complex network architectures tend to improve recognition performance. However, there is still room for improvement in the scalability of these approaches for the size of the training corpus. Both traditional i-vector systems and state-of-the-art DNNs aim to learn the mapping from speaker discourse to speaker representation or speaker identity. When there are insufficient training data, these data-driven modeling approaches frequently experience rapid performance erosion. Meanwhile, the overfitting issue caused by a tiny sample corpus decreases the model's capacity for generalization. Based on these facts, the method proposed in this research, known as SincNet-DCGAN, uses single-scale SincNet and DCGAN to recognize closed-set speakers without the need for text. To extract interpretable single-channel speaker features from the original waveform, it employs a single-scale SincNet layer as a feature extractor for the generator and discriminator and a modified deep convolutional generative adversarial network with a Wasserstein distance optimized objective function. The discriminator contains two types of outputs: true and false probability (adversarial output), and category labels of real samples. In addition, the discriminator is directly utilized as a speaker classifier (categorical output).

Our main contributions can be summed up as follows: (1) a single-scale SincNet-DCGAN architecture is designed for learning the speaker's FEATURE MAP from the one-dimensional raw waveform signal, and DCGAN is used to generate spurious samples that are closer to the real data distribution to improve the model's generalizability; (2) the loss function of DCGAN is proposed to be replaced using Wasserstein distance to stabilize the training environment of the network; and the training environment of the network.

The remainder of the essay is structured as follows. SincNet and deep convolutional generative adversarial networks are briefly reviewed in Sect. 2; the architecture of the strategy suggested in this paper is described in Sect. 3; experimental results and a detailed analysis are provided in Sect. 4; and the entirety of the paper is summarized in Sect. 5, along with recommendations for future research.

2 Related Work

2.1 Single-Scale SincNet Structure

A new CNN architecture, known as SincNet, was created in 2018 by Ravanelli [15] primarily for the network's first layer's feature extraction capabilities. it uses convolution based on the sinc function in the first layer, based on the traditional CNN. Rectangular band-pass filters are implemented to produce more meaningful CNN filters. Unlike traditional CNNs that learn all elements of each filter, SincNet only learns high and low cut-off frequencies from the data, so significantly reducing the number of parameters in the first convolutional layer.

Compared to other methods, the SincNet feature map obtained in the first convolutional layer has better interpretation and readability. The filter set only relies on parameters that have a clear physical meaning. Also, SincNet forces the network to focus only on the filter parameters that have a significant impact on performance, allowing the network to achieve fast convergence.

To extract shallow speaker features from the original speech waveform and to give the network a better chance of capturing significant narrowband speaker features, a single-scale SincNet layer is used in this paper as the first convolutional layer of the generator and discriminator, respectively. The SincNet layer used in this paper performs convolution using a predefined function g [15], with function g depending only on the learnable parameters θ. The input waveform signal and the filter bank function perform the convolution operation as shown in Eq. (1).

$$h[n] = x[n] * g[n, \theta] \tag{1}$$

where the parameter θ can be learned. A block of the waveform signal is denoted by $x[n]$, the filter bank function is denoted by $g[n, \theta]$, and the filtered output with shallow speaker features is denoted by $h[n]$.

The rectangular band-pass filter is used by the SincNet layer. The difference between two rectangular low-pass filters can be used to represent the frequency response of a band-pass filter in the frequency domain, as shown in Eq. (2).

$$G[f, f_1, f_2] = rect\left(\frac{f}{2f_2}\right) - rect\left(\frac{f}{2f_1}\right) \tag{2}$$

where f_1 and f_2 are the learned low and high cutoff frequencies, respectively. rect($\cdot$) is the frequency response of the rectangular low-pass filter, see Eq. (3).

$$rect(x) = \begin{cases} 0, & if |x| > 0.5, \\ 0.5, & if |x| = 0.5, \\ 1, & if |x| < 0.5, \end{cases} \tag{3}$$

The inverse Fourier transform of the filter function turns the g function into as shown in Eq. (4).

$$g_{f_1 f_2}[n] = 2f_2 \sin c(2\pi f_2 n) - 2f_1 \sin c(2\pi f_1 n), n = 1, 2, \ldots, L \tag{4}$$

The Sinc function is $\sin c(x) = \sin x / x$, and L is the filter length. To avoid abrupt breaks in the filter set function, the window function w is usually used. As expressed in Eq. (5), the filter function g and the window function we are multiplied to eliminate the abrupt discontinuity at the end of g.

$$g_{f_1 f_2}[n] = g_{f_1 f_2}[n] \cdot w[n] \tag{5}$$

where $w[n]$ stands for the Hamming window, which is very useful for achieving high frequency selectivity [23]. The definition of the Hamming window is shown in Eq. (6).

$$w[n] = 0.54 - 0.46 * \cos\left(\frac{2\pi n}{L}\right) \tag{6}$$

2.2 Deep Convolutional Generative Adversarial Networks

Deep Convolutional Generative Adversarial Network (DCGAN) [24] is a combination of Convolutional Neural Network (CNN) and Generative Adversarial Network (GAN) [25]. Compared to traditional generative adversarial networks, DCGAN improves on traditional GANs mainly in terms of network architecture, with both the generative and discriminative models constructed from CNNs. The DCGAN architecture based on the speaker recognition task is designed by eliminating all pooling layers, using transposed convolution for up sampling in the G-network, and adding stride's convolution instead of the polling layer in the D-network. The generative and discriminative models satisfy the relationship in Eq. (7).

$$\min_{G} \max_{D} V(D, G) = E_{x \sim P_r(x)}\left[\log(D(x))\right] + E_{z \sim P_z(z)}\left[\log(1 - D(G(z)))\right] \quad (7)$$

where discriminator D must distinguish between G(z) as false and x as true. Additionally, x corresponds to the actual sample taken from the in $P_r(x)$. Since the use of random noise z has no discernible impact on the trials, unlike the usual DCGAN, the real sample x is directly used as the input to G in this study [22].

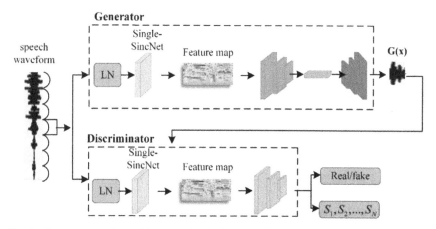

Fig. 1. Demonstrates the architecture of a single-scale SincNet and DCGAN-based network

3 The Proposed Speaker Identification System

Traditional GAN and DCGAN discriminators are solely used to forecast the input's true and false indications. Since GAN has excellent output in terms of generation and draws on the basic ideas of reference [26]. This paper uses a modified DCGAN for the speaker identification task. Figure 1 shows the architecture based on a single-scale SincNet and DCGAN network. As the samples generated by the adversarial are closer to the distribution of real data, the generalization capability of the SI network can be effectively improved.

The discriminator for this network needs not only to model the shallow features of the original speech waveform but also the deep network structure for the speaker classification task. The generator G uses real speech block shapes as input conditions to generate false samples of the same size. While the Wasserstein distance [27] gives the reason for the instability of GAN training, i.e., Jensen-Shannon divergence (JS)) is not suitable to measure the distance between the generated data distribution and the real data distribution, so the Wasserstein distance is used instead of JS scattering to optimize the network proposed in this paper.

Also, compared to GAN, the SincNet-DCGAN network can generate type-rich spurious speech samples, avoiding the problem of distortion of the generated speech signal caused by pattern collapse. $loss_G$ the loss function denoting G is shown in Eq. (8).

$$loss_G = E\left[(D(G(x)) - 1)^2\right] \tag{8}$$

This discriminator D takes as input the false samples generated by G and the real speech chunks from the corpus and outputs the true/false flags and N-category discriminators, i.e., x_{real}/x_{fake} an N-dimensional vector $\{S_1, S_2, ..., S_N\}$. Where S_k denotes the probability $P(y = k|x)$ that input x belongs to a category k. Thus, the discriminator's objective function consists of the classification loss and the adversarial loss, i.e., $loss_D = loss_s + loss_A$. $loss_s$ denotes the cross-entropy loss for all labeled data.

$$loss_s = -E_{x,y\sim P_r(x,y)} \sum_{i=1}^{N} y_i \log k_i \tag{9}$$

The adversarial loss function $loss_A$ is shown in Eq. (9).

$$loss_A = E_{x\sim P_r}\left[(D(G(x)) - 1)^2\right] \tag{10}$$

It is known from previous research that the configuration of a GAN is very important for the stability of its training environment. The network structure was designed in conjunction with the specific task of speaker recognition, and previous work [20] was consulted to configure the network parameters. Table 1 shows the network configuration of the proposed method in this paper in detail.

For the generator G network, the input real sample X_{real} is first normalized by layer and then fed into a single-scale SincNet layer to extract the shallow features of the speaker. It then passes through three convolutional layers and three transposed convolutional layers in turn, each with batch normalization and a Leaky ReLU activation function with a negative slope of 0.03. Finally, a one-dimensional convolution and a one-dimensional adaptive mean aggregation layer are passed to output a spurious speech block of the same size as the input X_{fake}. Meanwhile, the discriminator D in this paper acts as a multi-classifier to estimate the probability that a sample comes from real data. D outputs a large probability if the sample is from real data, and a small probability otherwise. d has two inputs, corresponding to X_{real}, X_{fake}.

The D-network utilizes layer normalization before the single-scale SincNet layer, same as the generator G. Five 2D convolutional layers and four fully linked layers are added after that in that order. To avoid gradient sparsity, all layers in D—aside from the output layer—use the Leaky ReLU activation function. In our tests, a waveform X_{real} is the original speech waveform divided into numerous speech chunks with an overlap of 10ms and a duration of 200ms.

Table 1 shows the network architectures of the generators and discriminators in single-scale SincNet and DCGAN networks for speaker identification tasks. Conv2d. Denotes two-dimensional convolution, FC denotes fully connected layer, BN denotes batch normalization, LN denotes layer normalization and LR denotes Leaky ReLU activation function.

Table 1. The network architecture of generators and discriminators in single-scale SincNet and DCGAN networks.

Discriminator D	Generator G
Input: X_{real},X_{fake}	Input: X_{real}
LN ([1, 3200])	LN ([1, 3200])
Single-SincNet Filter (K = 80, L = 251)	Single-SincNet Filter (K = 80, L = 251)
5 × 5 Conv2d. 64, BN, LR	15 × 1 Conv2d. 256, BN, LR
5 × 5 Conv2d. 128, BN, LR	5 × 1 Conv2d. 512, BN, LR
5 × 5 Conv2d. 256, BN, LR	5 × 1 Conv2d. 512, BN, LR
5 × 5 Conv2d. 512, BN, LR	4 × 1 ConvTrans2d. 512, BN, LR
5 × 5 Conv2d. 1024, BN, LR	4 × 1 ConvTrans2d. 256, BN, LR
AvgPool1d (3)	4 × 1 ConvTrans2d. 1, BN, LR
FC1 (2048)	squeeze a dimension 5 × 1 Conv1d.1
FC2 (512)	AdaptiveAvgPool1d (3200)
FC_NC (num_classes), FC_RF (2)	Output:(1,3200)
Output1:(num_classes), SoftMax	
Output2:(2), SoftMax (dim = -1)	

4   Experiment

4.1   Datasets

To test the recognition approach suggested in this research, train-clean-100 from the LibriSpeech corpus [28] was used. The raw speech signal was pre-processed using the standard methods for processing speech signals, including pre-emphasis, frame and window, and voice activity detection. All the speech was sampled at 16 kHz. The train-clean-100 corpus consists of 251 speakers (125 female and 126 male), with a randomly chosen training and test sample in a 3:2 ratio, employing 12–15 s of training utterances per speaker and 2–6 s of test utterances.

4.2   Experimental Setup

For the baseline system, we chose the discriminator D-network (D-network) and the state-of-the-art x-vector model, using L2 regularization, and dropout, respectively. And the x-vector was structured with the help of the model from the literature [29]. The small batch size was set to 128 and the learning rate was set to 0.001. The maximum learning period was set to 500. The Adam optimizer was used to optimize the network.

To improve the classification accuracy of this paper, a dropout with a random deactivation rate of 0.5 was added to the generator and discriminator respectively, and the waveform of each speech sentence was segmented into 200 ms chunks (with a 10 ms overlap) and fed into the first convolutional layer (SincNet layer) of the generator and discriminator of the proposed SincNet-DCGAN network. Layer (SincNet layer) to extract more interpretative features of the speaker.

The sinc-based convolution described in Sect. 2.1 is carried out by a single-scale SincNet layer as explained in Sect. 3, which employs 80 filters with a length $L = 251$ samples. SGD and Adam optimizers with a momentum of 0.9 were used to train the network. The learning rate was set to 0.0005, the epoch size to 1000, and the small batch size to 128.

4.3 Results Analysis

To evaluate the effectiveness of using SincNet for direct recognition of speech raw waveforms, the frequently tried hand-made features Fbank and MFCC were selected for ablation experiments and the size of the hand-made features was 64×240. Table 2, it can be found that compared with DCGAN (FBank) and DCGAN (MFCC), the recognition of SincNet-DCGAN accuracy (ACC) increased by 1.28% and 1.96%, respectively.

Table 2. Ablation experiments on the optimizer, and feature map of the proposed method (SincNet-DCGAN) in this paper in the LibriSpeech corpus.

Methods	optimizer	handcrafted features	ACC (%)
DCGAN	Adam	FBank	96.04
DCGAN	SGD	FBank	89.68
DCGAN	Adam	MFCC	95.36
DCGAN	SGD	MFCC	84.21
SincNet-CGAN	Adam	-	**97.32**
SincNet-CGAN	SGD	-	84.54

In addition, to evaluate the impact of different optimizers on the experimental results, this paper compares the recognition accuracy of the commonly used SGD with that of the Adam optimizer applied to the proposed model in this paper. The biggest drawback of SGD is its slow descent rate and its tendency to produce locally optimal solutions, while Adam is an adaptive learning rate method combining first-order momentum and second-order momentum algorithms. It is discovered that the outcomes produced by the Adam optimizer are superior to those produced by the SGD optimizer. This demonstrates that the model's performance is significantly influenced by the algorithm used to optimize it, and the Adam optimizer is more appropriate for the model used in this paper. The

SincNet-DCGAN network's recognition accuracy with Adam optimizer, meanwhile, was 97.32%.

In Table 3, the state-of-the-art recognition model i-vector is built on [7] for classification evaluation of a 20-dimensional Fbank. And CNN-Raw [30] is used for recognition based on the same original waveform of speech. Table 3 shows that the approach used in this research improves on the state-of-the-art i-vector and x-vector, respectively, by 79.62% and 55.11%. The recognition performance of CNN-Raw, however, is superior to the model suggested in this study, which offers guidance for our upcoming model optimization.

Table 3. Compares the methods the classification error rate for the Librispeech corpus using the approach from this paper and the most recent recognition model.

Methods	CER (%)
i-vector	13.15
x-vector	5.97
CNN-Raw	1.00
SincNet-DCGAN	**2.68**

Table 4. Comparison of the methods in this paper and the baseline system: SincNet-DCGAN method; D-network and x-vector method with L2 regularization, dropout.

Methods	CER (%)	F1-score (%)
x-vector + DP	5.97	81.76
x-vector + L2	8.14	89.91
D-network + DP	6.27	81.53
D-network + L2	7.37	80.42
SincNet-DCGAN	**2.68**	**90.74**

Table 4 shows the results for the methods in this paper and the baseline system. For the input features in the baseline D-network we choose the better-performing Fbank (see Table 2). The CER of the proposed SincNet-DCGAN is 2.68%, which is 55.11%, 67.08%, 57.26% and 63.64% higher relative to the x-vector + DP, x-vector + L2, D-network + DP and D-network + L2 baselines, respectively. Meanwhile, SincNet-DCGAN outscored all baseline models with an F1-score of 90.74%.

Table 4 shows that the baseline dropout setting is more effective than L2 regularization at increasing the model's recognition accuracy. However, classification performance utilizing the discriminator network D does not outperform the x-vector network as a reference. Therefore, the improvement of the method in this paper is due to the simulated samples generated by the generator network, which solves the overfitting problem of the network and thus improves the recognition performance of the model.

5 Conclusion

In this study, we propose a SincNet and DCGAN-based network architecture for the text-independent closed-set speaker identification task, called SincNet-DCGAN. it uses the discriminator of DCGAN to directly classify speaker identities. For the generator and discriminator of DCGAN, we first obtain single-channel speaker features from the original audio waveform using a single-scale SincNet filter, instead of using pre-computed manual features, such as MFCC. The convolutional and deconvolutional layers are then used to extract the embedding information of the speaker. The speaker ID is output from the last linear layer of the improved discriminator D. The method is easy to implement as it can automatically optimize and select the generated features to improve the regularization model for the classification task. In experiments, the SincNet-DCGAN method proposed in this paper achieves 97.32% classification accuracy on the LibriSpeech dataset, outperforming traditional speaker identification methods.

Although the focus of this study is solely speaker identification, we think the strategy presented in this paper enhances model performance in limited sample settings and is broadly applicable. As a result, in the future, the techniques presented in this study could be applied to other applications like speech recognition, speech classification, and music processing. Alternatively, for SincNet it can be extended to multi-scale conditions for more accurate recognition.

References

1. Beigi, H.: Fundamentals of Speaker Recognition. Springer US, Boston, MA (2011). https://doi.org/10.1007/978-0-387-77592-0
2. Abdel-Hamid, O., Mohamed, A.-R., Jiang, H., Deng, L., Penn, G., Yu, D.: Convolutional neural networks for speech recognition. IEEE/ACM Trans. Audio Speech Lang. Process. **22**(10), 1533–1545 (2014)
3. Jahangir, R., Teh, Y.W., Nweke, H.F., Mujtaba, G., AlGaradi, M.A., Ali, I.: Speaker identification through artificial intelligence techniques: a comprehensive review and research challenges. Expert Syst. Appl. **171**, 114591 (2021)
4. Reynolds, D.A., Quatieri, T.F., Dunn, R.B.: Speaker verification using adapted gaussian mixture models. Digital Signal Process. **10**(1–3), 19–41 (2000)
5. Campbell, W.M., Sturim, D.E., Reynolds, D.A.: Support vector machines using GMM supervectors for speaker verification. IEEE Signal Process. Lett. **13**(5), 308–311 (2006)
6. Kenny, P., Boulianne, G., Ouellet, P., Dumouchel, P.: Joint factor analysis versus eigenchannels in speaker recognition. IEEE Trans. Audio Speech Lang. Process. **15**(4), 1435–1447 (2007)
7. Dehak, N., Kenny, P.J., Dehak, R., Dumouchel, P., Ouellet, P.: Front-end factor analysis for speaker verification. IEEE Trans. Audio Speech Lang. Process. **19**(4), 788–798 (2010)
8. JiweiZhang, M., et al.: AntiConcealer: reliable detection of adversary concealed behaviors in EdgeAI-assisted IoT. IEEE Internet of Things J. **9**(22), 22184–22193 (2022). https://doi.org/10.1109/JIOT.2021.3103138
9. Zhang, J., Bhuiyan, M.Z.A., Yang, X., Singh, A.K., Hsu, D.F., Luo, E.: Trustworthy target tracking with collaborative deep reinforcement learning in EdgeAI-aided IoT. IEEE Trans. Industr. Inf. **18**(2), 1301–1309 (2021)
10. Prince, S.J., Elder, J.H.: Probabilistic linear discriminant analysis for inferences about identity. In: 2007 IEEE 11th International Conference on Computer Vision, pp. 1–8. IEEE (2007)

11. Variani, E., Lei, X., McDermott, E., Moreno, I.L., Gonzalez-Dominguez, J.: Deep neural networks for small footprint text-dependent speaker verification. In: 2014 IEEE International Conference on Acoustics, Speech and Signal Processing (ICASSP), pp. 4052–4056. IEEE (2014)

12. Snyder, D., Garcia-Romero, D., Povey, D., Khudanpur, S.: Deep neural network embeddings for text-independent speaker verification. In: InterSpeech, pp. 999–1003 (2017)

13. Chen, N., Qian, Y., Yu, K.: Multi-task learning for text-dependent speaker verification. In: Sixteenth Annual Conference of The International Speech Communication Association (2015)

14. Zhang, C., Koishida, K., Hansen, J.H.: Text-independent speaker verification based on triplet convolutional neural network embeddings. IEEE/ACM Trans Audio Speech Lang. Process. **26**(9), 1633–1644 (2018)

15. Ravanelli, M., Bengio, Y.: Speaker recognition from raw waveform with SincNet. In: 2018 IEEE Spoken Language Technology Workshop (SLT), pp. 1021–1028. IEEE (2018)

16. Adiga, N., Pantazis, Y., Tsiaras, V., Stylianou, Y.: Speech enhancement for noise-robust speech synthesis using Wasserstein GAN. In: Interspeech, pp. 1821–1825 (2019)

17. Fang, F., Yamagishi, J., Echizen, I., Lorenzo-Trueba, J.: High-quality nonparallel voice conversion based on cycle-consistent adversarial network. In: 2018 IEEE International Conference on Acoustics, Speech and Signal Processing (ICASSP), pp. 5279–5283. IEEE (2018)

18. Hono, Y., Hashimoto, K., Oura, K., Nankaku, Y., Tokuda, K.: Singing voice synthesis based on generative adversarial networks. In: ICASSP 2019–2019 IEEE International Conference on Acoustics, Speech and Signal Processing (ICASSP), pp. 6955–6959. IEEE (2019)

19. Springenberg, J.T.: Unsupervised and Semi-Supervised Learning with Categorical Generative Adversarial Networks. arXiv preprint arXiv:1511.06390 (2015)

20. Odena, A.: Semi-Supervised Learning with Generative Adversarial Networks. arXiv preprint arXiv:1606.01583 (2016)

21. Nidadavolu, P.S., Kataria, S., Villalba, J., Dehak, N.: Low-resource domain adaptation for speaker recognition using cycle-GANs. In: 2019 IEEE Automatic Speech Recognition and Understanding Workshop (ASRU), pp. 710–717. IEEE (2019)

22. Chen, L., Liu, Y., Xiao, W., Wang, Y., Xie, H.: SpeakerGAN: speaker identification with conditional generative adversarial network. Neurocomputing **418**, 211–220 (2020)

23. Rabiner, L., Schafer, R.: Theory and Applications of Digital Speech Processing. Prentice Hall Press, Hoboken (2010)

24. Fang, W., Zhang, F., Sheng, V.S., Ding, Y.: A method for improving CNN-based image recognition using DCGAN. Comput. Mater. Cont. **57**(1), 167–178 (2018)

25. Goodfellow, I., et al.: Generative adversarial nets. In: Advances in Neural Information Processing Systems, vol. 27 (2014)

26. Shen, P., Lu, X., Li, S., Kawai, H.: Conditional generative adversarial nets classifier for spoken language identification. In: Interspeech, pp. 2814–2818 (2017)

27. Gulrajani, I., Ahmed, F., Arjovsky, M., Dumoulin, V., Courville, A.C.: Improved Training of Wasserstein GANs. In: Advances in Neural Information Processing Systems, vol. 30 (2017)

28. Panayotov, V., Chen, G., Povey, D., Khudanpur, S.:Librispeech: An Asr corpus based on public domain audio books. In: 2015 IEEE international conference on acoustics, speech and signal processing (ICASSP), pp. 5206–5210. IEEE (2015)

29. You, L., Guo, W., Dai, L., Du, J.: Multi-task learning with high-order statistics for x-vector based text-independent speaker verification. arXiv preprint arXiv:1903.12058 (2019)

30. Muckenhirn, H., Magimai-Doss, M., Marcel, S.: On learning vocal tract system related speaker discriminative information from raw signal Using CNNs. In: Interspeech, pp. 1116–1120 (2018)

Genome-Wide Feature Selection of Robust mRNA Biomarkers for Body Fluid Identification

Guangyi He[1], Liming Xiao[2], Yingnan Bian[3(✉)], and Ence Yang[1,2(✉)]

[1] Department of Medical Bioinformatics, School of Basic Medical Sciences,
Peking University, Beijing 100191, China
yangence@pku.edu.cn
[2] Institute of Systems Biomedicine, School of Basic Medical Sciences,
Peking University, Beijing 100191, China
[3] Enlight Medical Technologies (Shanghai) Co., Ltd., Banxia Road,
Pudong New Area, Shanghai 201318, China
yingnan_bian@mitrallabs.com

Abstract. Tracing the origins of body fluids, which can provide information linking sample donors with criminal acts, is one of the primary challenges facing forensic medicine. Gene expression profiling methods have been widely developed to identify biomarkers for body fluid identification. In this study, we systematically investigated large-scale, multi-category, high-throughput gene expression data and identified 36 high potential body fluid-specific mRNAs with robust discriminability based on decision tree models. Robustly expressed reference genes were selected for normalization, which further improved the accuracy. Results on independent datasets suggested the robust performance and good generalizability of our biomarkers. In addition, simulated data indicated that our biomarkers could also be employed for accurate body fluid mixture deconvolution. We believe our methods may facilitate body fluid identification and provide insights into forensic crime scene reconstruction.

Keywords: Machine learning · Feature selection · Decision tree · Biomarker · Forensic medicine

1 Introduction

One of the challenges facing forensic medicine is tracing the origins of body fluids. Omics approaches, such as messenger RNA (mRNA) profiling analysis, have exhibited advantages in distinguishing among forensic-related body fluids in parallel [14,21,25,36,50]. However, robust performance of the developed mRNA biomarkers was not guaranteed [2,14,22,35,41], partially due to the small sample sizes, limited classes of included body fluids and the narrow range of mRNA targets utilized during biomarker development. Mining large-scale genome-wide mRNA data in a quantitative way has proven to be superior to traditional qualitative approaches [14].

© The Author(s), under exclusive license to Springer Nature Singapore Pte Ltd. 2022
Y. Tan and Y. Shi (Eds.): DMBD 2022, CCIS 1745, pp. 29–42, 2022.
https://doi.org/10.1007/978-981-19-8991-9_3

To mine biomarkers for body fluid identification with more robust performance, it is necessary to employ a dataset with a large sample size and multiple classes of sample sources to perform a genome-wide screening of robust mRNA biomarkers. The Genotype-Tissue Expression (GTEx) database, which contains genome-wide mRNA expression data (RNA-seq data) from 54 tissue sites across nearly 1000 individuals [10], provides an excellent opportunity to utilize its large sample size and genome-wide mRNA expression data, to seek potential body fluid-specific mRNA biomarkers.

In this study, we used machine learning methods to perform genome-wide mining of GTEx transcriptome data and identified the optimal combination of 36 mRNA biomarkers based on their tissue specificities. We also identified a set of three reference genes for normalization and built an interpretable model on top of them. Testing based on our identified candidate genes and normalization method was carried out on external datasets and exhibited good generalizability and a high accuracy of 100%. In addition, simulated data suggested that our biomarkers also have the potential to be applied to resolve body fluid mixtures and showed accurate predicted proportions.

2   Methods

2.1   Data Availability and Pre-processing

The expression datasets were downloaded from GTEx Portal [10]. The metadata, including the subject-level and sample-level information, were obtained through dbGaP. The genome annotation file was obtained from GENCODE. The gene-level read count and TPM (transcripts per million) values for 19,820 protein-coding genes were extracted from samples of the minor salivary gland, whole blood, prostate, testis, uterus and vagina. We then filtered the samples whose qualities were high (RINs > 6.0 by convention). Samples with SMTSISCH (total ischemic time for a sample) lower than zero or missing were also excluded from further analysis.

2.2   Tissue Specificity Index

The tau index is defined as:

$$\tau = \frac{\sum_{i=1}^{N}(1 - x_i)}{N - 1} \tag{1}$$

where x_i is the expression in the ith tissue normalized by the maximal expression value and N is the number of tissues [48]. It is a widely used method to measure the tissue specificity of the expression profile of each gene. It is a continuous value and varies from 0 for absolutely housekeeping genes to 1 corresponding to strictly one tissue-specific gene. Different thresholds depend on the different levels of stringency required.

2.3   Identification of Candidate Biomarkers

The Scikit-learn-0.22.1 machine learning library was used to evaluate the discriminability or specificity of genes based on decision tree classification models. In each run, we split out 80% of the samples for each tissue to build the model. For each tissue, genes whose minimum TPM values did not exceed 1 were excluded. Then, genes were retained if their mean expression was higher than that of other tissues. Next, to obtain the genes that are specific to each tissue, we used a "one-versus-all" model and labeled the target tissue as '1' and the remaining tissues as '0' when training the model. The Mean Decrease in Impurity (MDI) of genes was extracted to indicate tissue specificities. The higher the value is, the more discriminative this gene is during classification tasks. The bootstrap sampling, training and validation processes were run 20 times, and the average values of MDI in the 20 runs were used to rank the genes for each tissue. Next, the top G genes from each tissue were selected, and the median values of expression were combined into a signature matrix. We iteratively changed G from 1 to 100 across all tissues to obtain signature matrices and calculated their condition numbers (CNs). The signature matrix with the lowest condition number was retained (G = 6 and CN = 8.99).

2.4   Identification of Reference Genes

For each tissue type, we extracted 97 samples' TPM values to balance tissue proportions, and the 3,765 genes whose minimum TPM values exceeded 1 across all tissues were retained to identify reference genes. Several methods, including coefficient of variation (CV) [7,11,12], GLMM [49] and geNorm [45], were applied to assess their expression stabilities in related tissues. Then, analysis of similarities (ANOSIM) was performed to evaluate their effects.

Variation Measurement. The coefficients of variation (CV) of the TPM values of each gene was obtained. Genes with lower CVs were regarded as genes with stronger stabilities. The 13 traditional human housekeeping genes for comparison were selected according to the list of human housekeeping genes recommended for experimental calibration (https://www.tau.ac.il/~elieis/HKG/) [15]. Read counts were used to numerically quantify the stabilities using the common tool geNorm [45] and an iterative generalized linear mixed model (GLMM) method [49]. The M value in geNorm measures the arithmetic mean of all pairwise variations between a gene and other genes. The GLMM method provided the total variance as a stability measure and could decompose them into between-sample, between-treatment and between-experiment variance components. Notably, SMGEBTCH (batch when RNA from a sample was analyzed) and tissue type information were used to divide samples into different experimental and treatment groups.

Evaluation of Stability After Normalization by Reference Genes. We performed ANOSIM to verify how much our identified set of reference genes would help to reduce within-group (within-tissue) variations of our identified biomarkers for body fluid identification. ANOSIM is a kind of non-parametric statistical test with wide applications in ecology, and its R statistic compares the dissimilarities between groups and within groups. On this occasion, the smaller the distance between R and 1, the larger the similarity within tissues than between tissues. We calculated the differences in R statistics between raw count data and normalized data to display the improvement of the normalization methods. ANOSIM was conducted using the R package vegan (v2.5-6, https://cran.r-project.org/web/packages/vegan). Euclidean distance was chosen as the distance metric measuring the dissimilarity between every two samples.

2.5   Testing on Public Datasets

Combining related RNA sequencing raw data from GEO (accession numbers: GSE120795, GSE52665, GSE68229, and GSE69434) [17,27,28,42] and the Human Protein Atlas (HPA, ArrayExpress accession number: E-MTAB-2836) [20,44], a total of 43 RNA-seq samples were integrated. RNA sequencing fastq files were downloaded from the above datasets. Reads were aligned to the prebuilt human reference genome hg19 using STAR (v2.7.3a) [13] in the 'GeneCounts' model, and mapped read counts for all genes in all samples were extracted for further analysis. The Scikit-learn-0.22.1 machine learning library was used to build the random forest classification model (number of trees = 500) to evaluate the discriminability of our biomarker genes in the form of raw count and normalized data. Models were trained on all GTEx samples and evaluated on the testing dataset.

2.6   Deconvolution Analysis

To evaluate the practical value of our biomarker genes when applied to mixed body fluid samples, we performed deconvolution analysis on the testing dataset and simulated mixture samples. Except for semen samples, which were composed of prostatic fluid and spermatozoa, the known fractions of the samples were set to 50% for each, and all other samples were considered pure samples to confirm the reliabilities of the different methods. Simulated data of each gene were generated by randomly sampling the values of the gene in each tissue and adding them up according to the assigned fractions. Pearson correlation coefficients (R) and root mean square errors (RMSE) were used as metrics to assess the performance of the deconvolution methods.

3   Experimental Results

3.1   Principal Component Analysis of Six Body Fluid-related Tissues

Expression levels of 19,820 protein-coding genes (features) in RNA-seq data from 97 salivary gland, 223 blood, 118 prostate, 214 testis, 98 uterus and 106 vagina samples, corresponding to the most forensic-related body fluids, namely, saliva, blood, semen without sperm, normal semen, menstrual blood and vaginal secretions.

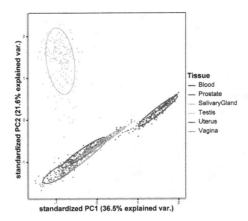

Fig. 1. Principal component analysis (PCA) of the transcriptome profiles. PC1 (which explained 36.5% of the variance) divided the whole blood (orange) from other tissues, and PC2 (which explained 21.6% of the variance) separated the testis from the remaining tissues. (Color figure online)

Principal component analysis (PCA) (Fig. 1) showed that whole blood and testis are the two most easily distinguished tissues, which was consistent with previous studies showing that blood and semen have more special patterns [21, 36]. Distributions of the tissue specificity index [48] also indicated that there were more tissue-specific genes in blood and testis. However, the remaining four tissues were less distinguishable, in keeping with previous observations that body fluids, except blood and semen, are more difficult to identify [41].

3.2   Feature Selection for Tissue-specific Biomarkers

To screen biomarkers for body fluid identification, we first ranked the genes by their specificity. For each tissue, 80% of the samples were randomly selected as the training set to build a series of decision tree models. The specificity of genes, which corresponds to the discriminability of each gene, was measured by the Mean Decrease in Impurity (MDI) [6,43]. For each tissue, potential biomarker genes were ranked in descending order based on their specificity. The downward trends of testis and whole blood were slower than those of other tissues, indicating more genes with strong discriminability within their transcriptome (Fig. 2A). We repeated the process of bootstrap sampling, training and validation to reduce sampling bias caused by randomly selected training sets. The overlapping biomarkers of the top 200 specific genes between runs tended to converge after 20 runs, suggesting a reduction in sampling bias.

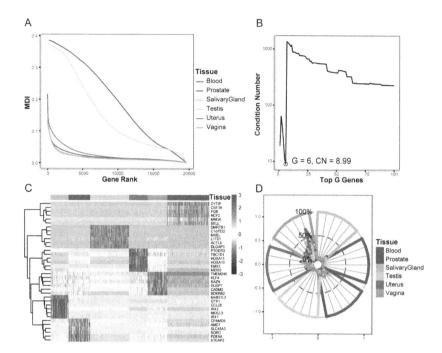

Fig. 2. Identification of tissue-specific biomarkers. (A) Discriminability or specificity of each gene measured by the Mean Decrease in Impurity (MDI) in the identification of each tissue. Genes are ranked in descending order. (B) CN of the signature matrix for different numbers of top candidate genes from each tissue. The red circle corresponds to the lowest condition number of the matrix composed of 6 genes for each tissue. (C) Heatmap of the biomarker gene expression across different tissues (normalized data). (D) Radar diagram of the expression patterns of signature genes in different tissues, where the radius is the percentage of expression relative to the maximum expression values. (Color figure online)

Next, we constructed expression signature matrices of different numbers of top-specific genes and determined the optimal amounts of biomarkers by condition numbers (CNs). The number of top genes was enumerated from 1 to 100, and the corresponding CNs for signature matrices were calculated to determine the optimal number of biomarkers, with lower CNs corresponding to matrices less affected by input variation or noise [1,34]. For each tissue, the optimal number of top genes was 6 (with the lowest CN = 8.99, G = 6, Fig. 2B). Based on these results, a robust signature matrix with 36 biomarkers was constructed (2C). The expression patterns exhibited the high specificity of these biomarkers (Fig. 2C, D).

The results of our analysis are aligned with previous findings, including NKX2-3, IRX1 and IRX2 for salivary glands [5,33,39,44], STEAP2 for prostates [30,37], and EMX2, HOXA11 and PTGER3 for endometrium [26,32,47]. These consistencies suggest the high tissue specificity of our biomarkers, thereby supporting their high discriminability for body fluid identification.

3.3   Identification of Reference Genes for Normalization

For the practical application of our screened biomarkers, a normalization method is important to accurately quantify the relative expression levels and remove within-group variations. We employed several methods to identify robustly expressed genes as reference genes for normalization in our particular forensic context and evaluated the potential improvement of normalization in body fluid identification.

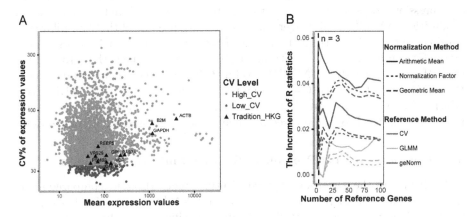

Fig. 3. Identification of reference genes. (A) Coefficient of variation (CV%) of expression values of different mean expression levels across all tissues. Each point represents a gene, and blue points indicate the top 5% of genes ranked by CV. Black triangles indicate the 13 traditional human housekeeping genes. Except for C1orf43, all other genes ranked below the top 5%. (B) The increment of R statistics in ANOSIM with different numbers of reference genes and different normalization methods. Different colors and line types denote different identification or normalization methods for the reference gene, respectively. The values of the y-axis were obtained by subtraction of the R statistics of non-normalized biomarker gene data. HKG, housekeeping gene. (Color figure online)

The coefficients of variation (CVs) were calculated on 3,765 genes whose minimum TPM values were >1.0 to measure the variability of the expression levels of these genes across all tissues [7,11,12]. We first identified 189 genes exhibiting CVs below the 5th percentile (CV% < 33.87%), which were considered good candidates for reference genes (Fig. 3A). Traditional human housekeeping genes recommended for calibration [15], such as GAPDH and ACTB, showed higher variabilities in expression levels than these 189 genes in the particular forensic context (except C1orf43, the CV% of which was 30.83% and ranked 76th). This result was in line with the previous view that typical housekeeping genes may not be appropriate as endogenous control genes for normalization in body fluids [19,41].

For comparison, we next employed two variance measure algorithms to assess the expression stability of each gene, including the generalized linear mixed model (GLMM) approach [49] and the geNorm algorithm [45]. Consistent with the CV results, the traditional housekeeping genes also showed relatively higher variabilities in expression levels and ranked after 100, except for C1orf43 (ranked 23rd in GLMM and ranked 18th in geNorm) and PSMB2 (ranked 41st in GLMM and ranked 76th in geNorm).

Next, potential improvements of different identification methods of reference genes (CV, GLMM method and geNorm algorithm) and different normalization methods (the arithmetic means of expression levels, the geometric means of expression levels, and normalization factors) were evaluated by analysis of similarities (ANOSIM) [9]. In general, normalization reduced the dissimilarities within each tissue. The arithmetic means of expression of the top 3 genes selected by the CV methods showed the strongest ability to reduce the within-group variation (Fig. 3B), including CNPPD1 (cyclin Pas1/PHO80 domain containing 1), BABAM1 (BRISC and BRCA1 A complex member 1) and ARF1 (ADP ribosylation factor 1). Therefore, in the following analysis, the arithmetic means of the expression levels of these three reference genes were used for normalization.

3.4   Comparison with Previously Reported mRNA Biomarkers

To further assess the performance of our identified biomarkers, we compared their expression patterns to previously identified mRNA biomarkers for body fluid identification. Sixty-one reported body fluid-specific mRNA biomarkers from several representative forensic mRNA panels were selected for comparison [21, 25,36]. These biomarkers consisted of 9 saliva biomarkers, 28 blood biomarkers, 10 semen biomarkers, 5 menstrual blood biomarkers and 10 vaginal secretion biomarkers (Fig. 4A).

The MDI, CV and R statistics from ANOSIM analysis suggested that our identified biomarkers exhibited lower variance within tissues and higher distinguishing ability on a large sample dataset than reported biomarkers. The clear separation observed via PCA also suggested the better performance of our biomarkers in representing the main intra-class variations than that of the previously reported biomarkers (Fig. 4B, C). The above results indicated that our identified candidate biomarkers were comparable to the previously reported mRNA biomarkers in identifying body fluids.

3.5   Generalization on External Datasets

To validate the forensic practicality of our candidate biomarker genes and our normalization method, we evaluated the prediction performance of these biomarkers on public datasets from the Gene Expression Omnibus (GEO) and the Human Protein Atlas. A total of 43 RNA-seq samples were collected as our external testing set, which consisted of 3 salivary gland, 6 whole blood nuclear

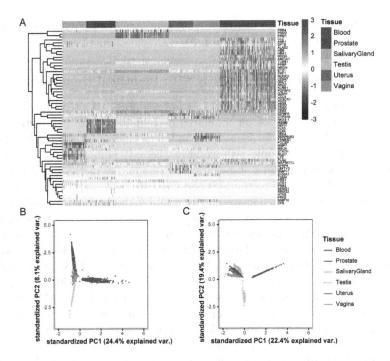

Fig. 4. Comparison with previously reported biomarkers. (A) Heatmap of the reported biomarker gene expression across different tissues (data normalized by our method in the GTEx dataset). (B) principal component analysis (PCA) of the expression of the reported biomarker genes. (C) principal component analysis (PCA) of the expression of our identified biomarkers.

cell, 8 prostate, 4 testis, 5 semen, 2 endometrium of cervix, 3 endometrium, 2 myometrium of uterus, 2 cervix and 8 vagina samples (see Methods).

We fitted a random forest model to all GTEx samples and evaluated the performance of the biomarkers on the testing set. As expected, the salivary gland, whole blood nuclear cells, prostates, semen, testes, myometrium and endometrium of uterus were assigned to their corresponding classes. Samples of endometrium of cervixes were predicted as uteruses, and samples of cervixes were predicted as vaginas, which is reasonable, considering the origins, histological characteristics and adjacent physiological positions of these tissues [38]. Under these assumptions, the model achieved a high accuracy of 100% on the testing set. Compared to raw count data, using normalized data improved the prediction accuracy and the probabilities of true labels, suggesting the advantage of our normalization method. In addition, the prediction accuracy of our identified biomarkers was slightly higher than that of the combination of reported biomarkers from several prior studies (100% to 97.7% under the same setting). In general, our model achieved a relatively high accuracy and generalizability across different datasets. The results described above indicated that our 36 candidate biomarkers together with the three reference genes could successfully distinguish those tissues from other RNA-seq datasets.

3.6   Mixture Component Analysis with Identified Biomarkers

Body fluid mixtures appear frequently in forensic analysis. Therefore, we conducted deconvolution analysis on simulated body fluid mixtures to further evaluate the practical value of our identified candidate biomarkers for resolving mixtures of body fluids. We employed several mathematical methods to deconvolve the mixtures, including the non-negative least squares method (NNLS) [46], DeconRNASeq [18], Chiu's method [8] and CIBERSORT [34]. Biomarker signature matrices for deconvolution were generated on the basis of the GTEx data (Methods). All methods were first applied to the testing set, from which the involved samples were considered mostly 'pure'. Most methods performed well and showed high Pearson correlation coefficients (R) and low root mean square errors (RMSE), confirming the reliability of these methods. Next, we simulated a series of admixed samples from the testing dataset, where 20%, 40%, 60%, 80% and 100% expression for different tissues was added (Fig. 5). All Pearson's correlation coefficients from the deconvolution results were above 0.9, and root mean square errors (RMSEs) were below 0.15, demonstrating high levels of consistency between the given proportions and the estimated fractions. The results indicated that our identified candidate biomarkers have the potential to resolve mixed body fluid samples.

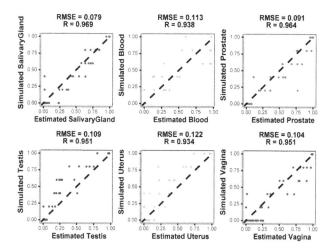

Fig. 5. Deconvolution analysis of simulated admixed samples. Deconvolution performance of different tissues using CIBERSORT on simulated admixed samples. R and RMSE values measured the concordance between the predicted proportions and the known fractions. R, Pearson's correlation coefficient; RMSE, root mean square error.

4   Discussion

Human body fluids represent the most common biological materials found at crime scenes. Precise identification of body fluids can provide significant insights into crime scene reconstructions. Many mRNA biomarkers have been identified for forensic body fluid identification [14, 21, 25, 36, 50]; however, non-robust performance of the mRNA biomarkers may still be observed, partly due to the relatively small sample sizes, the limited classes of included body fluids and the narrow range of mRNA targets utilized during biomarker development. To identify biomarkers with higher specificity, we performed a systematic gene expression analysis on GTEx, a large sample, multi-class dataset, to screen biomarkers for forensic body fluid identification. We identified a combination of 36 candidate biomarkers with a set of three robustly expressed reference genes. The high accuracy of our biomarkers across multiple datasets suggested the efficacy of utilizing such large sample, multi-class datasets.

Considering practical applications for forensic cases, a normalization method to remove experimental variations would be useful. Traditional housekeeping genes are usually used for normalization in related studies [29, 40, 41, 50]. However, some may exhibit low expression levels, in keeping with the view that they may not be appropriate as internal control genes in body fluids [19, 41]. Therefore, there is currently a lack of consensus on suitable housekeeping genes for the detection of all tested body fluids [19]. Our study systematically analyzed the variability of gene expression levels and identified a set of reference genes, including CNPPD1, BABAM1 and ARF1. These genes exhibit low tissue specificity, as the Human Protein Atlas project revealed [44], and exhibited the ability to reduce within-group variations to improve the performance of our biomarkers, suggesting considerable application potential.

Our study is based on the analysis of tissue samples, which might underestimate the differences in mRNA compositions among tissues and body fluids. However, a number of previously reported findings based on body fluids can also be verified in our results, including CCL28 for human saliva [23, 24], SLC45A3 and SORD for semen [3, 4, 16], and NCF2 and HOXA10 for blood and menstrual blood, respectively [31, 50], suggesting the consistency of highly expressed genes in body fluids. The results of this study indicate that our biomarkers could assist body fluid identification and provide insights into forensic crime scene reconstruction.

5   Conclusion

In this study, a genome-wide gene expression analysis was performed in large sample, multi-class RNA-seq datasets, and novel body fluid-specific mRNA biomarkers with reference mRNAs were identified with high and robust discriminability across large samples. The high accuracy of our mRNA biomarkers together with the reference genes, as demonstrated on independent datasets, indicated the robust performance and good generalizability of the identified biomarkers. It was also suggested that our biomarker development strategy would facilitate the unbiased identification of valid and robust forensic biomarkers, thereby aiding forensic scene investigation and providing insights into crime scene reconstruction.

Acknowledgements. We are grateful to all the participants in this study. This work was supported by Beijing Natural Science Foundation (No. 7212065). We are also grateful to the GTEx program, GEO, HPA database and corresponding data contributors for making their enormous database and resources available. The Genotype-Tissue Expression (GTEx) Project was supported by the Common Fund of the Office of the Director of the National Institutes of Health, and by NCI, NHGRI, NHLBI, NIDA, NIMH, and NINDS. The data used for the analyses described in this manuscript from GTEx were obtained from: the GTEx Portal on 05/04/2019 and dbGaP accession number phs000424.v7.p2 on 05/04/2019.

References

1. Abbas, A.R., Wolslegel, K., Seshasayee, D., Modrusan, Z., Clark, H.F.: Deconvolution of blood microarray data identifies cellular activation patterns in systemic lupus erythematosus. PLoS One **4**(7), e6098 (2009)
2. An, J.H., Shin, K.J., Yang, W.I., Lee, H.Y.: Body fluid identification in forensics. BMB Rep. **45**(10), 545–553 (2012)
3. Batruch, I., et al.: Proteomic analysis of seminal plasma from normal volunteers and post-vasectomy patients identifies over 2000 proteins and candidate biomarkers of the urogenital system. J. Proteome Res. **10**(3), 941–953 (2011)
4. Batruch, I., et al.: Analysis of seminal plasma from patients with non-obstructive azoospermia and identification of candidate biomarkers of male infertility. J. Proteome Res. **11**(3), 1503–1511 (2012)
5. Biben, C., Wang, C.C., Harvey, R.P.: NK-2 class homeobox genes and pharyngeal/oral patterning: Nkx2-3 is required for salivary gland and tooth morphogenesis. Int. J. Dev. Biol. **46**(4), 415–422 (2002)
6. Chicco, D., Rovelli, C.: Computational prediction of diagnosis and feature selection on mesothelioma patient health records. PLoS One **14**(1), e0208737 (2019)
7. Chim, S.S.C., et al.: Systematic selection of reference genes for the normalization of circulating rna transcripts in pregnant women based on RNA-seq data. Int. J. Mol. Sci. **18**(8), 1709 (2017)
8. Chiu, Y.J., Hsieh, Y.H., Huang, Y.H.: Improved cell composition deconvolution method of bulk gene expression profiles to quantify subsets of immune cells. BMC Med. Genomics **12**(Suppl 8), 169 (2019)
9. Clarke, K.R.: Non-parametric multivariate analyses of changes in community structure. Aust. J. Ecol. **18**(1), 117–143 (1993)
10. Consortium, G.T., et al.: Genetic effects on gene expression across human tissues. Nature **550**(7675), 204–213 (2017)
11. Czechowski, T., Stitt, M., Altmann, T., Udvardi, M.K., Scheible, W.R.: Genome-wide identification and testing of superior reference genes for transcript normalization in arabidopsis. Plant Physiol. **139**(1), 5–17 (2005)
12. Dekkers, B.J., et al.: Identification of reference genes for RT-qPCR expression analysis in arabidopsis and tomato seeds. Plant Cell Physiol. **53**(1), 28–37 (2012)
13. Dobin, A., et al.: STAR: ultrafast universal RNA-seq aligner. Bioinformatics **29**(1), 15–21 (2013)

14. Dorum, G., Ingold, S., Hanson, E., Ballantyne, J., Snipen, L., Haas, C.: Predicting the origin of stains from next generation sequencing mRNA data. Forensic Sci. Int. Genet. **34**, 37–48 (2018)
15. Eisenberg, E., Levanon, E.Y.: Human housekeeping genes, revisited. Trends Genet. **29**(10), 569–574 (2013)
16. Garcia-Herrero, S., Meseguer, M., Martinez-Conejero, J.A., Remohi, J., Pellicer, A., Garrido, N.: The transcriptome of spermatozoa used in homologous intrauterine insemination varies considerably between samples that achieve pregnancy and those that do not. Fertil. Steril. **94**(4), 1360–1373 (2010)
17. Georgiadis, A.P., et al.: High quality RNA in semen and sperm: isolation, analysis and potential application in clinical testing. J. Urol. **193**(1), 352–359 (2015)
18. Gong, T., Szustakowski, J.D.: DeconRNASeq: a statistical framework for deconvolution of heterogeneous tissue samples based on mRNA-seq data. Bioinformatics **29**(8), 1083–1085 (2013)
19. Haas, C., Hanson, E., Kratzer, A., Bar, W., Ballantyne, J.: Selection of highly specific and sensitive mRNA biomarkers for the identification of blood. Forensic Sci. Int. Genet. **5**(5), 449–458 (2011)
20. Habuka, M., Fagerberg, L., Hallstrom, B.M., Ponten, F., Yamamoto, T., Uhlen, M.: The urinary bladder transcriptome and proteome defined by transcriptomics and antibody-based profiling. PLoS One **10**(12), e0145301 (2015)
21. Hanson, E., Ingold, S., Haas, C., Ballantyne, J.: Messenger RNA biomarker signatures for forensic body fluid identification revealed by targeted RNA sequencing. Forensic Sci. Int. Genet. **34**, 206–221 (2018)
22. Hanson, E.K., Ballantyne, J.: Highly specific mRNA biomarkers for the identification of vaginal secretions in sexual assault investigations. Sci. Justice **53**(1), 14–22 (2013)
23. Hernandez-Molina, G., et al.: Absence of salivary CCL28 in primary Sjogren's syndrome. Rheumatol. Int. **35**(8), 1431–1434 (2015)
24. Hieshima, K., et al.: CCL28 has dual roles in mucosal immunity as a chemokine with broad-spectrum antimicrobial activity. J. Immunol. **170**(3), 1452–1461 (2003)
25. Ingold, S., et al.: Body fluid identification using a targeted mRNA massively parallel sequencing approach - results of a EUROFORGEN/EDNAP collaborative exercise. Forensic Sci. Int. Genet. **34**, 105–115 (2018)
26. Jiang, L., Zhang, M., Wang, S., Han, Y., Fang, X.: Common and specific gene signatures among three different endometriosis subtypes. PeerJ **8**, e8730 (2020)
27. Jodar, M., Sendler, E., Krawetz, S.A.: The protein and transcript profiles of human semen. Cell Tissue Res. **363**(1), 85–96 (2016)
28. Johnson, G.D., Jodar, M., Pique-Regi, R., Krawetz, S.A.: Nuclease footprints in sperm project past and future chromatin regulatory events. Sci. Rep. **6**, 25864 (2016)
29. Juusola, J., Ballantyne, J.: mRNA profiling for body fluid identification by multiplex quantitative RT-PCR. J. Forensic Sci. **52**(6), 1252–1262 (2007)
30. Korkmaz, K.S., Elbi, C., Korkmaz, C.G., Loda, M., Hager, G.L., Saatcioglu, F.: Molecular cloning and characterization of STAMP1, a highly prostate-specific six transmembrane protein that is overexpressed in prostate cancer. J. Biol. Chem. **277**(39), 36689–36696 (2002)
31. Liang, Q., et al.: Development of new mRNA markers for the identification of menstrual blood. Ann. Clin. Lab. Sci. **48**(1), 55–62 (2018)
32. May, K.E., Villar, J., Kirtley, S., Kennedy, S.H., Becker, C.M.: Endometrial alterations in endometriosis: a systematic review of putative biomarkers. Hum. Reprod. Update **17**(5), 637–653 (2011)

33. Michael, D.G., Pranzatelli, T.J.F., Warner, B.M., Yin, H., Chiorini, J.A.: Integrated epigenetic mapping of human and mouse salivary gene regulation. J. Dent. Res. **98**(2), 209–217 (2019)

34. Newman, A.M., et al.: Robust enumeration of cell subsets from tissue expression profiles. Nat. Methods **12**(5), 453–457 (2015)

35. Nussbaumer, C., Gharehbaghi-Schnell, E., Korschineck, I.: Messenger RNA profiling: a novel method for body fluid identification by real-time PCR. Forensic Sci. Int. **157**(2–3), 181–186 (2006)

36. Park, S.M., et al.: Genome-wide mRNA profiling and multiplex quantitative RT-PCR for forensic body fluid identification. Forensic Sci. Int. Genet. **7**(1), 143–150 (2013)

37. Porkka, K.P., Helenius, M.A., Visakorpi, T.: Cloning and characterization of a novel six-transmembrane protein STEAP2, expressed in normal and malignant prostate. Lab. Invest. **82**(11), 1573–1582 (2002)

38. Raffi, R.O., Moghissi, K.S., Sacco, A.G.: Proteins of human vaginal fluid. Fertil. Steril. **28**(12), 1345–1348 (1977)

39. Saitou, M., et al.: Functional specialization of human salivary glands and origins of proteins intrinsic to human saliva. Cell Rep. **33**(7), 108402 (2020)

40. Setzer, M., Juusola, J., Ballantyne, J.: Recovery and stability of RNA in vaginal swabs and blood, semen, and saliva stains. J. Forensic Sci. **53**(2), 296–305 (2008)

41. Song, F., Luo, H., Hou, Y.: Developed and evaluated a multiplex mRNA profiling system for body fluid identification in Chinese Han population. J. Forensic Leg. Med. **35**, 73–80 (2015)

42. Suntsova, M., et al.: Atlas of RNA sequencing profiles for normal human tissues. Sci. Data **6**(1), 36 (2019)

43. Tackmann, J., Arora, N., Schmidt, T.S.B., Rodrigues, J.F.M., von Mering, C.: Ecologically informed microbial biomarkers and accurate classification of mixed and unmixed samples in an extensive cross-study of human body sites. Microbiome **6**(1), 192 (2018)

44. Uhlen, M., et al.: Proteomics. Tissue-based map of the human proteome. Science **347**(6220), 1260419 (2015)

45. Vandesompele, J., et al.: Accurate normalization of real-time quantitative RT-PCR data by geometric averaging of multiple internal control genes. Genome Biol. **3**(7), RESEARCH0034 (2002)

46. Venet, D., Pecasse, F., Maenhaut, C., Bersini, H.: Separation of samples into their constituents using gene expression data. Bioinformatics **17**(Suppl 1), S279–S287 (2001)

47. Xu, B., et al.: Regulation of endometrial receptivity by the highly expressed HOXA9, HOXA11 and HOXD10 HOX-class homeobox genes. Hum. Reprod. **29**(4), 781–790 (2014)

48. Yanai, I., et al.: Genome-wide midrange transcription profiles reveal expression level relationships in human tissue specification. Bioinformatics **21**(5), 650–659 (2005)

49. Zhuo, B., Emerson, S., Chang, J.H., Di, Y.: Identifying stably expressed genes from multiple RNA-seq data sets. PeerJ **4**, e2791 (2016)

50. Zubakov, D., Hanekamp, E., Kokshoorn, M., van Ijcken, W., Kayser, M.: Stable RNA markers for identification of blood and saliva stains revealed from whole genome expression analysis of time-wise degraded samples. Int. J. Legal Med. **122**(2), 135–142 (2008)

HOS-YOLOv5: An Improved High-Precision Remote Sensing Image Target Detection Algorithm Based on YOLOv5

Hongren Wang[✉] [iD]

Shandong University of Science and Technology, Tai'an 271000, China
hongren.wang@sdust.edu.cn

Abstract. Object detection has made great strides in natural images over the past few years. However, due to the characteristics of small size, dense distribution, and different scales of remote sensing images, when they are directly applied to remote sensing images, the detection accuracy of their targets is too low. To this end, we propose HOS-YOLOv5, an improved high-precision remote sensing image target detection algorithm based on YOLOV5, construct the HOS backbone network, add multiple SPD modules and downsampling modules, and introduce the DotD algorithm to solve remote sensing images. The detection accuracy of the target is too low. HOS-YOLOv5 has conducted a large number of experiments on the public dataset DOTA. The experimental results show that compared with the traditional YOLOv5, the mAP of HOS-YOLOv5 is increased by 4.65%, and a good detection effect is achieved.

Keywords: Remote sensing images · Object detection · HOS-YOLOv5 · DotD · YOLOv5

1 Introduction

In recent years, with the significant progress made in the task of object detection using deep convolutional neural networks [1–3], research on remote sensing image processing has become increasingly popular, especially on some sensitive objects such as aircraft, vehicles, Ships, ports, etc. In the past few years, many researchers have proposed various object detection solutions in remote sensing images [4–8], but due to the small size, dense distribution, different scales of remote sensing images, and limited Interference from shadows, light, and other external factors can cause problems such as missed detections or even false detections. The traditional remote sensing target detection method is sensitive to the size of the target and has poor robustness; secondly, when there are small targets with high exposure and complex backgrounds in the image, the difficulty of detection will increase, so how to improve the accuracy of remote sensing image detection still remains, is a huge challenge.

At present, many solutions have been proposed to solve the above target detection problem, but they are not friendly to remote sensing images, especially small targets

© The Author(s), under exclusive license to Springer Nature Singapore Pte Ltd. 2022
Y. Tan and Y. Shi (Eds.): DMBD 2022, CCIS 1745, pp. 43–56, 2022.
https://doi.org/10.1007/978-981-19-8991-9_4

in remote sensing images, which are mainly reflected in the following aspects: excessive downsampling rate; excessive receptive field; contradiction between semantics and space; lack of feature fusion. The current remote sensing image detection mainly includes data augmentation [9–11], sliding window detection, etc. However, these optimization algorithms cannot fundamentally improve the detection effect of remote sensing images.

To this end, we propose an improved model HOS-YOLOv5 based on YOLOv5 to improve the performance of remote sensing image object detection. We borrow the idea of Hornet [12], construct a HOS backbone network, add SPD [13] module and downsampling module to realize input adaptation, long-range and high-order spatial interaction, and adopt multiple convolutions of different sizes The multi-scale information is encoded to provide rich features, and the relationship between channels is modeled through the precise position information of the feature map and the long-distance dependency is captured, so as to better solve the problem of remote sensing image target detection.

Our main contributions are summarized as follows:

(i)   We propose a new network model, HOS-YOLOv5, which aims to address the fundamental limitation of low perception intensity of dense small objects in the detection of remote sensing images in the past.
(ii) We introduce a new metric algorithm, DotD, which aims to improve the quality of NMS to overcome the weakness of traditional metrics in anchoring tiny targets.
(iii) Extensive experiments on the DOTA dataset show that our proposed HOS-YOLOv5 achieves 60.36% (mAP), which is 4.65% higher than the traditional model YOLOv5, with higher average model accuracy and a significant improvement in detection performance.

2   Related Work

2.1   Object Detection

At present, target detection is mainly divided into two-stage algorithms represented by the R-CNN series and one-stage algorithms represented by YOLO [2] and SSD [14].

The two-stage algorithm first generates candidate regions on the image, and then performs classification and boundary regression for each candidate region in turn. Girshick et al. [15] pioneered the R-CNN algorithm, but it has a lot of flaws in itself. Subsequently, a series of algorithms were proposed to improve it, and He et al. proposed SPP-Net, which accelerated the process of training and inference. Girshick later proposed Fast R-CNN on this basis. In order to truly achieve end-to-end training, Ren et al. improved Fast R-CNN and proposed the Faster R-CNN algorithm. Then researchers took Faster R-CNN as the prototype, and successively proposed algorithms such as R-FCN, FPN, and Mask R-CNN.

The one-stage algorithm directly completes the localization and classification of all targets on the entire image, omitting the generation of candidate regions. The earliest one-stage detector OverFeat was proposed by Sermanent et al. in 2013. It was not until Redmon et al. [2] proposed the YOLO algorithm that real-time target detection was truly realized. After the birth of YOLO, more one-stage detectors have come out one after another. Liu et al. inherited the core idea of YOLO and proposed the SSD algorithm.

Later, the original YOLO was improved and upgraded, and algorithms such as YOLOv2, YOLOv3, YOLOv4, and YOLOv5 were successively proposed to further improve the detection ability.

2.2 Tiny Object Detection

In complex environments, object detection in remote sensing images usually faces a large number of small objects. At present, methods on small object detection mainly include data augmentation, multi-scale feature learning, context-based feature detection and designing better training strategies.

Data augmentation. The technology of increasing the number of training sets by generating more equivalent data from limited data through algorithms can effectively overcome the problem of insufficient training data. On the basis of the existing data set, more equivalent data is generated, the distribution of training data is enriched, and the generalization ability of the obtained model is stronger. There are two main ways to implement this strategy. One is to increase the generalization ability of the model by increasing the amount of data in the training set; the other is to increase the robustness of the model by increasing the noise data of the training set.

Multiscale feature learning. Image pyramid is a classic scale transformation method, which can extract features of different scales based on input of different resolutions, but it also causes a lot of computation. Considering that the deeper the feature map of the convolutional neural network, the larger the receptive field, the SSD algorithm [14] and the MS-CNN algorithm [16] have been proposed successively, but due to the different depths of each feature layer, the feature representation capabilities are also different, the detection ability of its small target has not been improved. Since then, many scholars have improved this. Lin et al. proposed the famous Feature Pyramid Network FPN [17] by fusing the feature information of different depths inside the network. Then people searched for better construction schemes one after another, such as Liu et al. [18] proposed PANet, and multi-scale feature learning was further developed.

Context-based feature detection. A common approach to context-based feature detection is to utilize combined feature maps in convolutional networks for prediction. Pyramid [19] uses a semi-supervised approach to supervise high-order semantic feature learning and combines high-order semantic information with low-order geometric features. Chen et al. [20] used context patches in parallel with RPN-generated proposal patches and augmented R-CNN to improve the accuracy of tiny object detection.

Design better training strategies. In the past few years, more powerful classification networks such as R-CNN, FPN, OverFeat, and YOLO have come out one after another. The target detection algorithm based on deep learning is mainly divided into two-stage algorithm and one-stage algorithm. The two-stage algorithm first generates a series of candidate regions with potential targets, and then classifies and performs boundary regression for each region according to the features of the candidate regions. The one-stage algorithm omits the step of generating candidate regions, and only uses a convolutional neural network to directly complete the localization and classification of all objects on the entire image. Compared with the one-stage algorithm, the two-stage algorithm has higher positioning accuracy, and the one-stage algorithm is generally faster.

2.3 Evaluation Metric in Object Detection

IoU is the most widely used metric to measure the similarity between bounding boxes, however, IoU has limitations in evaluating the positional relationship between two bounding boxes, when two bounding boxes are adjacent or far apart. As a result, the IoU cannot accurately reflect the location relationship.

In order to solve this problem, GIoU [21] is proposed. Compared with IoU, GIoU not only pays attention to the overlapping area, but also pays attention to other non-overlapping areas, which can better reflect the degree of overlap between the two. However, when the detection frame and the real frame are included, GIoU will degenerate into IoU. And when the two boxes intersect, the convergence speed is slower in the horizontal and vertical directions.

Since then, based on the characteristics of IoU, considering the shortcomings of GIOU, overlapping area, center point distance, and aspect ratio, DIoU [22] and CIoU [22] have been proposed successively to overcome the limitations of IoU and GIoU. However, the aspect ratio describes a relative value, there is a certain ambiguity, and the balance of difficult and easy samples is not considered.

GIoU, DIoU, CIoU are IoU-based modification metrics that address some issues in IoU-based loss functions. However, when IoU detects small objects, there are still problems such as being sensitive to small offsets between bounding boxes. To this end, we introduce a new metric, DotD, to improve the accuracy of detecting tiny objects.

3 Method

3.1 Review of YOLOv5

YOLOv5 is an improved version based on YOLOv4. Compared with traditional detection methods, the accuracy and speed are greatly improved, and the real-time performance is stronger. Therefore, we use YOLOv5 for research and improvement. Among them, YOLOv5 includes four detection versions: YOLOv5s, YOLOv5m, YOLOv5l and YOLOv5x. The YOLOv5 detection model consists of four parts: the input layer, the backbone network, the neck network and the prediction layer. Taking YOLOv5s as an example, the structure is shown in Fig. 1.

In terms of data preprocessing, YOLOv5 follows the Mosaic data augmentation method proposed by YOLOv4, and performs splicing through random scaling, random cropping, and random arrangement to enrich the data diversity in the input part and increase the number of small targets in a single batch. Improve the network's ability to recognize small targets. YOLOv5 improves the accuracy and speed of image detection by adaptive anchoring and adaptive image scaling, and by using NMS to select the best anchor frame value. For data augmentation in the HOS-YOLOv5 network, we combine MixUp, Mosaic and traditional methods.

Use Focus and CSP modules in the backbone network. The Focus module reduces the size of the feature map by increasing its dimension. Taking the structure of YOLOv5s as an example, as shown in Fig. 1, the original $608 \times 608 \times 3$ image is input into the Focus structure, and after Slice and Concat operations, it outputs a $304 \times 304 \times 12$ feature map, and then after a convolution operation of 32 convolution kernels, a 304

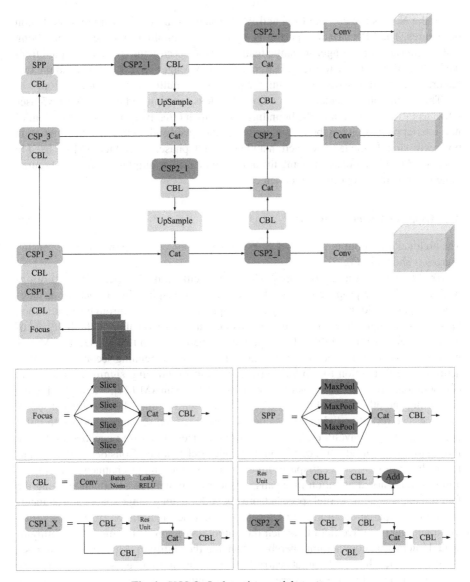

Fig. 1. YOLOv5s detection model structure.

× 304 × 32 feature map is output. YOLOv5 designs two CSP structures. Taking the YOLOv5s network as an example, the CSP1_X structure is applied to the Backbone network, which improves the gradient value of backpropagation between layers, thereby obtaining finer feature granularity.

In the Neck structure, the FPN and PAN structures are used for multi-scale fusion of features. The FPN structure performs top-down upsampling to make the underlying feature map contain stronger semantic features; the PAN structure is downsampled from the bottom up so that the top-level features contain stronger spatial features and the two features are finally fused, thus solving the problem of multi-scale object detection.

The prediction layer includes bounding box loss function and NMS. YOLOv5 uses GIoU as the loss function of the bounding box, which effectively solves the problem of non-overlapping bounding boxes and improves the speed and accuracy of the prediction box regression. In the target detection and prediction phase, a weighted NMS is used to select the bounding box, enhancing the ability to identify multiple targets and obscured targets to obtain the optimal target detection box.

3.2 HOS Backbone Network

The architecture of our proposed HOS-YOLOv5 for object detection in remote sensing images is shown in Fig. 2.

Traditional convolution operations do not explicitly consider spatial interactions as well, for which we propose HOS backbone networks. Inspired by Hornet, we achieve input adaptation, long-range, and high-order spatial interactions through self-attention operations, compatible with various variants of convolution, enabling a high degree of flexibility and customizability of the operation, where through two consecutive Matrix multiplication performs second-order spatial interactions, extending second-order interactions in self-attention to arbitrary orders without introducing significant additional computation. We draw on dynamic convolution [23], SimAM [24], SCNet [25], edge computing and other algorithm ideas [26, 27], in order to reduce the problem caused by the excessive receptive field and the contradiction between semantics and space Influence, a variety of convolution kernels of different sizes are used to encode multi-scale information through adaptive operations to provide rich features. Considering the dynamics in dimensions such as airspace, input channels, and output channels, we employ a multi-dimensional attention mechanism to learn complementary attention along the four dimensions of the kernel space, adaptively building long-range spaces and channels around each spatial location. The inter-dependency self-calibration operation is used to expand the receptive field to enrich the output and improve the modeling ability of spatial interaction convolution, thereby enhancing the ability to extract weak features.

We consider that small targets carry less information often leads to weaker feature representation and fewer features are extracted by multi-level convolution operations. In the Neck layer, we design a continuous downsampling convolution layer and introduce an SPD module to downsample the feature map while retaining feature information and eliminate spanwise distance operations and pooling operations, thus improving the performance of processing small target images.

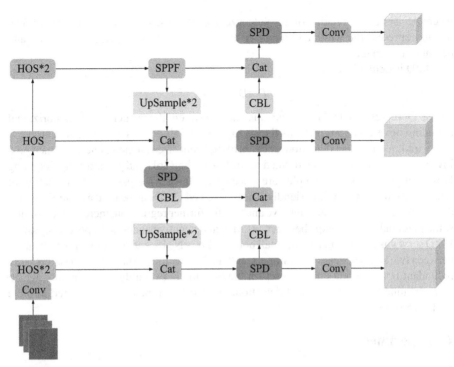

Fig. 2. Architecture of HOS-YOLOv5. Compared with the original version, HOS-YOLOv5 adds the HOS backbone network and multiple Upsample and SPD modules to improve performance.

3.3 Introduce DotD Algorithm

The GIoU [21] indicator is used in YOLOv5, and GIoU can be expressed as:

$$GIoU = IoU - \frac{|C - A \cup B|}{|C|}. \tag{1}$$

However, when the two prediction boxes have the same height and width and are on the same horizontal plane, GIOU degenerates into IoU. In addition, GIoU and IoU have two disadvantages: slower convergence and less accurate regression. To better fit our proposed network structure, we introduce a simple and effective new metric, called Dot Distance (DotD) [28], to improve the performance of detecting tiny objects in remote sensing images.

The absolute size and relative size of the definition object A of DotD are calculated as follows:

$$AS(A) = \sqrt{w_A \times h_A}. \tag{2}$$

$$RS(A) = \sqrt{\frac{w_A \times h_A}{W \times H}}. \tag{3}$$

where AS is the abbreviation of absolute size and RS is the abbreviation of relative size. w_A, h_A represent the width and height of the border A, W, H represent the width and height of the image.

DotD is defined as:

$$DotD = e^{-\frac{D}{S}}. \tag{4}$$

where D represents the Euclidean distance between the centers of two horizontal bounding boxes, and S represents the average size of all objects in a certain dataset.

In traditional object detection, anchors of different sizes are first generated, then positive and negative anchors are defined according to their IoU and ground-truth bounding boxes, and then positive samples are selected for further regression. The detection of remote sensing images is not friendly. The introduced DotD can be used as a threshold for determining the positive and negative anchors for further regression, thereby overcoming some potential relationships between positive and negative anchors. In post-processing, DotD serves as a better metric for small bounding box NMS, and the center point distance between two small boxes is more important than their width and height when suppressing redundant boxes. DotD only focuses on the position between the center points, which is more suitable for small object detection, and DotD can be easily integrated into the YOLOv5 framework.

4 Experiments

4.1 Dataset

To verify the effectiveness of our proposed HOS-YOLOv5, experiments are conducted on the remote sensing image dataset DOTA [29]. We select a small sample of data and use only one-fifth of the original data. According to the settings in the previous method, we use the training set and the validation set for training, and use the test set for testing, so as to train the model faster and get the experimental results. At the same time, in order to ensure the validity of the experiment, we choose the data according to the weights of various instances of the original data.

DOTA is the largest dataset for directional object detection in remote sensing images. DOTA-v1.0 contains 2806 large aerial images, ranging in size from 800×800 to 4000×4000, with a total of 188 instances in 15 common categories: aircraft, baseball diamonds, bridges, ground track and field, small vehicles, large Vehicles, boats, tennis courts, basketball courts, storage tanks, football fields, roundabouts, ports, swimming pools and helicopters.

4.2 Implementation Details

Since the original picture size is relatively large and most of the images in the dataset are of high resolution. Using the original size as the training dataset would result in too many parameters. Therefore, we choose to cut the original pictures in the training dataset according to the method of Van Etten A et al. [30] to form a new training dataset according to the pixel size of 640×640 and the overlap of 15%, which helps to avoid excessive Fitting occurs, thereby improving the generalization ability [31] of the trained network.

4.3 Experimental Results

To compare YOLOv5 and our proposed improved model HOS-YOLOv5, the processed images will be trained with the same number of epochs. First, we compare the loss values of the two models. Figure 3 shows a graph comparing the loss values of the YOLOv5 and HOS-YOLOv5 models. It can be seen that the loss value of HOS-YOLOv5 decreases faster than that of YOLOv5, and the loss value of HOS-YOLOv5 is closer to 0, indicating that HOS-YOLOv5 has better loss convergence ability.

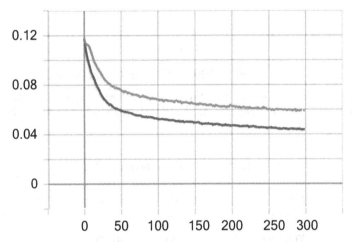

Fig. 3. Comparison of loss curves. The abscissa is the number of epochs, and the ordinate is the loss value. The orange and red lines represent the loss values of YOLOv5 and HOS-YOLOv5 respectively (Color figure online).

Figure 4 shows the mAP comparison plot of YOLOv5 and HOS-YOLOv5. Experiments show that the mAP of YOLOv5 is 55.71%, while the mAP of HOS-YOLOv5 reaches 60.36%. The mAP of the HOS-YOLOv5 model for detecting remote sensing images is significantly higher than that of YOLOv5, indicating the superiority of the HOS-YOLOv5 model for remote sensing image detection.

We also tested and compared the YOLOv3 and YOLOv4 models with HOS-YOLOv5. In Table 1, we record the mAP and Recall for each model separately. mAP is the mean of AP for each category, and Recall is the proportion of predicted positive actually positive to the overall positive sample, which is an important metric to evaluate the target detection ability. Analyzing the data in Table 1, it can be seen that the mAP and Recall of HOS-YOLOv5 are greatly improved compared with the traditional YOLO network, and HOS-YOLOv5 improves the ability to detect remote sensing images.

On the DOTA dataset, our proposed HOS-YOLOv5 achieves a mAP of 60.36%, and the mAP of HOS-YOLOv5 is much improved compared to other models, proving its effectiveness in detecting small objects on satellite images.

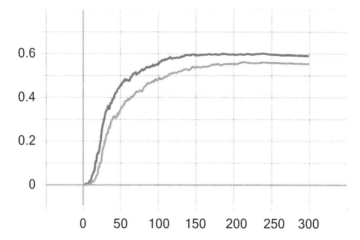

Fig. 4. Comparison of mAP curves. The abscissa is the number of epochs, and the ordinate is mAP. The orange and red lines represent mAP of YOLOv5 and HOS-YOLOv5 respectively (Color figure online).

Table 1. Comparisons of different models.

Models	mAP	Recall
YOLOv3	33.76	31.56
YOLOv4	43.35	41.79
YOLOv5s	55.71	53.10
HOS-YOLOv5	60.36	59.14

In addition, we use YOLOv5s and HOS-YOLOv5 for detection on remote sensing images, respectively, and compare the two models. The detection results of YOLOv5s and HOS-YOLOv5 are shown in Figs. 5 and 6, respectively. The experimental results show that our proposed HOS-YOLOv5 performs better in detecting images with complex backgrounds, less pixels occupied by objects and denser images. From the comparison of the pictures, it can be seen that YOLOv5s target detection has large problems of false detection and missed detection, while HOS-YOLOv5 not only improves the detection accuracy of remote sensing image targets, but also improves the false detection and missed detection.

4.4   Ablation Experiment

In this section, we conduct internal ablation experiments on the DOTA dataset to verify the contributions of each module in the HOS-YOLOv5 model. Taking YOLOv5s as the baseline, its mAP reaches 55.71%. Then, we study the fusion of the YOLOv5s framework and various modules. The experimental results are shown in Table 2. As can be seen from the experimental results, our proposed HOS-YOLOv5 achieves remarkable results.

Fig. 5. Detection results of YOLOv5. The left is the dense small target detection result, and the right is the small target detection result under the complex background (cloud layer).

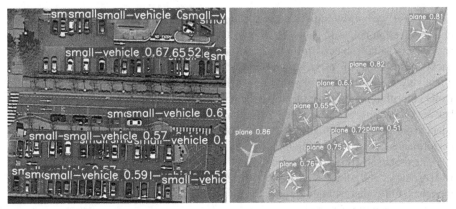

Fig. 6. Detection results of HOS-YOLOv5. The left is the dense small target detection result, and the right is the small target detection result under the complex background (cloud layer).

Table 2. Ablation study on the DOTA dataset. Taking YOLOv5s as the baseline, fused with various modules and trained separately for 300 epochs.

Models	mAP	Recall
YOLOv5s	55.71	53.10
YOLOv5s + Hornet	56.85	55.62
YOLOv5s + Hornet + DY-CNN	57.01	55.73
YOLOv5s + Hornet+DY-CNN + SimAM	57.53	55.75

(continued)

Table 2. (*continued*)

Models	mAP	Recall
YOLOv5s + Hornet + DY-CNN + SimAM + DotD	58.81	56.55
YOLOv5s + Hornet + DY-CNN + SimAM + DotD + SPD	59.46	56.63
HOS-YOLOv5	60.36	59.14

The results show that YOLOv5s is integrated with other modules, and its mAP and Recall have been improved to a certain extent. In remote sensing image target detection, both mAP and Recall of HOS-YOLOv5 are significantly improved. The experimental results show that HOS-YOLOv5 achieves better target detection results.

5 Conclusion

In this paper, we borrow some advanced techniques of object detection and propose a new object detection network, called HOS-YOLOv5, to solve the problem of low detection accuracy of small objects in high-precision remote sensing images. We improve the backbone network of YOLOv5 and add SPD module and downsampling module to effectively reduce the loss of small object feature information. At the same time, the DotD algorithm is introduced to solve the problem that IoU is sensitive to small offsets between bounding boxes when detecting small objects, so that the network can better adapt to the detection of small objects in remote sensing images and improve the detection performance of remote sensing images.

Our proposed HOS-YOLOv5 conducts extensive experiments on the widely used DOTA dataset and achieves a mAP of 60.36%, outperforming the performance of other models. It fully demonstrates the effectiveness of our proposed HOS-YOLOv5 for object detection on remote sensing images.

References

1. Ren, S., He, K., Girshick, R., Sun, J.: Faster R-CNN: towards real-time object detection with region proposal networks. IEEE Access **39**(6), 1137–1149 (2017)
2. Redmon, J., Divvala, S., Girshick, R., Farhadi, A.: You only look once: unified, real-time object detection. In: Proceedings of the IEEE Conference on Computer Vision and Pattern Recognition, pp. 779–788 (2016)
3. Lin, T.Y., Goyal, P., Girshick, R., He, K., Dollár, P.: Focal loss for dense object detection. In: Proceedings of the IEEE Conference on Computer Vision and Pattern Recognition, pp. 2980–2988 (2017)
4. He, K., Zhang, X., Ren, S., Sun, J.: Deep residual learning for image recognition. In: Proceedings of the IEEE Conference on Computer Vision and Pattern Recognition, pp. 770–778 (2016)
5. Li, Y., Li, S., Du, H., Chen, L., Zhang, D., Li, Y.: YOLO-ACN: focusing on small target and occluded object detection. IEEE Access. **8**, 227288–227303 (2020)

6. Dosovitskiy, A., et al.: An image is worth 16 × 16 words: transformers for image recognition at scale. arXiv:2010.11929 (2020)
7. Lin, T.Y., RoyChowdhury, A., Maji, S.: Bilinear CNN models for fine-grained visual recognition. In: Proceedings of the IEEE International Conference on Computer Vision, pp. 1449–1457 (2015)
8. Huang, Z., Pan, Z., Lei, B.: Transfer learning with deep convolutional neural network for SAR target classification with limited labeled data. Remote Sens. **9**(9), 907 (2017)
9. Guo, H., Mao, Y., Zhang, R.: Mixup as locally linear out-of-manifold regularization. In: Proceedings of the AAAI Conference on Artificial Intelligence, vol. 33, pp. 3714–3722 (2019)
10. DeVries, T., Taylor, G.W.: Improved regularization of convolutional neural networks with cutout. arXiv:1708.04552 (2017)
11. Yun, S., Han, D., Oh, S. J., Chun, S., Choe, J., Yoo, Y.: CutMix: regularization strategy to train strong classifiers with localizable features. In: Proceedings of the IEEE/CVF International Conference on Computer Vision, pp. 6023–6032 (2019)
12. Rao, Y., Zhao, W., Tang, Y., Zhou, J., Lim, S. N., Lu, J.: HorNet: efficient high-order spatial interactions with recursive gated convolutions. arXiv:2207.14284 (2022)
13. Sunkara, R., Luo, T.: No more strided convolutions or pooling: a new CNN building block for low-resolution images and small objects. arXiv:2208.03641 (2022)
14. Liu, W., et al.: Ssd: Single Shot Multibox Detector. In: Leibe, B., Matas, J., Sebe, N., Welling, M. (eds.) ECCV 2016. LNCS, vol. 9905, pp. 21–37. Springer, Cham (2016). https://doi.org/10.1007/978-3-319-46448-0_2
15. Girshick, R., Donahue, J., Darrell, T., Malik, J.: Rich feature hierarchies for accurate object detection and semantic segmentation. In: Proceedings of the IEEE Conference on Computer Vision and Pattern Recognition, pp. 580–587 (2014)
16. Cai, Z., Fan, Q., Feris, R.S., Vasconcelos, N.: A unified multi-scale deep convolutional neural network for fast object detection. In: Leibe, B., Matas, J., Sebe, N., Welling, M. (eds.) ECCV 2016. LNCS, vol. 9908, pp. 354–370. Springer, Cham (2016). https://doi.org/10.1007/978-3-319-46493-0_22
17. Lin, T.Y., Dollár, P., Girshick, R., He, K., Hariharan, B., Belongie, S.: Feature pyramid networks for object detection. In: Proceedings of the IEEE Conference on Computer Vision and Pattern Recognition, pp. 2117–2125 (2017)
18. Liu, S., Qi, L., Qin, H., Shi, J., Jia, J.: Path aggregation network for instance segmentation. In: Proceedings of the IEEE Conference on Computer Vision and Pattern Recognition, pp. 8759–8768 (2018)
19. Tang, X., Du, D.K., He, Z., Liu, J.: PyramidBox: a context-assisted single shot face detector. In: Ferrari, V., Hebert, M., Sminchisescu, C., Weiss, Y. (eds.) ECCV 2018. LNCS, vol. 11213, pp. 812–828. Springer, Cham (2018). https://doi.org/10.1007/978-3-030-01240-3_49
20. Chen, C., Liu, M.-Y., Tuzel, O., Xiao, J.: R-CNN for small object detection. In: Lai, S.-H., Lepetit, V., Nishino, Ko., Sato, Y. (eds.) ACCV 2016. LNCS, vol. 10115, pp. 214–230. Springer, Cham (2017). https://doi.org/10.1007/978-3-319-54193-8_14
21. Rezatofighi, H., Tsoi, N., Gwak, J., Sadeghian, A., Reid, I., Savarese, S.: Generalized intersection over union: a metric and a loss for bounding box regression. In: Proceedings of the IEEE/CVF Conference on Computer Vision and Pattern Recognition, pp. 658–666 (2019)
22. Zheng, Z., Wang, P., Liu, W., Li, J., Ye, R., Ren, D.: Distance-IoU loss: faster and better learning for bounding box regression. In: Proceedings of the AAAI Conference on Artificial Intelligence, vol. 34(07), pp. 12993–13000 (2020)
23. Chen, Y., Dai, X., Liu, M., Chen, D., Yuan, L., Liu, Z.: Dynamic convolution: attention over convolution kernels. In: Proceedings of the IEEE/CVF Conference on Computer Vision and Pattern Recognition, pp. 11030–11039 (2020)

24. Yang, L., Zhang, R.Y., Li, L., Xie, X.: SimAM: a simple, parameter-free attention module for convolutional neural networks. In: Proceedings of the International Conference on Machine Learning, pp. 11863–11874 (2021)

25. Liu, J.J., Hou, Q., Cheng, M.M., Wang, C., Feng, J.: Improving convolutional networks with self-calibrated convolutions. In: Proceedings of the IEEE/CVF Conference on Computer Vision and Pattern Recognition, pp. 10096–10105 (2020)

26. Zhang, J., Bhuiyan, M.Z.A., Yang, X., Singh, A.K., Hsu, D.F., Luo, E.: Trustworthy target tracking with collaborative deep reinforcement learning in EdgeAI-Aided IoT. IEEE Trans. Ind. Inform. **18**(2), 1301–1309 (2021)

27. Zhang, J., et al.: AntiConcealer: reliable detection of adversary concealed behaviors in EdgeAI assisted IoT. IEEE Internet Things J. (2021). https://doi.org/10.1109/JIOT.2021.3103138

28. Xu, C., Wang, J., Yang, W., Yu, L.: Dot distance for tiny object detection in aerial images. In: Proceedings of the IEEE/CVF Conference on Computer Vision and Pattern Recognition, pp. 1192–1201 (2021)

29. Xia, G.S., et al.: DOTA: a large-scale dataset for object detection in aerial images. In: Proceedings of the IEEE Conference on Computer Vision and Pattern Recognition, pp. 3974–3983 (2018)

30. Van Etten, A.: You only look twice: rapid multi-scale object detection in satellite imagery. arXiv:1805.09512 (2018)

31. Redmon, J., Farhadi, A.: Yolov3: an incremental improvement. arXiv:1804.02767 (2018)

A Multi-module 3D U-Net Learning Architecture for Brain Tumor Segmentation

Saqib Ali[1], Jianqiang Li[1], Yan Pei[2(✉)], and Khalil Ur Rehman[1]

[1] Faculty of Information Technology, Beijing University of Technology, Beijing 100124, China
{alisaqib,rehmankhalilur}@emails.bjut.edu.cn, lijianqiang@bjut.edu.cn
[2] Computer Science Division, University of Aizu, Aizuwakamatsu 965-8580, Japan
peiyan@u-aizu.ac.jp
http://www.u-aizu.ac.jp/~peiyan/

Abstract. Segmentation of gliomas is a crucial step in brain tumor surgical planning, and it serves as the foundation for further diagnosis of brain tumors. Tumor borders are usually unclear, and a significant amount of heterogeneity in the structure, causing brain tumor segmentation a tough task. However, for tumor segmentation, approaches based on deep learning have shown promising results. This study develops a multi-module U-Net system that utilizes multiple U-Net modules to collect spatial detail at varying resolutions. We use various up-inception and down-inception modules to extract and exploit enough features. Experimental results show that the dice scores of 0.95, 0.90, 0.84, and 0.91, 0.84, 0.77 were achieved for the whole tumor, core tumor, and enhancing tumor, using the BraTS 2018 and local private dataset, respectively. When compared to cutting-edge methods, this study achieves competitive segmentation results.

Keywords: Segmentation · Brain tumor · Residual inception modules · Biomedical imaging · Deep learning

1 Introduction

In the domain of medical image segmentation and classification, Convolutional Neural Networks (CNNs) are commonly used. This is especially true for tasks like brain tumor segmentation [1]. Owing to individual differences in body position, and shape, manually segmenting 3D images is a laborious process. Clinical diagnoses in urgent situations can be made more quickly with the use of an automatic segmentation system that achieves high levels of accuracy.

As stated in [2,3], a CNN is a set of operations that use a series of convolutions, pools, and non-linearities to learn important information. However, both 2D and 3D CNNs have difficulty achieving state-of-the-art performance. For instance, Havaei et al. [4] and Kamnitsas et al. [5] proposed multi-scale systems for both local and global features. The traditional models of 2D convolutions

© The Author(s), under exclusive license to Springer Nature Singapore Pte Ltd. 2022
Y. Tan and Y. Shi (Eds.): DMBD 2022, CCIS 1745, pp. 57–69, 2022.
https://doi.org/10.1007/978-981-19-8991-9_5

do not make use of all of the contextual information included in 3D medical images. Similarly, 3D filters offer superior performance than 2D filters. However, because of resource constraints, the depth of 3D CNNs is confined. Additionally, conventional 3D CNN's poor segmentation performance is due to the absence of end-to-end training techniques. Fully convolutional neural networks (FCNNs) like U-Net [6] and their variants [7,8] can overcome these drawbacks. U-Net consists of two parts: an encoder and a decoder. Contextual features are learned and the high resolution of medical images is reduced using the encoder's convolution and pooling processes. Contrarily, the decoder performs an upsampling procedure to restore the original quality of the images. At the same time, the decoder applies convolution operations to the aggregated features from the encoder and the upsampling function, giving them a more abstract representation. Concatenation [7] or addition [8] serve as aggregation functions in the skip-connection of the U-Net design.

The U-Net is used in many CNN approaches for segmenting medical images [9–11]. Though, these systems suffer from an enormous amount of parameters. Due to the overlapping labels, some authors have used cascaded techniques on U-Net, particularly for brain tumor segmentation [12–15]. To tackle the issue of segmentation, the cascaded model based on U-Net employs multiple encoder-decoder networks in parallel. For instance, researchers of [13] introduced a cascaded U-Net model in which the WT, TC, and ET were segmented by employing three U-Net networks. Nonetheless, the cascading U-Net topologies make it difficult to address a multi-class segmentation task. To avoid problems with vanishing gradients in a more complex network, cascaded U-Net [16] also makes use of residual connections. To obtain multi-scale contextual information, the U-Net requires a deep network. On the other hand, the residual U-Net utilizes multiple channels during training, leading to an increase in required parameters.

There are two possible constraints on the U-Net designs. Firstly, training residual-based U-Net topologies needs a huge number of parameters. In addition, the convolution layers in common residual blocks duplicate information. However, these layers do not incorporate the effective low-level features used by earlier layers. Second, it is difficult for existing U-Net structures to obtain the information of many receptive scales perfectly. To address this issue, numerous studies described potential approaches for doing so [17,18]. These approaches brought about a variety of scales of receptivity in feature maps. Unfortunately, these approaches are inadequate when faced with the wide range of variability seen in medical image modalities. Ideally, the decoder can retrieve attributes from the network's deep layers. Low-resolution features provide enough semantic details, while encoder layers provide abundant important information but a small global context. To optimize the combination of multi-scale features, high-level semantic details and low-level important details can be appropriately combined in the design.

Though several approaches have been presented for segmenting images of brain tumors, the U-Net structure remains the gold standard [19]. It serves as the basis for numerous advancements in segmentation technology. After passing via many convolutional and pooling layers, the input image resolution is reduced in the U-Net. As the upsampling process continues, the initial image size is recovered. Simultaneously, U-Net uses a skip connection to automatically construct feature mappings between the encoder and decoder networks. However, this is insufficient if only the deepest part of the U-Net architecture is used for upsampling. Since the shallow layer's encoding networks produce high-resolution feature maps, there is a wealth of data available for upsampling to acquire enough semantic understanding. To overcome this issue, the author of [20] created U-Net++, a deeply supervised network in which the sub-networks of the encoder and decoder are linked via many nested, dense skip routes. In addition, we offer a multi-module 3D U-Nets approach, which combines multiple U-Net modules at varying network depths to collect long-distance spatial features. We anticipate that the model's ability to retain the fine-grained properties of the foreground object improves when we gradually upsample the feature maps from the encoder side before merging them into the decoder side for extraction and usage of the necessary information. The following is a summary of this paper's major contributions:

1. First, to begin, we introduce multi-module 3D U-Nets, a novel approach that upsamples local features at various levels to gather and use sufficient information via residual inception modules.
2. Second, to resolve the issue of extreme class imbalance, we offer a combination of two loss functions. Our method achieve high segmentation performance without requiring fine-tuning of weight hyper-parameters.
3. Finally, when conducting our examinations, we use BraTS 2018 and local private datasets. In comparison to the advanced methods, such as cascaded and ensemble mechanisms, our suggested framework significantly outperformed.

2   Proposed Methods

This study designed a multi-module 3D U-Net technique for the segmentation of input units of 128 × 128 × 128 images, as depicted in Fig. 1. The input MRI brain scans are fed into a 3 × 3 × 3 Conv layer, and from there, 64 × 64 × 64 feature maps are generated. The input maps are then used by a Conv layer with a dimension of 3 by 3, yielding maps with a final resolution of 32 × 32 × 32. To get varying degrees of features, the feature maps of varying levels are filtered by a U-Net module and pooling layers to get diverse feature information. To ensure that the outputs are properly scaled for the ultimate softmax layer, trilinear interpolation is used to rescale the outputs to the size of the input scan. Our network can take MRI scans of any resolution as input, but to speed up the segmentation process and the problem of high experimental requirements, we reduce the original size to 128 × 128 × 128 pixels.

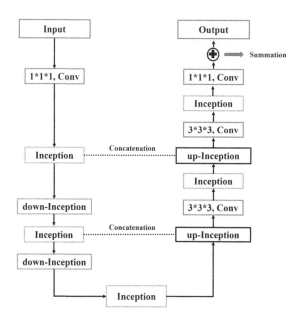

Fig. 1. Summary of our U-Net module.

The U-Net model trains from both ends and has a well-adjusted burden on the encoder and decoder units. Leveraging the benefits of the U-Net architecture, we develop a U-Net module that can simultaneously collect and transport context information across several scales to the decoder layers.

For the case of a $64 \times 64 \times 64$ input channel, our U-Net block operates as expected. To cut down on channels and computation time, the input maps first go through a $1 \times 1 \times 1$ kernel. The feature maps are then analyzed with inception units that alternate with down-inception units to provide the lowest resolution outputs, which is a departure from the standard U-Net. Thereafter, the up-inception unit alternate with the inception unit is used to return the maps to their original resolution. The Conv layer of dimension $1 \times 1 \times 1$ then restores the correct number of output maps. It is important to note that the features are concatenated between the encoding and decoding layers using the skip connection to fully exploit the deep features and retrieve additional feature information. To preserve as much information as possible, we have also decided to include the inputs themselves in the feature maps that will ultimately be generated. The number of parameters is greatly lower by using a set of residual connections similar to that used in ResNet [16]. In most cases, some data is lost during transmission from the conventional convolutional layer. The residual connection safeguards data by directly combining input and output attributes. Since the add operation is carried out on each element basis, no new parameters are introduced into the network. Our inception unit is mathematically calculated as:

$$y(X) = F(X) + X \tag{1}$$

where, the input and output feature maps of the inception unit are denoted as $y(x)$ and x, respectively. The learning of the residual mapping is represented by the function $F(x)$.

2.1 Residual Inception Blocks

It is a problem for deep learning systems to deal with both depth and width. Deep learning models suffer from a lack of multi-scale features, which reduces their effectiveness. Units containing residual connections [21,22] tackle these problems. Utilizing inception units, we can build incredibly complex designs without increasing the number of parameters. By using current inception modules, this design enables enough features for several receptive scales. Segmentation challenges benefit from the use of multiple receptive scales as they produce multi-background knowledge. Figure 2a represents a residual inception unit with three convolutional layers of various receptive fields. Additionally, the use of 1×1 convolution layers aids in minimizing the number of features. The next step is to combine the output feature maps from several receptive fields, resulting in multi-scale features. Figure 2b and Fig. 2c depict the building blocks of a down-inception and an up-inception.

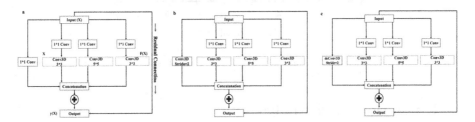

Fig. 2. Representation of the inception module. (a) A residual-inception module (b) a Down-inception module and (c) an Up-inception module.

2.2 Loss Function

In this study, the proposed architecture starts training after normalizing MRI modalities. Subsequently, patches of dimension $128 \times 128 \times 128$ are generated from the brain MRI training data. Throughout the proposed network training, we employed a fusion of two loss functions, which are as follows.

$$L^{tl} = -(L_{mdl} - L_{bcl}) \tag{2}$$

where multi-label dice loss is denoted by mdl [2] and bcl signifies the binary cross-entropy loss. Mathematically, both can be written as

$$loss^{mdl} = \sum_{c \epsilon C} \frac{\sum p_c t_c}{\sum p_c + \sum p_c t_c} \tag{3}$$

$$loss^{bcl} = -\frac{1}{T} \sum_{c \epsilon C} \sum (t_c.log(p_c)) + (1 - t_c).log(1 - p_c) \tag{4}$$

where p_c and t_c are used for the prediction and ground truth of class c. C is the total classes. T signifies the voxels in output.

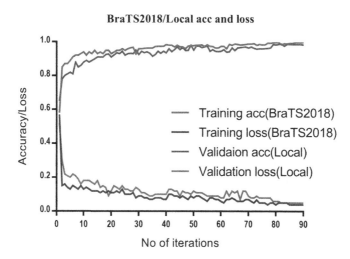

Fig. 3. Training accuracy and loss results of BraTS2018 and Private/local dataset.

3   Evaluations and Analyses

3.1   Method of Training

Python's deep learning framework and TensorFlow library are used to create our network, which runs on a graphics processing unit (GPU) powered by an NVIDIA GeForce GTX 1660Ti. By eliminating all possible zero voxels, we reduce the image size to $128 \times 128 \times 128$. We generate input images in a randomized order using a batch size of 1 for up to 90 iterations. In cases when the validation loss has not declined over the period of the previous five epochs, we resort to the Adam optimization technique, which begins with a learning rate of $1e^{-3}$ and is lowered at each iteration. Training is terminated in advance if the loss has not decreased over the previous few epochs. The proposed model training accuracy and loss performance for both the datasets is shown in Fig. 3.

3.2 Comparative Analysis of the Proposed Model and Standard U-Net and Without Inception Module

To evaluate the effectiveness of the inception module, we replaced it with a $3 \times 3 \times 3$ sized Conv layers on the 2018 BraTS and private dataset. The down-inception block was replaced by a Conv layer with $3 \times 3 \times 3$ dimensions and a stride of 2, while the up-inception module was substituted by a de-convolutional layer with the same parameters. The obtained results are presented in Table 1 and Table 2 for DATASET1 and DATASET2, respectively. Using inception blocks improves network performance, lowers the number of parameters greatly, and protects the data's integrity, as shown by the findings. It demonstrates that our network architecture is reasonable.

Table 1. Experimental performance on the DATASET1(BraTS 2018)

Method	Dice			Sen			Spec		
	WT	TC	ET	WT	TC	ET	WT	TC	ET
Without inception	0.845	0.756	0.698	0.902	0.783	0.758	0.994	0.995	0.999
Standard U-Net	0.881	0.840	0.778	0.910	0.839	0.816	0.990	0.993	0.995
Proposed	0.953	0.906	0.840	0.989	0.967	0.945	0.979	0.986	0.990

Table 2. Experimental performance on the DATASET2(Private dataset)

Method	Dice			Sen			Spec		
	WT	TC	ET	WT	TC	ET	WT	TC	ET
Without inception	0.773	0.715	0.640	0.851	0.812	0.756	0.996	0.998	0.999
Standard U-Net	0.843	0.769	0.710	0.851	0.795	0.736	0.994	0.997	0.998
Proposed	0.910	0.845	0.779	0.928	0.853	0.803	0.991	0.992	0.995

3.3 Ablation Study

To demonstrate the efficacy of our network, we contrast the results of the proposed approach to that of a standard U-Net architecture on the BraTS 2018 and private dataset and our "Standard U-Net" which we created to replace the U-Net block with common convolutional layers. Using a 4-layer U-Net architecture, we first downsampled the input image from its original dimensions to $16 \times 16 \times 16$ using a sequence of Conv layers with dimensions $3 \times 3 \times 3$ and stride value 2. Then we upsampled the image to its actual dimensions by concatenating the resolution maps of the encoding and decoding layers which were used as the input of the following layers. Table 1 and Table 2 show the outcomes of the experiments on the BraTS 2018 and private datasets, respectively. We can see that our network significantly boosts performance compared to the network without the inception block. We speculate that this is because of the U-Net block, which, thanks to its upsampling layers, can filter out some of the noise information while capturing a variety of context information. The output of the designed multi-module 3D U-Net network is higher than that of the conventional U-Net construction "Standard U-Net". We believe that the model can more effectively capture the fine-grained details of the ground truth when the feature maps from the encoder network are progressively upsampled before being fused into the decoder network. Figure 4 and Fig. 5 shows the segmentation results of Brats 2018 and private datasets using the proposed model along with "Standard U-Net" and without inception block models.

Flair Input   Without Inception   Standard U-Net   Proposed

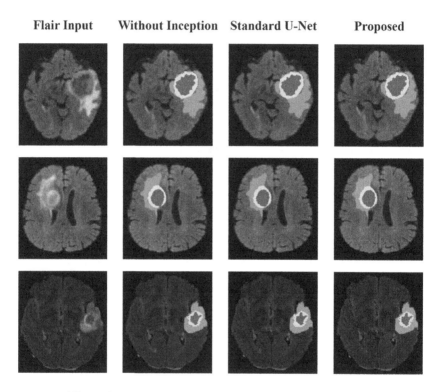

Fig. 4. Segmentation performance of BraTS 2018 dataset.

3.4   Comparative Analysis with Other Methods

In this study, we contrast the effectiveness of the proposed system with other existing approaches using the BraTS 2018 benchmarking dataset. The findings are presented in Table 3. When compared to other cutting-edge neural networks, our proposed model performs admirably. According to Table 3, our network outperforms all other existing and state-of-the-art approaches including [2,8,22–25]. Some previous studies also perform better like DeepMedic [8], Fidon et al. [23]. This is because our network uses 3D depth-wise separable convolution instead of a normal convolution, which drastically decreases time complexity and space complexity. Furthermore, we did not make use of any post-processing stages or ensemble of many networks, unlike [7] and [25]. We believe other post-processing algorithms, like CRF, can enhance the results of brain tumor segmentation. Some post-processing techniques will be incorporated into our future projects.

Flair Input   Without Inception   Standard U-Net   Proposed

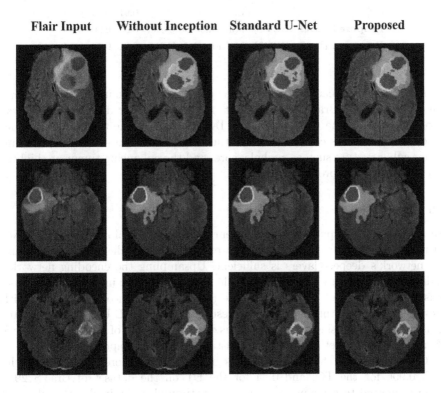

Fig. 5. Segmentation performance of Private dataset.

This study includes the comparison of our proposal with [24] which utilizes the hybrid framework, [25] implemented Filtered Output, and [26] employed Res U-Net. Moreover, our network is also compared with ensemble networks proposed by [23], and [12].

Table 3. Performance comparison with other existing approaches

Reference	Method	WT	TC	ET
[8]	DeepMedic + CRF	0.85	0.67	0.63
[24]	Guided attention	0.87	0.75	0.65
[22]	CNN	0.85	0.72	0.61
[23]	Deep learning	0.85	0.72	0.61
[24]	Filtered output	0.92	0.88	0.80
[25]	Res U-Net	0.92	0.89	0.75
[26]	Ensemble	0.93	0.87	0.79
[12]	Ensemble	0.91	0.83	0.79
Proposed (DATASET1)	Multi-module U-Net	0.95	0.90	0.84
Proposed (DATASET2)	Multi-module U-Net	0.91	0.84	0.77

All of these approaches, including the one we present (multi-module U-Net), are trained on the BraTS 2018 dataset. Additionally, our designed model was also evaluated on the private dataset. Table 3 displays the typical DSC rating for each strategy. As can be shown in the results, the dice values for the brain tumor sub-structure such as a whole, core, and the enhancing tumor are highest when we apply our proposed method.

3.5   Discussions

Among the several approaches to segmenting images of brain tumors, the U-Net structure stands out as a top choice. However, we do not believe that upsampling the network's deepest layers is sufficient. Upsampling the encoding network's high-resolution feature maps can provide enough semantic information to make sense of the data and also gives a more robust performance as compared with previous research in this study. We suggest multi-module 3D U-Net architectures as a means of addressing these issues; this design makes use of many U-Net blocks of varying sizes to better detain long-distance details of important features.

Our proposed architecture achieves improved dice scores of 0.953 for the WT, 0.906 for the TC, and 0.84 for the ET on the dataset of BraTS 2018 when compared to prior performance. This study also obtained little enhanced performance in terms of dice scores of 0.910, 0.845, and 0.779 for WT, TC, and ET, respectively for the private dataset. The improved performance is due to the up-sampling at various resolutions from the encoder network which can adequately retrieve features information at various levels sufficiently.

Unfortunately, our model produces segmentation results of less accuracy in TC and ET regions. We believe this problem is pervasive in nature owing to the class imbalance problem. Additionally, the enhancing region is not included in many LGG images, which lowers the optimization performance of the network. In the future attention must be paid to the class imbalance issue and improve the optimization quality of the algorithm by applying various augmentation techniques and evaluating the network for new and unseen images.

4   Conclusion

This research presents a new multi-module 3D U-Net model that is especially well-suited for segmenting medical images. The current study applied densely associated units in the proposed model to help with training parameter reduction and gradient flow efficiency. Likewise, dense connectivity eliminated extra information from the convolution layer by setting the growth rate to its minimum. That's why we handled the problem of excessively large learnable parameters. To learn from a variety of scales, the 3D U-Net made use of residual-inception blocks. We also presented two distinct down-inception and up-inception blocks in encoder-decoder paths. The 3D U-Ne efficacy was evaluated using the BraTS 2018 as well as private datasets. On the BraTS 2018 dataset, the suggested model had very good segmentation scores. Furthermore, using the private dataset, our proposed produced competitive segmentation scores. In the future, we plan to enhance the functionality of medical datasets by employing efficient postprocessing methods. Our research has led us to the conclusion that our designed method would also produce improved results on other medical image databases.

Acknowledgment. This study is partially supported by the National Key R&D Program of China with project no. 2020YFB2104402.

References

1. Qamar, S., Jin, H., Zheng, R., Ahmad, P.: 3D hyper-dense connected convolutional neural network for brain tumor segmentation. In: 2018 14th International Conference on Semantics, Knowledge and Grids (SKG), 12–14 September 2018, Guangzhou, China, pp. 123–130 (2018)
2. Sua, J.N., et al.: Incorporating convolutional neural networks and sequence graph transform for identifying multilabel protein Lysine PTM sites. Chemom. Intell. Lab. Syst. **206**(104171), 1–8 (2020)
3. Le, N.Q.K., Ho, Q.-T., Yapp, E.K.Y., Ou, Y.-Y., Yeh, H.-Y.: DeepETC: a deep convolutional neural network architecture for investigating and classifying electron transport chain's complexes. Neurocomputing **375**, 71–79 (2020)
4. Havaei, M., et al.: Brain tumor segmentation with deep neural networks. Med. Image Anal. **35**, 18–31 (2017)
5. Kamnitsas, K., et al.: Efficient multi-scale 3D CNN with fully connected CRF for accurate brain lesion segmentation. Med. Image Anal. **36**, 61–78 (2017)
6. Ronneberger, O., Fischer, P., Brox, T.: U-net: convolutional networks for biomedical image segmentation. In: Navab, N., Hornegger, J., Wells, W.M., Frangi, A.F. (eds.) MICCAI 2015. LNCS, vol. 9351, pp. 234–241. Springer, Cham (2015). https://doi.org/10.1007/978-3-319-24574-4_28
7. Isensee, F., Kickingereder, P., Wick, W., Bendszus, M., Maier-Hein, K.H.: Brain tumor segmentation and radiomics survival prediction: contribution to the BRATS 2017 challenge. In: Crimi, A., Bakas, S., Kuijf, H., Menze, B., Reyes, M. (eds.) BrainLes 2017. LNCS, vol. 10670, pp. 287–297. Springer, Cham (2018). https://doi.org/10.1007/978-3-319-75238-9_25

8. Khened, M., Kollerathu, V., Krishnamurthi, G.: Fully convolutional multi-scale residual DenseNets for cardiac segmentation and automated cardiac diagnosis using ensemble of classifiers. Med. Image Anal. **51**, 21–45 (2019)

9. Wang, W., Chen, C., Ding, M., Yu, H., Zha, S., Li, J.: TransBTS: multimodal brain tumor segmentation using transformer. In: de Bruijne, M., et al. (eds.) MICCAI 2021. LNCS, vol. 12901, pp. 109–119. Springer, Cham (2021). https://doi.org/10.1007/978-3-030-87193-2_11

10. Wang, G., Song, T., Dong, Q., Cui, M., Huang, N., Zhang, S.: Automatic ischemic stroke lesion segmentation from computed tomography perfusion images by image synthesis and attention-based deep neural networks. Med. Image Anal. **65**, 1–14 (2020)

11. Ghaffari, M., Sowmya, A., Oliver, R.: Automated brain tumour segmentation using cascaded 3D densely-connected U-net. In: Crimi, A., Bakas, S. (eds.) BrainLes 2020. LNCS, vol. 12658, pp. 481–491. Springer, Cham (2021). https://doi.org/10.1007/978-3-030-72084-1_43

12. Baid, U., Shah, N.A., Talbar, S.: Brain tumor segmentation with cascaded deep convolutional neural network. In: Crimi, A., Bakas, S. (eds.) BrainLes 2019. LNCS, vol. 11993, pp. 90–98. Springer, Cham (2020). https://doi.org/10.1007/978-3-030-46643-5_9

13. Vu, M.H., Nyholm, T., Löfstedt, T.: TuNet: end-to-end hierarchical brain tumor segmentation using cascaded networks. In: Crimi, A., Bakas, S. (eds.) BrainLes 2019. LNCS, vol. 11992, pp. 174–186. Springer, Cham (2020). https://doi.org/10.1007/978-3-030-46640-4_17

14. Kim, S., Luna, M., Chikontwe, P., Park, S.H.: Two-step U-nets for brain tumor segmentation and random forest with radiomics for survival time prediction. In: Crimi, A., Bakas, S. (eds.) BrainLes 2019. LNCS, vol. 11992, pp. 200–209. Springer, Cham (2020). https://doi.org/10.1007/978-3-030-46640-4_19

15. He, K., Zhang, X., Ren, S., Sun, J.: Deep residual learning for image recognition. In: Proceedings Of The IEEE Conference on Computer Vision and Pattern Recognition, Las Vegas, NV, USA, 27–30 June 2016, pp. 770–778 (2016)

16. Zhou, Z., Rahman Siddiquee, M.M., Tajbakhsh, N., Liang, J.: UNet++: a nested U-net architecture for medical image segmentation. In: Stoyanov, D., et al. (eds.) DLMIA/ML-CDS -2018. LNCS, vol. 11045, pp. 3–11. Springer, Cham (2018). https://doi.org/10.1007/978-3-030-00889-5_1

17. Szegedy, C., et al.: Going deeper with convolutions. In: Proceedings Of The IEEE Conference on Computer Vision and Pattern Recognition, Boston, MA, USA, 7–12 June 2015, pp. 1–9 (2015)

18. Szegedy, C., Ioffe, S., Vanhoucke, V., Alemi, A.: Inception-v4, inception-ResNet and the impact of residual connections on learning. In: Thirty-First AAAI Conference on Artificial Intelligence, San Francisco, California USA, 4–9 February 2017 (2017)

19. Kayalibay, B., Jensen, G., Smagt, P. CNN-based segmentation of medical imaging data. ArXiv Preprint ArXiv:1701.03056, pp. 1–24 (2017)

20. Chen, X., Liew, J., Xiong, W., Chui, C., Ong, S.: Focus, segment and erase: an efficient network for multi-label brain tumor segmentation. In: Proceedings of the European Conference on Computer Vision (ECCV), Munich Germany, 8–14 September 2018, pp. 654–669 (2018)

21. Zhao, X., Wu, Y., Song, G., Li, Z., Zhang, Y., Fan, Y.: A deep learning model integrating FCNNs and CRFs for brain tumor segmentation. Med. Image Anal. **43**, 98–111 (2018)

22. Zhou, C., Ding, C., Wang, X., Lu, Z., Tao, D.: One-pass multi-task networks with cross-task guided attention for brain tumor segmentation. IEEE Trans. Image Process. **29**, 4516–4529 (2020)
23. Fidon, L., Ourselin, S., Vercauteren, T.: Generalized wasserstein dice score, distributionally robust deep learning, and ranger for brain tumor segmentation: BraTS 2020 challenge. In: Crimi, A., Bakas, S. (eds.) BrainLes 2020. LNCS, vol. 12659, pp. 200–214. Springer, Cham (2021). https://doi.org/10.1007/978-3-030-72087-2_18
24. Zhao, Y.-X., Zhang, Y.-M., Liu, C.-L.: Bag of tricks for 3D MRI brain tumor segmentation. In: Crimi, A., Bakas, S. (eds.) BrainLes 2019. LNCS, vol. 11992, pp. 210–220. Springer, Cham (2020). https://doi.org/10.1007/978-3-030-46640-4_20
25. McKinley, R., Rebsamen, M., Meier, R., Wiest, R.: Triplanar ensemble of 3D-to-2D CNNs with label-uncertainty for brain tumor segmentation. In: Crimi, A., Bakas, S. (eds.) BrainLes 2019. LNCS, vol. 11992, pp. 379–387. Springer, Cham (2020). https://doi.org/10.1007/978-3-030-46640-4_36
26. Lachinov, D., Shipunova, E., Turlapov, V.: Knowledge distillation for brain tumor segmentation. In: Crimi, A., Bakas, S. (eds.) BrainLes 2019. LNCS, vol. 11993, pp. 324–332. Springer, Cham (2020). https://doi.org/10.1007/978-3-030-46643-5_32

A Better Linear Model Than Regression-Line for Data-Mining Applications

Sukhamay Kundu$^{(\boxtimes)}$

Computer Science Department, Louisiana State University,
Baton Rouge, LA 70803, USA
kundu@csc.lsu.edu

Abstract. The regression-line for a set of data-points $p_i = (x_i, y_i), 1 \leq i \leq N$ and $N > 2$, lacks the rotation-property in the sense that if each p_i is rotated by an angle θ around the origin then the regression-line does not rotate by the same angle θ except for the special case when all p_i's are collinear. This makes the regression-line unsuitable as a linear model of a set of data points for applications in data mining and machine learning. We present an alternative linear model that has the rotation property. In many ways, the new model is also more appealing intuitively as we show with examples. The computation of the new linear model takes the same $O(N)$ time as that for the regression-line.

Keywords: Perpendicular distance · Regression-line · Rotation property · Application to data mining

1 Introduction

For simplicity of exposition, we consider here only 2-dimensional data-points $p_i = (x_i, y_i)$. In many data mining and machine learning applications, one can partition a given set of data-points p_i into a small number of clusters, where each cluster has a simple structure. The simplest such structure is roughly a linear shape, i.e., where the points can be approximated closely by a straight line [2]. A key problem here is how to best approximate (or model) a set of data-points $S = \{p_i : 1 \leq i \leq N\}$, $N > 2$, by a straight line $L : y = mx + c$. We show that the commonly used regression-line (in short, RL) is not a suitable linear model for applications in machine learning and data mining, because it lacks the rotation-property in that if each p_i is rotated by an angle θ around the origin then the regression-line RL does not rotate by the same angle θ except for the very special case when all p_i's are collinear (and hence they all lie on the straight line RL). In data mining and machine learning, the clusters (and their shapes) should be independent of the orientation of the coordinates axes and depend only on the spatial relationship among the points themselves. We show that a variation of the RL based on the notion of perpendicular-distance of a

© The Author(s), under exclusive license to Springer Nature Singapore Pte Ltd. 2022
Y. Tan and Y. Shi (Eds.): DMBD 2022, CCIS 1745, pp. 70–79, 2022.
https://doi.org/10.1007/978-981-19-8991-9_6

point from a straight line gives a straight line L as a linear model of S which has the rotation-property and hence is a better linear model. More specifically, if q_i denotes the point on L such the line $p_i q_i$ is perpendicular to L (with $p_i = q_i$ if $p_i \in L$), then we define the average squared perpendicular-distance for S by $aspd(S, L) = (1/N) \sum_{i=1}^{N} ||p_i - q_i||^2$. We say L is an optimal perpendicular-distance line (in short, an $OPDL$) for S if it minimizes $aspd(S, L)$. We show that an $OPDL$ has the rotation-property.

For our purpose, we want the approximating line L to have the following two simple geometric properties in relation to the points S. The RL satisfies only the first property and an $OPDL$ satisfies both the properties.

- *Translation-invariance property*: If we translate each point $p_i = (x_i, y_i) \in S$ horizontally by a and vertically by b (in short, by (a, b)) to the point $\tau_{a,b}(p_i) = (x_i + a, y_i + b)$, which is equivalent to moving the origin $O = (0, 0)$ to $(-a, -b)$, then the approximating line for the points $S_{a,b} = \{\tau_{a,b}(p_i) : p_i \in S\}$ should be the corresponding translation of L, i.e., the line $\tau_{a,b}(L) : y - b = m(x - a) + c$. Note that $\tau_{a,b}(L)$ has the same slope m as L and goes through the point $\tau_{a,b}(0, c) = (a, c + b)$.
- *Rotation-invariance property*: If we rotate each point $p_i = (x_i, y_i) \in S$ by an angle θ around the origin $O = (0, 0)$ to the point $\rho_\theta(p_i)$, then the approximating line for the points $S_\theta = \{\rho_\theta(p_i) : p_i \in S\}$ should be the corresponding rotation of L around $(0,0)$ by the angle θ, i.e., the line $\rho_\theta(L) : y = m'x + c'$. where m' and c' are related to m and c as shown in Eqs. (1)–(2) below.

In what follows, we refer to both the angle $0 \leq \phi < \pi$ between $L : y = mx + c$ and the x-axis and $m = tan(\phi)$ as slope(L); this should not cause any confusion. Henceforth, we assume for simplifying the discussions that neither of L and L' is parallel to y-axis, unless specifically indicated otherwise.

$$m' = tan(\phi + \theta) = \frac{m + tan(\theta)}{1 - m.tan(\theta)} \tag{1}$$

$$c' = \frac{c.cos(\phi)}{cos(\phi + \theta)} = \frac{c\,sec(\theta)}{1 - m.tan(\theta)} \tag{2}$$

In Fig. 1, the points P' and Q' are obtained by rotating the points P and Q by the angle θ around the origin $O = (0, 0)$, and the point P'' is obtained by rotating P by the same angle θ around Q. If we write $x(P)$ for the x-coordinate of point P and similarly for the other points, then one can show $x(Q) - x(Q') = x(P'') - x(P)$ ($= h$ in Fig. 1) and similarly for the y-coordinates. For example, suppose θ_p, θ_q, and θ_{qp} are the slopes of the lines OP, OQ, and QP with x-axis and $d_p = \text{dist}(O, P)$, $d_q = \text{dist}(O, Q)$, and $d_{qp} = \text{dist}(Q, P)$ be the related distances. Then, $d_p cos(\theta_p) = d_q cos(\theta_q) + d_{qp} cos(\theta_{qp})$, both being equal to $x(P)$, and $d_p sin(\theta_p) = d_q sin(\theta_q) + d_{qp} sin(\theta_{qp})$, both being equal to $y(P)$. It follows that $x(Q) - x(Q') = d_q(cos(\theta_q) - cos(\theta_q + \theta)) = (d_q cos(\theta_q) + d_{qp} cos(\theta_{qp} + \theta)) - d_p cos(\theta_p + \theta) = x(P'') - x(P')$. This shows that a rotation by an angle θ around an arbitrary point $Q = (a, b)$ is equivalent to the rotation by the angle θ around the origin followed by the translation $\tau_{a-a',b-b'}$, where $(a', b') = \rho_\theta(Q)$. Note that $\tau_{a-a',b-b'}(\rho_\theta(Q)) = Q$. Thus, the translation-property and the rotation-property around origin together imply the rotation-property around an arbitrary point Q. Because both the RL and an $OPDL$ satisfy the translation-property (see Sect. 2 and Sect. 3), henceforth we will consider rotations only around the origin.

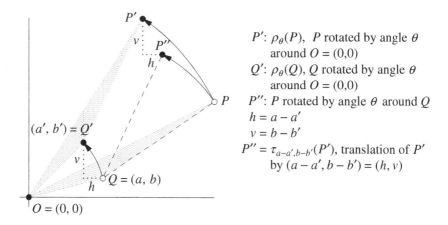

P': $\rho_\theta(P)$, P rotated by angle θ around $O = (0,0)$

Q': $\rho_\theta(Q)$, Q rotated by angle θ around $O = (0,0)$

P'': P rotated by angle θ around Q

$h = a - a'$

$v = b - b'$

$P'' = \tau_{a-a',b-b'}(P')$, translation of P' by $(a - a', b - b') = (h, v)$

Fig. 1. Relationship between the rotation about an arbitrary point Q by an angle θ and the rotation about the origin $O = (0, 0)$ by the same angle θ.

2   Translation-Invariance Property of an $OPDL$

Figure 2 shows a set of $N = 3$ points $S = \{p_1, p_2, p_3\}$ and the perpendicular projection q_i of each p_i onto a line L. It also shows the result of the horizontal translation $\tau_{a,0}: x \rightarrow x + a$ for some $a > 0$, with $p'_i = \tau_{a,0}(p_i)$, $q'_i = \tau_{a,0}(q_i)$, and $L' = \tau_{a,0}(L)$. Clearly, $||p_i - q_i|| = ||p'_i - q'_i||$ for each p_i and thus $aspd(S, L) = aspd(S', L')$, where $S' = \tau_{a,0}(S) = \{p'_i : p_i \in S\}$. In particular, L is an $OPDL$ for S if and only if L' is an $OPDL$ for S'. The same result hold if $a < 0$ and also for a vertical translation $\tau_{0,b}: y \rightarrow y + b$. Thus, $aspd(S, L) = aspd(S', L')$ for an arbitrary translation $\tau_{a,b}: (x, y) \rightarrow (x + a, y + b)$, which is a composition of $\tau_{a,0}$ and $\tau_{0,b}$. (In Sect. 3, we show that the translation-property also holds for the RL).

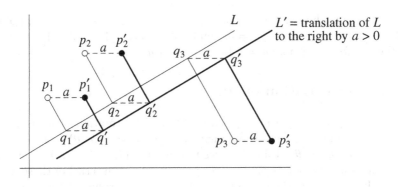

Fig. 2. Illustration of the invariance of perpendicular-distances and $aspd(S, L)$ under the translation $x \to x + \epsilon$.

We assume henceforth that the points $p_i = (x_i, y_i)$ have at least two distinct x_i's or two distinct y_i's, i.e., either the variance σ_x^2 of x_i's is > 0 or the variance σ_y^2 of y_i's is > 0. In particular, for regression-lines (RLs) we assume $\sigma_x^2 > 0$. We write $\bar{x}$, $\bar{y}$, and $\overline{xy}$ for the averages of x_i's, y_i's, and x_iy_i's, respectively.

3   Effect of Translation on *RL*

The regression-line $L : y = mx + c$ for the points $S = \{p_i : 1 \le i \le N\}$ is obtained by choosing m and c such that the average squared y-error $asye(S, L) = (1/N) \sum_1^N (y_i - mx_i - c)^2$ is minimized. The usual Eqs. (3)–(4) below are obtained by equating the partial derivatives of $asye(S, L)$ with respect to c and m to 0. Eq. (4) gives the slope m of *RL* in terms of the points S and then Eq. (3) gives the value of c in terms of the points in S. Eq. (3) also shows that *RL* goes through the centroid $(\bar{x}, \bar{y})$ of S. (If $\sigma_x^2 = 0$, i.e., all x_i are the same, in which case we also have $\overline{xy} = \bar{x}\,\bar{y}$, then the *RL* is considered undefined). If L is the *RL*, then we write $asye(S)$ or simply $asye$ for $asye(S, L)$ when S is clear from the context. It follows that $asye = (1/N) \sum [(y_i - \bar{y}) - m(x_i - \bar{x})]^2 = \sigma_y^2 + m^2\sigma_x^2 - 2m(\overline{xy} - \bar{x}\,\bar{y}) = \sigma_y^2 - m^2\sigma_x^2$, which gives us Eq. (5). Note that the righthand side of Eq. (5) is independent of m and c.

$$\bar{y} = m\bar{x} + c \tag{3}$$

$$\overline{xy} = m\bar{x}^2 + c\bar{x}, \text{ i.e., } \overline{xy} - \bar{x}\,\bar{y} = m\sigma_x^2 \tag{4}$$

$$asye = \sigma_y^2 - m(\overline{xy} - \bar{x}\,\bar{y}) = \sigma_y^2 - (\overline{xy} - \bar{x}\,\bar{y})^2/\sigma_x^2 \tag{5}$$

We show that Eqs. (3)–(4) imply the translation-property for *RL*. Let $\tau_{a,b}(p_i) = p_i' = (x_i', y_i') = (x_i + a, y_i + b)$. Then, $\bar{x}' = \bar{x} + a$, $\bar{y}' = \bar{y} + b$, $\overline{x'y'} - \bar{x}'\,\bar{y}' = \overline{xy} - \bar{x}\,\bar{y}$, $\sigma_{x'}^2 = \sigma_x^2$, and $\sigma_{y'}^2 = \sigma_y^2$. It follows that $\tau_{a,b}(L) = L' : y' = m'x' + c'$, with $m' = m$ and $c' = c + b - ma$, satisfies Eq. (3), i.e., $\bar{y}' = m'\bar{x}' + c'$; likewise, Eq. (4) also holds. This shows $\tau_{a,b}(L)$ is the *RL* for the points $\tau_{a,b}(S) = \{\tau_{a,b}(p_i) : p_i \in S\}$.

If all p_i are on a line $L_0 : y = m_0 x + c_0$, $-\infty < m_0 < +\infty$, then $\overline{y} = m_0 \overline{x} + c_0$ and $\overline{xy} - \overline{x}\,\overline{y} = m_0 \sigma_x^2$. Thus, $m = m_0$ and $c = c_0$ satisfy Eqs. (3)–(4) and hence L_0 is the RL for S, with $asye = 0$ because each $y_i - mx_i - c = 0$.

4   Effect of Rotation on RL

Let $\rho_\theta(p_i) = p_i' = (u_i,\ v_i)$ be the point obtained by rotation of $p_i = (x_i,\ y_i)$ around the origin $O = (0,\ 0)$ by an angle θ. Then, $u_i = x_i cos(\theta) - y_i sin(\theta)$ and $v_i = x_i sin(\theta) + y_i cos(\theta)$. Table 1 shows the relationship of the various averages and variances for the points $S_\theta = \rho_\theta(S) = \{p_i' : p_i \in S\}$ in terms of those for the points S. In particular, the centroid $(\overline{u}, \overline{v})$ of S_θ is the result of the rotation of the centroid $(\overline{x}, \overline{y})$ of S. The equations in Table 1 and Eqs. (3)–(5) above hold in the more general case when each p_i has associated with it a positive probability and the probability of p_i' is the same as that of p_i.

Table 1. The averages, variances, etc. for the points (u_i, v_i) obtained by rotation of points (x_i, y_i) by an angle θ.

$$\overline{u} = \overline{x}\,cos(\theta) - \overline{y}\,sin(\theta)$$
$$\overline{u^2} = \overline{x^2}\,cos^2(\theta) + \overline{y^2}\,sin^2(\theta) - 2\overline{xy}\,sin(\theta)cos(\theta)$$
$$\overline{v} = \overline{x}\,sin(\theta) + \overline{y}\,cos(\theta)$$
$$\overline{v^2} = \overline{x^2}\,sin^2(\theta) + \overline{y^2}\,cos^2(\theta) + 2\overline{xy}\,sin(\theta)cos(\theta)$$
$$\overline{u}\,\overline{v} = (\overline{x}^2 - \overline{y}^2)sin(\theta)cos(\theta) + \overline{x}\,\overline{y}\,cos(2\theta)$$
$$\overline{uv} = (\overline{x^2} - \overline{y^2})sin(\theta)cos(\theta) + \overline{xy}\,cos(2\theta)$$
$$\overline{uv} - \overline{u}\,\overline{v} = (\sigma_x^2 - \sigma_y^2)sin(\theta)cos(\theta) + (\overline{xy} - \overline{x}\,\overline{y})cos(2\theta)$$
$$\sigma_u^2 = \sigma_x^2\,cos^2(\theta) + \sigma_y^2\,sin^2(\theta) - (\overline{xy} - \overline{x}\,\overline{y})sin(2\theta)$$
$$\sigma_v^2 = \sigma_x^2\,sin^2(\theta) + \sigma_y^2\,cos^2(\theta) + (\overline{xy} - \overline{x}\,\overline{y})sin(2\theta)$$

From Eq. (4) and Table 1, we get the slope of the regression-line $L' : v = m'u + c'$ for S_θ is given by

$$m' = \frac{\overline{uv} - \overline{u}\,\overline{v}}{\sigma_u^2} = \frac{(\sigma_x^2 - \sigma_y^2)\,sin(\theta)cos(\theta) + (\overline{xy} - \overline{x}\,\overline{y})\,cos(2\theta)}{\sigma_x^2\,cos^2(\theta) + \sigma_y^2\,sin^2(\theta) - (\overline{xy} - \overline{x}\,\overline{y})\,sin(2\theta)}. \tag{6}$$

On the other hand, if the rotation of the points p_i to p_i' would cause a corresponding rotation of the regression-line $L : y = mx + c$, then from Eqs. (1) and (4) we would have,

$$m' = \frac{m + tan(\theta)}{1 - m.tan(\theta} = \frac{(\overline{xy} - \overline{x}\,\overline{y})cos(\theta) + \sigma_x^2\,sin(\theta)}{\sigma_x^2\,cos(\theta) - (\overline{xy} - \overline{x}\,\overline{y})sin(\theta)} \tag{7}$$

Lemma 1. *For the special case of $\theta = \pi$, the rotation of the points $p_i \in S$ by the angle π around the origin makes the regression-line RL also rotate by the angle π. Moreover, the asye remains unchanged.*

Proof. From Table 1, we have $\overline{u} = -\overline{x}$, $\overline{v} = -\overline{y}$, $\sigma_u^2 = \sigma_x^2$, $\sigma_v^2 = \sigma_y^2$ and $\overline{uv} - \overline{u}\,\overline{v} = \overline{xy} - \overline{x}\,\overline{y}$. Let $L : y = mx + c$ be the RL for the points S and $L' : v = m'u + c'$ be the RL for the points S_π. From Eqs. (1)–(2), we get the rotation of L by π gives the line $\rho_\pi(L) : y = mx - c$. From Eq. (3), we have $\overline{y} = m\overline{x} + c$, i.e. $\overline{v} = m\overline{u} - c$. and from Eq. (4), we have $m = (\overline{xy} - \overline{x}\,\overline{y})/\sigma_x^2 = (\overline{uv} - \overline{u}\,\overline{v})/\sigma_v^2 = m'$. This shows $L' : v = mu - c$ (with $c' = -c$) and this proves that RL is rotated by π around the origin as we rotate the points in S by π around the origin. That *asye* remains unchanged follows from Eq. (5) and the fact that $\sigma_y^2 - (\overline{xy} - \overline{x}\,\overline{y})^2/\sigma_x^2 = \sigma_v^2 - (\overline{uv} - \overline{u}\,\overline{v})^2/\sigma_u^2$.

Recall that $-\infty < m < +\infty$ and $\sigma_x > 0$. In what follows, we only consider $-\pi/2 < \theta < \pi/2$ and $\theta \neq 0$.

Theorem 1. *The regression-line for the points $S = \{p_i : 1 \leq i \leq N\}$ has the rotation-property if and only if p_i's are collinear. In that case, the regression-line equals the optimal perpendicular-distance line.*

Proof. Let L be the regression-line for S. First, we prove the "if" part. Assume that p_i's are collinear with the line $L_0 : y = m_0 x + c_0$, Then, $L = L_0$ and the points $p_i' = \rho_\theta(p_i)$ are collinear with line $\rho_\theta(L_0) = L_0' : y = m_0'x + c_0'$ obtained by rotation of L_0 by θ. Thus, the regression-line for p_i''s trivially rotates by θ. (Here, $\sigma_y^2 = m_0^2\sigma_x^2$ and $\overline{xy} - \overline{x}\,\overline{y} = m_0\sigma_x^2$ and thus the righthand side of Eq. (6) equals $(cos(\theta) - m_0 sin(\theta))(m_0 cos(\theta) + sin(\theta))/(cos(\theta) - m_0 sin(\theta))^2 = (m_0 + tan(\theta))/(1 - m_0 tan(\theta)) = m_0'$ as per Eq. (1)).

To prove the "only if" part, let m and m' be respectively the slopes of regression-line L for the points p_i and of regression-line $\rho_\theta(L) = L'$ for the points $p_i' = (u_i, v_i)$. Because the rotation of points p_i by the angle θ causes their centroid $(\overline{x}, \overline{y})$ also to rotate by θ to the centroid $(\overline{u}, \overline{v})$ of p_i''s and L and L' go through the corresponding centroids $(\overline{x}, \overline{y})$ and $(\overline{u}, \overline{v})$, the rotation-property of regression-line is equivalent to saying that the right hand sides of Eqs. (6) and (7) are the same when $1 - m.tan(\theta) \neq 0$. This gives after simplification $(\overline{xy} - \overline{x}\,\overline{y})^2 sin(\theta) = \sigma_x^2\sigma_y^2 sin(\theta)$ and hence $(\overline{xy} - \overline{x}\,\overline{y})^2 = \sigma_x^2\sigma_y^2$. This gives, by Eq. (5), *asye* $= 0$ and hence the points p_i are collinear with the regressions-line.

Equation (6) gives the following lemma and is illustrated in Example 1.

Lemma 2. *If $\sigma_x^2 = \sigma_y^2 = \sigma^2$ and $\overline{xy} = \overline{x}\,\overline{y}$, then $\sigma_u^2 = \sigma_v^2 = \sigma^2$ and $\overline{uv} = \overline{u}\,\overline{v}$. In particular, the regression-line does not rotate due to the rotation of the points and its slope remains 0.*

Example 1. Consider the points $S_{ET} = \{(0,0), (2,0), (1, \sqrt{3})\}$, consisting of the vertices of an equilateral triangle shown in Fig. 3(i), which also shows the various averages, variances, etc. and the regression-line. Figure 3(ii) shows the vertices of the same triangle after rotation by $\theta = \pi/6$ around the origin $O = (0,0)$ and the corresponding averages, variances, etc. and the associated regression-line. Here, the regression-line does not rotate along with the points S_{ET} because $\sigma_x^2 = \sigma_y^2$ and $\overline{xy} = \overline{x}\,\overline{y}$ (cf. Lemma 2). A similar situation arises for the points $S_{SQ} = \{(1,1), (-1,1), (-1,-1), (1,-1)\}$, the vertices of a square with sides of length 2 and parallel to the xy-axes. Here also we have $\sigma_x^2 = 1 = \sigma_y^2$ and $\overline{xy} = 0 = \overline{x}\,\overline{y}$, and the regression-line does not rotate if we rotate the points.

5   Effect of Rotation on an *OPDL*

We first derive the conditions for a line $L : y = mx + c$ to minimize the sum of perpendicular-distance squares $aspd(S, L)$ for a given set of points $S = \{p_i : 1 \le i \le N\}, N \ge 2$. We denote the minimum sum by $aspd(S)$ or simply by $aspd$ when S clear from the context.

5.1   Minimizing *aspd* When $m \ne \pm\infty$

Figure 4 shows the perpendicular-distance p of a point (x_0, y_0) from the line L. We take $p = x_0$ if L is the y-axis (with $m = \pm\infty$) and, more generally, $p = |x_0 - x_0'|$ if $L : x = x_0'$. Otherwise, $aspd(S, L) = f(m, c) = \frac{1}{N(1+m^2)} \sum_{i=1}^{N}(y_i - mx_i - c)^2$ and we want to minimize $f(m, c)$.

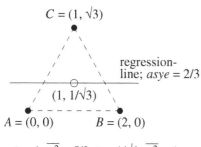

$C = (1, \sqrt{3})$

regression-line; *asye* = 2/3

$(1, 1/\sqrt{3})$

$A = (0, 0)$ $B = (2, 0)$

$\bar{x} = 1, \overline{x^2} = 5/3, \bar{y} = 1/\sqrt{3}, \overline{y^2} = 1,$
$\sigma_x^2 = 2/3 = \sigma_y^2, \overline{xy} = 1/\sqrt{3} = \bar{x}\bar{y}$

(i) The various averages, variances, etc. and the regression-line; the open circle is the centroid $(1, 1/\sqrt{3})$.

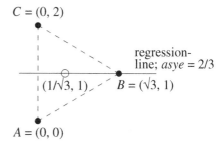

$C = (0, 2)$

regression-line; *asye* = 2/3

$(1/\sqrt{3}, 1)$ $B = (\sqrt{3}, 1)$

$A = (0, 0)$

$\bar{u} = 1/\sqrt{3}, \overline{u^2} = 1, \bar{v} = 1, \overline{v^2} = 5/3,$
$\sigma_u^2 = 2/3 = \sigma_v^2, \overline{uv} = 1/\sqrt{3} = \bar{u}\bar{v}$

(ii) The various averages, variances, etc. and the regression-line after rotating the points in (i) by $\theta = \pi/6$ around $(0, 0)$.

Fig. 3. Illustration of Lemma 2 for the points S_{ET} shown as solid circles, which form the vertices of an equilateral triangle.

Assume for the moment $-\infty < m < +\infty$. Equating the partial derivative $\partial f(m, c)/\partial c$ to 0, we get $\sum(y_i - mx_i - c) = 0$, which simplifies to Eq. (8) below (which is the same as Eq. (3)). It shows that an optimal perpendicular-distance line goes through the centroid $(\bar{x}, \bar{y})$ of the points $p_i = (x_i, y_i) \in S$, as is the case for the regression-line. Now, eliminating $c = \bar{y} - m\bar{x}$ in $f(m, c)$ we get $f(m) = \frac{1}{N(1+m^2)} \sum((y_i - \bar{y}) - m(x_i - \bar{x}))^2 = \frac{1}{1+m^2}[\sigma_y^2 + m^2\sigma_x^2 - 2m(\overline{xy} - \bar{x}\,\bar{y})]$. Equating the partial derivative $\partial f(m)/\partial m$ to 0, we get $(1 + m^2)[m\sigma_x^2 - (\overline{xy} - $

$\overline{x}\,\overline{y})] - m[\sigma_y^2 + m^2\sigma_x^2 - 2m(\overline{xy} - \overline{x}\,\overline{y})] = 0$, which simplifies to Eq. (9). This is the same equation we get when we equate $\partial f(m,c)/\partial m$ to 0 and then substitute $c = \overline{y} - m\overline{x}$.

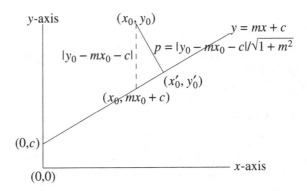

Fig. 4. Illustration of perpendicular distance.

For a vertical line $L : x = x_0'$, $aspd(S, L) = \sum(x_i - x_0')^2$ and this is minimized when $x_0' = \overline{x}$, with the minimum value $aspd = \sigma_x^2$. (For $m = \pm\infty$, we take $m/(1 + m^2) = 0 = 1/(1 + m^2)$ and $m^2/(1 + m^2) = 1$ and this gives $f(m) = \sigma_x^2$ as above).

$$\overline{y} = m\overline{x} + c \tag{8}$$

$$m(\sigma_x^2 - \sigma_y^2) + (m^2 - 1)(\overline{xy} - \overline{x}\,\overline{y}) = 0 \tag{9}$$

Theorem 2. *For a set S of N points, the computation of m and c from Eqs. (8)–(9) for an $OPDL$ takes $O(N)$ time, which is the same as that for the computation of m and c from Eqs. (3)–(4) for the regression line RL.*

Proof. This is immediate from Eqs. (8)–(9) because the computation of each of $\overline{xy}, \overline{x}, \sigma_x^2$, etc. takes $O(N)$ time [1]. Note that in the case of $\overline{xy} = \overline{x}\,\overline{y}$ and $\sigma_x^2 = \sigma_y^2$, m is not unique.

Theorem 3. *Let $S' : \{(u_i, v_i) : 1 \le i \le N\}$ be the points obtained by rotating the points $S = \{(x_i, y_i) : 1 \le i \le N\}$ ($N \ge 2$) by the angle θ around the origin $O = (0, 0)$. Also, let $L' : y = m'x + c'$ be the line obtained by rotating the line $L : y = mx + c$ by the angle θ around the origin O. Then, L' minimizes $aspd(S', L')$ if and only if L minimizes $aspd(S, L)$.*

Proof. From Eq. (1), after converting m' and $(m')^2 - 1$ to a form with a common denominator, we get

$$m' = \frac{m.cos(\theta) + sin(\theta)}{cos(\theta) - m.sin(\theta)} = \frac{m.cos(2\theta) - (m^2 - 1)\frac{sin(2\theta)}{2}}{(cos(\theta) - m.sin(\theta))^2} \tag{10}$$

$$(m')^2 - 1 = \frac{(m^2 - 1)cos(2\theta) + 2m.sin(2\theta)}{(cos(\theta) - m.sin(\theta))^2} \tag{11}$$

Substituting these values and the values for $\sigma_u^2 - \sigma_v^2$ and $\overline{uv} - \overline{u}.\overline{v}$ from Table 1 into the left side of Eq. (9) for L', we get

$$
\begin{aligned}
&m'(\sigma_u^2 - \sigma_v^2) + ((m')^2 - 1)(\overline{uv} - \overline{u}.\overline{v}) \\
&= m'[(\sigma_x^2 - \sigma_y^2)cos(2\theta) - 2(\overline{xy} - \overline{x}\,\overline{y})sin(2\theta)] + ((m')^2 - 1)[(\sigma_x^2 - \sigma_y^2)\frac{sin(2\theta)}{2} \\
&\quad + (\overline{xy} - \overline{x}\,\overline{y})cos(2\theta)] \\
&= m(\sigma_x^2 - \sigma_y^2) + (m^2 - 1)(\overline{xy} - \overline{x}\,\overline{y})
\end{aligned}
$$

and this immediately proves the theorem.

Substituting $m^2\sigma_x^2 = m^2\sigma_y^2 + (m - m^3)(\overline{xy} - \overline{x}\,\overline{y})$ from Eq. (9) into $f(m)$, we get the following lemma, which shows that the *aspd* for an *OPDL* has the same form as the *asye* for *RL*, except that the slope m for an *OPDL* can be different from the slope m of *RL*.

Lemma 3. *For an OPDL, aspd $= \sigma_y^2 - m(\overline{xy} - \overline{x}\,\overline{y})$, where $m = slope(OPDL)$ is given by Eq. (9).*

Example 2. For the points S_{ET} in Example 1, each of the points A, B, and C is at a distance $d = 2/\sqrt{3}$ from the centroid. It is easy to see that for an arbitrary line L through the centroid and slope$(L) = \theta$, we have $aspd(S_{ET}, L) = d^2[sin^2(\pi/6 - \theta) + sin^2(\pi/6 + \theta) + cos^2(\theta)] = 2$ because $sin(\pi/6 - \theta) = (1/2)cos(\theta) - (\sqrt{3}/2)sin(\theta)$, etc. Thus, any line going through the centroid is an *OPDL*. Eq. (9) is trivially satisfied here because $\sigma_x^2 - \sigma_y^2 = 0 = \overline{xy} - \overline{x}\,\overline{y}$.

Example 3. Consider the points $S_{RIT} = \{(0,0), (3,0), (3,3)\}$, the vertices of a right-angled isosceles triangle as shown in Fig. 5(i). We have $\overline{x} = 2$, $\overline{x^2} = 6$, $\sigma_x^2 = 2$, $\overline{y} = 1$, $\overline{y^2} = 3$, $\sigma_y^2 = 2$, and $\overline{xy} = 3$. For *OPDL*, this means $c = \overline{y} - m\overline{x} = 1 - 2m$, where m minimizes $f(m) = (\sigma_y^2 + m^2\sigma_x^2 - 2m(\overline{xy} - \overline{x}\,\overline{y}))/(1 + m^2) = (2 + 2m^2 - 2m)/(1 + m^2) = 2(1 - m/(1 + m^2))$. This happens at $m = 1$ and the optimal perpendicular-distance line PL going through $(\overline{x}, \overline{y})$ with $m = 1$ is shown as a thick line. The regression-line RL going through $(\overline{x}, \overline{y})$ with $m = 1/2$ is shown as a thin line in Fig. 5(i). The regression-line has $asye = 3/2$ and $aspd(RL) = 9/8 > 1 = aspd(PL)$. Figure 5(ii) shows the corresponding results for the points $\{(0,0), (3/\sqrt{2}, 3/\sqrt{2}), (0, 3\sqrt{2})\}$ obtained by rotating those in Fig. 5(i) by $\theta = \pi/4$ around $(0, 0)$. We have now $\overline{x} = 1/\sqrt{2}, \overline{x^2} = 3/2$, $\sigma_x^2 = 1$, $\overline{y} = 3/\sqrt{2}$, $\overline{y^2} = 15/2$, $\sigma_y^2 = 3$, and $\overline{xy} = 3/2$. This means $c = \overline{y} - m\overline{x} = (3 - 1m)/\sqrt{2}$, where m minimizes $f(m) = (\sigma_y^2 + m^2\sigma_x^2 - 2m(\overline{xy} - \overline{x}\,\overline{y}))/(1 + m^2) = (3 + m^2)/(1 + m^2) = 1 + 2/(1 + m^2)$. This happens at $m = \infty$ and the optimal perpendicular-distance line PL going through $(\overline{x}, \overline{y})$ with $m = \infty$ is shown as a thick line. Here, $aspd(PL) = 1$ as before and is $< 3 = aspd(RL)$.

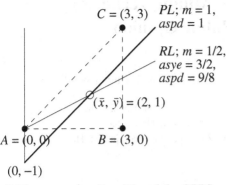

(i) The regression-line *RL* and the OPDL *PL* for the points given by the vertices of a right-angled isosceles triangle.

(ii) The regression-line *RL* and the OPDL *PL* for points obtained by rotating those in (i) by $\theta = \pi/4$ around (0, 0).

Fig. 5. Illustration of the rotation-property of the optimal perpendicular-distance line *PL*; here, the regression-line *RL* rotates in the opposite direction.

6   Conclusion

We have shown here that an optimal perpendicular-distance based regression-line (*OPDL*) has the important rotational-invariance property for data-mining applications that the usual regression-line does not. We have also given detailed techniques to find an *OPDL* and given the characterization of the case when the usual regression-line has the rotational-invariance property.

References

1. Garey, M.R., Johnson, D.S.: Computers and Intractability: A Guide to the Theory of NP-Completeness. W.H.Freeman & Co. (1979)
2. Tan, P.-N., Steinbach, M., Karpatne, A., Kumar, V.: Introduction to Data Mining. Addison-Wesley, Boston (2018)
3. Abott, D.: Applied Predictive Analysis. Wiley, Hoboken (2014)

Research on Hot Spot Mining Technology
for Network Public Opinion

Chengxin Xie[1], Yuxuan Han[1], Yingxue Mu[1(✉)], and Xiumei Wen[1,2(✉)]

[1] Hebei University of Architecture, Zhangjiakou, Hebei, China
526110454@qq.com, xiumeiwen@163.com
[2] Big Data Technology Innovation Center of Zhangjiakou, Zhangjiakou, Hebei, China

Abstract. The research on network public opinion has attracted more and more attention. To accurately find the hot spots in online public opinion data and analyze their heat, this paper studies the hot spot mining work of Weibo public opinion data. Considering the defects of the traditional K-means++ clustering algorithm in the initial point optimization, the Word2Vec model proposes a hot spot discovery improvement algorithm for the network public opinion data WPK-means++ (Word to vector Penalty factor K-means++). The algorithm introduces the penalty factor to make up for the problem that K-means++ is applied to the scattered text data of hot topics that are affected by outlier points, reduces the invalid coverage of the initial clustering center of the text clustering algorithm, and verifies the accuracy and efficiency of the final clustering results through the analysis of comparative experiments. The original dataset is preprocessed using Chinese word segmentation and removal of stopping words, and the text modeling of the preprocessed result set is carried out by a word embedding model. Finally, the Weibo public opinion data set was used as the corpus.

Keywords: Weibo public opinion dataset · Hot spot · WPK-means++ · Penalty factor · Clustering

1 Introduction

According to the Statistical Report on the Development of China's Internet in China, the number of Internet users reached 1.032 billion in December 2021. The real-time and high efficiency of the Internet is also not limited by distance, regional culture, and time. With the expansion of the network scale, the influence and importance of the network public opinion also continue to expand.

Nowadays, online public opinion has become an important form of social public opinion. It is characterized by the participation of the whole people and the rapid formation of hot spots, which can quickly gather massive public opinion data with real-time value and generate huge public opinion pressure. Therefore, the hot spot mining for network public opinion has become an indispensable preliminary work for the follow-up public opinion monitoring and monitoring work. The research on network public opinion in the information age has attracted more and more attention. To accurately find hotspots

© The Author(s), under exclusive license to Springer Nature Singapore Pte Ltd. 2022
Y. Tan and Y. Shi (Eds.): DMBD 2022, CCIS 1745, pp. 80–90, 2022.
https://doi.org/10.1007/978-981-19-8991-9_7

in the massive network public opinion data and analyze their popularity, this paper studies the hotspot mining of Weibo public opinion data. Weibo, the largest Internet platform in China, is full of various public opinion data. This paper conducts hot spot mining of Weibo public opinion data. This paper just takes Weibo data as an example to verify our work. An interactive platform like Weibo is essentially a real-time incremental data streaming platform. To realize the tracking and detection of hotspot information, it is necessary to realize real-time clustering. Weibo is an emerging social platform in recent years. Compared with traditional social platforms, it has higher timeliness. The hot spot discovery of Weibo text is naturally different from traditional news, it has many unique text characteristics. But not limited to Weibo, other platforms are also possible.

In this paper, the related technologies and related theoretical knowledge of text clustering technology are studied, combined with the Word2Vec word embedding model, aiming at the defects of the traditional K-means++ clustering algorithm in the initial point optimization, an improved algorithm WPK-means++ is proposed for the hot spot detection of network public opinion data. The algorithm introduces a penalty factor to make up for the problem that K-means++ applied to short text data with scattered hot words will be affected by outliers, and reduce the invalid coverage of the initial clustering center of the text clustering algorithm. This paper also verifies the superiority of the performance of the algorithm through the analysis of comparative experiments. On this basis, this paper designs the overall architecture of the hotspot discovery and tracking model. The design ideas and architecture diagrams are expounded, and the experimental analysis is carried out with the Weibo public opinion dataset as the corpus.

2 Related Work

The research on hotspot mining of network public opinion data is comprehensive research involving a variety of technologies. It includes preprocessing technology, natural language processing technology, text feature extraction, weight calculation, keyword extraction, text summarization, text vectorized representation, and data mining technology, etc. The rational use of this technology largely determines the efficiency and accuracy of data processing. The hot spot discovery for online public opinion is centered on text clustering technology. The current research status on the K-means algorithm can be divided into start optimization, algorithm combination, parameter adjustment, and other aspects.

Kolose [1] derived clustering features by the two-step method and combined clustering of K-means, and Solli, Bazin [2] used the VGG16 + K-means binding method to find high-purity clusters of proton events for real experimental data, and explored the application of clustering the potential space of the autoencoder neural network for the event separation. Chandel, Hot [3], et al. used k-mean classification spectral angle mapping to improve orchard block-scale mapping of RGB injective mosaic layers. Aoyama, [4], et al., designed sparse K-means clustering using algorithms with different representations. Amanowicz Marek [5], and others combined the K-means clustering algorithm and the hierarchical clustering algorithm for feature selection by applying the genetic algorithm method to obtain the best features. Alsuhaim, Azmi [6], et al., used an enhanced K-means clustering algorithm that uses the distances calculated from previous iterations to minimize the number of distance calculations. A K-means clustering algorithm for the latent Dirichlet assignment topic modeling approach was proposed by Alharbi, Hijji [7], et al.

Generally, although the technology applied to text mining has high maturity at home and abroad, and there are many related research papers, there is relatively little research on applying text mining technology to the early hot mining of public opinion data, especially for the public opinion hot mining of Chinese data sets. In the foreign language literature, Zhang, Liu [8], et al., proposed a modified K-means algorithm that slightly improves the F value of the clustering results for the comment text data of novel networks. Zhang, Lu [9], et al., proposed a text content similarity query algorithm and proposed a set of detection methods based on current network events, which can be applied to network events to reveal their evolution trends well.

3 Methodology

The purpose of hot spot discovery research of text information is to obtain the most important topics from massive data information. The core algorithm of the hot spot discovery model is to realize text clustering. This paper presents the WPK-means++ text clustering algorithm, combined with the Word2Vec model, and performs initial point optimization, introducing the penalty factor. The algorithm is suitable for massive sparse text data processing and can reduce the influence of outliers on the clustering effect. To realize the real-time clustering detection of hot spot information, this paper combines the WPK-means++ algorithm with the incremental Single-Pass algorithm to construct a text clustering model. The specific process shown in Fig. 1 mainly includes the following processes:

Step 1: Preprocess the experimental data set, including Chinese word segmentation and removal of stop words, where the stop word list is updated according to the characteristics of the data set. The above processing results are stored on the ground.

Step 2: Do Word2Vec modeling. The preprocessed data set is directly represented by the Word2Vec word embedding model for data vectorization, the input parameters involved in the model are given, and the modeling results are stored.

Step 3: Carry out the experimental design of the improved clustering algorithm proposed WPK-means++ algorithm, and verify the effectiveness and feasibility of the improved algorithm in text clustering research. First, compare the experimental data sets with the proposed algorithm. The improved algorithm and the K-means++ algorithm optimized by the initial point and the Word2Vec model combined with the K-means++ algorithm are compared with each other, and the precision, recall, and F1 value of the three algorithms are calculated, and the changes in the experimental results are given. Curve comparison chart.

Step 4: Apply the improved clustering algorithm proposed in the WPK-means++ algorithm to the hot spot discovery of the Weibo public opinion dataset, design experiments according to the model structure and algorithm flow, and give the results of the hot spot discovery experiment.

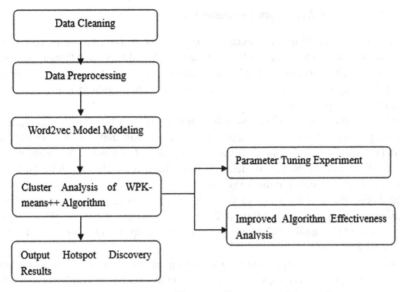

Fig. 1. Design diagram of hot spot discovery model experiment

3.1 Word2Vec

The process of the Word2Vec model can be simply summarized as one-hot encoding as input, adjusting the model parameters through neural network backpropagation, and then adjusting the form of one-hot encoding, adding adjacent word relationships to it, and obtaining a new vector representation through model training. The whole process can be seen as further optimization of one-hot encoding. Its specific implementation is divided into two training models: CBOW and Skip-gram.

3.2 Single-Pass Algorithm

This study uses the Single-Pass algorithm for the hotspot tracking phase. The algorithm abandons the traditional iterative method and adopts the mode of sequential processing of real-time samples to realize single processing of data. It requires the dataset to have a certain order. For the current samples to be processed, the classification is processed according to the algorithm judgment conditions. There is no need to iterate all samples, the simple thinking process is efficient, and the need to present a parameter to judge the conditions generated by the new category, and not the number of categories.

The proposed algorithm can be well used in both topic tracking and social media fields, especially for streaming short text data such as Weibo data. Its efficient characteristics make it well cope with the requirements of real-time data processing. The algorithm process can be simply described as the following: the similarity calculation of the current coming sample data, and the similarity calculation between texts can use the cosine distance or mutual information, and it can also use a similar Word2Vec model for vector representation. If the bar sample is sufficiently similar to the currently existing class cluster, it is placed into the class, otherwise, create a new category for it.

3.3 WPK-Means++ Algorithm Implementation

According to the algorithm introduced in the previous section, the core algorithm of the hotspot discovery model is the WPK-means++ (Word to vector Penalty factor K-means++) clustering algorithm. The WPK-means++ algorithm takes the preprocessing result set $D = \{x_1\ x_2, \ldots\ldots, x_m\}$, number of clusters k, and threshold λ as input.

The specific steps are as follows:

Step 1: Conduct the Word2Vec modeling of the result set $D = \{x_1, x_2, \ldots, x_m\}$.

See the previous section for the specific parameter setting, and store the model results as the dataset W. Extract any point from D, noted as μ 1; for any other point x in the sample set D, select the minimum distance from the nearest cluster center (selected), And all distances and saved in the array Sum (x).

Step 2: For any x, if the value of W (x) is greater than λ, the larger point of W(x) is given a higher selected probability. If W (x) is less than λ, the larger W (x) is given a higher selected probability of the points, and the corresponding sample point x is the selected probability p.

Step 3: Use the weighted probability distribution, and randomly select the new central points. Repeat steps 2–5 and stops the iteration after the termination condition is satisfied. Output result noted as $\{\mu_1, \mu_2, \ldots, \mu_k\}$.

Step 4: Calculate the distance between the remaining point x_i (i = 1,2,... m) and the current center point μ_j (j = 1,2,... k), Attach x_i to the smallest corresponding category, with the category number of λ_i, and update the class cluster set.

Step 5: Update the cluster center of each class cluster, If the cluster center stabilizes, perform step (5), otherwise, iterate the step above (3).

4 Experimental Setup

In this section, to verify the improvement effect of the algorithm, the following comparison experiment is designed: first, the WPK-means++ algorithm, K-means++ algorithm, Word2Vec model, and K-means++ combination algorithm of these three algorithms on the same area label experimental dataset for cluster experiment analysis, select accuracy, recall, F1 value as the evaluation indicators of the comparison experiment, give the display and analysis of the comparison experiment results.

4.1 Dataset

In this experiment, the 541.1 MB-sized Weibo data were used as the original dataset, The dataset includes 249,911 pieces of Weibo short text data, involving politics, military, science and technology, sports, finance and business, medicine and health, social life, and other seven aspects. Each piece of data includes information about id, content, picture_list, category, dateline, Comment, Repost, likes, new_label, fake_label, comment, comment_all, etc.

4.2 Data Pre-processing

Weibo has a new social platform recently. Compared with traditional social platforms, they have higher timeliness. The hot discovery of micro-blog text is naturally different from traditional news. It has the characteristics of non-standard text content and fast semantic update, which increases the difficulty in subsequent text word segmentation processing. This paper analyzes the characteristics of the text and describes the data preprocessing method of the text.

This paper firstly analyzes the characteristics of the Weibo public opinion dataset and extracts the content in the <context> tag as the main body of data mining. Then, the word segmentation selects the stuttering word segmentation, uses the default mode in it to process, and manually adds the network of new words with special meanings to the word segmentation dictionary. The tokenizer contains three modes, of which the default mode is more balanced. This mode can effectively eliminate ambiguity and obtain the most reasonable word segmentation results. In addition, this paper combines common stopwords such as cn_stopwords.txt, sc_stopwords.txt, hgb_stopwords.txt, baidu_stopwords.txt, etc., adds and deletes them appropriately, and adds meaningless new words and words that repeat more words that affect the results of subsequent analysis. The stop word list Chinesestopword.txt is sorted out in line with Weibo text, containing a total of 2429 stop words. In this paper, Chinesestopword.txt is used as the stop word list to filter the stop words, which can more effectively clean out the words that affect the text analysis. Finally, save the preprocessing result set.

4.3 Text Representation

The text representation adopts the Word2Vec model. The specific process of the experiment is as follows:

Step 1: Traverse the text information in the preprocessing result set, and count the word frequency to build a dictionary.

Step 2: Generate a Huffman tree structure.

Step 3: Generate the one-hot binary encoding of the current node as the input word vector.

Step 4: Initialize the intermediate vector of each non-leaf node and the word vector in the leaf node. The leaf node stores the word vector of each word with a length of m, which is used as the input vector of the neural network. The intermediate vector stores a set of vectors with a length of m, which corresponds to the parameters of the hidden layer in the three-layer network structure. The input layer and the hidden layer information jointly determine the output result of the classification.

Step 5: Start training.

5 Experimental Result

The input parameter K indicates the number of clusters, and its value has a significant influence on the clustering experiment results. For this paper, the K value selection

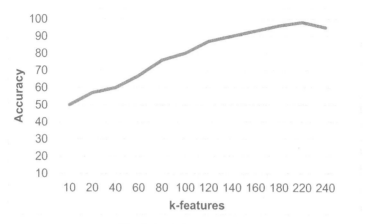

Fig. 2. Variation curve of K

experiment is analyzed between 10 and 240 values, and gives a curve trend diagram of the experimental results, as shown in Fig. 2.

It can be seen from the figure that when K takes 220, the clustering results have the highest accuracy, so in the hot spot discovery experiment in the Weibo public opinion data set, K takes 220.

To verify the efficiency of the above algorithm, the Single-Pass algorithm, K-means++ algorithm, improved K-means++ algorithm, Word2Vec model, K-means++ combined algorithm, and WPK-means++ algorithm are analyzed on the same Weibo public opinion dataset, and the time value spent in the clustering of each algorithm is shown in Fig. 3.

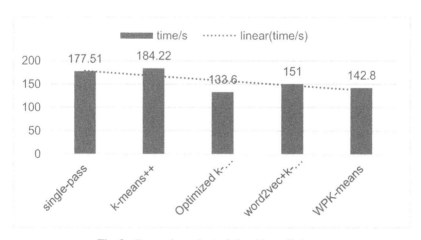

Fig. 3. Comparison chart of algorithm efficiency

To verify the effectiveness of the above algorithms in specific experiments, this paper designs a comparative experiment in the labeled Chinese topic data set to verify the text clustering. Recall, precision, and F1 value are the most commonly used to evaluate clustering An indicator of algorithm effectiveness. Precision and recall are commonly used indicators in clustering and classification, covering standards such as accuracy and coverage. The F1 values are the evaluation criteria for combining precision and recall. The combination of this evaluation index can better evaluate the clustering algorithm performance comprehensively. Therefore, this paper chooses the recall rate, precision rate, and F1 value as indicators to evaluate the effectiveness of the clustering algorithm.

In this paper, the proposed improved algorithm WPK-means++ algorithm, K-means++ algorithm optimized by initial point optimization, Word2Vec model + K-means++ algorithm is used on the experimental dataset to design the comparison experiment, and give the comparison test results according to the three indexes.

5.1 Check Accuracy Rate

The accuracy rate represents the ratio of the number of topic samples accurately judged as a certain category in the experimental results and the total number of all samples accurately judged as this category in the experimental results. See the calculation formula in (1).

$$Precision = \frac{|C_{it}|}{|C_i|} \tag{1}$$

Specifically, $|C_{it}|$ indicates the number of topic samples that the experiment had judged correctly in category I, and $|C_{it}|$ represents the full number of samples that the experiment had judged as a category i. Comparison experiments were designed for the IMP algorithm WPK-means++, K-means++, Word2Vec model + K-means++ algorithm, and the experimental results are shown in Fig. 4.

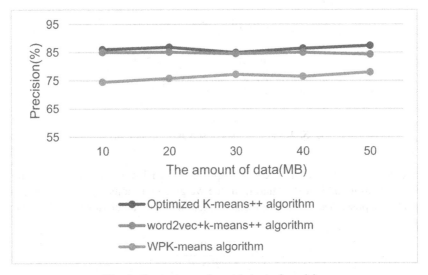

Fig. 4. Contrast experimental chart of precision

5.2 Check the Full Rate

The whole represents a proportion of the actual data amount of the category in the return result. See the calculation formula in (2).

$$Recall = \frac{|C_{it}|}{|D_i|} \qquad (2)$$

where, $|C_{it}|$ indicates the number of topic samples that the experiment has judged correctly in category I, and $|C_{it}|$ indicates the number of topic samples included in category i. Comparison experiments were designed for the modified algorithm WPK-means++ algorithm, K-means++ algorithm after initial point optimization, and Word2Vec model + K-means++ algorithm, and the experimental results are shown in Fig. 5.

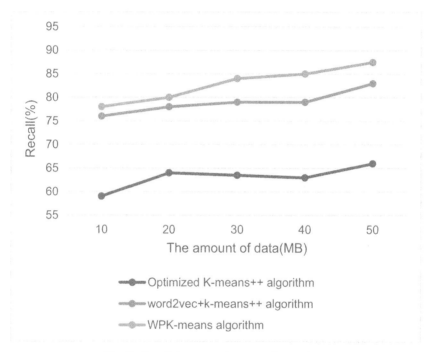

Fig. 5. Recall the comparison experiment chart

In some cases, precision and recall will appear, so the F1 value, the index is a comprehensive evaluation index, calculated from the weighted harmonic average of precision and recall, and possible contradictions can be excluded. The calculation formula is shown in (3).

$$F1 = \frac{2 \times P \times R}{P + R} \qquad (3)$$

where R represents recall and P represents accuracy. Comparison experiments were designed for the IMP algorithm WPK-means++ algorithm, K-means++ algorithm,

Word2Vec model + K-means++ algorithm, and the experimental results are shown in Fig. 6.

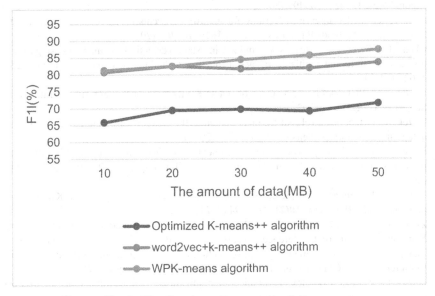

Fig. 6. F1 value comparison experiment diagram

In this paper, the model experimental design was conducted on anaconda3 to show the ten keywords in the top ten categories in the clustering results of the WPK-means++ algorithm on the public opinion dataset.

6 Conclusion

Because of the optimization shortcomings of the traditional clustering algorithm K-means++, this paper proposes a hot spot discovery and improvement algorithm (WPK-means++). By combining the idea of Single-Pass incremental clustering, the hotspot tracking model is built for the subsequent new data, which reduces the time of repeated clustering. This paper conducted comparative experiments on the Weibo public opinion dataset and reached a precision of 0.87, recall of 0.86, and F1 score of 0.83. In future studies, the WPK-means++ algorithm can be tested in a distributed architecture. Meanwhile, the performance of the proposed algorithm can be validated using newer data.

Acknowledgments. This work was supported in part by the Research Project of Fundamental Scientific Research Business Expenses of Provincial Colleges and Universities in Hebei Province 2021QNJS04.

Project Fund:. Research Project of Fundamental Scientific Research Business Expenses of Provincial Colleges and Universities in Hebei Province 2021QNJS04.

References

1. Kolose, S., et al.: Cluster size prediction for military clothing using 3D body scan data. Appl. Ergon. **96**(2), 103487–103497 (2021)
2. Solli, R., et al.: Unsupervised learning for identifying events in active target experiments. Nucl. Instrum. Methods Phys. Res., Sect. A **1010**, 165461 (2021)
3. Chandel, A.K., et al.: Apple powdery mildew infestation detection and mapping using a high-resolution visible and multispectral aerial imaging technique. Scientia Horticulturae **287**, 110228 (2021)
4. Kazuo, A.: CPI-model-based analysis of sparse K-means clustering algorithms. Int. J. Data Sci. Anal. **12**, 229–248 (2021)
5. Marek, A.: Detection and classification of malicious flows in software-defined networks using data mining techniques. Sensors. **21**(9), 2972 (2021)
6. Daoud, A.S. et al.: Improving arabic document clustering using k-means algorithm and particle swarm optimization. In: Conference 2017, IntelliSys, pp.879–885. IEEE Xplore (2017)
7. Alharbi, A.R.: Enhancing topic clustering for Arabic security news based on K-means and topic modeling. IET Netw. **10**(2), 278–294 (2021)
8. Zhang, H., Liu, C., Zhang, M., Zhu, R.: A hot spot clustering method based on improved K-means algorithm. In: Conference 2017, (ICCWAMTIP), pp. 32–35. IEEE (2017)
9. Zhang, W., Lu, J.: An online water army detection method based on network hot events. In: Conference 2018,ICMTMA, pp. 191–193. IEEE Computer Society (2018)
10. Huang, C., Zhu, Z.: Complex communication application identification and private network mining technology under a large-scale network. Neural Comput. Appl. **33**(9), 3871–3879 (2020). https://doi.org/10.1007/s00521-020-05442-0

Research Hotspots, Emerging Trend and Front of Fraud Detection Research: A Scientometric Analysis (1984–2021)

Li Zeng[1], Yang Li[2(✉)], and Zili Li[3]

[1] School of International Business and Management, Sichuan International Studies University,
Chongqing 400000, China

[2] Hunan Equastar Technology Co. Ltd., Hunan 410000, China
yang@sciradar.com

[3] Hunan Institute of Traffic Engineering, Hunan 421009, China

Abstract. This paper conducted a comprehensive scientometric review of Fraud Detection between 1984 and 2021 to depict the landscapes, research hotspots, and emerging trends in this field. Besides scientific outputs evaluation using statistical analysis and comparative analysis, scientometric methods such as co-occurrence analysis, cocitation analysis, and coupling analysis were used to analyze the knowledge structure of Fraud detection. Results showed that Fraud Detection research went up significantly in the past two decades, in addition to conventional scientometric results, keywords with the strongest citation burst such as Intrusion Detection, Audit Planning, Pattern Recognition, Data Mining, Insurance Fraud, Benfords Law, Business Intelligence, Outlier Detection, Genetic Algorithm, Big Data, and Deep Learning, demonstrate the emerging trends of Fraud Detection.

Keywords: Scientometric · Research hotspots · Citespace · Fraud detection

1 Introduction

Fraud Detection (FD) refers to the technology that uses specific algorithms, models, or tools to identify various suspicious fraudulent activities [1]. Fraud Detection is widely used in computer science [2], economics [3], business [4], management [5], Health [6] and so on.

In recent years, comprehensive reviews of the research related to Fraud Detection were conducted. Bolton, RJ et al. (2002) [7] described the tools available for statistical fraud detection and the areas in which fraud detection technologies are most used. Yufeng Kou et al. (2004) [8] have given a comprehensive review of different techniques to detect fraud and present a survey of current techniques used in credit card fraud detection, telecommunication fraud detection, and computer intrusion detection. West, Jarrod, et al. (2016) [9] and Ashtiani, Matin N. et al. (2022) [10] presented a comprehensive analysis of existing fraud detection literature based on key aspects such as detection algorithm used, fraud type investigated, and performance of the detection methods for

© The Author(s), under exclusive license to Springer Nature Singapore Pte Ltd. 2022
Y. Tan and Y. Shi (Eds.): DMBD 2022, CCIS 1745, pp. 91–102, 2022.
https://doi.org/10.1007/978-981-19-8991-9_8

specific financial fraud types. Callao, M. Pilar and I. Ruisanchez (2018) [11] describes the state of the art of multivariate qualitative analysis for determining food fraud and differentiates between authentication and adulteration. Omair, B and Alturki, A (2020) [12] gave a systematic literature review of fraud detection metrics in business processes. Pourhabibi, Tahereh, et al. (2020) [13] investigated the present trends and challenges that require significant research efforts to increase the credibility of graph-based anomaly detection. Gupta, Sonika, et al. (2021) [14] and Al-Hashedi et al. (2021) [15] made a systematic literature review of data mining based on financial fraud detection. Wang, Nana, et al. (2018) [16] made a comparative analysis of china and the world financial fraud research based on a knowledge map from the perspectives of hotspots and the evolution process. Mansour, A.Z. et al. (2021) [17] presented a bibliometric analysis of fraud detection based on Scopus database and VOSviewer [18]. Different from these methods, this paper conducts a scientific metrological review of fraud detection research by investigating scientific output, geographical distribution, and distribution of international cooperation, institutions, and journals, aiming to provide another perspective for research and development in the field of fraud detection. In addition, innovative methods such as co-citation analysis and burst detection are also applied, which can vividly describe the landscape, research trends, and fronts of this field.

2 Data and Method

2.1 Data

The data used for this paper were collected from Web of Science database on September 12, 2022, and the search strategy is as follows:

Topic = "Fraud Detection*", Timespan = 1984–2021.

Finally, 2688 bibliographic records were gathered for an in-depth analysis.

2.2 Method

After an ETL operation of the original data, a basic analysis of high-productive countries/regions and research institutes, highly cited references and highly cited authors is performed, then the H-index and other indicators are calculated by SciRadar [19], a self-developed scientometrics software; the geographical distribution of scholars is drawn by Bibliometrix [20] according to the author relationship; network analysis of different types of entities, such as countries/regions, research institutes, and categories and keywords are conducted by CiteSpace [21]. In addition, keyword burst detection is performed by the algorithm proposed by Kleinberg [22].

3 Result and Discussion

3.1 Scientific Outputs of Fraud Detection Research

Figure 1 shows the maturity forecasting result of Fraud Detection. The black curve represents documents per year published, it can be seen that substantial interest in Fraud

Detection research did not emerge until 1998. The red curve represents the cumulative publications growth. Finally, a green fitting curve using Logistic Growth Model [23] with formula (1) to evaluate and predict the maturity and the prospective growth of Fraud Detection publications.

$$y = 7061.129/(1 + \exp^{421.6617 - 0.2083x}) \tag{1}$$

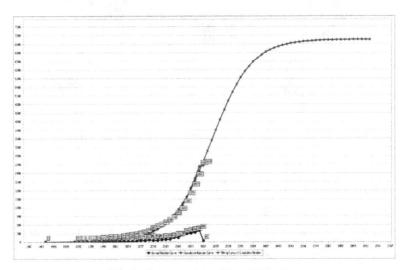

Fig. 1. Paper number of fraud detection.

Here, x and y represent the publication year and documents published per year respectively. According to formula (1), the development of Fraud Detection can be divided into four stages: infant period (before 2013), growth period (2013–2035), mature period (2035–2043), and stable period (after 2043). The above stage division shows the research of Fraud Detection in 2021 was in the mature period with a maturity of 38.07%.

3.2 Characteristics of International Collaboration

A collaboration map between countries/territories was generated by Bibliometrix [19] (Fig. 2). The color of the place in the collaboration map represents the number of papers. In total, there are 102 countries/territories and 418 links between them. Table 1 lists the top ten most productive countries/territories in the field of Fraud Detection. Overall, the USA is the first most productive and influential country, with a total number of 604 papers (361 independent papers, 243 internationally collaborated papers), 183 institutes, and 14509 citations, its H-Index is 57. China is the second most productive and influential country in this field, with a total number of 446 papers (278 independent papers, 168 internationally collaborated papers), 273 institutes, and 6287 citations, and its H-Index is 37. Other countries/territories such as England, Brazil, Spain, and Germany also make outstanding contributions in this field. Besides, the goal of Betweenness Centrality metrics [18] is to find pivotal points between countries/territories of Fraud Detection. Thus, high betweenness centrality nodes such as USA and England play a central role in this research field.

Fig. 2. Country/territories collaboration mapping of fraud detection

Table 1. Top ten countries/territories in fraud detection

No	C/T	TP	IP	CP	TC	HI	TI	BC
1	USA	604	361	243	14509	57	183	0.259
2	China	446	278	168	6287	37	273	0.057
3	India	278	248	30	2274	20	81	0.052
4	England	141	71	70	2975	28	73	0.118
5	Brazil	97	76	21	1091	18	67	0.035
6	Spain	95	66	29	3070	21	60	0.075
7	Germany	99	68	31	1081	17	47	0.076
8	Australia	107	54	53	1717	22	73	0.016
9	France	84	37	47	1205	17	40	0.074
10	Iran	67	56	11	608	13	70	0.010

No., Rank by TP; C/T, Country/Territory; TP, Total papers; IP, Independent papers; CP, Internationally collaborated articles; TC, Total citations counts; HI, H Index; TI, Total institutes numbers; BC, Betweenness centrality in Cooperation Networks.

3.3 Characteristics of Institutional Cooperation

Figure 3 shows the institute's collaboration network of Fraud Detection which was generated by Citespace. In general, there are 2462 institutes, 834 cooperative relationships and 23 clusters with 30 or more members. According to the details listed in Table 2, Carnegie Mellon Univ and Florida Atlantic Univ are the most influential institutes with

1065 and 1029 citations respectively; Florida Atlantic Univ and Arizona State Univ engaged in this field earliest since 1998; Alibaba Grp, Tongji Univ and Univ Chinese Acad Sci are the rising stars in this field.

Fig. 3. Institute collaboration map in the field of fraud detection.

Table 2. Top ten institutes in fraud detection

No.	Name	Frequent	Frequency burst	Citations	Year
1	Chinese Acad Sci	38	17.07	319	2006
2	Tongji Univ	38	9.39	508	2016
3	Florida Atlantic Univ	35	8.79	1029	1998
4	Carnegie Mellon Univ	31	3.85	1065	2004
5	Shanghai Jiao Tong Univ	27	5.68	436	2011
6	Tsinghua Univ	26	5.10	367	2004
7	Univ Chinese Acad Sci	22	0	100	2017
8	Univ Illinois	18	6.59	501	2006
9	Arizona State Univ	18	5.58	404	1998
10	Alibaba Grp	18	7.70	99	2018

3.4   Publication Distribution and Co-citation Network Analysis

Figure 4 shows the distribution of publication number of Fraud Detection. The red curve depicts the change in source publication number, it can be seen that the number of publications in the field of fraud detection is gradually increasing, and has stabilized at about 200 in the past three years. The green curve shows the change in cited publication

number which has an abrupt increase after 2017. Figure 5 is the Publication Cocitaion
Network of Fraud Detection generated by Citespace. The node in the network represents
a cited publication and the link between two nodes are calculated by their co-cited
frequents. After a pruning process by G-Index [24] and community detection process by
Louvain algorithm [25], a core network with 957 nodes, 1897 links, and 19 communities
with more than 30 members was generated.

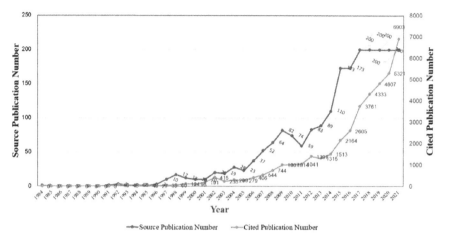

Fig. 4. Source publication number and cited publication number of fraud detection.

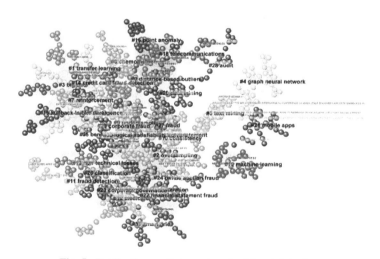

Fig. 5. Publication cocitaion network of fraud detection.

Cluster #0 is the largest one with 45 members, including publications such as
Machine Learning, CMC-Computers Materials & Continua, Information Processing &
Management, and its cluster labels are distance-based outliers, pattern recognition, etc.;
Cluster #4 is the newest one with 39 members, including publications such as ACM

SIGKDD, ICLR, CIKM, and its cluster labels are graph neural network, social network, etc.

3.5 Character of Subject Categories

Dual-map thematic overlays [26] can reveal the flow of knowledge about Fraud Detection (Fig. 6). The clusters on the left are the source journals, while the clusters on the right are the target journals. Journals are classified into several disciplines. Obviously, the essential knowledge flows are Systems-Computing-Computer and Economics-Economic-Political in fraud detection research.

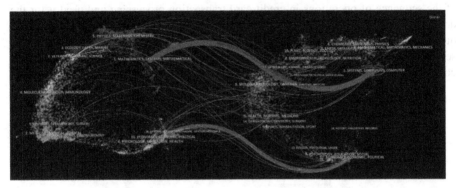

Fig. 6. Dual-map thematic overlay of fraud detection (1984–2021)

3.6 Research Hotspots and Emerging Trends of Fraud Detection

Table 3. Top 10 highly cited papers of fraud detection.

No.	Title	First Author	Journal Name	Year	DOI	Total Citations	Average Citations	Citation Distribution
1	Statistical fraud detection: A review	Bolton, RJ	STATISTICAL SCIENCE	2002	10.1214/SS/1042727940	501	23.86	
2	Adaptive fraud detection	Fawcett, T	DATA MINING AND KNOWLEDGE DISCOVERY	1997	10.1023/A:1009700419189	436	16.77	
3	The application of data mining techniques in financial fraud detection: A classification framework and an academic review of literature	Ngai, E. W. T.	DECISION SUPPORT SYSTEMS	2011	10.1016/j.dss.2010.08.006	435	36.25	
4	Distributed data mining in credit card fraud detection	Chan, PK	IEEE INTELLIGENT SYSTEMS & THEIR APPLICATIONS	1999	10.1109/5254.809570	216	9	
5	Corporate Lobbying and Fraud Detection	Yu, Frank	JOURNAL OF FINANCIAL AND QUANTITATIVE ANALYSIS	2011	10.1017/S0022109011000457	195	16.25	
6	Fraud detection system: A survey	Abdallah, Aisha	JOURNAL OF NETWORK AND COMPUTER APPLICATIONS	2016	10.1016/j.jnca.2016.04.007	171	24.43	
7	Credit card fraud detection using hidden Markov model	Srivastava, Abhinav	IEEE TRANSACTIONS ON DEPENDABLE AND SECURE COMPUTING	2008	10.1109/TDSC.2007.70228	158	10.53	
8	An overview of multivariate qualitative methods for food fraud detection	Pilar Callao, M.	FOOD CONTROL	2018	10.1016/J.foodcont.2017.11.034	151	30.2	
9	A cost-sensitive decision tree approach for fraud detection	Sahin, Yusuf	EXPERT SYSTEMS WITH APPLICATIONS	2013	10.1016/j.eswa.2013.05.021	150	15	
10	Learned lessons in credit card fraud detection from a practitioner perspective	Dal Pozzolo, Andrea	EXPERT SYSTEMS WITH APPLICATIONS	2014	10.1016/j.eswa.2014.02.026	146	16.22	

Table 3 lists the detail of the top 10 highly cited papers on Fraud Detection which can represent the main research hotspots in this field. Bolton, R. et al. (2002) [7] made a review of statistical fraud detection. Fawcett, T. et al. (1997) [27] applied an adaptive fraud detection framework to score possible fraud events. Ngai, E.W.T., et al. (2011) [28] constructed a classification framework for the application of data mining techniques in financial fraud detection. Chan, P. et al. (1999) [29] proposed methods of combining multiple learned fraud detectors under a "cost model" which can significantly reduce loss due to fraud through distributed data mining of fraud models. Yu, F. et al. (2011) [3] inspected the relationship between corporate lobbying and fraud detection. Abdallah, A. et al. (2016) [30] explored the state-of-the-art fraud detection systems, approaches, and techniques in five areas of fraud such as credit card fraud, telecommunication fraud, healthcare insurance fraud, automobile insurance fraud, and online auction fraud. Srivastava, A. et al. (2008) [31] build a hidden Markov model (HMM) to capture features of the sequence of operations in credit card transaction processing and used it for the detection of fraud. Pilar Callao, M. et al. (2018) [11] gave an overview of multivariate qualitative methods for food fraud detection. Sahin, Y. et al. (2013) [32] utilized a cost-sensitive decision tree approach for fraud detection. Dal Pozzolo, A. et al. (2014) [33] concluded the lessons in credit card fraud detection from a practitioner's perspective.

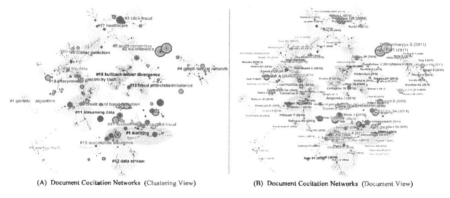

(A) Document Cocitation Networks (Clustering View)   (B) Document Cocitation Networks (Document View)

Fig. 7. Document cocitation network of fraud detection.

The role of document co-citation analysis [34] is to comprehend the intellectual infrastructure of the knowledge domain in Fraud Detection. After network pruning and community detection, it generated a core network that includes 1241 cited references, 586 co-citation links, and 18 co-citation clusters containing more than 30 members. The modularity of community division is 0.9509 (Fig. 7). Table 4 lists the details of the top 5 largest clusters. The oldest and largest cluster is cluster #0 with the average year of 2015. Its labels are sampling, imbalanced data, and credit card fraud detection, and its symbolic papers are [35–37]. Cluster #1 is the second largest one and its label are credit cards, transfer learning, transaction fraud detection, attention mechanisms, and individual behavior, and its representative papers are [38–40]. Cluster #2 is the third largest one and its label are big data, medicare, class imbalance, and random undersampling, its representative papers are [41–43]. Cluster #3 is the fourth largest one and its label are outlier detection, fraud management, suspicion score and click fraud, and its representative papers are [44–46]. Cluster #4 is the fifth largest one and its labels are graph neural network, graph convolution network, laplacian matrix, and aggregates, and its representative papers are [47–49].

Figure 8 shows the timeline graph of Fraud Detection. In this graph, Keywords indicate the micro-scale emerging trends in Fraud Detection are: Intrusion Detection, Audit Planning, Pattern Recognition, Data Mining, Insurance Fraud, Benfords Law, Business Intelligence, Outlier Detection, Genetic Algorithm, Big Data, and Deep Learning.

Table 4. Top 5 largest clusters

#	Size	Mean year	Labels (Labeled by LLR)	Representative papers
0	42	2015	Sampling; imbalanced data; credit card fraud detection; credit scoring	[35–37]
1	38	2018	Credit cards; transfer learning; transaction fraud detection; attention mechanisms	[38–40]
2	37	2016	Big data; medicare; class imbalance; random undersampling	[41–43]
3	37	2005	Outlier detection; fraud management; suspicion score; click fraud	[44–46]
4	33	2018	Graph neural network; graph convolution network; laplacian matrix; aggregates	[47–49]

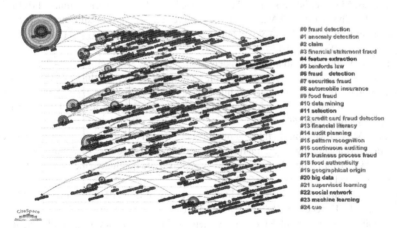

#0 fraud detection
#1 anomaly detection
#2 claim
#3 financial statement fraud
#4 feature extraction
#5 benfords law
#6 fraud   detection
#7 securities fraud
#8 automobile insurance
#9 food fraud
#10 data mining
#11 selection
#12 credit card fraud detection
#13 financial literacy
#14 audit planning
#15 pattern recognition
#16 continuous auditing
#17 business process fraud
#18 food authenticity
#19 geographical origin
#20 big data
#21 supervised learning
#22 social network
#23 machine learning
#24 cue

Fig. 8. Timeline graph of the keyword co-occurrence network of fraud detection.

4 Conclusion

In this paper the prospects, research hotspots, and emerging trends in fraud detection research are evaluated with quantitative methods. Based on the comprehensive sciento-metric analysis, the publication data in the field of fraud detection were analysed using data sets from 1984 to 2021 from the Web of Science database. The analytics mainly focuses on scientific achievements, geographical distribution, institutions, journals, and subject categories. In addition, co-citation analysis and burst detection are also applied. The conclusions of this paper can well reveal the research prospects and emerging trends of fraud detection from multiple perspectives.

References

1. Fraud: Detection, Prevention, and Analytics! In: Fraud Analytics Using Descriptive, Predictive, and Social Network Techniques, pp. 1–36. John Wiley and Sons, Inc., Hoboken (2015)
2. Sun, C., Li, Q., Cui, L., Yan, Z., Li, H., Wei, W.: An effective hybrid fraud detection method. In: Zhang, S., Wirsing, M., Zhang, Z. (eds.) KSEM 2015. LNCS (LNAI), vol. 9403, pp. 563–574. Springer, Cham (2015). https://doi.org/10.1007/978-3-319-25159-2_51
3. Yu, F., Yu, X.: Corporate lobbying and fraud detection. J. Financ. Quant. Anal. **46**, 1865–1891 (2011)
4. Viaene, S., Derrig, R.A., Baesens, B., Dedene, G.: A comparison of state-of-the-art classification techniques for expert automobile insurance claim fraud detection. J. Risk Insur. **69**, 373–421 (2002). https://doi.org/10.1111/1539-6975.00023
5. Cecchini, M., Aytug, H., Koehler, G.J., Pathak, P.: Detecting management fraud in public companies. Manage. Sci. **56**, 1146–1160 (2010). https://doi.org/10.1287/mnsc.1100.1174
6. Bauder, R., Khoshgoftaar, T.M., Seliya, N.: A survey on the state of healthcare upcoding fraud analysis and detection. Health Serv. Outcomes Res. Method. **17**(1), 31–55 (2016). https://doi.org/10.1007/s10742-016-0154-8
7. Bolton, R., Hand, D.: Statistical fraud detection: a review. Stat. Sci. **17**, 235–249 (2002)
8. Kou, Y., et al.: Survey of fraud detection techniques. In: Proceedings of the 2004 IEEE International Conference on Networking, Sensing and Control, vol. 2, pp. 749–754 (2004)
9. West, J., Bhattacharya, M.: Intelligent financial fraud detection: a comprehensive review. Comput. Secur. **57**, 47–66 (2016)
10. Ashtiani, M.N., Raahemi, B.: Intelligent fraud detection in financial statements using machine learning and data mining: a systematic literature review. IEEE Access **10**, 72504–72525 (2022)
11. Callao, M.P., Ruisanchez, I.: An overview of multivariate qualitative methods for food fraud detection. Food Control **86**, 283–293 (2018)
12. Omair, B., Alturki, A.: A systematic literature review of fraud detection metrics in business processes. IEEE Access **8**, 26893–26903 (2020)
13. Pourhabibi, T., et al.: Fraud detection: a systematic literature review of graph-based anomaly detection approaches. Decis. Support Syst. **133**, 113303 (2020)
14. Gupta, S., Mehta, S.K.: Data mining-based financial statement fraud detection: systematic literature review and meta-analysis to estimate data sample mapping of fraudulent companies against non-fraudulent companies. Glob. Bus. Rev. (2021). 097215092098485
15. Al-Hashedi, K.G., Magalingam, P.: Financial fraud detection applying data mining techniques: a comprehensive review from 2009 to 2019. Comput. Sci. Rev. **40**, 100402 (2021)

16. Nana, W., Wang, F.: Comparative analysis on domestic and foreign financial fraud research based on knowledge map-web of science core collection. In: Proceedings of the 2017 4th International Conference on Management Innovation and Business Innovation (ICMIBI 2017), vol. 81, no. 2017, pp. 81–90 (2017)

17. Mansour, A.Z., Ahmi, A., Popoola, O.M.J., Znaimat, A.: Discovering the global landscape of fraud detection studies: a bibliometric review. J. Financ. Crime **29**, 701–720 (2021). https://doi.org/10.1108/jfc-03-2021-0052

18. van Eck, N.J., Waltman, L.: VOS: a new method for visualizing similarities between objects. In: Decker, R., Lenz, H.-J. (eds.) Advances in Data Analysis. SCDAKO, pp. 299–306. Springer, Heidelberg (2007). https://doi.org/10.1007/978-3-540-70981-7_34

19. Li, Z., Li, Z., Zhao, Z., et al.: Landscapes and emerging trends of virtual reality in recent 30 years: a bibliometric analysis. In: Proceedings of the 2018 IEEE SmartWorld, Ubiquitous Intelligence & Computing, Advanced & Trusted Computing, Scalable Computing & Communications, Cloud & Big Data Computing, Internet of People and Smart City Innovation (SmartWorld/SCALCOM/UIC/ATC/CBDCom/IOP/SCI). IEEE (2018)

20. Aria, M., Cuccurullo, C.: Bibliometrix : an R-tool for comprehensive science mapping analysis. J. Informet. **11**(4), 959–975 (2017)

21. Chen, C.: CiteSpace II: detecting and visualizing emerging trends and transient patterns in scientific literature. J. Am. Soc. Inform. Sci. Technol. **57**(3), 359–377 (2006)

22. Kleinberg, J.: Bursty and hierarchical structure in streams. In: Proceedings of the Eighth ACM SIGKDD International Conference on Knowledge Discovery and Data Mining - KDD 2002. ACM Press (2002)

23. Rogosa, D., Brandt, D., Zimowski, M.: A growth curve approach to the measurement of change. Psychol. Bull. **92**(3), 726–748 (1982)

24. Egghe, L.: Theory and practise of the g-index. Scientometrics **69**, 131–152 (2006)

25. Blondel, V.D., Guillaume, J.-L., Lambiotte, R., Lefebvre, E.: Fast unfolding of communities in large networks. J. Stat. Mech: Theory Exp. **2008**(10), P10008 (2008)

26. Chen, C., Leydesdorff, L.: Patterns of connections and movements in dual-map overlays: A new method of publication portfolio analysis. J. Am. Soc. Inf. Sci. **65**(2), 334–351 (2013)

27. Fawcett, T., Provost, F.: Adaptive fraud detection. Data Min. Knowl. Discovery **1**, 291–316 (1997). https://doi.org/10.1023/A:1009700419189

28. Ngai, E.W.T., Hu, Y., Wong, Y.H., Chen, Y., Sun, X.: The application of data mining techniques in financial fraud detection: a classification framework and an academic review of literature. Decis. Support Syst. **50**, 559–569 (2011). https://doi.org/10.1016/j.dss.2010.08.006

29. Chan, P., Fan, W., Prodromidis, A., Stolfo, S.: Distributed data mining in credit card fraud detection. IEEE Intell. Syst. Their Appl. **14**, 67–74 (1999). https://doi.org/10.1109/5254.809570

30. Abdallah, A., Maarof, M.A., Zainal, A.: Fraud detection system: a survey. J. Netw. Comput. Appl. **68**, 90–113 (2016). https://doi.org/10.1016/j.jnca.2016.04.007

31. Srivastava, A., Kundu, A., Sural, S., Majumdar, A.K.: Credit card fraud detection using hidden Markov model. IEEE Trans. Dependable Secure Comput. **5**, 37–48 (2008). https://doi.org/10.1109/TDSC.2007.70228

32. Sahin, Y., Bulkan, S., Duman, E.: A cost-sensitive decision tree approach for fraud detection. Expert Syst. Appl. **40**, 5916–5923 (2013). https://doi.org/10.1016/j.eswa.2013.05.021

33. Dal Pozzolo, A., Caelen, O., Le Borgne, Y.-A., Waterschoot, S., Bontempi, G.: Learned lessons in credit card fraud detection from a practitioner perspective. Expert Syst. Appl. **41**, 4915–4928 (2014). https://doi.org/10.1016/j.eswa.2014.02.026

34. Small, H.: Co-citation in the scientific literature: a new measure of the relationship between two documents. J. Am. Soc. Inform. Sci. **24**, 265–269 (1973). https://doi.org/10.1002/asi.4630240406

35. Correa Bahnsen, A., Aouada, D., Stojanovic, A., Ottersten, B.: Feature engineering strategies for credit card fraud detection. Expert Syst. Appl. **51**, 134–142 (2016). https://doi.org/10.1016/j.eswa.2015.12.030

36. Van Vlasselaer, V., et al.: APATE: A novel approach for automated credit card transaction fraud detection using network-based extensions. Decis. Support Syst. **75**, 38–48 (2015). https://doi.org/10.1016/j.dss.2015.04.013

37. Jurgovsky, J., et al.: Sequence classification for credit-card fraud detection. Expert Syst. Appl. **100**, 234–245 (2018). https://doi.org/10.1016/j.eswa.2018.01.037

38. Nami, S., Shajari, M.: Cost-sensitive payment card fraud detection based on dynamic random forest and k-nearest neighbors. Expert Syst. Appl. **110**, 381–392 (2018). https://doi.org/10.1016/j.eswa.2018.06.011

39. Rushin, G., Stancil, C., Sun, M., Adams, S., Beling, P.: Horse race analysis in credit card fraud—deep learning, logistic regression, and gradient boosted tree. In: Proceedings of the 2017 Systems and Information Engineering Design Symposium (SIEDS). IEEE (2017)

40. Zheng, L., Liu, G., Yan, C., Jiang, C.: Transaction fraud detection based on total order relation and behavior diversity. IEEE Trans. Comput. Soc. Syst. **5**, 796–806 (2018). https://doi.org/10.1109/tcss.2018.2856910

41. Chen, T., Guestrin, C.: XGBoost. In: Proceedings of the 22nd ACM SIGKDD International Conference on Knowledge Discovery and Data Mining. ACM, New York, NY, USA (2016)

42. Herland, M., Khoshgoftaar, T.M., Bauder, R.A.: Big Data fraud detection using multiple medicare data sources. J. Big Data **5**(1), 1–21 (2018). https://doi.org/10.1186/s40537-018-0138-3

43. Wang, Y., Xu, W.: Leveraging deep learning with LDA-based text analytics to detect automobile insurance fraud. Decis. Support Syst. **105**, 87–95 (2018)

44. Hodge, A.: A survey of outlier detection methodologies. Artif. Intell. Rev. **22**, 85–126 (2004). https://doi.org/10.1007/s10462-004-4304-y

45. Maranzato, R., Pereira, A., Neubert, M., do Lago, A.P.: Fraud detection in reputation systems in e-markets using logistic regression and stepwise optimization. ACM SIGAPP Appl. Comput. Rev. **11**, 14–26 (2010)

46. Cleary, R., Thibodeau, J.C.: Applying digital analysis using Benford's law to detect fraud: the dangers of type I errors. Auditing J. Pract. Theory **24**, 77–81 (2005). https://doi.org/10.2308/aud.2005.24.1.77

47. Liu, Z., Chen, C., Yang, X., Zhou, J., Li, X., Song, L.: Heterogeneous graph neural networks for malicious account detection. In: Proceedings of the 27th ACM International Conference on Information and Knowledge Management. ACM, New York (2018)

48. Wang, D., et al.: A semi-supervised graph attentive network for financial fraud detection. In: Proceedings of the 2019 IEEE International Conference on Data Mining (ICDM). IEEE (2019)

49. Liu, Z., Dou, Y., Yu, P.S., Deng, Y., Peng, H.: Alleviating the inconsistency problem of applying graph neural network to fraud detection. In: Proceedings of the 43rd International ACM SIGIR Conference on Research and Development in Information Retrieval. ACM, New York (2020)

Optimization Methods

An Algorithm of Set-Based Differential Evolution for Discrete Optimization Problem

Michiharu Maeda$^{(\boxtimes)}$ and Yuta Chikuba

Department of Computer Science and Enginnering, Fukuoka Institute of Technology,
3-30-1 Wajirohigashi, Higashi-ku, Fukuoka, Fukuoka 811-0295, Japan
maeda@fit.ac.jp

Abstract. This paper presents an algorithm of set-based differential evolution for discrete optimization problem. Differential evolution has been hitherto studied for continuous optimization problem. Extending approaches in continuous space to these in discrete space with set-based representation schemes, differential evolution can adopt to discrete optimization problem. A candidate solution is defined by a crisp set and all arithmetic operations in mutation are redefined by new operators. The mutation operator of our algorithm adds two different solutions selected randomly to the current solution and our algorithm constructs the solution probabilistically. In order to evaluate the validity of our algorithm, we examine numerical experiments compared to existing algorithms.

Keywords: Differential evolution · Discrete space · Optimization problem · Set-based scheme · Traveling salesman problem

1 Introduction

For optimization problem, it is generally difficult to find an optimal solution and it takes a huge amount of time to solve the problem. In this situation, metaheuristics have focused attention for solving optimization problems [1]. Metaheuristics involve, for example, genetic algorithm (GA) [2] that imitates the evolutionary process of biology, ant colony optimization (ACO) [3] that does the foraging behavior of ants, particle swarm optimization (PSO) [4] which imitates the simple social model such as birds flocking and fish schooling, and differential evolution (DE) [5] that has the mutation, crossover, selection in evolutionary computation. For optimization problem, there are continuous optimization problem in continuous space and discrete optimization problem in discrete space. Typical examples of optimization problems in discrete space include traveling salesman problem [6], which searches for the shortest possible route that one visits each given city once and returns to the start city. Though the traditional PSO which particles have a position and velocity is designed to work only in continuous space, discrete particle swarm optimization (DPSO) [7] operates in

© The Author(s), under exclusive license to Springer Nature Singapore Pte Ltd. 2022
Y. Tan and Y. Shi (Eds.): DMBD 2022, CCIS 1745, pp. 105–117, 2022.
https://doi.org/10.1007/978-981-19-8991-9_9

binary space by using sigmoid function. Memory binary particle swarm optimization (MBPSO) [8] based on DPSO decides the position according to the previous position, and its mechanism is simple and effective. Set-based comprehensive learning and particle swarm optimization (SCLPSO) [9] is based on a set-based representation scheme. SCLPSO can solve discrete optimization problems with high quality and is successfully applied to large-scale problems. For knapsack problem, set-based particle swarm optimization with status memory has been suggested and shown significant results [10]. For an attempt to traveling salesman problem, set-based comprehensive learning and particle swarm optimization with memory has been discussed [11,12].

In this paper, an algorithm of set-based differential evolution is presented for discrete optimization problem. Our algorithm has a set-based representation scheme and extends the application of differential evolution to discrete optimization problem. For applying differential evolution of continuous problems to discrete problems, a candidate solution is defined on a crisp set and all arithmetic operators in mutation are redefined by new operators. We modify the procedure that the mutation and the population sets generate the trial set satisfied constraints of traveling salesman problem. Experimental results are compared our algorithm to Max-min ant system (MMAS) that improved ACO [13], MBPSO and SCLPSO for traveling salesman problem.

2 Preliminary

2.1 Particle Swarm Optimization

Particle swarm optimization (PSO) is an optimization approach that achieves the social model of birds flocking and fish schooling. N_p particles cooperate to search for the global optimum in D-dimensional space. Each particle $i(i = 1, 2, ..., N_p)$ has position $X_i(x_i^1, x_i^2, ..., x_i^D)$ and velocity $V_i(v_i^1, v_i^2, ..., v_i^D)$ which are a candidate solution and a vector constructed by the current position and the best position, respectively. Each particle stores the base position previously encountered by itself and the best position of all particles. The traditional PSO algorithm is only operated in continuous space. Updating rule of a velocity and position of the i-th particle are defined as follows:

$$v_i^j = wv_i^j + c_1r_1(P_i^j - x_i^j) + c_2r_2(G^j - x_i^j) \tag{1}$$

$$x_i^j = x_i^j + v_i^j \tag{2}$$

where $P_i(P_i^1, P_i^2, ..., P_i^D)$ is the best-so-far solution obtained by the i-th particle and $G(G^1, G^2, ..., G^D)$ is the best solution yielded by the whole swarm. w, c_1, and c_2 are positive coefficients, r_1 and r_2 are random uniform values in $[0.0, 1.0]$, and $j(j = 1, 2, ..., D)$ represents the j-th dimension.

2.2 Set-Based Particle Swarm Optimization

PSO extends to set-based particle swarm optimization (SPSO) for solving combinatorial optimization problem in discrete space. SPSO adopts a set-based representation scheme and redefines a position and velocity and all arithmetic operators for the discrete space by new operators and procedures.

A. Representation Scheme

For combinatorial optimization problem, a universal set and a candidate solution in SPSO are described in the following characteristics.

- Universal set E can be divided into D dimensions, $E = E^1 \cup E^2 \cup ... \cup E^D$ is a set corresponding to the j-th dimension of the searching space. In traveling salesman problem, universal set E is composed of all arcs connecting every two cities, and the j-th dimension of the searching space E is the set of arcs that connects with node j.
- Candidate solution X corresponds to a subset of E, where $X = X^1 \cup X^2 \cup ... \cup X^D$ is a crisp set with two arcs. X is a feasible solution only if X satisfies constraints Ω.

According to the above description, a candidate solution is converted into a solution that optimizes the objective function. Figure 1 shows an example of 4 cities in symmetric traveling salesman problem. Each arc (k, l) can be viewed as an element, and $(k, l) \in E^k$ between node k and l are assigned length d_{kl}. Note that arc (k, l) is equal to arc (l, k).

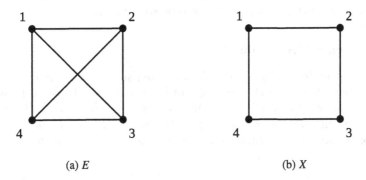

(a) E (b) X

Fig. 1. Example of the representation scheme for the symmetric traveling salesman problem

In Fig. 1(a), there exists $E = \{(1,2), (1,3), (1,4), (2,3), (2,4), (3,4)\}$. For example, $E^1 = \{(1,2), (1,3), (1,4)\}$ has only arcs connected to node 1. In Fig. 1(b), $X = \{(1,2), (1,4), (2,3), (3,4)\}$ forms a circuit of the graph. In this solution, $X^1 = \{(1,2), (1,4)\}$ has two arcs connected to node 1. Similarly, each dimension E^j and X^j have arcs connecting to node j.

B. Procedure of the Algorithm

In SPSO, the position is defined as the candidate solution for discrete optimization problems, and the velocity is defined as a set with possibilities as follows:

$$V_i^j = \{e/p(e) \mid e \in E^j\} \tag{3}$$

where V_i^j is the set with possibility of the j-th dimension of the i-th particle. V_i^j has possibility $p(e) \in [0.0, 1.0]$ of each element $e \in E$.

SPSO generates solutions that are similar to the current solutions. If the swarm size is small, the algorithm is more likely to be trapped in local optima. To avoid this situation, SCLPSO uses the velocity updating of comprehensive learning PSO (CLPSO) [14]. The velocity updating rule denotes as follows:

$$V_i^j = wV_i^j + cr^j(P_{best}{}_{f_i(j)}^j - X_i^j) \tag{4}$$

where X_i^j is position of the j-th dimension of the i-th particle. The position is given by a crisp set. c and w are positive coefficients, r^j is random uniform values in $[0.0, 1.0]$. $P_{best}{}_{f_i(j)}^j$ is the best solution of the j-th dimension of the i-th particle. $f_i(j)$ is given as the following description [14]. First, a uniform random value R in $[0.0, 1.0]$ is generated. If R is larger than a parameter with the i-th particle, $f_i(j)$ is substituted into i otherwise the algorithm applies position of particle of high fitness to two randomly selected particles.

After updating the velocity, particle i use the updated velocity V_i to adjust its current position X_i and builds a new position. Unlike in continuous space, positions in discrete space must satisfy constrains. Particle i updates its position according to the new position updating procedure in [9].

2.3 Differential Evolution

Differential evolution (DE) is a population-based stochastic technique of evolutionary computation. The characteristic of DE is simple and easy to implement without complicated computations. DE uses the difference vector of randomly selected two different vectors in the population. In DE, an individual x is D-dimensional real-valued parameter vector $x_i = [x_i^1, x_i^2, ..., x_i^D]$ in the population of N_p.

A. Mutation
There are some kinds of mutation strategies in DE. For example, DE/rand/1 strategy is selected, a mutant vector $v_i = [v_i^1, v_i^2, ..., v_i^D]$ is generated by the mutation operator as follows:

$$v_i^j = x_{r_1}^j + F \cdot (x_{r_2}^j - x_{r_3}^j) \tag{5}$$

where x_{r_1}, x_{r_2} and x_{r_3} indicate different three individuals in the population. Random numbers $r_1, r_2, r_3 \in 1, 2, ..., N_p$ which are $i \neq r_1 \neq r_2 \neq r_3$. $x_{r_1}^j$ is called the parent vectors, and $(x_{r_2}^j - x_{r_3}^j)$ is called the differential vector. F is a positive control parameter used to scale the differential vector.

B. Crossover
The crossover operator implements a recombination of the mutant vector and

the parent vector to produce the trial vector $u_i = [u_i^1, u_i^2, ..., u_i^D]$. The crossover operator is defined as follows:

$$u_i^j = \begin{cases} v_i^j & \text{if}(\text{rand}^j[0.0, 1.0] \leq C_r \text{ or } j = j_{rand}) \\ x_i^j & \text{otherwise} \end{cases} \tag{6}$$

where $C_r \in [0.0, 1.0]$ is the crossover rate and appears as a control parameter of DE. $\text{rand}^j \in [0.0, 1.0]$ is a random number and $j_{rand} \in [1, 2, ..., D]$ is a randomly chosen index that ensures u_i gets at least one parameter in v_i.

C. Selection

The selection operator is used to select the next population x^{new} between the trial vector and the target vector. The selection operator is defined as follows:

$$x_i^{new} = \begin{cases} u_i & \text{if}(f(u_i) \leq f(x_i)) \\ x_i & \text{otherwise} \end{cases} \tag{7}$$

where $f()$ is the fitness function for minim solution.

3   Set-Based Differential Evolution

In this section, we present an algorithm of set-based differential evolution (SBDE). In this study, a new mutation operator is defined to enable DE to complete the transformation and DE extends to SBDE for solving combinatorial optimization problem in discrete space. Individual $x_i(i = 1, 2, ..., N_p)$ that is the candidate solution is a crisp set. Arithmetic operators for mutation and the procedure are redefined by new operators and procedure. The structure of SBDE is similar to the original DE, which is shown in Algorithm 1.

Algorithm 1. Pseudo-code for SBDE

---
procedure SBDE
    Initialization:
        Set paramters.
        Generate solutions $x_i(i = 1, 2, ..., N_p)$, randomly.
        Select solutions in order of the nearest city.
    while terminal condition not met **do**
        for each individual $x_i(i = 1, 2, ..., N_p)$ **do**
            Mutation;
            Crossover;
            Selection;
        end for
    end while
end procedure

In SBDE, for accelerating the search speed, N_p initial solutions are constructed randomly and selected in order of the nearest city. We start searching iteratively and optimize solutions by repeating iteration, mutation, crossover, and selection every iteration.

A. Mutation

In SBDE, the mutation operator generates the mutant set $v_i = v_i^1 \cup v_i^2 \cup ... \cup v_i^D$. The mutation operator of SBDE is defined as follow:

$$v_i^j = \begin{cases} (x_{r_2}^j - x_{r_3}^j) & \text{if}(\text{rand}^j[0.0, 1.0] \leq F) \\ x_{r_1}^j & \text{otherwise} \end{cases} \tag{8}$$

where x_{r_1}, x_{r_2} and x_{r_3} indicate different three individual sets in the population. F is a positive control parameter to scale the differential set. The redefined arithmetic operators in Eq. (8) are described below.

Individual set - Individual set: The minus operator between two crisp sets A and B is defined as follows:

$$(A - B) = \{e \mid e \in A \text{ and } e \notin B\}. \tag{9}$$

For example, if $A = \{(1, 2), (1, 4), (2, 3), (3, 4)\}$ and $B = \{(1, 3), (1, 4), (2, 3), (2, 4)\}$, then we obtain $A - B = \{(1, 2), (3, 4)\}$. Differential set $(A - B)$ is to find elements including A but not B.

Mutation Set: This operator inherits a differential set or an individual set according to parameter F for each dimension. We defined this operator that generates a mutation set as follows:

$$v^j = \begin{cases} S^j & \text{if}(\text{rand}^j[0.0, 1.0] < F) \\ x^j & \text{otherwise} \end{cases} \tag{10}$$

where $F \in [0.0, 1.0]$. S^j is the j-th dimension of the differential set. For example, $S^1 = \{(1, 2)\}$, $x^1 = \{(1, 3), (1, 4)\}$, F is set as 0.5, rand$[0.0, 1.0] = 0.3$. In this case, $v^1 = \{(1, 2)\}$. But if rand$[0.0, 1.0] = 0.7$, the result will be $v^1 = \{(1, 3), (1, 4)\}$. The mutation set is generated based on the above two operations.

To help us understanding, the candidate solutions in the case of 4 cities are shown in Fig. 2. In this case, we obtain a differential set $(x_{r_2} - x_{r_3}) = S = \{(1, 2), (3, 4)\}$. In addition, for example, F is set as 0.5. If rand$^1[0.0, 1.0] = 0.7 > F$, rand$^2[0.0, 1.0] = 0.2 < F$, rand$^3[0.0, 1.0] = 0.9 > F$, and rand$^4[0.0, 1.0] = 0.4 < F$, then we obtain $v^1 = X_1^1 = \{(1, 2), (1, 4)\}$, $v^2 = S^2 = \{(1, 2)\}$, $v^3 = X_1^3 = \{(2, 3), (3, 4)\}$, $v^4 = S^4 = \{(3, 4)\}$. Finally, we obtain the mutation set $v = \{(1, 2), (2, 3), (3, 4)\}$.

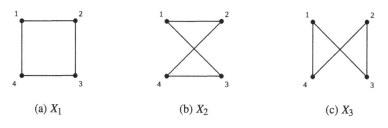

(a) X_1 (b) X_2 (c) X_3

Fig. 2. The candidate solutions in the symmetric TSP with 4 cities

B. Crossover

To enhance the potential diversity of the population, the crossover operator performs after generating the mutation set. The mutant set exchanges its components with the individual set under the crossover operator to form the trial set $u_i = u_i^1 \cup u_i^2 \cup ... \cup u_i^D$, which is also feasible solution.

DE family of algorithms can use two kinds of crossover [15]. In SBDE, we adopt exponential crossover. The effect of exponential crossover becomes a continuous path of inherited mutation and population sets. The procedures are shown in Algorithm 2 and Algorithm 3. In Algorithm 3, trial sets are empty and we first choose two variables n and L. n denotes the starting point of dimension number that the trial set inherits the mutant set. L denotes the number of components the trial set inherits the mutant set. We first choose an integer n randomly among the numbers $[1, D]$ and another integer L in the interval $[1, D]$. After choosing n and L, the trial set is obtained as follows:

$$u_i^j = \begin{cases} v_i^j & \text{if} (j = \langle n \rangle_D, \langle n+1 \rangle_D, ..., \langle n+L-1 \rangle_D) \\ x_i^j & \text{otherwise} \end{cases} \quad (11)$$

where $\langle \rangle_D$ denote a modulo function with modulus D. The integer L is formed according to the following pseudo-code:

$L = 1;$
while(rand$[0.0, 1.0] < C_r$ and $L < D$){
$\quad L = L + 1;$
}

C_r is the crossover rate. For each mutant set, n and L must be chosen randomly as shown above.

Algorithm 2. Pseudo-code of crossover procedure.

---

    procedure CROSSOVER(x_i, v_i)
        $u_i = \phi$
        Choose a random index $n \in [1, D]$;
        $L = 1;$
        while (rand$[0.0, 1.0] < C_r$ and $L < D$) **do**
            $L = L + 1;$
        end while
        for each dimension $j(j = 1, 2, ..., D)$ **do**
            if $(j = \langle n \rangle_D, \langle n+1 \rangle_D, ..., \langle n+L-1 \rangle_D)$ **then**
                construct(u_i^j, v_i^j)
            else
                construct(u_i^j, x_i^j)
            end if
        end for
    end procedure

Algorithm 2 constructs candidate solutions. Algorithm 3 shows the procedure for selecting arcs among candidate solutions in Algorithm 2. For each dimension, u_i^j first learns elements in s^j and adds the candidate set to one element. In TSP, for example, we can employ the length of each arc as the heuristic information and select the shortest arc in the candidate set. If there is no one element in the candidate set, one element is added in the universal set to construct a feasible solution.

For example, we assume that the dimension is 4, and given the mutation set $v_i = \{(1,2),(2,3),(3,4)\}$ and the individual set $x_i = \{(1,2),(1,3),(2,4),(3,4)\}$. Here we assume $n = 2$, $L = 2$. Then we start with the 1-st dimension. Since $j \neq \{\langle 2 \rangle_4, \langle 3 \rangle_4\}$, u_i^1 learns x_i^1 and add the arc (1,2). Then we turn to the 2-nd dimension. Since $j = \{\langle 2 \rangle_4, \langle 3 \rangle_4\}$, u_i^1 learns v_i^1 and add the arc (2,3). We repeat this procedure to complete the construction of u_i that is a feasible solution.

Algorithm 3. Pseudo-code of construct procedure.

---

procedure CONSTRUCT(u_i, s_i)
    $Candidate\_Set = \{e \mid e \in s_i^j$ and e satisfies $\Omega\}$
    if $Candidate\_Set_i^j \neq \phi$ **then**
        select an element in $Candidate\_Set_i^j$ and add it to u_i^j;
    else
        $Candidate\_Set = \{e \mid e \in E^j$ and e satisfies $\Omega\}$
        if $Candidate\_Set_i^j \neq \phi$ **then**
            select an element in $Candidate\_Set_i^j$ and add it to u_i^j;
        end if
    end if
end procedure

C. Selection

The selection operator is similar to Eq. (7). In the selection operator, evaluates the trial set u_i and the individual set x_i by the fitness and remains the set with smaller fitness for the next generation, which is expressed as follows.

$$x_i^{new} = \begin{cases} u_i & \text{if}(f(u_i) \leq f(x_i)) \\ x_i & \text{otherwise} \end{cases} \tag{12}$$

where $f()$ is the fitness function for minimize optimization.

4   Numerical Experiments

We examine numerical experiments for MMAS, MBPSO, SCLPSO, and our algorithm (SBDE). Traveling salesman problem instances are eil51, berlin52, st70, eil76, kroA100, eil101, ch130, kroA150, d198 and tsp225 in TSPLIB [16]. We give parameters: the number of cities D, population size $N_p = 20$, number of maximum iteration $I_{max} = 500D$, generation counter $k \in [1 : I_{max}]$, and run times $T = 30$ for each algorithm. Other parameters are chosen as follows: $\alpha = 1$, $\beta = 2$, and evaporation coefficient $\rho = 0.98$ in MMAS, weighting constant $c_1 = c_2 = 4$ in MBPSO, inertia weight $w = 0.9 - 0.5*k/I_{max}$ and weight constant $c = 2.0$ in SCLPSO, scale parameter $F = 0.5$ and crossover rate $C_r = 0.9$ in SBDE, and probability generated by a uniform random value r in $[0.0, 1.0]$.

Results are given in Table 1. In the instances with a small of cities for eil76, the fitness difference among the existing algorithms and SBDE is not large. As the number cities increases, the difference among the average of SBDE and other algorithms becomes larger. SBDE is only able to find the optimal solution or the best approximate solution for all instances.

Table 1. Experimental results.

Instance	Best known	MMAS			MBPSO			SCLPSO			SBDE		
		Best	Average	Worst	Best	Average	Worst	Best	Average	Worst	Best	Average	Worst
eil51	426	**426**	427.93	430	427	427.60	429	**426**	426.97	428	**426**	426.93	427
berlin52	7542	**7542**	**7542**	7542	**7542**	**7542**	**7542**	**7542**	**7542**	7542	**7542**	**7542**	7542
st70	675	**675**	682.30	699	**675**	679.23	686	**675**	675.40	677	**675**	675.33	677
eil76	538	**538**	539.83	545	**538**	539.43	547	**538**	538.27	542	**538**	538.30	**541**
kroA100	21282	**21282**	21429.50	21783	**21282**	21342.20	21396	**21282**	21301.47	21468	**21282**	21287.23	21383
eil101	629	631	639.87	652	**629**	633.57	640	**629**	629.40	633	**629**	629.30	630
ch130	6110	6148	6195.73	6252	6140	6191.00	6271	**6110**	6146.17	6194	**6110**	6128.53	6159
kroA150	26524	26771	27029.70	27429	26525	26730.27	27279	26579	26687.73	26894	**26524**	26563.03	26766
d198	15780	15835	15892.53	16037	15812	15905.20	16571	15789	15825.17	15919	**15782**	**15793.17**	15806
tsp225	3916	3924	3958.07	3996	3925	3952.43	4024	3918	3936.17	3955	**3916**	**3923.90**	3950

Table 2 is shown the result of wilcoxon signed rank test with a significance level of 5% between SBDE and other algorithms in 10 instances. Three symbols "$+, -, =$" indicate that SBDE exhibits significantly better, worse than, and equal to the competitor, respectively. Table 2 shows that there are significant differences in all cases for our algorithm.

Table 2. Comparison results of SBDE with other algorithms.

Algorithms	+	=	−
MMAS	8	2	0
MBPSO	8	2	0
SCLPSO	4	6	0

We investigate the convergence speed for each algorithm. Figure 3, 4, 5, and 6 show the convergence speed of each algorithm for eil51, st70, kroA100 and kroA150. The convergence speeds of SBDE are the fastest compared to that of other algorithms for all instances.

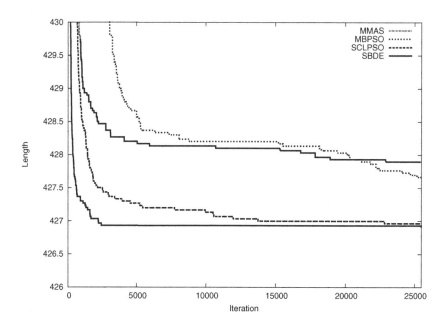

Fig. 3. Convergence speed of each algorithm of eil51

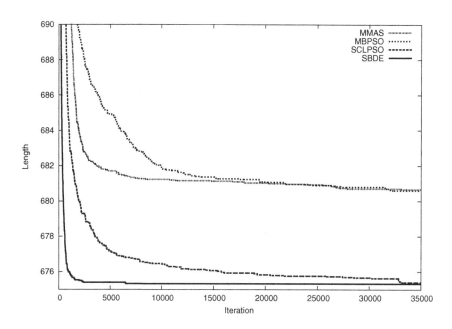

Fig. 4. Convergence speed of each algorithm of st70

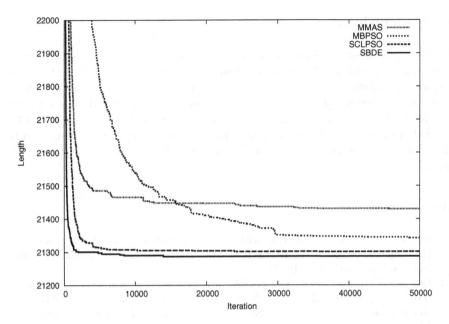

Fig. 5. Convergence speed of each algorithm of kroA100

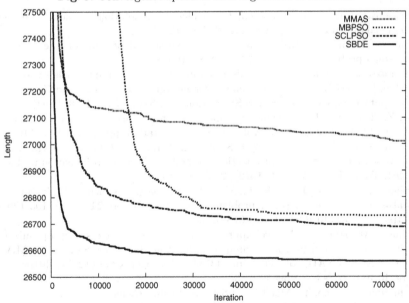

Fig. 6. Convergence speed of each algorithm of kroA150

5   Conclusions

We have presented an algorithm of set-based differential evolution for discrete optimization problem. Our algorithm had a set-based representation scheme for discrete optimization problem. For applying differential evolution of continuous problems to discrete problems, a candidate solution was defined on a crisp set and all arithmetic operators in mutation were redefined by new operators. Our algorithm showed the effectiveness through numerical experiments compared to the existing algorithms. For the future work, we will study theoretical considerations.

References

1. Aiyoshi, E., Yasuda, K.: Metaheuristics and Applications. Ohmsha, Japan (2007)
2. Golberg, D.E.: Genetic Algorithms in Search, Optimization, and Machine Learning. Addison Wesley, Boston (1989)
3. Dorigo, M., Maniezzo, V., Colorni, A.: Ant system: optimization by a colony of cooperating agents. IEEE Trans. Syst. Man Cybern. Syst. **26**(1), 29–41 (1996)
4. Kennedy, J., Eberhart, R.: Particle swarm optimization. In: Proceedings of ICNN 1995-International Conference on Neural Networks, vol. 4, pp. 1942–1948. IEEE (1995)
5. Price, K., Storn, R.M., Lampinen, J.A.: Differential evolution: a practical approach to global optimization. Springer, Heidelberg (2006)
6. Lin, S., Kernighan, B.W.: An effective heuristic algorithm for the traveling-salesman problem. Oper. Res. **21**(2), 498–516 (1973)
7. Kennedy, J., Eberhart, R.C.: A discrete binary version of the particle swarm algorithm. In: 1997 IEEE International Conference on Systems, Man, and Cybernetics. Computational Cybernetics and Simulation, vol. 5, pp. 4104–4108. IEEE (1997)
8. Ji, Z., Tian, T., He, S., Zhu, Z.: A memory binary particle swarm optimization. In: 2012 IEEE Congress on Evolutionary Computation, pp. 1–5. IEEE (2012)
9. Chen, W.N., Zhang, J., Chung, H.S., Zhong, W.L., Wu, W.G., Shi, Y.H.: A novel set-based particle swarm optimization method for discrete optimization problems. IEEE Trans. Evol. Comput. **14**(2), 278–300 (2009)
10. Hino, T., Ito, S., Liu, T., Maeda, M.: Set-based particle swarm optimization with status memory for knapsack problem. Artif. Life Robot. **21**(1), 98–105 (2016). https://doi.org/10.1007/s10015-015-0253-6
11. Maeda, M., Hino, T.: A novel approach of set-based particle swarm optimization with memory state. In: Phon-Amnuaisuk, S., Ang, S.-P., Lee, S.-Y. (eds.) MIWAI 2017. LNCS (LNAI), vol. 10607, pp. 437–449. Springer, Cham (2017). https://doi.org/10.1007/978-3-319-69456-6_36
12. Chikuba, Y., Hino, T., Maeda, M.: Set-based comprehensive learning and particle swarm optimization with memory for discrete optimization problem. Nonlinear Theory Appl. IEICE **13**(2), 452–458 (2022)
13. Stuzle, T., Hoos, H.: Max–Min ant system. Future Gener. Comput. Syst. **16**(9), 889–914 (2004)
14. Liang, J.J., Qin, A.K., Suganthan, P.: Comprehensive learning particle swarm optimizer for global optimization of multimodal. IEEE Trans. Evol. Comput. **10**(3), 281–295 (2006)

15. Das, S., Suganthan, P.N.: Differential evolution: a survey of the state-of-the-art. IEEE Trans. Evol. Comput. **15**(1), 4–31 (2011)
16. TSPLIB: http://comopt.ifi.uni-heidelberg.de/software/TSPLIB95/

Multi-objective Optimization Technique for RSU Deployment

Zecheng Kang[1], Dongyang Li[2(✉)], Weian Guo[2,3(✉)], Zhenyao Hua[1],
Guangcao Liu[4], and Yanfen Mao[2]

[1] Department of Electronics and Information Engineering, Tongji University,
Caoan Road, Shanghai 201804, China
{2130806,2032976}@tongji.edu.cn
[2] Sino-German College of Applied Sciences, Tongji University, Caoan Road,
Shanghai 201804, China
lidongyang0412@163.com, {guoweian,maoyanfen}@tongji.edu.cn
[3] Shanghai Institute of Intelligent Science and Technology, Tongji University,
Caoan Road, Shanghai 201804, China
[4] Fuzhou Polytechnic, Longjiang Road, Fujian 350300, China

Abstract. Due to its short latency, low transmission cost, and benefit
in data security, the vehicle to roadside-units (V2R) technology is growing in importance in the VANET. Roadside unit (RSU) complicated
location, however, has an impact on the RSU network in terms of time
delay, transmission efficiency, etc., making it challenging to use large-
scale RSU networks. In view of this, a cooperative transmission framework is devised for data transmission in VANET. The number of RSU
and the time delay are used as the metrics for measuring the economy
and network transmission performance, respectively, in order to create
the RSU deployment optimization model in this article, which addresses
the issue. A multi-objective evolutionary algorithm is then used to carry
out the RSU deployment's optimization. The results of experiments are
based on taxi data from ShenZhen. The findings show that the suggested
technique can reduce the number of RSU while enhancing the RSU network's transmission capabilities.

Keywords: V2R · RSU deployment · Multi-objective optimization ·
Network performance · Economy

1 Introduction

In response to the rapid development of the transportation infrastructure and
the problems raised by the increasing number of vehicles, the Internet of Vehicles
technology has been proposed and iteratively developed for traffic control, vehicle
safety, information services, and smart city construction, et al. [1–3].

Intelligent Vehicle Infrastructure Cooperative Systems(IVICS) is a hot topic
in the field of Internet of Vehicles, where vehicle to roadside unit (V2R) is a
key technique and road side unit (RSU) network is the intermediate medium

© The Author(s), under exclusive license to Springer Nature Singapore Pte Ltd. 2022
Y. Tan and Y. Shi (Eds.): DMBD 2022, CCIS 1745, pp. 118–132, 2022.
https://doi.org/10.1007/978-981-19-8991-9_10

between vehicles and cloud servers. Furthermore, RSU can also be adopted as a part of the cloud-edge collaboration system for special tasks [4–6]. In comparison to the traditional cellular networks, first, the transmission data of RSU are featured with low communication cost, better message transmission capability, lower end-to-end delay and flexible deployment et al. [7]. Second, transmitting the vehicle data with RSU can reduce the data traffic load of the 4G/5G cellular networks. Third, edge computing can be adopted based on RSU to provide real-time services for vehicles [8].

When it comes to RSU deployment, data transmission delay and RSU deployment cost are two optimization factors that are often considered, and there have been a lot of studies to optimize based on one or both of these indicators. It is well known that most research work focuses on reducing the transmission delay to optimize the location of RSU deployment because time delay is an important indicator to measure network performance. In order to overcome the time delay problem of signal propagation, Fogue et al. propose a genetic algorithm for RSU deployment [9]. Ahmed et al. formulate the RSU deployment problem as an integer linear programming model and propose an RSU placement strategy called the Delay Minimization Problem (DMP) [10]. Anbalagan et al. propose a meme-based RSU (M-RSU) placement algorithm to minimize communication latency and increase coverage area between IoV devices by optimizing RSU deployment [11]. Shi et al. propose a V2X network-based RSUD message propagation model and a central-rule-based neighborhood search algorithm (CNSA) [12].

Most deployment optimization algorithms only evaluate vehicle density and intersection attractiveness, ignoring the impact of map obstructions like buildings on RSU deployment. Ghorai et al. suggest a CDT-based algorithm [13]. Wang et al. deduce a connectivity analysis model considering the RSU deployment problem in one-way road scenarios, and analyzed the relationship between the number of RSUs and network connectivity [14]. Liu et al. establish a network model containing vehicle clusters for mathematical analysis [15]. Ni et al. investigate the deployment problem of minimizing the number of RSUs for two-dimensional IoV networks, using a utility-based maximization problem to solve the RSU deployment problem [16]. Ma et al. propose a multi-objective artificial bee colony optimizer (H-MOABC) to optimize a two-level Radio frequency identification networks planning (RNP) model based on hierarchical decoupling [17,20]. Yeferny et al. propose Minimum Mobile Mode Coverage (MPC) as a spatiotemporal coverage method to optimize RSU deployments. MPC mines vehicle trajectory data to describe its travel pattern, then extracts minimal transversals of a hypergraph to calculate the optimal RSU position [18]. Some researchers consider both factors when deploying RSU. Cao et al. construct a six-objective RSU deployment optimization model, including time delay and number of RSU deployments. This paper proposes a clustering method in which the cluster radius varies according to the number of RSUs in the cluster [19]. At the same time, an improved algorithm based on PCMLIA-ADE (PCMaLIA) is proposed to optimize the ES deployment model and achieve the tradeoff between conflicting objectives.

Despite the success of the existing work, few studies can be found for RSU deployment to simultaneously investigate the optimal delay and number of RSUs. First, the communication performance of the RSU networks is affected by the distribution of RSUs, since the traffic flow characteristics are different across areas [21]. Generally, the RSU network's performance should be good if enough RSUs are deployed. For instance, dense traffic commonly brings heavy data transmission load. Consequently, the data packets are crowded in the channel and need to be queued to enter the route for processing, resulting in increasing data transmission delay [22,23]. To this end, it is necessary to adopt more RSUs to reduce the delay and improve the network's performance. However, increasing costs are needed to deploy large-scale RSUs, which results in unexpected budgets and difficulties in implementation [24]. In places with sparse traffic, only small-scale data needs to be processed. Therefore, the density of RSUs can be curtailed to reduce the cost of building the RSU networks [25].

In order to balance the budget and performance of the RSU network, this article proposes a framework for cooperative transmission, based on which a multi-objective system model is built by considering the transmission delay time and the number of RSUs. In the proposed model, the transmission delay and the RSU deployments reflect the performance of the network and the economy of the system, respectively. In comparison to the single-objective based system model, the proposed model can get rid of the prior knowledge of weighting the importance for different objectives.

In summary, this paper makes the following contributions:

1. This paper proposes a hybrid framework for data transmission in the Internet of Vehicles. Vehicles can choose one of the channels for data transmission, so that resources can be fully integrated, and vehicles can be adjusted to select an appropriate channel for data transmission.
2. This paper introduces a multi-objective optimization model based on the time delay and the number of RSUs to optimize the deployment location of RSUs from the perspective of economics and network performance for the first time. We divided the area into grids and selected appropriate grids to deploy RSUs. This simplifies calculations and converges faster for better results.
3. In order to realize the model, we select a suitable multi-objective joint optimization algorithm, conducted experimental analysis, and obtained ideal results on the indicators we set.

The rest of this paper is organized as follows. Section 2 describes the proposed RSU deployment model. Section 3 provides a brief overview of the adopted optimization algorithm. Section 4 presents the experimental results and discussions. Finally, we conclude this paper and provide several future study directions in Sect. 5.

Table 1. Key terms in the model.

Key terms	Descriptions
D	Length of a data frame
R	RSU transmission radius
K	The number of RSUs
A	RSU set, A = $\{A_1, A_2,...,A_K\}$
B	Transmission bandwidth
x	Distance from vehicle to RSU
$RI(x)$	Data transfer rate
D_c	Critical data packet size
n_p	Number of packet received by RSU
T_Q	Queuing delay of packet
μ	Service rate
D_{en}	Packet arrival rate
η	Single RSU computing power
T_{ij}	Communication delay between RSU and vehiclex
$Gi(x)$	Channel gain
N_0	Noise power spectral density
β_1	Communication path loss constant
β_2	Communication path loss index
n_v	Vehicles number in a certain range
RS	Road resource (area)
T_c	Critical delay of transmission

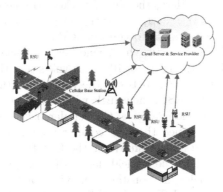

Fig. 1. Transmission network framework of RSU.

2   Problem Description and System Model

For better understanding, the key terms involved in the proposed model are listed in Table 1.

2.1   Multi-RSU Cooperative Data Transmission Network Framework

In current data transmission systems, RSUs are adopted to assist data transmission and relieve the transmission burden of cellular networks. Strong support for intelligent transportation can be furnished by the RSU data transmission paradigm with low latency and low communication cost.

This paper considers a vehicular network with multi-RSU and cellular base stations, which helps to connect vehicles to the cloud servers and transmit data with Internet. Figure 1 illustrates a RSU cooperative data transmission framework, where RSU and cellular networks receive data packets from vehicles and upload them to the cloud servers. Each vehicle has two communication interfaces of RSU and cellular base station. Vehicles can independently choose which interface to connect to. Compared with the cellular base station, vehicles prefer to transmit data with RSU due to its low communication cost, low time delay, and high data security. However, if a vehicle is out of communication range of the RSU or the RSU that a vehicle connects with is overloaded, the vehicle will upload data through the cellular base station. This strategy is capable of reducing the overall communication delay and cost. The RSUs, which are denoted as $A = \{A_1, A_2, ..., A_K\}$, are utilized to receive data packets from vehicles and forward them to the cloud servers, where K represents the number of RSU. Communication base stations are arranged to divert a part of vehicle's data and relieve RSU data transmission pressure to enhance the service efficiency. Suppose that N vehicles, which are denoted as $V = \{V_1, V_2, ..., V_N\}$, are required to upload the collected data to the edge nodes; each vehicle is of the same rate of producing and collecting data, and the collected data will be integrated (Referred as a data packet) and transmitted out when the data stored in the vehicle cache reach a critical value D_C. Here, the set of packets transmitted from vehicles is denoted as $M = \{M_1, M_2, ..., M_N\}$. For the data transmission, vehicles need to select what kind of edge node to connect with, since each vehicle has two choices as mentioned above. First, check whether a vehicle is in the range of RSUs. If the vehicle is in the range of RSUs, it will select the nearest RSU for data transmission. If the distance between the vehicle and the RSU exceeds the communication range of the RSU, the vehicle will transmit data with the cellular base station. The transmission range of the cellular base station is larger than that of the RSU. It is assumed that the cellular base stations fully cover the map and can transmit data successfully for the first time. If the transmission delay with RSU is less than the critical delay, the transmission is considered successful. However, vehicles are constantly moving, or huge amounts of data packets are crowded into one RSU, which will result in the time delay exceeding the critical delay T_c. Therefore, the vehicle will choose the cellular base station for the second time. Here, denote x as the distance between the vehicle V_n and the corresponding selected RSU; R is the transmission cover radius of RSU.

2.2   Transmission Delay Model

As shown in the Fig. 2, transmission delay commonly consists of four parts, i.e., the propagation delay of data packets between different nodes, the transmission delay of devices for pushing out data packets, the processing delay of routers for data checking, and the delay of data packets entering the queue.

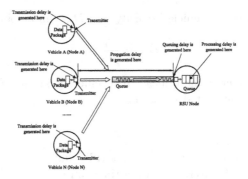

Fig. 2. Time delay model.

In this model, the distance between the roadside unit node and the vehicle is less than 1,000 m, and the speed of data propagation corresponds to the speed of electromagnetic wave propagation through the air. Consequently, the theoretical propagation speed is within 0.003 milliseconds, which is significantly less than the queueing delay and transmission delay of over 100 milliseconds. Therefore, the propagation delay can be disregarded in this model. Additionally, the processing delay is generally considered negligible [26].

The sending delay T_{ij} is calculated by (1):

$$T_S = \frac{D}{RI(x)} \tag{1}$$

where T_S represents the data transmission time of the ith vehicle in the jth time slot, $RI(x)$ is the transmission rate of the current location, and $RI(x)$ is calculated according to

$$RI(x) = B \cdot \log_2\left(1 + \frac{Gi(x) \cdot P_N}{B \cdot N_0}\right) \tag{2}$$

$$Gi(x) = \beta_1 \cdot x^{\beta_2} \tag{3}$$

where $Gi(x)$ and x are the channel gain and distance between vehicle V_N and the RSU, respectively; β_1 and β_2 represent the path loss constant and path loss exponent in the communication, respectively; P_N is the RSU's transmission power; B is the bandwidth and N_0 represents the noise power spectral density [8]. In order to calculate the waiting time of a packet to be received by the RSUs, the queuing theory of M/M/1 model is adopted in this paper with assuming that the arrival rate is λ and the service rate of the RSU is μ. λ can be calculated according to

$$\lambda = \frac{D_{en}^k}{m \cdot k!} e^{-D_{en}} \tag{4}$$

where D_{en} represents the vehicles' density and D_{en} can be obtained by

$$D_{en} = \frac{n_v}{RS} \tag{5}$$

where n_v is the number of the vehicles in specific regions and RS represents the road resources. μ is calculated according to

$$\mu = \frac{\eta}{S} \tag{6}$$

where η is the computing power of a single RSU and S is the average length of packets. Afterwards, the average waiting time can be obtained according to (7) to (8).

$$n_v = \frac{\rho}{1-\rho} = \frac{\lambda}{\mu - \lambda} \tag{7}$$

$$T_Q = \frac{n_v}{\lambda} = \frac{\rho}{(1-\rho)\lambda} = \frac{1}{\mu - \lambda} \tag{8}$$

where T_Q is the waiting time. Then, the total transmission delay of one packet is calculated by

$$T_{ij} = T_S + T_Q \tag{9}$$

where T_{ij} is the total delay of the ith vehicle in the jth time slot. Note that the RSU-based transmission of the ith vehicle in the jth time slot is successful only if $T_{ij} \leq T_c$, or the ith vehicle will transmit data with cellular stations in the jth time slot. When sending data packets with the cellular base station, since the cellular base station has a longer delay and higher communication cost, we set a larger delay time for the data packets transmitted with the cellular base station as punishment.

2.3   RSU Number Model

All the RSUs in the model share the same characteristics, such as performance and deployment costs. Therefore, the cost of building the RSU network depends on the number of RSUs. In this paper, the map is divided into multiple refined grid areas G_R and each grid only includes one RSU or not. Accordingly, the number of RSUs deployed in the entire model can be calculated by

$$G_R(n) = \begin{cases} 1, & \text{if } RSU \text{ depolyed in this area } n \\ 0, & \text{none } RSU \text{ depolyed in this area } n \end{cases} \tag{10}$$

$$K_{RSU} = \sum_1^n G_R \tag{11}$$

In order to reduce the overall deployment cost, the number of RSUs in the model should be reduced. Note that this objective is conflict to minimize the overall delay mentioned above.

2.4   Problem Formulation

This paper aims at minimizing the average time delay of RSU data transmission and reducing the number of deployed RSUs by optimizing the location distribution of the RSUs. These two objectives can be formulated as

$$min f_1 = \left\{ \sum_{n=1}^{K} T_{ij} \right\} \tag{12}$$

$$min f_2 = \{ K_{RSU} \} \tag{13}$$

3   Algorithm Background

The goal of this work is to minimize the transmission delay and the number of RSUs to achieve an efficient RSU network. NSGA-II is a powerful tool in solving multi-objective optimization problems [28], which are briefed as follows.

1. Initialization
   Given that MG is the maximum number of iterations, P_{size} is the population size, P_{size} individuals are randomly generated, according to the characteristics of the problem. f_1 and f_2 are calculated for each individual.
2. Pareto sorting
   Execute the non-dominated sorting according to the fitness [27].
3. Selection
   Select P_{size} individuals to participate the crossover and mutation operations [28].
4. Crossover
   The standard NSGA-II algorithm adopts an analog binary crossover operator, and the new individuals in generation k are generated based on the selected individuals (See Step 2) according to

$$p_{1,k+1} = \frac{1}{2} \left[(1 - \beta_{qi}) p_{1,k} + (1 + \beta_{qi}) p_{2,k} \right] \tag{14}$$

$$p_{2,k+1} = \frac{1}{2} \left[(1 + \beta_{qi}) p_{1,k} + (1 - \beta_{qi}) p_{2,k} \right] \tag{15}$$

where $p(1, k+1)$ and $p(2, k+1)$ are the individuals generated at generation k with the crossover operation; $p(1, k)$ and $p(2, k)$ are the selected individuals at k generation; β_{qi} is calculated according to

$$\beta_{qi} = (2\mu_i)^{\frac{1}{\tau+1}} \quad \mu_i \leq 0.5 \tag{16}$$

$$\beta_{qi} = \frac{1}{[2(1 - \mu_i)]^{\frac{1}{\tau+1}}} \mu_i \geq 0.5 \tag{17}$$

where μ_i is a random number within $[0, 1)$; τ is the cross-distribution index, which will affect the distance between the generated individuals and the parent individuals.

5. Mutation

The mutation operation is to simulate the genetic mutation behavior. This paper adopts the polynomial mutation operator, which is shown as

$$p_{k+1} = p_k + \left(p_k^{\max} + p_k^{\min}\right) \delta_k \tag{18}$$

where p_k is the individuals to be mutated at generation k; p_k^{max} and p_k^{min} are the upper and lower bounds of the decision variables; δ_k is calculated according to

$$\delta_k = \begin{cases} (2r_k)^{\frac{1}{i_m+1}} - 1 & r_k < 0.5 \\ 1 - [2(1 - r_k)]^{\frac{1}{i_m+1}} & r_k \geq 0.5 \end{cases}, \tag{19}$$

where r_k is the uniformly distribute random number in $[0, 1]$; i_m is the mutation index.

6. Termination criterion checking

If the termination criterion has been satisfied, output the individuals; If not, select P_{size} individuals as $P(k+1)$ from $P(k) \cup P_{child}(k)$ and return to Step 2, where $P(k)$ and $P_{child}(k)$ are the populations and the newly generated individuals at generation k, respectively [27].

The NSGA II's time complexity is $O(MN^2)$, where M represents the number of objectives and N represents the size of the population. The NSGA II's space complexity is $O(BTN)$, where B represents the number of blocks in the map and T represents the number of time periods.

4   Experiment and Simulation

4.1   Simulation Set up

In the experimental part, all the simulations are run with Intel i7-11800H; Table 2 lists the key parameters in the experiment.

Where P_N is the RSU transmit power, N_0 is the noise power spectral density, β_1 is the communication path loss constant and β_2 is the communication path loss index, these four parameters are cited from reference [8]. In order to balance the solution quality and computation time, this paper sets the max generation G_{max} and the population size of one generation P_{size} as 200 and 50, respectively. i_m is the mutation index and τ is the cross-distribution index, which are cited from reference [28].

4.2   Experiment Data

The experiments are conducted based on a Shenzhen taxi dataset which records the travel coordinates of 602 taxis in Shenzhen on October 22, 2014, and the coordinate data are updated about every 20–40 s. The following criterion is adopted for data processing: Data interpolation. We divided the whole day into 12 time periods in chronological order. Every time period contains 2 h and the sampling is performed every 30 s in each time period.

Table 2. The value of key terms.

Key terms	Descriptions	Value
D	Length of a data frame	1 Mb
R	RSU transmission radius	1000 m
D_c	Critical data packet size	5 Mb
P_N	RSU transmit power	23 dBm
N_0	Noise power spectral density	-174 dBm/Hz
β_1	Communication path loss constant	0.0007
β_2	Communication path loss index	2
T_c	Critical delay of transmission	5S
G_{max}	Max generation	200
P_{size}	Population size of one generation	50
i_m	The mutation index	20
τ	The cross-distribution index	20

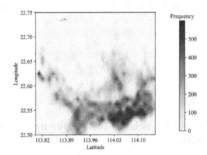

Fig. 3. Frequency of RSU's likely location

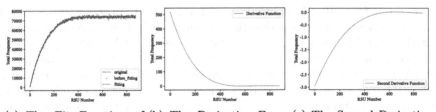

(a) The Fit Function of Statistics Curve

(b) The Derivative Function of Fit Function

(c) The Second Derivative Function of Fit Function

Fig. 4. Fit function of RSU frequency statistics curve and derivative function

In this paper, we apply the multi-objective optimization algorithm to optimize taxi trajectory data for each time period to find the pareto optimal surface of RSU deployment positions and numbers. RSU deployment locations vary each time period due to taxi trajectories. The frequency heat map of RSU possible sites is obtained by stacking RSU likelihood locations over all time periods, as illustrated in Fig. 3. Then we sort and count the frequency of the possible positions of each RSU, accumulate from the high frequency to the low frequency, and obtain the change curve of the frequency and quantity shown in the Fig. 4, and then fit the curve to obtain the fitted continuous function.

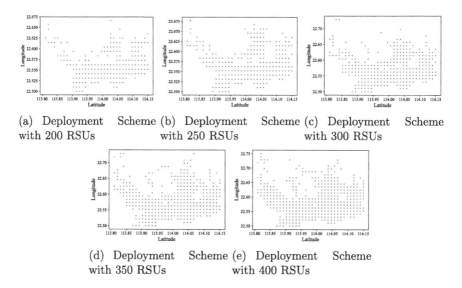

(a) Deployment   Scheme (b) Deployment   Scheme (c) Deployment   Scheme
with 200 RSUs   with 250 RSUs   with 300 RSUs

(d) Deployment   Scheme (e) Deployment   Scheme
with 350 RSUs   with 400 RSUs

Fig. 5. RSU depolyment scheme with different number of RSUs

Since the derivative of the fitted function is greater than zero and the second derivative is less than zero within the domain of definition (0, 875), it can be seen that the fitted function is a concave function, and because there are no inflection points and stagnation points, we cannot find the only optimal point. According to the derivative function, when the number of RSUs is 200, the value of the derivative is 136.548, when the number of RSUs is 400, it is 16.388, and in this interval, the total frequency of RSUs is close to the maximum point. It can be seen that in this interval, the two indicators of economic activity and delay are balanced. Therefore, we obtain a series of new RSU deployment schemes in the interval of 200–400. The delays of these schemes are shown in Fig. 7, and the deployment position of RSU is shown in Fig. 5. Additionally, the time delay distribution in each block is shown in Fig. 6, one can see that the number of the areas with high time delay decreases with the increasing number of RSU.

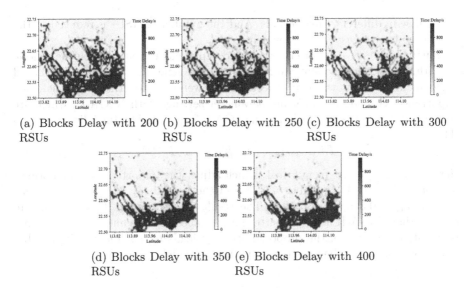

(a) Blocks Delay with 200 RSUs (b) Blocks Delay with 250 RSUs (c) Blocks Delay with 300 RSUs

(d) Blocks Delay with 350 RSUs (e) Blocks Delay with 400 RSUs

Fig. 6. Time delay distribution in each block with different number of RSUs

NSGA-II is applied to find the proper solutions to (12) and (13). The performance of the population with respect to these two objectives are shown in Fig. 7, indicating that with the increasing of the system delay (from about 1,148,176s to 1,245,795s), the number of RSUs decreases from 200 to 400. In comparison to the original delay of 4,054,000s and the original RSU number of 450, the delay is reduced by about 69.3% to 71.7% and the number of RSUs is reduced by 11.2% to 55.6%.

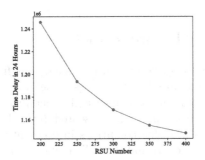

Fig. 7. Total time delay in 24 h of each scheme

By counting the frequency of RSUs' usage positions in different regions in different time periods of the Pareto optimal surface, and selecting the appropriate number and location of RSUs according to the total frequency changing curve, we can obtain 5 highly robust RSU deployment schemes which can adapt to the traffic flow in different time periods. And the number of RSUs is reduced at the same time to decrease the deployment cost.

Furthermore, we compare the proposed deployment strategy with the genetic algorithm-based deployment method [9]. In the genetic algorithm (GA) based deployment strategy, the two objectives are weighted together with the same importance. GA adopts the same parameter settings with NSGA-II, which are shown in Table 2. The fitness function of GA is formulated by the follow equation [11]:

$$Fitness_{GA} = w_1 n_{RSU}^{norm} + w_2 T_{total}^{norm}. \tag{20}$$

Here, w_1 and w_2 range from 0 to 1, which adjust the importance of the normalized objectives: RSU's number n_{RSU}^{norm} and the time delay T_{total}^{norm}, respectively. We set $w_1 = 0.5$ and $w_2 = 0.5$. The results are shown in Table 3. One can observe that NSGA-II achieves better performance in the same traffic-flow environment. Furthermore, the proposed strategy leads to a reduced RSU number in comparison to GA-based strategy with similar delay performance.

Table 3. Comparison results on two algorithm.

Algorithm	Time delay/seconds	RSU's number
GA	1.246×10^6	472
NSGA-II	$1.148 \times 10^6 - 1.245 \times 10^6$	200–400

In summary, the experimental results demonstrate that the adopted algorithm on proposed framework is effective in simultaneously reducing the time delay and RSU number, which is beneficial to the application of the large-scale RSU network.

5   Conclusion and Future Work

This paper proposes a cooperation data transmission framework-based RSU deployment model to minimize data transmission delay and RSU number. These objectives measure network performance and economy. By adopting a multi-objective optimization algorithm, the presented RSU deployment strategy is capable of adapting to the traffic conditions in different regions. Experimental results show that both the delay and the RSU number can be effectively reduced with respect to a real-world dataset.

In our future work, we will investigate more factors in the RSU network, including the RSU work/sleep strategy and the multiple retransmission strategy, to continue improving the performance of the RSU network.

Acknowledgements. This work is supported by the National Natural Science Foundation of China under Grant Number 71771176 and 61503287; Natural Science Foundation of Shanghai, China under Grant Number 19ZR1479000, 20692191200; Shanghai

Municipal Science and Technology Major Project (2022-5-YB-09); Education research and reform project of Tongji University: Research on talent training program and model of Sino-German international factory.

References

1. Siegel, J.E., Erb, D.C., Sarma, S.E.: A survey of the connected vehicle landscape— architectures, enabling technologies, applications, and development areas. IEEE Trans. Intell. Transp. Syst. **19**(8), 2391–2406 (2017)
2. Contreras-Castillo, J., Zeadally, S., Guerrero-Ibañez, J.A.: Internet of vehicles: architecture, protocols, and security. IEEE Internet Things J. **5**(5), 3701–3709 (2017)
3. Lu, Z., Qu, G., Liu, Z.: A survey on recent advances in vehicular network security, trust, and privacy. IEEE Trans. Intell. Transp. Syst. **20**(2), 760–776 (2018)
4. Zhao, J., Li, Q., Gong, Y., Zhang, K.: Computation offloading and resource allocation for cloud assisted mobile edge computing in vehicular networks. IEEE Trans. Veh. Technol. **68**(8), 7944–7956 (2019)
5. Yang, Z., Yang, K., Lei, L., Zheng, K., Leung, V.C.: Blockchain-based decentralized trust management in vehicular networks. IEEE Internet Things J. **6**(2), 1495–1505 (2018)
6. Xiao, L., Lu, X., Xu, D., Tang, Y., Wang, L., Zhuang, W.: UAV relay in VANETs against smart jamming with reinforcement learning. IEEE Trans. Veh. Technol. **67**(5), 4087–4097 (2018)
7. Zhao, C., Wang, T., Yang, A.: A heterogeneous virtual machines resource allocation scheme in slices architecture of 5G edge datacenter. Comput. Mater. Contin **69**, 423–437 (2019)
8. Cui, J., Wei, L., Zhong, H., Zhang, J., Xu, Y., Liu, L.: Edge computing in VANETs-an efficient and privacy-preserving cooperative downloading scheme. IEEE J. Sel. Areas Commun. **38**(6), 1191–1204 (2020)
9. Fogue, M., Sanguesa, J.A., Martinez, F.J., Marquez-Barja, J.M.: Improving roadside unit deployment in vehicular networks by exploiting genetic algorithms. Appl. Sci. **8**(1), 86 (2018)
10. Ahmed, Z., Naz, S., Ahmed, J.: Minimizing transmission delays in vehicular ad hoc networks by optimized placement of road-side unit. Wireless Netw. **26**(4), 2905–2914 (2020). https://doi.org/10.1007/s11276-019-02198-x
11. Anbalagan, S., et al.: Machine-learning-based efficient and secure RSU placement mechanism for software-defined-IoV. IEEE Internet Things J. **8**(18), 13950–13957 (2021)
12. Shi, Y., Lv, L., Yu, H., Yu, L., Zhang, Z.: A center-rule-based neighborhood search algorithm for roadside units deployment in emergency scenarios. Mathematics **8**(10), 1734 (2020)
13. Ghorai, C., Banerjee, I.: A constrained Delaunay Triangulation based RSUs deployment strategy to cover a convex region with obstacles for maximizing communications probability between V2I. Veh. Commun. **13**, 89–103 (2018)
14. Wang, Y., Zheng, J.: Connectivity analysis of a highway with one entry/exit and multiple roadside units. IEEE Trans. Veh. Technol. **67**(12), 11705–11718 (2018)
15. Liu, C., Huang, H., Du, H.: Optimal RSUs deployment with delay bound along highways in VANET. J. Comb. Optim. **33**(4), 1168–1182 (2017). https://doi.org/10.1007/s10878-016-0029-5

16. Ni, Y., He, J., Cai, L., Pan, J., Bo, Y.: Joint roadside unit deployment and service task assignment for Internet of Vehicles (IOV). IEEE Internet Things J. **6**(2), 3271–3283 (2018)

17. Ma, L., Wang, X., Huang, M., Lin, Z., Tian, L., Chen, H.: Two-level master-slave RFID networks planning via hybrid multiobjective artificial bee colony optimizer. IEEE Trans. Syst. Man Cybern. Syst. **49**(5), 861–80 (2017)

18. Yeferny, T., Allani, S.: MPC: a RSUs deployment strategy for VANET. Int. J. Commun Syst **31**(12), 3712 (2018)

19. Cao, B., et al.: Large-scale many-objective deployment optimization of edge servers. IEEE Trans. Intell. Transp. Syst. **22**(6), 3841–3849 (2021)

20. Ma, L., Huang, M., Yang, S., Wang, R., Wang, X.: An adaptive localized decision variable analysis approach to large-scale multiobjective and many-objective optimization. IEEE Trans. Cybern. **52**(7), 6684–6696 (2022)

21. Song, C., Wu, J., Yang, W.-S., Liu, M., Jawhar, I., Mohamed, N.: Exploiting opportunities in V2V transmissions with RSU-assisted backward delivery. In: 2017 IEEE Conference on Computer Communications Workshops (INFOCOM WKSHPS), pp. 271–276. IEEE (2017)

22. Xu, X., Zhang, X., Liu, X., Jiang, J., Qi, L., Bhuiyan, M.Z.A.: Adaptive computation offloading with edge for 5G-envisioned internet of connected vehicles. IEEE Trans. Intell. Transp. Syst. **22**(8), 5213–5222 (2020)

23. Sahebgharani, S., Shahverdy, M.: A scheduling algorithm for downloading data from RSU using multicast technique. In: 2012 Ninth International Conference on Information Technology-New Generations, pp. 809–814. IEEE (2012)

24. Lamb, Z.W., Agrawal, D.P.: Data-driven approach for targeted RSU deployment in an urban environment. In: 2017 IEEE Intelligent Vehicles Symposium (IV), pp. 1916–1921. IEEE (2017)

25. Lin, X., Lu, R., Liang, X., Shen, X.: STAP: a social-tier-assisted packet forwarding protocol for achieving receiver-location privacy preservation in VANETs. In: 2011 Proceedings IEEE INFOCOM, pp. 2147–2155. IEEE (2011)

26. Xu, X., et al.: Edge server quantification and placement for offloading social media services in industrial cognitive IoV. IEEE Trans. Industr. Inf. **17**(4), 2910–2918 (2020)

27. Deb, K., Pratap, A., Agarwal, S., Meyarivan, T.: A fast and elitist multi-objective genetic algorithm: NSGA-II. IEEE Trans. Evol. Comput. **6**(2), 182–197 (2002)

28. Deb, K., Agrawal, S., Pratap, A., Meyarivan, T.: A fast elitist non-dominated sorting genetic algorithm for multi-objective optimization: NSGA-II. In: Schoenauer, M., et al. (eds.) PPSN 2000. LNCS, vol. 1917, pp. 849–858. Springer, Heidelberg (2000). https://doi.org/10.1007/3-540-45356-3_83

Knowledge Learning-Based Brain Storm Optimization Algorithm for Multimodal Optimization

Xueping Wang, Yue Liu, and Shi Cheng[✉] [iD]

School of Computer Science, Shaanxi Normal University, Shaanxi 710119, China
{wxp,liuyuemelody,cheng}@snnu.edu.cn

Abstract. Using swarm intelligence to obtain multiple optima in a single run simultaneously proved efficient for solving multimodal optimization problems (MOPs). However, the existing studies fail to resolve the contradiction between the required solution accuracy and the number of solutions. In this paper, an improved brain storm optimization (BSO) algorithm based on knowledge learning (KLBSO) is proposed as a solution to the problem. The properties of the improved algorithm and the domain knowledge of the problem are combined during the search process. Two factors need to be taken into account to solve a MOP: the accuracy and the diversity of the solution set. In the proposed algorithm, there are two learning approaches. Firstly, improving the learning method by replacing the perturbation operator of the random solution with the inter-solution learning of the worst solutions, improves the optimization ability of the algorithm. Secondly, by analyzing the MOPs, adding an archive set guarantees the solution's diversity. To assess the efficiency of KLBSO, eight benchmark functions with various sizes and complexities were used. Comparing the results of KLBSO with those of state-of-the-art methods which are brain storm optimization algorithm (BSO), brain storm optimization algorithm in objective space (BSOOS), two kinds of pigeon-inspired optimization algorithms (PIO, PIOr), the comparison results show that the KLBSO is able to solve the contradiction between required solution accuracy and the number of solutions, and improves the outcomes where BSO is ranked first followed by the test algorithms.

Keywords: Brain storm optimization · Learning · Multimodal optimization · Knowledge acquisition · Knowledge utilization

1 Introduction

Many real-world engineering optimization problems are both dynamic and multimodal. Multimodal optimization aims to locate all or most of the multiple

This work is partially supported by National Natural Science Foundation of China (Grant No. 61806119), Fundamental Research Funds for the Central Universities (No. GK202201014), and Graduate innovation team project of Shaanxi Normal University (No. TD2020014Z).

© The Author(s), under exclusive license to Springer Nature Singapore Pte Ltd. 2022
Y. Tan and Y. Shi (Eds.): DMBD 2022, CCIS 1745, pp. 133–143, 2022.
https://doi.org/10.1007/978-981-19-8991-9_11

solutions in a single search and maintain these solutions during the entire search [10]. The challenge for solving multimodal optimization problems (MOPs) is the trade-off between solution accuracy and the number of solutions required [8]. If the accuracy requirements are met blindly, the algorithm is likely to fall into a single solution, and the number of solutions is insufficient; If too much focus is placed on the number of solutions, it will be impossible to obtain satisfying accuracy. An effective approach for solving MOPs is the intelligent optimization algorithm.

Swarm intelligence optimization methods, as a class of methods that could effectively solve complex large-scale optimization problems, have become a research hotspot in many fields [9]. Traditional swarm intelligence optimization methods, such as particle swarm optimization algorithm, differential evolution algorithm, etc., are mainly model-driven and based on simple iterative formulas, these algorithms use the same parameter settings and structure to address various optimization problems. These methods have the benefits of being simple to implement and not requiring prior knowledge of the problem, but failing to obtain high accuracy and performance guarantee for specific problems.

Brain storm optimization (BSO) algorithm incorporates data analysis [2, 3]. The solution set is directed to the area with the highest fitness value by classifying or clustering the data from the solution set, iteratively searching the solution space, and using the current solution information discovered by the search. To address MOPs, it is crucial to enhance the diversity of the output solutions and improve the solution accuracy.

This paper proposes an improved BSO based on knowledge learning and applies it to solve MOPs. This paper is organized as follows. Section 2 introduces the preparatory knowledge of this paper, including the basic knowledge of the BSO algorithm and multimodal optimization. Section 3 introduces the knowledge-driven strategy and basic algorithm flow for improving the BSO algorithm. Section 4 discusses and analyzes the experimental results. Section 5 is the conclusion of this paper and future research directions.

2   Background Knowledge

2.1   Brain Storm Optimization Algorithm

BSO is a swarm intelligence optimization algorithm inspired by the human social activity—brainstorming process [14]. The algorithm is based on the prototype of everyone's brainstorming to solve the problem, extracts the mode of solving the problem, and abstracts it into an optimization algorithm [3]. Algorithm 1 presents the basic flow of the BSO algorithm.

2.2   Multimodal Optimization Problem

MOP is characterized by two or more very different solutions that have the same or very close values. Multimodal optimization is to solve MOPs and hold these

---

Algorithm 1: The basic process of BSO algorithm

Input: Initialize n individuals with random values, and evaluate the individuals

1 **while** *not find satisfied solutions or not reach the pre-determined maximum number of iterations* **do**

2 | **Solution grouping operation**: Diverge n individuals into m groups by a clustering/classification algorithm ;

3 | **New solutions generation operation**: Randomly select solutions from one or two sets of solutions to generate new solution individuals;

4 | **Solution disruption operation**: Randomly choose a solution, reinitialize the value of a dimension, and update the function value of the new solution accordingly;

5 | **Solution selection operation**: Compare the newly generated solution and the existing solution with the same index; the better one is kept and recorded as the new individual;

---

optima during the entire search. Figure 1 shows an example of a MOP. With the decision variable $x \in [0, 1]$, exist four solutions 0.125, 0.375, 0.625, and 0.875, as shown in Eq. (1).

$$f(x) = 1 - \sin^4(4 \times \pi \times x) \tag{1}$$

Generally, there are two indicators to measure the optimization results of MOPs, which are the number of optima found (NPF) and the ratio of the found optimal solutions to all the global optimal solutions (optima ratio, PR) [4]. For MOPs, the larger the NPF, the closer the PR is to 1; when the NPF value is equal to the number of global optimal solutions, that is, all global optimal solutions are found, and PR is 1. During the experiment, the Eq. (2) is used to update the PR:

$$PR = \frac{\sum_{i=1}^{NR} NPF_i}{NKP \times NR} = \frac{NPF}{NKP \times NR} \tag{2}$$

where NPF_i refers to number of the found optima in ith run, NR is the number of runs of the algorithm, NKP is the number of known optima for the benchmark function.

3 Knowledge Learning for Brain Storm Optimization

3.1 Knowledge-Driven Strategies for Optimization Algorithms

Knowledge in the context of swarm intelligence optimization refers to information that is useful for solving problems. The primary challenge in developing knowledge-driven optimization algorithms, according to various information classifications, is how to leverage the knowledge acquisition mechanism to extract valuable knowledge from crowded data.

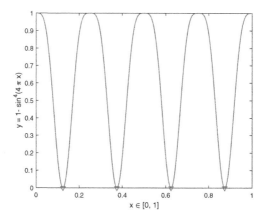

Fig. 1. Example of a multimodal optimization problem.

From the perspective of algorithm design, the solution set information that needs to be processed by the knowledge acquisition strategy could be simply classified into several categories during the search.

- From the accuracy of the information, information could be divided into definite information and uncertain information.
- From the trend of information changes, it could be divided into static information (offline information) and dynamic information (online information)
- From the timeliness of information, it could be divided into historical information and current information.
- From the way of information acquisition, it could be divided into direct information and indirect information.

In swarm intelligence optimization algorithms, designing algorithms in accordance with the characteristics of the problem is a research hotspot [12]. Considering the characteristics of the problem in the optimization process, the information could be divided into optimization strategy knowledge, population distribution knowledge, and domain knowledge. Optimization strategy knowledge refers to the frame design of the algorithm, the selection of optimization operators and optimization parameters, etc. According to the population distribution knowledge, which is dynamically changing, the optimization information of the algorithm could be obtained in real-time and the optimization strategy could be adjusted.

The knowledge of optimization algorithms refers to choosing the appropriate optimization operator and efficient operator structure, parameter settings, etc., for the problem. To choose the appropriate setting, it needs to be based on the characteristics of the problem and leverage knowledge of optimization algorithms. A hyper-heuristic algorithm is a class of optimization methods that utilize algorithmic knowledge, using the results of multiple attempts to select a suitable setting among a variety of settings [6].

Knowledge of intelligent optimization algorithms could be analyzed and obtained a priori from the properties of the algorithm and the solved problem. While the distribution information of the population needs to be obtained dynamically during the optimization process. Based on the distribution information of the population, the status of the current population search could be obtained, and trends for the next search could be judged, such as the emphasis on exploration or exploitation capabilities. Convergence and diversity as two indicators to measure population distribution information could guide the direction of the search.

In this paper, knowledge is defined as the valuable structured information that swarm intelligence methods could be used to solve optimization problems. Decomposing complex problems into simple, previously learned sub-problems, and acquiring knowledge based on a hierarchical approach, could be used to design algorithms to deal with complex system problems [7].

3.2   Knowledge Learning Strategy of Brain Storm Optimization

To design the learning strategy of the algorithm, it is necessary to combine the search characteristics of the algorithm and the problem. In terms of algorithm characteristics, improve the optimization ability of the algorithm by improving the worst solution at each iteration; in terms of problem characteristics, use the archive set method to enhance the diversity of optimized solutions. The learning of algorithmic search features and problem features are combined in the KLBSO algorithm.

Algorithmic Search Features. BSO is divided into two categories, the classical method based on solution set clustering BSO algorithm [14] and BSO in objective space (BSOOS) algorithm [15]. Classic BSO algorithm has some disadvantages like premature convergence and high time complexity; while BSOOS algorithm has the characteristics of fast convergence speed, low computational resource consumption, and low search accuracy. In this paper, the method needs to find multiple solutions that meet the accuracy requirements after 500 iterations. Taking advantage of BSOOS algorithm in the diversity of computing resources and solutions, this study will increase the optimization ability of BSOOS algorithm to address MOPs. The BSOOS algorithm with learning ability, in which the disturbance operator of the random solution is removed and the worst solution is updated by learning from the optimal solution, could increase the optimization ability of the original BSOOS algorithm.

In each iteration of the BSOOS algorithm, all solutions in the current population set need to be sorted according to the fitness value, and divided into elitist class and normal class. A specific optimization is performed for the worst solution in the solution set to improve the optimization ability of the algorithm. The optimal solution and the worst solution of the current solution set are changed from the original BSOOS. It is generated by the fitness value sorting operation in the algorithm and does not consume extra computing resources. Drawing on the new solution generation method of the differential evolution algorithm, the worst solution is proposed according to the Eq. (3) to update.

$$\mathbf{x}_{worst}^{t+1} = \mathbf{x}_{worst}^{t} + F(\mathbf{x}_{best}^{t} - \mathbf{x}_{rand}^{t}) \tag{3}$$

where $\mathbf{x}_{worst}$, $\mathbf{x}_{best}$, $\mathbf{x}_{rand}$ are the worst solution, optimal solution and random solution in the current solution set, respectively, t is the number of iterations, and F is the scaling factor.

Problem Characteristics. To solve MOPs, it is required to locate as many solutions as feasible in a single search. Under the condition of satisfying search accuracy, the number and diversity of solutions are particularly important. Increasing the variety of the current solution set in the population is required to increase the diversity of the output solution set. However, increasing the diversity of the population will slow down the process of optimization. As a result, based on the characteristics of the problem, the algorithm search is separated from the diversity of the solution set. Therefore an additional archive set is utilized to store and maintain the solution set. Algorithm 2 specifies the update strategy for the archive set. For MOPs, the algorithm is required to consider optimization efficiency and solution diversity. During the search, the archive set is used to store the intermediate solutions that meet the requirements, which could maintain the diversity of the solution set. After executing k iterations, KLBSO employs Algorithm 2 to update the archive set. Only the distance between the current solution and the solutions in the archive is required.

Algorithm 2: Archive set update strategy

    Input: The size of the archive set, the fitness value of the current solution set

1 **for** *All solutions in the current solution set that satisfy the fitness requirement* **do**

2   **if** *Archive set is not full* **then**

3   save the solution into the archive;

4   **else**

5   Calculate the distance between the solution and the solution stored in the archive, and replace the solution closest to the current solution in the archive with the current solution;

The archive set strategy based on problem features does not change the search process, so it does not affect the optimization process. However, through the archive set strategy, the diversity of the output solutions could be effectively increased. Change once evaluation at the end of the search process to several judgments in the search process, and store and maintain multiple solutions that meet the requirements. Thereby improving the quality of the output solution.

4 Experimental Results and Analysis

Eight multimodal benchmark functions are used to test the proposed KLBSO algorithm in this experiment, and the selected functions are consistent with the setting in the paper [1].

4.1 Algorithm Parameter Settings

In the experiment, we used five algorithms including the KLBSO algorithm proposed in this paper, brain storm optimization algorithm (BSO) [13,14], brain storm optimization algorithm in objective space (BSOOS) [15], 2 kinds of pigeon-inspired optimization algorithms (PIO, PIOr) [5].

In the experiment, the algorithms all use the same parameter settings: number of iterations is set to 500 ; PIO and PIOr are both composed of two operators, map and compass operator and landmark operator with the same methods; initial population size is set to 100. And all optimization problems will be executed 50 times.

4.2 Results

Table 1 shows the benchmark functions of multimodal optimization used in the experiment [1,11]. All algorithms iterate 500 times, and the solution accuracy $\epsilon = 1.0E - 03$.

Table 1. Benchmark functions of multimodal optimization.

Func	Function name	Optima (global/ /local)	Niche radius r	Maximum	Number of Known Optima (NKP)
f_1 (1D)	Five-Uneven-Peak Trap	2/3	0.01	200.0	2
f_2 (1D)	Equal Maxima	5/0	0.01	1.0	5
f_3 (1D)	Uneven Decreasing Maxima	1/4	0.01	1.0	1
f_4 (2D)	Himmelblau	4/0	0.01	200.0	4
f_5 (2D)	Five-Uneven-Peak Trap	2/4	0.5	4.126513	2
f_6 (2D)	Shubert	$D \times 3^D$	0.5	186.73090	18
f_6 (3D)		/ many		2709.09350	81
f_7 (2D)	Vincent	$6^D/0$	0.2	1.0	36
f_7 (3D)			0.2	10.0	216
f_8 (2D)	Modified Rastrigin	$\prod_{i=1}^{D} k_i/0$	0.01	−2.0	12
f_8 (8D)	- All Global Optima			−8.0	12

Table 2 shows optima ratio (PR) on eight maximum benchmark functions. For the same benchmark problem, the larger PR the algorithm obtains, the better the performance of the algorithm for solving multimodal problems will be. Table 3 shows the solution results of the algorithm. In the table, the bolded parts of the results are the optimal results of the 5 algorithms in the experiment.

Table 2. The optima ratio (PR) on eight maximum benchmark functions ($\epsilon = 1.0E - 03$).

Algorithm	NPF	PR	NPF	PR	NPF	PR	NPF	PR
Function	f_1 (1D)		f_2 (1D)		f_3 (1D)		f_4 (2D)	
$NKP \times NR$	100		250		50		200	
BSO	64	0.64	88	0.352	50	1	51	0.255
BSOOS	86	0.86	**250**	1	50	1	103	0.515
PIO	77	0.77	54	0.216	49	0.98	50	0.25
PIOr	97	0.97	248	0.992	50	1	59	0.295
KLBSO	**99**	0.99	133	0.532	**50**	1	**191**	0.855
Function	f_5 (2D)		f_6 (2D)		f_6 (3D)		f_7 (2D)	
$NKP \times NR$	100		900		4050		1800	
BSO	50	0.5	100	0.1111	72	0.0177	51	0.045
BSOOS	**96**	0.6	136	0.5111	1	0.0002	72	0.04
PIO	50	0.5	100	0.1111	62	0.0153	50	0.2777
PIOr	82	0.82	4	0.4444	0	0	**272**	0.1511
KLBSO	50	0.5	**303**	0.3366	**367**	0.0906	111	0.0616
Function	f_7 (3D)		f_8 (2D)		f_8 (8D)			
$NKP \times NR$	1800		600		600			
BSO	50	0.0046	53	0.0883	**50**	0.08333		
BSOOS	75	0.006	206	0.3433	0	0		
PIO	50	0.0046	50	0.0833	0	0		
PIOr	63	0.0058	114	0.9	1	0.00166		
KLBSO	**91**	0.0084	**215**	0.3583	0	0		

Table 2 shows that on most multimodal functions (except f_6 (3D)), the PIOr algorithm is better than the PIO algorithm, indicating that the algorithm with a ring structure can find more optima and obtain solutions with better diversity. And the results in Table 3 show that KLBSO achieves the best search accuracy on most functions. Meanwhile, in contrast to the other four algorithms, BSOOS has the worst effect on obtaining results that meet the accuracy requirements in the search. Compared with the BSOOS algorithm, the improved BSOOS with learning ability, KLBSO algorithm, significantly improves the solution accuracy, thereby increasing the number of satisfying solutions.

Table 3 presents the solution data after 500 iterations. It can be seen that for the same type of algorithm, the algorithms that rely on the global optimal

Table 3. Search results comparisons on eight multimodal optimization problems.

Algo.	Best	Mean	Std. dev.	Best	Mean	Std. dev.
	f_1 (1D)			f_2 (1D)		
BSO	200	**200**	0	1	**1**	0
BSOOS	200	194.197	24.611	0.99812	0.78158	0.26884
PIO	200	199.531	1.8298	1	**1**	9.4E-17
PIOr	200	198.786	3.9477	1	0.99999	1.5E-11
KLBSO	200	**200**	0	1	0.99999	9.4E-17
	f_3 (1D)			f_4 (2D)		
BSO	0.99999	**0.99999**	6.6E-16	200	**200**	0
BSOOS	0.99320	0.58414	0.35828	199.998	171.927	130.92
PIO	0.99999	0.99995	0.00032	200	199.999	3.5E-11
PIOr	0.99999	0.99931	0.00468	199.999	199.999	0.00145
KLBSO	0.99999	**0.99999**	4.9E-16	200	**200**	6.2E-14
	f_5 (2D)			f_6 (2D)		
BSO	4.12651	**4.12651**	2.0E-15	186.730	**186.730**	9.9E-14
BSOOS	4.12295	3.13253	2.77107	186.611	159.776	50.4790
PIO	4.12651	**4.12651**	2.2E-15	186.730	**186.730**	6.9E-13
PIOr	4.12651	4.12645	0.00012	186.730	186.569	0.46379
KLBSO	4.12651	**4.12651**	3.3E-14	186.730	**186.730**	4.0E-12
	f_6 (3D)			f_7 (2D)		
BSO	2709.09	2450.38	498.75	1	**1**	0
BSOOS	2704.14	2118.15	915.29	0.99997	0.95072	0.16910
PIO	2709.09	**2647.77**	207.89	1	**1**	1.0E-16
PIOr	2707.52	2510.00	220.96	0.99999	0.99998	1.6E-05
KLBSO	2709.09	2458.35	472.56	1	0.99999	2.3E-15
	f_7 (3D)			f_8 (2D)		
BSO	1	**1**	1.0E-16	−2	−2	0
BSOOS	0.99992	0.97781	0.08327	−2.15886	−5.75254	4.27077
PIO	1	0.99996	0.00013	−2	−2.00000	4.23E-06
PIOr	0.99999	0.99917	0.00103	−2.00000	−2.00020	0.00032
KLBSO	0.99999	0.99999	3.3E-12	−2	**−2**	2.28E-12
	f_8 (8D)					
BSO	−8	**−8**	9.33E-08			
BSOOS	−8.74641	−14.2320	5.55439			
PIO	−8.00030	−8.29651	0.33122			
PIOr	−8.41504	−10.27624	1.04460			
KLBSO	−8.00011	−8.00018	4.73541			

value information for search (such as PIO algorithm) are more efficient than those that rely on the local extremum information (such as PIOr algorithm) for better convergence accuracy. Compared with the BSOOS algorithm, the BSO algorithm could effectively improve the search accuracy of the solution by using the location information, but it consumes a lot of extra computing resources due to the continuous clustering. It can be seen that the overall performance of the PSO-type algorithm is better, while the BSO-type algorithm performs better on complex problems. On most multimodal functions (except f_6 (3D)), the solution accuracy is almost indistinguishable between KLBSO and BSO. On f_6 (3D), KLBSO algorithm shows better results than BSO algorithm. Also, by improving the BSOOS algorithm, the search accuracy of the algorithm can be effectively improved. This also illustrates the effectiveness of the algorithmic learning strategy.

5   Conclusion and Future Work

This paper studies a knowledge learning-based brain storm optimization algorithm that improves algorithm characteristics and learns problem knowledge, optimizes the algorithm's solution structure and parameter settings and applies the improved algorithm to solve MOPs. The experimental results show that the proposed KLBSO algorithm is superior to the original algorithm in terms of both search accuracy and solution diversity, which also shows the effectiveness of the algorithm and knowledge-learning strategy. Future research work will mainly focus on: (1) Research on the BSO algorithm for learning problem knowledge with an adaptive mechanism, and adaptively selection operators for different search stages; (2) Research on combining both the search solution accuracy and diversity to improve the search efficiency of the algorithm in MOPs.

References

1. Cheng, S., Lei, X., Lu, H., Zhang, Y., Shi, Y.: Generalized pigeon-inspired optimization algorithms. Science China Inf. Sci. **62**(7), 1–3 (2019). https://doi.org/10.1007/s11432-018-9727-y
2. Cheng, S., Ma, L., Lu, H., Lei, X., Shi, Y.: Evolutionary computation for solving search-based data analytics problems. Artif. Intell. Rev. **54**(2), 1321–1348 (2020). https://doi.org/10.1007/s10462-020-09882-x
3. Cheng, S., Qin, Q., Chen, J., Shi, Y.: Brain storm optimization algorithm: a review. Artif. Intell. Rev. **46**(4), 445–458 (2016). https://doi.org/10.1007/s10462-016-9471-0
4. Cheng, S., Zhang, M., Shi, Y., Lu, H., Lei, X., Wang, R.: Generalized pigeon-inspired optimization algorithm for balancing exploration and exploitation. SCIENTIA SINICA Technologica (2022). https://doi.org/10.1360/SST-2021-0371
5. Duan, H., Qiao, P.: Pigeon-inspired optimization: a new swarm intelligence optimizer for air robot path planning. Int. J. Intell. Comput. Cybern. **7**(1), 24–37 (2014). https://doi.org/10.1108/IJICC-02-2014-0005

6. Epitropakis, M.G., Burke, E.K.: Hyper-Heuristics, pp. 1–57. Springer International Publishing, Cham (2018). https://doi.org/10.1007/978-3-319-07153-4_32-1

7. Eppe, M., Gumbsch, C., Kerzel, M., Nguyen, P.D.H., Butz, M.V., Wermter, S.: Intelligent problem-solving as integrated hierarchical reinforcement learning. Nat. Mach. Intell. **4**, 11–20 (2022). https://doi.org/10.1038/s42256-021-00433-9

8. Hua, Y., Liu, Q., Hao, K., Jin, Y.: A survey of evolutionary algorithms for multi-objective optimization problems with irregular pareto fronts. IEEE/CAA J. Autom. Sinica **8**, 303 (2021). https://doi.org/10.1109/JAS.2021.1003817

9. Kennedy, J., Eberhart, R., Shi, Y.: Swarm Intelligence. Morgan Kaufmann Publisher, San Francisco (2001)

10. Li, X.: Niching without niching parameters: particle swarm optimization using a ring topology. IEEE Trans. Evol. Comput. **14**(1), 150–169 (2010). https://doi.org/10.1109/TEVC.2009.2026270

11. Li, X., Engelbrecht, A., Epitropakis, M.G.: Benchmark functions for CEC 2013 special session and competition on niching methods for multimodal function optimization. Evolutionary Computation and Machine Learning Group, RMIT University, Australia, Technical report (2013)

12. Lu, H., Shi, J., Fei, Z., Zhou, Q., Mao, K.: Analysis of the similarities and differences of job-based scheduling problems. Eur. J. Oper. Res. **270**(3), 809–825 (2018). https://doi.org/10.1016/j.ejor.2018.01.051

13. Shi, Y.: Brain storm optimization algorithm. In: Tan, Y., Shi, Y., Chai, Y., Wang, G. (eds.) ICSI 2011. LNCS, vol. 6728, pp. 303–309. Springer, Heidelberg (2011). https://doi.org/10.1007/978-3-642-21515-5_36

14. Shi, Y.: An optimization algorithm based on brainstorming process. Int. J. Swarm Intell. Res. (IJSIR) **2**(4), 35–62 (2011). https://doi.org/10.4018/jsir.2011100103

15. Shi, Y.: Brain storm optimization algorithm in objective space. In: Proceedings of 2015 IEEE Congress on Evolutionary Computation (CEC 2015), pp. 1227–1234. IEEE, Sendai, Japan (2015). https://doi.org/10.1109/CEC.2015.7257029

Market Investment Methods

Non-local Graph Aggregation for Diversified Stock Recommendation

Zhihan Yue[1] and Ying Tan[1,2(✉)]

[1] Key Laboratory of Machine Perception (MOE), School of Artificial Intelligence, Institute for Artificial Intelligence, Peking University, Beijing 100871, China
{zhihan.yue,ytan}@pku.edu.cn
[2] Nanjing Kangbo Intelligent Health Academy, Nanjing 211100, China

Abstract. Stock prediction plays a key role in stock investments. Despite the promising achievements of existing solutions, there are still limitations. First, most methods focus on mining the local features from node neighbors, while ignoring non-local features in the stock market. Second, most existing works form the portfolio with the stocks with the highest predicted return, exposed to some risk factors that cause common price movements. To reduce the risk exposure, it is crucial to learn a diversified portfolio. To address the shortage of existing methods, this paper proposes a novel stock recommendation framework that enables both local and non-local feature learning for stock data. Different from the existing methods, the stocks are selected locally according to the ranks within each independent group. This strategy diversifies the recommended stocks effectively. Experimental results on multiple datasets from the U.S. and Chinese stock markets demonstrate the superiority of the proposed method over existing state-of-the-art methods.

Keywords: Stock prediction · Non-local aggregation · Graph neural networks

1 Introduction

Stock prediction, aiming to predict the future movements of stock prices, plays a key role in active stock investments. It helps investors to select the stocks with the best profitability. Sequential models based on recurrent neural networks (RNNs) [8,14,23] and convolutional neural networks (CNNs) [1,3,4] have been widely applied to stock prediction tasks. These methods forecast each stock time series independently, without incorporating the correlations between stocks. Recent studies have focused on modeling the stock relationships with graph neural networks (GNNs) [9,18]. GNN-based methods represent the stock relationships as a graph and enable features learning from relevant stocks with local aggregation. However, there are still notable limitations in these methods.

First, few of the existing methods mine the non-local representations of the market to enhance the prediction of individual stocks. Most existing works leverage local operators to aggregate features from node neighbors. However, the price

© The Author(s), under exclusive license to Springer Nature Singapore Pte Ltd. 2022
Y. Tan and Y. Shi (Eds.): DMBD 2022, CCIS 1745, pp. 147–159, 2022.
https://doi.org/10.1007/978-981-19-8991-9_12

movement correlations over different stocks are both local and non-local. Empirical studies have proven that capitalization, industry, liquidity, and many other non-local factors have a significant impact on the price movements of individual stocks. [7] Therefore, learning non-local features is crucial for making accurate stock predictions.

Second, most existing works form the portfolio with the stocks with the highest predicted returns. The resulting portfolio may be exposed to some risk factors that cause common price movements on different stocks, which contributes to the overall risk of the portfolio. To reduce the risk exposures, it is crucial to learn a diversified portfolio.

To address these issues, this paper proposes a novel stock recommendation framework, which enables both local and non-local feature learning for stock data. It assigns the stocks into diversified portfolios and learns non-local states for each portfolio. These non-local states are attended by the stock embeddings with the attention mechanism, which injects global features into node-level representations. Different from the existing methods, the stocks are selected locally according to the ranks within each independent group. This strategy diversifies the recommended stocks effectively. Extensive experiments on multiple datasets demonstrate the superiority of our method.

The major contributions of this paper are summarized as follows:

– This paper proposes a novel framework that utilizes both local and non-local features for diversified stock recommendation. To the best of our knowledge, it is one of the first few studies exploring the role of non-local features in stock recommendation.
– To achieve the above goal, two novel designs are leveraged in the framework. First, the non-local aggregation module is proposed to capture the non-local market states and inject the non-local states into the stock embeddings. Second, a diversity loss is introduced to learn independent groups for diversified stock recommendation.
– The proposed method outperforms existing state-of-the-art baselines on three real-world datasets. For example, our method improves the Sharpe Ratio by 61.1% on ACL18, 9.7% on KDD17, and 2.6% on CH compared to the best baseline methods.

2   Related Work

2.1   Stock Prediction

There is a rich history of studies about stock prediction. Most classical methods are based on time series analysis models, such as Auto-Regressive Moving Average (ARMA) [2], Vector Auto-Regression (VAR) [16], and Generalized Auto-Regressive Conditional Heteroskedasticity (GARCH) [6]. However, these methods are based on specific linear assumptions about the stochastic processes, facing difficulties when dealing with complex time series tasks such as stock prediction.

To address the limitations of classical methods, there have been many efforts bringing in deep learning to predict the stock trends, which outperform classical models in precision. For some concrete examples, [23] decomposes the hidden states of memory cells with discrete Fourier transform and captures multi-frequency trading patterns from market data to predict stock prices. [8] leverages adversarial training to improve the generalization of neural networks for stock prediction. [5] proposes multi-scale Gaussian prior to enhance the locality of vanilla transformer and applies fixed temporal windows to learn hierarchical features of market data. In addition, there have been a few attempts utilizing graph neural networks to model the cross-sectional relationship. [9] extracts cross-sectional features by graph convolution on the predefined industry and company graphs. [18] leverages multi-graph interaction to learn stock correlations dynamically, showing competitive performance on various datasets. Despite they have achieved promising results, few of them explored non-local feature learning for the stock graph, which is crucial to stock prediction tasks.

2.2 Graph Neural Networks

In recent years, a wide variety of graph neural networks has been proposed. Most of these models adopt the framework of "message passing" [11], in which the GNN aggregates features from neighbors and updates the node representation. For example, GCN [19] aggregates the linearly transformed features from each node's neighbors to update its representation; GAT [17] performs masked attention to adaptively aggregate features from neighbors; GraphSAGE [12] introduces a sampling strategy for local aggregation to scale to large graphs. Pooling methods have also been proposed for graphs to coarsen features of a group of nodes. [21] proposes a differentiable graph pooling module that enables hierarchical representation learning of graphs in an end-to-end fashion. [15] proposes a sparse pooling method that captures coarse information hierarchically with better edge connectivity. [10] introduces not only a pooling operator (gPool) but also its inverse operation (gUnpool) to inject coarse features into the original graph. Unlike these previous approaches, this paper focuses on risk-aware coarsening of the stock relation graph, which is underexplored.

3 Method

3.1 Problem Statement

Given a set of historical stock time series $\mathcal{X} = \{X_1, X_2, \cdots, X_N\}$ from N correlated stocks, the target is to learn a mapping function $f_\theta(\mathcal{X})$ that predicts the future price movements of these stocks based on observed historical features. Each input time series X_i is a multivariate time series that has dimension $T \times F$, where T is the time series length and F is the feature dimension. To enable the cross-sectional feature interaction between latent stock embeddings, this paper further introduces a stock graph $\mathcal{G}$. The graph $\mathcal{G}$ can be represented by $\mathcal{G} = (\mathcal{V}, \mathcal{E}, \mathcal{A})$, where $\mathcal{V}$ is the set of stock nodes, $\mathcal{E}$ is the set of edges, and $\mathcal{A} \in \mathbb{R}^{N \times N}$ is the adjacent matrix representing the stock correlations.

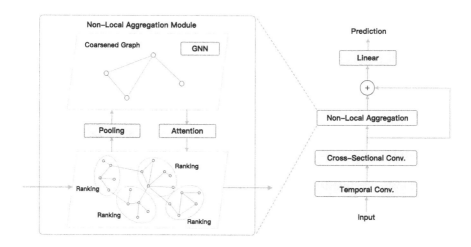

Fig. 1. The overall framework of the proposed method.

3.2   Architecture

Figure 1 shows the overall framework of the proposed method. The input time series $\mathcal{X}$ are firstly fed into a temporal convolution module to encode temporal dynamics for individual stocks. Then, a cross-sectional convolution module is applied to enable cross-sectional feature learning that aggregates features from local neighbors. Finally, a non-local aggregation module is developed, which has the capability of capturing the global correlations between stocks. Therefore, both local and non-local dependency learning are incorporated in the framework. The final predictions are produced with a linear mapping layer. The details of the framework are described in the following subsections.

3.3   Spatial-Temporal Embedding

To capture both non-linear temporal dependencies and cross-sectional correlations in stock time series, this paper introduces the temporal and cross-sectional convolution modules, respectively.

Temporal Convolution Module. The temporal convolution module consists of several dilated CNN blocks to extract high-level temporal features for individual stocks. The l-th block contains two 1-D convolution layers with a dilation parameter of 2^l. The dilated convolutions enable a large receptive field for temporal encoding [1]. This module contains 3 hidden building blocks. Each block has the structure of "GatedGELU $\rightarrow$ DilatedConv $\rightarrow$ GELU $\rightarrow$ DilatedConv" with skip connections between adjacent blocks. The kernel size is set to 5 in order to encode the original daily observations into weekly features. The input gate (GatedGELU) is designed to filter the noise of the financial data, which can be formulated as:

$$Z' = \text{SIGM}(w \cdot Z + b) \odot \text{GELU}(Z), \tag{1}$$

where $Z, Z' \in \mathbb{R}^{N \times T \times H}$ is the input and output respectively, $w, b \in \mathbb{R}^H$ is the learnable weights, SIGM is the sigmoid activation function, and GELU is the Gaussian Error Linear Unit activation function.

Cross-Sectional Convolution Module. The cross-sectional convolution module is applied after the temporal convolution module to aggregate time series embeddings from local neighbors. The SAGE convolution [12] is selected as the building block in the module, for its capability of encoding large graphs. This module is comprised of three SAGE convolutional layers. To exploit contextual information from multiple hops, the concatenation of these three SAGE layers is passed to a fully connected layer to produce spatial embedding. The encoding process of the cross-sectional convolution module is as follows:

$$E_i = \text{ReLU}(\text{SAGEConv}_i(E_{i-1}, \mathcal{A})), \tag{2}$$
$$E = \tanh(\text{FC}([E_1, E_2, E_3])), \tag{3}$$

where $E_i \in \mathbb{R}^{N \times H}$ represents the embedding from i-th SAGE convolutional layer, H is the hidden dimension, E_0 is the output of temporal convolution module at the last time point, and E is the final spatial embedding.

3.4 Non-local Graph Aggregation

This subsection proposes the non-local aggregation module that injects global market states into stock nodes. The assignment matrix is required to coarsen the local embeddings to global market states. This paper adopts an adaptive way for learning assignment matrix due to the dynamic nature of the market states. For example, although the industry of a stock is relatively fixed, varied themes still emerge over time. Inspired by this, the assignment matrix is defined as the sum of a dynamic assignment matrix, that changes over time, and a learnable static assignment matrix:

$$S_{\mathcal{G}} = \text{softmax}(\tilde{S} + f_{assign}(E, \mathcal{A})), \tag{4}$$

where $\tilde{S} \in \mathbb{R}^{N \times G}$ is the learnable static assignment matrix that mines intrinsic properties of the stocks, f_{assign} is a cross-sectional convolution module with an output dimension of G, G is the number of the pooled nodes, and $S_{\mathcal{G}} \in \mathbb{R}^{N \times G}$ is the final assignment matrix for graph $\mathcal{G}$.

Following [21], the hidden features of the stock nodes are mapped into the coarse high-level graph with:

$$E_c = S_{\mathcal{G}}^T E, \tag{5}$$
$$\mathcal{A}_c = S_{\mathcal{G}}^T A S_{\mathcal{G}}, \tag{6}$$

where $E_c \in \mathbb{R}^{G \times H}, \mathcal{A}_c \in \mathbb{R}^{G \times G}$ are the node features and the adjacent matrix of the coarse graph respectively.

Then, a GNN module is applied to aggregate global features in the coarse graph:

$$E'_c = f_c(E_c, \mathcal{A}_c), \tag{7}$$

where f_c is a cross-sectional convolution module applied in the coarse graph with an output dimension of H.

To unpool the coarse features into the original graph, a scaled dot-product attention layer is introduced, which queries the aggregated node features in the coarse graph E'_c by the original graph embeddings E:

$$Q = EW_q, \quad K = E'_c W_k, \quad V = E'_c W_v, \tag{8}$$

$$E' = \text{softmax}\left(\frac{QK^T}{\sqrt{H}}\right) V, \tag{9}$$

where $W_q, W_k, W_v \in \mathbb{R}^{H \times H}$ are learnable weights for linear transformation.

3.5 Diversified Stock Recommendation

Stock ranking [24] serves as an effective way for stock recommendation. It aims to predict the relative rank of investment revenues in a cross-section. It is required to learn a function f_θ that gives better rank predictions. To achieve this, the Information Coefficient metric is used as a training objective. The corresponding loss function can be formulated as:

$$L_{IC}^{(t)} = -\frac{\sum_i(\hat{r}_{i,t} - \mu_{\hat{r}_{:,t}})(r_{i,t} - \mu_{r_{:,t}})}{(N-1)\sigma_{\hat{r}_{:,t}}\sigma_{r_{:,t}}}, \tag{10}$$

where $r_{i,t}$ denotes the i-th stock return at the time point t, $\hat{r}_{i,t}$ denotes the predicted ranking score of i-th stock at the time point t, and μ, σ represents the sample mean and standard deviation respectively.

After getting the rank predictions, one may select the stocks with the highest ranking scores as the portfolio. However, the portfolio produced by this rule may be risky due to the common price movements of different stocks. Hence this paper proposes a risk parity strategy aiming to select stocks from several independent groups. This strategy is based on a loss function that enforces the non-local aggregation module to learn a diversified assignment matrix. Note that the nodes in the coarse graph can be seen as portfolios weighted by the assignment matrix, and their returns can be calculated by:

$$R = S_{\mathcal{G}}^T r, \tag{11}$$

where $r \in \mathbb{R}^{N \times T_f}$ represents the return matrix of the future T_f time points for all stocks.

The goal is to minimize the covariance between these portfolios. Because of $\text{Var}\left(\frac{1}{G}\sum_{i=1}^{G} R_i\right) = \frac{1}{G^2}\sum_i\sum_j \text{Cov}(R_i, R_j)$, it is feasible to optimize the variance of the mean of these portfolio returns. Therefore, we propose the diversity loss as follows:

$$\mathcal{L}_D = \text{Std}\left(\frac{1}{G}\sum_{i=1}^{G} R_i\right), \tag{12}$$

where Std represents the sample standard deviation function.

The final loss is the weighted sum of these two losses balanced by a factor α:

$$\mathcal{L} = \alpha\mathcal{L}_D + \frac{1}{T_{train}}\sum_t \mathcal{L}_{IC}^{(t)}. \tag{13}$$

To select diversified stocks, the stock nodes are divided into groups using the assignment matrix. For each stock, the group it belongs to is defined as the group with the largest assignment weight for this stock. The stock that ranks in the top k_1 in its group will be selected as a candidate. The stocks with top k_2 ranking scores in all candidate stocks form the final portfolio.

4 Experiments

4.1 Settings

Datasets. The proposed method is evaluated on three datasets: ACL18 [20], KDD17 [23], and CH. KDD17 and ACL18 are widely used public datasets for stock prediction, and CH is a real-world dataset from Chinese markets.

- ACL18 collects the historical time series of 88 stocks in NASDAQ and NYSE markets, which ranges from 2012-09 to 2017-09. The data from 2012-09 to 2016-02 are used for training, 2016-03 to 2016-08 for validation, and 2016-09 to 2017-09 for testing.
- KDD17 contains 50 stocks in U.S. markets ranging from 2007-01 to 2016-12. The data from 2007-01 to 2014-12 are used for training, 2015-01 to 2015-12 for validation, and 2016-01 to 2016-12 for testing.
- CH includes the constituent stocks of the SH50 index of the Chinese market. It contains 49 stocks ranging from 2013-01 to 2020-12. The data from 2013-01 to 2018-12 are used for training, 2019-01 to 2019-12 for validation, and 2020-01 to 2020-12 for testing.

Features. To evaluate the end-to-end performance without feature engineering, only the price and volume features are used for the prediction model. To avoid drifting, the unit roots are removed from the original k-line data by:

$$x_t^{open} = \text{open}_t/\text{close}_t - 1, \tag{14}$$

$$x_t^{high} = \text{high}_t/\text{close}_t - 1, \tag{15}$$

$$x_t^{low} = \text{low}_t/\text{close}_t - 1, \tag{16}$$

$$x_t^{close} = \text{close}_t/\text{close}_{t-1} - 1, \tag{17}$$

$$x_t^{vol} = \text{volume}_t/\text{Mean}(\text{volume}_{t-41:t}) - 1, \tag{18}$$

where $\text{open}_t, \text{high}_t, \text{low}_t, \text{close}_t$ and volume_t denote the open price, the highest price, the lowest price, the close price and the trading volume at day t respectively, and $\text{Mean}(\text{volume}_{t-41:t})$ is the average volume of the data from last 42 trading days (about two months).

Graph Construction. The common movements of the stock prices often reflect the inherent characteristics of stocks. For example, the prices of stocks belonging to the same industry often rise and fall at the same time. Hence this paper adopts a predefined graph in which the edge weights are defined as the Pearson correlation coefficients between stocks:

$$\mathcal{A}_{i,j} = \frac{\sum_t (r_{i,t} - \mu_{r_i})(r_{j,t} - \mu_{r_j})}{(T_{train} - 1)\sigma_{r_i}\sigma_{r_j}}, \tag{19}$$

where $r_{i,t}$ denotes the i-th stock return at the time point t, and μ, σ represents the sample mean and standard deviation respectively. The adjacent matrix $\mathcal{A}$ is calculated using the training set with T_{train} trading days.

Evaluation Metrics. Multiple metrics are used to evaluate the performance of all methods, including Information Coefficient (IC), Annual Return, Sharpe Ratio, and Calmar Ratio [13]. IC is the Pearson correlation between the predicted signals and the ground-truth returns. The Annual Return is the annualized return of the backtesting result for trading strategies. The Sharpe Ratio and Calmar Ratio are the expected return per unit of risk measured by the standard deviation and the maximum drawdown respectively.

Hyperparameters. The number of training epochs is set to 5 empirically. α is set to 1.0. The model inputs time series data of the previous 21 trading days (about one month). T_f is set to 63. H is set to 64. G is set to 30. k_1 is set to 1 for ACL18 and CH, and 2 for KDD17. k_2 is set to 10 for ACL18 and KDD17, and 5 for CH. All experiments are conducted on a NVIDIA GeForce RTX 3090.

4.2 Performance Comparison

Extensive experiments on stock recommendation are conducted to evaluate our method, compared with other state-of-the-art methods, including SFM [23], ALSTM [14], Adv-ALSTM [8], GCN [19], TGC [9], G-Transformer [5], and DTML [22]. The evaluation results are presented in Table 1, 2 and 3. Overall, the proposed method achieves substantial improvement over existing baselines on ACL18, KDD17, and CH datasets. Specifically, our method improves the Sharpe Ratio by 61.1% on ACL18, 9.7% on KDD17, and 2.6% on CH compared to the best result of baseline methods. We also note that our method achieves a similar annual return as GCN on the KDD17 dataset. However, our method substantially improves the Sharpe and Calmar ratios over GCN. This implies the proposed method effectively reduces the risk while ensuring the return.

Table 1. Performance comparison results on ACL18 dataset.

Method	IC	Annual return	Sharpe	Calmar
SFM	−0.22%	−8.29%	−0.734	−0.473
ALSTM	−0.31%	0.24%	0.019	0.012
Adv-ALSTM	0.00%	−1.21%	−0.111	−0.156
GCN	1.61%	21.87%	1.730	2.143
TGC	1.69%	28.51%	1.734	2.880
G-Transformer	0.26%	5.82%	0.463	0.396
DTML	−0.44%	−8.49%	−0.723	−0.400
Ours	**2.49%**	**37.6%**	**2.795**	**5.142**

Table 2. Performance comparison results on KDD17 dataset.

Method	IC	Annual return	Sharpe	Calmar
SFM	−0.44%	12.56%	1.231	1.358
ALSTM	0.47%	17.96%	1.582	2.722
Adv-ALSTM	1.58%	24.21%	1.858	2.226
GCN	1.35%	25.81%	1.552	2.964
TGC	−0.01%	16.16%	1.366	2.477
G-Transformer	0.95%	21.35%	1.699	2.708
DTML	2.14%	12.72%	0.868	1.609
Ours	**2.63%**	**26.24%**	**2.039**	**5.199**

Table 3. Performance comparison results on CH dataset.

Method	IC	Annual return	Sharpe	Calmar
SFM	1.48%	10.73%	0.423	0.367
ALSTM	1.63%	−2.60%	−0.095	−0.063
Adv-ALSTM	0.77%	10.93%	0.404	0.295
GCN	**4.32%**	35.71%	1.334	2.663
TGC	3.81%	34.28%	1.261	2.501
G-Transformer	4.18%	46.01%	1.880	2.770
DTML	2.81%	37.91%	1.524	1.313
Ours	**4.32%**	**70.84%**	**1.930**	**5.841**

4.3   Ablation Study

Table 4. Ablation results on ACL18 dataset.

	IC	Annual return	Sharpe	Calmar
Ours	**2.49%**	**37.6%**	**2.795**	**5.142**
w/o ST Embedding	1.73%	7.99%	0.598	0.607
w/o Non-Local Aggregation	1.50%	24.80%	1.993	4.550
w/o Diversity Loss	1.67%	27.90%	1.896	4.839

To verify the effectiveness of the proposed components in our method, the ablation study is conducted. The proposed method is compared with its three variants on ACL18 dataset, where (1) **w/o ST Embedding** removes the temporal and cross-sectional convolution modules, (2) **w/o Non-local Aggregation** removes the non-local aggregation module, and (3) **w/o Diversity Loss** sets α to 0. As shown in Table 4, all the above components are indispensable.

4.4   Signal Analysis

The objectives of diversified stock recommendation are twofold. First, the predicted signals of the model should be capable of distinguishing the levels of stock returns. This provides a basis for recommending the top-ranked stocks. Second, the recommended stocks should be as diversified as possible, which reduces the portfolio risk and improves investment performance. These two aspects are analyzed respectively below.

Discrimination. For each trading day, the stocks are divided into 5 levels according to the quantile of their predicted scores. For example, top 0%–20% means always recommending the top-20% ranked stocks for each trading day. The backtesting results over different signal quantiles on the ACL18 dataset for our method are shown in Fig. 2. Among these quantiles, the top quantile (0%–20%) achieves the best cumulative return, and the bottom quantile (80%–100%) achieves the worst cumulative return. This shows that the proposed model is able to distinguish the stocks with different returns clearly.

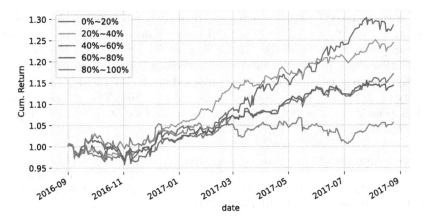

Fig. 2. Backtesting results over different signal quantiles on ACL18 dataset.

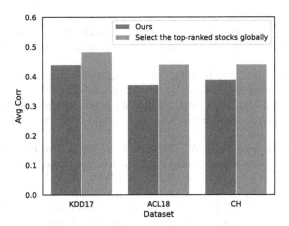

Fig. 3. The average correlation of the daily selected stocks with different strategies.

Diversification. To assess the portfolio diversity, we calculate the average correlation coefficient between the return series of daily recommended stocks. The proposed strategy in Sect. 3.5 is compared to the vanilla strategy that selects the top-ranked stocks globally. Figure 3 shows that the proposed model is able to improve the diversity of recommended stocks on all the datasets, thus achieving better performance.

5   Conclusion

This paper proposes a novel framework for diversified stock recommendation. Inside the framework, the spatial-temporal embedding is leveraged for capturing both temporal and cross-sectional dependencies, the non-local graph aggregation module is proposed for learning global market states, and the IC and diversity losses are introduced for stock ranking and diversification respectively. Extensive experiments on ACL18, KDD17, and CH datasets demonstrate the superiority of the proposed method over the existing state-of-the-art methods. Furthermore, the ablation study proves the effectiveness of the proposed components. Signal analysis validates the capability of the proposed method to distinguish the profitability of stocks and recommend a diversified portfolio. The proposed framework is generic and has the potential to be applied for other spatial-temporal prediction tasks.

Acknowledgements. This work is supported by Science and Technology Innovation 2030 - 'New Generation Artificial Intelligence' Major Project (Grant Nos.: 2018AAA0100302) and partially supported by the National Natural Science Foundation of China (Grant No. 62076010 and 62276008).

References

1. Bai, S., Kolter, J.Z., Koltun, V.: An empirical evaluation of generic convolutional and recurrent networks for sequence modeling. arXiv preprint arXiv:1803.01271 (2018)
2. Box, G.E., Jenkins, G.M., Reinsel, G.C., Ljung, G.M.: Time Series Analysis: Forecasting and Control. John Wiley & Sons, Hoboken (2015)
3. Chen, W., Jiang, M., Zhang, W.G., Chen, Z.: A novel graph convolutional feature based convolutional neural network for stock trend prediction. Inf. Sci. **556**, 67–94 (2021)
4. Deng, S., Zhang, N., Zhang, W., Chen, J., Pan, J.Z., Chen, H.: Knowledge-driven stock trend prediction and explanation via temporal convolutional network. In: Companion Proceedings of The 2019 World Wide Web Conference, pp. 678–685 (2019)
5. Ding, Q., Wu, S., Sun, H., Guo, J., Guo, J.: Hierarchical multi-scale gaussian transformer for stock movement prediction. In: IJCAI, pp. 4640–4646 (2020)
6. Engle, R.F.: Autoregressive conditional heteroscedasticity with estimates of the variance of united kingdom inflation. Econometrica: J. Econ. Soc., 987–1007 (1982)
7. Fama, E.F., French, K.R.: A five-factor asset pricing model. J. Finan. Econ. **116**(1), 1–22 (2015)
8. Feng, F., Chen, H., He, X., Ding, J., Sun, M., Chua, T.S.: Enhancing stock movement prediction with adversarial training. IJCAI (2019)
9. Feng, F., He, X., Wang, X., Luo, C., Liu, Y., Chua, T.S.: Temporal relational ranking for stock prediction. ACM Trans. Inf. Syst. (TOIS) **37**(2), 1–30 (2019)
10. Gao, H., Ji, S.: Graph u-nets. In: International Conference on Machine Learning, pp. 2083–2092. PMLR (2019)
11. Gilmer, J., Schoenholz, S.S., Riley, P.F., Vinyals, O., Dahl, G.E.: Neural message passing for quantum chemistry. In: International Conference on Machine Learning, pp. 1263–1272. PMLR (2017)
12. Hamilton, W., Ying, Z., Leskovec, J.: Inductive representation learning on large graphs. Adv. Neural Inf. Process. Syst. **30** (2017)
13. Ma, T., Tan, Y.: Stock ranking with multi-task learning. Expert Syst. Appl. **199**, 116886 (2022)

14. Qin, Y., Song, D., Cheng, H., Cheng, W., Jiang, G., Cottrell, G.W.: A dual-stage attention-based recurrent neural network for time series prediction. In: Proceedings of the 26th International Joint Conference on Artificial Intelligence, pp. 2627–2633 (2017)
15. Ranjan, E., Sanyal, S., Talukdar, P.: Asap: Adaptive structure aware pooling for learning hierarchical graph representations. In: Proceedings of the AAAI Conference on Artificial Intelligence, vol. 34, pp. 5470–5477 (2020)
16. Sims, C.A.: Macroeconomics and reality. Econometrica: J. Econ. Soc., 1–48 (1980)
17. Veličković, P., Cucurull, G., Casanova, A., Romero, A., Lio, P., Bengio, Y.: Graph attention networks. arXiv preprint arXiv:1710.10903 (2017)
18. Wang, H., Li, S., Wang, T., Zheng, J.: Hierarchical adaptive temporal-relational modeling for stock trend prediction. In: IJCAI, pp. 3691–3698 (2021)
19. Welling, M., Kipf, T.N.: Semi-supervised classification with graph convolutional networks. In: International Conference on Learning Representations (ICLR 2017) (2016)
20. Xu, Y., Cohen, S.B.: Stock movement prediction from tweets and historical prices. In: Proceedings of the 56th Annual Meeting of the Association for Computational Linguistics, vol. 1: Long Papers, pp. 1970–1979 (2018)
21. Ying, Z., You, J., Morris, C., Ren, X., Hamilton, W., Leskovec, J.: Hierarchical graph representation learning with differentiable pooling. Adv. Neural Inf. Process. Syst. **31** (2018)
22. Yoo, J., Soun, Y., Park, Y.c., Kang, U.: Accurate multivariate stock movement prediction via data-axis transformer with multi-level contexts. In: Proceedings of the 27th ACM SIGKDD Conference on Knowledge Discovery & Data Mining, pp. 2037–2045 (2021)
23. Zhang, L., Aggarwal, C., Qi, G.J.: Stock price prediction via discovering multi-frequency trading patterns. In: Proceedings of the 23rd ACM SIGKDD International Conference on Knowledge Discovery and Data Mining, pp. 2141–2149 (2017)
24. Zhang, X., Tan, Y.: Deep stock ranker: a lstm neural network model for stock selection. In: International Conference on Data Mining and Big Data, pp. 614–623. Springer, Heidelberg (2018). https://doi.org/10.1007/978-3-319-93803-5_58

Novel Sentiment Analysis from Twitter for Stock Change Prediction

Yang Cui[1(✉)], Yucen Jiang[2], and Haisong Gu[1]

[1] VisionX LLC., San Jose, USA
forcuiyang@gmail.com
[2] Birmingham Business School, University of Birmingham, Birmingham, UK

Abstract. Literature in behavioral economics and socioeconomics tells us that the public's sentiment expression affects individual decision-making and hence the market collective decision-making. In this paper, we investigate whether public sentiment drives stock market performance. To be specific, we look at whether there is an association between changes in the Dow Jones Industrial Average (DJIA) and sentiment expression by using a large-scale comprehensive dataset of emotional state swings obtained from Twitter. We analyze relevant textual content on daily Twitter feeds using two sentiment quantification tools: FinBert, which is a categorical indicator that captures positive, neutral, and negative sentiment, and XLNet, which quantifies public sentiment from three types of moods (Positive, Neutral and Negative). Based on the time series dataset of the sentiment indicators, the relationship between public sentiment and DJIA index value is studied through Granger causal analysis and self-organizing fuzzy neural network. In addition, the changes in DJIA closing prices are predicted. Our results show that the accuracy of DJIA predictions can be significantly improved by including information on public sentiment. We have achieved state-of-the-art accuracy when predicting the daily up and down movement of the Dow Jones Industrial Average closing prices.

Keywords: Stock market · Sentiment analysis · Time series prediction · Machine learning

1 Introduction

Prediction of stock market performance has always been a hot topic and research direction. The Efficient Market Hypothesis (EMH) states that stock market prices in an efficient market follow a random walk pattern since prices reflect all historical and current information. Stock price changes are due to unforeseen future events [1]. The movement of stock prices largely depends on new information coming to the market, such as news posted on the internet and information reported in the financial press. However, future news is highly unpredictable. Hence, stock prices should follow a random walk movement and should never be predicted.

© The Author(s), under exclusive license to Springer Nature Singapore Pte Ltd. 2022
Y. Tan and Y. Shi (Eds.): DMBD 2022, CCIS 1745, pp. 160–172, 2022.
https://doi.org/10.1007/978-981-19-8991-9_13

The concept of an "efficient market" has been empirically proved in several early studies [2–5]. The popularity of EMH reached its peak in the eighties [6]. However, the random walk theory has gradually received numerous critics while studies reveal that markets are inefficient in terms of predictability, raising doubts about the assumptions of an "efficient market". Among these, numerous papers show that existing market anomalies arise from the irrationality of market participants, and stock prices are to some extent predictable due to pattens [6–12].

In addition, recent studies have shown that economic and corporate outcomes can be predicted by early signals could be extracted from online social media, such as Facebook, Twitter feeds, blogs and forums. Empirical evidences demonstrate that online public sentiment are useful in predicting book sales [13], movie sales [14], box-office revenues [15] and a variety of economic indicators [16]. Several studies supports that public sentiment has predictive power of stock price movement [17–19].

In this paper, we test the hypothesis, based on the premise of behavioral economics, that individuals' emotions influence their decision-making process, leading to a strong correlation between "public sentiment" and "market sentiment." We perform sentiment analysis on publicly available Twitter data to validate the association between the two. By adopting a model of self-organizing fuzzy neural network (SOFNN), we predict future stock price movements based on the previous days' Dow Jones Industrial Average (DJIA) index values and sentiment indicators.

Our work is based on the well-received study by Bollen et al. [19]. The authors predict the closing prices of the DJIA by analyzing the sentiment arising from feeds on Twitter (namely, tweets). The sample dataset of the study includes daily Twitter feeds containing terms that explicitly express users' mood states. The sample period ranges from February 28th, 2008 to December 19th, 2008. The authors adopt OpinionFinder and Google Profile of Mood States to convert public sentiment into quantifiable values. The resulting time series of mood swings were cross-validated by comparing public sentiment responses to specific cultural events. Then, after verifying the correlation between the sentiment value time series and the DJIA value time series by using Granger causal analysis, the authors used a self-organizing fuzzy neural network, based on sentiment data and historical DJIA data, to predict the direction of changes in the Dow Jones Industrial Index with an accuracy of 86.7%.

Our research combines the experimental results obtained by XLNet and FinBert to fully exploit the respective advantages of these two algorithms. Get the sentiment label (positive, natural, or negative) of each tweet through each algorithm, and the positive, natural, and negative sentiment values under each algorithm. We use these sentiment labels and sentiment values to predict the up and down trend of the DJIA.

2   Related Work

2.1   System Design

Please note that the first paragraph of a section or subsection is not indented. The first paragraph that follows a table, figure, equation etc. does not need an indent, either.

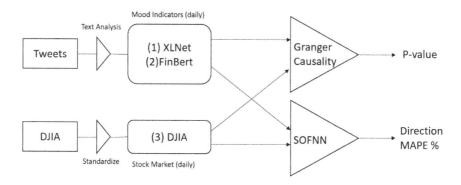

Fig. 1. Diagram outlining 3 phases of methodology and corresponding data sets.

As shown in Fig. 1, after the dataset is processed, we proceed in three stages. In the first stage, we use 3 sentiment assessment tools on the daily tweet dataset: (1) XLNet, which measures positive, neutral, and negative sentiment from textual content; (2) FinBert, which measures 3 different sentiments (positive, negative, and neutral) from a textual content dimension; and (3) calculation of the daily sentiment label score. These processes resulted in a total of 12 public sentiment time series, 6 generated by XLNet and 6 generated by FinBert, each representing a quantified value of public sentiment on a specific date. In addition, we extracted a time series of daily DJIA closing prices from Yahoo Finance. In the second stage, we investigate the hypothesis that public sentiment measured by XLNet and FinBert can predict future trends in the DJIA. We used Granger causality analysis to correlate DJIA values with the obtained sentiment values. In the third stage, we build a self-organizing fuzzy neural network model to test the hypothesis that the prediction accuracy of the DJIA prediction model can be improved by including public sentiment.

2.2   Data Collection

We obtained a dataset of public tweets from January 1st to December 25th, 2010. This data provides the username of the post, the date and time the content was published (GMT+0), and the text content of the tweets (text length is limited to 140 characters). In the Twitter text dataset, we only consider tweets that contain explicit subjective feelings of their authors' emotional states, such as "I feel", "I am feeling", "I'm feeling", "I don't feel", "I'm", " Im", "I am" and "makes me" [18,20].

2.3   Pre-processing

Text data contains more "noisy" words, which do not contribute towards classification [21]. We need to drop those words. In addition, text data may contain tabs, emojis, more white spaces, punctuation characters, stop words, etc [22]. We also need to remove these words. For this purpose, we create our own stop words list, which specifically contains stop words related to finance and general English. After removing stop words, we group all tweets submitted on the same date. To avoid spam, we filter out tweets that contain hyperlinks such as "http:" or "www". In addition, in order to avoid repeated posts affecting the expression of the overall sentiment value, we also remove the tweets with the same content sent by the same users and retain the content and time point of the initial posts. At the same time, we remove the content part of the original tweet in the reposts and retain the text information of the comments left by the users when reposting. Since this study mainly considers the US market, we convert the times of the posts in other time zones to the time zone of the New York Stock Exchange (GMT-8). After processing, the dataset contains 6,809,329 tweets.

2.4   Tokenizing Text Mood by XLNet

XLNet uses Transformer XL as a feature extracting architecture, since Transformer XL added recurrence to the Transformer [23,24], which can give the XLNet a deeper understanding of the language context. XLNet is a pretrained model, so we only need to use a fine-tuning method to update the pre-trained model to fit the next task needed.

We randomly select 1000 items from the Twitter data in 2.3 from January 2010 to February 2010 to manually label sentiment labels (Negative, Neutral, Positive). Then we jointly build a training set with the Financial Phrasebank [25] to train the classifier. The Financial Phrasebank is a dataset of sentences from financial news. The dataset consists of 4,840 sentences from English-language financial news categorized by sentiment (Negative, Neutral, Positive) [26,27].

The Twitter Sentiments Dataset [28] is a public dataset. It contains two fields for the tweet and the sentiment label. There are a total of 162,981 sets of data. We randomly select 1,000 of them as the test set to evaluate the performance of the XLNet model. In order to prevent data distortion, the epoch of XLNet is set as 1. The results show that the test accuracy is 0.861, the test loss is 0.23, and the F1-score is 0.87. It meets the needs of our next task.

2.5   Sentiment Analysis by FinBert

Although XLNet has excellent features in context understanding and language recognition, more training is required for a larger number of subdivisions in financial-related fields. In order to obtain the accuracy of sentiment value in more subdivided directions, we introduce FinBert [29]. FinBERT is a pre-trained NLP model to analyze the sentiment of financial text. It is built by further training the BERT [30] language model in the finance domain, using a large financial corpus and thereby fine-tuning it for financial sentiment classification. FinBert [31] uses data from Financial Web (6.38B words), Yahoo Finance (4.71B words), and Reddit Finance QA (1.62B words) for pre-training, and related research shows that its text analysis in the financial segment is more accurate. FinBert quantifies the sentiment of tweets in terms of positive, negative, and neutral.

2.6   Comparing Sentiment Analysis Results of XLNet and FinBert

To enable the comparison of XLNet and FinBert time series, we standardized them to z-scores on the basis of a local mean and standard deviation within a sliding window of k days before and after the particular date [32,33]. The principle and mechanism are the same as Gallup's Economic Confidence Index. The z-score of time series X_t, denoted Z_{x_t}, is defined as:

where $\bar{x}(x_{t\pm k})$ and $\sigma(x_{t\pm k})$ represent the mean and standard deviation of the time series within the period [t-k, t+k]. This standardization ensures all time series' factors to fluctuate around a zero mean and be expressed on a scale of unit standard deviation.

$$z_{x_t} = \frac{x_t - \bar{x}(x_{t\pm k})}{\sigma(x_{t\pm k})} \tag{1}$$

2.7   Cross-Validation of XLNet and FinBert Time Series for High-Impact Sociocultural Events

We first validate the ability of XLNet and FinBert to capture various aspects of public sentiment. For this we will apply tweets published during the March period from October 5th to December 5th, 2010. This interval was chosen because it may contain public sentiment reflected by cultural events with significant or complex social impact, namely the US Presidential Midterm Election (November 2, 2010) and Thanksgiving (November 27, 2011). Therefore, the emotion quantification results of XLNet and FinBert can be cross-validated according to the expected responses to these specific events. The time series of emotion values obtained are shown in Fig. 2 and Fig. 3, and expressed as z-score. The formula is shown in Eq. 2.

where X represents the emotional time series obtained from the 4 groups, which are the sentiment label score of XLNet, the sentiment value of XLNet, the sentiment label score of FinBert, and the sentiment value of FinBert.

$$Y_{Djia} = a + \sum_{i=1}^{n} \beta_i X_{i-t} \tag{2}$$

From Fig. 2 and Fig. 3, we can see that the sentiment values of XLNet and FinBert can both respond to the major social events introduced in the study by Bollen et al. [18] and respond to public sentiment.

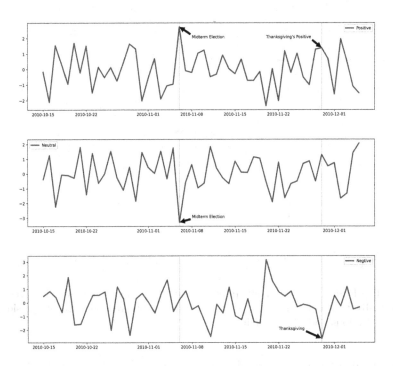

Fig. 2. The XLNet model shows public sentiment swings from tweets posted from October 2010 to December 2010, which can reveal public responses to the presidential midterm elections and Thanksgiving.

Table 1. The SSR for each emotion dimension combination is in this table.

Emotion Dimensions	SSR
XLN_score - XLN_value	344.6979244
XLN_score - FinB_value	334.8667083
FinB_score - FinB_value	338.9763747
FinB_score - XLN_value	335.5207981
All	337.9401028

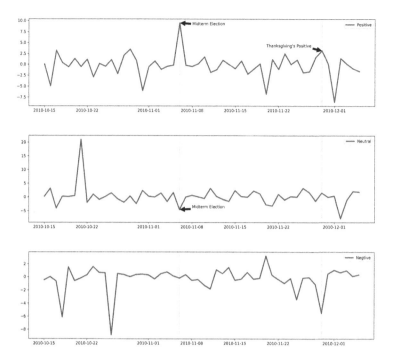

Fig. 3. The FinBert model shows public sentiment swings from tweets posted from October 2010 to December 2010, which can reveal public responses to the presidential midterm elections and Thanksgiving.

The multiple regression results are shown in Table 1. From this table, we conclude that the emotional performance of some FinBerts is not all consistent with the emotional changes provided by XLNet. The expression of events by the sentiment analysis of a single algorithm cannot well reflect the correlation between public sentiment and special events. If taking all dimensions of emotional changes into account does not give the optimal result, interleaving various dimensions would achieve relatively better results.

2.8   The Lag of Public Sentiment on Events

Changes in sentiment values are continuous over time. However, the DJIA series is discontinuous because of the presence of a market closure. We consider the impact of public sentiment on economic changes to be continuous during the market closure. In other words, when the market is closed, the DJIA index just does not show up in the form of data, but the impact of public sentiment is still there. This part of the impact of public sentiment accumulates until the market opens. Alternatively, the DJIA value on the first day after the market opens is not just influenced by one day of public sentiment, but a cumulated expression of public sentiment over several days. Therefore, the average change of the DJIA value from the day before the market closure to the first day of the market opening is calculated. This average change is used to compute the DJIA value on market closure days. At the same time, a dummy variable is added, with the date of having the actual DJIA recorded as 0 and the date of using the calculated DJIA recorded as 1.

We apply the econometric technique of Granger causality analysis to make a preliminary test on the correlation between DJIA index movement and the daily time series produced by XLNet and FinBert. Granger causality analysis rests on the assumption that the past value of one time series influencing the present and future value of another time series [34]. Granger [35] proposed that the variance of the optimal prediction error of time series X is reduced by including the historical data of time series Y. In fact, this notion is based mainly on predictability but not causality of Y on X [36]. Following Hiemstra and Jones [34], we use linear Granger causality test on the dynamic relationship between daily Twitter sentiment and DJIA index movement.

We thus expect that the lagged values of X exhibit a statistically significant correlation with Y. Correlation however does not prove causation [18]. We are not testing actual causation but whether one time series has predictive information about the other or not. Our DJIA time series, denoted D_t, is defined to reflect daily changes in stock market value, i.e. its values are the delta between day t and day t 1: $D_t = DJIA_t\text{-}DJIA_{t-1}$. To test whether our sentiment time series predicts changes in stock market values, we compare the variance explained by two linear models as shown in Eq. 3 and Eq. 4. The first model (L1) uses only n lagged values of D_t, i.e. $(D_{t-1}, \cdots, D_{t-n})$ for prediction, while the second model L2 uses the n lagged values of both D_t and the XLNet with the FinBert sentiment time series denoted as $X_{t-1}, \cdots, X_{t-n}$. Based on Bollen et al. [18], we add the second lag to the sixth lag of D_t and X_t in our model L1 and L2.

$$L_1 : D_t = \alpha + \sum_{i=1}^{n} \beta_i D_{t-i}-_t \tag{3}$$

$$L_2 : D_t = \alpha + \sum_{i=1}^{n} \beta_i D_{t-i} + \sum_{i=1}^{n} \gamma_i x_{t-i}+_t \tag{4}$$

It can be seen from the results of the Granger causality analysis (Table 2), there is a strong correlation between the time series of emotional values and DJIA values. Among them, when t=3, the correlation between sentiment series and the DJIA value series is the highest. In order to show the viewing results more intuitively, we visualize the time series of emotions and the time series of DJIA at t=3. To maintain the same scale, we convert the DJIA delta values D_t and sentiment value X_t to z-scores as shown in Eq. 1. And, since the verification shows that the result is better when t=3, we use the data with a lag of 3 days in the model in the subsequent prediction.

Table 2. The p-values of each sentiment value.

Lag	$XLNet\_value$			$FinBert\_value$		
–	Negative	Neutral	Positive	Negative	Neutral	Positive
1 day	0.2087	0.0476	0.3504	0.2897	0.3279	0.4833
2 day	0.1276	0.0005	0.0986	0.3626	0.1341	0.3373
3 day	0.0092	0.0025	0.0354	0.0062	0.1088	0.1101
4 day	0.0150	0.0789	0.0584	0.1690	0.0305	0.1247
5 day	0.1479	0.1835	0.2543	0.1041	0.1258	0.0757
6 day	0.3533	0.2959	0.4661	0.3409	0.0178	0.4400

2.9 Model Training and Prediction

Since the correlation between sentiment value and DJIA closing prices is non-linear [18], after determining the correlation between lags of Twitter sentiment, lags of DJIA index value and the present DJIA index value, we established a SOFNN model based on the sentiment value and the closing price of the day with a lag of 3 days and 4 days, respectively. We have taken January 8th, 2010 to November 30th, 2010 as the training set, and December 1st, 2010 to December 17th, 2010 as the test set.

The Self Organizing Fuzzy Neural Network (SOFNN) [37] is a 5-layer fuzzy neural network which uses ellipsoidal basis function (EBF) neurons consisting of a center vector and a width vector. Based on the relevant literature, we establish the SOFNN algorithm model. Neural networks have been considered to be a very effective learning algorithm for decoding nonlinear time series data, given that financial markets often follow nonlinear trends [18,38] (Fig. 4).

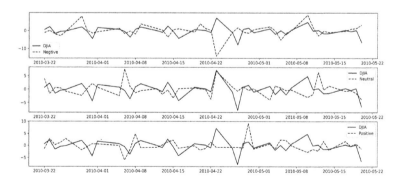

Fig. 4. A panel consisting of three charts. The graph above shows the daily difference in DJIA values (blue: ZDt) versus XLNet's sentiment values, i.e. negative, neutral, positive, with a lag of 3 days. (Color figure online)

We constructed an online algorithm for SOFNN following the method of paper [39], where neurons are added or pruned from the existing network when new samples arrive. In order to compare the effects of different algorithms on the prediction of the direction of change of DJIA. In contrast to SOFNN, we used logistic regression and SVM. In order to find higher prediction accuracy, we studied 7 permutations and combinations of the input variables of the models, as shown in Eq 5. We finally obtain the prediction results as shown in Table 3.

$$I_{A,B...} = DJIA_{t-k,k-1,k-2,...,1}, X_{A_{t-k,k-1,k-2,...,1}}, X_{B_{t-k,k-1,k-2,...,1}} \cdots$$

DJIA t-k,k-1,k-2,. . .,1 represents the DJIA values and its lagged values. XA,t-k,k-1,k-2,. . .,1 represents the values of the sentiment dimension and its lagged values. k represents the values of lag days. A, B, C, D represent the dimension of sentiments: the sentiment label score of XLNet, the sentiment value of XLNet, the sentiment label score of FinBert, and the sentiment value of FinBert. I represent the input dataset [40].

Although we can see from Fig. 2 that the changes of each individual dimension of sentiment deviates from the changes of DJIA index values, from the results shown in Table 3, each dimension of sentiment to some degree has contributed on the predictability of the closing values of DJIA. When all sentiment indicators are included, the prediction accuracy reaches the highest, 88.30%. We compute the MAPE value to further test on the accuracy [18], and the results show that the MAPE value is significantly improved.

Table 3. The model predicts the upward or downward change direction of the closing price of DJIA compared with the previous day, and compares it with the actual change direction to obtain the accuracy rate.

I	Logistic regression dirction(%)	SVM dirction(%)	SOFNN	
−			Dirction(%)	MAPE(%)
$XLNet\_score-XLNet\_value$	62.40	67.97	76.21	1.91
$XLNet\_score-FinB\_value$	62.40	73.26	88.30	1.55
$FinB\_score-FinB\_value$	62.40	64.35	75.86	2.06
$FinB\_score-XLNet\_value$	62.40	68.60	85.89	1.73
All	62.40	70.47	80.65	1.59

3 Conclusions and Future Work

In this paper, we verify the relationship between public sentiment and DJIA values by surveying a large number of tweets on Twitter. Our results show that, first, public sentiment can indeed be obtained from large-scale tracking through natural language processing techniques in specific situations. Second, the correlation between changes in public sentiment and changes in DJIA values after 3 days was obtained through Granger causality analysis. Third, it is more helpful to improve the prediction accuracy of the DJIA's closing price by the comprehensive inclusion of various sentiment values, rather than just looking at a single dimension of sentiment. Fourth, it verifies the feasibility of XLNet and FinBert in dealing with the influence of text sentiment on market public opinion.

Finally, it is worth mentioning that there are many factors that our analysis did not take into account. First, we observed and screened datasets in specific regions and periods. With the progress of the times and changes in people's lifestyles, further research and verification are needed on the changed Twitter user population and expressions. Second, although we get the results of evaluating public sentiment after validation, there is no objective fact that it can directly reflect public sentiment. That is, we only proved the correlation between emotional state and the prediction result of DJIA value, and there is no data information on the causal mechanism between these two. Third, we currently only consider the one-way effect of public sentiment on changes in DJIA values to make predictions. And the market is complex, and its impact is not just one-way.

About the future work, due to the strong randomness in the expression of public sentiment, more targeted sentiment expression can better reflect the volatility of the stock market. Moreover, there is a certain time lag between public sentiment and stock price volatility, and our results show that an average 3-day lag can best reflect the impact of public sentiment on the market. But this is not the optimal lag period. We find that when public sentiment is more volatile, it takes less time to affect stock prices. Further adjustments to the forecasting model may improve the forecasting accuracy for a wider range of time periods. Therefore, the impact of changes in public sentiment on the market, as well as on investment decisions, remains an area of future research.

References

1. Fama, E.F.: Efficient capital markets: a review of theory and empirical. J. Finan. **25**(2), 383–417 (1970)
2. Kendall, M.G., Hill, A.B.: The analysis of economic time-series-part I: prices. J. Roy. Stat. Soc. **116**(1), 11–34 (1953)
3. Larson, A.: Measurement of a random process in futures prices. Proc. Annual Meet. **33**, 101–112 (1960)
4. Fama, E.F.: Efficient capital markets: II. J. Finan. **46**(5), 1575 (1991). https://doi.org/10.2307/2328565
5. Sewell, M. (2022) History of the Efficient Market Hypothesis. Research Note, 11 (04): 04, UCL Computer Science. https://www.ucl.ac.uk/computer-science/. Accessed 30 Oct 2022
6. Shiller, R.J.: From efficient markets theory to behavioral finance. J. Econ. Perspect. **17**(1), 83–104 (2003)
7. Butler, K.C., Malaikah, S.J.: Efficiency and inefficiency in thinly traded stock markets: Kuwait and Saudi Arabia. J. Bank. Finan. **16**(1), 197–210 (1992). https://doi.org/10.1016/0378-4266(92)90085-E

8. Kavussanos, M.G., Dockery, E.: A multivariate test for stock market efficiency: the case of ASE. Appl. Finan. Econ. **11**(5), 573–579 (2001). https://doi.org/10.1080/09603100010013006

9. Schwert, G.W.: Analomies and market efficiency. Handb. Econ. Finan. **1**, 939–974 (2003). http://www.nber.org/papers/w9277. Accessed 30 Oct 2022

10. Bouman, S., Jacobsen, B.: The halloween indicator, "Sell in May and Go Away": another puzzle. Am. Econ. Rev. **92**(5), 1618–1635 (2002)

11. Bailey, W., Kumar, A., Ng, D.: Behavioral biases of mutual fund investors. J. Finan. Econ. **102**(1), 1–27 (2011). https://doi.org/10.1016/j.jfineco.2011.05.002

12. Bartram, S.M., Grinblatt, M.: Global market inefficiencies. J. Finan. Econ. **139**(1), 234–259 (2021). https://doi.org/10.1016/j.jfineco.2020.07.011

13. Gruhl, D., Guha, R., Kumar, R., et al.: The predictive power of online chatter. Proceedings of the ACM SIGKDD International Conference on Knowledge Discovery and Data Mining, pp. 78–87 (2005). https://doi.org/10.1145/1081870.1081883

14. Mishne, G., Glance, N.: Predicting movie sales from blogger sentiment. In: AAAI Spring Symposium - Technical Report, SS-06-03, pp. 155–158 (2006)

15. Asur, S., Huberman, B.A.: Predicting the future with social media. In: Proceedings - 2010 IEEE/WIC/ACM International Conference on Web Intelligence, WI 2010, vol. 1, pp. 492–499 (2010). https://doi.org/10.1109/WI-IAT.2010.63

16. Choi, H., Varian, H.: Predicting the present with google trends. Econ. Rec. **88**(SUPPL.1), 2–9 (2012). https://doi.org/10.1111/j.1475-4932.2012.00809.x

17. Gilbert, E., Karahalios, K.: Widespread worry and the stock market. In: ICWSM 2010 - Proceedings of the 4th International AAAI Conference on Weblogs and Social Media, pp. 58–65 (2010)

18. Bollen, J., Mao, H., Zeng, X.: Twitter mood predicts the stock market. J. Comput. Sci. **2**(1), 1–8 (2011). https://doi.org/10.1016/j.jocs.2010.12.007

19. Goel, A., Mittal, A.: Stock prediction using twitter sentiment analysis. Cs229.Stanford.Edu, (December), pp. 1–5 (2012). http://cs229.stanford.edu/proj2011/GoelMittal-StockMarketPredictionUsingTwitterSentimentAnalysis.pdf. Accessed 30 Oct 2022

20. Gokulakrishnan, B., Priyanthan, P., Ragavan, T., Prasath, N., Perera, A.: Opinion mining and sentiment analysis on a Twitter data stream. In: International Conference on Advances in ICT for Emerging Regions (ICTer2012), pp. 182–188 (2012). https://doi.org/10.1109/ICTer.2012.6423033

21. Choy, M.: Effective listings of function stop words for Twitter. Int. J. Adv. Comput. Sci. Appl. **3**(6) (2012). https://doi.org/10.14569/ijacsa.2012.030602

22. Kharde, V., Sonawane, S.S.: Sentiment analysis of twitter data: a survey of techniques. Int. J. Comput. Appl. **139**(11), 5–15 (2016). https://doi.org/10.5120/ijca2016908625

23. Yang, Z., et al.: XLNet: generalized autoregressive pretraining for Language Understanding (2020). arXiv.org. https://arxiv.org/abs/1906.08237?source=techstories.org. Accessed 30 Oct 2022

24. Mustapha, M., Krasnashchok, K., Al Bassit, A., Skhiri, S.: Privacy policy classification with XLNet (Short Paper). In: Garcia-Alfaro, J., Navarro-Arribas, G., Herrera-Joancomarti, J. (eds.) DPM/CBT -2020. LNCS, vol. 12484, pp. 250–257. Springer, Cham (2020). https://doi.org/10.1007/978-3-030-66172-4_16

25. Malo, P., et al.: Good debt or bad debt: detecting semantic orientations in economic texts. J. Assoc. Inf. Sci. Technol. **65**(4), 782–796 (2013). https://doi.org/10.1002/asi.23062

26. Babu, N.V., Rawther, F.A.: Multiclass sentiment analysis in text and emoticons of twitter data: a review. Trans. Comput. Sci. Comput. Intell., 61–68 (2021). https://doi.org/10.1007/978-3-030-49500-8_6

27. Adoma, A.F., Henry, N.-M., Chen, W.: Comparative analyses of Bert, Roberta, Distilbert, and xlnet for text-based emotion recognition. In: 2020 17th International Computer Conference on Wavelet Active Media Technology and Information Processing (ICCWAMTIP) (2020). https://doi.org/10.1109/iccwamtip51612.2020.9317379

28. Hussein, S.: Twitter Sentiments Dataset. Mendeley Data, V. 1 (2021). https://doi.org/10.17632/z9zw7nt5h2.1

29. Colacicchi, L.: Comparison and fine-tuning of methods for financial sentiment analysis (2022). https://dke.maastrichtuniversity.nl/jan.niehues/wp-content/uploads/2022/01/Colacicchi-Thesis.pdf. Accessed 30 Oct 2022

30. Gao, Z., Feng, A., Song, X., Wu, X.: Target-dependent sentiment classification with BERT. IEEE Access **7**, 154290–154299 (2019). https://doi.org/10.1109/ACCESS.2019.2946594

31. Liu, Z., et al.: Finbert: A pre-trained financial language representation model for financial text mining. In: Proceedings of the Twenty-Ninth International Joint Conference on Artificial Intelligence [Preprint] (2020). https://doi.org/10.24963/ijcai.2020/622

32. Gadri, S., et al.: Sentiment analysis: developing an efficient model based on machine learning and deep learning approaches. In: Intelligent Computing & Optimization, pp. 237–247 (2022). https://doi.org/10.1007/978-3-030-93247-3_24

33. Dusane, P., Sujatha, G.: Events of interest extraction from forensic timeline using Natural Language Processing (NLP). In: Proceedings of International Conference on Deep Learning, Computing and Intelligence, pp. 83–94 (2022). https://doi.org/10.1007/978-981-16-5652-1_7

34. Hiemstra, C., Jones, J.D.: Testing for linear and nonlinear granger causality in the stock price-volume. J. Finan. **49**(5), 1639–1664 (1994)

35. Granger, C.W.J.: Investigating causal relations by econometric models and cross-spectral methods. Econometrica **37**, 424–38 (1969)

36. Shojaie, A., Fox, E.B.: Granger causality: a review and recent advances. Ann. Rev. Stat. Appl. **9**, 289–319 (2022). https://doi.org/10.1146/annurev-statistics-040120-010930

37. Kuremoto, T., Obayashi, M., Kobayashi, K.: Forecasting time series by SOFNN with reinforcement learning (2015). https://www.semanticscholar.org/paper/Forecasting-Time-Series-by-SOFNN-with-Reinforcement-Kuremoto-Obayashi/8a5ce65e52077303b8dcbe39a3953219e910ca3f/figure/12. Accessed 30 Oct 2022

38. Leng, G., Ray, A., Mcginnity, T.M., Coleman, S., Maguire, L., Vance, P.: An Interval Type-2 Fuzzy Neural Network for Cognitive Decisions (2014). https://www.researchgate.net/publication/266849980_An_Interval_Type-2_Fuzzy_Neural_Network_for_Cognitive_Decisions. Accessed 30 Oct 2022

39. Leng, G., Prasad, G., McGinnity, T.M.: An on-line algorithm for creating self-organizing fuzzy neural networks. Neural Netw. **17**(10), 1477–1493 (2004). https://doi.org/10.1016/j.neunet.2004.07.009

40. Nofer, M., Hinz, O.: Using twitter to predict the stock market. Bus. Inf. Syst. Eng. **57**(4), 229–242 (2015). https://doi.org/10.1007/s12599-015-0390-4

A Novel Investment Strategy for Mixed Asset Allocation Based on Entropy-Based Time Series Prediction

Xuemei Yao, Jiahui Long, Longyun Wang, Binglin Wang, Maidi Liu, and Kewei Yang[✉]

National University of Defense Technology, Changsha 410073, China
kayyang27@nudt.edu.cn

Abstract. In recent years, the combinational investment of gold and Bitcoin has become a hot spot, and it is expected to achieve a balance between risk aversion and maximum income. Some existing methods lack of timeliness. Hence, this article proposes an Objective Empowerment Multi-Objective Programming Investment strategy based on ARIMA, which can increase the income obtained on the premise of minimizing investment risk. Firstly, the Autoregressive Integrated Moving Average (ARIMA) model is used to predict the price changes. Then, based on the forecast curve of prices, a Multi-Objective Nonlinear Programming model is adopted to find the optimal transaction strategy. This method achieves to maximize the cumulative income and chooses the strategy of investment by identifying different market trends. According to the precise data indicators of the US Gold Market and the Bitcoin Market from 2016–2021, this article introduces the Entropy Weight method to evaluate the adopted strategy of the previous period, so as to timely adjust the next investment strategy. Finally, through the sensitivity test, it is found that the method proposed in this article is robust.

Keywords: ARIMA model · Multi-objective programming model · Entropy weight method

1 Introduction

1.1 Background

Nowadays, the combination of traditional investment and alternative assets has become a hot spot. Gold has more stable investment value. Its precious metal attributes and scarcity have been recognized as risk aversion assets since ancient time. With the development of block-chain technology, virtual currency gradually enters the vision of asset allocation. Among them, Bitcoin is the most important currency. It was first issued in November 2008. Due to its privacy and scarcity, it reached a single $ 69,000 in 2021. Compared with gold, although Bitcoin has greater risks, its yields, large volatility, and supervision exemption have attracted

© The Author(s), under exclusive license to Springer Nature Singapore Pte Ltd. 2022
Y. Tan and Y. Shi (Eds.): DMBD 2022, CCIS 1745, pp. 173–190, 2022.
https://doi.org/10.1007/978-981-19-8991-9_14

investors' vision. The combination of gold and Bitcoin is conducive to the pursuit of maximum benefits while maintaining the security of assets. Due to the violent fluctuations in the two aspects and high complexity, the research on the process of allocation of assets is carried out.

Researchers have introduced a variety of methods for research on asset quantification. In recent years, many scholars have used DEA (Data Envelopment Analysis) model [1] to obtain the best investment. Yun introduced DEA model in the Multi-Objective Genetic Algorithm to compare the solution. This model can consider classic DEA models such as CCR and BCC through different parameter values [2]. Tavana proposed the NSGA -II and Multi -Objective Particle Algorithm based on the reference point, and then used the DEA model to evaluate the solution. Finally, the TOPSIS method was used to adopt the optimal solution [3]. Cheng and Vincent used the DEA model to determine the relative efficiency of each operator in the Genetic Algorithm [4].

The time series method attracts the attention of researchers [6]. Various methods are applied such as the VaR-APARCH model [7], VEC model [8], ARIMA [5]. The mechine learning methods are also introduced to assist the time series analysis [9]. Besides, the safety of Bitcoin and gold is compared [10]. During the research process, the designed algorithm need to be flexible and robust. The computation time needs to be low for the timely determination.

Due to the dynamic changes in gold and Bitcoin, the daily optimal trading strategy is also constantly updated, and the requirement for timeliness for the algorithm is much higher. The above algorithm has more iteration and the operating efficiency is low. Therefore, investment analysis methods with low calculation costs and fast adjustment speed are required. This article conducts market price predictions based on ARIMA, combined with Entropy Weight method to conduct investment strategies and perception evaluations, and proposes an Objective Empowerment Multi-Objective Programming method based on ARIMA. The process is transformed into a Real-Time Multi-Objective Nonlinear Programming problem, and carried out the research on the hybrid investment of gold and Bitcoin. At the same time, because gold and Bitcoin are representative in the field of futures and virtual currency, the research methods of this article can also be expanded to investment in multi-futures and multi-currencies.

1.2   Problem Analysis

Based on the goal mentioned above, following points are considered:

– To determine the specific operation (buy, hold, or sell) performed on a certain day, we need to first judge the price trend of that day or even a period of time in the future. From the data, we can see that both assets have a certain growth, but the final change trend does not tend to be linear, so it can be roughly considered that the time series of the two assets are not stable. We introduce the prediction model ARIMA to explore the changing tendency of gold and Bitcoin prices.

- We use the price change data before the day to predict the price of this day, and the price of a period of time after that, and then analyze the price of this day and the price changes in the period of time before and after, if it is the lowest price, then make a purchase; if the price is the highest point, sell it; if the price is between the lowest and the highest, we need to consider the commission we have to pay for each transaction and make a decision later. After identifying the daily trend of price changes, we further consider the optimal trading strategies for each day. Our primary goal is to make the final total return as high as possible. However, in reality, traders may sell assets not for profit, but to avoid more losses. Therefore, we use a Multi-Objective Programming model to maximize profits and reduce losses as the overall goal, and adjust the value of the factor, so as to find the corresponding optimal trading strategy.
- The output of the Multi-Objective Programming model is not unique, so we select the optimal trading strategy through comparison. In order to find the best trading strategy, we use Entropy Weight method, which is more objective, set evaluation indicators, and find the same indicator data of the gold market and Bitcoin market in the same period, and obtain the optimal transaction through the first question. The strategy and the actual data are scored, and we end up with the best strategy.
- To determine how sensitive the strategy is to transaction cost, we analyze the sensitivity by changing the values of gold trading commission α and Bitcoin trading commission β and observe changes in total assets as well as transaction frequency.

The flow chart is shown in Fig. 1:

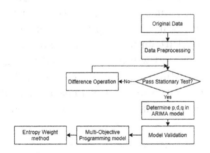

Fig. 1. Flow chart

2 Objective Empowerment Multi-objective Programming Investment Strategy Based on ARIMA

2.1 Symbol, Definitions and Assumptions

- Symbol and Definitions
  For ease of calculation, the symbols are defined as follows:

Name	Symbol	Name	Symbol
Total value of assets held	z	Hold gold weight	m
Gold daily price	g	Buy gold weight	m+
Gold forecast price	g'	Sell gold weight	m-
Change in the value of gold held	Δg	Hold Bitcoin weight	n
Bitcoin daily price	b	Buy Bitcoin weight	n+
Bitcoin forecast price	b'	Sell Bitcoin weight	n-
Change in the value of bitoin held	Δb	Gold trading commission	α
Amount of dollars held	d	Bitcoin trading commission	β

- Assumptions

    In order to simplify the model and grasp the essence of the problem, we make the following assumptions:

    First, each transaction is executed at the closing price of the day, and the closing price is known. Second, as actual transaction, gold trading is suspended on statutory holidays, assuming that the daily price of gold during the period when the market is not open is consistent with the last business day before the suspension. Third, whether it is gold or Bitcoin, it can only be traded in US dollars and cannot be directly converted. Last but not the least, gold and Bitcoin can only be held, purchased or sold on that day.

2.2   Data Preprocessing

- Gold is regarded as Actual in this article, including gold nuggets (bricks), gold ingots, gold bars and gold coins, needs to rely on relevant platforms and institutions for trading, so it is necessary to consider the situation that these trading platforms and institutions stop trading on statutory holidays.
- Unlike gold, as futures, Bitcoin has no entity and no issuing institution, so it can be traded every day and will not be affected by legal holidays.
- We use the method of Min-Max scaling to process the daily prices of gold and Bitcoin, and convert the method of linearization of the original data to the range of [0,1]. The normalization formula is as follows:

$$X_{norm} = \frac{X - X_{min}}{X_{max} - X_{min}} \tag{1}$$

Among them, X_{norm} is the normalized data, X is the original data, X_{max} and X_{min} are the maximum and minimum values of the original data set, respectively.

2.3   ARIMA Model

Autoregressive Integrated Moving Average model, ARIMA for short, regards the data sequence formed by the predicted object as a random sequence, and uses a certain mathematical model to approximate this sequence. ARIMA model has three parameters:p,d and q, p represents the lags of the time-series data itself adopted in the prediction model,d represents the orders of difference that the time series data needs to undergo to be stable and q represents the lags of the prediction error adopted in the prediction model. Once this model is recognized, the future value can be predicted from the past values and current values of the time sequence. The modeling steps are as follows:

Stationary Test. In order to explore whether the trends of historical data and future data obey similar tendency, we need to test the stationarity of the time series. The p-values corresponding to the unit root statistics of Bitcoin and gold are 0.9614 and 0.9042 respectively, both of which are significantly greater than 0.05.

Therefore, it is judged that the sequence is a non-stationary sequence. In order to improve the stationarity of the data, we perform a first-order difference operation on the two data. The p-values for Bitcoin and gold outputs are $2.3078e^{-11}$ and $9.2697e^{-13}$, which are far less than 0.05. In Fig. 2, the X-axis represents the number of days, and the Y-axis represents the first-order difference.

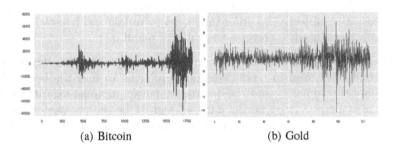

(a) Bitcoin   (b) Gold

Fig. 2. Stationary test

We can see the relatively average random oscillation of the white noise sequence around zero. Therefore, the sequence of the first difference is stable. Compared with the first difference, the improvement of the stationarity from the second difference is limited. Hence, it is more appropriate to use the first difference for this sequence that d=1.

ACF and PACF Test. The Autocorrelation Coefficient(ACF) measures the correlation between the same event in two different periods, The q-value can be roughly judged by the maximum lag point of ACF plot. When calculating the influence or correlation degree of a certain element on another element, the influence of other elements is not considered temporary, and the close degree of mutual relationship between those two elements is studied separately, which is called Partial Correlation. The p-value can be roughly judged by the maximum lag point of the Partial Autocorrelation Coefficient (PACF) plot. The plots are shown in Fig. 3.

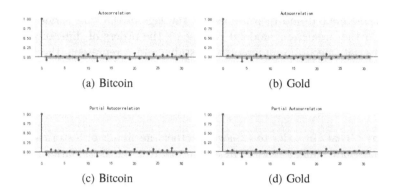

Fig. 3. ACF and PACF Plot

The price of gold and Bitcoin in the previous 30 days are selected for the analysis. As can be seen from Fig. 3, the trend sequence ACF and PACF of Bitcoin experiences a shape increase in the first order, which is called the first-order truncation, so we could choose p=1,q=1. Similarly, the trend sequence ACF and PACF of gold has second-order truncation, so we could choose p=2,q=2.

However,it is subjective to order the model by tailing and truncation. Therefore, BIC is introduced to traverse the value of p and q.

Model Ordering. Bayesian information criterion originates from Bayesian theory and is mainly used in model selection problems to find the best balance between model complexity and the descriptive power of model logarithmic data sets. Let $x = \{x_1, \cdots , x_N\}$ be the data set and M be the parameter model to be selected. To maximize the maximum likelihood function $L(x, M)$, the BIC of model M can be defined as:

$$BIC(M) = \log L(x, M) - \lambda \frac{m}{2} \log N \tag{2}$$

The first part represents the matching quality between model and data, the second part is the penalty factor of model complexity, λ represents the penalty factor, which can be set according to different model selection situations, and M represents the number of parameters. [11]

The order of p and q in the ARIMA model generally does not exceed 5 orders, so we use the traversal method, p, q take values from 0 to 5 respectively, train the data, and draw a heat map, as shown in Fig. 4. The X-axis represents the q-value, and the Y-axis represents the p-value.

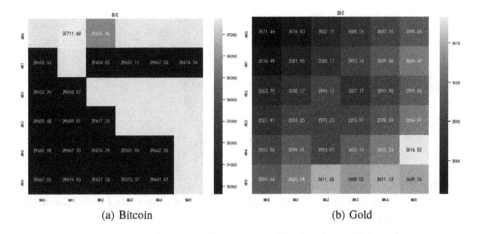

(a) Bitcoin   (b) Gold

Fig. 4. Heat Map

In the heat map of Bitcoin and gold, the minimum values of BIC are 29617.20 and 3571.46, which $(p,q)=(3,2)$ and $(0,0)$ respectively.

Model Validation. To confirm the correctness of the model, we conduct autocorrelation test of model residuals. The test results of Bitcoin and gold are shown in Fig. 5. The shaded area represents the standard deviation. It is obvious that the autocorrelation coefficients of the residuals are all within 2 times the standard deviation, so the test is passed.

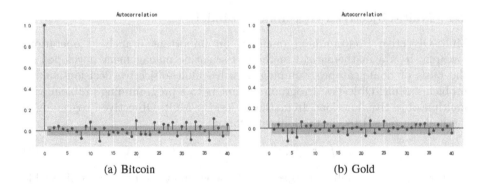

(a) Bitcoin   (b) Gold

Fig. 5. Residual Analysis

Model Prediction. The data is predicted with the new parameters, and the result is shown in Fig. 6.

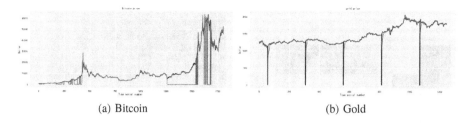

(a) Bitcoin   (b) Gold

Fig. 6. Model Output

The X-axis represents the number of days since September 11, 2016 and the Y-axis represents the price of Bitcoin and gold in US dollar. Red is the predicted curve, black is the original curve.

It can be seen in Fig. 6 that the fitting effect is good.

Computing Prediction Accuracy. In order to ensure that our prediction model is sufficient to support the completion of the follow-up work, we calculate the accuracy of the price changes of gold and Bitcoin predicted by the ARIMA model. By observing the difference between the predicted value and the true value, we count the number of prediction errors, and thus calculate the prediction accuracy of gold and Bitcoin to be 97.896% and 96.126%, respectively. At the same time, we calculate the standard deviations of gold and Bitcoin respectively, and the results are 1.302 and 101.471, and the average daily prices are 1464.549 and 12206.068. The standard deviations are more reasonable under the vertical comparison. Therefore, our prediction model can support the following work.

2.4   Multi-objective Programming Model

Multi-Objective Programming model is an important branch of operations research. It is a mathematical method of scientific management developed on the basis of nonlinear programming to solve multi-objective decision-making problems. Multi-Objective Programming refers to a programming problem with multiple objective functions. In mathematics, the Multi-Objective Programming method can be written in the following form:

$$\min\left(f_1(x), f_2(x), \cdots, f_k(x)\right), \quad s.t \quad x \in X \tag{3}$$

$k > 1$, refers to the number of objective functions, and the set X is a set of feasible decision vectors. Feasible sets are usually defined by some constraint functions. Furthermore, a vector-valued objective function is usually defined as:

$$f : X \to R^k, f(x) = (f_1(x), \cdots, f_k(x))^T \tag{4}$$

$x^* \in X$ is a workable solution or a workable decision. Vector obtained for feasible solutions X^* is $z^* := f(x^*) \in R^k$, which is called the target vector or the result.

For each objective $k(k \in K)$in multi-objective optimization, if there are two sets of parameters $\theta = (\theta_s, \theta_k)$ and $\theta^* = (\theta_s^*, \theta_k^*)$, such that $L_k(\theta_s, \theta_k) \geq$

$L_k(\theta_s^*, \theta_k^*)$ and $L(\theta_s, \theta_k) \neq L(\theta_s^*, \theta_k^*)$, then the parameter $\theta^* = (\theta_s^*, \theta_t^*)$ is called Pareto optimal [12]. In multi-objective optimization, there is usually no feasible solution that minimizes all objective functions simultaneously. Therefore, attention should be paid to Pareto optimal that cannot be improved in any objective without compromising at least one objective. The modeling steps are as follows.

– **Determine the objective function**
  According to the requirement, the total return should be as large as possible, but considering the actual transaction, the prices of gold and Bitcoin may continue to rise or fall for a certain period of time, that is, the extreme point is not reached. Therefore, we should take into account the eagerness of traders, and let traders make as much as possible in an uptrend and lose as little as possible in a downtrend. The expressions for the three targets are as follows:

$$z = g'\left(m + m^+ - m^-\right) + b'\left(n + n^+ - n^-\right) + d - g\left(m^+ - m^-\right) - b\left(n^+ - n^-\right)$$
$$- \alpha * g * \left(m^+ + m^-\right) - \beta * b * \left(n^+ + n^-\right) \tag{5}$$

$$\Delta g = g'\left(m + m^+ - m^-\right) - g * m - g\left(m^+ - m^-\right) - \alpha * g * \left(m^+ + m^-\right) \tag{6}$$
$$\Delta b = b'\left(n + n^+ - n^-\right) - b * n - b\left(n^+ - n^-\right) - \beta * b * \left(n^+ + n^-\right) \tag{7}$$

  Coordinate and compromise among the three objective functions, so that each sub-objective can be optimized as much as possible.
– **Determine constraints**
  The amount of gold and Bitcoin cannot be negative after each transaction:

$$m - m^- \geq 0, n - n^- \geq 0 \tag{8}$$

  Every trade uses USD, so the USD that the trader has before the trade must be higher than the price of the newly purchased asset plus the commission paid:

$$d - g * \left(m^+ - m^-\right) - \alpha * g * \left(m^+ + m^-\right) - b * \left(n^+ - n^-\right) - \beta * b * \left(n^+ + n^-\right) \geq 0 \tag{9}$$

  The amount of buying and selling gold and Bitcoin cannot be negative:

$$m^+ \geq 0, m^- \geq 0, n^+ \geq 0, n^- \geq 0 \tag{10}$$

2.5 Entropy Weight Method

In information theory, entropy is a measure of uncertainty. According to the characteristics of entropy, the randomness and disorder degree of an event can be judged by calculating the entropy value, and the dispersion degree of an index can also be judged by the entropy value. The greater the dispersion degree of the index, the greater the impact of the index on the comprehensive evaluation. Entropy weight method can determine the weight of each evaluation index, which can effectively reduce the influence of human subjective factors on the weight size [13]. The modeling steps are as follows:

Determine and calculate evaluation indicators

a. $Annualized\,Rate\,of\,Return = \dfrac{Annual\,Profit}{Initial\,Assets\,of\,the\,year}$

b. $Annualized\,Maximum\,Drawdown\,Rate = Max\dfrac{Z_j - Z_i}{Z_i}$

c. $Annualized\,Sharpe\,Ratio = \dfrac{Expected\,Rate\,of\,Return - Risk\,Free\,Rate}{Portfolio\,Standard\,Deviation}$

We make a portfolio investment of gold and Bitcoin, and its expected rate of return is 5.90% ; The risk-free interest rate is an asset investment without credit risk and market risk, which refers to the interest rate of treasury bonds whose maturity date is equal to the investment period. By looking up the data, we find that the risk-free interest rate in the United States from 2016 to 2021 is 1.56%. The formula for the portfolio standard deviation is:

$$\sigma_P = \sqrt{w_A^2 \sigma^2\left(k_A\right) + w_B^2 \sigma^2\left(k_B\right) + 2w_A w_B R\left(k_A, k_B\right)\sigma\left(k_A\right)\sigma\left(k_B\right)} \qquad (11)$$

w_i is the weight of each element in the combination, $\sigma(i)$ represents the standard deviation of each element, and the calculation formula is as follows:

$$\sigma = \sqrt{\dfrac{\sum_{t=1}^{n}(R, -\bar{R})^2}{t-1}} \qquad (12)$$

Among them, R_t and R are the actual rate of return and the average rate of return in each period, respectively, and t is the number of historical rates of return.

$R(K_a, K_b)$ represents the correlation coefficient of elements a and b, and the calculation formula is:

$$R(X,Y) = \dfrac{\sum(x-\bar{x})(y-\bar{y})}{\sqrt{\sum(x-\bar{x})^2\sum(y-\bar{y})^2}} \qquad (13)$$

x is the daily price and $\bar{x}$ is the average daily price.

d. $Calmer = \dfrac{Annualized\,Rate\,of\,Return}{Annualized\,Maximum\,Drawdown\,Rate}$

However, in our actual operation, the Sharpe ratio does not apply, and the specific reasons are expected rate of return and risk-free rate of return are mainly for portfolio investment of different stocks, we did not find data on portfolio investment. Also, when calculating the standard deviation, since gold cannot be traded every day, the price of gold will have no data for some days, and it cannot correspond to the price of Bitcoin one-to-one, so the correlation coefficient cannot be calculated. Furthermore, the investment ratio of gold and Bitcoin changes dynamically, so there is no fixed weight. If the first and last values are forced to replace the weight, a large error may occur.

Local analysis of indicators for each year

Construct a judgment matrix for each evaluation index in each year, where rows 0 to 4 represent September 11, 2016 to September 10, 2017, September 11, 2017 to September 10, 2018, and so on. Columns 0 to 2 represent three indicators: Annualized Rate of Return, Annualized Maximum Drawdown Rate and Calmer. First, adopt the normalization formula:

$$z_{i,j} = \frac{x_{i,j} - \min\left(x1, j, x2, j, \cdots, x3, j\right)}{\max\left(x_{1,j}, x_{2,j}, \cdots, x_{3,j}\right) - \min\left(x_{1,j}, x_{2,j}, \cdots, x_{3,j}\right)} \tag{14}$$

to make matrix X non-negative, which includes 5 samples and 3 indicators:

$$X = \begin{pmatrix} x_{1,1} & x_{1,2} & \cdots & x_{1,\ 3} \\ x_{2,1} & x_{2,2} & \cdots & x_{2,\ 3} \\ \vdots & \vdots & \ddots & \vdots \\ x_{5,1} & x_{5,1} & \cdots & x_{5,3} \end{pmatrix} \tag{15}$$

The normalized matrix is in Fig. 7.

```
Annualized rate of return      Annualized maximum drawdown rate    Calmer
0        0.271065                           0                          1
1        0.407391                           0                          1
2        0.237504                           0                          1
3        0.003785                           0                          1
4        0.313107                           0                          1
```

Fig. 7. Normalized Judgment Matrix

The normalized matrix obtained after the first step is Z:

$$Z = \begin{pmatrix} z_{1,1} & z_{1,2} & \cdots & z_{1,\ 3} \\ z_{2,1} & z_{2,2} & \cdots & z_{2,\ 3} \\ \vdots & \vdots & \ddots & \vdots \\ z_{5,1} & z_{5,1} & \cdots & z_{5,3} \end{pmatrix} \tag{16}$$

Second, calculate the proportion of the i_{th} sample under the $j - th$ index, and regard it as the probability used in the calculation of relative entropy p.

$$p_{i,j} = \frac{z_{i,j}}{\sum_{1=1}^{5} z_{i,j}} \tag{17}$$

Third, calculate the information entropy of each index, the information utility value, and obtain the entropy weight of each index by normalization. For the j_{th} index, the information entropy is calculated as follows:

$$e_j = -\frac{1}{\ln 5} \sum_{i=1}^{5} p_{i,j} \ln p_{i,j} \tag{18}$$

The entropy values of the three indicators are 0.7713, 0, 0.8924. The definition of information utility value is:

$$d_j = 1 - e_j \tag{19}$$

Therefore, the greater the utility value of information is, the more information it corresponds to. The entropy weight of each index can be obtained by normalizing the information utility value:

$$\omega_j = \frac{d_j}{\sum d_j} \tag{20}$$

The actual weights of the three indicators are 0.1719, 0.7516, 0.07648. Based on the entropy weights, the scores of each year are 3.4000, 1.3676, 0.6137, 0.3991, 1.7660 and the first year has the highest score. Therefore asset growth in the first year is the fastest.

3   Results and Analysis

To make the results more specific and persuasive, we assume that the initial asset is $1000, 0 troy ounces, 0 bitcoins.

3.1   Case Study

Based on the prediction result of ARIMA model, we use the data of the first twenty-five days as the initial sample size for prediction, and obtain the trend chart of the daily value of US dollar, gold and Bitcoin owned by traders. Since this model is a Multi-Objective Programming model, the solution sets are various. After running the model multiple times, we obtain an optimal solution set, select

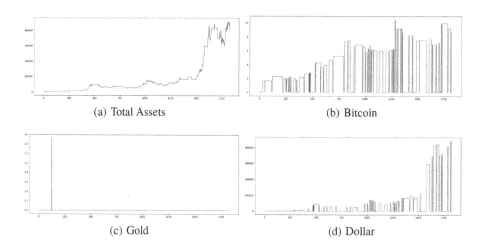

(a) Total Assets   (b) Bitcoin

(c) Gold   (d) Dollar

Fig. 8. Total Changing Tendency

the optimal trading strategy through comparison, and choose the final trading strategy according to the optimal trading strategy. The specific analysis is carried out based on Fig. 8. The X-axis reprsents days, and the Y-axis represents value.

In the first month, the prediction accuracy is low, the prediction model is poorly fitted, and the investment risk is high.

On October 11, 2016, it is predicted that Bitcoin will appreciate by 2.54%, so spend all US dollars to buy 1.59 bitcoins. Over the next 4 months, Bitcoin's daily price volatility will increase evenly, with an increase in total assets. By January 3, 2017, it is predicted that in the next four days, the price of Bitcoin will drop sharply, and the loss rate is as high as 22.5%, so all the existing Bitcoins are sold.

A week later, it is forecast that gold will increase by 3.4% in a short period of time, so it will hold about 1,800 US dollars to buy all gold, and only 1.53 ounces of gold will be held at this time. On the second day, it is predicted that gold has reached its peak in the next week, and then it will drop by 2.7%, and Bitcoin has reached the lowest value in the past two months, so after all the gold is sold, all the dollars will be used to buy Bitcoin. In the ensuing three months, the Bitcoin price fluctuates little and grows steadily, and the total assets double. By April 16, 2017, it is predicted that Bitcoin suddenly dropped, so all Bitcoins are sold. The price of gold is relatively stable, so it is not traded. Half a month later, it is predicted that Bitcoin will surge by 11.7%, so all US dollars are used to buy nearly 2 bitcoins. By July 8, 2017, the price of Bitcoin is growing rapidly and steadily. On this day, it is predicted that the price of Bitcoin will drop dramatically, so all Bitcoins owned are sold.

After 20 days, a large increase in the value of Bitcoin is predicted, and all the funds are used to buy Bitcoin. In the following six months, the price of Bitcoin surges. On January 6, 2018, it is predicted that the price of Bitcoin will fall sharply, so all Bitcoins are sold. The price of gold remains relatively stable, so it is not traded and the total assets have already increased significantly.

On February 17, 2018, it is predicted that the growth trend of Bitcoin is obvious, and all US dollars are used to buy Bitcoin. In the ensuing year, the market rebounds, and the value of Bitcoin continues to decline slowly. In January 2019, it is predicted that the price of Bitcoin will increase significantly in a short period of time, so Bitcoin is sold. The price of gold remains relatively stable, so it is not traded.

By March 2019, the price of Bitcoin have recovered, and a large increase is predicted, and all funds are used to buy Bitcoin. In the following three months, the volatility of Bitcoin increases, so the Bitcoin held is not sold. By June 28, 2019, the value of Bitcoin has dropped significantly in a short period of time, so we choose to sell all Bitcoin. A month later, predicting an imminent rise in Bitcoin price, buy Bitcoin with all your liquid assets. By September 28, 2019, the price of Bitcoin has fallen sharply, and the total assets have declined relatively when they choose to announce the sale. On October 20, 2019, it is predicted that the price of Bitcoin will skyrocket in the short term, so buy Bitcoin with all US dollars. But 4 months later, Bitcoin rebounds sharply, so sell all Bitcoins. The price of gold remains relatively stable, so it is not traded.

After the low price lasts for a month, the price begins to recover. Because of the short-term interest, Bitcoin is purchased near the lowest point of the price forecast. By May 2021, Bitcoin price fluctuates greatly, but there is a substantial increase in value and total assets increase. But after 14 months of volatile growth, there is a notable drop in the short-term forecast, so all Bitcoins are sold. The price of gold fluctuates in a small range, so it is not bought or sold.

By July 2021, the price has seen its lowest value in nearly 1 year, so use all the funds to buy Bitcoin. In the following two months, the price volatility of Bitcoin increases, and by the end of the five-year period, 8.7 bitcoins are still held, and the total assets are 401896.2854 US dollars. From the change trend of total assets, it can be found that the total assets have an increasing trend, and the values of the last five days are 451530.4769, 459453.0313, 408270.2462, 401896.2854, 0. It can be seen that the final total assets are 401896.2854 US dollars.

According to Entropy Weight method, we build a judgment matrix of evaluation indicators to prove that our model provides the best investment strategy, in which rows 0 to 2 represent the optimal strategy we found, the gold market, and the Bitcoin market. Columns 0 to 2 represent three indicators: Annualized Rate of Return, Annualized maximum drawdown rate and Calmer. The normalized matrix is in Fig. 9:

```
   Annualized rate of return   Annualized maximum drawdown rate   Calmer
0          0.534304                            0                     1
1          0.081314                            0                     1
2          0.258889                            0                     1
```

Fig. 9. Normalized Judgment Matrix

The entropy values of the three indicators are 0.6364, 0, 0.7925. The actual weights of the three indicators are 0.2314, 0.6365, 0.1321. Using the formula to score the optimal trading strategy in the first question, the actual investment strategy in the gold market, and the actual investment strategy in the Bitcoin market, the results are 192.16, 0.5589, 54.6426. We find that the score of our proposed trading strategy is much higher than the other two, so we can consider our trading strategy as the best trading strategy.

3.2   The Discussion of Optimal Strategy

In the above calculation, total assets after five years would be 401896.2854 US dollars. Chen Xinyu [14] use the Gray Forecast model to predict the price of gold and bitcoin the next day respectively. Next, compare the absolute value of the rise or fall to the absolute value of the median to determine the sell and buy operations. Then, establish a dynamic programming model to avoid risks, and use the Monte Carlo Method to determine the transaction time and transaction amount. Finally, the total value after five years was obtained by referring to the literature and recalculating the proportion of fixed investment. By comparing the sizes of the two, the optimal strategy is proved. The total assets are calculated to be 3636.259 US dollars, which is much smaller than the result of this paper, so this paper adopts the optimal investment strategy.

3.3 Sensitivity Analysis

In order to study the sensitivity of the strategy to the transaction cost, the article adjusts the value of the transaction commission and records the changes of the transaction strategy and transaction frequency. Due to the fact that the actual investment has many disturbances, the market fluctuates greatly, and the model predicts the future price in a limited number of days, the planned trading strategy pays more attention to short-term interests, and realizes the appreciation of assets under large price fluctuations, which is likely to cause frequent transactions. However, the increase in transaction commissions will inevitably increase transaction costs. Be more cautious when buying and selling, and avoid frequent transactions.

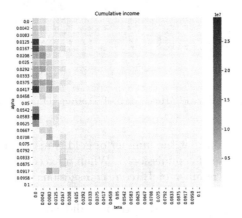

Fig. 10. Heat Map

Typical transaction commissions are 1%, 0.5%, or less. In our tests, the trading commission for gold and the trading commission for Bitcoin are chosen as 25 discrete values evenly distributed between 0 and 0.1%. The trading strategy of each pair (α, β) combination is calculated by traversal, and the total assets accumulated in each pair (α, β) under 5 years are visualized through Fig. 10.

It can be seen that the cumulative total income is more sensitive to the changes in commissions. With the increase of transaction costs, the overall trend of cumulative total returns is decreasing; At the same time, it can be found that the changes of α and β have different effects on cumulative total returns. When

α remains the same, with the increase of β value, the cumulative total return is generally reduced, and the change of β will have a greater impact on the cumulative total return. If the value of β remains the same, only looking at the value of α, the cumulative total return first increases and then decreases with the increase of α, and the change range is relatively small.

To illustrate the effect of commission changes on transaction frequency, the number of transactions under different (α, β) combinations in the experiment is counted. Figure 11 is the transaction times of gold and Bitcoin under different (α, β), respectively.

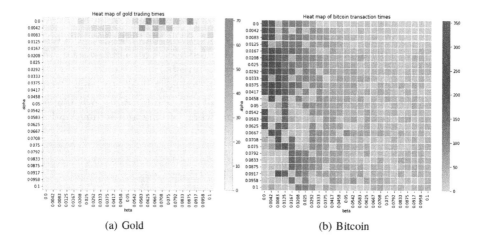

(a) Gold   (b) Bitcoin

Fig. 11. Heat Map of Trading Time

It can be clearly seen that the number of gold transactions decreases significantly with the increase of commission α. When α exceeds 2.08%, gold basically does not traded. The number of Bitcoin transactions also decreases with the increase in commissions, but the decrease is not as significant as gold. Even with the 10% commission on trades, trading did not stop completely. This is also related to the characteristics of the two products. The price of gold is relatively stable, the price fluctuation is small, and the expected return is relatively low. When the commission reaches a certain level, gold has no investment value. However, the price of Bitcoin rises and falls are relatively drastic, Bitcoin fell to an one-month low as Russian President Vladimir Putin's decision to launch a military operation in eastern Ukraine followed the cryptocurrency's plunge. At the time of writing, Bitcoin was trading at \$35,478.13, down 7.1%. Wang Juan, secretary general of the digital economy Committee of Beijing Computer Society, thinks that under the situation in Russia and Ukraine, Ukraine's second largest hub as COINS mining machine, digital currency supply scarce, high dependence on the network environment, exchange instability, poor trading convenience, led directly to the capital to convert them into real liquidity, the threshold is too high, too slow, and the timeliness and availability than anonymity, So gold, which is easy to exchange, is once again in demand.

To sum up, the combination of traditional assets and new assets can increase returns, but its own and the uncertainty of the environment also brings greater risks. In the actual investment process, we should maintain a cautious and objective attitude, and reasonably arrange the investment strategy of gold and Bitcoin.

4 Conclusion

For the problem of portfolio investment, in order to maximize the total investment return, the idea of first predicting the future market price and then figuring out the investment strategy and total assets is adopted. First, according to historical data, the ARIMA model is used to predict the closing prices of gold and Bitcoin on the next trading day, respectively. From the perspective of prediction accuracy, the fitting effect is good. Then, according to the forecast results of the price of the current day and the forecast price of the next day, the Multi-Objective Programming model is used to figure out the optimal investment strategy and obtain the maximum profit. According to Entropy Weight method, the article compare the strategy proposed with other two known strategies and finally prove that the optimal investment strategy is provided.

Acknowlegements. This research is supported by the Science and Technology Innovation Program of Hunan Province (No. 2020RC4046) and the National Natural Science Foundation of China (No. 72071206).

References

1. Sohraiee, S., Hosseinzadeh, L.F.: Selective convexity in extended GDEA model. Math. Methods Appl. Sci. **5**(77–80), 3861–3873 (2011)
2. Yun, Y.B., Nakayama, H., Tanino, T.: A generalized model for data envelopment analysis. Eur. J. Oper. Res. **157**(1), 87–105 (2004)
3. Tavana, M., Li, Z., Mobin, M., et al.: Multi-objective control chart design optimization using NSGA-III and MOPSO enhanced with DEA and TOPSIS. Expert Syst. Appl. **50**(15), 17–39 (2016)
4. Lu, C.C., Vincent, F.Y.: Data envelopment analysis for evaluating the efficiency of genetic algorithms on solving the vehicle routing problem with soft time windows. Comput. Industr. Eng. **63**(2), 520–529 (2012)
5. Poongodi, M., Vijayakumar, V., Chilamkurti, N.: Bitcoin price prediction using Arima model. Int. J. Internet Technol. Secur. Trans. **10**(4), 396–406 (2020)
6. Amjad, M., Shah, D.: Trading Bitcoin and online time series prediction. In: NIPS Time Series Workshop, pp. 1–15. PMLR 2017 (2016)
7. Kasse, I., Mariani, A., Utari, S., Didiharyono, D.: Investment risk analysis on Bitcoin with applied of VAR-APARCH model. JTAM (Jurnal Teori dan Aplikasi Matematika) **5**(1), 1–13 (2021)
8. Wang, J., Xue, Y., Liu, M.: An analysis of Bitcoin price based on VEC model. In: International Conference on Economics and Management Innovations, pp. 180–186. Atlantis Press 2016 (2016)

9. Gupta, A., Nain, H.: Bitcoin price prediction using time series analysis and machine learning techniques. In: Joshi, A., Khosravy, M., Gupta, N. (eds.) Mach. Learn. Predict. Anal., pp. 551–560. Springer Singapore, Singapore (2021)
10. Shahzad, S.J.H., Bouri, E., Roubaud, D., Kristoufek, L., Lucey, B.: Is Bitcoin a better safe-haven investment than gold and commodities? Int. Rev. Financ. Anal. **63**, 322–330 (2019)
11. Xiao, J., Auger, F., Jing, Z., Houidi, S.: Non-intrusive load event detection algorithm based on Bayesian information criterion. Power Syst. Protect. Control. **46**(22), 8–14 (2018)
12. Zhang, B., Xu, L., Huang, Z., Yao, X.: Multi-objective GANs pareto optimal solution algorithm with gradient strategy. Comput. Eng. Appl. **57**(9), 89–95 (2021)
13. Zhang, B.: Surrounding rock classification method for tunnel construction based on entropy weight method. J. Yangtze River Sci. Res. Inst. **39**(4), 122–127 (2022)
14. Chen, X., Hong, W.: Best plans for gold and bitcoin portfolios. Adv. Appl. Math. **11**(4), 2187–2203 (2022)

The Framework of Hammer Credit Rating System for Enterprises in Capital Markets of China with International Standards

George Xianzhi Yuan[1,2,3,4]([✉]), Hua He[4], Haiyang Liu[4], Chengxing Yan[4], Yunpeng Zhou[4], and Eric Chen[4]

[1] Business School , Chengdu University, Chengdu 610106, China
george_yuan99@yahoo.com
[2] Business School, Sun Yat-sen University, Guangzhou 510275, China
[3] Business School , East China University of Science and Technology, Shanghai 200237, China
[4] Shanghai Hammer Digital Technology Co., Ltd. (Hammer), Shanghai 200093, China

Abstract. The goal of this paper is to discuss how we establish the "Hammer Credit System" by applying Gibbs sampling algorithm under the framework of bigdata approach to extract features in depicting proxy default (bad) samples or illegal behaviors by following the "five step principle". Our study shows that the Hamer Credit System is able to resolve three problems of the current credit rating market in China which rate: "1) the rating is falsely high; 2) the differentiation of credit rating grades is insufficient; and 3) the poor performance of predicting early warning and related issues"; and in addition the CAFÉ credit is supported by clearly defining the "BBB" as the basic investment level with annualized rate of default probability in accordance with international standards in the practice of financial industries, and the credit transition matrix for "AAA-A" to "CCC-C" credit grades.

JEL Classification: C53 · C58 · G21 · G24 · G32

Keywords: Credit rating · Hammer (CAFÉ) system · Five step principle · Default matrix · Credit transition matrix · Proxy default sample · ROC and AUC testing · Non-structured feature · Risk gene · Default probability · Credit Rating Agencies (CRAs)

1 The Background and Related Issues

The credit rating is one of the most important parts for today's financial market economy (Altman [1, 2], Altman and Sabato [3], Hull [8, 9]). After nearly 30 years of rapid development in the domestic financial industry, the current domestic credit rating market in China is now facing at least three main problems (PBC [4, 5]), they are:

© The Author(s), under exclusive license to Springer Nature Singapore Pte Ltd. 2022
Y. Tan and Y. Shi (Eds.): DMBD 2022, CCIS 1745, pp. 191–211, 2022.
https://doi.org/10.1007/978-981-19-8991-9_15

1. **The rating is falsely high;**
2. **The differentiation of credit rating grades is insufficient; and**
3. The poor performance of predicting early warning.

Since the world's first Credit Rating agency was established by U.S. Moody's in the early 20th century, the Credit Rating industry with a century of development, has played an important intermediate role in promoting market development, revealing and preventing credit risks, reducing transaction costs, and assisting the government in financial supervision, and of course, has faced many adjustments (Dun and Bradstreet [6], FICO [7], Anderson [14], Chi et al. [15], Thomas et al. [16], Witzling [17], Yuan and Wang [18]). The Securities and Exchange Commission of the U.S. also believes that Credit Rating results have become more and more important to investors and other market participants in recent years, affecting issuers' access to the capital market, funding costs, financial transaction structure, trustee's investment capabilities, and so on. At the same time, the development and growth of the Credit Rating industry and the formation of a system depend to a large extent on the development of the financial market, especially the bond and securities market (Jing et al. [10], Du [11], Zhang [12], Ministry [19], PBC [4, 5]).

Thanks nearly 30 years of development, China's rating business includes almost all aspects of China's financial market. However, there are still a few many existing problems summarized as follows: First, the understanding of the Credit Rating industry needs to be deepened; Second, the legislative work on Credit Rating is obviously lagging behind; Third, the failure to form an effective supervision system; Fourth, the imbalance between supply and demand in the Credit Rating market is prominent, which is, on the one hand, there are many credit rating agencies (CRAs), on the other hand, the credit rating industry has few quality professional products available for rating and poor business stability, which makes many credit rating companies rely on non-credit main business support; Fifth, the independence and impartiality of credit rating agencies needs to be enhanced, and they are subject to more administrative interventions in the process of conducting credit ratings and lack objective independence; Sixth, there is a lack of objective and credible rating behavior, and this is the most deadly problem at present, especially in the objective assessment and handling of the actual situation of China's financial market itself, generally existing immature professional rating technologies, and the problem that the quality of credit ratings urgently needs to be improved professionally (Du [11], Feng [13], PBC [4, 5], Yuan [21]).

From the perspective of modern rating theory and approach in the practice from international credit rating agencies (CRAs), China's credit rating companies are gradually exploring credit rating methods and technologies that are suitable for China's national conditions, and have initially formed rating methods that can cover basic rating theories, Credit Rating models, and credit rating system based on classification of industries, products, and subjects. Nevertheless, the gap between China's Credit Rating companies and its international counterparts is also very prominent: for instance, credit rating is a necessary disclosure factor to promote the issuance of credit bonds in our country, and an important reference basis for bond issuance pricing, but during the rapid development of China's bond market, a large number of potential risks have been accumulated, and default events have occurred frequently, and the risks have shown normalization of default events, diversification of the nature of the subject, diversification of bond varieties, diffusion of industry distribution, and diversification of default area distribution and so on often happened. A typical incredible case is that the ratings of most China's companies by domestic rating agencies are still high with the rating grades from "AA" to "AAA" levels mostly, for example, according to the data provided by the platform "Wind"[1] at the end of year 2020, almost more than 90% of issuers and their bonds/debts' rating are in the range of AA and above, compared with the Credit Ratings of international rating agencies, the overall rating in Chinese capital markets is so higher and the distribution is more concentrated, which is not conducive to domestic and foreign investors to identify different risk of bond/debts in guiding investment decisions. If the quality of current credit rating market for domestic financial market in China is not improved and adjusted in time, this will affect the healthy development of China's financial market, especially the capital market for ever (see, PBC [4, 5]).

Taking into account a simple fact that the available samples of default (also, called "bad" sample) events observed for defaulted entities (the issuers being companies or enterprises) in the market is very small, we must consider to find a new path to establish reasonable credit rating method suitable to Chinese markets with international standards. On the other hand, in the current era of digital economy (ecology), especially in today's rapid development of big data with the financial technology (Fintech), under the premise of fully considering the information provided by both traditional structure and unstructured data, using new approach in dealing with non-structure data which is called "Hologram" approach (Yuan and Wang [18]) as a fundamental tool, we are able to extract (non-structured) risk feature factors based on un-structured data (instead of only traditional structure data) as breakthroughs to establish the so-called "Hammer (CAFÉ) Risk Assessment System" (in short, "Hammer (CAFÉ) Credit System", or "Hammer", or "CAFÉ Credit") to conduct rating for almost 10,000 companies in China by including all listed companies and bonds/debts' issuers (Yuan [20, 21], Yuan et al.[22, 23]). At the same time, combining the international standards that must be considered in the financial credit market, the basic investment level recognized in the financial industry is with "BBB" grade as the starting level, we are able to resolve the issue for the problem without enough default events (i.e., the "default", or "bad samples") by creating enough required proxy bad samples under the twelve categories of non-structured relevant penalty data released by CSRC (China Securities Regulatory Commission) on listed companies in A-share capital markets of China (see more from Yuan [20, 21]). In this way, it would help us to establish a so-called "Hammer (CAFÉ) Credit Rating system" for China's corporate entities and bonds (debts) that are in the line with international standards (e.g., see Yuan [20, 21], Yuan et al. [23]).

In this paper, we first discuss the existing problems of the current rating system used by the capital markets in China, then discuss the idea how the framework of "Hammer (CAFÉ) System" is established by applying the Hologram approach, then as applications of the "CAFÉ System" (reflected as the "Hammer", or "CAFÉ Credit" when related to the capital markets' risk assessment) (Yuan [20, 21]). The foundation of our Hammer (CAFÉ) system is a multi-dimensional risk assessment under the framework of bigdata

---

[1] A data service company in China for the information of financial market activities.

analysis by using the so-called Hologram approach (Yuan and Wang [18]) applying to "heterogeneous" data with combining the concept so-called "dynamic ontology" to extract entities' risk genes[2] by using AI algorithms (mainly, the Gibbs sampling method) as the proxy default (bad) samples to resolve the issue "not sufficient defaulted (bad) samples" (Yuan et al. [25, 26], or Yuan [21]. In this way, we are able to achieve comprehensive dynamic assessments for companies' credit risk from the four dimensions which consists of "Corporate structure hologram" (denoted by "C"), "Accounting behavior hologram" (denoted by "A"), "Financial behavior hologram" (denoted by "F") and "Ecosystem Hologram" (denoted by "E"), in short, "CAFÉ system" to form the "CAFÉ Risk Assessment System" for the (credit) risk assessment for entities in financial markets of China in the practice.

The goal of this paper is to discuss how we establish the "Hammer (CAFÉ) Credit System" by applying Gibbs sampling algorithm under the framework of bigdata approach to extract features in depicting bad or illegal behaviors by following the "five step principle" descried below with a full picture to readers at the first time in this paper. Then by using a number of case studies, we show that the Hammer (CAFÉ) Credit System discussed in this paper is able to resolve three problems of the current credit rating market in China which rate: "1) the rating is falsely high; 2) the differentiation of credit rating grades is insufficient; and 3) the poor performance of predicting early warning and related issues", and in addition the Hammer (CAFÉ) credit is supported by clearly defining the "BBB" as the basic investment level associated with the (annualized) rate of default probability in accordance with international standards in the practice for financial markets, and the credit transition matrix for "AAA-A" to "CCC-C" credit grades in describing (forecasting) the change of entities' crediting rating.

This paper consists of three parts: The first section is for an introduction and background and issues we face in current Chinese markets. The second section discuss the general framework and the key ideas of our "Hammer (CAFÉ) Risk Assessment System" established under the big data approach by applying the method for the extraction of risk features based on Gibbs algorithms (Yuan et al. [23]) and Hologram (Yuan and Wang [18]). Finally, the third Section is for the conclusion with brief discussion related CRAs for emerging markets on rating business in the practice related to financial industries in China, and possible impact and influence to the East Asian Economics.

2 The Framework of CAFÉ Risk Assessment System by Using Bigdata Method

As the world's second largest economy, China needs to establish a risk assessment system suitable for its national conditions and in line with the international credit rating system. In order to achieve this goal, the first work is to build a credit evaluation model by scientific means, and enough bad samples are needed to realize modeling, model proofreading and testing. Then, according to the international credit rating standard,

---

[2] Here, "Risk Gene" is basically a general term, which mainly represents various kinds of risk features in describing bad behaviors of entities such as financial anomalies, breaking compliance, business rules in the practice required by CSRC, PBC, or related regulatory agencies.

return to the most basic through the professional definition of "AAA" to "C", and take "BBB credit rating as the most basic investment grade" as the standard to establish the credit rating system for issuers (and bonds/debts): That is by applying the following "five Steps" (called "Five Step Principle") to establish a scientific and consistent standard system for credit rating with the default rates as the base criteria and bonds (debts) (Yuan [20, 21]):

Step 1: defining credit rating standards with default rate as the base criteria;
Step 2: constructing the "default matrix" required by credit risk;
Step 3: construct the "credit transfer matrix" of the change of subject (company) and debt credit qualification;
Step 4: supporting the "ROC" (and "AUC")[3] testing for credit model performance in Steps 2 and 3 above;
Step 5: build the necessary "proxy default (bad) samples to support Steps 2, 3 and Step 4 above (so allow us to complete the construction of the credit rating system in Step 1).

Here, we like to point out that the most difficult part is to construct enough "proxy bad samples for default events", and in addition, the information from actual default (bad) samples collected in Chinese capital market is not regular, thus not able to provide necessary risk information to support the modeling and related testing performance for credit risk modelling by comparing with those from capital markets in North America or West European regions. Indeed, for example, from 2007 to the end of year 2021, the sample size of all true default entities in China was only about 210 cases, and moreover, most of their basic risk information and related data are not disclosed. This difficulty situation forces us to find a new way to solve the issue on the shortage of default (bad) samples by constructing enough "proxy bad samples" for default events (in depicting (default) bad events or illegal behaviors of entities in the capital market of China), that is, China's credit evaluation system must build a description of proxy bad samples suitable for Chinese market! Fortunately, the bigdata analysis in Fintech supports us to realize this goal by taking, for example, the penalty data released by CSRC, and related regulatory agencies as the "proxy default (bad) samples" for listed companies using such as the Gibbs sampling algorithm to extract corresponding features which describe the possible bad behaviors in the capital markets by listed companies, as discussed by Yuan [20, 21].

Today, the capital markets in China maintains of more than 50,000 bonds (or debts), plus near around 5,000 listed companies, but around 92% of the bonds and issues are rated as "AA" or even higher credit rating. From the perspective of international standard in the practice, this is obviously inconsistent with the real market situation, which means that most of companies rated as "AA" or "AAA" are actually not true! On the other hand, since 2018, a number of companies (enterprises) rated as "AA" or "AAA" with

---

[3] The term "ROC" stands for Receiver Operating Characteristic (Fawcett [30]). The ROC curves are frequently used to show in a graphical way the connection/trade-off between clinical sensitivity and specificity for every possible cut-off for a test or a combination of tests. In addition, "AUC" is the area under ROC curve which gives an idea about the benefit of using the test(s) in question, often used in the testing of (default) bad samples in financial credit risk assessments for loan application by either individual or companies for their business development (Handley and McNeil [29]).

their bonds/debts with "AAA" credit ratings (such as the state-owned platforms) directly went to bankrupt or announcing no plan to pay back the face amount and or accrued interest of bonds/debts, these events absolute are against the current domestic credit rating system in China. Therefore, it is so urgently to have an internationally accepted Credit Assessment System suitable for China's financial market. In order to achieve this goal, as mentioned above, our starting point is first to find a scientific way to construct enough bad samples that required by the credit rating modelling to identify good or bad companies with the clear definition for the standard being "BBB" credit rating as the fundamental investment level associated with criteria consisting of the "Default Probability" and the "Credit Transition Matrix" for all classes from "C" to "AAA" credit rating grades. In this way, we first construct around more 1,200 bad samples for years since 2017 which was around 20% of listed companies in China's exchange stock markets, which support us to give a clear definition for the standards being "BBB" credit rating grade as the fundamental investment level; and finally we are able to establish a genera framework called "CAFÉ Risk Assessment", with its application in credit rating, called "CAEF Credit" (Yuan [20], Yuan et al. [22]).

In summary, our "CAFÉ Credit" uses "BBB" (instead of current "AA" rating by current most rating agencies inside China) as the starting point for the basic investment-grade standard by against the international standard under Five Steps principle listed above, and our CAFÉ credit system is able to solve three problems discussed above, which is also verified by a number of case studies below (see the work given by Yuan et al., 2022a; Yuan et al., 2022b). We like to point out that this is the first time in this paper to give a full picture how he framework of CAFÉ System (also maybe reflected as "CAFÉ Credit", or "Hammer System" when related to the applications in the practice) by applying five step principle mentioned above as discussed by Sects. 2.1, 2.2, 2.3 and 2.4 below.

2.1 The Framework for the Construction of CAFÉ Risk Assessment System

In the process of implementation, our starting point is to define the credit rating of entitles (companies, and also their bonds/debts) from the following four dimensions: First, the company's financial performance; Second, whether the company has fraud and how good or bad of the corresponding financial management quality; Third, how health of the company in terms of financial assets and liabilities, immediately indicating the degree of risk of company failure or default; and the fourth: The quality of the company's ecological environment and business risk (i.e., how good of the companies' ecosystems). This is done by using our Hologram approach (Yuan and Wang [18]), which leads us to conduct the rating distinction more clearly, and the credit rating assessments can better reflect the company's actual credit status in the market.

Our "CAFÉ" is indeed the system that integrates all kind of information including the management structure of the corporation itself, the operational and business disclosure information, and related parts in terms of networks. All of these are done by classifying as four dimensions:

1. **Corporate structure hologram (denoted by "C"); and**
2. **Accounting behavior hologram (denoted by "A"); and**

3. **Financial behavior hologram (denoted by "F"); and**
4. **Ecosystem Hologram (denoted by "E").**

In short, denoted by "**CAFÉ**" to represent the "CAFÉ Risk Assessment System" for financial markets in China. For the convenience of our discussion, the both terms "**CAFÉ**" and "**Hammer**" are used interchangeably in this paper.

The two major features of this system are that it does not only include static analysis, but also the dynamic analysis, and then combine dynamic analysis with corporate ecology to build a more objective characterization of corporate ratings, but also allow us to form corresponding characterizations which integrate heterogeneous and heterogeneous big data by using the hologram approach developed since year 2015 as a tool to implement the "data fusion" to extract (risk) features with the concept called the "Risk Genes" embedded in the complex network of entities with associated related parties as discussed by Yuan and Wang [18].

We like to specifically share with the readers that in order to have a good performance of risk assessment system for entitles in Chinese market, it is essentially to first establish the criteria for the modelling of listed companies financial fraud risk indicators (risk features), which should be the integration of financial statement analysis, the performance analysis on the enterprise management and associated governance structure, audit and internal control analysis, based on the general framework of the so-called "fraud triangle theory" as the starting point, and then to extract reliable risk characteristics (features) which include at least the following three types, which are either in traditional structured or unstructured data forms in our CAFÉ system: 1) the pressure/motivation dimension includes financial stability, external pressure, personal needs and financial goals; 2) the opportunity/vulnerability dimension including industry attributes, invalid supervision, organizational structure; and 3) the excuse/attitude dimension includes the auditing dimension.

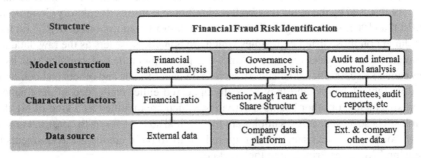

Fig. 1. The framework Identification for company's financial fraud risk under the Hammer (Café) Assessment

Indeed, we follow the structure as illustrated by the Fig. 1 to conduct the risk identification for company's performance on its financial fraud behaviors to build our reliable risk features in supporting dynamic credit risk assessment for listed companies.

Actually, as discussed in next Section, based on the data from 2016 to 2020 from China's listed companies, we first classify all bad (i.e., not-good) events as twelve kinds raised from capital markets of China, they are: 1) occupation of company assets; 2) false disclosures (other); 3) illegal guarantees; 4) fraudulent listings; 5) unauthorized changes to the use of funds; 6) general accounting mishandling; 7) false records (or misleading statements); 8) postpone disclosure; 9) fictitious profits; 10) major material omissions; 11) false listings of assets; and 12) the other case. By the fact that these twelve types of bad events can be used to explain the 8 types of financial fraud behaviors, which thus allow us to construct around 1,000 bad cases as the "proxy (default) bad samples for default events". In this way, by combining with audit information and internal control performance on the enterprise's management and governance structure, which help us to establish a dynamic and ecological enterprise risk assessment (see more by Yuan [20, 21], Yuan et al. [22–26]) and related references wherein), by using Gibbs sampling algorithms to extract risk features as discussed in next section briefly.

2.2 The Extraction of Risk Features Based on AI Algorithm Under the Bigdata Framework

The quality for the construction of China's credit system is actually essentially with one key thing: how to deal with the situation where well-defined default (bad) samples are normally not available? That is, how we "construct" a reasonable number of proxy default or bad samples (as around 20% of total listed companies) based on the alternative data (i.e., the unstructured samples) which are mainly illegal behaviors caused by some of entities and related parties from among around 5,000 listed companies, and they may be issuers for debts in the capital markets of China.

As discussed above, based on around 5,000 listed companies, we like to have around 1000 (=20% × 5000) default bad samples. However, the actual situation is that until the end of year 2021 (from year 2007), the total number of default entitles (samples) that can be used to describe company failures in China is not more than 210 cases, so the possible way we can do is to consider around 2,700 events (which are mainly non-structure data) issued or released by the regulatory bodies of "China Securities Regulatory Commission (CSRC)" and "China Banking and Insurance Regulatory Commission (CBIRC)" for their punishment on those listed companies which are bond/debt issuers as the raw data, and by taking these raw data regarded a kinds of "proxy (default) bad samples" for listed (companies) issuers' illegal behaviors such as financial frauds and others bad behaviors listed in Table 1 below, and they basically appeared either embedded in the financial report statements, or other business activities, which are qualified as a kind of big data samples. These around 2,700 samples are the original sources for us to construct at least 1,000 around proxy bad samples as required for us to build credit risk assessments by following Five Steps Principle in the practice.

By using framework for the extraction of risk features based by Gibbs algorithms established by Yuan et al. [22]), we will discuss below how we extract the risk characteristics embedded in these 12 kinds of category for bad events (see Table 1 below) in explaining 8 types of financial fraud behaviors (see Table 2) to construct around 1,000 proxy (default) bad samples to establish the modeling of our Hammer (CAFÉ) credit rating system.

The Extraction of Features Highly Correlated to the Behavior of Financial Fraud Events

During time period from January 2017 to December 2018, the data results show that there were around 2,700 bad events happened by around 383 listed companies as given by Table 1 below for twelve categories of bad events by applying the general principle of CSRC's compliance in the practice for capital markets in China.

Table 1. The Summary of 12 classes of violation events from listed companies from Jan. /2017 to Dec. /2018

Appropriation of company assets	Unauthorized change of use of funds	Breach of warranty	Fraudulent listing	False disclosure (other)	Sequence assets
87	17	60	0	32	4
General accounting is not handled properly	Misrepresentation (misleading statement)	Deferred disclosure	Fictitious profits	Material omissions	Other
30	233	306	15	143	117

On the other hand, In the light of China's capital market, Huang et al. [27] conducted analysis based on 175 financial fraud behaviors caused by 113 listed companies from the time period between 2010 to 2019, and one key conclusion they find is that almost all of financial fraud behaviors by listed companies in the past 10 years in China can be classified as eight types: Including such as Income and cost fraud (including cost fraud and expense fraud), monetary capital, investment income, asset impairment, non-operating revenue, expenditure and related other ways.

Through sorting, the following is the distribution of fraud by listed Companies in China's capital market in eight categories (see Table 2):

Table 2. The list of financial fraud types in the capital markets of China

Fraud type	# of Events	Ratio	Fraud type	# of Events	Ratio
1) Revenue fraud	77	44%	5) impairment fraud	13	7%
2) Expense fraud	25	14%	6) non-operating revenue and expenditure fraud	10	6%
3) Cash fraud	24	14%	7) investment income fraud	7	4%
4) Cost fraud	17	10%	8) Other fraud	2	1%

In this way, we are able to construct around 1,000 proxy samples of issuers' financial anomalies which would be regarded as the "proxy samples" for (default) bad behaviors under the eight types of financial fraud behaviors based on around 2,700 bad events (as shown by Table 1.), this allows us to reach the ratio level around 20% for proxy (default) bad samples among the total 5,000 listed companies, which would provide truly strong supporting for the modelling of the CAFÉ credit system as we will discuss below.

In order to achieve this highly related risk feature extraction that characterizes fraudulent embedded from the un-structured data, we use the one so-called Gibbs sampling algorithm (see the related application by Yuan [20, 21], Yuan et al. [24–26]). The Gibbs sampling method indeed is a Monte Carlo algorithm based on the Markov framework (MCMC) in statistics, which is also listed as one of the top ten human algorithms in the 20th century (Geman and Geman [33]), which is, in particular, important and useful in deal with simulation in the practice for high dimensional complex systems. Since the launch of its basic algorithm prototype for Gibbs algorithm in the 1950s, starting in the 1970s and 1980s, the integration of the AIC (Akaike Information Criteria) (Akaike [31]), and BIC (Bayesian Information Metrics) (Schwarz [32]) test standards for the amount of information were used and developed, the Gibbs algorithm is currently a very effective method to support feature extraction from high dimensional complex systems.

Based on the framework and proxy bad samples discussed above, we are able to obtained following 8 characteristic factors in depicting the risk of financial fraud were screened out by using the Gibbs sampling method as shown by Table 3. below (see also Yuan et al. [23], Yuan [20, 21] for more in details), which is based on the pool of 183 initial features given by Table 4. below.

Table 3. The 8 features highly correlated to the behavior of financial fraud events

Numbers	Description of features	Coefficients	p-value	Significant	Odds ratio
0	Constant term	− 2.49	0.00%	N/A	0.08
1	Deduction of non-net profit growth rate	− 0.41	0.00%	82.30%	0.67
2	Growth rate of works under construction	− 0.16	0.89%	87.40%	0.85
3	Advance payment growth rate	− 0.15	1.05%	59.70%	0.86
4	Where: interest expense (finance expense)/total operating income	0.30	0.00%	97.90%	1.36
5	Net income from investments/total operating income	− 0.15	0.24%	52.90%	0.86
6	Other income/total operating income	− 0.20	0.06%	98.45%	0.82

(*continued*)

Table 3. (*continued*)

Numbers	Description of features	Coefficients	p-value	Significant	Odds ratio
7	Other receivables (including interest and dividends)/total assets	0.20	0.00%	99.80%	1.22
8	Long-term borrowings/total assets	− 0.17	0.14%	65.05%	0.84

The Table 4. is the pool of initial characteristic factors (in part) in supporting to describe the behaviors of financial fraud and related financial anomalies, which helps jus to extract 8 key features given by Table 3. above.

Table 4. The pool of initial characteristic factors for the behavior of financial frauds & related financial anomalies

Numbers	Description of features	Significance of related parties
1	Paid-in capital (or equity)/total assets	31.95%
2	Days of non-current asset turnover	25.70%
3	Capital leverage	20.15%
4	Net worth EBIT rate	18.45%
5	Short-term borrowings/total assets	15.55%
...	...	...
181	Accounts receivable turnover days	0.05%
182	Growth rate of other payables	0.05%
183	Absorption of cash received from investments/Subtotal of cash inflows from financing activities	0.05%

The sample data with ratio of 80% as the training set and 20% as the test set (keep the proportion of black and white samples in the training set and the test set the same, i.e., the proxy "bad" samples account for around 20% of the total training set as mentioned above), by using the Logistic regression model and combining with OR (Odds Ratios) criteria, we extracted 8 features to describe the behaviors of financial fraud risk for listed companies, and the corresponding AUC values based on the training set and test set are 0.771 and 0.766, respectively (as shown in the area under the AUC curve in Fig. 2 below), which means that the features we screened can be more effective in characterizing the financial fraud risk of listed companies.

For the meaning of the ROC testing in a simple way, if the ROC test result is 0.7 or above, it indicates that the features used have strong discrimination and interpretation capabilities (see Yuan et al. [20, 21], Yuan et al. [22–26]) for the supporting the claim

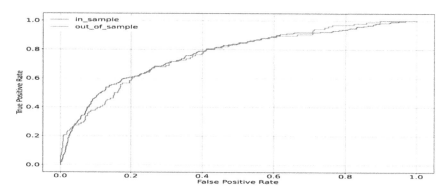

Fig. 2. The AUC (ROC) test for features in depicting financial fraud risk model

here, which thus supports our CAFÉ system has the ability to evaluate companies and debts more effectively.

Next, we discuss the extraction of features for fraud indicators from the framework of corporate governance structure as need for the construction of our CAFÉ credit system.

The Extraction of Fraud Indicators from the Framework of Corporate Governance Structure

Now considering the classification analysis of the company's major shareholders, management, board of directors and supervisory board according to the shareholding ratio, the identity of the position, and the proportion of internal and external, the CART classification method and the corresponding XGBoost algorithm (combined with the Weight of Evidence (WOE), and Information Value (IV) to explain the impact on the risk of possible fraud on the assessment for listed companies, then we obtain an unstructured feature assessment index that characterizes the quality of the corporate governance structure (Yuan [20, 21] and references wherein).

By the fact that the heart of corporate governance is the company's ownership structure, which indeed plays a key role which affects the behavior of financial fraud in the practice. This can be described in terms of the following four features from the perspective of corporate governance framework to be used to provide early warning for the performance that may lead to fraudulent behavior. Indeed, the company's shareholding structure affects the company's financial fraud risk important factors, and the following four characteristics can be used to warn the typical performance characteristics that may lead to fraud from the perspective of the corporate governance framework (Yuan et al. [24]):

1. The ratio of major shareholders, and legal representatives of companies is between 5% and 50%;
2. The cumulative ratio of the major shareholder shall not exceed 60%, that is, the sum of the shares of all major shareholders shall not exceed 60%; and
3. The shareholding of senior management is less than 1%; and
4. The proportion of major shareholders in the board of directors is not exceed 12%.

Now put all together on the two types of features extracted and developed by last two parts, combining with the performance analysis on internal and external audit-related data, we just have established a comprehensive characteristic system that could portray the company's financial fraud behavior (see the illustration by Fig. 1 above).

In addition, in terms of the construction for features from characterizing indicators of corporate (financial) fraud, we may think about a basic question: Why is there always fraud event happened by the listed companies? In view of above question, actually by combining the business situation, violations, cooperation of the audit institution, as well as auditor's education experience, work experience, etc. together to conduct a comprehensive sorting and analysis, and use WOE and IV criteria (Yuan et al. [24], Yuan [21]), we actually have the following core findings (which seem never been discussed by the existing literature before):

1. The number of inconsistencies from company's audit committee has a corresponding impact on the company's fraud behavior; and
2. The linear performance of the ROC curve test for audit performance also shows that in general, external audits can only find whether the company has fraudulent behavior, but cannot form a preventive effect against the company's financial fraud (because if the external audit work can form a preventive effect, the ROC corresponding to the audit effectiveness test curves should be nonlinear convex functions rather than linear states); and
3. In the study of the relationship between the number of directors and structure of senior management team for companies, it is found that regardless of the company's rating, the number of board committees as long as it is within the prescribed reasonable range (i.e., in principle, the number of directors is between 5 and 9 people), the number of directors does not constitute a special impact on the company's operation.

Here we also like to point out that for more discussion related above 1), 2) and 3) in details, see Yuan et al. [24] and reference wherein.

We also refer to Yuan et al. [22] for the comprehensive case studies in support how the Hammer (CAFÉ) credit system is able to identify the financial fraud behavior in the practice of capital markets in China in last a few years.

2.3 The Construction of Credit Transition Matrix by Hammer (CAFÉ) System for Financial Markets in China

Credit rating adjustment is one of the most important rating actions of credit rating agencies. Credit rating adjustment behaviors include upscaling, downscaling, and maintenance. In a certain period (inspection period), the result of credit rating agency's adjustment of the debt issuer's credit rating can form the debt issuer's credit migration path, which reflects the change in the debt issuer's credit quality, this is done through the so-called Credit Transition Matrix (Hull, [8, 9]; Jarrow et al. [28]). In order to do so, we first discuss the mapping rules for the construction of the Hammer (CAFÉ) credit transition matrix with the following two parts below.

The Definition for BBB Rating Associated with Default Probability Criteria for CAFÉ (Hammer) Credit Risk Assessment

As discussed in the beginning of this paper, one of major reasons for credit rating systems in financial markets used and developed by the most Credit Rating Agencies (CRAs) in China associated with three typical issues such as "the rating is falsely high; the differentiation of credit rating grades is insufficient; and the poor performance of predicting early warning and related issues", is mainly due to one face that the shortage of (default) bad samples as not many CRAs paid the attention to solve this problem.

Under the framework above in Sect. 1 and using algorithms for the extract of features discussed based on the proxy bad samples above in Sect. 2, we are able to derive its default (model) rate for the BBB credit rating with its annualized default probability as shown by Table 5 below (for the default of probability rate in the physical measure, i.e., the rates observed from markets):

Table 5. The criteria of annualized default probability for BBB rating for hammer (CAFÉ) system (2020)

Rank	CAFÉ (Model)	CAFÉ (observed from market)	Moody's	CRAs in China
AAA	0.004%	0.000%	0.000%	0.152%
AA	0.008%	0.000%	0.020%	0.369%
A	0.021%	0.000%	0.060%	0.502%
BBB	0.113%	0.113%	0.180%	2.825%
BB	0.631%	0.733%	0.910%	8.261%
B	1.987%	1.944%	3.440%	12.177%
CCC-C	10.641%	12.139%	10.140%	28.701%

P.S.: CAFÉ (Hammer)'s (Annualized) Default Probability Rate is from 2020; Moody's is the average from 1983 to 2017; CRAs in China is from 2014 to 2020

Based the results given by Table 6., it is clearly for the generic "BBB" credit rating in capital market of China for non-financial industry, its annualized default probability (PD) is 0.113% based on the data collected as December 31,2020, which is comparable with 0.180% used by Moody's. The criterion being 0.113% for BBB grade was actually validated by the market data we observed in year 2020, and the corresponding annualized default probabilities for "AAA" to "CCC-C" are determined under the help of our default rate model, as shown by the Table 5., too.

In another word, in order to resolve three issues faced by credit rating markets in China, it is done by first clearly defining (determining) the "BBB" as the basic investment level accordance with international practice with consideration of features from the capital markets in China with reasonable default probability. We also obtained that the default rate of hammer and Moody's rating at "AAA-BBB" is generally lower than 1.000%, which is consistent with the default rate of investment grade "BBB and above" bonds (assets), which is significantly lower than those given by CRAs in China. We also observed that our Hammer and Moody's results show that the default rate for "CCC-C" grade is significantly different from that of "AAA-B" level.

The Mapping Rules for CAFÉ (Hammer) Credit Transition Matrix

By following Yuan et al. [22, 23], take the criteria for "BBB" rating as the base with help for the annualized default probability rates from "AAA" to "CCC-C", which allow us to construct transition matrices.

In order to make the credit transition matrix useful, we need first consider its stability of Hammer (CAFÉ) credit system, so the construction of the rating transition matrix is completed by the mapping consisting of three steps below (see the Table 6 below):

The First Step: Divide the default model into one-year and two-year periods, and conduct ROC verification to determine the final model;

The Second Step: Give different rating results based on the 1-year and 2-year default models;

The Third Step: Integrate the 1-year and 2-year rating results to give the initial rating. The rules are as follows:

Table 6. CAFÉ's initial rating mapping table based on 1 year and 2 year period data

Items	Credit rating in 1 year						
Credit rating in 2 years	AAA	AA	A	BBB	BB	B	CCC-C
AAA	A	A	A	BBB	BB	BB	CCC-C
AA	A	A	A	BBB	BB	BB	CCC-C
A	A	A	A	BBB	BB	B	CCC-C
BBB	A	BBB	BBB	BBB	BB	B	CCC-C
BB	BBB	BBB	BBB	BBB	BB	B	CCC-C
B	BB	BB	BB	BB	BB	B	CCC-C
CCC-C	BB	B	B	B	CCC-C	CCC-C	CCC-C

The CAFÉ'S (Hammer) Credit Transition Matrix

Taking into account the limitation of data acquisition, the observation limit of CAFÉ on the sample of listed companies is limited to the period from 2014 to 2019. We have obtained 3,000 companies with complete annual financial information from 2014, and 4,500 companies in 2019. Taking the 31st of December, 2020 as the observation day, the number of default samples returned for one year was 44; the number of default samples returned for the second year was 89 (here, we emphasize that we have actually observed "three years of return the number of default samples in this report is 115", but in the construction and analysis of the credit transition matrix in this report, the reason is that other sample information needs to be improved when the default samples of three years backed back are used for feature extraction. Therefore, only the backed One-year and two-year default samples) (Jarrow et al. [28]).

Based on the use of the above mapping rules, after integrating the rating results with the one-year and two-year default models, we will observe the following basic conclusion: the basis of the credit transition matrix from rating "AAA-A" to "CCC-C" (see **Appendix b**elow, also given by Yuan et al. [23]) for the definitions of Hammer (CAFÉ) Risk assessment system in details). Basically with "BBB" as the center, this maintains good stability, thereby solving the problem of instability of the "AAA", "AA" and "A"-level migration matrix (especially for emerging markets like China). Therefore, from the perspective of the credit transition matrix, if we classify "AAA" to "A" into the "AAA-A" category, after adjusting the mapping threshold, we have the following credit transition matrix results as shown by Table 7. below (see also Yuan et al. [22, 23]):

Table 7. Summary information of BBD 2015–2020 transition matrix

	AAA-A	BBB	BB	B	CCC-C
AAA-A	71.55%	24.76%	3.24%	0.39%	0.04%
BBB	15.11%	69.19%	13.77%	1.76%	0.15%
BB	3.68%	22.62%	55.66%	16.52%	1.51%
B	2.05%	8.94%	36.30%	42.93%	9.74%
CCC-C	1.52%	5.05%	16.41%	39.39%	37.37%

It can be seen from the results of the transition matrix that the "AAA-A" grades maintain better stability after merging, and the transition matrix also reflects the monotonic decrease in the stability of "AAA-CCC" at each level, which supports the relative stability of our CAFÉ system Stability issues, and thus play a role in supporting the industry.

Put all together, by following five step principle given above, we now establish the Hammer (CAFÉ) credit system for capital markets in China to have a reasonable performance for credit rating in the practice with the international standards in the practice, which help us to give a clear classifications for credit grades from "AAA" to "C" given by Appendix A (below) associated with credit risk information with (annualized) rate of default probability, and credit transition matrix, which are requited by PBC [4, 5] effectively on January 1, 2023!

Now as applications of Hammer (CAFÉ) Credit assessment, our case studies will show Hammer (CAFÉ) credit system's capability in resolving three issues: "1) the rating is falsely high; 2) the differentiation of credit rating grades is insufficient; and 3) the poor performance of predicting early warning and related issues" in the current capital market by comparing with true market performance provided by the most of CRAs in China, and see more given by Yuan [20, 21] in details and the Sect. 2.4 below.

2.4 The Applications of Hammer (CAFÉ) Assessment System on Capital Markets in China

By following the previous studies established by Yuan et al. [22–24], which are as applications of the CAFÉ Risk Assessment based on around 5,000 listed companies in China with information before the end of 2020, we actually have the following main conclusions incorporating by a number of case studies in this section and Yuan et al. [22] for the comprehensive analysis by covering at least 8 sectors of listed companies. they are:

1. The domestic listed companies with a credit rating being "AA" or above accounted for about 10% of listed companies, and companies with a rating of "AAA" accounted for only about 1% of listed companies. By compared with foreign countries such as USA, the proportion of "AAA" level is about 2%-4%, and the corresponding proportion of "AAA" level in Japanese listed companies is 3%-6%;
2. From the credit rating grades distribution of listed companies, the term structure of default probability, and the performance for the detection results in terms of testing by the ROC curve, our CAFÉ Credit is more able to characterize the credit risk of China's companies, and at the same time has better predictive capabilities.

The above general conclusions show that the CAFÉ credit system for capital markets in China conduct a reasonable performance for credit rating for all listed companies.

3 The Conclusion with Brief Discussion and Remark

As mentioned in the beginning of this paoer, under the help of proxy bad samples for default events which are based on the penalty data released by CRSC for listed companies and issuers of debts in financial markets in China, this paper first discusses how we establish the so-called "Hammer (CAFÉ) Credit System" by applying Gibbs sampling algorithm under the framework of bigdata analysis for the extract of features in depicting bad or illegal behaviors by following "five step principle". The Hammer (CAFÉ) credit rating assessment system allows us to resolve three problems of the current credit rating market in China which are: "1) the rating is falsely high; 2) the differentiation of credit rating grades is insufficient; and 3) the poor performance of predicting early warning and related issues". In addition, the CAFÉ credit is developed by clearly defining the "BBB" as the basic investment level in accordance with international standards in the practice of financial industries with annualized rate of default probability, and the credit transition matrix.

Second, by considering a simple fact that the reasonable size for default samples with basic necessary information of issuers directly observed from the capital markets would not be improved in a short term in China, we are able to develop a bigdata approach to establish the "Hammer (CAFÉ) Risk Assessment System" which seems suitable to financial markets in China under the framework by extracting risk features incorporating Gibbs sampling method to identify and obtain reliable risk factors from the proxy default (bad) samples. For related applications with more discussion in details, see Yuan [20, 21], Yuan et al. [22–26] and reference wherein.

Third, we realize that though Hammer (CAFÉ) Credit System established under the framework of big data in this paper is capable to reveal the company's risks, and the comprehensive case studies given by the paper and those given by Yuan et al. [22] show that the Hammer (CAFÉ) system is able to provide risk assessments of issues in China's capital market in the line with international standards to support the development of the credit rating system for domestic financial industry, however, the term structure of default probability rate established is only for one year long, and the credit transition matrix of CAFÉ credit is still needed to be improved for "AAA", "AA", "A" and "CCC-C" grades during to the development of capital markets in China by looking forward.

Before the ending of this paper, we also like to make a few remarks for a brief discussion on what might happen from the perspective of credit rating agencies (CRAs) on rating business in the practice related to financial industries in China, and even the impact and influence to the East Asian Economics (see also, related discussion by Oh [34], Joe and Oh [35], and Tian et al. [36]).

First, we like to point out that as No.2 position for the economy size in the world, China must have a reliable credit rating system under a framework of financial way in the line with the international standards accepted by international financial communities in the practice, such as the "five step principle" discussed above in this paper. Thus there exists a "competitive" environment on credit rating markets in China should be first beneficial for the development of financial markets in Credit risk assessment by emphasizing the quality on the financial risk assessments on issues and debts with such as the exposure on the rates of default probability must be released by CRAs, which is required to apply to all CRAs' starting on January 1, 2023 by People's Bank of China (PBC) (the main regulatory body on financial markets in China) based on its official announcement on Aug 6/2021 and Aug 18/2021 (see PBC [4, 5]), it seems to us this is indeed a huge step!

Second, China began to start its open door policy on the credit business since around 2018/2019 to allow foreign ownership of CRAs, and currently only a few international agencies ones like S&P and Fitch hold general credit rating licenses for business on corporate and debt credit rating inside China, but we do think this is also the opportunity for CRAs inside China, too as they always are facing the challenge raised by the practice from the dynamic behavior of financial markets in China with rapid changes in daily basis with Chinese characteristics (see the discussion by Tian et al. [36] and references wherein for more discussion).

Overall, we are sure that the current practice of credit rating market in China with three problems will be improved to meet the international standards with the risk exposure such as the term structure of default probability rates, and associated credit transition matrix, this would also be the driving force to promote the healthy development of financial markets globally.

Acknowledgements. This work is supported in part by National Natural Science Foundation of China (NNSFC) with Project # U1811462; and #71971031. All authors have no conflict of interest related to project funding.

Appendix: The Framework for the Extraction of Features Based on Gibbs Algorithms

The following is the framework for the extraction of risk features by using Gibbs sampling algorithms (see Yuan et al. [23] for more in details).

Step 1: Assuming that the characteristic indicators depicting financial fraud follow the Bernoulli distribution, the characteristic space formed by the characteristic factors is initialized. Based on random sampling, the characteristics are classified according to whether the coefficient is 0: those who are not 0 are recorded as 1:

$$A_0 = (0, 1, 1, \ldots, 0) \in \{0, 1\}^m. \tag{1}$$

where, m represents the number of features in the initialized feature space, and represents A_0 a subset in the initialized feature space.

Step 2: Via BIC (Bayesian Information Criterions) construct a standard that supports random sample counting, and construct a distribution function for features, to:

$$P_{BIC}(i_n = 1|I_{-n}) = \frac{exp(-BIC(i_n = 1|I_{-n}))}{exp(-BIC(i_n = 0|I_{-n})) + exp(-BIC(i_n = 1|I_{-n}))} \tag{2}$$

where $P_{BIC}(i)$ the indicator transfer probability function, representing the nth feature, I_{-n} is in addition to i_n the other feature sets, the number of features in the initialized feature space, I_0 represents a subset in the initialized feature space, using the formula to ensure that the feature subset shifts to a higher degree of fit, As a result, the salience of the characteristic indicators that ultimately characterize financial fraud behavior can be revealed.

Step 3: Determine the number of sample counts for the sample. The number of sampling calculations is determined to reduce the computational complexity and ensure that the results of the final indicator significance are achieved within the tolerable margin of error. At this point, we need to set the error range due to the sample size. In order to ensure the significance of the extracted feature calculation results, the sample size error is usually recommended to be no more than 5%, and the corresponding formula is as follows:

$$Std(p) = \sqrt{\frac{p(1-p)}{M}} < \sqrt{\frac{1}{4M}}. \tag{3}$$

When the analog error is controlled within 2 times of $Std(p)$ by not bigger than 5% (for 2 standard deviations (i.e., 2 $Std(p)$), the number of sampling counts can be obtained by the above formula M is 400 (times), In this way, the number of sample counts can have the effect of reducing the computational complexity and ensuring the distinctiveness of the features.

References

1. Altman, E.I.: Financial ratios, discriminant analysis and the prediction of corporate bankruptcy. J. Finance **23**(4), 589–609 (1968)
2. Altman, E.I.: Corporate Financial Distress. A Complete Guide to Predicting, Avoiding, and Dealing with Bankruptcy. John Wiley and Sons Inc., New York (1983)
3. Altman, E.I., Sabato, G.: Modeling credit risk for SMEs: evidence from the US market. Abacus **43**(3), 332–357 (2007)
4. Notice on promoting the high-quality and healthy development of the credit rating industry in the bond market (Exposure Draft). People's Bank of China. http://www.pbc.gov.cn/tiaofasi/144941/144979/3941920/4215457/index.html
5. Notice of PBC, NDRC, MOF, CBIRC, and CSRC on Promoting the Sound Development of the Credit Rating Industry for the Bond Market. People's Bank of China. http://www.pbc.gov.cn/en/3688253/3689009/4180845/4530539/index.html
6. Dun and Bradstreet on credit rating. http://www.dandb.com/glossary/d-b-rating
7. What is a credit score? https://www.myfico.com/credit-education/credit-scores
8. Hull, J.: Options, Futures and Other Derivatives, 10th edn. Pearson, New York (2017)
9. Hull, J.: Risk Management and Financial Institutes, 5th edn. Pearson, New York (2018)
10. Jing, X.C., Li, D., Wang, J.H.: Current situation and development prospect of China's credit rating agencies. China Financ. Bimonthly **21**, 47–48 (2003)
11. Du, L.H.: Plan ahead: the internationalization challenge of Chinese rating agencies. Financ. Mark. Res. **62**(7), 119–127 (2017)
12. Zhang, H.: Review and Prospect of the Development of China's Credit Rating Market. Financ. Dev. Res. **29**(10), 29–352018 (2018)
13. Feng, G.H., et al.: Principles and Pragmatism of Credit Rating. China Finance Press, Beijing (2019)
14. Anderson, R.: The Credit Scoring Toolkit: Theory and Practice for Retail Credit Risk Management and Decision Automation, 1st edn. Oxford University Press, UK (2007)
15. Chi, G.T., Yu, S.L., Yuan, G.X.: Facility rating model and empirical for small industrial enterprises based on LM test. J. Ind. Eng. Eng. Manage. **33**, 170–181 (2019)
16. Thomas, L., Crook, J., Edelman, D.: Credit Scoring and Its Applications, 2nd edn. SIAM, Philadelphia (2017)
17. Witzling, D.: Financial complexity: accounting for fraud. Science **352**(6283), 301 (2016)
18. Yuan, G.X., Wang, H.Q.: The general dynamic risk assessment for the enterprise by the hologram approach in financial technology. Int. J. Finance Eng. **6**(1), 1–48 (2019)
19. Ministry (for Ministry of Finance, People's Republic of China): Accounting standards for business enterprises No. 36 - disclosure by related parties (2008)
20. Yuan, G.X.: The CAFÉ risk assessment by applying Hologram approach for Chinese market, TGES, 22 February 2021. https://mp.weixin.qq.com/s/RwP6UTtk3hMF9gYkImqD7A
21. Yuan, G.X.: Using big data approach to improve the quality of credit rating in China: the CAFÉ risk assessment system. Tsinghua Financ. Rev. **98**, 70–74 (2022)
22. Yuan, G.X., Yan, C.X., Zhou, Y.P., Liu, H.Y., Qian, G.Q., Shi, Y.K.: Credit risk analysis of Chinese companies by applying the CAFÉ approach. In: Wang, Y., Zhu, G., Han, Q., Zhang, L., Song, X., Lu, Z. (eds.) Data Science, ICPCSEE 2022. Communications in Computer and Information Science, vol. 1629, Part II, pp.475–502. Springer, Singapore (2022). https://doi.org/10.1007/978-981-19-5209-8_33
23. Yuan, G.X., Zhou, Y.P., Yan, C.X., et al.: The framework of CAFE credit risk assessment for financial markets in China. Procedia Comput. Sci. **202**, 33–46 (2022)
24. Yuan, G.X., Zhou, Y.P., Yan, C.X., et al.: The framework for the risk feature extraction method on corporate fraud. China J. Manage Sci. **30**(3), 47–58 (2022)

25. Yuan, G.X., Zhou, Y.P., Yan, C.X., et al.: New method for corporate financial fraud early warning and risk feature screening: based on artificial intelligence algorithm. In: Proceedings of the 15th (2020) China Annual Management Conference, pp. 709–724 (2020)

26. Yuan, G.X., Liu, H.Y., Zhou, Y.P., et al.: The extraction of risk features by applying stochastic search algorithm FOF under the framework of bigdata. Manage. Sci. **33**(6), 41–53 (2020)

27. Huang, S.Z., Ye, Q.H., Xu, S., et al.: Analysis of financial fraud of Chinese listed companies from 2010 to 2019. Financ. Acc. Monthly **14**, 153–160 (2020)

28. Jarrow, R.A., Lando, D., Turnbull, S.M.: A Markov model for the term structure of credit risk spreads. Rev. Financ. Stud. **10**(2), 481–523 (2004)

29. Hanley, J.A., McNeil, B.J.: A method of comparing the areas under receiver operating characteristic curves derived from the same cases. Radiology **148**(3), 839–843 (1983)

30. Fawcett, T.: An introduction to ROC analysis. Pattern Recogn. Lett. **27**(8), 861–874 (2006)

31. Akaike, H.: A new look at the statistical model identification. IEEE Trans. Autom. Control **19**(6), 716–723 (1974)

32. Schwarz, G.: Estimating the dimension of a model. Ann. Stat. **6**(2), 461–464 (1978)

33. Geman, S., Geman, D.: Stochastic relaxation, gibbs distributions, and the Bayesian restoration of images. IEEE Trans. Pattern Anal. Math. Intell. **6**, 721–741 (1984)

34. Oh, F.D.: Assessing competitive conditions in Korea's credit rating industry after the 1997 financial crisis. Economics Bulletin. **34**, 1114–1121 (2014)

35. Joe, D.Y., Oh, F.D.: Credit ratings and corporate cash holdings: Evidence from Korea's corporate reform after the 1997 Asian financial crisis. Jpn. World Econ. **45**, 9–18 (2018)

36. Tian, W., Zhou, X., Tian, Y., Meng, W.: Short-term competition and long-term convergence between domestic and global rating agencies: evidence from China. PLoS ONE Public Libr. Sci. **15**(5), 1–15 (2020)

Community Detection and Diagnosis Systems

A Self-adaptive Two-Stage Local Expansion Algorithm for Community Detection on Complex Networks

Hui Shan, Bin Li, Haipeng Yang, and Lei Zhang[✉]

Key Laboratory of Intelligent Computing and Signal Processing of Ministry of Education,
School of Computer Science and Technology, Anhui University, Hefei, China
zl@ahu.edu.cn

Abstract. Community detection is of great importance to find hidden information in complex networks. For this problem, local expansion algorithms are becoming popular due to the low time complexity. However, most of them depend heavily on seed selection or require setting some thresholds in advance, leading to inaccurate partition. To this end, this paper proposes a self-adaptive two-stage local expansion algorithm (SALEA) for community detection. Specifically, we propose a self-adaptive strategy that can be used in SALEA for finding communities spontaneously. In the first stage, we apply the self-adaptive strategy for nodes to conduct local expansion and get coarse community structures. In the second stage, we apply the self-adaptive strategy for weak communities obtained in the first stage to refine the coarse community structures and get more accurate partitions. Finally, the experimental results on real and synthetic networks demonstrate that SALEA is superior over several state-of-the-arts.

Keywords: Complex network · Community detection · Local expansion algorithm · Self-adaptive strategy · Two-stage framework

1 Introduction

Complex networks have been used in numerous fields to describe many kinds of complex systems, such as Internet networks and social networks. In these complex networks, there are always community structures which means the nodes in the same community have dense connection while the nodes between different communities have sparse connection [1]. Detecting community structures accurately can find hidden information in complex networks effectively. Therefore, community detection has drawn the attention of numerous academics and it has emerged as a key tool in several fields, including social science, network science, biological science, and so on [2].

Based on the different network information required, community detection algorithms can be divided into two kinds generally. One kind is global algorithms which apply information from the entire network to detect communities. Global algorithms, such as hierarchical clustering [3,4], spectral clustering [5–7], and evolutionary computation [8–11], can always get accurate and reasonable results according to the global information obtained. However, due to their high time complexity, the majority of them

© The Author(s), under exclusive license to Springer Nature Singapore Pte Ltd. 2022
Y. Tan and Y. Shi (Eds.): DMBD 2022, CCIS 1745, pp. 215–230, 2022.
https://doi.org/10.1007/978-981-19-8991-9_16

cannot be employed for large-scale complex networks. Another kind is local algorithms which utilize local information instead of global information to detect communities. Local algorithms, including random walks [12,13], label propagation [14,15], and so on, can detect communities in a short time because of their acceptable time complexity.

Local expansion [16–23] is one kind of popular local algorithm. Two main ways can achieve local expansion. One way is expanding from specific seeds. It requires selecting one seed node by computing the local property index first. Then, to optimize the partition, it merges nearby nodes of the seed node using the predetermined rules or metrics. As a result, the local expansion process end and the final partition can be created. It is obvious that local expansion algorithms can make full use of local information and reduce computational time effectively. The other way is connecting all pairs of nodes which are based on local similarity. Instead of finding the seeds and conducting local expansion based on the seeds, they pay more attention to the local property for each node. They select the closest or the most similar node for each node and make them a pair. Based on these pairs of nodes, they can reconstruct a simpler network and find connected component in the network, where each connected components can be viewed as a community.

The aforementioned local expansion algorithms for community detection have shown their good performance in complex networks. However, for the first method of local expansion, their performances depend heavily on the position of seeds. A sound method for choosing seeds can select nodes that may exist in its community more accurately and completely, whereas a poor method is likely to produce subpar results. Meanwhile, most of them require setting some thresholds and metrics in advance at the local expansion process, such as the threshold of fitness [16] and modularity [24], which may influence the precision of partition. Moreover, nodes that are far from the center of the network can easily be ignored [25]. For the second method of local expansion, there may exist many communities which only contain small amounts of nodes because of lack of global knowledge. Hence, most of them require setting a parameter λ in advance for the community size to merge these incomplete communities into complete ones. However, these two methods also exist some weaknesses. For one thing, the parameter may influence the results greatly and an inappropriate setting may lead to inaccurate partition. For another, if we merely care about the community size, the internal topological structure of the community will be neglected.

To this end, in this paper, we propose a self-adaptive two-stage local expansion algorithm for community detection. In the algorithm, we suggest a self-adaptive strategy for local expansion and global merger in the two stages. Note that the proposed self-adaptive strategy can detect communities spontaneously without any parameter. Specifically, in the first stage, we apply the self-adaptive strategy for local expansion. Thus, we mainly take account of the property of the last added nodes and the center of the community can keep updated. As a result, the nodes at the edge of networks can also be easily checked and accurately determined whether to add a community without any thresholds and extra metrics, which can get coarse community structures quickly. However, it may form weak communities which are incomplete and only contain small amounts of nodes. To refine these coarse community structures, the same self-adaptive strategy can be applied in the second stage and weak communities can merge accurately and effectively. In the global merger process, we not only need to consider the internal topological structures of the communities but also compute the local similarity between weak communities and neighboring communities. Specially, the main contributions of this paper can be summarized as follows.

1. A self-adaptive local expansion strategy is suggested for local expansion and global merger two stages. The local expansion process can start from any node or weak community and put its closest neighbor into the same community with it. Then the closest neighbor can be viewed as the new start node and continue to conduct expansion. The process will be repeated until the size of the community achieves the maximum. Different from existing algorithms, the process of local expansion with the rule of local similarity is self-adaptive and can stop spontaneously. By the self-adaptive process, we can get a reasonable and accurate network partition.

2. Based on the proposed self-adaptive local expansion strategy, a two-stage algorithm named SALEA is suggested for community detection. In the first stage, we apply the proposed self-adaptive strategy and traverse each node so that we can form coarse community structures in a short time. Then we select weak communities that have no real sense of community structure. By traversing weak communities and applying the self-adaptive strategy for them, we can refine coarse community structures in the second stage. Thus, we get more accurate community structures.

3. The effectiveness of the proposed SALEA is verified on both real-world networks and synthetic networks. Experimental results demonstrate that the proposed SALEA performs better than several state-of-the-art and representative local expansion algorithms for community detection on complex networks.

2   The Proposed Algorithm SALEA

In this section, we will present the proposed SALEA method for community detection on complex networks. First, we present the general framework of the self-adaptive two-stage algorithm, and then elaborate how the self-adaptive strategy is used in the two stages.

2.1   The General Framework of SALEA

In the proposed SALEA, a self-adaptive strategy is proposed to detect communities spontaneously. Based on the proposed self-adaptive strategy, the SALEA consists of a self-adaptive local expansion stage and a self-adaptive global merger stage. In the first stage, we randomly select nodes and apply the proposed self-adaptive strategy so that can form one community. Then we choose another node from the rest nodes which are not traversed and also apply a self-adaptive strategy which can form another community. The process will be repeated until each node is traversed. In this way, we can get initial communities and isolated nodes. Next, we consider the local property of the isolated nodes and find their nearest nodes with greater centrality (NGC node) [26]. Then we need to merge the isolated nodes into the communities containing their NGC nodes. Thus, we can get coarse community structures quickly.

However, most initial communities only contain small amounts of nodes and are viewed as weak communities that have no real sense of real community structure. To

---

Algorithm 1: General Framework of SALEA

Input: Network $G(V, E)$
Output: F: Final solutions;
1: $C \leftarrow \emptyset$; //store initial communities and isolated nodes in the first stage
2: $F \leftarrow \emptyset$
    Stage1: Self-Adaptive Local Expansion Stage
3: **while** $V \neq \emptyset$ **do**
4:      $[V_1] \leftarrow$ LocalExpansion(V, E);
5:      $V \leftarrow V - V_1$;
6:      $C \leftarrow C \cup \{V_1\}$
7: **end while**
8: $I \leftarrow$ get all isolated nodes;
9: $C \leftarrow$ merge isolated nodes I into initial communities C which contain their NGC nodes;
    Stage2: Self-Adaptive Global Merger Stage
10: **while** $C \neq \emptyset$ **do**
11:     $[C_1] \leftarrow$ GlobalMerger(C, G);
12:     $C \leftarrow C - C_1$;
13:     $F \leftarrow F \cup \{C_1\}$
14: **end while**

---

refine the coarse community structures, we view all weak communities as seed nodes in the second stage. Specifically, each seed node is required to be traversed and the self-adaptive strategy is used again. As a result, we can get more accurate community structures. Algorithm 1 presents the main procedure of the proposed SALEA. In the following, we present the proposed self-adaptive strategy and illustrate how to apply it in the two stages.

2.2   Self-adaptive Strategy

In this section, a self-adaptive strategy is proposed for local expansion and global merger. The strategy can be used for nodes and weak communities. The self-adaptive strategy for nodes can be applied in the first stage and the self-adaptive strategy for weak communities can be applied in the second stage.

Self-adaptive Strategy for Node.   In the local expansion stage, each node can be viewed as a seed node. Thus, we can randomly choose one node v_0 from the network as a start node and put the node into a new local community. Then we select the start node's closest node v_1 and include it into the newly created community. However, if node v_0 do not have the closest node, the node will be identified as an isolated node. Next, we view the closest node as a new start node and continue to find its closest node v_2. If v_2 and v_0 are the same nodes, the local expansion process will stop. Otherwise, node v_2 will also be included in the newly created community. When the next closest node v_n has been in the newly created community, we are unable to find new nodes and the process should stop.

When a community has formed, we may find that the closest nodes of other untraversed nodes exist in the community. If this happens, let these nodes be included in the

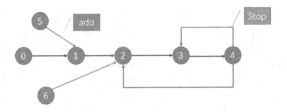

Fig. 1. An illustrative example of the proposed self-adaptive strategy.

newly created community so that the partition can be completed. In this way, we can get the coarse community structures. Figure 1 gives an example of illustrating the self-adaptive strategy. In this figure, the directed edge between node v_0 and v_1 means node v_1 is the closest node to node v_0. The process will stop until the closest node of node v_4 has existed in the newly created community, just like node v_3 or node v_2. If there exist nodes like v_5 and v_6 which are not included in the community at first, we need to merge them into the community.

Self-adaptive Strategy for Weak Community. We randomly select set C of nodes in a weak community that has no real sense of community structure as a seed and create a new final community F_1 to store it. Next, we get the set NB of all its neighboring initial communities' nodes and choose the pair of nodes (v_C, v_{NB}) that are the most similar nodes between set C and NB, where v_C is a node in set C and node v_{NB} is another node in set NB. Then, we put the community C_{NB} which contains node v_{NB} into final community F_1 and community C_{NB} is considered as the closest community of C. In this way, we can refine coarse community structures and get more accurate community structures. If community C_{NB} and other subsequent communities satisfy

- **Condition 1**: The community is a weak community.
- **Condition 2**: The community does not exist in the newly created community F_1.

then they can be viewed as a new seed and continue to merge with other initial communities. Otherwise, the process of merger for community C will stop.

In summary, we can conclude that the proposed self-adaptive strategy can detect communities spontaneously without setting any parameter.

2.3 Self-adaptive Local Expansion Stage

Similarity Evaluation. To evaluate the similarity between two nodes, we use the definition of the common neighbors [27] of adjacent nodes v_i and v_j, shown in formula 1.

$$CN_{ij} = |\Gamma(i) \cap \Gamma(j)| \tag{1}$$

where $\Gamma(i)$ and $\Gamma(j)$ are the sets of neighbors of node v_i and v_j, respectively. Remarkably, the value of CN_{ij} represents the sharing neighbors' number of node v_i and v_j. We find that the more neighbors two nodes share, the higher local similarity of the two nodes has. When node v_k has the highest local similarity with node v_i among all the neighbors of node v_i, we call v_k is the closest node of v_i and both nodes always exist in the same community.

Self-adaptive Local Expansion. Since we have computed the similarity between adjacent nodes, we can apply the above-mentioned self-adaptive strategy for nodes to form initial communities. However, the closest node of a node requires to be similar to the node and has good centrality. If one node has several candidate closest nodes which share the same number of neighbors with it, we choose the node which has the largest value of degree as the closest node of the node, because the node which has the most number of neighbors has a better centrality comparing other nodes. Algorithm 2 summarizes the details of local expansion in complex networks.

Algorithm 2: LocalExpansion

Input: Network $G(V, E)$
Output: VC: Nodes exist in one community;
 1: $v \leftarrow$ randomly select one node from the network;
 2: $VC \leftarrow v$;
 3: $NB \leftarrow$ get neighbors of node v;
 4: $v^{CN} \leftarrow$ get the closest node of v from NB;
 5: **while** $v^{CN} \neq \emptyset$ **do**
 6:    $v \leftarrow v^{CN}$;
 7:    $VC \leftarrow v \cup VC$;
 8:    $NB \leftarrow$ get neighbors of node v;
 9:    $Candidate_1 \leftarrow$ get the closest node of v from NB;
10:    $v^{CN} \leftarrow Candidate_1 - VC$;
11: **end while**
12: $Candidate_2 \leftarrow$ find other nodes which aren't in the community but their closest nodes in it;
13: $VC \leftarrow VC \cup Candidate_2$

Isolated Nodes Merger. After the self-adaptive local expansion stage, we can get initial communities and isolated nodes. It is obvious that one isolated node cannot be viewed as one community. Therefore, we require to merge these isolated nodes into neighboring initial communities. The community which contains the high centrality node can always appeal to the isolated nodes. To measure the centrality of one node, we adopt the formula [26]

$$centrality(v) = deg(v) + \sum_{u \in \Gamma(v)} \left(deg(u) + \sum_{w \in \Gamma(u)} deg(w) \right) \tag{2}$$

where $deg(x)$ is the degree of node x and $\Gamma(x)$ is the set of neighbors of x. When centrality values of all neighbors of an isolated node have been calculated, we choose the maximum among them as its nearest nodes with greater centrality (NGC node) and merge the isolated node into the community which contains the NGC node. Thus, we can get the coarse community structures. Figure 2 describes what is isolated node and how to merge it into initial communities. Nodes $\{v_1, v_2, v_3\}$ and nodes $\{v_4, v_5, v_6, v_7\}$ are identified as two communities. Since no nodes share common neighbors with node v_0, it is identified as an isolated node. We calculate the centrality of node v_2 and v_4, and get the values of 26 and 52, respectively. Therefore, we merge nodes v_0 into the community $\{v_4, v_5, v_6, v_7\}$.

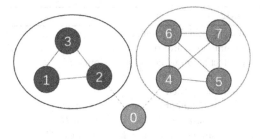

Fig. 2. An illustrative example of an isolated node and its merger process.

2.4 Self-adaptive Global Merger Stage

After self-adaptive local expansion, the coarse community structures can be obtained quickly. However, we find that some initial communities not only have dense connections internally but also have close connections externally. We call these initial communities weak communities which are required to global merge in the second stage. The reason why weak communities are formed is that they have very dense connections in the local areas and are unable to expand further.

Seeds Selection. Since any weak community can be chosen as a seed, we need to identify what is weak community quantitatively. Thus, we define the index of *weak community extent* (WCE)

$$WCE = \beta \times outdegree(C) - indegree(C) \tag{3}$$

where $outdegree(x)$ is the number of edges between community x and other neighboring nodes and $indegree(x)$ is the number of edges in community x. The parameter β can evaluate the quality of C and a higher value of β means that more communities can be chosen as seeds, which is always set as 2. If the value of WCE is greater than zero, we think the community does not have a good community structure and is identified as a weak community. All weak communities among communities will be viewed as seeds in the second stage.

Self-adaptive Global Merger. Since the seeds of the second stage have been chosen, a self-adaptive strategy for weak communities can be applied in the second stage. However, if there exist two or more pairs of nodes (v_{NB1}, v_{C1}), $(v_{NB2}, v_{C2}), ..., (v_{NBn}, v_{Cn},)$ which share the same number of common neighbors, we are supposed to find the pair that the node in set NB has the most centrality to the node in set C. The index to evaluate the centrality has been given

$$centrality(x, y) = \frac{degree(x)}{degree(y)} \tag{4}$$

Algorithm 3: GlobalMerger

Input: Network $G(V, E)$; Initial Communities $C_i, i = 1, 2, ..., n$
Output: F: a final community partition;
1: $IC \leftarrow$ randomly select an initial community from C;
2: $F \leftarrow IC$;
3: **if** IC is a weak community **then**
4:     $NB \leftarrow$ get nodes of neighboring communities of IC;
5:     $IC^{CN} \leftarrow$ get the closest node in NB of nodes in IC;
6:     $IC^{NB} \leftarrow$ get the initial community which contains IC^{CN};
7:     $F \leftarrow F \cup IC^{NB}$;
8:     **while** $IC^{NB} \neq \emptyset$ and IC^{NB} is a weak community **do**
9:         $IC \leftarrow IC^{NB}$;
10:        $NB \leftarrow$ get nodes of neighboring communities of IC;
11:        $IC^{CN} \leftarrow$ get the closest node in NB of nodes in IC;
12:        $Candidate_1 \leftarrow$ get the initial community which contains IC^{CN};
13:        $IC^{NB} \leftarrow Candidate_1 - F$
14:        $F \leftarrow F \cup IC^{NB}$;
15:    **end while**
16:    $Candidate_2 \leftarrow$ find other communities which aren't in the set but their closest communities in it;
17:    $F \leftarrow F \cup Candidate_2$
18: **end if**

---

where $degree(x)$ denotes the degree of node x. In this part, x is the node in set NB while y is the node in set C. The pair (v_{NBi}, v_{Ci}) having the largest $centrality(x, y)$ is chosen and v_{NBi} is viewed as the closest node of v_{Ci}.

Isolated Communities Merger. When we traverse all the weak communities and get several new final communities $F_i, i = 1, 2, 3, ..., n$, there exist the rest of the initial communities which are not traversed. These k initial communities called isolated communities will be put into newly created final communities $F_i, i = n+1, n+2, ..., n+k$ respectively, which do not need extra merger. Thus, we can refine the coarse community structures and get more accurate community structures. Algorithm 3 presents the details of the global merger stage.

2.5   Complexity Analysis

Let the number of nodes in the network G be n and the number of edges in the network G be m. The computational complexity of SALEA consists of two main stages (i.e. self-adaptive local expansion stage and self-adaptive global merger stage). In the first stage, each node is viewed as a seed node so that neighbors of them and neighbors of neighbors of them require to be checked. Therefore, we suppose the largest node degree is d and the complexity of the first stage is $O(n \times d \times d)$. After the first stage, we can get the initial communities. Let the number of these communities be k. Thus, the average size of initial communities is n/k. If the maximum number of initial communities' surrounding communities is k_1, the complexity of the second stage is $O(k \times (k_1 \times n/k)^2)$. However, the local similarity between nodes in adjacent communities has been calculated in the first stage so that the complexity of checking each community can be simplified from $O(n/k)$ to $O(1)$. Thus, the complexity of the second stage is $O(k \times k_1^2)$. Hence, the computational complexity of SALEA is $O(n \times d^2 + k \times k_1^2)$.

3   Experimental Results

In this section, we empirically verify the performance of the proposed SALEA by comparing it with several state-of-the-art and representative local expansion algorithms on both real-world and synthetic networks. In the following, we introduce experimental settings including five baseline algorithms, test data sets and evaluation metrics and then analyze the experimental results of the proposed SALEA.

3.1   Experimental Settings

Comparison Algorithms. In this paper, five local expansion algorithms have been chosen to be comparison algorithms, namely Louvain [28], label propagation algorithm (LPA) [29], LSMD [19], ASOCCA [23] and BLI [22]. Note that Louvain, LPA and LSMD are algorithms that use the first way of local expansion, while ASOCCA and BLI are algorithms that use the second way of local expansion. With the exception of BLI, all compared algorithms' source codes were obtained from the authors of those algorithms. For BLI, we have tried our best to optimize the code and make it run as effectively as we can to allow for a fair comparison. All experiments in this paper are conducted on Legion Y7000 2020 with an Intel(R) Core(TM) CPU i5-10300H, 2.50GHz, 16GB memory.

Test Data Set. Experiments are conducted on both real-world and synthetic networks. We adopt four real-world networks as test data sets including Zachary's [30] karate club, dolphin social network [31], American college football [32] and books about U.S. politics [32], which all have ground truth community structures. The characteristics of the four real-world networks are given in Table 1.

Table 1. Real-world networks with different characteristics.

Real networks	#Nodes	#Edges	Ave. Degree	Real clusters
karate	34	78	4.59	2
dolphin	62	159	5.13	2
football	115	613	10.66	12
polbook	105	441	8.4	3

Since LFR networks developed by Lancichinetti *et al.* [33] can reflect several significant characteristics of complex networks, we also adopt them as synthetic networks

Table 2. LFR networks with different characteristics.

Group	LFR networks	#Nodes	Mixing parameters
Group1	LFR1	1,000	0.35
	LFR2	2,000	0.35
	LFR3	3,000	0.35
	LFR4	4,000	0.35
	LFR5	5,000	0.35
	LFR6	10,000	0.35
Group2	LFR7	10000	0.1
	LFR8	10,000	0.2
	LFR9	10,000	0.3
	LFR10	10,000	0.4
	LFR11	10,000	0.5
	LFR12	10,000	0.6

to test the performance of algorithms in community detection. LFR networks include much information determined by kinds of parameters, such as node number N, average node degree k, mixing parameter μ and so on. We can adjust these parameters to synthesize networks having different properties. Two groups of LFR networks are used as test data sets. The first group of LFR networks have different node numbers including 1,000, 2,000, 3,000, 4,000, 5,000 and 10,000. The mixing parameter of the first group is set to 0.35. The second group of LFR networks has different mixing parameters including 0.1, 0.2, 0.3, 0.4, 0.5 and 0.6. The node number of the second group is set to 10,000. For the two groups of LFR networks, the remaining important parameters are set as follows. The average node degree k is set to 50, the maximal node degree $maxk$ is set to 100, the clustering coefficient is set to 0.55 and other parameters not mentioned remain default values. The characteristics of these LFR networks are given in Table 2.

Evaluation Metrics. To assess the performance of algorithms, two widely used metrics are adopted. The first one is normalized mutual information (NMI) [34], which can measure the similarity between the true community partition and the result detected by an algorithm. Formally, it can be defined as

$$NMI = \frac{-2 \sum_{i=1}^{m(X)} \sum_{j=1}^{m(Y)} n_{ij} log(\frac{n_{ij} * N}{n_{X_i} * n_{X_j}})}{\sum_{i=1}^{m(X)} n_{X_i} * log(\frac{n_{X_i}}{N}) + \sum_{j=1}^{m(Y)} n_{X_j} * log(\frac{n_{X_j}}{N})} \quad (5)$$

where the number of communities in partition X can be denoted as $m(X)$, the nodes number in the network can be denoted as N and the number of sharing nodes between community i in partition X (i.e. X_i) and community j in partition Y (i.e. Y_j) can be denoted as n_{ij}. Meanwhile, the number of nodes in X_i can be denoted as n_{X_i} and the number of nodes in Y_j can be denoted as n_{Y_j}. The more similar between the ground truth and community structure detected by an algorithm are, the larger value of NMI

is. The range of NMI value is supposed to be in $[0,1]$. If partition A detected by an algorithm is the same as the ground truth B, $NMI(A, B) = 1$, while if A is completely different from B, $NMI(A, B) = 0$.

The second metric is adjusted rand index ARI [35]. Formally,

$$ARI = \frac{\sum_{i=1}^{m(X)} \sum_{j=1}^{m(Y)} \binom{n_{ij}}{2} - \Omega}{\left[\sum_{i=1}^{m(X)} \binom{n_{X_i}}{2} + \sum_{j=1}^{m(Y)} \binom{n_{Y_j}}{2}\right]/2 - \Omega} \tag{6}$$

where Ω can be denoted as

$$\Omega = \sum_{i=1}^{m(X)} \binom{n_{X_i}}{2} * \sum_{j=1}^{m(Y)} \binom{n_{Y_j}}{2} \Big/ \binom{N}{2} \tag{7}$$

Like NMI, ARI is another kind of metric which can measure the accuracy of the partition results. The range of ARI value is supposed to be in $[-1,1]$. A large value of ARI always means the good performance of an algorithm.

Table 3. NMI and ARI of the six algorithms by averaging over 10 runs on the real-world networks.

Network	Metric	Lovain	LPA	LSMD	BLI	ASOCCA	SALEA
karate	NMI_avg	0.66	0.82	1	0.83	0.83	**1**
	NMI_std	0.03	0.11	0	0	0	0
	ARI_avg	0.52	0.84	1	0.88	0.88	**1**
	ARI_std	0.03	0.11	0	0	0	0
dolphin	NMI_avg	0.52	0.62	0.88	0.32	0.54	**1**
	NMI_std	0.04	0.11	0	0	0	0
	ARI_avg	0.34	0.50	0.93	0.29	0.39	**1**
	ARI_std	0.03	0.16	0	0	0	0
football	NMI_avg	0.86	0.87	0.85	0.88	0.75	**0.88**
	NMI_std	0.01	0.03	0	0	0	0
	ARI_avg	0.73	0.74	0.66	0.77	0.51	**0.77**
	ARI_std	0.04	0.09	0	0	0	0
polbook	NMI_avg	0.50	0.39	0.45	0.45	0.50	**0.54**
	NMI_std	0.01	0.20	0	0	0	0
	ARI_avg	0.59	0.46	0.59	0.50	**0.62**	0.60
	ARI_std	0.03	0.24	0	0	0	0

3.2   Experiments on Real-World Networks

In this section, we test the effectiveness of the proposed SALEA on real-world networks. Table 3 lists the averages and standard deviations of NMI and ARI of the six algorithms for community detection averaging over 10 runs on the four real-world networks. As shown in the table, the SALEA achieves the best average values of NMI among all the algorithms on all test data sets while it achieves the best average values of ARI on the three test data sets and the second best average value of ARI on the one test data set.

To further illustrate the effectiveness of the proposed SALEA, we take the karate network as an example. As shown in Fig. 3(a), the karate network can be divided into four communities by Louvain. Although nodes in the same community have close connection, some nodes between different communities also have dense connection. Since Louvain pursues modularity-based optimization, the partition results may be different from the ground truth community structure. Hence, they cannot achieve a high value of both NMI and ARI.

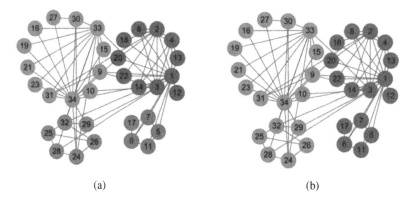

(a)   (b)

Fig. 3. The karate network detected by Louvain and SALEA. Nodes having the same colour are in the same community. (a) The partition result detected by Louvain. (b) The partition result detected by the proposed SALEA.

As shown in Fig. 3(b), we can clearly find that SALEA can merge four communities into two communities, because it makes full use of the local property of each node and doesn't need to set extra metrics for community in advance, which can improve the partition accuracy. For BLI and ASOCCA, both of them can also expand further and form two communities, but they ignore the neighbors' properties of the isolated nodes and are unable to deal with them accurately. In other data sets, both of them are also unable to solve small size communities problem just like Louvain because the parameter λ for community size cannot be set accurately in advance. For LPA, the algorithm has large randomness and the result is not stable so it cannot always have an accurate partition.

3.3   Experiments on LFR Networks

Since the proposed SALEA has the best performance among all comparison algorithms on the four small real-world networks, to further verify the effectiveness of SALEA on large networks, we conduct experiments on LFR networks. Since the ASOCCA has an enumeration process which makes him run out of memory, we exclude it in the LFR network experiment. The results of five algorithms averaging over 10 runs on the first group have been presented in Fig. 4. It is obvious that the NMI and ARI values of the proposed SALEA are always the best compared to other algorithms no matter the size of node's number in the networks. Thus, the effectiveness of the proposed SALEA in LFR networks which have different node numbers can be verified.

The results of the five algorithms averaging over 10 runs on the second group have been presented in Fig. 5. As shown in the figure, the larger mixing parameter value becomes, the more difficult detecting community structure accurately is, namely the smaller NMI and ARI value is. Nonetheless, the NMI and ARI of the proposed SALEA can take the lead in all cases.

In summary, we can conclude that the proposed SALEA can detect communities accurately on both real-world and LFR networks.

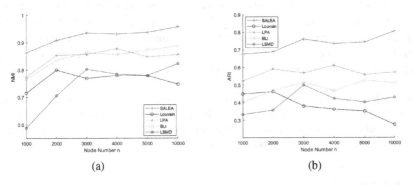

(a)   (b)

Fig. 4. NMI and ARI of the five algorithms by averaging over 10 runs on the LFR networks having different node numbers. (a) NMI of the five algorithms. (b) ARI of the five algorithms.

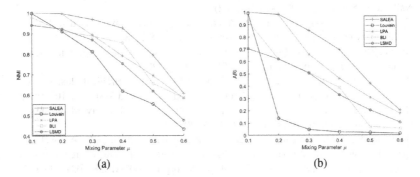

(a)   (b)

Fig. 5. NMI and ARI of the five algorithms by averaging over 10 runs on the LFR networks having different mixing parameters. (a) NMI of the five algorithms. (b) ARI of the five algorithms.

4 Conclusion and Future Work

In this paper, we proposed a self-adaptive two-stage local expansion algorithm named SALEA for community detection. In SALEA, a self-adaptive strategy has been suggested to form accurate and reasonable partitions, which can be applied in the two stages. Specifically, the proposed self-adaptive strategy was applied for traversing each node so that the coarse community structures can be found in a short time. Then, in the second stage, the self-adaptive strategy was also applied for traversing each weak community to refine the obtained coarse community structures. Thus, we can get more accurate community structures. The effectiveness of the proposed SALEA for community detection has been demonstrated by the experimental results on real-world and synthetic networks.

There still exists SALEA-related work that deserves to be looked into more thoroughly. For simplicity, we only detect the non-overlapping communities on unsigned networks in this paper, in the future, we would like to extend SALEA by exploring other kinds of networks, such as dynamic networks and signed networks. Moreover, it is also interesting to extend SALEA for detecting overlapping communities. Last but not least, it is very interesting to exploit the community structure obtained by SALEA to further improve the performance of other tasks in complex network analysis such as link prediction [36] and influence maximization [37].

Acknowledgments. This work was supported in part by the National Natural Science Foundation of China (61976001, 61876184), the Key Projects of University Excellent Talents Support Plan of Anhui Provincial Department of Education (gxyqZD2021089), and the Natural Science Foundation of Anhui Province (2008085QF309).

References

1. Girvan, M., Newman, M.E.: Community structure in social and biological networks. Proc. Natl. Acad. Sci. **99**(12), 7821–7826 (2002)
2. Cai, Q., Ma, L., Gong, M., Tian, D.: A survey on network community detection based on evolutionary computation. Int. J. Bio-Inspired Comput. **8**(2), 84–98 (2016)
3. Xu, Q., Zhang, Q., Liu, J., Luo, B.: Efficient synthetical clustering validity indexes for hierarchical clustering. Expert Syst. Appl. **151**, 113367 (2020)
4. Wu, C., Peng, Q., Lee, J., Leibnitz, K., Xia, Y.: Effective hierarchical clustering based on structural similarities in nearest neighbor graphs. Knowl.-Based Syst. **228**, 107295 (2021)
5. Hu, F., Liu, J., Li, L., Liang, J.: Community detection in complex networks using node2vec with spectral clustering. Phys. A **545**, 123633 (2020)
6. Berahmand, K., Mohammadi, M., Faroughi, A., Mohammadiani, R.P.: A novel method of spectral clustering in attributed networks by constructing parameter-free affinity matrix. Clust. Comput. **25**(2), 869–888 (2022). https://doi.org/10.1007/s10586-021-03430-0
7. Berahmand, K., Nasiri, E., Li, Y., et al.: Spectral clustering on protein-protein interaction networks via constructing affinity matrix using attributed graph embedding. Comput. Biol. Med. **138**, 104933 (2021)
8. Zhang, L., Pan, H., Su, Y., Zhang, X., Niu, Y.: A mixed representation-based multiobjective evolutionary algorithm for overlapping community detection. IEEE Trans. Cybern. **47**(9), 2703–2716 (2017)

9. Zhang, X., Zhou, K., Pan, H., Zhang, L., Zeng, X., Jin, Y.: A network reduction-based multi-objective evolutionary algorithm for community detection in large-scale complex networks. IEEE Trans. Cybern. **50**(2), 703–716 (2020)

10. Luo, Y., et al.: A reduced mixed representation based multi-objective evolutionary algorithm for large-scale overlapping community detection. In: IEEE Congress on Evolutionary Computation, pp. 2435–2442 (2021)

11. Ma, H., Yang, H., Zhou, K., Zhang, L., Zhang, X.: A local-to-global scheme-based multi-objective evolutionary algorithm for overlapping community detection on large-scale complex networks. Neural Comput. Appl. **33**(10), 5135–5149 (2021). https://doi.org/10.1007/s00521-020-05311-w

12. Carletti, T., Fanelli, D., Lambiotte, R.: Random walks and community detection in hypergraphs. J. Phys.: Complex. **2**(1), 015011 (2021)

13. Guo, K., Wang, Q., Lin, J., Wu, L., Guo, W., Chao, K.-M.: Network representation learning based on community-aware and adaptive random walk for overlapping community detection. Appl. Intell. **52**, 1–19 (2021). https://doi.org/10.1007/s10489-021-02999-8

14. Xu, G., Guo, J., Yang, P.: TNS-LPA: an improved label propagation algorithm for community detection based on two-level neighbourhood similarity. IEEE Access **9**, 23526–23536 (2020)

15. El Kouni, I.B., Karoui, W., Romdhane, L.B.: Node importance based label propagation algorithm for overlapping community detection in networks. Expert Syst. Appl. **162**, 113020 (2020)

16. Lancichinetti, A., Fortunato, S., Kertész, J.: Detecting the overlapping and hierarchical community structure in complex networks. New J. Phys. **11**(3), 033015 (2009)

17. Lee, C., Reid, F., McDaid, A., Hurley, N.: Detecting highly overlapping community structure by greedy clique expansion. arXiv preprint. arXiv:1002.1827 (2010)

18. Cheng, F., Wang, C., Zhang, X., Yang, Y.: A local-neighborhood information based overlapping community detection algorithm for large-scale complex networks. IEEE/ACM Trans. Networking **29**(2), 543–556 (2020)

19. Bouyer, A., Roghani, H.: LSMD: a fast and robust local community detection starting from low degree nodes in social networks. Futur. Gener. Comput. Syst. **113**, 41–57 (2020)

20. Ma, T., Liu, Q., Cao, J., Tian, Y., Al-Dhelaan, A., Al-Rodhaan, M.: LGIEM: global and local node influence based community detection. Futur. Gener. Comput. Syst. **105**, 533–546 (2020)

21. Pan, Y., Li, D.H., Liu, J.G., Liang, J.Z.: Detecting community structure in complex networks via node similarity. Phys. A **389**(14), 2849–2857 (2010)

22. Wang, T., Yin, L., Wang, X.: A community detection method based on local similarity and degree clustering information. Phys. A **490**, 1344–1354 (2018)

23. Pan, X., Xu, G., Wang, B., Zhang, T.: A novel community detection algorithm based on local similarity of clustering coefficient in social networks. IEEE Access **7**, 121586–121598 (2019)

24. Zhou, Y., Sun, G., Xing, Y., Zhou, R., Wang, Z.: Local community detection algorithm based on minimal cluster. Appl. Comput. Intell. Soft Comput. **2016** (2016)

25. Eustace, J., Wang, X., Cui, Y.: Community detection using local neighborhood in complex networks. Phys. A **436**, 665–677 (2015)

26. Luo, W., Yan, Z., Bu, C., Zhang, D.: Community detection by fuzzy relations. IEEE Trans. Emerg. Top. Comput. **8**(2), 478–492 (2017)

27. Newman, M.E.: Clustering and preferential attachment in growing networks. Phys. Rev. E **64**(2), 025102 (2001)

28. Blondel, V.D., Guillaume, J.L., Lambiotte, R., Lefebvre, E.: Fast unfolding of communities in large networks. J. Stat. Mech: Theory Exp. **2008**(10), P10008 (2008)

29. Raghavan, U.N., Albert, R., Kumara, S.: Near linear time algorithm to detect community structures in large-scale networks. Phys. Rev. E **76**(3), 036106 (2007)

30. Zachary, W.W.: An information flow model for conflict and fission in small groups. J. Anthropol. Res. **33**(4), 452–473 (1977)
31. Lusseau, D.: The emergent properties of a dolphin social network. In: Proceedings of the Royal Society of London. Series B: Biological Sciences 270(suppl_2), pp. S186–S188 (2003)
32. Newman, M.E.: Modularity and community structure in networks. Proc. Natl. Acad. Sci. **103**(23), 8577–8582 (2006)
33. Lancichinetti, A., Fortunato, S., Radicchi, F.: Benchmark graphs for testing community detection algorithms. Phys. Rev. E **78**(4), 046110 (2008)
34. Press, W.H., Teukolsky, S.A., Vetterling, W.T., Flannery, B.P.: Numerical Recipes 3rd Edition: The Art of Scientific Computing. Cambridge University Press, Cambridge (2007)
35. Rand, W.M.: Objective criteria for the evaluation of clustering methods. J. Am. Stat. Assoc. **66**(336), 846–850 (1971)
36. Zhang, W., Li, B., Zhang, H., Zhang, L.: Community and local information preserved link prediction in complex networks. In: International Joint Conference on Neural Networks, pp. 1–7 (2022)
37. Zhang, L., Liu, Y., Cheng, F., Qiu, J., Zhang, X.: A local-global influence indicator based constrained evolutionary algorithm for budgeted influence maximization in social networks. IEEE Trans. Netw. Sci. Eng. **8**(2), 1557–1570 (2021)

Supervised Prototypical Variational Autoencoder for Shilling Attack Detection in Recommender Systems

Xinhao Wang[1], Huiju Zhao[2(✉)], Youquan Wang[1], Haicheng Tao[1], and Jie Cao[1]

[1] School of Information Engineering, Nanjing University of Finance and Economics, Nanjing 210046, China
1120201146@stu.nufe.edu.cn, jie.cao@nufe.edu.cn
[2] Department of Informatization Construction and Management, Nanjing University of Finance and Economics, Nanjing 210046, China
871103999@qq.com

Abstract. Collaborative filtering-based recommender systems are vulnerable to shilling attacks. How to detect shilling attacks has become a popular research direction. Some recent works have applied deep learning to the field of shilling attack detection. However, most of the existing deep learning-based shilling attack detection models are based on user-item scoring matrices, which do not apply manual scoring features well and cannot be used to detect cold-start shilling attackers. Thus, we propose a shilling attack detection algorithm based on Supervised Prototypical Variational Auto-Encoder (SP-VAE). Specially, SP-VAE can obtain a unified user-profile representation that can be easily used to down-stream applications of shilling attack detection classifiers. Then, the algorithm constructs the prototype representation of various shilling attacker, and a classifier is used to classify various shilling attack users and normal users. The experimental results show that our method consistently outperforms the traditional method in the case of cold-start profile of the shilling attack.

Keywords: Recommendation system · Shilling attack detection · Prototype network · Variational auto-encoder · Neural networks

1 Introduction

With the rapid development of e-commerce technology, the data and information on the Internet have shown an explosive growth trend. Faced with such a large amount of information, it is often difficult for users to select a service or product and find the target they need. Ordinary search engines can no longer meet users' needs for accurate and fast access to information. In order to solve this problem, the recommendation systems are generated. Recommender systems are technologies that filter and push information based on users' own characteristics,

© The Author(s), under exclusive license to Springer Nature Singapore Pte Ltd. 2022
Y. Tan and Y. Shi (Eds.): DMBD 2022, CCIS 1745, pp. 231–245, 2022.
https://doi.org/10.1007/978-981-19-8991-9_17

and are an important tool to solve the information explosion problem. Collaborative filtering [1] is one of the most widely used and mature algorithms in recommendation systems. Many well-known e-commerce recommendation systems are designed based on collaborative filtering algorithms, such as Amazon, YouTube and Facebook [2].

However, due to the characteristics of the collaborative filtering algorithm itself, there are serious security issues with the recommender system. Some fraudulent users influence the recommendation results of the system by injecting fake user profiles into the recommendation system. An attacker may increase or decrease the frequency of recommendations for certain products to change the product sales according to his own purpose. This kind of attack performed by fraudulent users is called shilling attack [3]. Shilling attacks not only mislead users' choice of products, but also cause unfair competition to normal merchants, resulting in large economic losses and seriously affecting the healthy development of e-commerce. Therefore, how to detect attacking users and ensure the security and recommendation quality of collaborative filtering recommendation system has become an important research direction.

In order to resist the impact of shilling attacks on recommendation systems, many researchers in China and abroad have been working on shilling attack detection methods and robust recommendation algorithms [4–6]. According to the degree of use of prior knowledge, shilling attack detection methods can be divided into supervised learning, unsupervised learning and semi-supervised learning. For supervised learning-based models, this is considered as a classification problem. That is, normal users and different shilling attack types are regarded as different categories, and then the shilling attack user detection is realized by constructing multi-classifiers with manually constructed features. For the unsupervised model of shilling attack detection, it is usually implemented based on a user-item rating matrix and must satisfy certain priori assumptions to complete the detection of shilling attacks. Semi-supervised learning usually starts with classifier learning based on the training dataset, and then tunes the classifier by analyzing the distribution characteristics of the test dataset. With the increasing use of deep learning in the field of data mining and recommender systems, there are several approaches to improve the detection accuracy of shilling attack by applying deep learning techniques [7,8].

Although new advances have been made in shilling attack detection through deep neural network models, current approaches do not address how to learn a set of manually constructed features. Unsupervised learning, such as variational autoencoder (VAE) [9] has achieved excellent performance in capturing outliers in the outlier detection domain. However, if applied directly to shilling attack, which could lead to reduce the detection effect with the unsupervised VAE model, especially when the number of manually constructed features is small. That is, the VAE model does not adequately express the classification between normal user profiles and shilling attack user profiles. In addition, some sophisticated shilling attackers escape detection by existing shilling attack detection algorithms by scoring only a small number of items, and the class of users is known as cold-start shilling attackers [10]. It is difficult to construct effective behavioral profiles for new coming shilling attackers, especially for cold-start shilling attackers.

To address this problem, we propose a Supervised Prototype Variational AutoEncoder (SP-VAE) based detection method in a recommender system. First, we construct features of attacking users and normal users based on the attack model of the shilling attack, and then inject them into the dataset to construct a training set and a test set to numerically label normal users and multiple attacking users. Next, we compute 11 feature values for all users, including the injected fake users, and form feature vectors using the user labels and these feature values. Moreover, we train the feature vectors for all users in the training set using the supervised variational autoencoder model and the prototype network approach. On the MovieLens dataset, we verify that the SP-VAE shilling attack detection method improves detection performance and demonstrate the effectiveness of the detection algorithm in the face of multiple shilling attacks. Our major contributions are summarized as follows:

- We design a supervised variational autoencoder method, which is an end-to-end learning process using a supervised variational autoencoder function for characterizing the feature representation of the training set.
- We propose a multi-task SP-VAE model for shilling attack detection, in which the feature representation and the prototype representation of the classification are learned, respectively.
- We conduct experiments on the real-world datasets to demonstrate the effectiveness and efficiency of our proposed method.

2   Related Works

2.1   Traditional Maching Learning-Based Models

The problem of resisting the impact of shilling attack detection is essentially a classification problem, which classifies users into normal users and shilling attack users. Traditional machine learning-based models can be classified into three categories: supervised-based models, unsupervised-based models, and semi-supervised-based models.

Supervised learning-based detection methods require analyzing features that can effectively describe an attack, extracting a set of feature values, constructing a classification model by traditional machine learning-based methods, and then using that classification model to detect a shilling attack. Chirita et al. [11] first proposed to detect shilling attacks based on various features of the labeled user, and detect average and random attacks, respectively. Williams et al. [12] systematically defined detection metrics based on previous work and proposed a shilling attack detection method based on decision trees and feature attributes. The method further analyzes the feature differences between shilling attack user profiles and real user profiles, and extracts a series of high-performance detection attributes.

Unsupervised learning-based detection methods are good for detecting unknown shilling attacks, but the methods rely on prior knowledge and need to satisfy the assumption that shilling attack users are extremely similar. Ohmahony et al. [13] first used clustering methods to detect shilling attacks. They modified the clustering method used in reputation reporting systems to detect fraudulent users of attack target items. Then several scholars proposed various unsupervised algorithm-based methods for shilling attack detection, Bhuamik [14] proposed a method based on K-mean classification, and Cheng and Hurley [15] proposed a method based on PCA, which has been shown to outperform other unsupervised methods. Yang et al. [16] proposed an unsupervised method based on graph mining to detect shilling attackers.

Semi-supervised learning-based detection methods combine the information of labeled users with the distribution pattern of unlabeled user data, providing better detection performance than supervised and unsupervised methods. Wu et al. proposed a semi-supervised learning-based shilling attack detection method, HySAD [17]. The core part of the learning process is based on a semi-supervised plain Bayesian approach, which uses maximum likelihood to estimate parameter values and iterative solutions using a similar EM algorithm. Cao et al. [18] and Wu et al. [19] proposed a new semi-supervised learning-based detection method, semi-SAD, which can use both labeled and unlabeled user profiles. And then, they proposed another semi-supervised hybrid learning model hPSD [20], which combines user features with user-product relationships for shilling attack detection and achieves good detection results.

2.2 Deep Neural-Based Models

In recent years, deep neural network learning techniques have achieved great success in natural language processing, computer vision, personalized recommendation [21, 22]. Currently, many scholars have applied these techniques to the attack detection of recommendation systems.

Tong et al. proposed a new method CNN-SAD [8] based on convolutional neural network and social perception network (SAN). Because the deep features implemented can describe the user's rating behavior more accurately than the features designed manually, the proposed method can detect the attack more effectively. Hao et al. [7] analyzed the user's behavior from the user rating matrix, user adjacency matrix and other angles. The stacked denoising autoencoder was used to automatically extract user features. On the basis of principal component analysis, the features extracted from multi-view were effectively combined, and SVM was used as a classifier to generate detection results. Xu et al. designed a double-attention recurrent neural network (HDAN) [23] for the behavior of defamatory users to give opposite evaluations between scores and comments, and used the improved GRU network to calculate whether the comments were positive or negative. Hao et al. [24] proposed an integrated attack detection method using deep sparse autoencoder to automatically extract features based on the time preference information of user rating items.

2.3   Prototypical Network

Jake Snell et al. [25] proposed a prototype network that can be used for few-shot learning. The network can recognize new categories that have never been seen during the training process, and only a small amount of sample data is needed for each category. The prototype network maps the sample data from each category into a space, and extracts their mean value to represent the prototype of the category. Using Euclidean distance as the distance metric, the training makes the distance of this type of data to the prototype of this type the closest, and the distance to other types of prototypes is farther. When testing, it uses *softmax* to process the distance from test data to the prototype of each category to determine the category label of test data. We apply this method combined with the VAE method to detect the shilling attacks with cold-start conditions.

3   Preliminaries

In this section, we first introduce the background of shilling attacks against collaborative filter-based recommender systems.

3.1   Problem Definition

Suppose there are M users $\mathcal{U} = \{u_1, u_2, \cdots, u_M\}$ and N items $\mathcal{I} = \{I_1, I_2, \cdots, I_N\}$ (e.g. products, service, check-ins) in the e-commerce platforms, $R_{ui} = \{0, 1, 2, 3, 4, 5\}$ denotes user u has rated item i and $\mathcal{R} \in \mathbb{R}^{M \times N}$ is the rating matrix. The positive feedback rating 1–5 indicates that the user has rated the item, while the rating 0 is an unknown entry. A rating usually accompanied by this other information, such as comments, rating time, etc. The goal of recommender system model is used to build a model to predict the scores of unknown entries with positive feedback ratings and obtain the top-k items for the user that would be interested in.

The goal of shilling attackers is to promote or suppress a set of target items with many attack strategies and destroy the actual recommendation effectiveness of the recommendation systems. Each attack profile is divided into four parts: selected items, filler items, unrated items and target item [26]. To be specific, the selected items and the filler items are used to the selected items for specific attack purposes and the randomly selected items, while the target item is the items that need to attack. Meanwhile, for each injection attack, the attackers usually choose one or many attack strategy to fix each attack profile. The basic attack strategies are random attack, average attack, bandwagon attack, segment attack, and etc.

In this paper, the objective of our shilling attack detection task is to spot various attackers with different attack strategies. In a recommender system, the user's behavior footprints, user rating time, rating strategies, etc. all indirectly reflect whether the user is an attack user. Thus, it is common to define a number of statistical characteristics for each user to indicate their own characteristics. For user u, we can generate K-dimension dense feature vector $X_u \in \mathbb{R}^K$ to construct their pre-defined behavior property. We utilize $\mathcal{X}$ to denote the feature matrix of all users. Based on these preliminaries, the shilling attack detection task can be defined as follow:

Definition 1. Shilling Attack Detection. *Given a training set $\mathcal{X}_{train}$ and its label set $\mathcal{Y}_{train}$, the aim of shilling attack detection is to detect the shilling attackers in the test set $\mathcal{X}_{test}$, where $\mathcal{X} = \mathcal{X}_{train} \cup \mathcal{X}_{test}$ and $\mathcal{Y}_{train} = \{0, 1\}_{j=1}^{|\mathcal{Y}_{train}|}$ (0 is the normal user and 1 is the shilling attacker).*

3.2 Feature Generation

According to the differences in scoring methods between trust attack users and normal users, We choose 11 features to describe the differences between shilling attack users and normal users in total, including Entropy, DegSim, LengthVar, RDMA, WDMA, WDA, FMD, MeanVar, FMV, FMTD, and TMF. The above feature indicators describe the differences between normal users and shilling attack users from different attack types, and achieve good results.

4 Approach

4.1 Framework

In this section, we detect the shilling attacker with the SP-VAE model. Figure 1 shows the framework of proposed model, where N and S is the classification of normal users and shilling attackers. It consists of two modules: 1) Variational auto-encoder embedding module which is used to obtain the robust representation of manual marking features. 2) A supervised prototypical model is used to learn a classifier for shilling attack detection.

4.2 Variational Auto-encodering Embedding

In this subsection, we formulate the training set $\mathcal{X}_{train}$ representation from a variational auto-encoding (VAE) perspective. VAE combines Bayesian inference and simple neural networks to learn a robust representation of the training set [27]. By optimizing the neural network parameters in the encoding and decoding steps, the VAE can be optimized by back propagation using continuous random variables. Given a latent hidden variable z randomly sampled from some prior distribution $p_\theta(z)$, VAE can be expressed as an encoder $enc(x) = q_\phi(z|x)$ and a decoder $dec(z) = p_\theta(x|z)$, where $x \in \mathcal{X}_{train}$. Using the variational inference, the task is to maximize the evidence lower bound (ELBO) [28]:

$$\mathcal{X}(p_\theta, q_\phi) = \mathbb{E}_{q_\phi(z|x)}[\log p_\theta(x, z) - \log q_\phi(z|x)] \tag{1}$$

$$= \mathbb{E}_{q_\phi(z|x)}[\log p_\theta(x|z)] - KL(q_\phi(z|x)\|p_\theta(z)) \tag{2}$$

$$= -\mathcal{L}_{VAE} \tag{3}$$

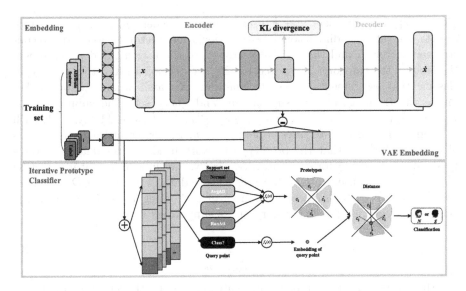

Fig. 1. The framework of our proposed method.

where $KL(\cdot\|\cdot)$ is the Kullback-Leibler (KL) divergence, $p_\theta(z) = \mathcal{N}(0,1)$, $\mathcal{X}_{VAE}$ is the loss function that we need to minimize in the VAE model. Specifically, we can formulate the encoder and decoder process through a neural network. Under this scenario, VAE is commonly used to first transform the input vector into a low-dimensional representation $z \in \mathcal{Z}$ for the downstream models in the unsupervised learning domain. To apply VAE to the domain of supervised learning, we construct a shared forward model $\phi : \mathcal{X} \to \mathcal{Z}$, a decoding function $r : \mathcal{Z} \to \mathcal{X}$ and a prediction function $d : \mathcal{Z} \to \mathcal{Y}$, where d is the downstream of the prediction task, and then the new loss function can be calculated as:

$$\mathcal{L}_1 = \frac{1}{|\mathcal{X}_{train}|} \sum_{j=1}^{|\mathcal{X}_{train}|} [l_{VAE}(\widetilde{x}_j, x_j) + l_d(\widetilde{y}_j, y_j)] \tag{4}$$

where $\widetilde{x}_j$ is the reconstructed vector of the user u_j, $\widetilde{y}_j$ is the prediction label of the user u_j. By construction, we can obtain the reconstruction loss function with $l_{VAE}(\widetilde{x}_j, x_j)$, and then we train the prediction loss with $l_d(\widetilde{y}_j, y_j)$ by optimizing a binary cross-entropy loss,

$$l_d(\widetilde{y}_j, y_j) = -y_j \log(\widetilde{y}_j) + (1 - y_j) \log(1 - \widetilde{y}_j). \tag{5}$$

4.3   Iterative Prototype-Classification Assignment

During the variational auto-encoder embedding processing, the user profile can be obtained with the training set $D = \{(p_1, y_1), (p_2, y_2), ...(p_n, y_n)|p_j \in \mathbb{R}^D, y_i \in$

$\{1, 2, ...k\}\}$, with n users and k user categories, where $p_j = |\widetilde{x}_j - x_j|$ represents the latent d-dimensional feature deviation vector between the reconstructed vector $\widetilde{x}_j$ and the original vector x_j of the user u_j, and y_i represents the label of the category. Motivated by [29], we develop an iterative prototype-classification assignment process to maintain K-classification attributes. We divide the training set into support set and query set. The support set is $D_{sup} = \{(p_1, y_1), (p_2, y_2), \cdots, (p_{|\mathcal{D}_{sup}|}, y_{|\mathcal{D}_{sup}|}) | x_i \in \mathbb{R}^D, y_i \in \{1, 2, ...K\}\}$, with m users and K user categories, where $m < n$. S_k represents the set of users of category k. Note that the prototype network needs to calculate the prototype representation c_k for each category. Firstly, the embedding feature function $f_\varphi : \mathbb{R}^D \to \mathbb{R}^M$ is used to map the user feature data of dimension : D to dimension M. The prototype representation c_k of each category is the mean of the embedding features of each category in the support set.

$$c_k = \frac{1}{|S_k|} \sum_{(p_l, y_l) \in S_k} f_\varphi(p_l) \tag{6}$$

After getting the prototype of each category, we use the *softmax* function to calculate the probability of each user in the query set being classified into each category:

$$f_\varphi(y_l = k \mid p_l) = \frac{\exp\left(-d\left(f_\varphi(p_l), c_k\right)\right)}{\sum_{k'} \exp\left(-d\left(f_\varphi(p_l), c_{k'}\right)\right)}, \tag{7}$$

where $f_\varphi(p_l)$ is the embedding feature representation vector, and $d(f_\varphi(p_l), c_k)$ is the Euclidean distance between $f_\varphi(p_l)$ and c_k. The real category label corresponding to the user profile is k. The training process uses the random gradient descent method, and the loss function is defined as follows:

$$\mathcal{L}_2 = -\frac{1}{|\mathcal{D}_{sup}|} \sum_{l=1}^{|\mathcal{D}_{sup}|} \log f_\varphi(y_l = k \mid p_l). \tag{8}$$

Putting all the components of the loss function in the variational auto-encoder embedding processing and the interactive prototype-classification assignment processing together, supervised prototypical variational autoencoder can be obtained with an end-to-end manner with the following loss:

$$\mathcal{L} = \mathcal{L}_1 + \lambda \mathcal{L}_2, \tag{9}$$

where λ is used to weight the contribution of the variational auto-encoder embedding processing and the interactive prototype-classification assignment processing.

4.4   Summary and Implementation Details

We summarie our method in Algorithm 1. Given a support set, it contains four categories of user profiles: normal users, love/hate attack users, random attack users and average attack users profile. For the classification task, we have four categories: normal users, love/hate attack users, random attack users and average attack users. The established process is as follows:

Algorithm 1. Proposed Method

Input: Training set $\mathcal{X}_{train}$, label set $\mathcal{Y}_{train}$, test set $\mathcal{X}_{test}$, the weight parameter λ
1: initialization parameter Θ
2: obtain the feature set of each user in Section 3.2
3: **for** $t = 1, 2, \cdots$ MaxIter **do**
4:     train the supervised VAE by Eq. (4)
5:     train the iterative prototype-classification model by Eq. (8)
6:     obtain the global loss function by Eq. (9)
7:     gradient ascent with $\triangledown_\Theta \mathcal{L}$
8: **end for**
9: Return the Learned Θ

First, given each user profile, we can calculate the feature information of each user according to the feature calculation formula using the supervised VAE method $f_\varphi(x)$ to encode each user sample, and use the auto-encoding operation to extract the user coding information with Eq. (4). Next, after learning the coding representation of each sample, we sum and average all the sample codes under each classification, and take the results as the prototype representation of the classification. When a new user profile sample in the test set $\mathcal{X}_{test}$ is input into the network, what we need is to predict its classification label. In the same way, we use $f_\varphi(x)$ to generate its coded representation for this new data sample. Then, the Euclidean distance formula is used to calculate the distance between the coded representation of the new sample and the prototype representation, and judge which classification the query sample belongs to through the nearest distance. Finally, after calculating the distance between the new data sample and all the classifications, we use softmax function to convert the distance into the form of probability and then get the distance of different categories.

5   Experiments

5.1   Dataset

Most of the data sets used in the research of shilling attack detection are the MovieLens data set[1], which is a non-commercial public data set for research purposes. The MovieLens data set has three levels of ratings of 100K, 1M, and 10M,which contains users' ratings of movies.

The dataset we selected is the *Movielens-100k* dataset, which is the most widely used in these three datasets. The data set records a total of 100,000 ratings information for 1682 movies by 943 users, among which the rating value

---

[1] http://movielens.umn.edu/.

is between 1 and 5 points, 5 points means like this movie most and 1 point means like this movie least. The higher the rate, the higher the user's preference for the movie. This data set also contains information about the time of user rating, movie types and user attributes. We mainly use users' rating information for these movies.

In the Movielens-100k dataset, we first select u1.base, and then we construct the profile of the attack users according to the attack model of shilling attack. We select three types of attacks: random attack, average attack and love/hate attack in our experiment processing. Finally, the attacking users are injected into u1.base with different attack size to form our training set. We set the filler size and attack size of multiple different orders of magnitude. The filler size is set to 0.5%, 1%, 2%, 3%, 5%, and the attack size is set to 5%, 10% and 15%, respectively. The filling rate and attack size are combined in pairs to construct 32 kinds of user profiles of shilling attacks, which are injected into u2.base to generate 32 kinds of test sets.

5.2 Evaluating Metrics

In order to objectively and accurately evaluate the experimental results of this algorithm, we selected three evaluation metrics widely used in information retrieval and statistical classification, *Precision* and *Recall* and *F1*. Since there will be a contradiction between *Precision* and *Recall* in some cases. For example, if only one result is detected and correct, the Precision will be 100%, but the recall is very low. In order to avoid the contradiction between the two indicators, we use *F-measure* to weigh and average them. This indicator integrates *Precision* and *Recall*, which can more accurately reflect the detection ability of the algorithm. The higher the *F1* value, the better the detection effect.

$$F1 = \frac{2 \times Precision \times Recall}{Precision + Recall} \tag{10}$$

5.3 Baselines

K-Nearest Neighbors Classifier (KNN): KNN classifier is a supervised learning with top-K nearest neighbors. First, extract the features of the new data and compare them with each data feature in the test set. Then k nearest (similar) data feature labels are extracted from the training set, and the classification with the most frequent occurrence in the K nearest data is counted as a new data category.

Naive Bayes Classifier (NB): It is a classification algorithm based on the Bayesian theorem and the assumption of independence of feature conditions. For a given training data set, it first learns the joint probability distribution of input and output, and then based on this model, use Bayes' theorem to find the output with the highest probability.

Decision Tree Classifier (DT): DecisionTree Classifier uses a tree structure to build a classification model. Each node represents an attribute. According to the division of this attribute, it enters the child nodes of this node until the leaf nodes. Each leaf node represents a certain category, so as to achieve the purpose of classification.

SVM Classifier (SVM): SVM Classifier is a supervised learning method. It maps the vector to a higher dimensional space and establishes a maximum spacing hyperplane in this space. Two parallel hyperplanes are built on both sides of the hyperplane separating the data. Separating the hyperplane maximizes the distance between the two parallel hyperplanes. The greater the distance between the parallel hyperplanes, the smaller the total error of the classifier.

MLPClassifier (MLP): It is a classifier based on multi-layer neural network, including three layers: input layer, hidden layer and output layer. There can be multiple hidden layers and different layers of MLP neural network are fully connected. Any neuron in the upper layer is connected to all neurons in the next layer. The classifier is trained by reading the training set, and then the test set is classified.

Supervised-VAE Classifier (SVAE): It is a simplified version of our algorithm and only variational auto-encoding is used to classify the different user profiles.

CNN Classifier [30] (CNN): The CNN classifier is used a deep Convolutional neural network-based method which used the user rating profiles only and does not use the artificially designed features.

5.4 Experimental Details

We implement the MLP, SVAE, CNN and our model based on Pytorch[2] and other baselines with python machine learning library Scikit-learn[3]. We adopt Adam with default parameter setting to optimize our objective functions. the embedding size, learning rate and batch size are set to 64, 0.001, and 64 for MLP, SVAE, CNN and our model. Our proposed method and all baselines are training on a Windows server with 3.6 GHz Intel I7-11700KF CPU and 10 GB Nvidia GeForce RTX 3080 GPU.

5.5 Results

Impact of the Hyper-Parameters. In this section, we mainly illustrate the influence of two hyper-parameters: *filler size* and the contribution weight of variational auto-encoding and the interactive prototype-classification λ. In order to verify the accuracy of the prototype network-based method with different filler size, we conduct an experiment with different size and a fixed attack size 10%. The filler size is range from 0.2% to 1%, with a total of 5 levels of 0.2%, 0.4%, 0.6%, 0.8%, 1%. In Fig. 2, we depict how the change of different filler size in terms

---

[2] http://www.pytorch.org.
[3] https://scikit-learn.org/stable/.

of *precision, recall* and *F1*. As can be seen in Fig. 2, in terms of *precision, recall* and *F1*, our proposed SP-VAE model performs an upward trend with increasing filling size with a fixed attack size 10%. Moreover, the upward trend of *precision* is some of the most pronounced.

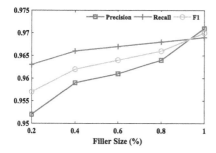

Fig. 2. Performance of different filler sizes.

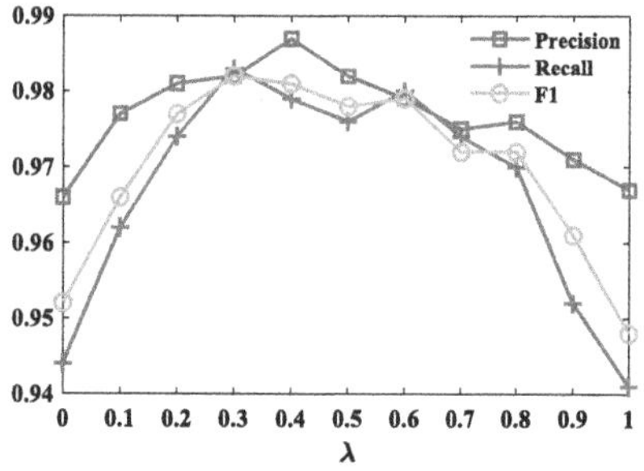

Fig. 3. Performance of contribution weight λ.

The second experiment is used to investigate the impact of the contribution weight of variational auto-encoding and the interactive prototype-classification λ. We set the filler size 1% and attack size 10, and the injected attack are random attack, average attack and love/hate attack, respectively. Figure 3 shows the performance of our model with different contrition weight from 0 to 1 with 0.1 interval. As can be seen, when the contrition weight $\lambda = 0.3$, the maximum recall and F1 are obtained for the MovieLen dataset. Therefore, $\lambda = 0.3$ is the relatively good choice, and becomes the default setting in our next experiments.

The Comparison of Different Detectors. In order to verify the accuracy of our proposed SP-VAE method, we designed several groups of comparative experiments. We mainly adjust the two parameters of filling size and attack size. The filling sizes range 0.5%, 1%, 2%, 3%, and 5%, and the attack size is set to 5% and 15%. We conducted experiments on 8 groups of test sets and recorded the precision, recall rate and F1 values, and used the comparison method described in the previous section to compare with our method: KNN, NB, DT, SVM, MLP, SVAE, and CNN.

Table 1 lists the evaluation results in the terms of precision, recall and F1, where the best results are highlight in bold type. As shown in Table 1, we observe that: (1) We can find that the shilling attack detection method based on the prototype network has better detection effect in most of the cases when the filling rate is low. When the filling rate increases, the detection effect also becomes better and tends to be stable. In the case of cold start, especially when the filling rate is less than 1%, our method has a better detection effect, which verifies the effectiveness of our method in the face of cold start attack detection. This clearly

Table 1. Overall performance comparisons with different filler sizes under 5% and 15% attack sizes

Measure	Method	Filler size									
		0.5%	1%	2%	3%	5%	0.5%	1%	2%	3%	5%
Precision	KNN	0.958	0.964	0.965	0.968	0.987	0.861	0.919	0.941	0.968	0.983
	NB	0.941	0.927	0.931	0.942	0.943	0.782	0.821	0.823	0.824	0.831
	DT	0.945	0.981	0.985	0.988	0.983	0.911	0.923	0.933	0.940	0.967
	SVM	0.941	0.972	0.975	0.978	0.985	0.885	0.896	0.921	0.955	0.976
	MLP	0.958	0.968	0.969	0.968	0.972	0.863	0.908	0.914	0.922	0.961
	SVAE	0.908	0.920	0.925	0.933	0.935	0.852	0.856	0.860	0.863	0.870
	CNN	0.963	0.967	0.972	0.979	0.983	0.872	0.906	0.911	0.920	0.948
	SP-VAE	**0.977**	**0.988**	**0.990**	**0.991**	**0.992**	**0.924**	**0.968**	**0.981**	**0.990**	**0.989**
Recall	KNN	0.967	0.976	0.977	0.980	**0.985**	0.887	0.910	0.938	0.967	0.983
	NB	0.964	0.963	0.965	0.966	0.967	0.884	0.885	0.886	0.889	0.895
	DT	0.969	**0.989**	**0.989**	**0.987**	0.984	0.911	0.932	0.923	0.940	0.971
	SVM	0.965	0.971	0.973	0.977	0.982	0.885	0.896	0.930	0.955	0.981
	MLP	0.969	0.971	0.972	0.972	0.975	0.893	0.917	0.920	0.921	0.946
	SVAE	0.912	0.931	0.972	0.952	0.951	0.851	0.865	0.868	0.874	0.877
	CNN	0.973	0.974	0.942	0.983	0.986	0.898	0.915	0.918	0.922	0.958
	SP-VAE	**0.977**	0.976	0.979	0.981	**0.985**	**0.929**	**0.963**	**0.975**	**0.985**	**0.985**
F1	KNN	0.962	0.968	0.971	0.973	0.986	0.873	0.914	0.939	0.967	0.983
	NB	0.947	0.945	0.947	0.951	0.955	0.830	0.832	0.853	0.840	0.862
	DT	0.956	**0.984**	**0.987**	**0.985**	0.981	0.880	0.900	0.933	0.926	0.969
	SVM	0.948	0.972	0.974	0.977	0. 983	0.852	0.901	0.925	0.956	0.978
	MLP	0.963	0.969	0.970	0.970	0.973	0.877	0.912	0.917	0.922	0.953
	SVAE	0.909	0.923	0.933	0.943	0.943	0.852	0.861	0.964	0.868	0.973
	CNN	0.964	0.970	0.974	0.981	0.984	0.884	0.911	0.915	0.922	0.953
	SP-VAE	**0.977**	0.982	0.984	**0.985**	**0.988**	**0.925**	**0.965**	**0.978**	**0.986**	**0.987**

demonstrates the benefit of our SP-VAE model which integrates the supervised prototype network and the variational auto-encoding. (2) The performance is followed by DT and KNN methods. In particular, the DT algorithm obtained some best results with the attack size 5% as the filler size increased. However, when the attack size is set to 15%, the best results are our method. This indirectly illustrates the stability of our proposed algorithm and the instability of other baseline algorithms. (3) The MLP and SVAE methods, as the module of our model, our model significantly outperforms MLP and SVAE models in the terms of precision, recall and F1, indicating that MLP and SVAE should be considered to integrate them together with the prototype module.

6 Conclusion

In this paper, we investigated the shilling attack detection in recommender systems, and presented a novel supervised prototypical variational autoencoder model named SP-VAE for shilling attack detection. Specifically, to obtain the robust representation of user profiles with manual marking features, we used the supervised variational autoencoder to aggregate the feature values for all users. To obtain the classes of each user, we construct the prototype representation of various shilling attackers and normal users. The experiments on the real-world datasets confirmed the effectiveness of our proposed SP-VAE model.

Acknowledgments. This work was supported in part by the National Natural Science Foundation of China (NSFC) under Grant Nos. 72172057, 71701089, 92046026, in part by the Fundamental Research on Advanced Leading Technology Project of Jiangsu Province under Grant BK20192004C, BK20202011.

References

1. Zhang, F., Sun, X., Zhao, G.: Research on privacy-preserving two-party collaborative filtering recommendation. Acta Electron. Sinica **37**(1), 84–89 (2009)
2. Linden, G., Smith, B., York, J.: Amazon.com recommendations: item-to-item collaborative filtering. IEEE Internet Comput. **7**(1), 76–80 (2003)
3. Lam, S.K., Riedl, J.: Shilling recommender systems for fun and profit. In: Proceedings of the 13th International Conference on World Wide Web, pp. 393–402 (2004)
4. Gunes, I., Kaleli, C., Bilge, A., Polat, H.: Shilling attacks against recommender systems: a comprehensive survey. Artif. Intell. Rev. **42**(4), 767–799 (2014)
5. Williams, C.A., Mobasher, B., Burke, R.: Defending recommender systems: detection of profile injection attacks. SOCA **1**(3), 157–170 (2007)
6. Cheng, Z., Hurley, N.: Robustness analysis of model-based collaborative filtering systems. In: Coyle, L., Freyne, J. (eds.) AICS 2009. LNCS (LNAI), vol. 6206, pp. 3–15. Springer, Heidelberg (2010). https://doi.org/10.1007/978-3-642-17080-5_3
7. Hao, Y., Zhang, F., Wang, J., Zhao, Q., Cao, J.: Detecting shilling attacks with automatic features from multiple views. Secur. Commun. Netw. **2019**, 1–13 (2019)
8. Sandvig, J.J., Mobasher, B., Burke, R.D.: A survey of collaborative recommendation and the robustness of model-based algorithms. IEEE Data Eng. Bull. **31**(2), 3–13 (2008)
9. Xu, H., et al.: Unsupervised anomaly detection via variational auto-encoder for seasonal KPIs in web applications. In: Proceedings of the 2018 World Wide Web Conference, pp. 187–196 (2018)
10. You, Z., Qian, T., Liu, B.: An attribute enhanced domain adaptive model for cold-start spam review detection. In: Proceedings of the 27th International Conference on Computational Linguistics, pp. 1884–1895 (2018)
11. Chirita, P.A., Nejdl, W., Zamfir, C.: Preventing shilling attacks in online recommender systems. In: Proceedings of the 7th Annual ACM International Workshop on Web Information and Data Management, pp. 67–74 (2005)
12. Burke, R., Mobasher, B., Bhaumik, R., Williams, C.: Segment-based injection attacks against collaborative filtering recommender systems. In: Fifth IEEE International Conference on Data Mining (ICDM 2005), pp. 1–4. IEEE (2005)
13. O'Mahony, M.P., Hurley, N.J., Silvestre, G.C.M.: Collaborative filtering – safe and sound? In: Zhong, N., Raś, Z.W., Tsumoto, S., Suzuki, E. (eds.) ISMIS 2003. LNCS (LNAI), vol. 2871, pp. 506–510. Springer, Heidelberg (2003). https://doi.org/10.1007/978-3-540-39592-8_72
14. Bhaumik, R., Mobasher, B., Burke, R.: A clustering approach to unsupervised attack detection in collaborative recommender systems. In: Proceedings of the International Conference on Data Science (ICDATA), pp. 1–7. Citeseer (2011)

15. Cheng, Z., Hurley, N.: Effective diverse and obfuscated attacks on model-based recommender systems. In: Proceedings of the third ACM Conference on Recommender Systems, pp. 141–148 (2009)
16. Yang, Z., Cai, Z., Guan, X.: Estimating user behavior toward detecting anomalous ratings in rating systems. Knowl.-Based Syst. **111**, 144–158 (2016)
17. Wu, Z., Wu, J., Cao, J., Tao, D.: HySAD: a semi-supervised hybrid shilling attack detector for trustworthy product recommendation. In: Proceedings of the 18th ACM SIGKDD International Conference on Knowledge Discovery and Data Mining, pp. 985–993 (2012)
18. Cao, J., Wu, Z., Mao, B., Zhang, Y.: Shilling attack detection utilizing semi-supervised learning method for collaborative recommender system. World Wide Web **16**(5–6), 729–748 (2013)
19. Wu, Z., Cao, J., Mao, B., Wang, Y.: Semi-SAD: applying semi-supervised learning to shilling attack detection. In: Proceedings of the Fifth ACM Conference on Recommender Systems, pp. 289–292 (2011)
20. Wu, Z., Wang, Y., Wang, Y., Wu, J., Cao, J., Zhang, L.: Spammers detection from product reviews: a hybrid model. In: 2015 IEEE International Conference on Data Mining, pp. 1039–1044. IEEE (2015)
21. Zhang, S., Yao, L., Sun, A., Tay, Y.: Deep learning based recommender system: a survey and new perspectives. ACM Comput. Surv. (CSUR) **52**(1), 1–38 (2019)
22. Yu, L., Zhang, W., Wang, J., Yu, Y.: SeqGAN: sequence generative adversarial nets with policy gradient. In: Proceedings of the AAAI Conference on Artificial Intelligence, pp. 2852–2858 (2017)
23. Hao, Y., Zhang, F., Chao, J.: An ensemble detection method for shilling attacks based on features of automatic extraction. China Commun. **16**(8), 130–146 (2019)
24. Hao, Y., Zhang, F.: Ensemble detection method for shilling attacks based on deep sparse autoencoder. Comput. Eng. Appl. (2019)
25. Snell, J., Swersky, K., Zemel, R.: Prototypical networks for few-shot learning. In: Proceedings of the 31st International Conference on Neural Information Processing Systems, pp. 4080–4090 (2017)
26. Pang, M., Gao, W., Tao, M., Zhou, Z.H.: Unorganized malicious attacks detection. In: Advances in Neural Information Processing Systems, pp. 1–10 (2018)
27. Diederik, P., Welling, M.: Information constraints on auto-encoding variational bayes. In: International Conference on Learning Representation, pp. 1–14 (2014)
28. Kingma, D.P., Welling, M.: Auto-encoding variational bayes. In: 2014 International Conference on Learning Representations, pp. 1–14 (2014)
29. Wang, X., Zhang, Z., Wu, B., Shen, F., Lu, G.: Prototype-supervised adversarial network for targeted attack of deep hashing. In: Proceedings of the IEEE/CVF Conference on Computer Vision and Pattern Recognition, pp. 16357–16366 (2021)
30. Tong, C., et al.: A shilling attack detector based on convolutional neural network for collaborative recommender system in social aware network. Comput. J. **61**(7), 949–958 (2018)

Knowledge Graph Based Chicken Disease Diagnosis Question Answering System

Shushu Gu[1], Jing Wang[2], Shaoqiu Zheng[2], Yanling Pan[3](✉), Guoxin Jiang[3], Wenwen Dai[3], Ziqi Cheng[3], and Delong Chen[3]

[1] Nanjing Animal Husbandry and Veterinary Station, Nanjing, China
[2] Nanjing Research Institute of Electronic Engineering, Nanjing, China
[3] Hohai University, Nanjing, China
yanling@hhu.edu.cn

Abstract. With the rapid development of natural language processing technology and knowledge graph technology, knowledge graph based intelligent question answering systems are being increasingly applied in various fields and industries. In the poultry industry, it is of great importance for farmers to promptly obtain scientific information of poultry disease diagnosis and curing measurements, where knowledge graph based question answering systems can contribute richly. In this paper, we design and implement Knowledge Graph based Chicken Disease Diagnosis Question Answering System (CDD-QAS) via deep learning models. We build a knowledge graph for chicken disease diagnosis, which contains 28 common chicken diseases and their corresponding symptoms, prevention and curing measures. In the construction of intelligent question answering system, we use BERT-TextCNN to realize the task of intention recognition and use BiLSTM-CRF to realize the task of entity recognition. Experimental results show that our proposed system can achieve better performance than other models, and possess great interactivity and accuracy. The proposed system can make great contribution to poultry industry and sets a good example of applying knowledge graph and deep learning methods in building question answering system.

Keywords: Intelligent question answering system · Knowledge graph · Intent recognition · Entity recognition

1 Introduction

Poultry farming occupies a very important position in modern agriculture. It plays an increasingly important role in meeting the increasing demand for meat products caused by the improvement of people's material life. However, affected by many factors such as breeding environment, poultry are prone to diseases. If effective measures are not taken in time to prevent and control diseases, flocks

This work was supported by Key Laboratory of Information System Requirements, No: LHZZ 2021-M04.

© The Author(s), under exclusive license to Springer Nature Singapore Pte Ltd. 2022
Y. Tan and Y. Shi (Eds.): DMBD 2022, CCIS 1745, pp. 246–259, 2022.
https://doi.org/10.1007/978-981-19-8991-9_18

of poultry may die, resulting in serious economic losses and biosafety problems. Therefore, obtaining accurate poultry disease classification, pathological symptoms, treatment measures, preventive measures and other information has become an urgent need for farmers.

Nowadays, based on the rapid development of artificial intelligence, there are some intelligent approaches for poultry disease diagnosis, early warning and breeding safety risk assessment [1,2]. These methods can effectively improve the diagnostic effects of poultry diseases and minimize the risky factors of poultry breeding. However, with the popularization of information technology in recent years, a large amount of poultry data has been accumulated. In this way, the intrinsic knowledge in massive data cannot be effectively utilized by the traditional methods, for they lack the abilities of learning knowledges from big data.

In this paper, we construct a Knowledge Graph based Chicken Disease Diagnosis Question Answering System (CDD-QAS), including 28 common chicken diseases and their corresponding symptoms, prevention and curing measures. The pipeline of the question answering system is shown in Fig. 1. Firstly, BERT [3] and TextCNN [4] are used to identify the intent of the input question. Then, we use Bidirectional LSTM-CRF [5] for entity recognition (ER). Finally, the identified information is filled into the pre-designed semantic slot to get the query statement, which is used to obtain relevant information in the chicken diseases knowledge graph. The main contributions of this paper can be concluded below.

– We take advantage of the vast amount of data on chicken disease through knowledge graph technology. The constructed knowledge graph includes 28 common chicken diseases and their corresponding symptoms, prevention and curing measures.
– We use deep learning and knowledge graph technology to build our Chicken Disease Diagnosis Question Answering System (CDD-QAS). It can achieve high accuracy, great interactivity and efficiency for intelligent chicken disease diagnosis. Hence, it can contribute to the poultry industry and knowledge graph application.

2 Related Works

2.1 Automated Poultry Disease Diagnosis

The diagnosis of poultry diseases requires a large amount of relevant domain knowledge, which leads to a large investment of human resources. However, with the development of artificial intelligence, more intelligent diagnostic methods have emerged in the past decade. For example, Wang et al. [1] proposed a back propagation neural network based on genetic algorithm. The genetic algorithm is used to search the optimal solution of weight and threshold in global space, and the auxiliary diagnosis system of avian diseases is implemented. Zhou et al. [2] used AHP-DS model to establish a risk early warning index system for

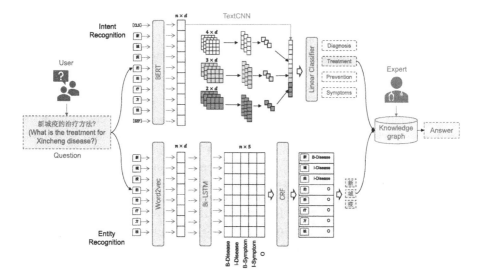

Fig. 1. Overview of the proposed model.

poultry industry, which was used to analyze the impact of many risks such as epidemic situation, feeding management, market risk and product risk. Mbelwa et al. [6] used convolutional neural networks to identify the most common chicken diseases from the images of chicken droppings. Although these methods reduce manual efforts, the poultry disease diagnosis is slightly less efficient and effective because knowledge from the massive amount of data cannot be fully utilized.

2.2   Intelligent Question Answering System

Question answering has been successfully applied in various domains. The commonly used methods are based on template, semantic parsing or deep learning. Systems based on template method has the disadvantages of difficult maintenance and poor portability because the template is manually designed by hundreds of experts. The question answering system based on semantic parsing first analyzes the questions syntactically. Then the question information is converted into logical expressions, which are combined with the semantic information in the knowledge graph to generate the query statements. For instance, Liu et al. [7] implemented a question answering system based on semantic parsing for college entrance examination consultation. With respect to question answering system based on deep learning method, it currently has two directions: module-level question answering system and end-to-end question answering system. The former one uses deep learning technology to improve each module, including intent recognition module, entity recognition module, entity normalization module and so on. The latter one vectorizes the information, maps it to the low-dimensional space using neural network model, then calculates the similarity and finally returns the answer with the pre-designed scoring mechanism. Since deep learning has achieved great success in many tasks, there are more and more deep learning based QA system [8–10] emerging in last decade.

2.3   Knowledge Graph Based QA System

Knowledge graph is a kind of semantic network based on graph model, which aims to use graph structure to store and express natural language sentences [11]. This makes it great potential to build intelligent question answering applications and many scholars have studied the construction method of knowledge graph [12–16]. The previous question answering system is based on database retrieval and keyword matching. But they could not accurately identify the question intent, resulting in poor accuracy of the output answers. Sometimes users are required to manually filter answers, and may even get answers unrelated to the question. However, the knowledge graph can solve these defects and has greater advantages than the traditional methods. For the questions and answers with diversified expression, the QA system based on knowledge graph can perform quite well in recognizing these varied expression. In addition, the usage of knowledge graph can solve the problems of large storage space and low query efficiency due to the large pool of expertise in intelligent question answering systems. Li et al. [17] proposed a reading comprehension model, which can fully take advantage of the structural medical knowledge and the reference medical plain text. Park et al. [18] proposed a graph-based QA system on electronic health records. And they demonstrated that graph-based datasets perform better than table-based datasets and the state of the art QA models at that time.

3   Knowledge Graph Construction

In this paper, we first construct a knowledge graph containing 28 common chicken diseases, and then use deep learning methods to implement an intelligent Chicken Disease Diagnosis Question Answering System (CDD-QAS) for these 28 poultry diseases. In order to construct a comprehensive and reliable knowledge graph of chicken diseases, we use a variety of data sources in Chinese, including relative websites, books and domain experts knowledge. Specifically, for the data source of knowledge graph, we collect the structured and semi-structured data related to chicken diseases from relevant websites and combine the structured chicken disease information organized by experts. Table 1 shows the structural symptom information of highly pathogenic avian influenza as an example. Since our dataset is in Chinese, we add translations to make this table understandable. Then we preprocess the data to extract the entities and entity relationships, and manually fuse the knowledge. Finally, we build our chicken disease knowledge graph, example of which can be shown in Fig. 2. The entity and relationship information of the map is described as shown in Table 2.

Table 1. Clinical information of highly pathogenic avian influenza. (The notes of symptoms refer to the diagnostic index out of 100.)

Category	Discription	Score
Symptoms	脚鳞出血 (Hemorrhage of foot scales)	10
	胸部皮肤出血 (Skin hemorrhage of chest)	10
	鸡冠出血或发绀 (Hemorrhage or cyanosis of comb)	10
	呼吸道症状，如咳嗽、喷嚏，呼吸困难 (Respiratory symptoms such as cough, sneezing and dyspnea)	2
	病鸡流泪，头和面部水肿 (Ears and facial edema in sick chickens) . . .	2 . . .
Treatment	鸡发生高致病性禽流感时，因发病急、发病和死亡率很高，目前尚无好的治疗办法。 (At present, there is no good treatment for highly pathogenic avian influenza in chickens because of its acute onset and high mortality.) . . . 非疫区的养殖场应及时接种疫苗,从而防止禽流感发生。 (Chickens in farms in non-epidemic areas should be vaccinated in time to prevent the occurrence of avian influenza.)	
Precaution	不从疫区或疫病流行情况不明的地区引种或调入鲜活鸡产品。 (Do not introduce or transfer fresh chicken products from epidemic areas or areas with unknown epidemic situation.) . . . 控制外来人员和车辆进入养鸡场，确需进入则必须消毒。生产中的运饲料和运鸡产品的车辆要分开专用。 (Control outside personnel and vehicle to enter chicken farm, and entering one must be sterilized. Vehicles for transporting feed and chicken products should be separately used.)	

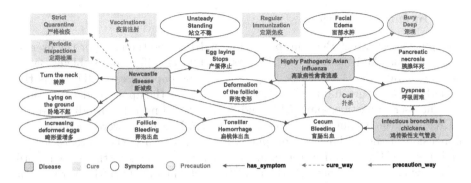

Fig. 2. Chicken disease knowledge graph.

Table 2. Entity information of the knowledge graph.

Name	Description
Disease	Disease entity
Pathology	Pathological entity
Symptoms	Symptom entity
Cure	Treatment entity
Precaution	Preventive entity

4 Question Answering System Based on Knowledge Graph

4.1 Overview

In the design of the intelligent question answering system for chicken disease diagnosis, we first integrate BERT [3] model and TextCNN [19] model to identify the intent of the question. Next, we use BiLSTM-CRF [5] to recognize the poultry symptoms and disease entities in the questions. Then, the recognized information is filled into the pre-designed semantic slots to answer the user's questions based on the template. At the same time, since one symptom may associate with multiple diseases, we use confidence-based uncertainty inference to solve the problem, in which we rank the weights according to the degree of association between each symptom and disease, infer the top 4 sets of data with the highest probability, and return their disease names and the inferred probabilities to the user.

The method proposed in this paper not only constructs a comprehensive knowledge graph for chicken diseases diagnosis, but also realizes a scientific and interactive intelligent poultry disease diagnosis system, which can offer great assistance for poultry management and treatment. In the following, we will elaborate on the concrete implementation of the system, including Intent Recognition (IR) model and Entity Recognition (ER) model.

4.2   Intent Recognition

The purpose of Intent Recognition (IR) is to determine the need for the user to ask questions. And the essence of IR task is a text classification problem. Based on the characteristics of the poultry disease, this paper uses BERT [3] as the underlying structure and the TextCNN [19] model as the upper model structure.

The user's questions plus [CLS] and [SEP] are fed into the encoding layer of BERT with the output of 768-dimensional token. Hence, the word vector matrix dimension of the BERT layer output is $n \times d$, where n is the sentence length and d is 768. Each word in the input question corresponds to the output word vector, which are then put into the next TextCNN model. Then the word vector matrix is convolutionally pooled using convolutional kernels with the width of 768 and the heights of 2, 3, and 4. Finally, we can obtain the 768-dimensional feature vector. In order to retain the advantages of BERT for better classification of obscure sentences and TextCNN for more sensitive keywords, our IR model concatenates the 768-dimensional token of CLS and the output of TextCNN, which are then sent to the fully-connected layer as the features of sentences and output the category and confidence level of each sentence.

4.3   Entity Recognition

The task of the Entity Recognition (ER) in this paper is to extract the disease entities and symptom entities from the input question. In our method, we leverage BiLSTM-CRF [5] model to train the dataset annotated by the BIO annotation system. Our ER model is consist of three layers: the embedding layer, the BiLSTM layer, and the CRF layer. The pipeline of this model can be summarized in three stages.

First, in the embedding layer, this paper uses the Word2Vec [20] pre-trained model from Python's gensim library to encode the poultry disease corpus, embedding each word in the user's question into a 200-dimensional vector space to generate a sequence of word vectors.

Second, we adopt BiLSTM to extract the semantic expression vector of each word in its context, and then uses softmax activation to decode the word semantic vector, which performs multiple classifications for each word. In this paper, we use the BIO annotation system [21] to annotate the entities, where B tag represents the beginning of entities, I tag represents non-beginning characters of entities, and O tag represents non-entities. In ER task, we focus on recognizing two types of entities, disease entities and symptom entities, which are the key entities to retrieve related information. Hence, in the proposed CDD-QAS, there are five candidate categories for each word, including B-Disease, I-Disease, B-Symptom, I-Symptom, and O.

Finally, the output of the BiLSTM is fed into the CRF layer, where the state transition matrix is used to predict the current label, and the softmax function is used to obtain the conditional probability of the final sequence. The sequence with the highest score is used as the final labeling result of the model using the Viterbi algorithm [22]. The role of the CRF layer is to take into account the context of the current character. The individual sequence labels become more logical through the CRF layer, because CRF can increase the label restrictions and reduce the unreasonable sequence labels.

5 Experiments

5.1 Datasets

Intent Recognition. According to the types of entities in the knowledge graph, the CDD-QAS in this paper design four kinds of question intents: disease diagnosis, treatment method, prevention method and related symptoms. For these four kinds of question intents, this paper crawls question statements in Huaxia Veterinary Website and Baidu Post Poultry Bar, and generates these question statements into the dataset by using question template and dictionary method with ratio of 2:8.

After obtaining the data, we clean the data and label the dataset according to the intent categories to do multi-classification task training of supervised learning. Finally, we get a IR dataset with 526 samples. The information of each intent category in our dataset is shown in Table 3.

Table 3. The information of each intent category in Intent Recognition dataset.

Category	Amount	Corpus examples
Diagnosis	97	鸡为什么会啄蛋? (Why do chickens peck eggs?)
Treatment	152	你好，鸡精神沉郁怎么治? (Hello, how to treat mental depression in chicken?)
Prevention	177	怎么避免我家的鸡得鸡痘? (How to avoid chicken pox in my chickens?)
Symptoms	100	如果家鸡得了新城疫会怎么样? (What will happen if a domestic chicken gets Newcastle disease?)

Entity Recognition. Since there is no public dataset in the field of poultry diseases, this paper modifies the open source Chinese Medical Question and Answer NER (cMedQANER) dataset in ChineseBLUE [23] to fit into our task. We replace the symptom entities and disease entities in the cMedQANER dataset with those in poultry diseases and convert other types of entity labels to non-entity labels.

Based on the questions in the IR dataset, the nonstandard words and stop words are first cleaned. And then the sentences are manually labeled with five types of tags, namely B-Disease, I-Disease, B-Symtom, I-Symtom, and O. After the labeling is completed, we clean the data again and split the statement with punctuation marks such as full stops or spaces. If a segment has all "O" tags, the segment is removed from the sentence in order to improve recognition performance. The training set of this dataset has 206,836 words, the validation set has 17,033 words, and the test set has 23,374 words, which are shown in Table 4.

Table 4. Entity recognition dataset

Number	Word	Label
1	治	O
2	疗	O
3	鸡	B-Disease
4	马	I-Disease
5	立	I-Disease
6	克	I-Disease
7	氏	I-Disease
8	病	I-Disease
...	...	...
247,239	咳	B-Symptom
247,240	嗽	I-Symptom
247,241	，	O
247,242	苍	B-Symptom
247,243	白	I-Symptom

5.2   Experiment Setup

Our experimental environment is Python3.6, keras 2.3.1, tensorflow 1.14.0. And the detailed experimental setup of each task are briefly displayed below.

Intent Recognition. After continuously tuning the hyperparameters, a group of hyperparameters which make the model have best performance are finally obtained. The model uses BERT for parameter initialization. In this task, the size of epoch is set to 10, the batch size is set to 32, the maximum sentence length is set to 60.

Entity Recognition. When comparing the performance of various models for entity recognition, the size of epoch is set to 50. The output vector dimension of each neuron in LSTM is set to 128, the learning rate is set to 0.001, the batch size is set to 8, and the optimizer is set to Adam.

5.3   Evaluation Metrics

In our experiments of IR task and ER task, we mainly use the precision, recall and F1-Score as our experimental metrics.

$$Precision = \frac{TP}{TP + FP} \times 100\% \tag{1}$$

$$Recall = \frac{TP}{TP + FN} \times 100\% \tag{2}$$

$$F1 - Score = \frac{2TP}{2TP + FP + FN} \times 100\% \tag{3}$$

where TP is an outcome where the model correctly predicts the positive class, TN is an outcome where the model correctly predicts the negative class, FP is an outcome where the model incorrectly predicts the positive class, FN is an outcome where the model incorrectly predicts the negative class.

5.4   Experimental Results

The overall experimental tasks can be divided into 2 subtasks, Intent Recognition and Entity Recognition.

Intent Recognition. In order to verify whether BERT is helpful to the improvement of intention recognition accuracy, this paper makes a comparison experiment between BERT-TextCNN model (adopted in this paper) and TextCNN model. The overall performance of the two methods is shown in Table 5. From the experimental results, we can see that the added BERT model can contribute to improving the accuracy of IR task, and BERT-TextCNN model performs much better than TextCNN on the chicken disease question dataset.

Entity Recognition. Table 6 comparing the model used in this paper with other baselines shows that BiLSTM-CRF model has the best performance. On this basis, we use the model to identify disease entities and symptom entities. From the table, we can see that the overall performance of the model to classify different entities is quite prominent.

Table 5. Experimental results of the Intent Recognition task.

Model	Precision	Recall	F1-Score
TextCNN	83	79	80
Bert-TextCNN	**92**	**90**	**90**

Table 6. Experimental results of the Entity Recognition task.

Model	Precision	Recall	F1-Score
HMM	79.26	75.66	77.28
CRF	85.48	81.53	83.42
LSTM	82.93	55.09	66.12
LSTM-CRF	83.64	81.97	82.97
BiLSTM	84.97	81.86	83.34
BiLSTM-CRF	84.98	82.63	**83.77**

5.5   Demonstration

In this paper, we build an executable QA system of our CDD-QAS. With the knowledge graph as the data source, our CDD-QAS provides users with convenient functions such as chicken disease information retrieval, disease diagnosis, disease treatment, epidemic prevention, and risk assessment. The visualization of the CDD-QAS can be seen in Fig. 3.

In the demonstration demo, we use 6 questions with different intents to test our CDD-QAS, including inquiring chicken disease diagnosis, treatment methods, prevention methods, disease symptoms, irrelevant question and aimless question. According to the output answers of our CDD-QAS, this system can accurately recognize the intents of the questions and answer the user accurately and interactively.

Our CDD-QAS set a great example of applying knowledge graph and deep learning methods in poultry disease diagnosis QA system, which is of great significance for advanced application of knowledge graph and the development of intelligent poultry industry.

6   Conclusion

In this paper, we construct a comprehensive knowledge graph of 28 common chicken diseases and realize a intelligent Chicken Disease Diagnosis Question Answering System (CDD-QAS) based on the knowledge graph. We obtain massive data of chicken diseases from varied ways to build up a scientific and comprehensive knowledge graph. And we resolve our target into two tasks to solve respectively, intent recognition task carried out by Bert-TextCNN and entity recognition task carried out by BiLSTM-CRF. With the recognized intent and entities of the input question, we then fetch information from the chicken disease knowledge graph to form the final answer. Based on experimental results, it is proved that this system is highly accurate, effective, intelligent and interactive, which realizes a scientific chicken disease diagnosis system for poultry industry and contributes to the intelligent poultry development. In the future, we will consider utilizing data in different languages and adopting multi-modal methods to improve our system.

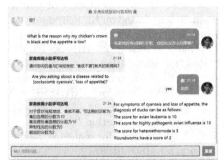

(a) Dialogues of chicken disease diagnosis with the output of four most likely diseases and their possibilities.

(b) Dialogues of chicken disease diagnosis with the output of the most likely disease and its treatment measures.

(c) Dialogues of inquiring possible symptoms and treatment measures for a chicken disease.

(d) Dialogues of inquiring prevention for a specific chicken disease.

(e) Dialogues of recognizing irrelevant question.

(f) Dialogues of recognizing missing entity in the question.

Fig. 3. Visualization examples of our CDD-QAS.

References

1. Wang, H., Xiao, J., Gao, X., Wang, H.: Design and implementation of poultry disease diagnosis and information management system based on BP neural network optimized by genetic algorithm. Heilongjiang Anim. Sci. Vet. Med. **2**, 1–4 (2017)
2. Zhou, Y.: Study on risk warning of poultry industry based on AHP-DS - a case study of Jiangxi Province. China Poultry **40**(19), 60–63 (2018)
3. Devlin, J., Chang, M.W., Lee, K., Toutanova, K.: Bert: pre-training of deep bidirectional transformers for language understanding. arXiv preprint arXiv:1810.04805 (2018)
4. Kim, Y.: Convolutional neural networks for sentence classification (2014)
5. Huang, Z., Xu, W., Yu, K.: Bidirectional LSTM-CRF models for sequence tagging. CoRR abs/1508.01991 (2015). https://arxiv.org/abs/1508.01991
6. Mbelwa, H., Machuve, D., Mbelwa, J.: Deep convolutional neural network for chicken diseases detection (2021)
7. Liu, Y., Li, J., Zhao, J.: Design and implementation of domain question-answering system based on semantic analysis. Comput. Appl. Softw. **38**(11), 42–48 (2021)
8. Zhu, M., Ahuja, A., Wei, W., Reddy, C.K.: A hierarchical attention retrieval model for healthcare question answering. In: The World Wide Web Conference, pp. 2472–2482 (2019)
9. Mollá, D.: Macquarie university at BioASQ 6b: deep learning and deep reinforcement learning for query-based multi-document summarisation (2018)
10. Pappas, D., Stavropoulos, P., Androutsopoulos, I., McDonald, R.: BIOMRC: a dataset for biomedical machine reading comprehension. In: Proceedings of the 19th SIGBioMed Workshop on Biomedical Language Processing, pp. 140–149 (2020)
11. Qi, G., Gao, H., Wu, T.: The research advances of knowledge graph. Technol. Intell. Eng. **3**(1), 4–25 (2017)
12. Ion, R., et al.: An open-domain QA system for e-governance. arXiv preprint arXiv:2206.08046 (2022)
13. He, G., Lan, Y., Jiang, J., Zhao, W.X., Wen, J.R.: Improving multi-hop knowledge base question answering by learning intermediate supervision signals. In: Proceedings of the 14th ACM International Conference on Web Search and Data Mining, pp. 553–561 (2021)
14. Akbari, H., Karaman, S., Bhargava, S., Chen, B., Vondrick, C., Chang, S.F.: Multi-level multimodal common semantic space for image-phrase grounding. In: Proceedings of the IEEE/CVF Conference on Computer Vision and Pattern Recognition, pp. 12476–12486 (2019)
15. Qing Zhou, Y., Liu, X.J., Dong, Y.: Build a robust QA system with transformer-based mixture of experts. arXiv e-prints pp. arXiv-2204 (2022)
16. Faisal, F., Keshava, S., Anastasopoulos, A., et al.: SD-QA: spoken dialectal question answering for the real world. arXiv preprint arXiv:2109.12072 (2021)
17. Li, D., Hu, B., Chen, Q., Peng, W., Wang, A.: Towards medical machine reading comprehension with structural knowledge and plain text. In: Proceedings of the 2020 Conference on Empirical Methods in Natural Language Processing (EMNLP), pp. 1427–1438 (2020)
18. Park, J., Cho, Y., Lee, H., Choo, J., Choi, E.: Knowledge graph-based question answering with electronic health records. In: Machine Learning for Healthcare Conference, pp. 36–53. PMLR (2021)
19. Kim, Y.: Convolutional neural networks for sentence classification. CoRR abs/1408.5882 (2014). https://arxiv.org/abs/1408.5882

20. Mikolov, T., Corrado, G., Chen, K., Dean, J.: Efficient estimation of word representations in vector space, pp. 1–12 (2013)
21. Wal, D., et al.: Biological data annotation via a human-augmenting AI-based labeling system. NPJ Digit. Med. **4** (2021). https://doi.org/10.1038/s41746-021-00520-6
22. Akkidas, D.: Viterbi algorithm. J. Exp. Algorithmics (2015)
23. Zhang, N., Jia, Q., Yin, K., Dong, L., Gao, F., Hua, N.: Conceptualized representation learning for Chinese biomedical text mining. In: WSDM 2020 Health Day (2020)

Therapeutic Effects of Corticosteroids for Critical and Severe COVID-19 Patients

Yuhan Gao[1,2] , Yaoqi Sun[1,2], Jinlan Bi[3], Shengying Wang[3], Jiyong Zhang[2], and Mang Xiao[4(✉)]

[1] Lishui Institute of Hangzhou Dianzi University, Hangzhou, Zhejiang, China
[2] Department of Automation, Hangzhou Dianzi University, Hangzhou, Zhejiang, China
[3] Tsinghua Shenzhen International Graduate School, Shenzhen, Guangdong, China
[4] Sir Run Run Shaw Hospital, Hangzhou, Zhejiang, China
joelxm@zju.edu.cn

Abstract. The rapid spread of severe acute respiratory syndrome coronavirus 2 (SARS-CoV-2) infection has led to an unprecedented public health, economic, and social crisis worldwide. Since no therapeutic treatment is yet available to effectively clear the virus and terminate transmission, supportive therapy is the primary clinical approach for coronavirus disease (COVID-19). The role of corticosteroids as one of the main means of anti-inflammatory adjuvants in the treatment of COVID-19 is controversial. Here, we retrospectively evaluated the therapeutic effects of corticosteroids by comparing clinical data of patients treated with or without a corticosteroids therapy at different severity levels. Kaplan-Meier curves shows that therapy with methylprednisolone and cortico-steroids increases the risk of death in patients with critical COVID-19 pneumonia. For patients in the critical group, the risk of death was slightly higher in males receiving corticosteroids therapy, while hypertension and trauma history reduced the hazard ratio.

Keywords: SARS-CoV-2 · COVID-19 · Corticosteroids therapy · Methylprednisolone · Dexamethasone

1 Introduction

COVID-19 is caused by SARS-CoV-2, which is responsible for global public health emergencies. Although the World Health Organization (WHO) and many countries/regions provide guidelines for COVID-19 at different clinical stages, no pharmaceutical products or measures have yet been developed to safely and effectively treat COVID-19. Supportive therapy is the surrogate prior to the emergence of specific therapeutics [1]. Most patients have mild illness, but the elderly and those with underlining comorbidities may progress to severe illness requiring hospitalization and care in the intensive care unit (ICU) [2]. The pathological progression of severe COVID-19 in patients includes a host inflammatory cytokine storm that leads to immunopathological lung injury, diffuse alveolar damage that accompanies the development of acute respiratory distress syndrome (ARDS), and death [3].

© The Author(s), under exclusive license to Springer Nature Singapore Pte Ltd. 2022
Y. Tan and Y. Shi (Eds.): DMBD 2022, CCIS 1745, pp. 260–287, 2022.
https://doi.org/10.1007/978-981-19-8991-9_19

Cytokine storm, as well as viral evasion of cellular immune responses, play an equally important roles in disease progression [4]. Thus, tackling the immune response with immunomodulatory agents is as important as addressing viral replication to prevent progression to multiorgan dysfunction [5]. Among the drugs that received early attention were corticosteroids due to their prominent broad-spectrum of anti-inflammatory and immunomodulatory effects via both the innate and adaptive immune system [6]. Corticosteroid monotherapy has been reported for the treatment of SARS-CoV-2 with an underlying ill-ness such as renal transplantation [7]. Corticosteroids may improve the dysregulated immune response caused by ARDS and sepsis. However, its adverse effects are partly due to suppression of normal host immune responses and impeded viral clearance [8]. High doses of corticosteroids are closely associated with adverse events such as secondary infections, inhibition of glucose uptake, delayed viral clearance, and emergence of viral resistance [9, 10]. Thus, the debate regarding the use of corticosteroids in COVID-19 patients is controversial [11].

Observational studies in patients with SARS and MERS have demonstrated that cortico-steroid therapy delays viral clearance and increases the high risk of complications, including hyperglycemia, psychosis, and avascular necrosis [12]. Patients with moderate-to-severe COVID-19 pneumonia are likely to benefit from moderate-dose corticosteroid therapy relatively late in the course of the disease, especially when patients require mechanical ventilation. Early treatment in milder disease seems to be harmful [13]. Low-dose corticosteroid therapy or pulse corticosteroid therapy appears to have a beneficial role in the management of severely ill COVID-19 patients. WHO recommends systemic cortico-steroids for the treatment of patients with severe and critical COVID-19, and recommends short courses of corticosteroids at low-to-moderate dose, used prudently, for critically ill patients with COVID-19 pneumonia [14].

More recently, systemic corticosteroids in the form of dexamethasone have been shown to reduce mortality in patients with severe COVID-19 requiring oxygen therapy or using a mechanical ventilator [15]. Nonetheless, more studies are needed to replicate the otcome shown in the RECOVERY trial to draw a substantive conclusion [16]. Intravenous methylprednisolone (1–2 mg/kg/day) is recommended for 3–5 days, but not for long-term use [17]. Methylprednisolone (dose and regimen not reported) reduces the risk of death in patients with COVID-19-associated ARDS [18]. However, corticosteroids in severe COVID-19–related acute respiratory distress syndrome (ARDS) have also been reported to be associated with increased mortality and delayed viral clearance. Corticosteroids may have both potentially deleterious and beneficial effects during the different stages of infection, lung injury, and ARDS. In Wuhan, the use of corticosteroids was not associated with a beneficial effect in reducing in-hospital mortality in severe or critical cases [19]. Here, we aimed to estimate the effects of corticosteroid use on mortality in a large cohort of COVID-19 patients with severe or critical illness.

2 Materials and Methods

2.1 Study Design and Participants

This retrospective study was based on clinical data collected from January 2020 to April 2020 at Tongji Hospital in Wuhan, China. All subjects were diagnosed with COVID pneumonia according to WHO interim guidance. Patients were risk-stratified according to the severity of mild, moderate, severe or critical COVID-19 symptoms presented at the hospital. Patients without hypoxia or exertional dyspnea were considered to have mild COVID-19. Patients with mild COVID-19 received only symptomatic relief and were not admitted to the hospital. Patients presented with infiltrates on chest radiography and required supplemental oxygen by nasal cannula or high-flow nasal cannula were classified as having moderate COVID-19. Patients were classified as having severe COVID-19 if they had hypoxia (oxygen saturation $\leq 93\%$ in room air) or tachypnea (respiratory rate > 30 breaths/min). Patients with respiratory failure requiring mechanical ventilation were classified as having critical COVID-19.

2.2 Data Collection

Data were determined from the hospital's electronic medical record and recorded on a standardized electronic case report form. Demographic data, information on clinical symptoms or signs at presentation, and laboratory and radiological examinations during the admission were collected for all COVID-19 patients. Patients with multiple admissions were included. All laboratory tests and radiological assessments, including plain chest radiography and computed tomography of the chest, were performed at the discretion of the attending physician. We collected demographic data (gender, date of birth, age, ancestral home, time of death, date of visit, discharge date, length and duration of hospitalization), history of present illness, history of past illnesses (infectious diseases, history of allergies, history of blood transfusion, previous surgeries, hypertension, coronary artery, diabetes, chronic obstructive pulmonary disease (COPD), malignant diseases, cerebrovascular diseases, hepatitis, tuberculosis, history of trauma, and cardiovascular disease), physical examination, specialist examination, chest X-ray examination, chest CT examination, routine blood tests, biochemical tests, coagulation tests, blood gas analysis, and treatment (ventilator, intubation, oxygen therapy, hemodialysis, extracorporeal membrane oxygenation (ECMO), continuous renal replacement therapy (CRRT), gamma globulin therapy, traditional Chinese medicine (TCM), corticosteroids therapy, immunotherapy, antiviral therapy, and antibacterial therapy). The main evaluation parameter was the mortality rate of severely and critically ill patients after hospital admission.

2.3   Inclusion and Exclusion Criteria

Cases with missing clinical information, mild and moderate symptoms were excluded. The survival analysis model estimated the association between corticosteroids use and in-hospital mortality in patients with COVID-19. The parameters used in univariate and multivariable Cox regression were laboratory test values, including routine blood, bio-chemical tests, coagulation tests, and blood gas analysis.

2.4   Statistical Analysis

We aimed to evaluate the therapeutic effect of corticosteroids in patients with or without corticosteroids therapy in different severity categories. Patients were divided into four groups (mild, moderate, severe, and critical) according to their severity. Survival analysis is the analysis of time-to-event data, which describe the length of time from a time origin to an endpoint of interest. Kaplan-Meier curve analysis is a univariate analysis and is useful when the predictor variable is categorical. Therefore, we performed Kaplan-Meier curve analysis for patients with and without corticosteroids therapy in the severe and critical illness groups, starting from the date of visit to the date of discharge or death.

The Kaplan-Meier curve analysis describes the survival rate based on one of the factors under investigation, but ignores the impact of other factors. The Cox model is an alternative that extends survival analysis methods to simultaneously assess the effect of several risk factors on survival time. The Cox model is a survival analysis regression model used for investigating the association between patients' survival time or mortality and multiple predictor variables in the medical field. The survival time used in Cox regression is the time from hospital admission (usually coinciding with the start of the first treatment ad-ministered) to the last visit. The Cox model is applicable to both quantitative predictor variables and categorical variables. Univariate Cox regression analyses were performed to identify individual factors significantly associated with mortality. The multivariable Cox regression model was used to describe how these factors jointly affected survival time. In the multivariate Cox proportional hazard model, only univariate analysis variables with $p < 0.05$ or speculative associations with the event were included to avoid overfitting. All variables with significance < 0.05 in the univariate study plus age and gender were included in the multivariate study [20]. The baseline characteristics of participants with and without corticosteroids therapy, including routine blood, biochemical tests, coagulation tests, cytokines, and vital signs, were compared. Descriptive data are presented as means with standard deviations. Categorical variables are expressed as percentages. All statistical analyses were performed using R Studio. Research manuscripts reporting large datasets that are deposited in a publicly available database should specify where the data have been deposited and provide the relevant accession numbers. If the accession numbers have not yet been obtained at the time of submission, please state that they will be provided during review. They must be provided prior to publication.

Interventionary studies involving animals or humans, and other studies that require ethical approval, must list the authority that provided approval and the corresponding ethical approval code.

3 Results

3.1 Characteristic and K-M Survival Curves

As at April 2020, 3337 patients had been admitted to Tongji Hospital. All patients were classified into four groups (mild, moderate, severe, and critical) according to the severity of COVID-19, except for 30 of them who had no accurate diagnosis (Table 1). 49.9% of the patients were males, which was slightly less than females. For critically ill cases, males ac-counted for 59.6% of cases, indicating that males are more susceptible to COVID-19. For the patients with a mean age of 58.39 years (Standard Deviation (SD) = 16.12), the mean age was highest in the critical group (64.95, SD = 16.66). The immune response was poorer in the elderly. Ageing is associated with endothelial dysfunction, which can lead to vascular pathologies and cardiovascular diseases in the elderly patients. The systematic use of corticosteroids therapy was higher in critically ill COVID-19 patients, with up to 80.6% of them receiving corticosteroids therapy. A lower percentage of patients with underlining comorbidities received corticosteroids therapy. 65% of patients receiving corticosteroids therapy used methylprednisolone, while 14% used dexamethasone (Fig. 5(c) and Fig. 1).

Of the 3337 patients admitted to the hospital, 294 patients with mild and moderate dis-ease and cases without an accurate diagnosis were excluded. Our analysis included 2243 (67%) patients with severe pneumonia and 800 (24%) patients with critical pneu-monia (Fig. 2). Cases with various complications, which may interfere with the thera-peutic effect of corticosteroids, are also listed. In the severe group, 1037 (46%) of the patients were male and 857 (38%) received corticosteroids therapy, with an average age of 57 years. In the critical group, 477 (60%) of the participants were male and 645 (81%) received cortico-steroids therapy, with an average age of 65 years. The survival analysis was performed on participants in both groups starting from the date of admission until discharge or death. The survival analysis, including Kaplan–Meier survival curves and Cox regression, was performed for our severe (2243) and critical (800) groups. The Kaplan–Meier survival curves showed that in the critical group, control therapy had bet-ter efficacy compared to corticosteroids and methylprednisolone, while in the absence of the severe group, there was no significant difference between the corticosteroid-treated and control groups (Figs. 3 and 4). In both the severe and critical groups, there was no significant difference between patients treated with dexamethasone compared to the control group (Fig. 5). We controlled the therapy variables except for corticosteroids ther-apy and compared the laboratory test values between patients treated with and without corticosteroids in the severe (728) and critical (88) groups.

Table 1. Characteristic distribution for collected COVID-19 patients

	Level	Total	Mild	Moderate	Severe	Critical	P
N		3337	2	262	2243	800	
Gender (%)	Male	1664 (49.9)	1 (50.0)	132 (50.4)	1037 (46.2)	477 (59.6)	< 0.001
	Female	1673 (50.1)	1 (50.0)	130 (49.6)	1206 (53.8)	323 (40.4)	
Age (mean (SD))		58.39 (16.12)	59.00 (25.46)	49.33 (14.68)	57.22 (15.07)	64.95 (16.66)	< 0.001
BMI (mean (SD))		23.89 (8.89)	NaN (NA)	25.52 (23.44)	23.78 (4.02)	23.25 (3.39)	0.038
Corticosteroids therapy (%)	No	1784 (53.4)	2 (100.0)	219 (83.6)	1386 (61.8)	155 (19.4)	< 0.001
	Yes	1553 (46.5)	0 (0.0)	43 (16.4)	857 (38.2)	645 (80.6)	
Past disease (%)	No	1468 (44.0)	1 (50.0)	146 (55.7)	1077 (48.0)	237 (29.6)	< 0.001
	Yes	1845 (55.3)	1 (50.0)	112 (2.7)	1155 (51.5)	556 (69.5)	
Infectious disease (%)	No	3225 (96.6)	2 (100.0)	250 (95.4)	2175 (97.0)	769 (96.1)	0.614
	Yes	112 (3.4)	0 (0.0)	12 (4.6)	68 (3.0)	31 (3.9)	
Allergic history (%)	No	3070 (92.0)	2 (100.0)	244 (93.1)	2043 (91.1)	751 (93.9)	0.047
	Yes	267 (8.0)	0 (0.0)	18 (6.9)	200 (8.9)	49 (6.1)	
Blood transfusion History (%)	No	3307 (99.1)	2 (100.0)	262 (100.0)	2224 (99.2)	790 (98.8)	0.234
	Yes	30 (0.9)	0 (0.0)	0 (0.0)	19 (0.8)	10 (1.2)	
Past surgery (%)	No	2759 (82.7)	2 (100.0)	217 (82.8)	1870 (83.4)	644 (80.5)	0.385
	Yes	578 (17.3)	0 (0.0)	45 (17.2)	373 (16.6)	156 (19.5)	
Hypertension (%)	No	2338 (70.1)	1 (50.0)	221 (84.4)	1638 (73.0)	459 (57.4)	< 0.001
	Yes	999 (29.9)	1 (50.0)	41 (15.6)	605 (27.0)	341 (42.6)	

(*continued*)

Table 1. (*continued*)

	Level	Total	Mild	Moderate	Severe	Critical	P
Coronory (%)	No	3100 (92.9)	1 (50.0)	256 (97.7)	2098 (93.5)	716 (89.5)	< 0.001
	Yes	237 (7.1)	1 (50.0)	6 (2.3)	145 (6.5)	84 (10.5)	
Diabetes (%)	No	2881 (86.3)	1 (50.0)	241 (92.0)	1951 (87.0)	662 (82.8)	0.001
	Yes	456 (13.7)	1 (50.0)	21 (8.0)	292 (13.0)	138 (17.2)	
COPD(%)	No	3292 (98.7)	2 (100.0)	261 (99.6)	2222 (99.1)	777 (97.1)	0.001
	Yes	45 (1.3)	0 (0.0)	1 (0.4)	21 (0.9)	23 (2.9)	
Malignoncy (%)	No	3243 (97.2)	2 (100.0)	258 (98.5)	2191 (97.7)	763 (95.4)	0.01
	Yes	94 (2.8)	0 (0.0)	4 (1.5)	52 (2.3)	37 (4.6)	
Cerebrovascular disease (%)	No	3220 (96.5)	2 (100.0)	257 (98.1)	2197 (97.9)	736 (92.0)	< 0.001
	Yes	117 (3.5)	0 (0.0)	5 (1.9)	46 (2.1)	64 (8.0)	
Hepatitis (%)	No	3278 (98.2)	2 (100.0)	254 (96.9)	2208 (98.4)	784 (98.0)	0.423
	Yes	59 (1.8)	0 (0.0)	8 (3.1)	35 (1.6)	16 (2.0)	
Tuberculosis (%)	No	3275 (98.1)	2 (100.0)	257 (98.1)	2206 (98.4)	781 (97.6)	0.716
	YES	62 (1.9)	0 (0.0)	5 (1.9)	37 (1.6)	19 (2.4)	
Trauma history (%)	No	3263 (97.8)	2 (100.0)	261 (99.6)	2197 (97.9)	773 (96.6)	0.04
	Yes	74 (2.2)	0 (0.0)	1 (0.4)	46 (2.1)	27 (3.4)	
Cardiovascular (%)	No	2185 (65.5)	1 (50.0)	210 (80.2)	1545 (68.9)	410 (51.2)	< 0.001
	Yes	1152 (34.5)	1 (50.0)	52 (19.8)	698 (31.1)	390 (48.8)	

Abbreviation: Body Mass Index, BMI; Body Surface Area, BSA; Extracorporeal Membrane Oxygenation, ECMO; Continuous Renal Replacement Therapy, CRRT; Chronic Obstructive Pulmonary Diseases, COPD; Chronic Kidney Disease, CKD.

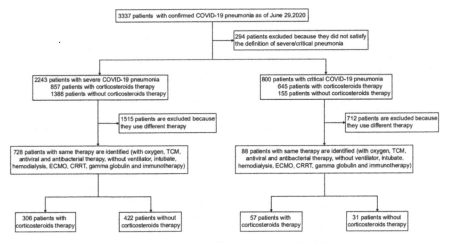

Fig. 1. Flow chart of patient group selection

The small sample for the previous analysis and the relatively young (median age of 39 years) and mild disease of the patients included in the study limited the generalizability of the findings to patients without ARDS, which is a major threat and challenge in clinical practice. The observational nature implies that many confounding factors may have influenced our results [21]. For patients in the severe group, univariate Cox regression results showed that gender ($p < 0.05$), infectious disease ($p < 0.05$), hypertension ($p < 0.05$) and cardiovascular history ($p < 0.05$) were significantly associated with mortality. COVID-19 patients had diverse complications, of which different complications contributed differently to survival time. COPD had a greater impact on mortality than other complications.

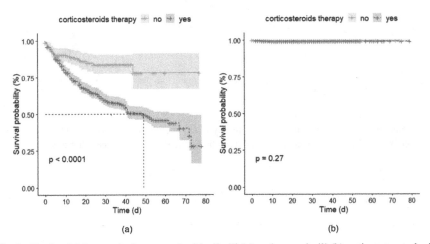

Fig. 2. Kaplan-Meier survival curves of critically ill (a) and severely ill (b) patients treated with corticosteroids

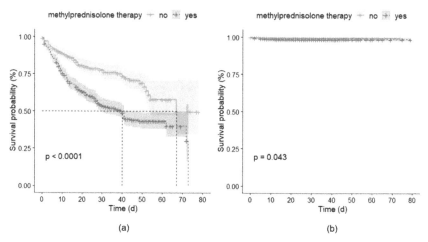

Fig. 3. Kaplan-Meier survival curves of critically ill (a) and severely ill (b) patients treated with methylprednisolone

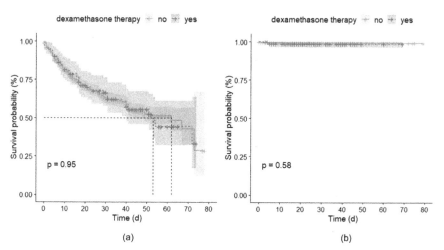

Fig. 4. Kaplan-Meier survival curves of critically ill (a) and severely ill (b) patients treated with dexamethasone. Yellow and blue shaded areas indicate the 95% confidence interval (CI).

Table 2. Univariate Cox regression of severely ill patients

	Beta	HR (95% CI)	Wald test	p value
Age	0.04	1 (1–1.1)	3.8	0.052
Gender	1.2	3.2 (1–10)	4	0.045
Corticosteroids therapy	0.57	1.8 (0.64–4.9)	1.2	0.27
Past disease	1.2	3.4 (0.95–12)	3.5	0.061
Infectious disease	1.6	5.1 (1.1–22)	4.6	0.033
Allergic history	– 17	3.6e-08 (0-Inf)	0	1
Blood transfusion history	– 15	3e-07 (0-Inf)	0	1
Past surgery	0.6	1.8 (0.58–5.7)	1	0.31
Hypertension	1.1	3.1 (1.1–8.4)	4.6	0.031
Coronory	0.024	1 (0.13–7.8)	0	0.98
Diabetes	0.019	1 (0.23–4.5)	0	0.98
COPD	2	7.6 (1–58)	3.8	0.05
Malignoncy	1.1	3 (0.39–23)	1.1	0.29
Cerebrovascular disease	1.2	3.4 (0.45–26)	1.4	0.24
Hepatitis	1.6	4.7 (0.62–36)	2.2	0.13
Tuberculosis	1.4	4.2 (0.56–32)	1.9	0.16
Trauma history	1.2	3.4 (0.45–26)	1.4	0.24
Cardiovascular	1.2	3.3 (1.2–9.2)	5.1	0.024

HR: hazard ratios; CI: confidence interval.

3.2 Univariate and Multivariable Cox Regression

A univariate Cox proportional-hazards model was used to estimate the association between medical history and in-hospital mortality. Administration of corticosteroids in severe COVID-19–associated ARDS was not associated with increased 78-day mortality and delayed SARS–CoV-2 coronavirus RNA clearance (Table 2). However, corticosteroids in critically ill COVID-19 were associated with increased 78-day mortality (Tables 4 and 5). According to multivariable Cox regression results, having infectious diseases increased the hazard ratio for death in the severe group (Table 3). Corticosteroids are hazardous during recovery because the virus not only persists, but also prevents the body from generating protective antibodies. Previous reports have demonstrated the beneficial effects of corticosteroids on critically ill COVID-19 patients [21]. Compared to the non-corticosteroids group, the systemic use of corticosteroids was not associated with any beneficial effect in reducing in-hospital mortality in both severe cases (HR = 1.8, 95% CI: 0.64–4.9, p = 0.27) and critical cases (HR = 2.7, 95% CI: 1.8–4.2, p < 0.001).

Table 3. Multivariable Cox regression of severely ill patients

	coef	exp (coef)	Lower 95%	Upper 95%	se (coef)	z	Pr(>|z|)	
Gender = Male	1.0989	3.001	0.9489	9.49	0.5874	1.871	0.0614	
Infectious disease = yes	1.5683	4.799	1.0683	21.56	0.7665	2.046	0.0407	*
Hypertension = yes	0.2367	1.267	0.1582	10.15	1.0614	0.223	0.8236	
Cardiovascular = yes	1.0218	2.778	0.3345	23.08	1.0801	0.946	0.3441	
Concordance = 0.749 (se = 0.059)								
Likelihood ratio test = 12.74 on 4 df, p = 0.01								
Wald test = 13.5 on 4 df, p = 0.009								
Score (logrank) test = 15.76 on 4 df, p = 0.003								

* P-values between 0.01 and 0.05. coef: coefficient. coef > 0 means higher hazard and worse prognosis. Exp (coef): exponential coefficients, known as hazard ratios, give the effect size of covariates. Exp (coef) > 1 means higher hazard. se(coef): standard error of coefficients. z: Wald statistic value. z = coef / se (coef).

For patients in the critical group, the results of univariate Cox regression showed that age (p < 0.001), gender (p < 0.001), corticosteroids therapy (p < 0.001), hypertension (p < 0.05) and history of trauma (p < 0.05) were significantly associated with mortality. Hypertension was a common factor contributing to mortality rate in both severe and critical COVID-1 groups. Males had a higher risk of death, and corticosteroids therapy increased the hazard. According to multivariable Cox regression results, a history of trauma reduced the hazard ratio for death. Corticosteroids increased mortality in critically ill patients with COVID-19, in contrast to previous reports.

Table 4. Univariate Cox regression in critically ill patients

	Beta	HR (95% CI)	Wald test	p value
Age	0.018	1 (1–1)	18	1.70E-05
Gender	0.42	1.5 (1.2–1.9)	12	0.00053
Corticosteroids Therapy	1	2.7 (1.8–4.2)	21	4.00E-06
Past disease	− 0.2	0.82 (0.64–1)	2.7	0.1
Infectious disease	0.34	1.4 (0.82–2.4)	1.5	0.22
Allergic history	0.028	1 (0.64–1.7)	0.01	0.91
Blood transfusion history	0.72	2.1 (0.97–4.3)	3.5	0.061
Past surgery	− 0.2	0.82 (0.61–1.1)	1.8	0.18

(continued)

Table 4. (*continued*)

	Beta	HR (95% CI)	Wald test	p value
Hypertension	− 0.28	0.75 (0.6–0.95)	5.8	0.016
Coronory	0.17	1.2 (0.84–1.7)	0.93	0.33
Diabetes	− 0.29	0.75 (0.55–1)	3.2	0.072
COPD	− 0.047	0.95 (0.47–1.9)	0.02	0.9
Malignoncy	0.32	1.4 (0.88–2.2)	2	0.16
Cerebrovascular disease	− 0.16	0.85 (0.56–1.3)	0.56	0.45
Hepatitis	− 0.064	0.94 (0.39–2.3)	0.02	0.89
Tuberculosis	0.063	1.1 (0.53–2.1)	0.03	0.86
Trauma history	− 1	0.35 (Table 4 Univariate Cox regression of critical patients 0.13–0.95)	4.3	0.039
Cardiovascular	− 0.2	0.82 (0.66–1)	3	0.081

HR: hazard ratios; CI: confidence interval.

Table 5. Multivariable Cox regression in critically ill patients

	coef	Exp(coef)	Lower 95%	Upper 95%	se(coef)	Z	Pr(>|z|)	
Age	0.02377	1.0241	1.015	1.0332	0.004515	5.264	1.41E−07	***
Gender = Male	0.426075	1.5312	1.2073	1.9421	0.121273	3.513	4.42E−04	***
Corticosteroids therapy = yes	0.997764	2.7122	1.7701	4.1557	0.21771	4.583	4.58E−06	***
Hypertension = yes	−0.400641	0.6699	0.5317	0.844	0.117894	-3.398.	6.78E−04	***
Trauma history = yes	−1.005674	0.3658	0.1363	0.9815	0.503583	−1.997	0.045821	*

Concordance = 0.642 (se = 0.017)

Likelihood ratio test = 81.55 on 5 df, p = 4e-16

Wald test = 69.86 on 5 df, p = 1e-13

Score (logrank) test = 71.34 on 5 df, p = 5e-14

* P-values between 0.01 and 0.05. ** P-values between 0.001 and 0.01. *** P-values less than 0.001. Coef: coefficient. Coef > 0 means higher hazard and worse prognosis. Exp (coef): exponentiated coefficients, known as hazard ratios, give the effect size of covariates. Exp (coef) > 1 means higher hazard. Se (coef): standard error of coefficients. z: Wald statistic value. Z = coef / se (coef).

3.3 Differences in Physiological Indicators

Furthermore, we controlled for other therapy variables since treatment is always tailored to the individual patient and the combinations of different treatments are indeed diverse. We selected patients who received the following treatments, including oxygen therapy, traditional Chinese medicine, antiviral therapy, antibacterial therapy, but not ventilator, intubation, hemodialysis, ECMO, CRRT, gamma globulin therapy, and immunotherapy. There were 728 cases in the severe group and 88 cases in the critical care group who met the above conditions. We compared all available indicators between the two groups of patients treated with and without corticosteroids and found numerous differences, including reduced Baso% in both groups and reduced Baso# in the critical group. The box plot shows the difference in Baso% and Baso# between corticosteroid-treated and control groups (Fig. 5). For severe patients, the results showed higher WBC#, LDH, Neut# and Neut%, and lower UA, ALB, TP, Lymph% in patients treated with corticosteroids (p < 0.001) (Tables 6 and 7; Fig. 6).

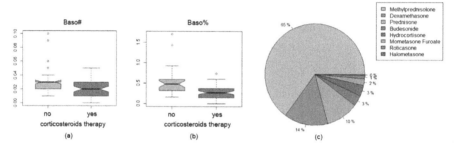

Fig. 5. Boxplot of indicators with significant differences in the critical group and distribution of corticosteroids therapy. Patients treated with corticosteroids have (a) lower basophil counts and (b) lower basophil percentage in the critical group.

Table 6. Descriptive statistics of parameters in the severely ill patient group

	Level	Overall	No corticosteroids therapy	Corticosteroids therapy	p
N		728	422	306	
Gender (%)	Male	353 (48.5)	207 (49.1)	146 (47.7)	0.778
	Female	375 (51.5)	215 (50.9)	160 (52.3)	
WBC #(mean (SD))		6.06 (1.75)	5.80 (1.53)	6.41 (1.96)	< 0.001
RBC #(mean (SD))		4.10 (0.53)	4.12 (0.51)	4.08 (0.55)	0.444
MCV (mean (SD))		89.81 (4.72)	89.85 (4.65)	89.75 (4.82)	0.777

(continued)

Table 6. (*continued*)

	Level	Overall	No corticosteroids therapy	Corticosteroids therapy	p
MCHC (mean (SD))		342.42 (12.59)	342.99 (10.87)	341.63 (14.61)	0.152
MCH (mean (SD))		30.76 (2.11)	30.82 (1.89)	30.68 (2.38)	0.378
RDW-CV (mean (SD))		12.80 (1.52)	12.67 (1.49)	12.99 (1.53)	0.005
RDW-SD (mean (SD))		41.38 (3.93)	40.97 (3.73)	41.95 (4.12)	0.001
Lymph % (mean (SD))		26.62 (8.01)	28.27 (7.97)	24.33 (7.51)	< 0.001
Lymph # (mean (SD))		1.52 (0.50)	1.57 (0.48)	1.46 (0.51)	0.003
Mono % (mean (SD))		9.27 (2.30)	9.35 (2.24)	9.16 (2.38)	0.278
Mono # (mean (SD))		0.54 (0.17)	0.53 (0.15)	0.56 (0.18)	0.003
Neut % (mean (SD))		61.63 (9.01)	59.72 (8.72)	64.25 (8.76)	< 0.001
Neut # (mean (SD))		3.85 (1.53)	3.56 (1.32)	4.25 (1.69)	< 0.001
Hct (mean (SD))		36.70 (4.03)	36.85 (4.03)	36.49 (4.02)	0.235
Eos % (mean (SD))		1.71 (1.30)	1.78 (1.27)	1.57 (1.36)	0.528
Baso % (mean (SD))		0.45 (0.24)	0.49 (0.24)	0.40 (0.23)	< 0.001
Eos # (mean (SD))		0.12 (0.09)	0.12 (0.08)	0.11 (0.10)	0.081
Baso # (mean (SD))		0.03 (0.01)	0.03 (0.01)	0.02 (0.01)	0.002
Hb (mean (SD))		125.60 (14.75)	126.44 (14.82)	124.44 (14.61)	0.072
PLT # (mean (SD))		243.99 (70.08)	246.07 (70.08)	241.11 (70.10)	0.348

(*continued*)

Table 6. (*continued*)

	Level	Overall	No corticosteroids therapy	Corticosteroids therapy	p
MPV (mean (SD))		10.53 (0.81)	10.50 (0.82)	10.56 (0.80)	0.375
PDW (mean (SD))		12.12 (1.84)	12.09 (1.89)	12.16 (1.77)	0.635
PCT (mean (SD))		0.25 (0.07)	0.26 (0.07)	0.25 (0.07)	0.216
P-LCR (mean (SD))		28.83 (6.61)	28.66 (6.74)	29.06 (6.44)	0.432
ALT (mean (SD))		30.22 (21.12)	28.63 (20.02)	32.41 (22.40)	0.017
AST (mean (SD))		25.20 (11.65)	24.29 (10.41)	26.44 (13.09)	0.014
GGT (mean (SD))		41.77 (37.14)	38.80 (34.41)	45.85 (40.31)	0.012
TBIL (mean (SD))		9.57 (5.49)	9.56 (4.89)	9.57 (6.23)	0.979
DBIL (mean (SD))		4.09 (3.97)	3.98 (2.98)	4.25 (5.02)	0.36
IBIL (mean (SD))		5.54 (2.60)	5.64 (2.76)	5.40 (2.36)	0.226
ALB (mean (SD))		37.12 (3.89)	37.77 (4.02)	36.23 (3.53)	< 0.001
GLO (mean (SD))		30.42 (4.07)	30.32 (4.27)	30.56 (3.79)	0.435
TP (mean (SD))		67.54 (4.47)	68.09 (4.44)	66.78 (4.40)	< 0.001
ALB/GLO (mean (SD))		1.26 (0.25)	1.29 (0.27)	1.22 (0.23)	0.001
PA (mean (SD))		239.71 (61.70)	244.05 (56.80)	234.17 (67.22)	0.143
TBA (mean (SD))		5.31 (11.50)	4.93 (8.19)	5.78 (14.62)	0.491
Crea (mean (SD))		70.49 (19.04)	70.52 (18.47)	70.45 (19.82)	0.965

(*continued*)

Table 6. (*continued*)

	Level	Overall	No corticosteroids therapy	Corticosteroids therapy	p
Urea (mean (SD))		4.48 (1.43)	4.44 (1.32)	4.54 (1.57)	0.323
UA (mean (SD))		275.14 (79.31)	285.96 (78.73)	260.23 (77.78)	< 0.001
TC (mean (SD))		4.14 (0.87)	4.11 (0.87)	4.17 (0.86)	0.373
TG (mean (SD))		1.66 (0.95)	1.64 (1.00)	1.67 (0.89)	0.759
HDL-C (mean (SD))		1.04 (0.28)	1.04 (0.27)	1.03 (0.28)	0.739
LDL-C (mean (SD))		2.61 (0.78)	2.61 (0.78)	2.60 (0.77)	0.921
K + (mean (SD))		4.25 (0.37)	4.25 (0.37)	4.25 (0.37)	0.904
Na + (mean (SD))		140.03 (2.33)	140.23 (2.30)	139.76 (2.34)	0.007
Cl- (mean (SD))		101.43 (2.56)	101.63 (2.41)	101.15 (2.73)	0.013
Ca (mean (SD))		2.18 (0.10)	2.19 (0.10)	2.17 (0.10)	0.006
P (mean (SD))		1.09 (0.17)	1.10 (0.17)	1.08 (0.17)	0.273
Mg2 + (mean (SD))		0.86 (0.07)	0.86 (0.06)	0.85 (0.08)	0.062
Glu (mean (SD))		6.31 (2.26)	6.08 (1.87)	6.63 (2.69)	0.001
LDH (mean (SD))		221.87 (61.19)	213.85 (59.91)	232.91 (61.30)	< 0.001
ALP (mean (SD))		72.11 (25.86)	70.35 (24.58)	74.52 (27.37)	0.032
ChE (mean (SD))		7246.98 (1831.97)	7407.12 (1959.45)	7048.08 (1644.60)	0.068
AFU (mean (SD))		24.68 (8.37)	24.07 (6.16)	25.43 (10.46)	0.13
Cys-C (mean (SD))		1.06 (0.32)	1.06 (0.30)	1.07 (0.33)	0.796

(*continued*)

Table 6. (*continued*)

	Level	Overall	No corticosteroids therapy	Corticosteroids therapy	p
Amy (mean (SD))		67.81 (33.12)	64.86 (21.47)	71.67 (43.71)	0.07
CKD-EPI (mean (SD))		91.86 (17.20)	92.20 (17.06)	91.40 (17.40)	0.534
TT (mean (SD))		16.66 (1.25)	16.68 (1.25)	16.65 (1.26)	0.749
PT (mean (SD))		13.70 (0.97)	13.68 (1.07)	13.72 (0.82)	0.542
APTT (mean (SD))		38.94 (4.63)	39.03 (4.45)	38.82 (4.88)	0.568
AT:A (mean (SD))		93.65 (12.17)	93.76 (11.90)	93.47 (12.64)	0.783
PT-INR (mean (SD))		1.05 (0.10)	1.05 (0.11)	1.05 (0.08)	0.921
D-Dimer (mean (SD))		1.04 (1.25)	0.99 (1.40)	1.10 (1.00)	0.273
FDP (mean (SD))		6.45 (7.73)	6.46 (7.62)	6.43 (7.91)	0.975
Fbg (mean (SD))		4.36 (1.16)	4.24 (1.17)	4.53 (1.13)	0.001
PTA (mean (SD))		93.79 (10.00)	93.91 (9.90)	93.64 (10.16)	0.729
IL-6 (mean (SD))		12.17 (20.86)	9.68 (15.28)	14.97 (25.47)	0.005
IL-10 (mean (SD))		8.79 (5.18)	8.77 (5.18)	8.81 (5.22)	0.969
IL-8 (mean (SD))		18.27 (30.76)	18.10 (35.29)	18.45 (24.82)	0.9
TNF-α (mean (SD))		8.35 (3.91)	8.34 (4.23)	8.37 (3.50)	0.928
IL-1β (mean (SD))		11.31 (10.62)	13.10 (14.27)	9.62 (4.87)	0.101
IL-2R (mean (SD))		532.05 (330.07)	496.89 (311.32)	575.53 (347.59)	0.004
IgA (mean (SD))		2.43 (0.99)	2.38 (0.89)	2.48 (1.07)	0.511

(*continued*)

Table 6. (*continued*)

	Level	Overall	No corticosteroids therapy	Corticosteroids therapy	p
IgG (mean (SD))		11.44 (2.45)	11.46 (2.17)	11.42 (2.68)	0.921
IgM (mean (SD))		1.08 (0.46)	1.13 (0.49)	1.04 (0.44)	0.232
C3 (mean (SD))		0.86 (0.16)	0.85 (0.14)	0.86 (0.18)	0.549
C4 (mean (SD))		0.23 (0.08)	0.23 (0.07)	0.23 (0.09)	0.999
temperature (mean (SD))		36.85 (8.30)	36.43 (1.98)	37.41 (12.55)	0.118
breathe (mean (SD))		19.79 (1.63)	19.75 (1.92)	19.84 (1.10)	0.431
diastolic (mean (SD))		76.61 (11.41)	76.54 (9.12)	76.70 (13.90)	0.849
systolic (mean (SD))		125.39 (13.53)	125.52 (13.25)	125.22 (13.92)	0.772
Pulse-rate (mean (SD))		80.42 (8.93)	80.20 (9.51)	80.73 (8.08)	0.434
SpO2 (mean (SD))		97.12 (5.51)	97.11 (6.13)	97.13 (4.54)	0.958

WBC#: white blood cell count; RBC: red blood cell count; MCV: mean red blood cell volume; MCHC: mean red blood cell hemoglobin concentration; MCH: average red blood cell hemoglobin; RDW: red blood cell volume distribution width; Lymph %: lymphocyte percentage; Lymph #: lymphocytes count; Mono%: monocyte percentage; Mono#: monocyte count; Neut%: neutrophil percentage; Neut#: neutrophil count; Hct: hematocrit; Eos%: eosinophils percentage; Eos#: eosinophils count; Baso%: basophils percentage; Baso#: basophils count; Hb: hemoglobin; PLT#: platelet count; MPV: mean platelet volume; PDW: platelet distribution width; PCT: platelet hematocrit; P-LCR: percentage of large platelets; ALT: alanine aminotransferase; AST: aspartate aminotransferase; GGT: gamma-glutamyl transferase; TBIL: total bilirubin; DBIL: direct bilirubin; IBIL: indirect bilirubin; ALB: albumin; GLO: globulin; TP: total protein; PA: prealbumin; TBA: total bile acid; UA: uric acid; TC: total cholesterol; TG: triglycerides; HDL-C: high density lipoprotein cholesterol; LDL-C: low density lipoprotein cholesterol; Glu: glucose; LDH: lactate dehydrogenase; ALP: alkaline phosphatase; ChE: cholinesterase; AFU: α-L-fucosidase; Cys-C: cystatin; Amy: amylase; TT: thrombin time; PT: prothrombin time; APTT: activated partial thromboplastin time; AT:A: antithrombin activity; FDP: fibrinogen degradation products; Fbg: fibrinogen; PTA: prothrombin time activity; IL: interleukin; TNF: tumor necrosis factor; Ig: immunoglobulin; SpO2: SpO2 oxygen saturation.

Table 7. Descriptive statistics of parameters in the critically ill patient group

	Level	Overall	No corticosteroids therapy	Corticosteroids therapy	p
N		88	31	57	
Gender (%)	Male	40 (45.5)	13 (41.9)	27 (47.4)	0.791
	Female	48 (54.5)	18 (58.1)	30 (52.6)	
WBC #(mean (SD))		7.34 (2.69)	6.62 (2.03)	7.73 (2.93)	0.063
RBC #(mean (SD))		3.90 (0.57)	3.84 (0.58)	3.93 (0.57)	0.471
MCV (mean (SD))		89.49 (5.40)	89.08 (6.74)	89.71 (4.56)	0.604
MCHC (mean (SD))		338.87(12.08)	339.83 (13.83)	338.34 (11.10)	0.585
MCH (mean (SD))		30.35 (2.40)	30.31 (3.05)	30.37 (2.00)	0.909
RDW-CV (mean (SD))		13.40 (1.51)	13.25 (1.46)	13.49 (1.54)	0.491
RDW-SD (mean (SD))		43.09 (5.05)	42.55 (5.47)	43.39 (4.84)	0.46
Lymph % (mean (SD))		19.79 (8.27)	21.65 (7.04)	18.78 (8.75)	0.12
Lymph # (mean (SD))		1.26 (0.59)	1.38 (0.81)	1.20 (0.41)	0.183
Mono % (mean (SD))		8.49 (2.72)	9.71 (2.88)	7.82 (2.41)	0.002
Mono # (mean (SD))		0.57 (0.20)	0.61 (0.18)	0.56 (0.21)	0.244
Neut % (mean (SD))		69.48 (10.31)	65.39 (8.10)	71.70 (10.76)	0.005
Neut # (mean (SD))		5.37 (2.60)	4.44 (1.55)	5.87 (2.91)	0.013
Hct (mean (SD))		34.72 (4.74)	33.90 (4.08)	35.16 (5.05)	0.238

(*continued*)

Table 7. (*continued*)

	Level	Overall	No corticosteroids therapy	Corticosteroids therapy	p
Eos % (mean (SD))		2.31 (1.23)	2.13 (0.85)	2.48 (1.65)	0.727
Baso % (mean (SD))		0.37 (0.26)	0.53 (0.34)	0.28 (0.16)	< 0.001
Eos # (mean (SD))		0.12 (0.13)	0.17 (0.17)	0.09 (0.08)	0.003
Baso # (mean (SD))		0.02 (0.02)	0.03 (0.02)	0.02 (0.01)	< 0.001
Hb (mean (SD))		117.20(17.65)	115.17 (14.91)	118.30 (19.01)	0.43
PLT # (mean (SD))		234.50(75.56)	223.80 (72.08)	240.32 (77.38)	0.33
MPV (mean (SD))		10.83 (0.94)	11.11 (0.94)	10.69 (0.92)	0.047
PDW (mean (SD))		12.77 (2.14)	13.33 (2.11)	12.47 (2.12)	0.075
PCT (mean (SD))		0.25 (0.06)	0.25 (0.06)	0.25 (0.07)	0.638
P-LCR (mean (SD))		31.18 (7.45)	33.43 (7.60)	29.99 (7.16)	0.04
ALT (mean (SD))		36.48(86.20)	23.25 (21.56)	43.68 (105.56)	0.291
AST (mean (SD))		32.30(47.35)	28.90 (17.56)	34.15 (57.52)	0.622
GGT (mean (SD))		45.35(35.40)	32.09 (22.01)	52.56 (39.20)	0.009
TBIL (mean (SD))		10.90 (8.85)	12.38 (13.54)	10.10 (4.65)	0.25
DBIL (mean (SD))		5.30 (6.73)	6.27 (10.56)	4.78 (3.14)	0.324
IBIL (mean (SD))		5.66 (2.78)	6.13 (3.85)	5.40 (1.96)	0.245

(*continued*)

Table 7. (*continued*)

	Level	Overall	No corticosteroids therapy	Corticosteroids therapy	p
ALB (mean (SD))		34.64 (3.57)	35.01 (3.88)	34.44 (3.40)	0.481
GLO (mean (SD))		31.67 (5.17)	32.15 (5.85)	31.41 (4.79)	0.523
TP (mean (SD))		66.27 (4.75)	67.16 (5.67)	65.78 (4.14)	0.194
ALB/GLO (mean (SD))		1.15 (0.26)	1.14 (0.27)	1.15 (0.25)	0.875
PA (mean (SD))		221.13(69.33)	225.86 (84.86)	218.68 (61.34)	0.749
TBA (mean (SD))		5.78 (8.53)	8.17 (13.95)	4.52 (2.72)	0.143
Crea (mean (SD))		72.01(29.72)	75.11 (33.43)	70.33 (27.67)	0.474
Urea (mean (SD))		6.10 (3.52)	6.30 (3.30)	6.00 (3.65)	0.705
UA (mean (SD))		248.85(78.71)	262.74 (78.17)	241.30 (78.66)	0.224
TC (mean (SD))		4.01 (0.91)	3.80 (0.86)	4.13 (0.92)	0.106
TG (mean (SD))		1.54 (0.77)	1.43 (0.70)	1.61 (0.81)	0.382
HDL-C (mean (SD))		0.99 (0.35)	1.04 (0.45)	0.96 (0.28)	0.392
LDL-C (mean (SD))		2.41 (0.72)	2.32 (0.78)	2.47 (0.69)	0.461
K + (mean (SD))		4.31 (0.42)	4.31 (0.47)	4.31 (0.40)	0.983
Na + (mean (SD))		139.88 (3.13)	139.94 (2.98)	139.86 (3.24)	0.909
Cl- (mean (SD))		101.14 (3.67)	101.70 (3.71)	100.84 (3.64)	0.295

(*continued*)

Table 7. (*continued*)

	Level	Overall	No corticosteroids therapy	Corticosteroids therapy	p
Ca (mean (SD))		2.16 (0.11)	2.19 (0.12)	2.14 (0.10)	0.052
P (mean (SD))		1.04 (0.21)	1.03 (0.26)	1.04 (0.17)	0.863
Mg2 + (mean (SD))		0.83 (0.10)	0.81 (0.08)	0.84 (0.11)	0.251
Glu (mean (SD))		7.00 (2.13)	6.79 (2.48)	7.12 (1.92)	0.491
LDH (mean (SD))		294.41(212.48)	251.62 (73.04)	317.68 (256.36)	0.165
ALP (mean (SD))		72.94 (23.15)	70.67 (25.78)	74.17 (21.73)	0.501
ChE (mean (SD))		6027.11(1742.86)	6235.45 (2075.83)	5916.80 (1561.53)	0.536
AFU (mean (SD))		24.06 (7.64)	23.54 (6.93)	24.34 (8.08)	0.724
Cys-C (mean (SD))		1.28 (0.61)	1.44 (0.73)	1.19 (0.51)	0.152
Amy (mean (SD))		70.58 (28.27)	77.22 (22.26)	66.59 (31.00)	0.211
CKD-EPI (mean (SD))		87.83 (21.83)	80.76 (22.30)	91.67 (20.77)	0.024
TT (mean (SD))		16.73 (1.72)	16.81 (1.34)	16.68 (1.91)	0.734
PT (mean (SD))		14.37 (1.91)	14.69 (2.37)	14.20 (1.60)	0.253
APTT (mean (SD))		40.01 (5.67)	41.49 (6.46)	39.15 (5.03)	0.068
AT:A (mean (SD))		91.09 (14.46)	90.86 (15.10)	91.21 (14.28)	0.923
PT-INR (mean (SD))		1.12 (0.20)	1.15 (0.24)	1.10 (0.17)	0.22

(*continued*)

Table 7. (*continued*)

	Level	Overall	No corticosteroids therapy	Corticosteroids therapy	p
D-Dimer (mean (SD))		1.81 (1.62)	1.84 (1.47)	1.80 (1.72)	0.915
FDP (mean (SD))		8.35 (7.60)	9.03 (5.73)	7.97 (8.52)	0.605
Fbg (mean (SD))		4.65 (1.23)	4.72 (1.37)	4.61 (1.15)	0.686
PTA (mean (SD))		88.58 (14.72)	85.24 (15.99)	90.40 (13.79)	0.117
IL-6 (mean (SD))		42.59 (140.08)	30.29 (40.50)	50.13 (175.50)	0.566
IL-10 (mean (SD))		15.14 (22.57)	21.50 (38.96)	12.25 (8.57)	0.29
IL-8 (mean (SD))		21.92 (23.02)	25.26 (29.54)	20.02 (18.46)	0.368
TNF-α (mean (SD))		10.41 (5.52)	11.54 (6.96)	9.73 (4.37)	0.173
IL-1β (mean (SD))		16.35 (17.99)	12.67 (9.51)	19.79 (23.17)	0.295
IL-2R (mean (SD))		732.42 (495.55)	748.50 (541.31)	722.15 (469.81)	0.822
IgA (mean (SD))		2.37 (1.10)	2.74 (1.40)	2.20 (0.92)	0.163
IgG (mean (SD))		13.18 (4.78)	11.90 (3.06)	13.78 (5.34)	0.265
IgM (mean (SD))		1.11 (0.58)	0.96 (0.42)	1.18 (0.64)	0.282
C3 (mean (SD))		0.87 (0.19)	0.94 (0.24)	0.85 (0.16)	0.188
C4 (mean (SD))		0.23 (0.09)	0.24 (0.10)	0.23 (0.08)	0.796

(*continued*)

Table 7. (*continued*)

	Level	Overall	No corticosteroids therapy	Corticosteroids therapy	p
temperature (mean (SD))		36.31 (2.26)	36.79 (1.31)	36.05 (2.61)	0.144
breathe (mean (SD))		20.37 (2.23)	19.70 (1.19)	20.73 (2.56)	0.037
diastolic (mean (SD))		150.19 (714.27)	73.35 (7.10)	191.98 (887.43)	0.46
systolic (mean (SD))		126.30 (12.93)	127.43 (12.74)	125.68 (13.10)	0.547
Pulse-rate (mean (SD))		81.46 (8.40)	81.60 (7.15)	81.39 (9.07)	0.913
SpO2 (mean (SD))		96.10 (5.87)	97.69 (2.14)	95.24 (6.99)	0.061

WBC#: white blood cell count; RBC: red blood cell count; MCV: mean red blood cell volume; MCHC: mean red blood cell hemoglobin concentration; MCH: average red blood cell hemoglobin; RDW: red blood cell volume distribution width; Lymph %: lymphocyte percentage; Lymph #: lymphocytes count; Mono%: monocyte percentage; Mono#: monocyte count; Neut%: neutrophil percentage; Neut#: neutrophil count; Hct: hematocrit; Eos%: eosinophils percentage; Eos#: eosinophils count; Baso%: basophils percentage; Baso#: basophils count; Hb: hemoglobin; PLT#: platelet count; MPV: mean platelet volume; PDW: platelet distribution width; PCT: platelet hematocrit; P-LCR: percentage of large platelets; ALT: alanine aminotransferase; AST: aspartate aminotransferase; GGT: gamma-glutamyl transferase; TBIL: total bilirubin; DBIL: direct bilirubin; IBIL: indirect bilirubin; ALB: albumin; GLO: globulin; TP: total protein; PA: prealbumin; TBA: total bile acid; UA: uric acid; TC: total cholesterol; TG: triglycerides; HDL-C: high density lipoprotein cholesterol; LDL-C: low density lipoprotein cholesterol; Glu: glucose; LDH: lactate dehydrogenase; ALP: alkaline phosphatase; ChE: cholinesterase; AFU: α-L-fucosidase; Cys-C: cystatin; Amy: amylase; TT: thrombin time; PT: prothrombin time; APTT: activated partial thromboplastin time; AT:A: antithrombin activity; FDP: fibrinogen degradation products; Fbg: fibrinogen; PTA: prothrombin time activity; IL: interleukin; TNF: tumor necrosis factor; Ig: immunoglobulin; SpO2: SpO2 oxygen saturation.

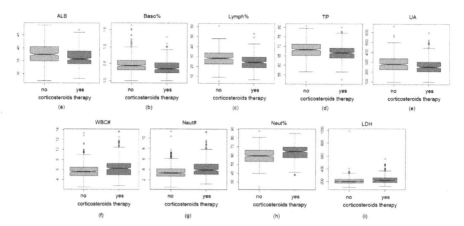

Fig. 6. Boxplot of indicators with significant differences in the severe group. Patients treated with corticosteroids have (a) lower alanine aminotransferase, (b) basophil percentage, (c) lymphocyte percentage, (d) total protein, (e) uric acid and higher (f) white blood cell count, (g) neutrophil count, (h) neutrophil percentage, and (i) lactate dehydrogenase in the severe group.

4 Discussion

Corticosteroids influence the inflammatory component of the inflammation–thrombosis–hypoxia interaction, which is beneficial in cases requiring mechanical ventilation and less effective after the development of a thrombus [22]. Corticosteroids are recommended in cases where intratympanic injections or oral medication given within a week result in a sudden hearing loss of more than 60 dB. Systemic or local corticosteroid therapy is not recommended for bacterial ENT infections [23]. Corticosteroid therapy should strike a balance between a small reduction in mortality and the potential impact of prolonged coronavirus shedding [24], and the duration of corticosteroid therapy should not be limited to 14 days [25].

While previous reports performed a 28-day survival analysis, we extended the mortality analysis to 78 days. In this prospective analysis, we collected and screened clinical data from 2243 severely ill patients and 800 critical cases among 3337 COVID-19 patients. Survival analysis demonstrates that corticosteroid therapy is not associated with a significant reduction in mortality in severely and critically ill patients. Corticosteroids should be considered in critically ill patients with severe COVID-19, but should be avoided in patients who do not require oxygen therapy [26]. Contrary to what was observed in the RECOVERY clinical trial, the absence of beneficial effects in this study may be due to biases in observational and indication data, differences in the clinical characteristics of patients, choice of corticosteroids, dose administered, concomitant antiviral or anti-inflammatory drugs, time of initiation and duration of treatment [18].

To address this controversy, efforts have been made to clarify the effectiveness of corticosteroids in ARDS through large-scale multi-center randomized controlled trials [27]. Characterization of the immune activation patterns of COVID-19 patients should provide additional insight into the timing and therapeutic effects of corticosteroids and help determine which COVID-19 patients will benefit or be harmed [28].

5 Limitations

This study has several limitations. First, sample size was large. However, many variables were involved, such as dosage, types of corticosteroid, initiation and duration of treatment, other concomitant treatments, underlining comorbidities, and demographic factors. The absence of stratification and incomplete information on certain factors associated with outcome may have led to an imbalance between the treated and control groups. Second, the study was retrospective in nature using real-world observational data outside the context of a random controlled trial. Third, small variations in standard clinical management of COVID-19 patients may not be completely excluded due to the emergency situation, which involves a wide spectrum of departments and physician specialists on ac-count of hospital reorganization and availability of resources. The data in this study are too sparse to draw any firm conclusions that may signal delayed viral clearance and in-creased secondary infection [29]. Finally, the daily evolution of inflammatory parameters during the first days after corticosteroid administration was documented in a limited number of included patients, which is insufficient to draw conclusions [30].

References

1. Naja, M., Wedderburn, L., Ciurtin, C.: COVID-19 infection in children and adolescents. Br. J. Hosp. Med. **81**(8), 1–10 (2020)
2. Rhee, E.J., Kim, J.H., Moon, S.J., et al.: Encountering COVID-19 as endocrinologists. Endocrinol. Metab. **35**(2), 197–205 (2020)
3. Fadel, R., Morrison, A.R., Vahia, A., et al.: Early short-course corticosteroids in hospitalized patients with COVID-19. Clin. Infect. Dis. **71**(16), 2114–2120 (2020)
4. Miao, Y., Fan, L., Li, J.Y.: Potential treatments for COVID-19 related cytokine storm-beyond corticosteroids. Front. Immunol. **11**, 1445 (2020)
5. Solinas, C., Perra, L., Aiello, M., et al.: A critical evaluation of glucocorticoids in the management of severe COVID-19. Cytokine Growth Factor Rev. **54**, 8–23 (2020)
6. Tlayjeh, H., Mhish, O.H., Enani, M.A., et al.: Association of corticosteroids use and outcomes in COVID-19 patients: a systematic review and meta-analysis. J. Infect. Public Health **13**(11), 1652–1663 (2020)
7. Johnson, K.M., Belfer, J.J., Peterson, G.R., et al.: Managing COVID-19 in renal transplant recipients: a review of recent literature and case supporting corticosteroid-sparing immunosuppression. Pharmacother. J. Human Pharmacol. Drug Therapy, **40**(6), 517–524 (2020)

8. Arabi, Y.M., Chrousos, G.P., Meduri, G.U.: The ten reasons why corticosteroid therapy reduces mortality in severe COVID-19. Intensive Care Med. **46**(11), 2067–2070 (2020)

9. Mattos-Silva, P., Felix, N.S., Silva, P.L., et al.: Pros and cons of corticosteroid therapy for COVID-19 patients. Respir. Physiol. Neurobiol. **280**, 103492 (2020)

10. Zhang, J., Xie, B., Hashimoto, K.: Current status of potential therapeutic candidates for the COVID-19 crisis. Brain Behav. Immun. **87**, 59–73 (2020)

11. Rizk, J.G., Kalantar-Zadeh, K., Mehra, M.R., et al.: Pharmaco-immunomodulatory therapy in COVID-19. Drugs **80**(13), 1267–1292 (2020)

12. Sanders, J.M., Monogue, M.L., Jodlowski, T.Z., et al.: Pharmacologic treatments for coronavirus disease 2019 (COVID-19): a review. JAMA **323**(18), 1824–1836 (2020)

13. Matthay, M.A., Wick, K.D.: Corticosteroids, COVID-19 pneumonia, and acute respiratory distress syndrome. J. Clin. Investig. **130**(12), 6218–6221 (2020)

14. Shang, L., Zhao, J., Hu, Y., et al.: On the use of corticosteroids for 2019-nCoV pneumonia. Lancet **395**(10225), 683–684 (2020)

15. Nicolau, D.V., Bafadhel, M.: Inhaled corticosteroids in virus pandemics: a treatment for COVID-19? Lancet Respir. Med. **8**(9), 846 (2020)

16. Singh, A., et al.: Role of corticosteroid in the management of COVID-19: a systemic review and a Clinician' perspective. Diab. Metab. Syndr. Clin. Res. Rev. **14**(5), 971–978 ((2020))

17. Yang, J.W., Yang, L., Luo, R.G., et al.: Corticosteroid administration for viral pneumonia: COVID-19 and beyond. Clin. Microbiol. Infect. **26**(9), 1171–1177 (2020)

18. Hasan, S.S., Capstick, T., Ahmed, R., et al.: Mortality in COVID-19 patients with acute respiratory distress syndrome and corticosteroids use: a systematic review and meta-analysis. Expert Rev. Respir. Med. **14**(11), 1149–1163 (2020)

19. Wu, J., Huang, J., Zhu, G., et al.: Systemic corticosteroids and mortality in severe and critical COVID-19 patients in Wuhan, China. J. Clin. Endocrinol. Metab. **105**(12), e4230–e4239 (2020)

20. Liu, Z., Li, X., Fan, G., et al.: Low-to-moderate dose corticosteroids treatment in hospitalized adults with COVID-19. Clin. Microbiol. Infect. **27**(1), 112–117 (2021)

21. Bartoletti, M., Marconi, L., Scudeller, L., et al.: Efficacy of corticosteroid treatment for hospitalized patients with severe COVID-19: a multicentre study. Clin. Microbiol. Infect. **27**(1), 105–111 (2021)

22. De Backer, D., Azoulay, E., Vincent, J.L.: Corticosteroids in severe COVID-19: a critical view of the evidence. Crit. Care **24**(1), 1–3 (2020)

23. Herman, P., Vincent, C., Winkler, C.P., et al.: Consensus statement. corticosteroid therapy in ENT in the context of the COVID-19 pandemic. Eur. Ann. Otorhinolaryngol. Head Neck Dis. **137**(4), 315–317 (2020)

24. Alijotas-Reig, J., Esteve-Valverde, E., Belizna, C., et al.: Immunomodulatory therapy for the management of severe COVID-19. Beyond the anti-viral therapy: a comprehensive review. Autoimmun. Rev. **19**(7), 102569 (2020)

25. Han, Y., Jiang, M., Xia, D., et al.: COVID-19 in a patient with long-term use of glucocorticoids: a study of a familial cluster. Clin. Immunol. **214**, 108413 (2020)

26. Pasin, L., Navalesi, P., Zangrillo, A., et al.: Corticosteroids for patients with coronavirus disease 2019 (COVID-19) with different disease severity: a meta-analysis of randomized clinical trials. J. Cardiothorac. Vasc. Anesth. **35**(2), 578–584 (2021)

27. Alexaki, V.I., Henneicke, H.: The Role of Glucocorticoids in the Management of COVID-19. Horm. Metab. Res. **53**(01), 9–15 (2021)

28. Gustine, J.N., Jones, D.: Immunopathology of Hyperinflammation in COVID-19. Am. J. Pathol. **191**(1), 4–17 (2021)

29. van Paassen, J., Vos, J.S., Hoekstra, E.M., et al.: Corticosteroid use in COVID-19 patients: a systematic review and meta-analysis on clinical outcomes. Crit. Care **24**(1), 1–22 (2020)

30. Kow, C.S., Hasan, S.S.: Glucocorticoid versus immunoglobulin in the treatment of COVID-19-associated fulminant myocarditis. Infection **48**(5), 805–806 (2020)

Big Data Analysis

Secure Cross-User Fuzzy Deduplication for Images in Cloud Storage

Xiaomei Liu[1], Xin Tang[1(✉)], Luchao Jin[1], Xiong Chen[1], Ziji Zhou[1],
and Shuai Zhang[2]

[1] School of Cyber Science and Engineering, University of International Relations,
Beijing 100091, China
xtang@uir.edu.cn
[2] Qi An Xin Technology Group Inc,
No. 334, Floor 3, Building 102, No. 28, Xinjiekou Wai Street, Xicheng District,
Beijing 10082, China

Abstract. In cloud storage, existing image fuzzy deduplication technology often adopts a cloud-based deduplication method, which, although it improves the image's deduplication efficiency, ignores the client's communication overhead. Therefore, to further reduce the bandwidth consumption caused by redundant image uploading, researchers use similar images to extract the same features and employ image features as encryption keys to achieve cross-user deduplication. Although this approach reduces the communication overhead, it increases the risk of side-channel attacks and threatens the image's privacy. Thus, this paper proposes a cross-user deduplication scheme based on image content decomposition to solve the privacy concern. Specifically, by acquiring the image's frequency characteristics, the base data representing the image's main contents and the deviation data representing the image's details are decomposed from the image. Then, we use the cross-user deduplication method for the base data deduplication and the cloud side deduplication method for the deviation data deduplication. The implementation demonstrates that the developed scheme improves the deduplication efficiency under the premise of effectively resisting side-channel attacks.

Keywords: Cloud storage · Image deduplication · Side channel attacks · Fuzzy deduplication

1 Introduction

Supported by advanced multimedia technology, much image data abounds in the applications and platforms [1–3]. As an essential storage method, cloud storage technology shelters massive image data. However, large scale of perceptually similar images, always considered duplicated or redundant, imposes high storage costs to cloud servers and huge redundant communication costs to users. Image fuzzy deduplication technologies [4–8] are effective solutions to the problem above. Since similar images share the same features, we can utilize an index which composes of various features of the image

© The Author(s), under exclusive license to Springer Nature Singapore Pte Ltd. 2022
Y. Tan and Y. Shi (Eds.): DMBD 2022, CCIS 1745, pp. 291–302, 2022.
https://doi.org/10.1007/978-981-19-8991-9_20

to identify whether it exists in the cloud. With the help of histogram [9], perceptual hash [10], and other feature extraction methods [11], the fuzzy deduplication method significantly promotes image deduplication efficiency. However, these methods bring great challenges to user privacy protection. Since the images uploaded to the cloud may contain sensitive information, such as the amount in the electronic invoice, the formula in the electronic prescription, or a person's photo identity, leakage of sensitive data leads to significant losses. To protect image security, researchers proposed a fuzzy deduplication scheme based on convergent key management [12]. However, this data encryption method imposes additional computing and storage overhead. Hence, cross-user deduplication effectively reduces communication costs [13–17], using image features as encryption keys and utilizing image ownership authentication technology to achieve cross-user deduplication of similar images. However, these algorithms cannot completely resist side-channel attacks which occurs in cross-user deduplication, where an attacker can infer content of sensitive data by monitoring the deduplication responses from the cloud.

Some researchers have recently proposed generalized deduplication methods and developed a set of secure deduplication frameworks [18–20]. Under this framework, raw data is decomposed into bases and deviations. In order to achieve confusion, only cross-user deduplication is performed on the base, while cloud side deduplication is performed on the deviation. Since the same base can be extracted from similar data with a certain probability, the attacker cannot judge the existence of the target data in the cloud according to the base's deduplication response. Thus the side-channel attack can be effectively resisted. However, such methods are only applicable to text data.

This paper proposes a cross-user generalized deduplication method appropriate for images to solve the above problems. Specifically, the suggested method uses a cross-user secure deduplication framework based on generalized deduplication and employs a perceptual hash algorithm for the base and deviation extraction to extract the same base from similar images with a high probability, improving the deduplication efficiency. Specifically, the main contributions of this paper are as follows:

1. Proposing a new image security deduplication framework. Indeed, the image is decomposed into base and deviation, where the base is deduplicated across the users, and the deviation is deduplicated in the cloud. In particular, the framework supports a base extraction scheme based on perceptual hashing. Under the proposed framework, the deterministic relationship between data existence and deduplication response is broken, and the deduplication efficiency can be effectively improved.
2. Conducting security analysis and performance verification on the proposed method and revealing that: (1) The proposed method can effectively resist side-channel attacks and protect image existing privacy. (2) The developed base extraction method can extract the same base from similar files with high probability, reducing the cloud storage overhead.

2   Related Work

In order to achieve image deduplication, Zhen et al. [7] considered an image as a binary file and then performed a sliding chunking strategy for image deduplication. This strategy is robust to image-level changes like noise but is sensitive to changes like picture resizing. Agarwala *et al.* [8] developed a secure near-identical image deduplication scheme using dual-integrity convergent encryption (DICE) protocol to improve deduplication efficiency. This scheme divides the image into chunks and applies the DICE protocol separately to each chunk instead of the whole image. However, the DICE protocol is vulnerable to offline dictionary attacks, a certain kind of side channel attack. Subsequent work suggested the fuzzy image deduplication scheme, based on the concept that the perpetually similar images are different in bit level but share the same feature vectors [9–11]. Nevertheless, these schemes cannot protect the images from the curious cloud system and malicious side channel attackers. Therefore, Li *et al.* [12] introduced a secure fuzzy image deduplication scheme. This scheme generates the signature of each image with the perceptual hash algorithm and determines the duplicate images by comparing the hamming distances between perceptual hash algorithm with a given distance. However, this scheme does not involve the ownership authentication of similar images. In paper [13], the authors proposed a client-side image fuzzy deduplication scheme that supports proof of ownership (PoW) authentication. This method achieves PoW-equipped deduplication relying on a novel similar image ownership authentication, which ensures that only the image owner can calculate the value of certain perceptual hash while the others cannot. However, the technique must set a trusted server and pay computing overhead for PoW. Takeshita *et al.* [14] designed a fuzzy deduplication scheme with a password-authenticated key exchange strategy and a secure locality-sensitive hash. Nevertheless, the deduplication should be assisted by other online users of limited availability. Li *et al.* [15] proposed SPSD, an AVG-phash based PoW-equipped fuzzy deduplication solution. AVG-phash largely reduces the computational overhead and can be easily extended to deduplication of multimedia data. However, the side channel attack threat still remains unsolved. The state-of-art fuzzy deduplication method is FuzzyDedup [16], where fuzzyMLE and fuzzyPoW are designed. FuzzyMLE cannot resist side-channel attacks, which is a potential threat inherent in client-based deduplication. However, relying on data encryption and ownership proof imposes additional computing and storage overhead and cannot entirely resist side channel attacks. Indeed, an attacker can infer sensitive data content by monitoring the traffic during deduplication.

Researchers have recently proposed a series of cross-user data deduplication techniques that resist side-channel attacks. These algorithms are primarily for text data but are employed for secure fuzzy image deduplication. For instance, Zuo *et al.* [17] proposed a chunk-level data deduplication scheme (RRCS), where one of the chunks uploaded by the client side contains sensitive information with low minimum entropy. Regardless of whether the sensitive chunk is duplicate, the cloud responds to the user side with a predefined number related to the number of the non-duplicate chunks. This strategy prevents the attacker from knowing whether the certain chunk is a duplicate or not. However, if the cloud side requires the user to upload chunks that does not contain the sensitive chunk, existential privacy will still be exposed. On this basis, Tang *et al.* [18] required the client to upload the XOR of all requested chunks regardless of sensitive chunks, achieving indistinguishable responses. In addition, the authors introduced MBOS [19], a deduplication scheme based on a marking strategy to resist side-channel attack. However, RRCS, RMDS, and MBOS cannot be applied to fuzzy image deduplication because they are sensitive to any image-level change, similar to paper [7, 8]. Some researchers have recently proposed generalized data deduplication schemes to decompose the original data into bases and deviations. For example, Tang *et al.* [20] suggested a generalized deduplication scheme--SRGDS. They proposed a detailed implementation at the content-coding level, ensuring the same template that contained generalized information could be extracted from similar files with non-negligible probability. Generalized deduplication is robust to text changes and is a potential approach to fuzzy image deduplication.

3   Proposed Secure Cross-User Fuzzy Deduplication Scheme

3.1   The Framework

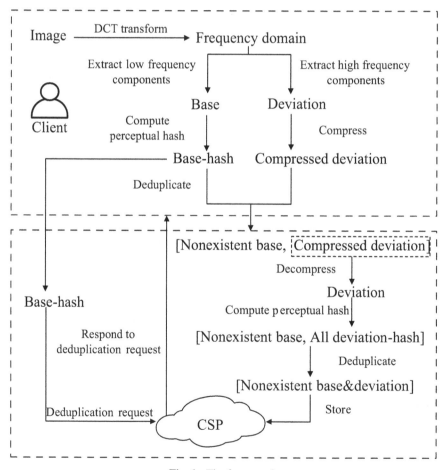

Fig. 1. The framework

This part first presents the cross-user fuzzy deduplication framework as a preparation before introducing the design in detail. Figure 1 illustrates that the client who launched the deduplication request first performs a DCT transform to the frequency domain for the original image. In the frequency domain of the original image, the low-frequency component is extracted as the base, and the high-frequency component is extracted as deviation. The base is converted to a binary sequence using a DCT-based perceptual hash algorithm, and the base hash is obtained. Next, the client sends the base hash as a deduplication request to the CSP, which receives the base hash and then checks its existence in the cloud. If this is the first request to upload an image in the whole image system, the CSP will ask the client to upload the base and deviation without deduplication. If the client requests to upload again, the CSP will return the deduplication response to the client based on the existence of the uploaded base hash in the cloud. After the client receives the deduplication response from the CSP, the client applies deduplication to the base and compresses the deviation, then uploads the deduplicated base and compressed deviations. After the CSP receives the uploaded content from the client, it first decompresses the deviation and divides the deviation into chunks of the same size as base. Then the deviation chunks converts into binary sequences by DCT-based perceptual hash algorithm to obtain deviation hash respectively, and the hash results used to compare with the deviation data already saved in the cloud. In the same way as base data processing, the cloud only retains one deviation data of a hash value. Finally, the CSP obtains the deduplicated base and deviation and stores them in the cloud.

3.2 The Proposed Scheme

The suggested deduplication process contains three key steps: (1) base extraction, (2) deviation computation, and (3) image deduplication, which will be introduced in detail.

(1) Base extraction: The DCT transform is first performed on the image, and the low-frequency component which represents the image's main data content is selected as the base data of the image. Since the perceptually similar images often having a similar data content, there's a high probability that our scheme can extract similar bases. Next, we further obfuscate the base data, using the DCT-based perceptual hashing algorithm (DCT-phash) to calculate the base data hash values. The DCT-phash algorithm first calculates the DCT mean value in the DCT matrix which derives from the whole image and compares it with each value in the matrix. If DCT mean value is less than or equal to DCT matrix value, it is recorded as '1'. Otherwise it is recorded as '0'. Thus, base data are converted into a binary sequence. Note that the dynamic base size is used in this paper, which is 1/80 of the original image.

(2) Deviation extraction: The left data after base extraction processing is deviation data. That is to say, the algorithm performs DCT transformation on image, and selects high-frequency components which represent the image's details as the deviation data. After receiving the deduplication response, the user compresses the deviation

and uploads it to the cloud. The Cloud decompresses it and dividing it into base-sized chunks. Similar to the base data, we also use the DCT-phash algorithm to calculate the deviation feature values of each chunks.

(3) Image deduplication: In our method, the base data deduplication occurs in the client side and the deviation data deduplication occur in the cloud side. The deduplication of base data can reduce communication overhead, while the deduplication of deviation data can further improve storage efficiency, under the premise of effective resistance to side channel attack. When cross-user deduplication occurs, the user first uploads the feature value of the base data to the cloud, and the cloud determines the existence of the image chunk through database retrieval. If the hash result of the feature value exists, it is determined to be a similar image, and the original base data will not be uploaded, while only the deviation data are uploaded after compression. To protect data privacy and resist side-channel attacks, the deviation data is not deduplicated in the client side. After uploading the data to the cloud, we compute the DCT-phash value of the deviation in the cloud. The results are compared in a cloud database to fuzzy deduplicate similar deviation data. In the fuzzy deduplication processing, we compare the hamming distance of DCT-phash computed with the data that have been stored on the cloud side. Here, the hamming distance parameter is set to 5.

4 Performance Evaluations

In this section, we introduce the evaluation of security and deduplication performance, comparing with the SPSD algorithm [15]. For the experiment, the server is equipped with two Intel CPU, 2 GB RAM, and a 40 GB SSD in a cloud virtual machine. Both perceptual hash and DCT functions rely on OpenCV 4.6 in Python 3.6.

4.1 Deduplication Performance

In these experiments, we specially generate an image data set that includes 1000 images originating from a template as shown in Fig. 2. We define that similar images means perceptually similar images, so every image in our data set are considered as non-similar images. For better analysis and comparison, we further apply salt noise to each original image and generate a perceptually similar image. Finally, A data set including 2000 images is formed and used in the following communication overhead and storage overhead experiments.

The communication overhead of our scheme and SPSD is illustrated in Fig. 3. It highlights that when the number of images tested increases, the deduplication rate in communication has a growing trend. Since our generalized deduplication scheme requires the uploading of all the deviations, the communication overhead in proposed scheme is less than SPSD (see Fig. 3). Despite the lower deduplication rate, our scheme is designed to ensure the security against the side channel attack at the expense of communication cost.

Next, the storage overhead is presented in Fig. 4. In this experiment, our scheme overcomes the disadvantage in communication cost because the cloud performs deduplication on the non-existent bases and the deviations uploaded additionally. In Fig. 4, our scheme deduplicates almost 60% data when more than 500 images are tested. In spite of the much lower deduplication rate than SPSD, the proposed scheme proves to be secure and efficient because the data we chose comes from two different bill patterns, one of which should not be deduplicated in our scheme. SPSD takes the two patterns as similar images, thus leading to a plausible but wrong result. Therefore, as we noticed the experiment results above, we additionally plot the error rate of SPSD. As shown in Fig. 5, the SPSD has a non-negligible possibility to be wrong in fuzzy deduplication.

xxx Corporation Company Fee Bill						
						Date: yyyy-MM-dd
Drawee	Name	xxxx	Payee	Name	xxxx	
	Account	xxxx-xxxx		Account	xxxx-xxxx	
Money	3266.25					
Remarks						

xxx Corporation Company Fee Bill						
						Date: yyyy-MM-dd
Drawee	Name	xxxx	Payee	Name	xxxx	
	Account	xxxx-xxxx		Account	xxxx-xxxx	
Money	6301.86					
Remarks						

Fig. 2. Images with sensitive message

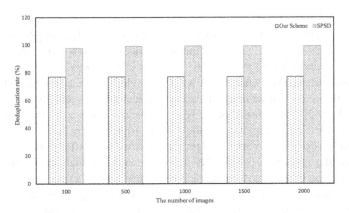

Fig. 3. Communication overhead

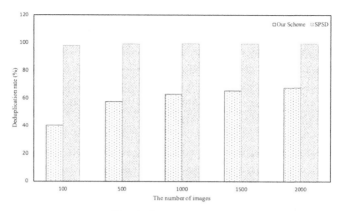

Fig. 4. Storage overhead

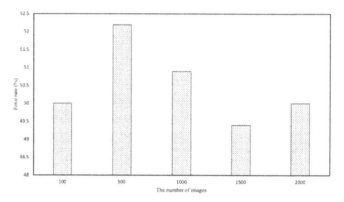

Fig. 5. Error rate of the SPSD algorithm

4.2 Security Evaluation

This part, we mainly test and verify the scheme can effectively resist the side channel attacks. We choose an employee record image and modify some sensitive information for experiments. Figure 6 shows the original image as well as the modified image, and marks the difference between two images with a red rectangle. Then, our scheme and the SPSD algorithm are used to extract image deduplication features respectively. Figures 7 and 8 compares the DCT-phash results of the base and the deviation extracted by our scheme with both images. While Fig. 9 shows the AVG-phash results by the SPSD algorithm of the two images. For the convenience of presentation, we sequentially encode every 8 bits into a block, the abscissa is the ID of each block, and the ordinate is the corresponding DCT-phash value in decimal form of each block. Due to the large size of the deviation data, Fig. 8 shows part of the results. As can be seen from Figs. 7 and 8, the same base results and different deviation results are extracted from the two images. Therefore, in the side-channel attack scenario, if the attacker only modifies the sensitive image in each deduplication request, he still needs to upload the deviation data. In the cloud side, the parted different deviation data are still retained after fuzzy deduplication processing. So, the attacker cannot obtain the existence privacy of the image. However, as shown in Fig. 9, the SPSD algorithm generate the same AVG-phash results between two images, which causes a side channel attack issue. Figure 10 shows the recovered results of two images, it proved that the image uploaded by the user can be recovered after the deduplication.

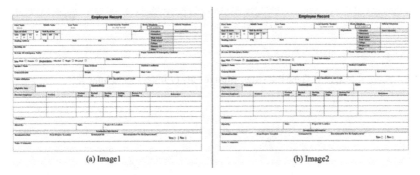

(a) Image1   (b) Image2

Fig. 6. Comparison of two images

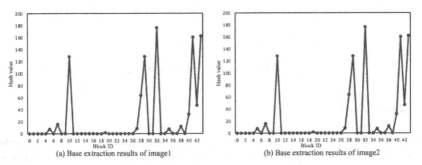

(a) Base extraction results of image1   (b) Base extraction results of image2

Fig. 7. The base extraction results of image1 and image2

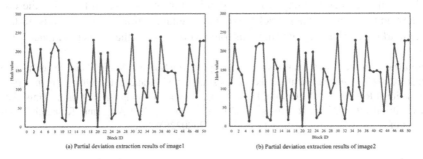

(a) Partial deviation extraction results of image1   (b) Partial deviation extraction results of image2

Fig. 8. The deviation extraction results of image1 and image2

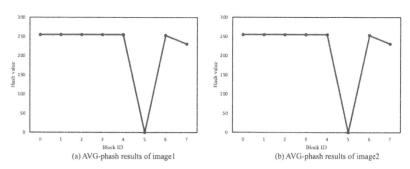

(a) AVG-phash results of image1   (b) AVG-phash results of image2

Fig. 9. The SPSD algorithm results of image1 and image2

(a) Recovered image1   (b) Recovered image2

Fig. 10. Recovered images

5   Conclusion

This paper proposes a novel cross-user deduplication scheme Specifically, we reduce the overhead and privacy protection according to the data characteristics by extracting the basis and deviation of the image content decomposition and conducting cross-user deduplication and cloud side deduplication. As the first scheme to apply the generalized deduplication theory to image fuzzy deduplication, we successfully verify the effectiveness in resisting channel attacks and image deduplication. Other methods of digital watermarking can be integrated into this framework to strengthen its performance further.

Acknowledgment. This work was specially supported by National Natural Science Foundation of China (62102113) and parted supported by Construction of advanced disciplines for University of International Relations (2021GA08), Fundamental Research Funds for the Central Universities, University of International Relations (3262022T20) and Student Academic Research Training Project of University of International Relations (3262022SWA01).

References

1. Shin, Y., Koo, D., Hur, J.: A survey of secure data deduplication schemes for cloud storage systems. ACM Comput. Surv. **49**(4), 1–38 (2017). https://doi.org/10.1145/3017428
2. Zhang, J., Bhuiyan, M., Yang, X., et al.: Trustworthy target tracking with collaborative deep reinforcement learning in EdgeAI-aided IoT. IEEE Trans. Industr. Inf. **18**(2), 1301–1309 (2022)
3. JiweiZhang, M., et al.: AntiConcealer: reliable detection of adversary concealed behaviors in EdgeAI-assisted IoT. IEEE Internet Things J. **9**(22), 22184–22193 (2022). https://doi.org/10.1109/JIOT.2021.3103138
4. Bellare, M., Keelveedhi, S., Ristenpart, T.: Message-locked encryption and secure deduplication. In: Johansson, T., Nguyen, P.Q. (eds.) Advances in Cryptology – EUROCRYPT 2013. LNCS, vol. 7881, pp. 296–312. Springer, Heidelberg (2013). https://doi.org/10.1007/978-3-642-38348-9_18
5. Gang, H., Yan, H., Xu, L.: Secure image deduplication in cloud storage. In: Khalil, I., Neuhold, E., Tjoa, A.M., DaXu, L., You, I. (eds.) Information and Communication Technology. LNCS, vol. 9357, pp. 243–251. Springer, Cham (2015). https://doi.org/10.1007/978-3-319-24315-3_25
6. Douceur, J., Adya, A., Bolosky, B., et al.: Reclaiming space from duplicate files in a server-less distributed file system. In: 22nd international conference on distributed computing systems (DCS), pp. 617–624, Vienna, Austria (2002)
7. Zheng, Y., Pan, J.: A duplicate data detection algorithm based on sliding blocking. Comput. Eng. **42**(2), 38–44 (2016)
8. Agarwala, A., Singh, P., Atrey, P.: Client side secure image deduplication using DICE protocol. In: IEEE Conference on Multimedia Information Processing and Retrieval (MIPR), pp. 412–417, Miami, USA (2018)
9. Ramaiah, P., Mohan, K.: De-duplication of photograph images using histogram refinement. In: IEEE Recent Advances in Intelligent Computational Systems (RAICS), pp. 391–395, Trivandrum, Kerala (2011)
10. Sun, Z., Lai, J., Chen, X., Tan, T. (eds.): Biometric Recognition. LNCS, vol. 7098. Springer, Heidelberg (2011). https://doi.org/10.1007/978-3-642-25449-9
11. Chen, M., Wang, Y., Zou, X., et al.: A duplicate image deduplication approach via Haar wavelet technology. In: IEEE 2nd International Conference on Cloud Computing and Intelligence Systems (CCIS), pp. 624–628, Hangzhou, China (2012)
12. Li, J., Chen, X., Li, M., et al.: Secure deduplication with efficient and reliable convergent key management. IEEE Trans. Parallel Distrib. Syst. **25**(6), 1615–1625 (2014)
13. Li, D., Yang, C., Jiang, Q., et al.: A client-based image fuzzy deduplication method supporting proof of ownership. Chinese J. Comput. **41**(6), 1267–1283 (2018)
14. Takeshita, J., Karl, R., Jung, T.: Secure single-server nearly-identical image deduplication. In: International Conference on Computer Communications and Networks (ICCCN), pp. 1–6, Honolulu, USA (2020)
15. Li, X., Li, J., Huang, F.: A secure cloud storage system supporting privacy-preserving fuzzy deduplication. Soft. Comput. **20**(4), 1437–1448 (2015). https://doi.org/10.1007/s00500-015-1596-6
16. Jiang, T., Yuan, X., Chen, Y., et al.: FuzzyDedup: secure fuzzy deduplication for cloud storage. IEEE Trans. Depend. Secur. Comput. 1–18 (2022)
17. Zuo, P., Hua, Y., Wang, C., et al.: Mitigating traffic-based side channel attacks in bandwidth-efficient cloud storage. In: IEEE International Parallel and Distributed Processing Symposium (IPDPS 2018) (2018)

18. Tang, X., Zhang, Y., Zhou, L., et al.: Request merging based cross- user deduplication for cloud storage with resistance against appending chunks attack. Chin. J. Electron. **30**(2), 199–209 (2021)
19. Tang, X., Chen, X., Zhou, R., et al.: Marking based obfuscation strategy to resist side channel attack in cross-user deduplication for cloud storage. In: IEEE International Conference on Trust, Security and Privacy in Computing and Communications (IEEE TrustCom), Wuhan, China (2022)
20. Tang, X., Liu, Z., Shao, Y., et al.: Side channel attack resistant cross-user generalized deduplication for cloud storage. In: IEEE International Conference on Communications (ICC), pp. 998–1003, Seoul, South Korea (2022)

Blockchain-Based Integrity Auditing with Secure Deduplication in Cloud Storage

Yuhua Wang[1], Xin Tang[2(✉)], Yiteng Zhou[2], Xiguang Chen[2], and Yudan Zhu[2]

[1] School of Information, Central University of Finance and Economics, Beijing 100081, China
[2] School of Cyber Science and Engineering, University of International Relations, Beijing 100091, China
xtang@uir.edu.cn

Abstract. Public auditing technology has currently been proposed to ensure the integrity of the cloud data and reduce users' overheads, which, enables users to hire a third-party auditor (TPA) for cloud data auditing. However, most existing public auditing schemes are exposed to security problems of not completely reliable TPAs, easily manipulated challenge messages, and the convenience for external adversaries to launch side-channel attacks based on audit parameters. Additionally, a large number of redundant integrity tags caused by the auditing mechanism increase the storage burden of cloud servers, and reduce the searching and auditing efficiency. Hence, aiming to solve the concern of data security and storage efficiency in cloud storage, this paper proposes a blockchain-based cloud storage integrity auditing with secure deduplication (BIAD). We distribute a random file key between different users by employing the ciphertext-policy attribute encryption (CP-ABE), and conduct secure public auditing through the blockchain combined with a bloom filter-based random challenge generation method. In particular, by applying the random key to encrypt ciphertext and integrity tags, the existence and ownership privacy of the requested file in the auditing process can be protected. The security analysis and experimental results demonstrate that compared with the state-of-the arts, the proposed scheme achieves public auditing and deduplication in a secure and lightweight way.

Keywords: Cloud storage service · Blockchain · Integrity auditing · Data deduplication · Side-channel attack

1 Introduction

Cloud storage, as a new storage mode, enables users to outsource data to remote servers, contributing to saving a lot of storage and management costs for users with limited resources [1]. However, cloud storage also presents many complications and challenges with all the convenience. Among them, the security of cloud storage is one of the key issues. Usually, users tend to delete local data to save space after outsourcing it, which indicates that users lose physical control over their data. Cloud storage data may be attacked by internal and external adversaries or damaged by uncontrollable factors [2, 3]. For example, cloud servers may delete data that is not frequently accessed to save

© The Author(s), under exclusive license to Springer Nature Singapore Pte Ltd. 2022
Y. Tan and Y. Shi (Eds.): DMBD 2022, CCIS 1745, pp. 303–318, 2022.
https://doi.org/10.1007/978-981-19-8991-9_21

cloud space. Once the user unknowingly uses incomplete data, a loss may be caused. Therefore, it is of practical significance to regularly check the integrity of cloud storage data.

In traditional public auditing schemes [4–9], users generally hire a third-party auditor (TPA) to audit their outsourced data regularly. However, these schemes have the following issues. ①TPA is not completely reliable. TPA may generate a good audit report without verifying the integrity proof for reducing the computation overhead. ②Single Point of Failure (SPoF). Once the centralized TPA is damaged by external attack or an internal failure, the auditing process cannot be normally conducted, and incorrect results may be produced [10]. Subsequently, researchers have investigated many public auditing schemes with the introduction of blockchain technology [11, 12]. Most of them adopt the Nonce value in the block to generate challenge messages and store the hash values of audit logs in the blockchain transactions. However, these methods only improve the reliability of TPA while failing to prevent collusion between malicious TPA and blockchain miners. As an improvement, a decentralized public auditing scheme based on blockchain (BDPA) [10] was proposed. It applies blockchain instead of centralized TPA and generates challenge messages relying on a smart contract. None of the above schemes considers the risk of side-channel attack [13–15]. After auditing, the auditor stores a log file that records the auditing process on the local server. In this case, the external adversary can launch a brute-force dictionary attack to predict the content of the data before using the challenge message, so as to verify the correctness of the integrity proof in the log file. The existence privacy of the file will be exposed once the verification is successful. Moreover, the ownership privacy will be compromised since the verification key used by these schemes is associated with the identity of the user.

At the same time, with the introduction of an auditing mechanism, the corresponding integrity tags will induce a considerable number of wasted storage space. In addition to the redundancy of the data itself [16, 17], due to different signature keys from distinct data owners. This inevitably increases the storage burden of the cloud server and reduces the efficiency of searching and auditing in the whole system. Therefore, the public auditing scheme with deduplication has become a research hotspot to solve the problem of storage efficiency. Then, a public auditing scheme based on Message-Locked Encryption (MLE) supporting deduplication [18] was proposed to improve storage efficiency. Nonetheless, users are required to monitor the identity of TPA by processing some audit parameters online. As a follow-up work, a novel strategy to support tag deduplication and integrity auditing [13] was designed through the aggregation strategy based on Lagrange interpolation. This scheme can resist the side-channel attack on the ownership privacy of the file. Nevertheless, it can neither perform public auditing and deduplication before the number of copies reaching the threshold nor protect the existence privacy of popular files.

Therefore, we focus on data security and storage efficiency in cloud storage services and present a blockchain-based integrity auditing with secure deduplication (BIAD). Our main contributions are summarized as follows:

- A secure public auditing framework is proposed. We replace the centralized TPA with a decentralized blockchain network to enhance the robustness of the whole auditing scheme. Moreover, to assure the randomness and reliability of the challenge message in auditing process, we combine the smart contract with a new random challenge generation method based on the bloom filter.

- The ciphertext-policy attribute encryption (CP-ABE) is introduced to support the secure deduplication of integrity tags as well as ciphertexts, thus enhancing the storage efficiency of the cloud server. Besides, the randomly generated file key is able to protect the existence and ownership privacy of files in the auditing mechanism.
- The security of BIAD is analyzed in detail and compared with the state-of-the arts in system overhead. Theoretical analysis and experimental results reveal that BIAD can lower the storage overhead of the cloud and reduce the computing and communication pressure of users. Concurrently, it further weakens the collusion risk between malicious participants in public auditing and successfully resists the side-channel attack.

2 Definitions and Preliminaries

2.1 System Model

The system model of the BIAD, as shown in Fig. 1, involves four different entities: key server (KS), user, cloud server (CS), and blockchain network.

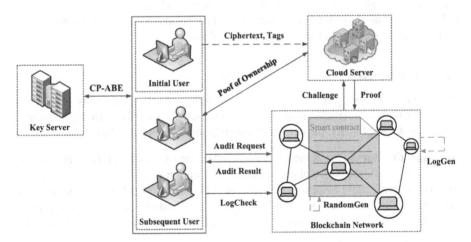

Fig. 1. System model of BIAD

- KS: The KS is a CP-ABE [19] Key Server, which is responsible for the management and issuance of each file key.
- User: The user is a data owner with limited storage and computing resources, who outsources local data to cloud server without backup. Furthermore, the user is able to entrust a TPA to audit the integrity of uploaded data and check the audit log.
- CS: The CS is an entity that provides storage services, with large storage space and strong computing power. It stores and maintains the complete outsourced data, as well

as limits the query rate of each user to reduce the risk of online brute-force dictionary attack by malicious adversaries.

- Blockchain: The blockchain is a transparent, tamper-proof distributed ledger, which provides immutable data logging services and platforms for the smart contract.

Definition 1. *BIAD mainly consists of 12 algorithms:*

- *DupDetect*. The algorithm is used to detect whether the requested file is duplicate in the cloud.
- *FileEnc*. The algorithm allows the initial user to encrypt the file with a randomly generated file key.
- *TagGen*. The algorithm generates integrity tags and the PoW tag.
- *Store*. The algorithm is used to verify and store data, and update the index list.
- *FkeyEnc*. The algorithm allows KS to encrypt the file key through CP-ABE.
- *PoWVerify*. The algorithm verifies the validity of the subsequent user.
- *RandGen*. The algorithm enables the smart contract to generate a random number.
- *ChallGen*. The algorithm generates the challenge message.
- *ProofGen*. The algorithm enables the CS to generate integrity proof.
- *ProofVerigy*. The algorithm allows the authorized verification node to verify integrity proof.
- *LogGen*. The algorithm generates the log file of the auditing process.
- *CheckLog*. The algorithm checks the behavior of the authorized verification nodes by checking the validity and correctness of log files.

2.2 Threat Model

The primarily security goal of BIAD is to protect the privacy and integrity of the data. We assume that communication between different entities cannot be externally truncated or tampered with. Finally, the current threat situation is summarized as follows:

Internal Adversary. One is the CS, a semi-honest entity, which enforces the protocol honestly, but will be curious about sensitive information of users. It tries to hide data loss by falsifying valid evidence, or delete data that users do not frequently access to save space. The other may be a blockchain node involved in generating the challenge message, which attempts to submit specially constructed values to control the final result.

External Adversary. Typically, this type of adversary is someone, who has access to the audit log files, launches brute-force dictionary attack to gain the target data privacy. Considering two scenarios now. One is that the legitimate users apply identity-related key before storing them in the cloud together with the original data. The other is they replace identity-related key with MLE key, and upload ciphertext and corresponding tags to the CS. In the first case, the adversary can directly put the predicted data into the parameter-generating equation, the privacy of the existence and ownership of the target file is compromised once the equation holds. In the second case, MLE key protects the identity of file owner, but the adversary can still steal the existence privacy by predicting the content to verify the specific equation.

2.3 Design Goals

To realize effective public auditing of cloud storage data in the above model, BIAD needs to achieve following objectives:

- Data correctness: CS must ensure that the data uploaded by the initial user is correct and complete.
- Public auditability: Only if the complete data of the user is stored correctly, can the CS pass the integrity auditing. The verification node in the blockchain cannot control the randomness of the challenge message.
- Side-channel attack resistance: The external adversaries without file key cannot launch side-channel attacks to steal the ownership privacy and the existence of target files on during the auditing.
- Robustness: By employing a blockchain instead of centralized TPA, the system is able to work properly even if some nodes in the blockchain fail unexpectedly.
- Efficiency: Not only the ciphertext, but also the corresponding integrity tag can be deleted, which further improves the efficiency of cloud storage.

3 The Proposed Scheme

3.1 Construction of BIAD

A KS, a user $\mathcal{U}$, a CS, and a blockchain are involved in setup phase, upload phase, audit phase and check phase of BIAD.

Setup Phase. Let $\mathbb{G}_1$ and $\mathbb{G}_2$ be two cyclic groups of prime order p, g and ω be two generators. Let $e : \mathbb{G}_1 \times \mathbb{G}_1 = \mathbb{G}_2$ denote a bilinear map. $H : \{0, 1\}^* \to \mathbb{G}_1$ is defined as a secure hash function and $h : \{0, 1\}^* \to \mathbb{Z}_p$ is defined as an encryption function. The system public parameter is $P = (e, p, \mathbb{G}_1, \mathbb{G}_2, g, \omega, H, h, l)$.

Upload Phase. Different upload processes are provided for different users.

– Initial user $\mathcal{U}$. The first one to upload a file F:

(1) *DupDetect*.

- $\mathcal{U}$ calculates a deduplication tag $h_F = h(F)$ and sends it to the CS.
- After receiving h_F, the CS looks for a match in an index list that records the deduplication tag and the PoW tag in the cloud. If there is no matching record, 0 is returned to indicate $\mathcal{U}$ is the first one to upload F.

(2) *FileEnc*.

- $\mathcal{U}$ chooses a random $\gamma \in \mathbb{Z}_p^*$ as a file key k_F to obtain the public key $Y = g^{k_F}$ and the ciphertext $C = E_{k_F}(F)$.

(3) TagGen.

- $\mathcal{U}$ divides C into n chunks: $C = c_1||c_2|| \cdots ||c_n$, for each chunk $c_j, j \in [1, n]$, $id_j \in \mathbb{Z}_p^*$ is the serial number. Then $\mathcal{U}$ computes S_j

$$S_j = \left(H\left(id_j\right) \cdot \omega^{c_j}\right)^{k_F} \tag{1}$$

as the id_j-chunk integrity tag and generatess a root node h_{root} (H_0) of the Merkle hash tree (MHT) [20] for F as the PoW tag. As shown in Fig. 2, MHT records hash values of plaintext chunks and connected nodes.

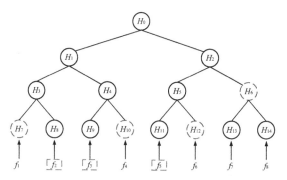

Fig. 2. The MHT of the file

- After processing all tags, $\mathcal{U}$ packs them into $\tilde{M} = \{C, \{S_j\}_{j \in [1,n]}, Y, h_F, h_{root}\}$ and uploads to the CS.

(4) *Store.*

- Upon receiving $\tilde{M}$, the CS verifies the correctness of the data according to a bi-linear equation as

$$e\left(\prod_{j=1}^{n} S_j, g\right) = e\left(\prod_{j=1}^{n} H\left(id_j\right) \cdot \omega^{c_j}, Y\right). \tag{2}$$

If holds, the CS stores C and $\{S_j\}$, and inserts h_F and h_{root} into the index list.

(5) *FkeyEnc.*

- KS maintains a CP-ABE access policy tree for each file, which takes the unique identity of a user as an attribute and assigns a private key $K_{cpabe} \in \mathbb{Z}_p^*$ related to its identity to each user. All of authorized users who possess the file are connected to the OR gate [19]. In particular, CP-ABE encrypts the random file key K_F after receiving it from the initial user and then assigns access key K_{cpabe} to each user, which enables authorized user to decrypt the encrypted K_F to assess the file.

– Subsequent user $\mathcal{U}'$. The user who uploads F later:

(1) *DupDetect.*

- This step is the same as that for the initial user. The only difference is that the CS can find a match in the index list and return 1 to claim the requested file has been stored in the cloud. That is to say, $\mathcal{U}$ needs to prove the ownership of F.

(2) *PoWVerify.*

- CS sends $\mathcal{U}'$ a challenge set $Chall_F$ of randomly selected elements from chunk indexes $[1, n]$, such as $\{2, 3, 5\}$ in Fig. 2.
- $\mathcal{U}'$ firstly generates a MHT of F and then returns the smallest set, which consists of the nodes of challenge set and auxiliary ones contributing to generate the root node. $\mathcal{U}'$ needs to return $PoW_F = \{H_6, H_7, H_8, H_9, H_{10}, H_{11}, H_{12}\}$ in Fig. 2.
- Then the CS calculates a root hash h'_{root} based on PoW_F and verifies whether h'_{root} equals to h_{root}. If so, the CS will notify the KS to distribute $\mathcal{U}'$ an identity-related private key to decrypt k_F.

Audit Phase. The blockchain performs the public auditing after receiving the audit request.

(1) *RandGen.*
- Collection of the hash value. The blockchain node who wants to participate in sends the hash of secret value [10] and a deposit to the smart contract within a specified time.
- Validation of the secret value. The node that successfully submits the hash needs to send the real secret value to the smart contract. Then the smart contract will calculate its hash value, which is compared with the previous submitted one. If they are not equal, the secret value will be deleted and the deposit will be confiscated.
- Construction of a random number. The smart contract calculates a random $\eta \in \mathbb{Z}_p$ from the valid secret value, and returns the deposit as well as reward to honest nodes respectively. At the end, the smart contract authorizes a node $\mathcal{N}$ with enough computational power depending on the random η to be the verification node [10].
(2) *ChallGen.*
- $\mathcal{N}$ selects k chunk indexes as a challenge set $L = \{l_1, l_2, \cdots, l_k\}$ according to η.
- $\mathcal{N}$ sets up k hash functions $h_i : \{0, 1\}^* \to \mathbb{Z}_p^*$, $i \in [1, k]$ based on the bloom filter [21], computes $h_i(\eta)$ to generate k challenges $v_j \in \mathbb{Z}_p^*, j \in L$, and then sends challenge message $Chall = \{(j, v_j)\}_{j \in L}$ to the CS, as shown in Fig. 3.

(3) *ProofGen.*
- CS generates integrity proof as

$$S = \prod_{j=l_1}^{l_k} S_j^{v_j} \in \mathbb{G}_1, \tag{3}$$

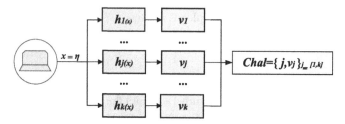

Fig. 3. The generation of challenge message based on bloom filter

$$\mu = \sum\nolimits_{j=l_1}^{l_k} v_j c_j \in \mathbb{Z}_p, \tag{4}$$

and sends $Proof = \{S, \mu\}$ to $\mathcal{N}$.

(4) *ProofVerify.*

- After receiving *Proof*, $\mathcal{N}$ verifies

$$e(S, g) = e\left(\prod\nolimits_{j=l_1}^{l_k} H(id_j)^{v_j} \cdot \omega^{\mu}, Y\right), \tag{5}$$

and returns 1 to indicate the data is complete if equation (5) holds. Otherwise, returns 0 to indicate the data is corrupted or the CS is malicious.

Check Phase. The user can check the behavior of the verification node.

(1) *LogGen.*
- $\mathcal{N}$ creates (*TaskID, Random, Bloomfilter, Chall, Proof*, 0/1) as an entry and stores all entries to a log file in chronological order as shown in Table 1, where *taskID* is the number of the smart contract. Then the hash value of the entry is calculated to store in the blockchain.

Table 1. Log file

TaskID	Random	Bloom filter	Chall	Proof	AuditResult
$taskID_1$	η_1	$h_i^1, i \in [1, k]$	$Chall_1$	(S_1, μ_1)	0/1
$taskID_2$	η_2	$h_i^2, i \in [1, k]$	$Chall_2$	(S_2, μ_2)	0/1
$\vdots$	$\vdots$	$\vdots$	$\vdots$	$\vdots$	$\vdots$

(2) *LogCheck*.

- $\mathcal{U}$ firstly checks whether the hash value stored in the blockchain matches that stored locally by $\mathcal{N}$. Secondly, it checks if the random η is the same one generated in the smart contract and verifies the challenge message. All parameters are valid only if they are validated.
- $\mathcal{U}$ selects a random subset of challenge message and generates an index set $B = \{b_1, b_2..., b_{k'}\}$ to the CS.
- CS returns integrity tags and ciphertexts of these challenged chunks.
- $\mathcal{U}$ calculates $S^{(B)} = \prod_{j=b_1,}^{b_{k'}} S_j{}^{v_j}, \mu^{(B)} = \prod_{j=b_1}^{b_{k'}} v_j C_j, j \in B$, and then verifies

$$e\left(S^{(B)}, g\right) = e\left(\prod_{j=b_1}^{b_{k'}} H\left(id_j\right)^{v_j} \cdot \omega^{\mu^{(B)}}, Y\right). \tag{6}$$

If Eq. (6) holds, $\mathcal{U}$ accepts the auditing process. Otherwise, $\mathcal{U}$ considers the auditing process is unqualified.

3.2 Security Analysis

Theorem 1. *CS must be responsible for the integrity and security of the data once the data is stored to the cloud.*

Proof. Before storing integrity tags and the data uploaded by the initial user, the CS is able to check whether the data is complete through Eq. (2):

$$
\begin{aligned}
e\left(\prod_{j=1}^{n} S_j, g\right) &= e\left(\prod_{j=1}^{n} \left(H\left(id_j\right) \cdot \omega^{c_j}\right)^{K_F}, g\right) \\
&= e\left(\prod_{j=1}^{n} H\left(id_j\right) \cdot \omega^{c_j}, g^{K_F}\right) \\
&= e\left(\prod_{j=1}^{n} H\left(id_j\right) \cdot \omega^{c_j}, Y\right).
\end{aligned}
\tag{7}
$$

If the verification holds, the CS stores the data with its related information.

Theorem 2. *BIAD is able to resist the control of random values by malicious blockchain nodes.*

Proof. As long as there is an honest blockchain node among participants when generating the random number by the smart contract, the final output is guaranteed to be unpredictable. Specifically, n involved nodes first submit the hash of the secret value, and disclose their secret value in the second step. Therefore, even if $(n - 1)$ malicious nodes collude, the secret value of the remaining node could not be predict, so the attack fails.

Theorem 3. *BIAD can prevent malicious adversaries from stealing the privacy of the specific user under side channel.*

Proof. Considering the two cases mentioned in Sect. 2.2, the root cause of the threat is that the adversary can verify whether the equation holds. Note that BIAD adopts a randomly generated file key independent from user's identity to generate integrity tags. Although the adversary has known the "v_j" in the challenge massage and the "μ" in the integrity proof through Eq. (4), the ciphertext C cannot be obtained since the file key K_F is not visible. Hence, it is hard for the adversary to steal the existence and ownership privacy of the specific file by verifying the equation.

Theorem 4. *BIAD can resist the collusion between malicious authorized verification node and the CS, and effectively check the integrity of cloud data.*

Proof. The authorized verification node obtains the challenge messages based on the bloom filter. Due to the unidirectional nature of the bloom filter, it is unable to pre-design challenge messages that satisfy malicious behavior, ensuring the strong randomness of the challenge message. During the proof verification, the node verifies the integrity proof generated by the CS according to bilinear Eq. (5):

$$
\begin{aligned}
e(S, g) &= e\left(\prod_{j=l_1}^{l_k} S_j, g \right) \\
&= e\left(\prod_{j=l_1}^{l_k} \left(\left(H\left(id_j\right) \cdot \omega^{c_j} \right)^{k_F} \right)^{v_j}, g \right) \\
&= e\left(\prod_{j=l_1}^{l_k} \left(H\left(id_j\right) \cdot \omega^{c_j} \right)^{v_j}, g^{k_F} \right) \\
&= e\left(\prod_{j=l_1}^{l_k} H\left(id_j\right)^{v_j} \cdot \omega^{\sum_{l=1}^{l_k} v_j c_j}, g^{k_F} \right) \\
&= e\left(\prod_{j=l_1}^{l_k} H\left(id_j\right)^{v_j} \cdot \omega^{\mu}, Y \right).
\end{aligned}
\tag{8}
$$

It indicates that the data is complete in the cloud once the verification is passed. Then, the node stores the hash value of the log file recording the auditing process in the block transaction. The log file is guaranteed not to be tampered with after the block is packaged and chained.

4   Performance Evaluation

All experiments are conducted on a workstation with Linux operating system Ubuntu 20.04 64-bit, CPU Intel(R) Core I5-8250U @ 3.40 GHz, memory 12 GB and hard disk 1 TB. We utilize PBC Library and Python 3.8 to code. Particularly, the length of the cyclic group $\mathbb{G}_1$ is denoted as $|\mathbb{G}_1|$ and that in $\mathbb{Z}_p$ as $|\mathbb{Z}_p|$. The system security level is chosen to be 160 bits.

We compare the performance of BIAD with One-Tag Checker [15] and ATDS [10] in terms of storage overhead, communication overhead, and computation overhead. Suppose there are $y(y > 0)$ users owning the same object file F, which is divided into n chunks of the equal size. Let k be the number of challenged chunks, s be the number of chunks within a chunk in the One-Tag Checker, and t be the threshold for triggering tag aggregation in the ATDS. To be fair, the storage and communication costs of F are not considered.

4.1 Storage Overhead

The storage overhead for these schemes is shown in Table 2. In BIAD, the CS needs to store integrity tags and related information. After subsequent users prove the ownership of the file, the KS will add an attribute to the file's access tree so that the new user will obtain the permission to access the file key. Set n to 300 and t to 40, the comparison of storage overhead is shown in Fig. 4. Compared with ATDS, BIAD and One-Tag Checker are not limited by the threshold. As we can see, there is no need to upload the auxiliary information or secondary tags to ensure private auditing before the threshold is reached, which significantly improves the storage efficiency of the CS. In addition, as the number of users increases, the storage overhead of One-Tag Checker rises, resulting in a gap with that of BIAD.

Table 2. Comparison of storage overhead

User Num	One-tag Checker [18]	ATDS [13]	BIAD
$y < t$	$n\lvert\mathbb{G}_1\rvert + 2y\lvert\mathbb{Z}_p\rvert$	$(2ny + t)\lvert\mathbb{G}_1\rvert$	$n\lvert\mathbb{G}_1\rvert + (3 + y)\lvert\mathbb{Z}_p\rvert$
$y \geq t$		$(n + t)\lvert\mathbb{G}_1\rvert$	

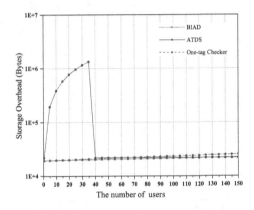

Fig. 4. Comparison of storage overhead

4.2 Communication Overhead

The communication overhead is considered during the upload and audit phase.

Upload Phase. Table 3 shows the total communication overhead of each user in this phase. Refer to the previous section for the analysis of communication overhead. Note that the PoW method is different for each scheme when subsequent users prove the ownership of files. We uniformly expressed as $\lvert PoW_F \rvert$ for the convenience since the size of PoW_F is smaller. After setting y to 1000 and 10000, n to 300, and t to 40, the communication overhead is visualized as shown in Fig. 5 (a) and (b), where the lines of BIAD and One-tag Checker almost coincide. It shows in Fig. 5(a) that when the number of users is fewer, two schemes are almost two orders of magnitude different from ATDS. And it is clear in Fig. 5(b) that as the number of users increases, two schemes gradually approach to ATDS and eventually tend to be parallel, but the communication overheads of them are always smaller than that of ATDS.

Audit Phase. The communication cost at this stage mainly depends on the size of the challenge message and the integrity proof as shown in Table 4, where special parameter in One-tag Checker is the sum of integrity tags signed by the product of the re-signed key and the challenge message. It should be noted that BIAD introduces blockchain to replace traditional TPA, so the random number $\eta \in \mathbb{Z}_p$ generated by the smart contract also needs to be transmitted.

Table 3. Comparison of communication overhead for upload phase

Comparison scheme	Total communication overhead
One-tag Checker [18]	$n\|\mathbb{G}_1\| + 2y\|\mathbb{Z}_p\| + \|PoW_F\|$
ATDS [13]	$(2nt + y)\|\mathbb{G}_1\| + \|PoW_F\|$
BIAD	$n\|\mathbb{G}_1\| + 2(1 + y)\|\mathbb{Z}_p\| + \|PoW_F\|$

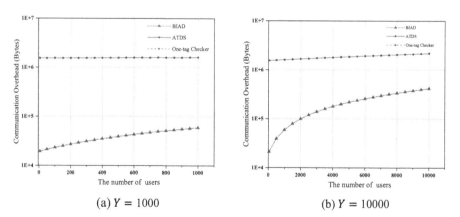

(a) $Y = 1000$ (b) $Y = 10000$

Fig. 5. Comparison of communication overhead for upload phase

Table 4. Comparison of communication overhead for audit phase

	One-tag Checker [18]	ATDS [13]	BIAD
Random	0	0	$|\mathbb{Z}_p|$
Challenge	$k(|n| + |\mathbb{Z}_p|)$	$k(|n| + |\mathbb{Z}_p|)$	$k(|n| + |\mathbb{Z}_p|)$
Proof	$k(2|\mathbb{G}_1| + s|\mathbb{Z}_p|)$	$k(|\mathbb{G}_1| + |\mathbb{Z}_p|)$	$k(|\mathbb{G}_1| + |\mathbb{Z}_p|)$
Special paras	$2|\mathbb{G}_1|$	0	0
Total	$2(k+1)|\mathbb{G}_1| + k(1 + s)|\mathbb{Z}_p| + k|n|$	$k|\mathbb{G}_1| + 2k|\mathbb{Z}_p| + k|n|$	$k|\mathbb{G}_1| + (2k+1)|\mathbb{Z}_p| + k|n|$

4.3 Computation Overhead

The notation is described as follows: $Exp_{\mathbb{G}_1}$ and $Mul_{\mathbb{G}_1}$ denote exponential operation and multiplication operation in $\mathbb{G}_1$. $Mul_{\mathbb{Z}_p}$ and $Add_{\mathbb{Z}_p}$ denote multiplication operation and addition operation in $\mathbb{Z}_p$. *Pair* denotes bilinear pairing operations. $Hash_{\mathbb{G}_1}$ and $Hash_{\mathbb{Z}_p}$ denote hash *function H* $: \{0, 1\}^* \rightarrow \mathbb{G}_1$ and $h : \{0, 1\}^* \rightarrow \mathbb{Z}_p$ respectively.

Upload Phase. The computation overhead in this phase is mainly from tag generation, as shown in Table 5. In BIAD, the MHT of the file for $(2n-1)$ times $Hash_{\mathbb{Z}_p}$. Additionally, the initial user needs to generate integrity tags. Set y to 10000, t to 40, and s to 40. The total computation overhead for 100 users is shown in Fig. 4. It is visualized that BIAD performs better, almost 1 order of magnitude less than that of One-tag Checker and almost 2 orders of magnitude less than that of ATDS (Fig. 6).

Table 5. Comparison of computation overhead on user side for upload phase.

Comparison scheme	Total computation overhead
One-tag Checker [18]	$n(s+1)Exp_{\mathbb{G}_1} + nsMul_{\mathbb{G}_1} + nHash_{\mathbb{G}_1} + 2yMul_{\mathbb{Z}_p} + yAdd_{\mathbb{Z}_p}$
ATDS [13]	$(2ny + 2nt + t)Exp_{\mathbb{G}_1} + (2ny - y + t)Mul_{\mathbb{G}_1} + n(y+t)Hash_{\mathbb{G}_1}$
BIAD	$2nExp_{\mathbb{G}_1} + nMul_{\mathbb{G}_1} + nHash_{\mathbb{G}_1} + 2yHash_{\mathbb{Z}_p}$

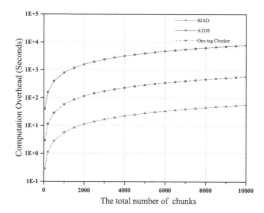

Fig. 6. Comparison of computation overhead for upload phase

Table 6. Comparison of computation overhead on user side for upload phase.

Comparison schemes	Proof generation	Proof verification
One-tag Checker [18]	$2kExp_{\mathbb{G}_1} + 2(k-1)Mul_{\mathbb{G}_1} + (2k+s)Mul_{\mathbb{Z}_p} + s(k-1)Add_{\mathbb{Z}_p}$	$2Pair + (k+s)Exp_{\mathbb{G}_1} + (k+s-1)Mul_{\mathbb{G}_1} + kHash_{\mathbb{G}_1}$
ATDS [13]	$kExp_{\mathbb{G}_1} + (k-1)Mul_{\mathbb{G}_1} + kMul_{\mathbb{Z}_p} + (k-1)Add_{\mathbb{Z}_p}$	$kExp_{\mathbb{G}_1} + (k-1)Mul_{\mathbb{G}_1} + kMul_{\mathbb{Z}_p} + (k-1)Add_{\mathbb{Z}_p}$
BIAD	$kExp_{\mathbb{G}_1} + (k-1)Mul_{\mathbb{G}_1} + kMul_{\mathbb{Z}_p} + (k-1)Add_{\mathbb{Z}_p}$	$kExp_{\mathbb{G}_1} + (k-1)Mul_{\mathbb{G}_1} + kMul_{\mathbb{Z}_p} + (k-1)Add_{\mathbb{Z}_p}$

Audit Phase. The computation overhead at this phase is mainly produced from auditing verification, as shown in Table 6. It should be noticed that during proof verification, One-tag Checker requires the user to generate key parameters for TPA online. In ATDS, the user can only perform private auditing to resist side-channel attack until the threshold is reached. While in BIAD, the auditing is always performed by the verification node, so as to the user's computation overhead keeps 0. Obviously, not only reducing the computational pressure, BIAD truly achieves public auditing, which is more practical.

5   Conclusion

In order to settle down the problem of data security and storage efficiency of cloud storage services, we propose a blockchain-based integrity auditing scheme with secure deduplication in cloud storage. On the one hand, the MHT-based PoW achieves secure deduplication at the user side, and CP-ABE controls the access to the file key. On the other hand, a combination of blockchain and bloom filter produces reliable challenge messages. It is worth mentioning that BIAD offers indirect protection against side-channel attack by employing the randomly generated file key. Finally, the security of

BIAD is analyzed in detail and its performance is evaluated comprehensively through comparative experiments. The results show that the scheme provides a strong security guarantee under cost-controllable condition.

Acknowledgements. This work was supported by National Natural Science Foundation of China (62102113), Student Academic Support Program of University of International Relations (3262022SWA02), and Research Funds for NSD Construction of University of International Relations (2021GA08).

References

1. Qi, Y., Tang, X., Huang, Y.: Enabling efficient batch updating verification for multi-versioned data in cloud storage. Chin. J. Electron. **28**(2), 377–385 (2019)
2. Zhang, J., et al.: AntiConcealer: reliable detection of adversary concealed behaviors in EdgeAI assisted IoT. IEEE Internet of Things Journal (2021)
3. Tang, X., Zhou, Y., Cheng, Y., Shao, Y.: Weighted average-based complexity calculation in block selection oriented reversible data hiding. Security and Communication Networks **2022**, 1–15 (2022)
4. Wang, Q., Wang, C., Li, J., Ren, K., Lou, W.: Enabling public verifiability and data dynamics for storage security in cloud computing. In: Backes, M., Ning, P. (eds.) ESORICS 2009. LNCS, vol. 5789, pp. 355–370. Springer, Heidelberg (2009). https://doi.org/10.1007/978-3-642-04444-1_22
5. Wang, C., Chow, S.S.M., Wang, Q., et al.: Privacy-preserving public auditing for secure cloud storage. IEEE Trans. Comput. **62**(2), 362–375 (2011)
6. Tang, X., Qi, Y., Huang, Y.: Reputation audit in multi-cloud storage through integrity verification and data dynamics. In: Proceedings of the IEEE 9th International Conference on Cloud Computing (IEEE CLOUD), San Francisco, CA, USA, pp. 624–631 (2016)
7. Qi, Y., Tang, X., Huang, Y.: Enabling efficient verification of dynamic data possession and batch updating in cloud storage. KSII Trans. Internet Inf. Syst. **12**(6), 2429–2449 (2018)
8. Tang, X., Qi, Y., Chang, C., Zhou, L.: Efficient real-time integrity auditing with privacy-preserving arbitration for images in cloud storage system. IEEE Access. **7**, 33009–33023 (2019)
9. Zhang, J., Bhuiyan, M., Yang, X., Singh, A.: Trustworthy target tracking with collaborative deep reinforcement learning in EdgeAI-Aided IoT. IEEE Trans. Industr. Inf. **18**(2), 1301–1309 (2022)
10. Shu, J., Zou, X., Jia, X., et al.: Blockchain-based decentralized public auditing for cloud storage. IEEE Trans. Cloud Comput. (2021). https://doi.org/10.1109/TCC.202-1.3051622
11. Zhang, Y., Xu, C., Lin, X., et al.: Blockchain-based public integrity verification for cloud storage against procrastinating auditors. IEEE Trans. Cloud Comput. **9**(3), 923–937 (2019)
12. Xue, J., Xu, C., Zhao, J., Ma, J.: Identity-based public auditing for cloud storage systems against malicious auditors via blockchain. Sci. China Inf. Sci. **62**(3), 1–16 (2019). https://doi.org/10.1007/s11432-018-9462-0
13. Tang, X., Zhou, L., Hu, B., et al.: Aggregation-based tag deduplication for cloud storage with resistance against side channel attack. Secur. Commun. Netw. **2021**, 1–15 (2021)
14. Tang, X., Chen, X., Zhou, R., Sui, L., Zhou, T.: Marking based obfuscation strategy to resist side channel attack in cross-user deduplication for cloud storage. In: Proceedings of the 21th IEEE International Conference on Trust, security and Privacy in Computing and Communications (IEEE TrustCom), Wuhan, China (2022)

15. Tang, X., Liu, Z., Shao, Y., Di, H.: Side channel attack resistant cross-user generalized deduplication for cloud storage. In: Proceedings of the IEEE International Conference on Communications (IEEE ICC), Seoul, South Korea, pp. 998–1003 (2022)
16. Tang, X., Zhou, L., Huang, Y., Chang, C.: Efficient cross-user deduplication of encrypted data through re-encryption. In: Proceedings of the 17th IEEE International Conference on Trust, Security and Privacy in Computing and Communications (IEEE TrustCom), New York, USA, pp. 897–904 (2018)
17. Tang, X., Zhang, Y., Zhou, L., Liu, D., Hu, B.: Request merging based cross-user deduplication for cloud storage with resistance against appending chunks attack. Chin. J. Electron. **30**(2), 199–209 (2021)
18. Liu, X., Sun, W., Lou, W., et al.: One-tag checker: message-locked integrity auditing on encrypted cloud deduplication storage. In: Proceedings of the IEEE Conference on Computer Communications (INFOCOM WKSHPS), Atlanta, GA, USA, pp. 1–9 (2017)
19. Bethencourt, J., Sahai, A., Waters, B.: Ciphertext-policy attribute-based encryption. In: 2007 IEEE Symposium on Security and Privacy (IEE S&P), California, USA, pp. 321–334 (2007)
20. Shai, H., Danny, H., Benny, P., Alexandra, S.: Proofs of ownership in remote storage systems. In: Proceedings of the 18th ACM Conference on Computer and Communications Security (ACM CCS), Chicago, Illinois, USA, pp. 491–500 (2011)
21. Byun, H., Lim, H.: Functional bloom filter, better than hash tables. In: Proceedings of 2018 International Conference on Electronics, Information, and Communication (ICEIC), Hawaii, USA, pp. 1–3 (2018)

Name Disambiguation Based on Entity Relationship Graph in Big Data

Gengsong Li[1], Hongmei Li[2], Yu Pan[3], Xiang Li[2], Yi Liu[2], Qibin Zheng[2(✉)], and Xingchun Diao[1]

[1] Defense Innovation Institute, Beijing 100071, China
[2] Academy of Military Sciences, Beijing 100091, China
Zhengqibin1990@163.com
[3] Command and Control Engineering College, Army Engineering University of PLA, Nanjing 210007, China

Abstract. Aiming at the problem of insufficient utilization of author information and low accuracy of the existing name disambiguation methods, a name disambiguation method based on commonly used author information entity relationship graph is proposed. The entity relationship graph is constructed according to the information of the co-authors and the authors' affiliated institutions, years of birth, gender and degrees, and the edges in the graph is divided into two categories: the vertices in the first type edges are the authors, and the vertices in the second type edges must include any one of the affiliated institution, year of birth, gender and degree. The connection strength of two authors with the same name in the graph is calculated by following steps: first, the length of the paths is limited; second, the first type edges and the second type edges are searched respectively in the graph; then, the connection strengths of different types of paths are calculated and normalized according to the number and the length of paths, and weighted summed to obtain the connection strength between two authors; finally, the obtained connection strength is compared with the threshold to realize name disambiguation. The experimental results show that the proposed method has higher accuracy than baselines.

Keywords: Data quality · Name disambiguation · Entity relationship graph · Accuracy · Big data

1 Introduction

In the era of big data, overwhelming data has brought a new challenge: there may be different representations of the same objective entity in the same or different data sets, causing a decrease in data quality. Entity Resolution is to distinguish different data object representations of the same objective entity [1–3]. Name Resolution is an important research content of entity resolution, which mainly focuses on human name resolution, place name resolution and organization name resolution. Human name resolution mainly includes the identification of the same name corresponding to different people, that is,

© The Author(s), under exclusive license to Springer Nature Singapore Pte Ltd. 2022
Y. Tan and Y. Shi (Eds.): DMBD 2022, CCIS 1745, pp. 319–329, 2022.
https://doi.org/10.1007/978-981-19-8991-9_22

Name Disambiguation, and the identification of multiple different names corresponding to the same person [4–6]. This paper mainly studies the problem of name disambiguation.

Due to China's large population, the problem of name disambiguation in Chinese people becomes very outstanding [7]. For example, when using "My Nanjing APP" to query the same name, the result shows that there are as many as 3190 people named "Zhang Wei" in Nanjing. In literature retrieval process, the ambiguity of the name easily leads to the decline of the retrieval accuracy, which troubles users a lot. And it will also affect the attribution of scientific research results. Therefore, identifying different author entities with the same name and correctly assigning their academic achievements to the corresponding author is very important, which can significantly improve the academic transparency of researchers and correctly evaluating their research ability.

Currently, existing name disambiguation methods can be divided into supervised methods and unsupervised methods [8–10]. The supervised methods mainly train a classification model to realize name disambiguation, and the unsupervised methods calculate the similarity between the authors with the same name to judge whether two authors are the same author. The DISTINCT method is a supervised method, it calculates the connection strengths of the paths between two authors through random walk probability according to the authors' information, such as the co-authors, research fields, journal or conference names and publication places, and then obtains the weights of different paths by training a Support Vector Machine (SVM) classifier. According to the weights of different paths, the connection strength between the two authors is calculated to realize name disambiguation [11, 12]. A GrapHical framewOrk for Name diStincTion (GHOST) method based on co-authors is an unsupervised method [13]. The GHOST method constructs a graph based on the cooperative relationship between authors, then searches the effective paths between the authors in the graph; and calculates the similarity between the authors according to the number and length of effective paths by using the parallel resistance similarity function, and compares the similarity with the set threshold to achieve the name disambiguation [14, 15]. Since GHOST only uses co-author information, if there is no co-author information in the literature, the method may not work. Therefore, Shang et al. proposed a Co-author and Affiliate Based Name Disambiguation (CoAAND) method based on the information of co-authors and affiliated institutions [16]. According to the cooperative relationship between authors and the membership relationship between authors and affiliated institutions in literature records, the connection strength between two authors with the same name is obtained by searching the effective paths of two authors in the graph [17], and the connection strength is compared with the set threshold to disambiguate the same name. In the above methods, if there are no co-authors in the two papers published by the same author and they belong to two different affiliated institutions in the two papers, the CoAAND method will judge that there are two people, which reduces the method accuracy.

In order to improve the accuracy of name disambiguation, this paper proposes a name disambiguation method based on commonly used author information. The entity relationship graph is constructed by using the information of the co-authors and the authors' affiliated institutions, years of birth, gender and degrees. The paths in the graph are divided into two types and searched respectively with a length constraint: the vertices in the first type paths are the authors, and the vertices in the second type paths include authors' affiliated institution, year of birth, gender and degree. The connection strengths of paths are calculated and normalized according to the number and the length of paths between the authors to be disambiguated. Then, the obtained connection strengths are weighted summed and compared with the set threshold value to judge whether the authors to be disambiguated are the same author entity. Compared with the methods mentioned above, NDAP can utilize the author information more effectively even when part of author information is missing.

Section 2 introduces the name disambiguation method based on commonly used author information, Sect. 3 carries out experiments, and Sect. 4 summarizes the work of this paper.

2 The Name Disambiguation Method Based on Commonly Used Author Information

To improve the accuracy of name disambiguation, we propose a Name Disambiguation method based on Author Profile (NDAP), which mainly use the commonly used information of the authors to disambiguate the same names.

2.1 Construct Entity Relationship Graph

The entity relationship graph is represented as $G = (V, E)$, where V is the set of vertices and $V = A \cup O \cup Y \cup D \cup S$, in which $A = \{a_1, a_2, ..., a_m\}$ is the set of all authors' names, and the authors to be disambiguated are distinguished by names with numbers; $O = \{o_1, o_2, ..., o_s\}$ is the set of authors' affiliated institutions, $Y = \{y_1, y_2, ..., y_k\}$ is the set of authors' years of birth, $D = \{$bachelor, master, doctor$\}$ is the set of authors' degrees, $S = \{$male, female$\}$ is the set of authors' gender, E is the set of edges. If there is a cooperative relationship between authors in a paper, then connect these two vertices of authors by the first type edge. And the vertex of an author is connected with the vertices of his affiliated institution, year of birth, gender, degree through the second type edges. This paper does not consider co-authors with the same name.

Assuming the paper information as in Table 1 and the author to be disambiguated is Li Na, then an entity relationship graph can be constructed as shown in Fig. 1.

Table 1. Author's common information and published papers

Paper	Authors with their affiliated institutions, years of birth, gender and degrees
p_1	Li Na(o_1, 1977, female, doctor), Ji Xiaobing((o_1, o_3), 1976, male, doctor), Zhang Lin(o_1, 1961, male, doctor)
p_2	Li Na(o_2, 1971, female, doctor), Chen Xiaohui(o_2, 1988, male, master)
p_3	Li Na(o_3, 1977, female, doctor), Ji Xiaobing(o_1, 1976, male, doctor), Zhang Lin(o_1, 1961, male, doctor)

(continued)

Table 1. (*continued*)

Paper	Authors with their affiliated institutions, years of birth, gender and degrees
p_4	Li Na(o_4, 1987, female, master), Li Yifan(o_4, 1966, male, doctor), Wang Hong(o_4, 1988, female, master)
p_5	Li Na(o_4, 1987, female, master), Li Yifan(o_4, 1966, male, doctor), Wang Hong(o_4, 1988, female, doctor), Zhang Yinxia(o_4, 1985, female, doctor)

In Table 1, p is the published paper, and other contents are the commonly used author information, where o represents the affiliated institutions of the authors.

In Fig. 1, vertex set V includes all authors' names, affiliated institutions, years of birth, degrees and gender, and two vertices are connected when they both are authors

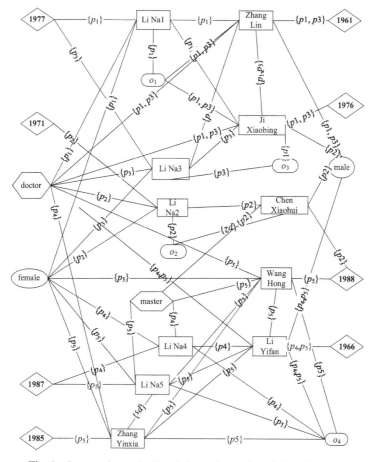

Fig. 1. Commonly used author information entity relationship graph

and have cooperated in a paper or one vertex is the author information of another author vertex.

If two authors to be disambiguated are the same author entity, their affiliated institutions, degrees, gender and years of birth are generally the same, and their co-authors are relatively fixed, that is, there are paths connected in the figure, and the more paths and shorter lengths, the more likely they are to correspond to the same author entity [18].

2.2 Calculate Connection Strength between Authors

In this section, the connection strength of two authors is calculated as follows:

1. Distinguish Path Types. As there are many types of vertices, one path may include vertices of different types. As shown in Fig. 1, there exists the path "Li Na 1 - Doctor - Ji Xiaobing - Li Na 3", which includes vertices of degree and co-author. Because different types of edges contribute differently to the authors' name disambiguation, the accuracy and efficiency of searching can be improved by limiting the edge type in a path. Meanwhile, for one author entity, he may have multiple co-authors, but his affiliated institution, year of birth, degree and gender may be relatively fixed. Therefore, this paper divides the paths into two categories. The first type path only contains the first type edges, namely the co-author type edges; and the second type path consists of the second type edges, that is the edge type of author name - affiliated institution, author name - year of birth, author name - gender, and author name - degree.
2. Path Length Limitation. For two authors to be disambiguated a_s and a_e, the breadth-first search strategy is adopted to search the paths between two vertices of a_s and a_e in the graph. As shown in Fig. 1, there are two paths from "Li Na 4" to "Li Na 5": "Li Na 4 - Li Yifan - Li Na 5" and "Li Na 4 - Li Yifan - Wang Hong - Zhang Yinxia - Li Na 5", and the latter one is obviously longer. The longer the path is, the less it can contribute to disambiguation, and the higher its search time complexity is. By limiting the path length, the search efficiency can be improved and has little influence on the disambiguation performance, so the path lengths of two path types are limited within a certain range respectively.
3. Calculation of Connection Strength. The connection strength is the sum of the path connection strength of all paths between two vertices. Suppose $R_1 = \{P_1, P_2, ..., P_L\}$ is the set of the first type paths between a_s and a_e whose length are not greater than 4, $R_2 = \{P'_1 P'_2, , ..., P'_M\}$ is the set of second type paths between a_s and a_e whose length are not greater than 2. P_i ($P_i \in R_1$) and P_j ($P_j \in R_2$) are the paths between a_s and a_e, N_{P_i} is the length of path P_i and N_{P_j} the length of path P_j. Then, the connection strength between a_s and a_e is calculated by following formulas.

$$cs(a_s, a_e) = \omega_1 \sum_{P_i \in R_1} \frac{1}{N_{p_i}} + \omega_2 \sum_{P_j \in R_2} \frac{1}{N_{p_j}} \tag{1}$$

$$\text{s.t. } \omega_1 + \omega_2 = 1 \tag{2}$$

$$\omega_1, \omega_2 \geq 0 \tag{3}$$

where, $cs(a_s, a_e)$ is the connection strength between a_s and a_e, ω_1 is the weight of the first type paths, $\sum_{P_i \in R_1} \frac{1}{N_{P_i}}$ is the sum of the connection strengths of the first type paths, ω_2 is the weight of the second type paths, $\sum_{P_j \in R_2} \frac{1}{N_{P_j}}$ is the sum of the connection strengths of the second type paths.

Assume that the path between two authors to be disambiguated, "Li Na 1" and "Li Na 3", is shown in Fig. 2. "Zhang Lin" and "Ji Xiaobing" are the co-authors of "Li Na 1" and "Li Na 3", and the affiliated institutions of "Li Na 1" and "Li Na 3" are o_1 and o_3 respectively.

In Fig. 2, the breadth-first search is conducted for the first type paths between "Li Na 1" and "Li Na 3", and the result paths are "Li Na 1 - Ji Xiaobing - Li Na 3", "Li Na 1 - Zhang Lin - Li Na 3" and "Li Na 1 - Ji Xiaobing - Zhang Lin - Li Na 3". Then the connection strength of each path is calculated as 1/2, 1/2, 1/3, respectively. The second type paths between "Li Na 1" and "Li Na 3" are "Li Na 1 - Doctor - Li Na 3", "Li Na 1 - female - Li Na 3" and "Li Na 1 - 1977 - Li Na 3". And the connection strength of each path is 1/2, 1/2, 1/2 respectively. After obtaining the connection strength of the two types of paths respectively, the connection strength between "Li Na 1" and "Li Na 3" is obtained by using Formula (4) to (5), and then compared with the set threshold to judge whether "Li Na 1" and "Li Na 3" are the same author.

The pseudo-code of NDAP is given in Algorithm 1:

Algorithm 1 The pseudo-code of NDAP.

Input：Paper record data, author profile information, threshold δ and number of authors to be disambiguated len

Output：Set of authors corresponding to the same author C

1. Graph G is constructed according to the information of co-authors, affiliated institutions, years of birth, gender and degrees
2. Set the length limitation of the first type path to 4 and the length limitation of the second type path to 2
3. For (i=1: len)
4.   For (j=(i+1): len)
5.   Search for the first type paths between a_i and a_j, and store them in path set R_1.
6.   Search for the second type paths between a_i and a_j, and store them in path set R_2.
7.   Use Formula (6) to (7) to calculate and normalize the connection strengths of paths in R_1 and R_2 respectively, and weighted sum the connection strengths of paths to obtain the connection strength $cs(a_i, a_j)$ between a_i and a_j
8.   If $cs(a_i, a_j) > \delta$
9.   Add a_i and a_j to the set of the same author C
10.   End
11.   End
12. End

In algorithm 1, step 1 constructs an entity relationship graph based on the paper record data and author profile information; step 2 defines the search limitations for the two types of paths in the graph; steps 3 to 7 search the two types of paths and obtain the normalized connection strengths of paths between each pair of two authors, and weighted sum the connection strengths of paths to get the connection strength between the two authors; steps 8 to 9 compare the connection strength between two authors with the set threshold, if the connection strength is larger than the threshold, then the two authors are the same author, otherwise not.

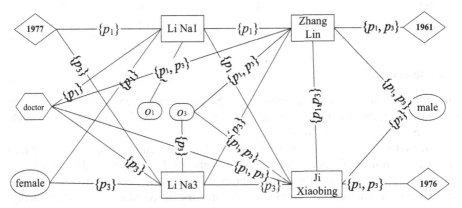

Fig. 2. Example of author information entity relationship

3 Experiments

3.1 Experiments Data Sets

In order to verify the effectiveness of the proposed method, the information of authors to be disambiguated is obtained from WanFang[1] database for test experiments.

The paper records of authors "Zhang Hui", "Li Wei", "Wang Wei", "Li Dan" and "Yang Jing" are obtained from WanFang database. The information of co-authors and affiliated institutions, years of birth, gender and degrees is derived according to the paper records. The detailed information is shown in Table 2.

---

[1] https://www.wanfangdata.com.cn.

Table 2. The statistical information of author information in paper records

Name	Number of papers	Number of authors	Number of co-authors	Number of affiliated institutions
Zhang Hui	50	9	574	158
Li Wei	71	10	1723	537
Wang Wei	146	13	1666	370
Li Dan	74	7	864	227
Yang Jing	150	6	1026	212

3.2 Baselines

To verify the effectiveness and superiority of NDAP method, a comparative experiment is conducted with DISTINCT method and CoAAND method. The settings of methods in the experiment are as follows:

Method A: DISTINCT method in reference [11]. The method constructs the data into a graph. Then it measures the connection strengths of the paths between two vertices in the graph by the random walk probability. Next, the weights of different types of paths between two vertices are obtained by training an SVM classifier. And finally, the connection strengths are weighted summed and compared with the set threshold to achieve the name disambiguation.

Method B: CoAAND method in reference [16]. This method first constructs entity relationship graph of authors by using the co-authors' names and affiliated institutions, then uses breadth-first search strategy to search the effective paths between the authors in the graph. According to the number and the type of effective paths, the connection strength between two authors is calculated and compared with the threshold, hence realizing the disambiguation of the same name.

Method C: the NDAP method proposed in this paper. In this method, the weight of the first type paths ω_1 is set to 0.4, and the weight of the second type paths is set to 0.6.

3.3 Evaluation Indicators

For name disambiguation, Recall, Precision and F1 values are commonly used to measure the disambiguation performance. Suppose N1 is the number of authors with the same name to be disambiguated in the dataset, N2 is the number of authors with the same name being disambiguated by the methods, and Nc is the number of authors with the same name being correctly disambiguated by the methods. Then, recall value R, precision value P and F1 value can be calculated by following formulas:

$$R = \frac{N_c}{N_1} \times 100\% \tag{8}$$

$$P = \frac{N_c}{N_2} \times 100\% \tag{9}$$

$$F_1 = \frac{2 \times P \times R}{P + R} \times 100\% \qquad (10)$$

where a greater indicator value represents a better method performance.

3.4 Results

DISTINCT, CoAAND and NDAP methods are used to disambiguate the author entities in the data sets in Table 2. And the mean and variance results of the methods are obtained and listed in Table 3.

Table 3. Experiment results

Name	Method	$R(\%)$	$P(\%)$	$F_1(\%)$
Zhang Hui	DISTINCT	60.93 ± 7.81	73.58 ± 9.22	66.66 ± 8.95
	CoAAND	73.47 ± 6.09	**100 ± 0**	84.68 ± 2.74
	NDAP	**87.1 ± 10.98**	**100 ± 0**	**92.95 ± 2.66**
Li Wei	DISTINCT	50.85 ± 8.58	67.42 ± 6.61	57.9 ± 8.24
	CoAAND	65.14 ± 3.22	84.07 ± 9.04	73.35 ± 5.93
	NDAP	**68.76 ± 13.3**	**100.00 ± 0**	**81.42 ± 10.8**
Wang Wei	DISTINCT	53.39 ± 4.22	62.02 ± 0.83	56.77 ± 1.32
	CoAAND	72.85 ± 12.11	75.00 ± 4.18	73.80 ± 6.91
	NDAP	**80.07 ± 4.29**	**82.01 ± 1.76**	**81.9 ± 3.08**
Li Dan	DISTINCT	33.69 ± 3.69	61.81 ± 11.12	44.19 ± 5.62
	CoAAND	47.63 ± 5.97	62.37 ± 5.66	53.99 ± 1.98
	NDAP	**66.3 ± 5.96**	**96.74 ± 14.24**	**78.66 ± 7.27**
Yang Jing	DISTINCT	30.57 ± 2.14	66.46 ± 2.49	41.88 ± 2.67
	CoAAND	52.06 ± 11.09	**95.78 ± 8.06**	67.9 ± 12.25
	NDAP	**95.42 ± 1.5**	95.75 ± 1.08	**95.2 ± 0.14**

It can be seen from Table 3 that the recall, precision and F_1 values of NDAP method are greater than those of CoAAND method and DISTINCT method, except that CoAAND has a better precision value on the data set of authors "Yang Jing", indicating the superiority and effectiveness of NDAP method over other methods.

Table 3 shows that NDAP method is better than CoAAND method and DISTINCT method. The reasons may be as follows:

1. The CoAAND method only utilizes the co-authors and affiliated institutions information of the authors with the same name, whose information amount is less than NDAP method. In addition, when the same author belongs to different institutions, CoAAND cannot judge that the authors are the same author entity, yet NDAP can overcome this problem.

2. The DISTINCT method needs more information such as research field, published journal, conference name, publication place and so on to achieve better performance. Besides, the method adopts the random walk probability to calculate the connection strength, which is insufficient to reflect the connection strength between the authors. The experiment results show that the NDAP method proposed in this paper needs less information while having better disambiguation performance than DISTINCT method, representing that NDAP has better applicability.

4   Conclusions

Aiming at the problem of inadequate utilization of author information and low accuracy of the existing name disambiguation methods, a name disambiguation method based on commonly used author information entity relationship graph, namely, NDAP is proposed. The NDAP method first constructs an entity relationship graph according to the information of the co-authors and the authors' affiliated institutions, years of birth, gender and degrees. Next, it divides the edges and paths in the graph into two categories: the vertices of the first type edge only contain the authors and the vertices of the second type edge must include any of the affiliated institutions, years of birth, gender and degrees; the first type path only consists of the first type edges and the second type path only consists of the second type edges. Then it limits the length of the different types of paths to reduce the time complexity of searching, and search the paths by using the breadth first searching strategy. At last, the connection strength of two authors with the same name in the graph is obtained by weighted summing the connection strengths of the paths between the two authors. The NDAP method is compared with CoAAND method and DISTINCT method, and the results show that the proposed method has a better performance. Further analyzing the results, NDAP has the following 3 advantages:

1. In the process of name disambiguation, author similarity cannot be measured directly, so the author information data is transformed into a graph, and the paths between the authors in the graph are found through the breadth first search method, which overcomes the influence of heterogeneous features of authors.
2. The corresponding entity relationship graph constructed according to the commonly used author information can effectively reflect the connection strength between two authors with the same name, which improves the accuracy when determining whether the two authors in the graph are the same entity.
3. The calculation efficiency is improved by setting the path length limitations of different path types in the graph, which makes the proposed name disambiguation method simpler and more efficient.

Acknowledgements. This work was supported by the National Science Foundation for Young Scientists of China (No. 62106281).

References

1. Tan, M.C., Diao, X.C., Cao, J.J.: Survey on entity resolution. computer. Science **41**(4), 9–12 (2017)
2. Simonini, G., Zecchini, L., Bergamaschi, S., et al.: Entity resolution on-demand. Proc. VLDB Endowment **15**(7), 1506–1518 (2022)
3. Li, B.-H., Liu, Y., Zhang, A.-M., Wang, W.-H., Wan, S.: A survey on blocking technology of entity resolution. J. Comput. Sci. Technol. **35**(4), 769–793 (2020). https://doi.org/10.1007/s11390-020-0350-4
4. Hussain, I., Asghar, S.: A survey of author name disambiguation techniques: 2010–2016. Knowl. Eng. Rev. **32**, E22 (2017)
5. Delgado, A.D., Montalvo, S., Unanue, R.M., et al.: A survey of person name disambiguation on the web. IEEE Access **6**, 59496–59514 (2018)
6. Kim, J., Owen-Smith, J.: Model reuse in machine learning for author name disambiguation: an exploration of transfer learning. IEEE Access **8**, 188378–188389 (2020)
7. Yao, Y., Wang, S.H.: The Author's name standard control and identification analysis and discussion of scientific journals. Chin. J. Sci. Tech. Periodicals **26**(1), 41–46 (2018)
8. Kim, J., Kim, J., Owen-Smith, J.: Generating automatically labeled data for author name disambiguation: an iterative clustering method. Scientometrics **118**(1), 253–280 (2018). https://doi.org/10.1007/s11192-018-2968-3
9. Rehs, A.: A supervised machine learning approach to author disambiguation in the Web of Science. J. Informet. **15**(3), 101166 (2021)
10. Alokaili, A., Menai, M.E.B.: SVM ensembles for named entity disambiguation. Computing **102**(4), 1051–1076 (2019). https://doi.org/10.1007/s00607-019-00748-x
11. Yin, X., Han, J., Yu, P.S.: Object distinction: distinguishing objects with identical names. In: 2007 IEEE 23rd International Conference on Data Engineering, pp. 1242–1246. IEEE, NJ, USA (2007)
12. Fakhri, M., Philipp, M.: Using Co-authorship networks for author name disambiguation. In: 2016 IEEE/ACM Joint Conference on Digital Libraries, pp. 261–262. IEEE, NJ, USA (2018)
13. Santini, C., Gesese, G.A., Peroni, S., et al.: A knowledge graph embeddings based approach for author name disambiguation using literals. Scientometrics **127**, 4887–4912 (2022)
14. Chen, Y., Jiang, Z., Gao, J., Du, H., Gao, L., Li, Z.: A supervised and distributed framework for cold-start author disambiguation in large-scale publications. Neural Comput. Appl. (2021). https://doi.org/10.1007/s00521-020-05684-y
15. Tan, M.C., Diao, X.C., Cao, J.J.: Relationship type based connection strength model for relationship-based entity resolution. J. Comput. Inf. Syst. **11**(16), 5947–5957 (2015)
16. Shang, Y.L., Cao, J.J., Li, H.M., et al.: Co-Author and affiliate based name disambiguation method. Comput. Sci. **45**(11), 227–232 (2018)
17. Xu, R.F., Gui, L., Lu, Q.: Incorporating multi-kernel function and internet verification for chinese person name disambiguation. Front. Comp. Sci. **10**(6), 1–13 (2018)
18. Li, Y.P.: Bibliometric analysis and name disambiguation research based on knowledge clustering. Nanjing Univ. Posts Telecommun., Nanjing (2019)

Ontology-Based Metadata Model Design of Data Governance System

Hong Yan[✉], Jing Wang, and Yu Zhou

Nanjing Research Institute of Electronics Engineering, Nanjing 210023, China
2428806758@qq.com

Abstract. Data as an important asset, its governance problem gradually high-lighted. Metadata as an important data technology means of data governance, its model is of great significance for sharing, exchanging, understanding, discovering, and interoperating data. This paper based on the ontology method, integrates various metadata models and proposes a metadata model system for the data governance lifecycle to promoting the construction of cross-domain data sharing space.

Keywords: Metamodel · Data governance · Ontology · Structure metadata · Discovery metadata

1 Introduction

Data, as an important asset, its governance, management, sharing and exchange are no longer limited to a certain enterprise or field, and have become an important issue faced by the country and the whole society. With the promotion and practice of the Open Government Data (OGD) in the global scope, data can be transferred and applied in a larger range. The influence and value of data gradually emerge [1], contributing to the development of social [2], political [3], economic [4] and environmental [5], etc. Data opening ability has become an important embodiment of national competitiveness [6].

With the development of big data, how to realize the discoverability, comprehension, and interoperability of massive data in the cross-domain data space, and how to support the understanding and automatic processing of humans and machines has become an urgent problem to be solved. Cloud, Big Data, Artificial Intelligence and other technologies cannot improve the capabilities of the data itself. Metadata, as the data to describe the data, is an important method and technical approach for the effective description and management of the data space and the goal of improving the capabilities of the data itself [7, 8]. In the construction of the portal website of open government data, the description and management of open data sets through metadata has become one of the core functions of the open data portal. Among them, metadata model, namely metamodel, is the core and key of metadata management system and metadata interoperability, such as the most famous W3C Open Data Metadata Cataloging DCAT standard [9].

Where there is data, there must be a need for metadata construction. Therefore, the governance and management of the data lifecycle also puts forward higher and

© The Author(s), under exclusive license to Springer Nature Singapore Pte Ltd. 2022
Y. Tan and Y. Shi (Eds.): DMBD 2022, CCIS 1745, pp. 330–342, 2022.
https://doi.org/10.1007/978-981-19-8991-9_23

more comprehensive requirements for metadata construction and management. From the perspective of ontology, facing the requirements for the description of data feature and the governance of data, this paper reorganizes and synthesizes the existing metadata models, and proposes a framework of metadata model system in governing data.

2 Metadata Model Technology

2.1 Metadata Model Classification

Metadata model is a model that describes metadata. With the construction and development of metadata in various fields, the research and achievements of metadata model are constantly improved and developed. There are also many methods for the classification of metadata.

United States Department of Defense divides metadata into structure metadata, discovery metadata and application metadata in its data strategy [7, 8].The companies like Huawei divides metadata into technical metadata, business metadata, and operational metadata [10].

In the ISO/IEC 19583-1:2019 (Information technology – Concepts and usage of metadata Part 1: Metadata concepts) [11] published by the International Organization for Standardization in 2019, metadata can be mainly divided into structure metadata, descriptive metadata and management metadata according to its different functions. So no matter which classification method, from a functional point of view, there are mainly three categories:

1) About the description of the data composition structure, the description of the semantic structure of the data to improve the understandability and interoperability of the data, this metadata is called structure metadata in this paper, such as Huawei's technical metadata, registered metadata object in ISO/IEC 11179-3 [12], metadata for digital still images in ANSI/NISO Z39.87 [13], geographic information metadata in ISO/IEC 19115-1 [14], etc., all belong to this type of metadata.

2) The description of the external characteristics and content of the data, the metadata used to discover and identify the content, this metadata is called the discovery metadata in this paper, such as the descriptive metadata in ISO/IEC 19583-1 [11], the famous DC metadata [15], the discovery metadata of the US military [7, 8], W3C's DCAT [9], etc., all belong to this kind of metadata.

3) Metadata required for data management and application, which is used for data exchange management, right confirmation management, value and quality evaluation, etc., this metadata is called management metadata in this paper, such as management metadata in ISO/IEC 19583-1 [11], and W3C's PROV-DM [16] for data provenance management are all belong to this kind of metadata.

2.2 Structure Metadata Model

Structure metadata models can generally be divided into two categories:

1) Dedicated structure metadata, usually such metadata models are released synchronously with specific data model standards, such as ①the metamodel used with Joint

C3 Information Exchange Data Model (JC3IEDM) of NATO Multilateral Interoperability Program (MIP) [17], which is specially used to describe the logical data model and physical data model of JC3IEDM; ②National Information Exchange Model (NIEM) [18, 19] jointly implemented by the US Department of Homeland Security and the Department of Justice, the structure domain of the model quotes common syntax and basic data types of XML Schema to support describing the generic, public and business domain of NIEM.

2) General structure metadata, this kind of metadata model is more abstract, such as ISO/IEC 11179-3:2013 (Information Technology Metadata Registry (MDR) Part 3: Metadata model and Basic Attributes of a Registry) [12] standards the conceptual model of a metadata registry and a set of basic attributes when a full registry solution is not required; And the not yet officially published ISO/IEC 11179-7:2019 Information technology – Metadata registries (MDR) Part 7: Dataset [20], extensions to the metadata model of the dataset package based on Part 3.

2.3 Discovery Metadata Model

Discovery metadata was first developed from Dublin metadata and developed in various fields; this brought about the problem of metadata interoperability and promoted the development of W3C standards for metadata cataloging.

Dublin Metadata Standard. The Dublin Core Element Set (DC) was jointly initiated by the Online Library Center (OCLC) and the National Center for Supercomputing Applications (NCSA) in March 1995 [21]. The members of the development team are computer scientists, network experts and library experts from the two institutions mentioned above, and the purpose is to establish a widely applicable set of metadata elements that can describe any network data asset and facilitate storage, retrieval, passing and retrieving data assets, and simple enough that any author can create metadata for their own files without specialized training.

W3C Open Data Metadata Catalog DCAT. W3C's   Data   Catalog   Vocabulary (DCAT) [9] is an RDF vocabulary designed to facilitate interoperability between data catalogs published on the Web. DCAT enables publishers to describe datasets and data services in catalogs using standard models and vocabularies, facilitating the consumption and aggregation of metadata from multiple catalogs to increase the discoverability of datasets and data services. It is also possible to use a distributed approach to publish data catalogs and use the same query mechanism and structure for federated searches of datasets in catalogs across multiple sites.

DCAT was earliest (2010) developed by the Digital Enterprise Research Institute (DERI) of the National University of Ireland Galway. DERI analyzed metadata of seven open data platforms including the United States, the United Kingdom, Australia, New Zealand, Ireland, London and San Francisco. Then, the initial framework of DCAT was built [22]. In 2012, it was further improved by the W3C's Government Linked Data Working Group. In 2014, DCAT was released as one of the three official W3C Recommendations on linked data (such as DCAT version 1.0); 2020 The 2nd edition of

DCAT 2 will be released in February 2020; the 3rd edition of DCAT 3 will be released in July 2022. According to the current OGD metadata standard, DCAT is the most widely used metadata vocabulary. The standards in the United States and Europe are designed based on DCAT, while the United Kingdom and Australia regard it as an important part of the standard and support the description of DCAT [23, 24].

2.4 Management Metadata Model

Provenance Metadata Standard. There are also several standards and models for the provenance metadata model, including ① the open provenance model (OPM) was first proposed in 2008 to solve the problem of source interoperability [25]; ②the Provenir model adopts an ontology-based approach to Expressing traceability information and using OWL-DL to define common traceability terms and relationships [26], Provenir has been widely used in biological sciences, oceans, sensors, and health care; ③In April 2013, the Provenance Working Group (Provenance Working Group, PWG) released the first traceability standard PROV [16], which became a key milestone in the global Internet information traceability specification. PROV-DM is the core document of PROV. It defines a general and domain-independent traceability model, including core structure and extension structure. The core structure is shown in Fig. 1.

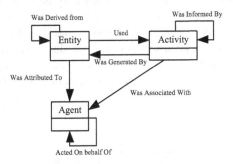

Fig. 1. The core structure of PROV data model

The core structure of PROV-DM includes 3 basic elements, namely, the identifiable Entity, the processing Activity and the involved Agent. And there may be seven kinds of relationships between these three elements, namely Generation, Usage, Communication, Derivation, Attribution, Association and Delegation. Through this model, the causal relationship of the development of things, the role of the participants, the attribution of responsibility, the derivative process, etc. can be explained.

Quality Metadata Standards. DCAT establishes a metadata model in the form of an ontology (that is, an RDF vocabulary). The revised version is based on the original ontology and draws on some practices from other metadata, and introduces new classes and new attributes, which not only integrates the W3C traceability ontology PROV-O, also introduces quality metadata. DCAT 1.1 introduces the dct:conformsTo attribute for dcat:Resource (including dcat:Dataset, dcat:Distribution, and dcat:DataService) to describe the consistency of data with standards (such as high-quality data), and its value filed is dcat:Standard. When describing richer quality information, it is necessary to introduce the "DataQualityVocabulary" (DQV) and the traceability ontology PROV-O. [27].

DQV is developed by the W3C "Web Data Best Practices Working Group" (Data on the Web Best Practices Working Group), which supplements the dcat:dataset class with attributes such as dqv:hasqualitymeasurement (quality measurement is), and introduces dqv:qualitymeasurement (quality measurement), dqv:metric (quality indicator) and new classes such as dqv:dimension (quality dimension).

2.5 The Data Reference Model of FEA

In 2002, the White House Office of Management and Budget (OMB) established the Enterprise Architecture Project Management Office (FEA-PMO) specializing in the development of federal enterprise architecture, and established and released the OMB "Enterprise Architecture Assessment Framework v3.0" to guide the federal government improves its investment in information technology toward sharing reusable information technology resources across the whole federal government. Among them, the FEA reference model is the core content of the entire enterprise architecture. The Data Reference Model (DRM) [28] framework model of FEA as shown in Fig. 2, combines the description of the data model, context information, and shared exchange management, etc. The data description model abstracts various products involved in the field of data description standards at a high level of abstraction, so that a consensus on the description of data is generated within the community of interests or among them. The data context

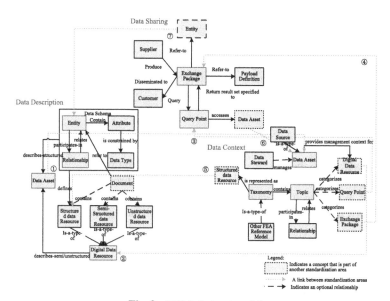

Fig. 2. DRM abstract model

(Context) is used to add information to the data related to the purpose for which it is used and created, so that it is convenient for data consumers to discover and use the data from different perspectives. Information exchange usually refers to a relatively fixed and frequently occurring information exchange process between information producers and information consumers, and for the use of information, in addition to the exchange of information, the information producers as information sources often need to externally provide interfaces and services for access various information, and this is the ability to access capability.

Throughout the development of metamodel technology at home and abroad, the metamodel shows a trend of integrative development based on ontology. First, the metamodel gradually returns to the ontology, such as the ontology extension in the W3C traceability standard PROV, metadata cataloging DCAT and other standards, which taking the data object as an entity, and treating it as an activity, etc. Second, the mutual integration, such as DCAT includes PROV and quality metadata, etc. In the ISO/IEC 11179-7 data sets is added, which reflects the mutual reference and integration development of different standard systems.

3 Metadata System Architecture

3.1 Data Governance System Requirements

The International Data Management Association (DAMA) released DAMA-DMBOK2 [29] in 2017, divides the data lifecycle into three major stages: Plan & Design, Enable & Maintain, and Use & Enhance, as shown in Fig. 3. At the same time, it also points out that metadata is an important technical means to manage the lifecycle of data.

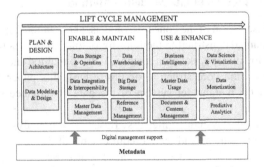

Fig. 3. Data lifecycle management functional framework

The data lifecycle governance and management is mainly divided into the following stages: the modeling stage is also the stage for develop the information system. The research unit of the information system establishes the structure metadata of the data and submits it for deployment and use as part of the information system; In the production stage, all kinds of sharable data generated by the information system are mainly extracted and converted by the data producer, and the discovery metadata is established, submitted for registration and published to the relevant data center of metadata registration and management system; In the registration stage, the main Data registration and management departments of various data centers at all levels and types, examine, check the conformity and approve the registration of data and its metadata; In the application stage, the requirements for exchanging data are mainly initiated by users of various types of data, and the data center examines and approves the use of the requirements for exchanging data; In the management stage, the data centers at all levels and various types of data evaluate and manage the quality and value of data, as shown in Fig. 4.

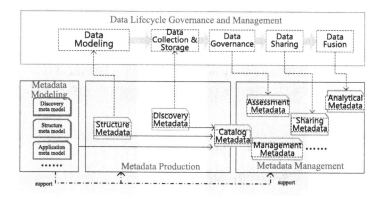

Fig. 4. Data lifecycle governance and management and its metadata relationship diagram

3.2 Based on Ontology Metadata Modeling Method

An ontology is a description of the concepts, objects, and relationships within a domain. Commonly used manual construction methods for ontology construction include TOVE method, Methontoloy method, skeleton method, IDEF-5 method and seven-step method [30–32],etc. Base on the core structure of PROV-DM, this paper adopts seven-step method to construct a metamodel system of the data governance system. The main steps include:

1) Establish a model system framework. Based on the analysis of metadata construction content requirements and model requirements of the data governance system, a metamodel architecture for the data governance is proposed.

2) Determine the professional field and category of ontology. The metamodel researched and proposed in this paper is a general core metamodel framework for the field of data governance.

3) Examine the possibility of reusing existing ontology or ontology fragments. The main function of ontology is to solve the problem of knowledge sharing and reuse. Through comparative analysis, the core meta-model of PROV-DM has great reference value and reusable value.

4) List important terms in the ontology. Important concepts in the field of data governance management include data entities, data agents, and data activities.

5) Define classes and class hierarchy. In the field of data governance, classes can be divided into data entities, data execution agents, data processing activities, etc. Data executive agents can be classified as people, organizations, or software services. Data processing activities can be classified as data modeling, data collection, data storage, data evaluation, etc.

6) Define the attributes of the class and the facets of the attributes. Establish the classification relationship of the concepts in the data governance field, and on this basis, add the attribute values of the classification concepts to the classification concepts; create the object instances that constitute the ontology. The main attributes of data entities include semantic structure, external data characteristics, data category, etc.

7) On the basis of the core model, it is evolved and derived for the specific process of data governance.

3.3 Metadata Model System

Focusing on data modeling, data collecting and storage, data governance and management, data sharing and exchange, and data fusing and applications, refer to PROV-DM to build core metamodel such as DataEntity, ExecuteAgent, and DataActivity, as shown in Fig. 5. DataEntity can be further derived as DataSet or DataService. StructureMetadata can describe the semantics and structure of structured or semi-structured DataSet, and DiscoveryMetadata can describe the external characteristics and data classification of DataEntity. DataActivity mainly includes attributes such as the time (DataTime), place(SpatialInfo), and related parameters(Params) of activities. And UserAgent can also be derived as Organization and AppSystem.

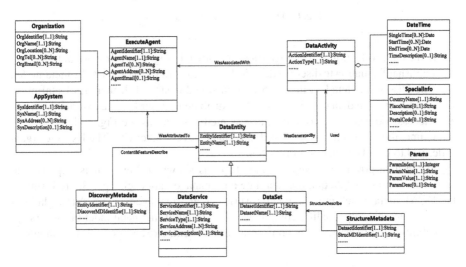

Fig. 5. Metadata model framework

In the data modeling stage, as shown in Fig. 4, it is important to describe the data model and register management. Referring to ISO/IEC 11179-3 [12] and NATO JC3IEDM metamodels [17], the StructureMetadata in Fig. 5 is refined and designed. It includes Entity (and its EntityRelationship), DataElement, and DataElementDomain (includes DomainValues), as the Fig. 6 shown. At the same time, the DataActivity is derived into DataModelingActivity. The ExecuteAgent is derived to be a Developer.

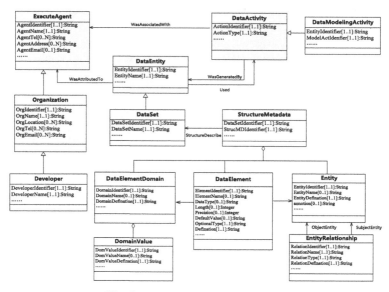

Fig. 6. Data structure metadata model

In the data collection and storage stage, as shown in Fig. 4, it is important to register and publish information to discover data. Referring to PORV-DM and DCAT metamodel, etc., the DiscoveryMetadata in Fig. 5 is refined and designed. It includes DataEntity-Content to describe data classification, DataAttribute to describe data external features, and AccessAddress to describe data access methods, etc. as the Fig. 7 shows. At the same time, the DataActivity is derived into DataCollectionActivity. The Execute Agent is derived to be a Provider and Publisher.

In the data governance and sharing stage, as shown in Fig. 4, it is important to assess and improve data quality, facilitate and manage data exchange. So, referring to the DCAT metamodel, etc., oriented governance and management for data right confirmation, traceability, quality, compliance, etc., to build the metamodel of ownership, traceability, quality assessment, conformity assessment, etc. and as the Fig. 8 shows.

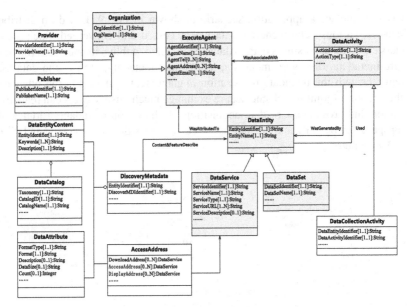

Fig. 7. Data discovery metadata model

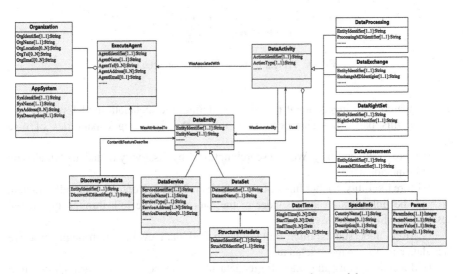

Fig. 8. Data governance management metadata model

4 Experimental Results and Analysis

Based on metadata model system, we have developed a metadata registry for data assets. The system can register the structure metadata and discovery metadata of data assets and evaluate the compliance of these metadata.

A typical metadata application scenario is shown in Fig. 9. Based on distributed data centers, various heterogeneous data was accessed and converged. Such as, data providers encapsulate business data to data assets. Then, publish its metadata (including structure metadata, discovery metadata, assessment metadata, etc.) to the data assets catalogue through the metadata registration management system. On the other hand, with the support of joint search and secure exchange mechanisms, users can realize data exploration and cross-network data acquisition. So based on metadata, a logical data sharing space can be built, and the data assets can be cross-domain accessed and utilized across data centers.

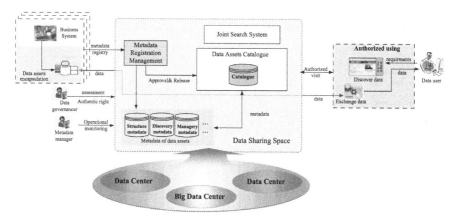

Fig. 9. Typical metadata application scenario

Compared with independent metadata modeling, the metadata model system proposed in this paper has significantly improved the following capabilities of data assets:

1) More discoverability. We can search not only by discovery metadata, but also by structure metadata.

2) More likability. Richer links can be established through ontology-based metadata, such as the link through the provider of the data assets, the link through the spatial description of the data assets, etc.

3) More understandability. Better understand data evolution through structure metadata and provenance metadata.

4) More data quality guarantee. Better data quality can be promoted through structure metadata for comparison with standards, etc.

5   Conclusion

Similar to the importance of the data model for data, the metadata model is also crucial to the construction and development of metadata. The early metadata was relatively simple, but in a continuous development environment of data governance and government data openness, metadata modeling faces higher and more comprehensive requirements, such as supporting the construction of networked data sharing space, traceability and manageable of data in its whole lifecycle (from data collection, cleaning and conversion, classification and cataloging, publishing and sharing, analysis and mining, etc.), and supporting the interoperability of cross-domain metadata. Basing on the ontology of management data resources with metadata, this paper presents a metadata model architecture, and explores the techniques and methods of metadata integration. So to support realizes data governance and management, and promote the construction of cross-domain data sharing space.

References

1. Fu, X., Zheng, L.: Value measurement of Open Government Data: comparative study of features and methods. Libr. Inf. Serv. **64**(19), 140–152 (2020)
2. Sunlight Foundation.: The social impact of open data. http://assets.sunlightfoundation.com. s3.amazonaws.com/policy/SocialImpactofOpenData.pdf
3. Open data barometer.: Open data barometer-global report 4th edition. http://opendatabaro meter.org/
4. McKinsey.: Open data: unlocking innovation and performance with liquid information. http://www.mckinsey.com/~/media/McKinsey/Business%20Functions/McKinsey%20Digi tal/Our%20Insights/Open%20data%20Unlocking%20innovation%20and%performance% 20with%liquid%information/MGI_Open_data_FullReport_oct2013.ashx
5. Carrara, W., Chan, W.S., Fischer, S., et al.: Creating value through open data: study on the impact of re-use of public data resources. http://www.europeandataportal.eu/sites/default/ files/edp_creating_value_through_open_data_0.pdf
6. Zhang, H., Wang, Z.: A comparative study of foreign Open Government Data. Intell. Mag. **34**(8), 142–146 (2015)
7. DoD Data Strategy. http://ipoipo.cn/post/10665.html, 2020/10/08
8. Department of Defense Net-Centric Data Strategy. http://www.researchgate.net/publication/ 235178063_Department_of_Defense_Net-Centric_Data_Strategy, 2003/05/09
9. Data Catalog Vocabulary (DCAT)-revised edition. https://www.w3.org/TR/vocab-dcat-2/
10. Huawei data management department.: Enterprise data at HUAWEI. 1st edn. China Machine Press, Beijing (2020)
11. ISO/IEC 19583-1:2019 Information technology – Concepts and usage of metadata Part 1: Metadata concepts. http://www.doc88/p-6827308980719.html
12. ISO/IEC 11179-3:2013 Information technology--Metadata registries (MDR)—Part 3: Registry metamodel and basic attributes. http://metadata-standards.org/11179/ (Part 3)
13. ANSI/NISO Z39.87-2006 (R2017) Data Dictionary-Technical Metadata for Digital Still Images. https://www.niso.org/publications/ansiniso-z3987-2006-r2017-data-dictionary-technical-metadata-digital-still-miages
14. ISO 19115-1/Amd 1:2018: Geographic information – Metadata – Part1: Fundamentals – Amendment 1. http://www.iso.org/standard/73118.html
15. Dublin Core. http://dublincore.org/documents/dces/
16. W3C Provenance Working Group.: Provenance Working Group Wiki Main Page. http://www. w3.org/2011/prov/wiki/Main_page
17. MIP JC3IEDM Metamodel. https://military-history.fandom.com/wiki/JC3IEDM
18. National Information Exchange Model. http://niem.github.io/reference/content/
19. Dai, J., et al.: Methods and Technologies of Cross Domain Information Exchange, 2nd edn. Publishing house of electronics industry, Beijing (2021)

20. ISO/IEC 11179-7:2019 Information technology — Metadata registries (MDR) — Part 7: Metamodel for data set registration. https://www.iso.org/standard/68766.html
21. Dublin core TM metadata element set. https://www.dublincore.org/specifications/dublin-core/dces/
22. Maali, F., Cyganiak, R., Peristeras, V.: Enabling interoperability of government data catalogues. In: 9th International Conference on Electronic Government, pp. 339–350. Lausanne, Switzerland (2010)
23. Wu, L., Huang, Y.: The development of study of metadata standards of open government data platform. Res. Libr. Sci. **6**, 14–21 (2017)
24. Xie, Z., Jun, Z., Li, H.: Construction progress of W3C metadata standard DCAT for open data and enlightenment. J. Intell. **38** (11) 167–174 (2019)
25. Moreau, L., Clifford, B., Freire, J., et al.: The Open provenance model core specification (v1.1). Futur. Gener. Comput. Syst. **27**(6), 743–756 (2011)
26. Provenir Ontology. http://wiki.knoesis.org/index.php/Provenir_Ontology
27. Data on the web best practices: Data quality vocabulary. https://www.w3.org/TR/vocab-dqv/
28. Federal Enterprise Architecure – The Data Reference Model Ver 2.0. https://www.doc88.com/p-696925718857.html
29. DAMA International.: The DAMA Guide to the Data Management Body of Knowledge. 2nd edn. Technics Publications (2017)
30. Ma, W.: Research on construction method of domain ontology. https://blog.csdn.net/u013263092/article/details/46327689
31. Wang, H., Kan, Y., Wu, W., et al.: Knowledge representation, representation learning and knowledge reasoning for multi-modal situational awareness. Command. Inf. Syst. Technol. **13**(3), 1–11 (2022)
32. Lan Chaozhen, L., Wanjie, L.L.: Construction and application of space object situation domain ontology Command. Inf. Syst. Technol. **12**(1), 34–54 (2021)

Ontology-Based Combat Force Modeling and Its Intelligent Planning Using Genetic Algorithm

Zhenya Li[1]([⊠]), Shaoqiu Zheng[2], Cunyang Song[1], Wei Wang[1], and Xiaojun Yang[1]

[1] Nanjing Research Institute of Electronic Engineering, Nanjing, China
300160227@163.com
[2] The Key Laboratory of Information System Requirement, Nanjing, China

Abstract. Modern warfare is under high-tech conditions, and joint operations of various services and arms have become the main combat form. It is necessary to make full use of the existing weapons and equipment of multiple services and arms, and display the overall combat effectiveness of the global joint force through mixed clusters. The effectively modeling of combat forces and intelligent planning by the task are core problems. In this paper, we proposed to use ontology technology to model the combat force, which defining the basic entity attributes, force relationships, and behaviors capabilities of combat forces from multiple dimensions. Then, the combat tasks framework is modeled by the vector and presented, thus the task oriented combat force planning is transferred into an optimization problems. On this basis, the genetic algorithm is proposed to get the "demand-capability" mapping matrix, which can quickly return the recommended combat force by different task.

Keywords: Ontology · Combat force · Force modeling · Intelligent planning · Genetic algorithm

1 Introduction

In modern warfare, the combat force is selected by the commanders with corresponding capabilities from the air, ground, sea, underwater and space to form a joint force based on the battlefield situation, and the mission. It is a kind of systematic warfare. It uses the combat forces from multi-dimensional (land, sea, air, space, and electricity) battlefield space, which has multiple combat styles and tactics [1]. The elements of the campaign constitute an interrelated, interdependent, and mutually synergistic combat system, exerting the overall power to defeat the enemy, giving it a functional amplification effect of "the whole is greater than the sum of its parts". However, how to represent the combat force form multi-dimensional space and effectively organize them to complete the combat mission is the great problem. In this paper, we propose an ontology-based combat force modeling method, which could characterize the combat force capabilities, combat behavior, combat rules, etc. Based on this, the genetic algorithm is used to deal with the organization of the combat forces for the mission, which could effectively return the combat force planning program.

© The Author(s), under exclusive license to Springer Nature Singapore Pte Ltd. 2022
Y. Tan and Y. Shi (Eds.): DMBD 2022, CCIS 1745, pp. 343–351, 2022.
https://doi.org/10.1007/978-981-19-8991-9_24

2 Related Works

In philosophy, Ontology is defined as "the systematic description of objective existence in the world" [2]. In the Oxford English Dictionary, the Ontology is defined as "a branch of philosophy that deals with the nature of existence" [3]. According to Webster dictionary, Ontology is a branch of metaphysics concerned with the nature and relations of being, or a particular theory about the nature of being or the kinds of things that have existence [4]. In the field of information systems, ontology is usually used to characterize knowledge in related fields, providing a common understanding of the concepts in the field, determine the commonly concepts and the relations with other concepts in the related fields.

Ontology is actually a formalized expression of a set of concepts in a specific field and the relationship between them. Ontology is a clear formal specification of shared conceptualization, with four meanings of conceptualization, clarity, formalization and sharing. It provides a knowledge model that describes domain knowledge and can support cross-domain sharing and reuse.

The ontology-based knowledge model can be represented by the five-tuple {C,R,P,A,I}. Among them, C refers to a concept, which can represent anything, such as entities, behaviors, functions, etc. R refers to relations, representing the interaction between domain concepts, defining the n-dimensional Cartesian product Subset R, C1 × C2 × … × Cn indicates that there is an n-array relationship R between concepts {C1,C2,…,Cn}; P refers to attributes, which are used to describe concepts; A refers to axioms, which are eternal truth descriptions, I denotes the instance, which refers to the specific examples in the concept. All instances in the field constitute the range of the domain concept in this field. The five-tuple {C,R,P,A,I} is also the modeling primitive of ontology.

Ontology-based knowledge modeling technology has been widely used in many fields. Specifically, ontology has incomparable advantages in knowledge acquisition, verification, reuse, knowledge sharing and system interoperability. Therefore, ontology has a lot of application value in military operations such as combat planning, combat situation, military training and so on. For example, in the field of battlefield environment analysis, literature [5] proposes a semantic similarity calculation method of battlefield environment elements based on combat mission ontology. According to the semantic correlation of combat missions, the battlefield environment elements are divided. The reasoning technology of combining rules and cases is used to establish semantic similarity calculation, quantify the entity semantics of battlefield environment elements, and greatly improve the efficiency and accuracy of battlefield environment data organization. In terms of operational planning analysis, literature [6, 8, 9] studied the construction of several general planning ontology, such as planning concept elements and knowledge representation technology, which provided sufficient and different model information for further study of operational action process and provided basic support for the interconnection of subsequent operational plans. In the field of new military, in order to achieve intelligent reasoning, real-time response and active early warning of space target behaviors and events, and protect space activities and space values, literature [7] proposed a space target situation ontology model for behaviors and events, which can establish a space target relationship model under a unified spatio-temporal framework, realize the dynamic deduction of space target behavior execution and event occurrence process, and provide effective technical support for space missions and space activities.

3 Ontology-Based Combat Force Modeling

Using the ontology as a tool to build a combat power model can provide a good definition of information such as combat power capabilities and provide a consistent understanding of the services and arms participating in the operation. At the same time, by applying the ontology combat force model to the combat command application system, the system's understanding of information can be upgraded from the grammatical layer to the semantic layer, and reasoning and analysis can be realized at the semantic layer, thereby enhancing the system's ability to assist decision-making and intelligence.

3.1 The Entity Modeling

Combat entities can be divided into troop entities and equipment entities. In the troop entities, they include military units, divisions, brigades, regiments, battalions, etc. The troop entities can also be clusters/formations divided by the combat missions and operations direction. In the equipment entities, they can be divided into sensor entities, weapon entities, and platform entities, as well as land, water, air, space, and underwater equipment entities.

To represent the capability of troop entities and equipment entities, the modeling methods are proposed for different kind of entities. The general attributes are mobility capabilities, strike capabilities, command capabilities, protection capabilities, etc. The entity model of the army mainly includes the name of the army, the type of the army, the level of the army, the type of the subordinate army, the establishment unit and the task. The equipment entity model mainly includes equipment name, equipment type, equipment quantity, military category and equipment performance (Fig. 1).

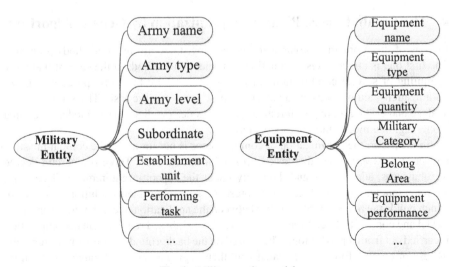

Fig. 1. Military entity model

3.2 The Relationship Modeling

According to the spatial analysis of power modeling, the relationships between entities mainly include command and control relationships and behavioral interactions between entities. For the command and control relationship, it is mainly used to express the command power and responsibility relationship between different force entities, such as the affiliation, affiliation, support, support, and coordination. For the behavioral interactions relationship, it is mainly used to express the distribution relationship between forces and equipment, including platform entities and supporting equipment Entity, mounting relationship, mounting plan, etc. (Fig. 2).

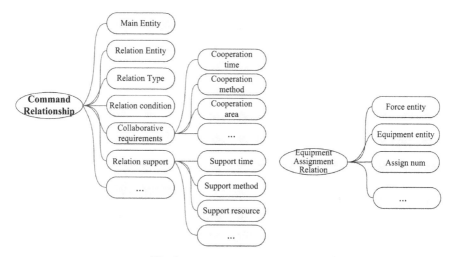

Fig. 2. Force relationship model

4 The Combat Force Planning Optimization by Genetic Algorithm

In view of the problem of combat force planning, there are many methods proposed. The first one is effectiveness evaluation and selection method. In the case of manually compiling of several combinations of power, the analytic hierarchy process or fuzzy optimization method is used to select the best for a specific task. The second one is analyze and choose among different structural modes (such as matrix mode, functional mode, regional mode, and flat mode, etc.).

In the paper, the optimization of combat forces is not for a specific combat mission, but for an appropriate combat task with similar background. There is a certain degree of robustness, adaptability and flexibility under the capacity requirements. Therefore, the main innovation of this paper is to present a general problems solutions framework which builds the mapping relationship between the application of combat force ontology model and combat task requirements. Firstly, the task-based requirement decomposition is carried out from top to bottom. Then based on the background capability requirements, the use of combat force is calculated, and then aggregate power through a bottom-up approach.

4.1 The Operational Task Modeling

The modeling of combat task requirements is the process of analyzing the requirements of joint combat missions and the aggregation of different types of forces of a certain scale to form combat capability requirements. For example, for joint landing combat missions, analyzing the reconnaissance perception of equipment required to complete the mission capabilities, intelligence processing capabilities, command and control capabilities, firepower strike capabilities, and combat support capabilities.

The main process is as follows:

4.1.1 Decomposition of Combat Tasks

The complex joint combat tasks are refined and decomposed according to the operational background categories, and the composite tasks and basic task requirements are obtained in turn, and the requirements of each task are analyzed to determine the possible subjects to complete the task and action, until the task is decomposed into associated with a single combat force type, the task requirement decomposition model is shown in the Fig. 3 below.

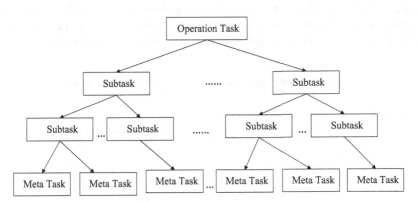

Fig. 3. Combat mission breakdown

4.1.2 Analysis of Combat Tasks Capability Requirements

When completing joint combat tasks through the joint use of multiple forces, the capability requirements that the combat forces need to achieve can be analyzed from multiple perspectives, including functional characteristic requirements, capability characteristic requirements and coordination characteristic requirements.

Functional characteristics requirements refer to the description of the externalized main function and secondary function requirements of the force combination, and are an unique functional characteristics that are different from other modules. For example, the functional characteristics of the rocket artillery brigade are long-range fire assault, and the functional characteristics of the mountain battalion are close-range offensive and defensive operations in the alpine mountains.

Capability characteristic requirements refer to the basic combat tasks that the force combination should complete and the description of the relevant requirements and conditions. For example, to accomplish a specific goal under a certain time condition.

The requirements for coordination characteristics refer to the functional requirements for the basic force units in order to realize the interconnection, interoperability, interoperability, mutual connection and mutual coordination of the main forces required for joint operations. Such as the coordination of information, the coordination of maneuverability, the coordination of carrying capacity, electromagnetic compatibility, etc. The force vector model is thus constructed.

Here, in order to facilitate the calculation, on the basis of task decomposition, only from the perspective of combat capabilities, including reconnaissance perception capabilities, intelligence processing capabilities, command and control capabilities, fire strike capabilities, combat support capabilities, etc. The combat capability requirements required to accomplish this complex joint combat mission. Aggregate and analyze tasks to obtain the set of combat capabilities required by joint combat tasks (Table 1).

Table 1. Modeling of combat tasks capability requirements

Combat task	Combat mission capability requirements									
	C1	C2	C3	C4	C5	C6	C7	C8	C9	...
T1	5	1	0	0	1	1	3	2	1	3
...	...	...	...	...	...	...	...	...	...	...
Tn	7	3	2	3	3	2	1	2	3	5
$\sum Tn$										

4.2 The Proposed Optimization Method Using Genetic Algorithm

For a specific operational background, on the basis of completing the decomposition of operational tasks and analysis of operational task capability requirements, the analysis work of "transformation from external demand to internal force composition" is carried out. As shown below (Fig. 4).

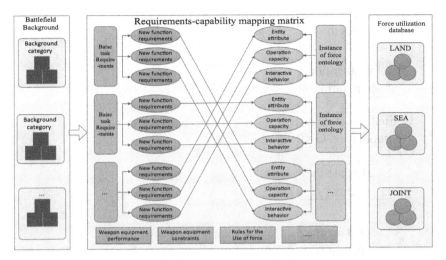

Fig. 4. Analysis of force utilization

The basic steps are as follows:

The first is to classify and merge the basic task requirements to form the overall requirements of functional characteristic requirements, capability characteristic requirements and coordination characteristic requirements.

The Second is to build a list of power ontology instances according to the basic operational data, weapon platform performance data, and the conceptual model of the ontology combat force. Each force ontology instance mainly includes entity attributes, combat capabilities, interactive behaviors, etc.

The third is to build a "requirement-capability" mapping matrix, according to the matching mapping relationship of "functional characteristics-entity attributes", "capability characteristics-combat capability", and "coordination characteristics-interaction behavior", combined with constraints such as power application rules to construct problems. The model is modeled as a multi-objective optimization problem.

The fourth is to solve the multi-objective optimization problem and calculate the composition and scale of the joint combat tasks.

According to the optimization problem obtained by using the optimization design modeling of combat forces, the genetic algorithm is used to solve the problem, and the solution process is shown in Fig. 5. We encode chromosomes into an array whose length is the size of the combat arsenal *D. The D value is coded in binary mode and is used to indicate the maximum number of selected troops. For example, $D = 4$ indicates that the maximum size of all combat troops does not exceed 1024. When chromosomes are crossed, it is necessary to ensure that the crossed chromosomes have physical meaning. Therefore, the selection at the crossover point needs to be an array position that is a multiple of 4. The chromosomal mutation is that each data bit on the array has a certain concept from 0 to 1, or 1 to 0.

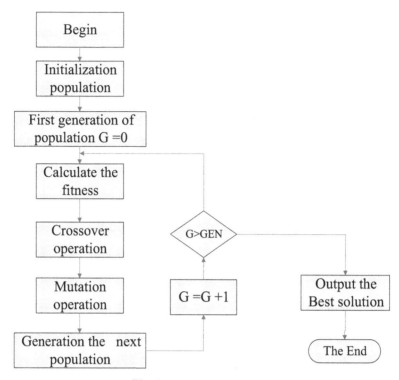

Fig. 5. The processing figure

5   Conclusion

In this paper, we proposed to use genetic algorithm for the optimization of combat force planning. The combat tasks framework is modeled by the vector and presented, thus the task oriented combat force planning is transferred into an optimization problems, and then the genetic algorithm is used to deal with it. The method proposed in this paper can provide effective reference for intelligent combat force planning and intelligent combat.

References

1. Gruber, T.R.: A translation approach to portable ontology specifications. Knowl. Acquis. **5**(2), 199–220 (1993)
2. Guo, F., Wang, S., Meng, F.: Mission planning model of synthetic Battalion's combat formation based on task breakdown. Command Control Simul. **39**(5), 18–21 (2017)
3. Chen, A., Mao, J.: Combat data architecture construction method and its key technologies. Command. Inf. Syst. Technol. **10**(6), 38–42 (2020)
4. Cai, L., Liu, G., Chen, Y.: Analysis method for target system. Command. Inf. Syst. Technol. **12**(2), 38–43 (2021)
5. Zhu, J., You, X., Xia, Q.: A semantic similarity calculation method for battlefield environment elements based on operational task ontology. Geomat. Inf. Sci. Wuhan Univ. **44**(9), 1407–1415 (2019)

6. Qian, M., Liu, Z., Yao, L., Zhang, W.: Survey of ontological modelling of military operation plans. J. Syst. Eng. Electron. **32**(5), 994–1000 (2010)
7. Lu, W., Xu, Q., Lan, C., Lv, L.: Design and construction of behavior and event oriented space object situation ontology. J. Astronaut. **41**(8), 1105–1114 (2020)
8. Alexander, K., Ray, B., Larry, G., Rebbapragada, V., Langston, J.: Building a tool for battle planning: challenges, tradeoffs, and experimental findings. Appl. Intell. **23**, 165–189 (2005)
9. He, H., Wang, W., Zhu, Y., Wang, T.: An operation planning generation and optimization method for the new intelligent combat SoS. IEEE Accessed 2019/7/1

Research on Multi-channel Retrieve Mechanism Based on Heuristic

Shiqi Ning⬤, Kun Liu, Chengjun Wang, Shan Jiang, and Qiang Wang(✉)

Advanced Institute of Big Data, Beijing, China
ningshiqi@hit.edu.cn, {liukun,wangq}@aibd.ac.cn
{chengjun110,jiangshan}@alumni.nudt.edu.cn

Abstract. Search system is a crucial component in information systems, that is to retrieve the relevant documents by the specific query. There are many search retrieve algorithms, almost all focus on a specific domain of retrieve algorithms, such as text matching, tag matching, semantic matching. However, in a real search system, the purpose of the retrieve module is to find the documents related to the specified query as fully as possible, so it requires that the search system should contain multiple forms of retrieve capability. In this paper, we propose a multi-channel retrieve model, including text channel, semantic channel and intention channel. In text channels, we propose heuristic two-stage query rewrite model, which can generate more semantically rich queries. In semantic channel, we present a novel sample dynamic construction method, which saves the manual annotation cost, and can train the model more fully. Finally, a brief general implementation of the retrieve methods based on intention channel is presented. The results show that the retrieve method based on multi-channel can significantly improve the retrieve number and accuracy of documents, and business indicators such as click-through rate are also significantly improved.

Keywords: Search system · Multi-channel · Heuristic two-stage query rewrite · Sample dynamic construction

1 Introduction

Search engines have become an important tool to help people access massive amounts of information online. With the development of deep learning technology, more and more search systems have introduced deep learning technology to improve the experience of search users. The core question of the search system is, how to retrieve as many documents related to the user query as possible.

In traditional text retrieve, for the same thing, based on different knowledge background, different people have different ways to describe. The vocabulary mismatch between query and document poses a critical challenge in search. Vocabulary gaps arise when documents and queries expressed as bags of words use different terms to describe the same concepts [20]. For vocabulary gap, there

© The Author(s), under exclusive license to Springer Nature Singapore Pte Ltd. 2022
Y. Tan and Y. Shi (Eds.): DMBD 2022, CCIS 1745, pp. 352–366, 2022.
https://doi.org/10.1007/978-981-19-8991-9_25

are many query-based rewriting methods to match the description of the document as much as possible [17,25]. However, the focus of different algorithms is different, and the results of rewriting are also different, so single model generated query coverage is not enough, not as far as possible more and more rich results. How to choose the query rewrite algorithm? Or how can we combine the results of the different algorithms? This remains a problem to be resolved.

In addition to text retrieve, there are many semantic retrieve studies based on embedding, and the core problem is how to model the correlation between query and document. The key idea is to represent query and document in finite dimensional vector space and learn their similarity in this space [9,10,24]. However, many methods give very complex model design, which can not be deployed in large-scale scenarios with high performance requirements, which is intolerable for retrieve systems with low latency time. Moreover, the sample processing techniques given by different papers vary greatly [7,12,18], and the sample size is insufficient for many search scenarios with small traffic, but we know that the sample determines the upper limit of the model. Sample acquisition is always an unavoidable topic, and how to use the existing training data to do more adequate training is a crucial problem.

So in this paper, we have three contributions: 1) We propose the concept of multi-channel retrieve to make a systematic design for as many retrieves as possible. Different channels can complement each other and have good expansibility. 2) In text channels, we propose a heuristic two-stage query rewrite model to solve the fusion problem of multiple rewriting models. 3) In semantic channel, we propose a general dynamic sample generation strategy, which is easy to implement in engineering, saves the cost of manual annotation, and can maximize the use of existing data to train the model more comprehensively.

2   Related Work

In order to retrieve more documents that match user query, there is a lot of work from the query side. Because different people have different ways of describing the same thing due to their different knowledge backgrounds, query rewrite is a natural solution. There are query rewrite methods based on the statistical approach. Based on log mining [4], the relationship between query and query is mined through user behavior data. Query click logs and query session logs are easy to think of. Click the query in the same document to establish the query co-occurrence relationship, and based on the query in the same session to establish the co-occurrence relationship. Gao et al. [8] exploits statistical translation model trained on clickthrough data for query rewrite. In general, the query-document with clicks is regarded as the source language and the target language, and the translation model is used to calculate the relationship between phrases of the two languages, so as to expand query and disambiguate it at the same time [1,2]. With the development of embedding technology, classic Word2vec [16] maps query as embedding. The classical expression *vector("king") -vector ("man") + vector("woman")* results in a vector that is closest to the *vector("queen")* [15].

Fasttext [3,14] improves word2vec, alleviates out-of-vocabulary(OOV) problem through n-gram, and can capture prefixes and suffixes better. However, the focus of different algorithms is different, and the results of rewriting are also different. How to combine the results of the different algorithms still is a problem to be resolved.

The above methods are essentially text-based retrieve. Currently, there are many embedding-based semantic retrieve technologies, among which twin tower model is the most popular, such as DSSM [13] and its variant CDSSM [21]. The twin tower model can better represent the semantics of query and document, so as to break through the traditional text matching retrieve method. Currently, based on the twin towers embedding retrieve, the network structure of the model is similar, and many papers have made a lot of efforts in terms of samples. Amazon [18] uses a very simple twin tower, which does embedding of words, then calculates avg pooling, and then calculates tanh and cosine. It uses point hinge loss distinguish the three cases of unexposed, exposed unclicked and clicked samples. In order to pay more attention to correlation, Baidu [7] uses active learning to treat the samples with low correlation score but high pctr score as bad cases. It uses click, unclick, bad case data to learn embedding. Facebook [12] uses a classic dssm model, with embedding as the bottom layer. In addition to text features, Facebook also includes user and context features. Query encoder and document encoder are both DNN, and the loss is triplet loss. For positive samples, there is little difference between using click samples or exposure samples. In the mining method of hard negative, each query generates the top k docs, finds the unclicked samples as negative examples, and actually selects the unclicked samples ranked in 101–500. The ratio of sample size for easy and hard was 100:1. We found that the sample processing techniques were completely different in each paper due to different business objectives. And the construction techniques they used are based on a large number of samples, but not every scene can obtain a large amount of training data. Baidu [26] once marked out 10 million samples to train the model, and the cost is undoubtedly huge. The cost of obtaining samples is always an unavoidable topic, for many search scenarios with small traffic, the sample size is not sufficient, and the mining of negative samples does not have too much data support.

3   Method

3.1   Text Retrieve Channel

Text retrieve channel is the main channel in retrieve module. Text retrieve is mainly through the literal matching of query and document, and the corresponding document is obtained by inverted index. In this section, we present a heuristic two-stage query rewriting model inspired by [11] and a evaluation standard. And we will give specific details in terms of model, implementation, and optimization.

Two-Stage Query Rewrite Model. The purpose of query rewriting is that different users have different ways of describing the same thing because of their different knowledge backgrounds. We rewrite one query into multiple queries with similar semantics, which can enhance the number of retrieves in the search system and enhance user experience.

Two-stage we proposed here means that in the first stage we use multiple models to generate the rewrite candidate set for query, and in the second stage we will use a unified semantic model to filter the candidate set generated in the first stage, as shown in Fig. 1.

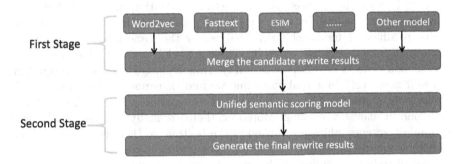

Fig. 1. Two-stage query rewrite model.

All previous methods on query rewrite only focus on a specific algorithm in the first stage, such as query rewrite method based on statistics [4], including log mining and user behavior data mining. Another example is based on classical embedding techniques, such as Word2vec [16], fastText [3,14], and even some deep neural network models, such as ESIM [5] and machine translation models. However, there are always five problems in the practice of query rewrite in industry.

1. Scenario restriction. Each algorithmic model of query rewriting is mostly applicable to a particular scenario. There are two common scenarios with inconsistent goals in the search system: 1) The precision of query rewrite is required to be high, but the semantic divergence is not. For example, some scenarios have low requirements on retrieve nums due to the consideration of performance. Due to low semantic divergence, rewrite query may have little difference from retrieve documents of original query. 2) High semantic divergence is required, but the rewriting accuracy is not required. For example, in some commercial advertising systems, there are higher requirements for revenue and advertising display. So rewrite query needs to retrieve a lot of additional documents. There are different solutions for the different scenarios described above. For example, for scenario 1, Fasttext uses N-gram, and the rewriting results are often very similar literally, so rewrite query is more accurate. However, rewrite query lacks semantic divergence. Although the

precision is high, the number of additional retrieved documents is small. For example, Fasttext argued that "colorful" can be thought of as highly similar to "colourful", but "colorful" is much less similar to "iridescent". Apparently, "iridescent" offers a lot more retrieves than "colourful". The classical skip-gram method of Word2vec uses words in nearby windows to generate the embedding of the current central word, so the rewriting result will be divergent, unlike the literal similarity pursued by Fasttext. Because of divergence, more additional documents can be retrieved, thus enriching the retrieve results.

2. Differences in distribution. The distribution of rewrite candidates generated by each model is inconsistent. In practical evaluation, we found that many reliable rewriting results may vary greatly in correlation order or suborder due to different model choices. That is, for the same rewriting result, the correlation and subplace given by different models are very different.

3. Selection criteria are difficult to unify. How to judge whether the rewriting result is correct? In actual modeling, we find that most of the rewrite model can only guarantee the reliability of the candidate query ranked first and second in relevance ranking. Moreover, there are many rewrited queries with good divergence which are ranked at the bottom, so there is no way to select reliable results by simple truncation according to correlation.

4. Lack of training samples. We know that in order to judge whether the rewriting result meets the requirements, it is essentially judged whether the mapping $query_1$ to $query_2$ meets the requirements. Therefore, we need more pairs of training samples such as $(query_1, query_2, label)$, but the cost of manual labeling is extremely high, which leads to the difficulty of sample acquisition and the scarcity of training samples, thereby affecting the accuracy of model training.

5. The evaluation criteria are not straightforward. In most studies, many of the proposed metrics are not generic. Many search systems indirectly evaluate the quality of query rewrite through online metrics such as click-through rate. This means uncontrollable, because the rewrite model can only evaluate quality after online A/B test.

Therefore, we propose the heuristic two-stage query rewrite model inspired by [11]. We decide to fuse the results of multiple models in the first stage, and make use of different algorithm models as many as possible to obtain rich candidate sets, including both similar literal and high divergence but similar semantic candidates. In the second stage, we use the unified semantic model to judge the candidate set in the first stage, so as to select the rewrited query that meets the requirements. This two-stage model can guarantee the accuracy of rewriting to the greatest extent and the divergence of rewriting at the same time, so as to guarantee the number of retrieved documents. In the first stage, we are no longer restricted by scenarios and can use different algorithms to generate rewrited query candidates as much as possible. In the second stage, we can construct unified selection criteria and no longer pay attention to the candidate distribution of a certain model.

In first stage, the original intention of our design is to choose the query rewrite model more freely and flexibly without requiring algorithm developers to pay too much attention to business scenarios. In second stage we use the well-optimized Bert [6, 22] model as the unified semantic model in the second stage to screen the candidates generated in the first stage. Since we need a unified semantic model, preferably with rich prior knowledge, and the ability to optimize the model for business scenarios, Bert was a natural choice for us. We will give the sample generation skills, a novel loss function optimization based on soft-argmax, and how to design a test set.

Sample Generation. Above, we introduced a problem that query rewrite faces in practice. Due to the high cost of manual annotation, the training samples are too few and the model cannot be fully trained. Then can we automatically obtain pair training data such as $(query_1, query_2, label)$ through business knowledge? The answer is yes. Here we present the training data generation method based on user behavior, and enrich the dataset through data enhancement. Suppose that if a document is frequently clicked by users searching for $query_1$ and $query_2$, then a high probability indicates that $query_1$ and $query_2$ are semantically similar. 1) We first get the click rate of each $query_1$ and $query_2$ jointly click on the document. If the value exceeds the set max threshold, we assume that the two query pairs are similar, that is, a $(query_1, query_2, 1)$ is generated; if the value is below the set min threshold, a $(query_1, query_2, 0)$ is generated. You need to manually configure the threshold based on the scenarios. 2) Since Bert's classification task input is position sensitive, we flip the samples generated in 1) to generate $(query_2, query_1, 1)$ and $(query_2, query_1, 0)$. In our search scenario, we simply filtered some data based on business rules and generated a total of about 600 thousand samples.

Loss Function Optimization. Now that we have generated the sample data, we are faced with two problems. 1) As we know, the Bert model has a huge number of parameters, Bert-Large has about 300 million parameters, and Bert-base has about 100 million parameters. However, we only have 600 thousand samples. According to experience, with such a huge number of parameters in a small sample, we cannot perform finetune for Bert well. 2) Bert uses the cross-entropy loss function. The sample has the problem of easy learning. Because truncation according to threshold is a rough sampling method, it is easy for the model to judge positive samples as 1 and negative samples as 0, and the predict output of the Bert is extremely close to 1 or 0, which will lead to minimal gradient change within a batchsize. In the face of the huge problem of insufficient parameters and samples, and the problem of easy learning, we creatively proposed to change Bert's loss function into the **Top1 Loss** function (see Eqs. 2, 3).

The original Bert loss function:

$$J = -\frac{1}{N}\sum_{i=1}^{N}(y_i \cdot \log(p_i) + (1 - y_i) \cdot \log(1 - p_i)) \tag{1}$$

where N is the size of a batch, p_i is the probability that the model considers the sample to be a positive sample, y_i is the label of the sample, which can only be 1 or 0.

The optimized **Top1 Loss** function:

$$J = -(y_{i_{max}} \cdot \log(p_{i_{max}}) + (1 - y_{i_{max}}) \cdot \log(1 - p_{i_{max}})) \tag{2}$$

$$i_{max} = \underset{1 \leq i \leq N}{\text{SoftArgmax}}(-y_i \cdot \log(p_i) - (1 - y_i) \cdot \log(1 - p_i)) \tag{3}$$

The SoftArgmax is:

$$\text{SoftArgmax}(\mathbf{x}) = \sum_{i=1}^{M}\frac{e^{\beta x_i}}{\sum_{j=1}^{}e^{\beta x_j}}i \tag{4}$$

where $\mathbf{x}$ is a vector, x_i, x_j is a scalar on one of the dimensions. M is the total number of vector dimensions and β is the regulator. We use SoftArgmax here because the traditional argmax is not differentiable.

It means that we only learn one sample with the largest loss in batchsize at a time, and replace the gradient of the whole batchsize with its gradient. Such method has the following advantages: 1) There is no need to manually select the hardest sample, and in the past, hard sample learning was always done offline in advance. Our approach can be dynamically generated during training. 2) Gradient change will increase batchsize times. Because the traditional Bert loss is calculated as the average of the loss of all samples, if the traditional Bert loss function is used on the easy sample, the batch gradient will be small, and the parameters cannot be adjusted quickly to adapt to the sample, and the specific business knowledge cannot be learned.

3.2 Semantic Retrieve Channel

In this section, we will introduce the implementation details of the semantic retrieve model and innovatively propose a dynamic training sample generation algorithm.

Model Selection. Let's first talk about the model selection of semantic retrieve channel. The vast majority of semantic retrieve in the industry adopts the twin tower model, as shown in Fig. 2. The CNN part, which can be flexibly selected according to scenes, such as RNN, and the current more popular transformer structures.

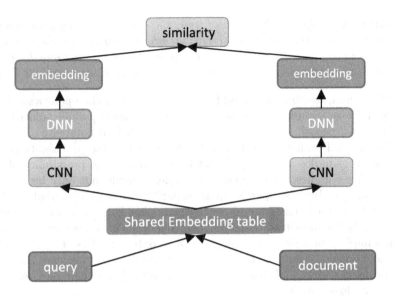

Fig. 2. A twin tower model example based on CNN.

Motivation of Dynamic Sample Generation. Let's recall how we trained before. We first have to prepare the positive and negative samples, and then send the positive and negative samples into the model [7,12,18]. If we generate both positive and negative samples in advance, then in each epoch, you have the same sample pair every time you train. So if we can make the query encounter different negative samples during the training process for each epoch, this is also equivalent to expanding the training sample. Compared to the big Internet companies like Facebook, Baidu [7,12], they spend great tricks on sample construction, which is certainly a very effective method. But the construction techniques they used are based on a large number of samples, and not every scene can obtain a large amount of training data. Baidu [26] once marked out 10 million samples to train the model, and the cost is undoubtedly huge. The cost of obtaining samples is always an unavoidable topic, so it is a more general idea to use the limited samples to train the model more fully. This is our motivation to propose a dynamic sample generation strategy.

Dynamic Sample Generation. Before introducing our dynamic training sample generation, let's first explain the application of pointwise and listwise in a real scenario. Let's first give the formal definitions of pointwise and listwise.

Definition 1. *Pointwise. If the form of the training sample is (query$_1$, document$_1$, 1), then query$_1$ and document$_1$ are related; If the form is (query$_1$, document$_1$, 0), then query$_1$ and document$_1$ are unrelated, then the training sample is pointwise.*

Definition 2. *Listwise. The form of training sample is (query₁, document₁+,*
document₂-, document₂-,..., documentₙ-), where query₁ and document₁ are
related, document₂-, document₂-,..., documentₙ- means query1 and document₂,
document₂,..., documentₙ are not related, then the training sample is listwise.

In the search scenario, we found that listwise is better than pointwise. For one
sample, listwise training refers to more training samples, while pointwise only
considers one. Below, we give the loss function based on pointwise and listwise
(see Eqs. 5, 6). It can be seen that listwise maximizes the probability of query
and positive samples and is equivalent to minimizing the probability of query
and negative samples, which means that query should not only be similar to
positive samples, but also open a gap in similarity with negative samples to better
distinguish between positive and negative samples. But the pointwise method,
which is only the most traditional, only considers the cross-entropy loss function
of one sample. For a single sample, pointwise only considers the probability of
query and one document, without reference to positive and negative documents,
so in terms of training efficiency, pointwise is much lower than listwise.

Listwise loss function:

$$p_+ = \frac{exp(\mathrm{R}(query, document+))}{\sum exp(\mathrm{R}(query, document'))} \tag{5}$$

$$loss = -\log(p_+) \tag{6}$$

where R is a similarity function.

With previous pointwise and listwise analysis, we will focus on how to introduce dynamic sample generation in listwise. Dynamic sample generation means
that different negative samples about a specific query will be generated every
time is trained. In this way, different *document*− can be encountered for the
same in different epochs, which will greatly expand the negative sample set of
training samples. In the following, we present the algorithm of dynamic sample
generation based on user click behaviors. See Algorithm 1.

The critical step is step 3 of Algorthm 1. How can negative samples be generated better, so that the model encounters more negative samples in different
epochs? We give a graphical interpretation (Fig. 3).

Let's explain Fig. 3. At the far left is the $< query, document+ >$ pair of
samples we generated from the user behavior log, all positive. We shifted the
positive samples in column 2 (in this case, only one unit was shifted, actually
implemented by a random offset) so that the original $< query_1, document_1+ >$
would become $< query_1, document_2- >$. It is clear that $document_2$ is a negative sample for $query_1$, that is $< query_1, document_2- >$. So we get $< query_1$
$document_1+, document_2- >$. Similarly, by shifting again we will get $< query_1$
$document_1+, document_2-, document_3- >$. After N_{neg} times we will get $<$
$query_1\ document+, document_1-, document_2-, ..., document_{N_{neg}} - >$.

Compared with the traditional offline generated samples, dynamic sample
generation has several advantages. 1) The acquisition cost of positive samples
is low, and it is easy to determine the selection method of positive samples

Algorithm 1. Dynamic sample generation.

Input: User click behaviors logs S_{log}; Click rate threshold for positive samples T_{max}; Negtive sampling nums N_{neg}; $batchnum$ for train;

Output: Samples like $< query, document_+, document_1-, document_2-, ..., document_{N_{neg}} - >$ on the current epoch;

1: Calculate the click rate of all documents in query from S_{log};
2: Click through rate greater than the T_{max} as a positive sample, then generate some $< query, document_+ >$ pairs;
3: **for** $i = 1$ to $batchnum$ **do**
4:    **for** $j = 1$ to N_{neg} **do**
5:       For specific each $< query, document_+ >$, a negtive sample $document-$ is generated;
6:    **end for**
7:    merge all negtive sample,generate $< query, document_+, document_1-, document_2-, ..., document_{N_{neg}} - >$
8: **end for**

according to the business. For example, the search scene query and the click rate of documents can be used as the criteria for the selection of positive samples. 2) It is no longer necessary to actively select negative samples. We know that negative samples are difficult to construct in many scenarios. For example, if you pick a document that is displayed but not clicked as a negative sample, this is problematic, because it is likely that the user has clicked on the document or that the document is similar to that clicked before. Not being clicked does not necessarily mean that the query is not relevant to the document. 3) It is not necessary to determine the generation of negative samples in the offline phase, but to generate negative samples in the training process. In this way, more negative samples can be generated more flexibly and the model can learn more information.

3.3   Intention Retrieve Channel

Imagine a scene in which a piece of text describes the appearance and lifestyle of a tiger, but the word "tiger" does not appear throughout. Do you think that text should be retrieved when a user searches for "tiger"? The answer for most people is "yes". This is often the case in a category system. For example, if a recruiter is looking for a chef and chooses the chef category before posting an article, it is likely that the recruiter will not include the word "chef" in the description because the chef category has been selected. In this case, traditional text-based retrieve will not retrieve the document.

For intent recognition, the key is how to formulate the set of intents based on the business scenario. The intent recognition can be implemented in many ways, but we present only one practical, simple way here, and will not spend much time on the specific technical implementation. The common pattern of retrieve based on intention recognition is to map query into multiple intents using a

query	postive doc		query	negtive doc		query	negtive doc
q_1	d_1 +		q_1	d_2 −		q_1	d_3 −
q_2	d_2 +	first translation	q_2	d_3 −	second translation	q_2	d_4 −
q_3	d_3 +		q_3	d_4 −		q_3	d_5 −
q_4	d_4 +		q_4	d_5 −		q_4	d_1 −
q_5	d_5 +		q_5	d_1 −		q_5	d_2 −

Fig. 3. A graphical interpretation for dynamic sample generation

multi-classification model, and document into multiple intents using a multi-classification model. Finally, the intention of query is used to match documents with corresponding intents.

4 Experiment

4.1 Text Retrieve Channel

We trained Word2vec and Fasttext with the titles and contents of 1.3 million documents. We use the Word2vec of spark [23] machine learning library and use Fasttext of Gensim [19] library. Experimental parameters are shown in Table 1. In two-stage with Bert, we use the Bert-base default parameters. We truncated the candidate queries for the test set to give labels of 0 or 1 based on the correlation threshold.

Table 1. Experimental parameters for Word2vec and Fasttext.

Method	minCount	maxNgram	minNgram	vectorSize	negativeSampleNum
Word2vec	1000	–	–	100	5
Fasttext	1000	3	2	100	5

In the search system, query is divided into two types: high frequency and long tail. Not only should we ensure that we measure the rewrite results at the query level, but we should also simulate the real online situation from the perspective of the real pv online. So we want to extract queries at random pv, although duplicate queries may be extracted. And we should also focus on the long-tailed query case, because that represents the generalization ability of our model. We tested the experiment on 1,700 samples like $(query_1, query_2, label)$ that we annotated ourselves. We did A/B test with search traffic of 2 million users, the experimental data are shown in Table 2.

Table 2. Test results on our manually labeled dataset.

Method	Rewrite num	Accuracy	Precision	$Recall_{pos}$	$Recall_{neg}$
Word2vec	2.3	68%	73%	61%	48%
Fasttext	3.6	61%	65%	68%	49%
Two-stage with Bert(no optimized)	**4.2**	81%	80%	79%	56%
Two-stage with Bert(optimized)	3.9	**90%**	**92%**	**89%**	**85%**

In the previous chapter, we raised the issue of evaluation criteria. Accuracy and Precision are both indicators related to positive samples. Also, we care about both $Recall_{pos}$ and $Recall_{neg}$. $Recall_{pos}$ represents the recall rate of positive samples. $Recall_{neg}$ represents the recall of negative samples, that is, our ability to screen negative samples. This is very important in the search system, because the search scenario is concerned with accuracy, try not to appear badcase, so the $Recall_{neg}$ index also needs to be concerned in the search scenario.

It should be noted that two-stage with Bert(optimized) not only shows improvement in Accuracy, Precision, $Recall_{pos}$ compared with two-stage with Bert(no optimized). The improvement is even more pronounced on $Recall_{neg}$. By analyzing the reasons, compared with before the loss function was optimized, when we encountered the wrong samples, we added punishment, and the gradient update range was larger, so that we could adjust Bert parameters faster.

4.2   Semantic Retrieve Channel

The online A/B test experimental data are shown in Table 3. After going online, the semantic retrieval channel increases click-through rate(Ctr) 5.5% of the overall search traffic and 10.9% of the average retrieval documents. The formula of **Average Retrieve documents** is as follow:

$$Average\ Retrieve\ Documents = \frac{D_{week}}{R_{week}} \tag{7}$$

where D_{week} is the number of documents retrieved by all search requests in a week, R_{week} is the number of all search requests in a week. Therefore, the index *Average Retrieve Documents* represents the retrieve ability of the search system.

Although the badcase rate increases by 0.8%, this is tolerable. It is a trade off between the retrieve num and the user experience. We found that although the documents retrieved by vector and the documents retrieved by text had some overlap, most of the additional recalled documents were related to query semantics, such as "cake maker" and "baker". This is also in line with the purpose of introducing semantic retrieve channel, which is not only to carry out text matching from a literal perspective, but also to retrieve from a semantic perspective.

After analyzing badcase, we find that the training samples of query corresponding to these badcases are very few and belong to long-tailed query. Therefore, it can be inferred that badcase of the model is mainly caused by insufficient training.

Table 3. semantic retrieve channel result

Method	AverageRetrieveDocuments	Ctr	OfflineAuc
Search without semantic retrieve	12.5	9.765%	0.671
Search with semantic retrieve(Pointwise)	**14.8**	6.527%	0.562
Search with semantic retrieve(Listwise)	13.86	**10.302%**	**0.714**

Meanwhile, we also conducted experiments on relationship between AUC and the number of negative samples, and the results are shown in Fig. 4. We found that the higher the number of negative samples, the higher the off-line auc. But beyond 20, the auc barely rises. The reason is probably that the number of negative samples has been enough, the model has seen enough samples, and the training has been sufficient.

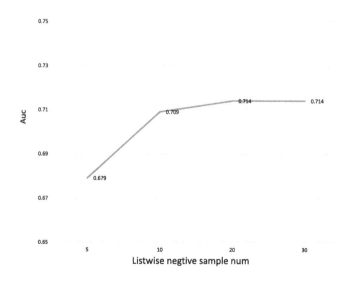

Fig. 4. Relationship between AUC and the number of negative samples.

5 Conclusion

In this study, in order to retrieve more documents related to the user query, we propose a multi-channel retrieve model based on heuristic, including text retrieve channel, semantic retrieve channel and intention retrieve channel. Text retrieve focuses on text matching, where we propose the heuristic two-stage query rewrite model, which can combine the advantages of various rewrites to give as many and semantically rich rewriting results as possible. Meanwhile, we use a new differentiable Top-1 loss function based on soft-argmax to optimize the model. In the semantic retrieve channel, we present a universal dynamic sample generation strategy which saves the manual annotation cost and can train the model more completely. In intention channel, because the type of intention is very dependent on the scene, we briefly give a general intention retrieve strategy. The channels are complementary to each other, and each channel has different retrieve focus.

References

1. Ali, A., Gao, J., He, X., Billerbeck, B.V., Ahari, S.: Enhanced query rewriting through statistical machine translation (2014)
2. Baoi, J.W., Zheng, D.Q., Bing, X., Zhao, T.J.: Query rewriting using statistical machine translation. IEEE (2013)
3. Bojanowski, P., Grave, E., Joulin, A., Mikolov, T.: Enriching word vectors with subword information. Trans. Assoc. Comput. Linguist. **5**, 135–146 (2017)
4. Cao, H., et al.: Context-aware query suggestion by mining click-through and session data. In: Li, Y., Liu, B., Sarawagi, S. (eds.) Proceedings of the 14th ACM SIGKDD International Conference on Knowledge Discovery and Data Mining, Las Vegas, Nevada, USA, 24–27 August 2008, pp. 875–883. ACM (2008). https://doi.org/10.1145/1401890.1401995
5. Chen, Q., Zhu, X., Ling, Z., Wei, S., Jiang, H., Inkpen, D.: Enhanced LSTM for natural language inference (2016)
6. Devlin, J., Chang, M.W., Lee, K., Toutanova, K.: BERT: pre-training of deep bidirectional transformers for language understanding (2018)
7. Fan, M., Guo, J., Zhu, S., Miao, S., Sun, M., Li, P.: Mobius: towards the next generation of query-ad matching in Baidu's sponsored search. In: Proceedings of the 25th ACM SIGKDD International Conference on Knowledge Discovery and Data Mining, pp. 2509–2517 (2019)
8. Gao, J., Nie, J.Y.: Towards concept-based translation models using search logs for query expansion. In: Proceedings of the 21st ACM international conference on Information and knowledge management, pp. 1–10 (2012)
9. Gonzalo, J., Li, H., Moschitti, A., Xu, J.: SIGIR 2014 workshop on semantic matching in information retrieval. In: International ACM SIGIR Conference on Research and Development in Information Retrieval, pp. 1296–1296 (2014)
10. Gysel, C.V., Rijke, M., Kanoulas, E.: Learning latent vector spaces for product search. ACM (2016)
11. He, Y., Tang, J., Hua, O., Kang, C., Yin, D., Yi, C.: Learning to rewrite queries. In: ACM (2016)
12. Huang, J.T., et al.: Embedding-based retrieval in Facebook search (2020)
13. Huang, P.S., He, X., Gao, J., Li, D., Heck, L.: Learning deep structured semantic models for web search using clickthrough data. In: Proceedings of the 22nd ACM International Conference on Information and Knowledge management (2013)
14. Joulin, A., Grave, E., Bojanowski, P., Mikolov, T.: Bag of tricks for efficient text classification. In: Proceedings of the 15th Conference of the European Chapter of the Association for Computational Linguistics: Volume 2, Short Papers (2017)

15. Mikolov, T., Yih, W.T., Zweig, G.: Linguistic regularities in continuous space word representations. In: North American Chapter of the Association for Computational Linguistics (2013)
16. Mikolov, T., Chen, K., Corrado, G., Dean, J.: Efficient estimation of word representations in vector space. Comput. Sci. (2013)
17. Mohankumar, A.K., Begwani, N., Singh, A.: Diversity driven query rewriting in search advertising (2021)
18. Nigam, P., et al.: Semantic product search. In: Proceedings of the 25th ACM SIGKDD International Conference on Knowledge Discovery and Data Mining. KDD 2019, pp. 2876–2885. Association for Computing Machinery, New York (2019). https://doi.org/10.1145/3292500.3330759
19. Řehůřek, R., Sojka, P.: Software framework for topic modelling with large corpora. In: Proceedings of the LREC 2010 Workshop on New Challenges for NLP Frameworks, pp. 45–50. ELRA, Valletta, Malta, May 2010. https://is.muni.cz/publication/884893/en
20. Sarvi, F., Voskarides, N., Mooiman, L., Schelter, S., Rijke, M.D.: A comparison of supervised learning to match methods for product search (2020)
21. Shen, Y., He, X., Gao, J., Deng, L., Mesnil, G.: A latent semantic model with convolutional-pooling structure for information retrieval. In: CIKM (2014)
22. Vaswani, A., et al.: Attention is all you need. In: arXiv (2017)
23. Zaharia, M., Chowdhury, M., Franklin, M.J., Shenker, S., Stoica, I.: Spark: cluster computing with working sets. In: 2nd USENIX Workshop on Hot Topics in Cloud Computing (HotCloud 2010) (2010)
24. Zhang, H., Wang, T., Meng, X., Hu, Y.: Improving semantic matching via multi-task learning in e-commerce. In: International ACM SIGIR Conference on Research and Development in Information Retrieval (2019)
25. Zheng, C., Xing, F., Yuan, L.: Pre-training for query rewriting in a spoken language understanding system. IEEE (2020)
26. Zou, L., et al.: Pre-trained language model based ranking in Baidu search. In: Proceedings of the 27th ACM SIGKDD Conference on Knowledge Discovery and Data Mining, pp. 4014–4022 (2021)

Big-Model Methods

PoetryBERT: Pre-training with Sememe Knowledge for Classical Chinese Poetry

Jiaqi Zhao[ID], Ting Bai, Yuting Wei[ID], and Bin Wu[✉][ID]

Beijing Key Laboratory of Intelligent Telecommunications Software and Multimedia,
Beijing University of Posts and Telecommunications, Haidian, Beijing 100876, China
{zhaojiaqibupt,baiting,yuting_wei,wubin}@bupt.edu.cn

Abstract. Classical Chinese poetry has a history of thousands of years and is a precious cultural heritage of humankind. Compared with the modern Chinese corpus, it is irrecoverable and specially organized, making it difficult to be learned by existing pre-trained language models. Besides, with the thousands of years of development, many words in classical Chinese poetry have changed their meanings or been out of use today, which further limiting the capability of existing pre-trained models to learn the semantics of classical Chinese poetry. To address these challenges, we construct a large-scale sememe knowledge graph of classical Chinese Poetry (**SKG-Poetry**), which connects the vocabularies in classical Chinese poetry and modern Chinese. By extracting the sememe knowledge from classical Chinese poetry, our model **PoetryBERT** not only enlarges the irrecoverable pre-training corpus but also enriches the semantics of the vocabularies in classical Chinese poetry, which enables PoetryBERT to be successfully used in downstream tasks. Specifically, we evaluate our model in two tasks in the field of Chinese classical poetry, which are poetry theme classification and poetry-modern Chinese translation. Extensive experiments are conducted on the two tasks to show the effectiveness of sememe knowledge based pre-training model.

Keywords: Natural language processing · Computational social science · Knowledge graph · Pre-training language model

1 Introduction

Classical Chinese poetry has inherited the Chinese civilization for thousands of years, reflecting the social ethos and cultural outlook at that time. In recent years, increasing attention has been attracted by researchers [20,34,50,58] to use artificial intelligence technology to analyze classical Chinese poetry, which is helpful to the promotion of traditional culture and cross-cultural communications. Existing studies in the field of classical Chinese poetry often provide solutions to a specific problem in a supervised way and cannot be generalized to other tasks. The labeled data of classical Chinese poetry is always obtained by manual methods, which is very time-consuming and requires the participation

ⓒ The Author(s), under exclusive license to Springer Nature Singapore Pte Ltd. 2022
Y. Tan and Y. Shi (Eds.): DMBD 2022, CCIS 1745, pp. 369–384, 2022.
https://doi.org/10.1007/978-981-19-8991-9_26

of a large number of experts in the field of classical Chinese poetry. General Pre-trained language models (PTMs), which can learn good semantic representations of language from a large amount of unsupervised corpus and generalize to the completion of various downstream tasks, have been urgently needed in the classical Chinese poetry area research.

Most of the existing PTMs [4,5,9,19] are trained on modern Chinese corpus and have been successfully utilized in many natural language processing tasks, such as text classification, reading comprehension, and intelligent question answering. While for classical Chinese poetry, due to the irrecoverable and specially organized structure, it is very difficult to be learned by existing pre-trained modern language models. Besides, with the thousands of years of development, many words in classical Chinese poetry have changed their meanings or been out of use today, For example, the sentences of classical Chinese poetry are concise and rhyming, and one word can usually express more than one meaning. In the poetry " 红豆生南国，春来发几枝。" translated as: the Ormosia born south, spring to hair a few branches.

Based on the context information, general pre-trained language models may learn that ormosia is a kind of plant. However, except for the meaning of a plant, ormosia is often used to express lovesickness in Chinese, which is also termed as "love pea". Pre-training language models only based on classical Chinese poetry suffers from the inherent drawback of the changing semantic of vocabularies in classical Chinese poetry.

The PTMs need to learn more external knowledge to enhance the model's ability to represent language [37], especially for the classical Chinese poetry area with limited and irrecoverable sentences. To address this challenge, we construct a large-scale sememe knowledge graph for classical Chinese Poetry (**SKG-Poetry**). We take full usage of the interpretation materials of one poetry, such as annotations, translations, and appreciation, and propose an automatic method with sememes[1] to connect the fragmented information of vocabularies in diverse forms in modern Chinese and classical Chinese poetry. As shown in Hownet[2], we can see that ormosia is not only an edible vegetable but also often used to express lovesickness.

With the sememe knowledge from classical Chinese poetry, we propose a novel sememe knowledge based PTMs, termed as **PoetryBERT**, to be trained on the classical Chinese poetry in an unsupervised way. We design two stage encoders to fuse the information from the poetry sentence and the sememe knowledge graph. Specifically, the "T-Encoder" with multi-head attentions encodes the texts and extracts the lexical and syntactic feature information of the poetry sentence, which is further jointly learned with the sememe knowledge in "K-Encoder" to obtain the representation of a word. Then we feed all the encoded

---

[1] In linguistics, sememes are defined as the smallest semantic unit of language. Linguists believe that the meaning of all words can be described by a limited set of meanings.

[2] Ormosia belong to seven sememes: think of, vegetable, part, tree, eat, mean, embryo.

information of words in a poetry into the Chinese language based the BERT-wwm [8] to get the final representations.

Our sememe knowledge based pre-training model PoetryBERT enlarges the irrecoverable pre-training corpus, as well as enriches the semantics of the vocabularies in classical Chinese poetry, enabling PoetryBERT to have deep understanding of ancient poetry and leading to its superior performance on downstream tasks. We evaluate the performance of our pre-trained model in two common tasks, i.e., poetry theme classification (PTC) [34] and poetry-modern Chinese translation (PMCT) [28], showing the effectiveness of sememe knowledge based PTM in classical Chinese poetry field.

The main contributions of this paper are:

- We automatically construct a large-scale sememe knowledge graph SKG-Poetry, which bridges the gap between classical Chinese poetry and modern Chinese, and provides a way to enlarge the irrecoverable corpus of classical Chinese poetry.
- We propose a specific sememe knowledge based pre-training model for classical Chinese poetry. Two stage encoders "T-Encoder" and "K-Encoder" are used to fuse the encoded information of the poetry and sememe knowledge for further pre-training. The specific large-scale pre-training model PoetryBERT will be open-sourced to promote the research in the classical Chinese poetry area.
- We evaluate our pre-training model on two downstream tasks, i.e., poetry theme classification and poetry-modern Chinese translation. The experimental results demonstrate that our sememe knowledge based pre-training model PoetryBERT owns superior performance in classical Chinese poetry field.

2   Related Work

2.1   Pre-training Language Models

A lot of research work [4,9,24] has shown that PTMs can learn universal language representations and are beneficial to downstream NLP tasks. GPT [41], BERT [9], MASS [43], UniLM [10], XLNet [54] have emerged one after another. They learn more contextual information of words, and use various language tasks to train PTM to support a wider range of applications. Since BERT, fine-tuning on PTMs has become a conventional paradigm in the NLP field. Many subsequent studies are improved based on BERT, such as SpanBERT [21], RoBERTa [33], ALBERT [25], etc. These models have greatly promoted the progress of the NLP field.

The PTMs of general domain lack domain-specific knowledge and are difficult to directly apply in special domain. Some studies have proposed PTMs for specific domains or tasks, such as BioBERT [27], SciBERT [2], Clinical-BERT [1] and CINO[3]. For many tasks in the field of classical Chinese poetry, we urgently needs a special pre-training model to support relevant work.

---

[3] https://github.com/ymcui/Chinese-Minority-PLM.

Recently, a new paradigm prompting has become more and more popular [7,31,36]. It transforms the input and output form of downstream tasks into the form of pre-training tasks needed. But designing prompt templates for downstream tasks requires a lot of time and experience. And prompt tuning has poor performance when the amount of data is small [14].

2.2   Knowledge-Enriched Pre-training Models

In order to improve the performance of PTMs, some studies introduce external knowledge into PTMs, including semantic [22,26,38], common sense [15], factual [51] and domain-specific knowledge [16] etc. ERICA [40] models the relational facts in the text to enhance the language model's understanding of entities and relations, and designs two pre-training tasks, entity discrimination and relational discrimination, to better capture the relational facts in the text. In addition, ERNIE(THU) [57], CoLAKE [44], GLM [42], and JAKET [56] all achieved certain results by introducing knowledge into PTM.

ERNIE (Baidu) [45] learn language representation enhanced by entity-level masking and phrase-level masking. KnowBERT [37] introduces structured data into the pre-training process through entity recognition and entity connection. KEPLER [49] is a unified model for knowledge embedding and pre-trained language representation, which can produce effective text-enhanced knowledge embedding. K-BERT [32] directly introduces relevant triples into sentences in the process of fine-tuning downstream tasks. ChineseBERT [46] introduced glyph and pinyin information of Chinese during pre-training. KLMo [17] proposed to combine the entities in KG and the relations between them into the process of language learning to obtain a knowledge enhancement pre-training model. [6] introduce entity-relationship constraints into the prompt learning framework and propose KnowPrompt, an efficient knowledge-embedded prompt learning method.

2.3   Ancient Chinese Domain Tasks

In the field of classical Chinese poetry, there has been some work on the generation of poetry [55,58], poetry sentiment and theme classification, the translation of poetry [52,53] and the knowledge graph of poetry [18,34,50]. [35] studied the new word detection in ancient Chinese corpus, and used a semi-automated method to construct a classical Chinese poetry knowledge graph (CCP-KG) [34]. They use BERT and GAT to encode the nodes in the text and knowledge graph respectively to classify the sentiment and theme of classical Chinese poetry. However, there is a large amount of artificial participation in the construction of the classical Chinese poetry knowledge graph, and the scale of the graph is difficult to expand. [13] studied the translation of English poetry. [30] create a new large-scale Ancient-Modern Chinese parallel corpus. In terms of poetry generation, [58] has launched the 'Jiuge'. [53] used an unsupervised method to study the generation of classical Chinese poetry from modern Chinese. [39] proposes a famous saying recommendation model, which aims to automatically recommend famous sayings (including English, modern Chinese and ancient poetry) suitable for the current context.

AnchiBERT [47] is a pre-trained language model based on ancient Chinese, but its performance in ancient Chinese poetry has not been verified. In short, there is still a lack of a pre-training model that can be used for various downstream tasks.

3 PoetryBERT

3.1 Overall Architecture

PoetryBERT is a sememe knowledge based pre-training model. As shown in Fig. 1, PoetryBERT is consist of four components, i.e., the sememe knowledge graph component, the two stage component: "(T-Encoder)" encodes text and extracts the lexical and syntactic feature information of the poetry sentence, and the K-Encoder fuses the information from both sememe knowledge graph and classical Chinese poetry sentence.

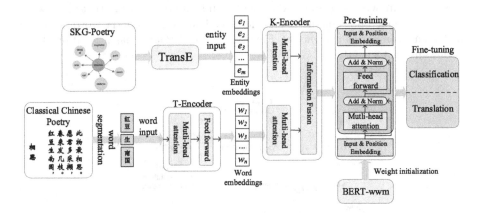

Fig. 1. The process of pre-training and fine-tuning of PoetryBERT.

3.2 Construction of SKG-Poetry

To enlarge the irrecoverable pre-training corpus of classical Chinese poetry and enrich the semantics of the vocabularies, we construct a large-scale sememe knowledge graph of classical Chinese Poetry (**SKG-Poetry**), which bridges the gap between classical Chinese poetry and modern Chinese. Specifically, we crawl the classical Chinese poetry dataset from *Gushiwen*[4] and *Soyun*[5] websites, which provide service of the full texts and appreciation of classical Chinese poetry. We collect 905,675 poetry from the pre-Qin (1000 BC: Before the Common Era)

---

[4] https://www.gushiwen.cn/.
[5] https://sou-yun.cn/.

to the Qing dynasty (1800 AD: Anno Domini), with a range of about three thousand years. We adopt the new word detection method in [35] for the word segmentation of poetry, and keep the words that used more than 5 times in poetry as the candidate words (145,800 words) to build the sememe knowledge graph.

To bridge the gap between classical Chinese poetry and modern Chinese, we crawl the modern Chinese definitions of candidate words from *HanDian*[6]. We find that a total number of 139,820 words are defined with modern Chinese in *HanDian*. Considering that in modern Chinese linguistics, sememes are defined as the smallest semantic unit of language and it is believed that the meaning of all words can be described by a limited set of meanings [11,12], we use the sememe knowledge to make semantic connections among the words in classical Chinese poetry. We find the number of words in *HanDian* with sememe annotations is 21,683. For other words in *HanDian*, we predict the sememes by Sememe Correlation Pooling Model (ScorP) [12], which is trained by the corpus from *Modern Chinese Dictionary*, and predict the scores of sememes that a specific word would belong to. Hence we use the candidate words in classical Chinese poetry (145,800 words) and sememes in *HowNet* (1400 sememes) as the nodes in sememe knowledge graph SKG-Poetry, and an edge is constructed between the poetry node and sememe node when the definition of poetry word is similar to sememe semantics in *HowNet*. Finally, the SKG-Poetry has a total of 91,152 nodes and 203,395 edges.

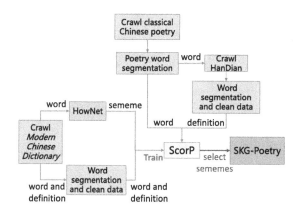

Fig. 2. Construction process of SKG-Poetry

The construction process of SKG-Poetry is shown in Fig. 2. By constructing the large scale sememes knowledge graph, we enlarge the irrecoverable pre-training corpus of classical Chinese poetry and enrich the semantics of the vocabularies.

---

[6] https://www.zdic.net/.

3.3 Two Stage Encoder Components

In order to introduce the entity information of SKG-Poetry into the pre-training model, we design two stage encoders to fuse the information from the poetry sentence and the sememe knowledge graph. Specifically, the "(T-Encoder)" with multi-head attentions encodes text and extracts the lexical and syntactic feature information of the poetry sentence. K-Encoder fuses the knowledge information in the sememe knowledge graph into the text information extracted by T-Encoder.

Formally, given a poetry sentence, denoted as $\{w_1, w_2, \ldots, w_n\}$, where n is the length of the word sequence. The corresponding entity sequence in SKG-Poetry is $\{e_1, e_2, \ldots, e_m\}$, where m is the length of the entity sequence. Note that m and n may not be equal, because the word may not be aligned to a sememe entity in the SKG-Poetry. T-Encoder is a multi-layer bidirectional Transformer encoder. By summing the word embedding, segment embedding, positional embedding for each word, the lexical and syntactic features of word sequence can be represented as $\{\mathbf{w}_1, \mathbf{w}_2, \ldots, \mathbf{w}_n\}$. The entity embeddings learned in SKG-Poetry are calculate [3] as $\{\mathbf{e}_1, \mathbf{e}_2, \ldots, \mathbf{e}_m\}$. Both words and entities information are fed into K-Encoder to get the semantic representations by learning from both the poetry sentence and sememe knowledge graph.

K-Encoder consists of two multi-head self-attentions (MH-ATTs) and an information fusion layer. In K-Encoder, word embeddings and entity embeddings are fed into a MH-ATTs respectively, formulated as:

$$
\begin{aligned}
\{\tilde{\mathbf{w}}_1, \ldots, \tilde{\mathbf{w}}_n\} &= \text{MH-ATTs}\left(\{\mathbf{w}_1, \ldots, \mathbf{w}_n\}\right), \\
\{\tilde{\mathbf{e}}_1, \ldots, \tilde{\mathbf{e}}_m\} &= \text{MH-ATTs}\left(\{\mathbf{e}_1, \ldots, \mathbf{e}_m\}\right).
\end{aligned}
\tag{1}
$$

The information fusion layer is composed of a fully connected network. Given the word w_j and its aligned entity e_k, $\mathbf{o}_j$ is the output embedding calculated by the information fusion layer. The information fusion operation is formulated as follows:

$$
\mathbf{o}_j = \sigma\left(\mathbf{W}_t \tilde{\mathbf{w}}_j + \mathbf{W}_e \tilde{\mathbf{e}}_k + \mathbf{b}\right),
\tag{2}
$$

where $\sigma(\cdot)$ represents the GELU function. $\mathbf{W}_t$, $\mathbf{W}_e$ and $\mathbf{b}$ are the parameters to be learned by the model.

For the words without corresponding entities, the information fusion layer computes the output embeddings as follows:

$$
\mathbf{o}_j = \sigma\left(\mathbf{W}_t \tilde{\mathbf{w}}_j + \mathbf{b}\right).
\tag{3}
$$

The output embeddings in the information fusion layer in K-Encoder are used as the input embeddings in the Chinese pre-training framework.

3.4 Pre-training of Classical Chinese Poetry

After obtaining the fused sentence information from K-Encoder, we use BERT-wwm[7], to obtain the pre-training representation of words in our classical Chinese

---

[7] https://github.com/ymcui/Chinese-BERT-wwm.

poetry corpus. BERT-wwm is a variant of BERT-base-Chinese, which is officially released by Google. In BERT-base-Chinese, Chinese is segmented at the granularity of characters, and the Chinese word segmentation in traditional NLP is not considered. While BERT-wwm applies the word mask method to Chinese, which is more suitable for our classical Chinese Poetry pre-trained model.

To inject semantic relations between entities in SKG-Poetry into language representations and enhance the robustness and generalization ability of the model, we add a new training task. Our task is similar to training a denoising auto-encoder(DEA), which randomly masks some token-entity alignments and then requires the system to predict all corresponding entities based on aligned tokens. The probability that the word w_i corresponds to the entity in the knowledge graph is e_j can be calculated as follows:

$$p\left(e_j \mid w_i\right) = \frac{\exp\left(\text{linear}\left(\boldsymbol{w}_i^o\right) \cdot \boldsymbol{e}_j\right)}{\sum_{k=1}^{m} \exp\left(\text{linear}\left(\boldsymbol{w}_i^o\right) \cdot \boldsymbol{e}_k\right)} \tag{4}$$

The linear (.) represents the linear layer.

Similar to BERT, ERNIE also adopts the masked language model (MLM) as pre-training tasks to enable ERNIE to capture lexical and syntactic information from tokens in text. We do not use next sentence prediction (NSP) task because previous work shows this objective does not improve downstream task performance [33]. The overall pre-training loss is the sum of the DEA and MLM loss.

4   Experiments

4.1   Pre-training Dataset

The pre-training datasets of PoetryBERT consist of classical Chinese poetry and ancient Chinese prose. Classical Chinese poetry corpus and ancient Chinese prose are collected from *Gushiwen*and *Soyun* websites. classical Chinese poetry covers the history of ancient China from the pre-Qin to the Qing dynasty for about three thousand years (1000 BC to 1800 AD). The size of classical Chinese poetry is 54.6M, and the size of ancient Chinese prose is 32.4M.

4.2   Parameter Settings of PoetryBERT

In the MLM task, we randomly mask 15% of the words in a sentence. During pre-training, 80% of those masked words are replaced with [MASK], 10% are replaced with random words, and 10% are unchanged. The training objective is to predict the masked words with cross entropy loss.

In the DEA task, we perform the following operations: 1) In 5% of the time, for a given token-entity alignment, we replace the entity with another random entity; (2) In 15% of the time, we mask the token-entity alignment; (3) In the rest 80% of the time, we keep the marker entity alignment unchanged.

We follow the pre-training hyper-parameters used in BERT. We use H_w, H_e represent the hidden dimension, A_w, A_e represent the number of self-attention heads of word embeddings and entity embeddings respectively. M and N represent the number of T-Encoder layers and K-Encoder layers respectively. In our pre-training model, we set: $H_w = 768$, $H_e = 100$, $A_w = 12$, $A_e = 4$, $M = 6$, $N = 6$. The parameters of BERT-wwm model we used are: 12-layer, 768-hidden, 12-heads, 110M parameters. In the pre-training process, the maximum sentence length is 256, the batch size is 64, and the learning rate is $5e^{-5}$.

4.3 Fine-Tuning on Downstream Tasks

We evaluate the performance of our pre-trained model in two widely used tasks, i.e., poetry theme classification (PTC) [34] and poetry-modern Chinese translation (PMCT) [28].

Poetry Theme Classification. The goal of PTC is to compute the corresponding themes label of poetry. We use a fully connected layer after the PoetryBERT and then calculate the probability of each label through the softmax function. The model finally outputs the label with the largest probability value. We conduct experiments on a publicly released labeled dataset[8], which contains 3.2K classical Chinese poetry combined with themes and keywords. We apply a batch size of 64 and use Adam optimizer with a learning rate of 2e−5.

Table 1. Performance Comparison of Different Methods on PTC task.

Model	Acc	F1
TextRCNN [23]	78.79	71.23
Transformer [48]	77.85	70.41
BERT-base-Chinese [9]	79.42	71.94
Roberta-zh [33]	80.58	72.88
ERNIE(Baidu) [45]	80.92	73.11
ChineseBERT [46]	82.16	75.64
AnchiBERT [47]	82.30	75.51
BERT-CCPoem[a]	82.35	75.54
BERT+GAT [34]	82.94	76.69
K-BERT [32]	83.79	77.75
Our model	**84.86**	**78.46**

[a] https://github.com/THUNLP-AIPoet/ BERT-CCPoem.

---

[8] https://github.com/shuizhonghaitong/classification_GAT/tree/master/data.

As shown in Table 1, our model shows the best performance on the PTC task. TextRCNN and Transformer have not been pre-trained to learn the language representation, so the performance is not as good as the pre-trained models. BERT-base-Chinese, Roberta-zh, ERNIE (Baidu) and ChineseBERT are pre-trained models with modern Chinese corpus, and they perform better than the general language models, such as Transformer. With the ancient Chinese corpus, the pre-training models AnchiBERT and BERT-CCPoem perform better than modern Chinese pre-training model, which have a better understanding of the semantics of classical Chinese poetry. The performance of BERT+GAT and the K-BERT is better, showing the usefulness of adding the knowledge graph information of ancient Chinese to the pre-training language model. Our model introduces a large scale sememe knowledge graph SKG-Poetry to learn the semantic connections of different words in classical Chinese poetry and bridges the gap between classical Chinese poetry and modern Chinese. By enlarging the learning corpus and enriches the semantic of words, our model achieves the best results in PTC task.

Poetry-Modern Chinese Translation. The goal of PMCT is to translate classical Chinese poetry into modern Chinese. For PMCT task, we adopt the encoder-decoder framework. We initialize the encoder with PoetryBERT and use a randomly initialized decoder. We conduct experiments on the Chinese Classical Poetry Matching Dataset (CCPM)[9], which contains 24,498 classical Chinese poetry-modern Chinese sentence pairs. The translation quality is evaluated by BLEU score. We apply BLEU-4 to evaluate the performance of models in this task. The training batch size is 64 and the layer number of the decoder is 6. We use Adam to optimize the network with weight-decay = 0.0001, and the dropout rate is 0.1.

Table 2. Performance Comparison Of Different Methods on PMCT task.

Model	BLEU
Transformer [48]	25.85
BERT-base-Chinese [9]	26.96
Roberta-zh [33]	27.15
ChineseBERT [46]	27.55
mRASP [29]	27.68
BERT+GAT [34]	27.89
BERT-CCPoem	28.21
AnchiBERT [47]	28.78
K-BERT [9]	29.32
Our model	**30.07**

---

[9] https://github.com/THUNLP-AIPoet/CCPM.

We can see that our model shows the best performance on the PMCT task in Table 2. The simple transformer model can't generate smooth and coherent modern Chinese. The PTMs with modern Chinese can't represent the semantics of classical Chinese well, so it is difficult to significantly improve the performance on the PMCT task. Although mRASP has been pre-trained on a multilingual corpus, it is still difficult to apply it to the PMCT task through fine-tuning. It might be because classical Chinese poetry is quite different from train corpus of mRASP. Compared with BERT-CCPoem, AnchiBERT has learned a lot of ancient Chinese corpus. Classical Chinese poetry and ancient Chinese prose have a certain similarity, so it surpasses BERT-CCPoem in the PMCT task. BERT+GAT performed better on the PTC task, but lacked on the PMCT task. This may be because CCP-KG only involves some ancient image and emotional vocabulary, but it does not correspond to modern Chinese. PoetryBERT not only learned a wide range of classical Chinese poetry and ancient prose corpus but also learned the sememe knowledge of SKG-Poetry. Thus PoetryBERT can generate smooth and coherent modern Chinese.

5   Experimental Analysis

5.1   Ablation Study

As shown in Table 3, we can see that both the classical Chinese poetry corpus and sememe knowledge graph improve the performance of Chinese pre-training model BERT-wwm. In addition, the addition of DEA loss function also improves the robustness and generalization ability of the model.

As shown in Table 4, our model with sememe knowledge graph SKG-Poetry performs better than hierarchical knowledge graph CCP-KG. CCP-KG is constructed manually and the entities in KG is much less than SKG-Poetry, showing the advantages of our large-scale sememe knowledge graph SKG-Poetry constructed by an automatical way. We also compare our model with other KG based pre-training model, the results are presented in Table 4, we can see that compared with K-BERT, using K-Encoder to encode the relationship between entities in the knowledge graph can make the pre-training models show better performance on downstream tasks.

5.2   Case Study of Poetry Translation

For the sentence "山青灭远树，水绿无寒烟。" (The green color of the mountains shades the trees in the distance,and the color of the water is green and there is no cold smoke.), PoetryBERT translates it as "山色青翠看不到远处的树木，水色碧绿没有寒烟。" (The mountains are verdant and you can't see the trees in the distance,and the water is green and there is no cold smoke.). "灭" in modern Chinese means "destroy, extermination, turn off", but in the context of describing scenery, "灭" means "conceal, cover". Neither BERT, AnchiBERT nor BERT-CCPoem can accurately understand the meaning of "灭". Only PoetryBERT can accurately translate "灭" into "Invisible".

Table 3. The ablation experimental results of PoetryBERT. '+Poetry' represents add classical Chinese poetry in the pre-training process; '+SKG' represents add SKG-Poetry in the pre-training process; '-DEA' represents removed DEA loss in the pre-training process.

Model	PTC		PMCT
	Acc	F1	BLEU
BERT-wwm	80.36	72.81	27.09
+Poetry	82.65	76.17	28.56
+Poetry +SKG	84.86	78.46	30.07
−DEA	83.91	77.19	29.86

Table 4. Ablation experimental results on PTC and PMCT tasks using different knowledge graphs and different pre-training frameworks.

Evaluate task		PTC		PMCT
Model	Knowledge graph	Acc	F1	BLEU
K-BERT	CCP-KG	82.16	76.55	28.23
	SKG-Poetry	83.79	77.75	29.32
Our model	CCP-KG	83.22	77.47	28.95
	SKG-Poetry	84.46	78.46	30.07

It can be seen from the examples that PoetryBERT can accurately learn the semantics of classical Chinese poetry and generate smooth and coherent modern Chinese. Because Transformer has not been pre-trained to learn language representation, it can't generate coherent and meaningful modern Chinese sentences for more complex sentences. BERT-Base-Chinese learns representation from modern Chinese corpus, but many words have different meanings in modern Chinese and ancient Chinese, so they may have wrong understandings. Although AnchiBERT and BERT-CCPoem have been trained on classical Chinese poetry and ancient poetry corpus, it is still difficult to accurately distinguish the meaning of these words.

6   Conclusion

In this paper, we propose the method of sememe prediction to construct a knowledge graph of classical Chinese poetry based on the word definition and their sememe annotation. We train the PoetryBERT by add a K-Encoder module to integrate SKG-poetry knowledge in the pre-training process. Besides, we evaluated the language understanding and generation ability of PoetryBERT on the task of PTC and PMCT. Our model showed optimal performance on two downstream tasks. We have open sourced the pre-training model, which can be used for downstream tasks in a variety of ancient poetry fields.

We have developed a knowledge graph intelligent service platform based on classical Chinese poetry, which not only analyzed the poetry but also analyzed the relationship between time and space and the relationship between characters. We will also introduce multi-modal information such as pictures, videos, and audio, develop a multi-modal PTM of classical Chinese poetry. Based on PoetryBERT, we will develop more interesting apps, such as classical Chinese poetry intelligent question answering system, poetry generation, etc. We will establish a complete ancient Chinese intelligent service system, restore the social and cultural sentiments of the time and allow more people to realize the richness and diversity of civilization.

References

1. Alsentzer, E., et al.: Publicly available clinical BERT embeddings. In: Proceedings of the 2nd Clinical Natural Language Processing Workshop, pp. 72–78 (2019)
2. Beltagy, I., Lo, K., Cohan, A.: SciBERT: a pretrained language model for scientific text. In: Proceedings of the 2019 Conference on Empirical Methods in Natural Language Processing and the 9th International Joint Conference on Natural Language Processing (EMNLP-IJCNLP), pp. 3615–3620 (2019)
3. Bordes, A., Usunier, N., Garcia-Duran, A., Weston, J., Yakhnenko, O.: Translating embeddings for modeling multi-relational data. In: Advances in Neural Information Processing Systems, vol. 26 (2013)
4. Brown, T.B., et al.: Language models are few-shot learners. arXiv preprint arXiv:2005.14165 (2020)
5. Chen, C., et al.: bert2BERT: towards reusable pretrained language models. In: Proceedings of the 60th Annual Meeting of the Association for Computational Linguistics (Volume 1: Long Papers), pp. 2134–2148 (2022)
6. Chen, X., et al.: Knowprompt: knowledge-aware prompt-tuning with synergistic optimization for relation extraction. In: Proceedings of the ACM Web Conference 2022, pp. 2778–2788 (2022)
7. Cui, G., Hu, S., Ding, N., Huang, L., Liu, Z.: Prototypical verbalizer for prompt-based few-shot tuning. arXiv preprint arXiv:2203.09770 (2022)
8. Cui, Y., et al.: Pre-training with whole word masking for Chinese BERT. arXiv preprint arXiv:1906.08101 (2019)
9. Devlin, J., Chang, M.W., Lee, K., Toutanova, K.: BERT: pre-training of deep bidirectional transformers for language understanding. In: Proceedings of the 2019 Conference of the North American Chapter of the Association for Computational Linguistics: Human Language Technologies, Volume 1 (Long and Short Papers), pp. 4171–4186 (2019)
10. Dong, L., et al.: Unified language model pre-training for natural language understanding and generation. In: Proceedings of the 33rd International Conference on Neural Information Processing Systems (2019)
11. Dong, Z., Dong, Q., Hao, C.: HowNet and its computation of meaning. In: COLING 2010: Demonstrations, pp. 53–56 (2010)
12. Du, J., Qi, F., Sun, M., Liu, Z.: Lexical sememe prediction by dictionary definitions and localsemantic correspondence. J. Chin. Inf. Process. **34**, 1–9 (2020)

13. Ghazvininejad, M., Choi, Y., Knight, K.: Neural poetry translation. In: Proceedings of the 2018 Conference of the North American Chapter of the Association for Computational Linguistics: Human Language Technologies, Volume 2 (Short Papers), pp. 67–71 (2018)

14. Gu, Y., Han, X., Liu, Z., Huang, M.: PPT: pre-trained prompt tuning for few-shot learning. arXiv preprint arXiv:2109.04332 (2021)

15. Guan, J., Huang, F., Zhao, Z., Zhu, X., Huang, M.: A knowledge-enhanced pre-training model for commonsense story generation. Trans. Assoc. Comput. Linguist. **8**, 93–108 (2020)

16. He, B., et al.: BERT-MK: integrating graph contextualized knowledge into pre-trained language models. In: Findings of the Association for Computational Linguistics: EMNLP 2020, pp. 2281–2290 (2020)

17. He, L., Zheng, S., Yang, T., Zhang, F.: KLMo: knowledge graph enhanced pre-trained language model with fine-grained relationships. In: Findings of the Association for Computational Linguistics: EMNLP 2021, pp. 4536–4542 (2021)

18. Hong, L., Hou, W., Zhou, L.: Knowpoetry: A knowledge service platform for tang poetry research based on domain-specific knowledge graph. In: Library Trends, vol. 69, pp. 101–124 (2020)

19. Hsu, C.J., Lee, H.Y., Tsao, Y.: XdBERT: distilling visual information to BERT from cross-modal systems to improve language understanding. arXiv preprint arXiv:2204.07316 (2022)

20. Hu, R., Li, K., Zhu, Y.: Knowledge representation and sentence segmentation of ancient Chinese based on deep language models. J. Chin. Inf. Sci. **35**, 8 (2021)

21. Joshi, M., Chen, D., Liu, Y., Weld, D.S., Zettlemoyer, L., Levy, O.: SpanBERT: improving pre-training by Representing and Predicting Spans. Trans. Assoc. Comput. Linguist. **8**, 64–77 (2020)

22. Ke, P., Ji, H., Liu, S., Zhu, X., Huang, M.: SentiLARE: sentiment-aware language representation learning with linguistic knowledge. In: Proceedings of the 2020 Conference on Empirical Methods in Natural Language Processing (EMNLP), pp. 6975–6988 (2020)

23. Lai, S., Xu, L., Liu, K., Zhao, J.: Recurrent convolutional neural networks for text classification. In: Proceedings of the AAAI Conference on Artificial Intelligence, pp. 2267–2273 (2015)

24. Lample, G., Conneau, A.: Cross-lingual language model pretraining. In: Proceedings of the Advances in Neural Information Processing Systems, pp. 7057–7067 (2019)

25. Lan, Z., Chen, M., Goodman, S., Gimpel, K., Sharma, P., Soricut, R.: AlBERT: a lite BERT for self-supervised learning of language representations. In: Proceedings of the International Conference on Learning Representations (2020)

26. Lauscher, A., Vulic, I., Ponti, E.M., Korhonen, A., Glavas, G.: Specializing unsupervised pretraining models for word-level semantic similarity. In: Proceedings of the 28th International Conference on Computational Linguistics, pp. 1371–1383 (2020)

27. Lee, J., et al.: BioBERT: a pre-trained biomedical language representation model for biomedical text mining. Bioinformatics **36**, 1234–1240 (2019)

28. Li, W., Qi, F., Sun, M., Yi, X., Zhang, J.: CCPM: a Chinese classical poetry matching dataset. arXiv preprint arXiv:2106.01979 (2021)

29. Lin, Z., et al.: Pre-training multilingual neural machine translation by leveraging alignment information. In: Proceedings of the 2020 Conference on Empirical Methods in Natural Language Processing (EMNLP), pp. 2649–2663 (2020)

30. Liu, D., Yang, K., Qu, Q., Lv, J.: Ancient-modern Chinese translation with a new large training dataset. In: ACM Transactions on Asian and Low-Resource Language Information Processing, vol. 19, pp. 1–13 (2019)

31. Liu, P., Yuan, W., Fu, J., Jiang, Z., Hayashi, H., Neubig, G.: Pre-train, prompt, and predict: a systematic survey of prompting methods in natural language processing. arXiv preprint arXiv:2107.13586 (2021)

32. Liu, W., et al.: K-BERT: enabling language representation with knowledge graph. In: Proceedings of the AAAI Conference on Artificial Intelligence, vol. 34, pp. 2901–2908 (2020)

33. Liu, Y., et al.: RoBERTa: a robustly optimized BERT pretraining approach. arXiv preprint arXiv:1907.11692 (2019)

34. Liu, Y., Wu, B., Bai, T.: The construction and analysis of the knowledge graph of classical Chinese poetry. In: Computer Research and Development, vol. 57, p. 1252 (2020)

35. Liu, Y., Wu, B., Xie, T., Wang, B.: New word detection in ancient Chinese corpus. J. Chin. Inf. Process. **33**, 46–55 (2019)

36. Mahabadi, R.K., et al.: Perfect: prompt-free and efficient few-shot learning with language models. arXiv preprint arXiv:2204.01172 (2022)

37. Peters, M.E., et al.: Knowledge enhanced contextual word representations. In: Proceedings of the 2019 Conference on Empirical Methods in Natural Language Processing and the 9th International Joint Conference on Natural Language Processing (EMNLP-IJCNLP), pp. 43–54 (2019)

38. Qi, F., Lv, C., Liu, Z., Meng, X., Sun, M., Zheng, H.T.: Sememe prediction for babelnet synsets using multilingual and multimodal information. arXiv preprint arXiv:2203.07426 (2022)

39. Qi, F., Yang, Y., Yi, J., Cheng, Z., Liu, Z., Sun, M.: Quoter: a benchmark of quote recommendation for writing. arXiv preprint arXiv:2202.13145 (2022)

40. Qin, Y., et al.: ERICA: improving entity and relation understanding for pre-trained language models via contrastive learning. In: Proceedings of the 59th Annual Meeting of the Association for Computational Linguistics, pp. 3350–3363 (2021)

41. Radford, A., Narasimhan, K., Salimans, T., Sutskever, I.: Improving language understanding by generative pre-training. OpenAI Blog (2018)

42. Shen, T., Mao, Y., He, P., Long, G., Trischler, A., Chen, W.: Exploiting structured knowledge in text via graph-guided representation learning. In: Proceedings of the 2020 Conference on Empirical Methods in Natural Language Processing (EMNLP), pp. 8980–8994 (2020)

43. Song, K., Tan, X., Qin, T., Lu, J., Liu, T.Y.: MASS: masked sequence to sequence pre-training for language generation. In: Proceedings of the 36th International Conference on Machine Learning, vol. 97, pp. 5926–5936 (2019)

44. Sun, T., Shao, Y., Qiu, X., Guo, Q., Hu, Y., Huang, X., Zhang, Z.: CoLAKE: contextualized language and knowledge embedding. In: Proceedings of the 28th International Conference on Computational Linguistics, pp. 3660–3670 (2020)

45. Sun, Y., et al.: Ernie: enhanced representation through knowledge integration. arXiv preprint arXiv:1904.09223 (2019)

46. Sun, Z., et al.: ChineseBERT: Chinese pretraining enhanced by glyph and Pinyin information. In: Proceedings of the 59th Annual Meeting of the Association for Computational Linguistics, pp. 2065–2075 (2021)

47. Tian, H., Yang, K., Liu, D., Lv, J.: AnchiBERT: a pre-trained model for ancient Chinese language understanding and generation. In: 2021 International Joint Conference on Neural Networks (IJCNN), pp. 1–8 (2021)

48. Vaswani, A., et al.: Attention is all you need. In: Advances in Neural Information Processing Systems, vol. 30 (2017)
49. Wang, X., et al.: KEPLER: a unified model for knowledge embedding and pre-trained language representation. Trans. Assoc. Comput. Linguist. **9**, 176–194 (2021)
50. Wei, Y., Wang, H., Zhao, J., Liu, Y., Zhang, Y., Wu, B.: Gelaigelai: a visual platform for analysis of classical Chinese poetry based on knowledge graph. In: 2020 IEEE International Conference on Knowledge Graph (ICKG), pp. 513–520 (2020)
51. Xiong, W., Du, J., Wang, W.Y., Stoyanov, V.: Pretrained encyclopedia: weakly supervised knowledge-pretrained language model. In: International Conference on Learning Representations (2020)
52. Yang, K., Liu, D., Qu, Q., Sang, Y., Lv, J.: An automatic evaluation metric for ancient-modern Chinese translation. Neural Comput. Appl. **33**, 3855–3867 (2021)
53. Yang, Z., et al.: Generating classical Chinese poems from vernacular Chinese. In: Proceedings of the Conference on Empirical Methods in Natural Language Processing. Conference on Empirical Methods in Natural Language Processing, vol. 2019, p. 6155 (2019)
54. Yang, Z., Dai, Z., Yang, Y., Carbonell, J., Salakhutdinov, R.R., Le, Q.V.: Xlnet: generalized autoregressive pretraining for language understanding. In: Proceedings of the Advances in Neural Information Processing Systems, vol. 32 (2019)
55. Yi, X., Li, R., Yang, C., Li, W., Sun, M.: Mixpoet: diverse poetry generation via learning controllable mixed latent space. In: Proceedings of the AAAI Conference on Artificial Intelligence, vol. 34, pp. 9450–9457 (2020)
56. Yu, D., Zhu, C., Yang, Y., Zeng, M.: Jaket: joint pre-training of knowledge graph and language understanding. arXiv preprint arXiv:2010.00796 (2020)
57. Zhang, Z., Han, X., Liu, Z., Jiang, X., Sun, M., Liu, Q.: ERNIE: enhanced language representation with informative entities. In: Proceedings of the 57th Annual Meeting of the Association for Computational Linguistics, pp. 1441–1451 (2019)
58. Zhipeng, G., et al.: Jiuge: a human-machine collaborative Chinese classical poetry generation system. In: Proceedings of the 57th Annual Meeting of the Association for Computational Linguistics: System Demonstrations, pp. 25–30 (2019)

Image Hide with Invertible Network and Swin Transformer

Yuhuan Feng[1] [iD], Yunjie Liu[2] [iD], Hongjuan Wang[1] [iD], Jin Dong[1] [iD], Rujia Wang[1] [iD], and Chunpeng Tian[1(✉)] [iD]

[1] Shandong University of Science and Technology, Tai'an 271019, China
tianchunpeng@sdust.edu.cn
[2] The Taishan College of Science and Technology, Tai'an 271021, China

Abstract. Image hiding is a way of hiding information by hiding a secret image in a carrier image in an imperceptible way and recovering it. How to effect better hiding of images in images is a problem that is still being studied. In this paper, we propose an invertible neural network based model using the Swin Transformer module to hide images. According to the properties of invertible neural networks, image hiding and revealing can be done by the same network of forward and backward processes. Since image hiding and recovery are forward and backward of the same network, sharing the same set of parameters, a lot of resources are saved accordingly. It is found that hiding secret information in wavelet domain can improve the concealment, so we transform the image to wavelet domain for hiding.

Keywords: INN · Image hiding · Swin transformer

1 Introduction

Image hiding is the hiding of a secret image in a cover image to hide the presence of data [1, 2] making it imperceptible for purposes such as encrypted communication or content protection. In contrast, cryptography focuses on the protection of secret information from being broken without hiding the act of secret communication. Nowadays, image hiding has been used in various fields not limited to covert communication, copyright protection, e-commerce, etc. The most important applications are covert communication and privacy protection [1].

Two of the more important metrics for image hiding are the stealthiness of the covert image transmission and the quality of the recovered image. Stealthiness requires that the secret image is not perceived as hidden data by steganalysis tools and the human eye. Recovered image quality: The recovered secret image is required to be more similar to the original secret image. Traditional image hiding methods use separate neural networks in the image hiding stage and the image recovery stage [3–8], so it is difficult to guarantee both the generation of highly concealed laden images and the recovery of high-quality secret images.

© The Author(s), under exclusive license to Springer Nature Singapore Pte Ltd. 2022
Y. Tan and Y. Shi (Eds.): DMBD 2022, CCIS 1745, pp. 385–394, 2022.
https://doi.org/10.1007/978-981-19-8991-9_27

In this paper, we propose an image hiding method based on INN, (Invertible Neural Network) and Swin Transformer. Our network views image hiding and recovery as two directions of the network, sharing the same set of parameters, thus reducing the training time to enhance the model effect.

The main contributions of this work can be summarized in two points:

- Referencing INN effectively uses a single network to solve image hiding and recovery problems.
- Use the Swin Transformer module in INN.

2 Related Work

2.1 Steganography and Image Hiding

Steganography is the hiding of textual information, audio, graphics, or video in a carrier information, and the carrier can make any of the previously mentioned. Image steganography is one of the steganography techniques [9, 10], which refers to the hiding of information in an image. Earlier, researchers have hidden information by modifying certain pixels, such as Least Significant Bit (LSB) [11, 12]. Such pixel-modified steganographic algorithms hide limited image information and usually cause changes in the statistical properties of the stego images that are easily identified by steganographic analysis methods [13, 14]. In contrast to LSB which hide messages in the spatial domain, some models point their attention to the frequency domain, such as Discrete Fourier Transform (DFT) domain [15] Discrete Cosine Transform (DCT) [16] Discrete Wavelet Transform (DWT) [17]. JSteg [2] hides the information into the least significant bit of the DCT of the carrier [16]. In general, these methods are more stealthy compared to LSB, but all have a relatively low steganographic load capacity and can only hide bit-level information.

With the development of deep learning, various models have made breakthroughs in the fields of image processing and natural language processing, and possible attacks can also be detected in advance by deep learning in the field of security [18], and researchers hope to use deep learning to break through the bottlenecks encountered in image steganography. Hayes [19] proposed HayesGAN, an image steganography framework for hiding text with images, which was the first time to implement images to hide secret information using coding networks. To increase the robustness of steganography, Zhu [20] proposed the HiDDeN (hiding data with deep networks) model, adding a noise layer to the network to simulate various situations in the image transmission process, and achieved better results.

Image hiding is an important part of image steganography. Image steganography is the hiding of image information in another carrier image. Baluja [4] first applied CNN to the field of image hiding. The network model proposed by Baluja [4] has a poor quality of the carrier image and the recovered secret image, and there is a noise problem in the image smoothing area, which can easily cause statistical data anomalies and even be detected by human eyes. Based on this, Wu [6] proposed the network model of StegNet (steganography with deep convolutional network) to modify the loss function based on the previous one so that the noise is uniformly distributed in the image, which effectively improves the above problem. Duan [7] modified the structure of the encoding network and also the image hiding results were improved. U-Net [7] can preserve the shallow and deep features of the image because the network structure of upsampling and downsampling has a connection operation, and the network structure as an encoder can make the recovered secret image more shaped with the secret image, which is improved compared to Baluja's method.

In addition to hiding color images in color images, some researchers hide black and white images in color images. Zhang [8] proposed the ISGAN (invisible steganography via generative adversarial networks) model. This model decomposes the color image into 3 channels, U/V/Y, where the U/V channel contains the chromaticity signal of the original image and the Y channel contains the luminance signal of the image. The model hides the secret image in the Y channel because the human body is not sensitive to the luminance information, so the secret image is hidden in the Y channel, and the similarity of the stego image is increased compared to the cover image in the case of human eye judgment, which enhances the concealment of the image hidden information.

2.2 Invertible Neural Network

Dinh [21] first proposed reversible neural networks. Dinh [22] introduced the introduction of convolute and multiscale layers in the model, which enabled the model to achieve superior results in image processing problems, while also reducing computational costs. Kingma [23] applied invertible 1×1 convolution and Glow to INN, which made it synthesize realistic images with good results [24] provides a further explanation of the invertible nature of INN [25] constructed a more flexible INN using convolution with masking, and the INN was also used in various tasks due to its excellent performance [26] applied INN to the field of image hiding.

2.3 Swin Transformer

Convolutional neural networks (CNN) have a relatively large advantage in focusing on and extracting local features, but are not as good as Transformer in focusing on global information [27–29]. The Transformer model, which recently originated in the field of natural language processing, is frequently used in the CV field [30]. Various approaches to applying the Transformer to computer vision tasks are emerging and achieving good results, even beyond convolutional neural networks. Vision Transformer (VIT) first applied the Transformer architecture directly to the image domain, decomposing images into a series of image block inputs [31].

The Swin Transformer (Shifted Windows Transformer) not only has the ability of the Transformer to focus on global information modeling, but also uses the method of moving windows to achieve cross-window connection, so that the model can focus on the relevant information of other adjacent windows. The aim is to introduce a hierarchical Transformer with the same hierarchical construction method commonly used in CNNs, and to perform self-attentive computation in the window region without overlap, and to model the relationship only locally in each layer, while being able to continuously reduce the feature map width and height to expand the perceptual field [32]. Compared with ViT, the computational complexity of Swin Transfomer is substantially reduced.

3   Approach

3.1   Network Architecture

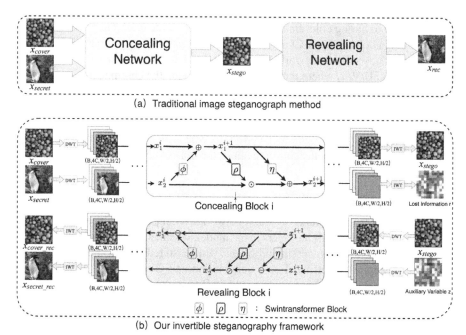

(a) Traditional image steganograph method

(b) Our invertible steganography framework

Fig. 1. Network architecture. In contrast to the conventional method (a), which deals with the conceal and reveal processes of the image separately, we use INN (b). The cover image and the secret image are used as the forward input to the invertible network, and several conceal blocks with the same structure are used to generate the stego image. Conversely, the backward goes through the reveal block to effectively recover the hidden image from the stego image. Where ϕ, ρ is the Swin Transformer block.

Table 1. Summary of notations in this paper.

Notation	Description
x_{secret}	Secret image: the image to be hidden
x_{cover}	Cover image: the image to hide secret information
x_{stego}	Stego image: the cover image with secret image inside
x_{rec}	Recovery image: the secret image recovered from the stego image
r	Lost information: the information lost in concealing process
z	Auxiliary variable: the variable to help recover secret image

Figure 1(a) shows the structure of the conventional network, processing the conceal and reveal processes of the image separately. Figure 1(b) shows the overall framework of our network. The cover image x_{cover} and the secret image x_{secret} are decomposed by DWT transform as the forward input of the network, and the stego image x_{stego} and the lost information r are generated by several concealing modules with the same structure. In the concealing process, a large amount of secret information hidden in the cover image will inevitably cause information loss, and also the secret information in the embedded secret image will destroy the cover image information, and the lost information r is composed of the lost information and the cover image destroyed information together. In turn, the inverse network can effectively recover high-quality hidden images from the stego image based on the stego image and the auxiliary variable z. Here the auxiliary variable z is sampled from the Gaussian distribution.

We view image hiding and recovery as a pair of invertible problems, and the process is formulated as follows:

$$\begin{aligned} x_{steo} &= f(x_{cover}, x_{secret}) \\ (x_{cover_{rev}}, x_{secre_{rev}}) &= f^{-1}(x_{stego}) \end{aligned} \tag{1}$$

where x_{stego} denotes the stego image, x_{cover} denotes the cover image, x_{secret} denotes the secret image, $x_{secre_{rec}}$ denotes the secret image recovered from the stego image, and $x_{cover_{rec}}$ denotes the cover image recovered from the stego image. We apply the network forward mapping to fit the steganography function $f(\cdot)$. The inverse mapping is used to fit the image recovery function $f^{-1}(\cdot)$.

In the model, for the ith conceal/recover block, we input the tensor x_1^i representing the carrier image and the tensor x_2^i representing the secret image, respectively, and the corresponding outputs are x_1^{i+1}, x_2^{i+1}, respectively. In the forward network:

$$\begin{aligned} x_1^{i+1} &= x_1^i + \phi(x_2^i) \\ x_2^{i+1} &= x_2^i \odot \exp(\alpha(\rho(x_1^{i+1}))) + \eta(x_1^{i+1}) \end{aligned} \tag{2}$$

where $\exp(\cdot)$ and $\alpha(\cdot)$ are exponential and sigmoid functions multiplied by a constant factor, and $\rho(\cdot), \eta(\cdot), \varphi(\cdot)$ n is an arbitrary function, Here the Swin Transformer module is used. $\odot$ is the dot product operation.

Corresponding in the backward network:

$$\begin{aligned} x_1^i &= x_1^{i+1} - \phi(x_2^i) \\ x_2^i &= (x_2^{i+1} - \eta(x_1^{i+1})) \odot \exp(-\alpha(\rho(x_1^{i+1}))) \end{aligned} \tag{3}$$

The $\exp(\alpha(\cdot))$ function of the concealed/revealed block in Fig. 1(b) for $\rho(\cdot)$ is omitted in the figure.

3.2   Wavelet Domain Hiding

Hiding images in the pixel domain is prone to a number of problems, such as texture-copying artifacts and color distortion [13, 33]. In contrast, those in the frequency domain, especially after the DWT, can be divided into low-frequency and high-frequency signals. The low-frequency signal is important, and it often contains the characteristics of the signal, while the high-frequency signal gives the details or differences of the signal, which is more suitable for image hiding [4]. In addition, the excellent performance of wavelets in reconstruction can help improve the quality of the recovered images [28]. After the DWT transformation, the feature map changes from (B, C, H, W) to (B, 4C, H/2, W/2), where B is the batch size, H is the height, W is the width, and C is the channel number. We use the Haar wavelet kernel to perform DWT and IWT because it is simple and effective. Moreover, the wavelet transform is biaxially symmetric and it does not affect the end-to-end training of our network.

3.3 Loss Function

The loss function is composed of three sub-functions together, which include conceal loss, extract loss, and low-frequency wavelet loss. The three losses together form the loss function.

Concealing Loss. In order to ensure the quality of hiding, the following loss function is designed in the forward network.

$$L_{con} = \sum_{n=1}^{N} \updownarrow_c \left(x_{cover}^{(n)}, x_{stego}^{(n)} \right) \tag{4}$$

where N represents the training sample size and $\updownarrow c$ is used to compare the difference between the cover image and the stego image, using either $\updownarrow 1$ or $\updownarrow 2$ norm.

Recoverling Loss. To ensure the quality of the recovered image. Where the auxiliary variable z is extracted from the Gaussian distribution $p(z)$. The loss function is as follows:

$$L_{rev} = \sum_{n=1}^{n} \mathbb{E}_{z \sim p(z)} \left[\ell_R \left(x_{secret}^{(n)}, x_{rec}^{(n)} \right) \right] \tag{5}$$

Among them, $\updownarrow_R$, like the $\updownarrow_c$ function, is responsible for measuring the difference between the secret image and the recovered secret image.

Low Frequency Wavelet Loss. We can hide the secret information in high-frequency subbands to improve image steganography [4]. To ensure that the image information is hidden in the high-frequency region, the low-frequency sub-bands of the carrier image and the carrier image should be similar, and we use $\mathcal{H}(\cdot)_{LL}$ to represent the low-frequency sub-bands after the wavelet transform. The formula is defined as follows:

$$L_{ferq} = \sum_{n=1}^{N} \ell_F \left(\mathcal{H}\left(x_{cover}^{(n)} \right) LL, \mathcal{H}\left(x_{stego}^{(n)} \right) LL \right) \tag{6}$$

where $\updownarrow_{\mathcal{F}}$ to measure the difference between the low-frequency wavelet subbands of the cover image and the stego image.

Total Loss Function. The total loss function consists of concealing loss, recovering loss and low frequency wavelet loss.

$$L_{total} = \lambda_c L_{con} + \lambda_r L_{rev} + \lambda_f L_{freq} \tag{7}$$

where λ_c, λ_r and λ_f are the weights used to balance the loss function.

4 Experiment

In that section, we conducted experiments on the dataset based on the model proposed above. And the results are derived.

4.1 Database and Experimental Setting

The dataset we use is DIV2K [34], where the training set consists of 800 photos with 2k resolution and the test set consists of 100 photos with 2k resolution. We randomly divide the testing set into two parts the cover image and the secret image respectively. Where the test images are cropped using a central cropping strategy. The number of concealing and recovered intervals is set to 2. The size of the trained patch is 224 × 224 and the parameters λ_c, λ_r and λ_f f are set to 1.0, 5.0 and 1.0, respectively. The mini-batch size is set to 2. The Adma optimizer is used with standard parameters and an initial learning rate of $1 \times 10^{-4.5}$, which is halved every 10K iterations.

4.2 Evaluation Metrics

We use two metrics to measure the quality of the hidden and recovered images. These include peak signal-to-noise ratio (PSNR), and structural similarity index (SSIM) [35]. The higher the value of PSNR and SSIM, the better the hidden and recovered images are.

Cover Image   Secret Image   Stego Image   Recovery Image

Fig. 2. The graph of the results obtained using our model

From Table 3, it can be seen that our method has the least loss relative to the previous algorithms in hiding and recovering secret information. In Fig. 2 we achieve better results than LSB in terms of PSNR.

Table 2. Results of Cover/Stego image pair.

Method	Cover/Stego image pair	
	PSNR	SSIM
4bit-LSB	33.19	0.9453
HiDDeN [20]	35.21	0.9691
Baluja [36]	36.77	0.9654
Our	34.32	0.9350

Table 3. Results of Secret/Recovery image pair.

Method	Secret/Recovery image pair	
	PSNR	SSIM
4bit-LSB	30.81	0.9020
HiDDeN [20]	36.43	0.9696
Baluja [36]	35.88	0.9377
Our	44.05	0.9911

5   Conclusion

In this paper, we adapt the invertible neural network and use the Swin Transformer module for the invertible neural network for image hiding. The network needs to be trained only once to obtain the network parameters needed for image hiding and recovery. Three loss functions are used to jointly constrain the network convergence. Experiments show that our network model yields good results.

References

1. Cheddad, A., Condell, J., Curran, K., Mc Kevitt, P.: Digital image steganography: survey and analysis of current methods. Signal Processing. **90**(3), 727–752 (2010)
2. Provos, N., Honeyman, P.: Hide and seek: an introduction to steganography. IEEE Secur. Priv. **1**(3), 32–44 (2003)
3. Ronneberger, O., Fischer, P., Brox, T.: U-Net: convolutional networks for biomedical image segmentation. In: International Conference on Medical Image Computing and Computer-Assisted Intervention, pp. 234–241. Springer (2015)
4. Baluja, S.: Hiding images in plain sight: deep steganography. Adv. Neural Inf. Process Syst. **30** (2017)
5. Rahim, R., Nadeem, S.: End-to-end trained CNN encoder-decoder networks for image steganography. In: Proceedings of the European Conference on Computer Vision (ECCV) Workshops, pp. 0–0 (2018)
6. Wu, P., Yang, Y., Li, X.: Stegnet: mega image steganography capacity with deep convolutional network. Future Internet. **10**(6), 54 (2018)

7. Duan, X., Jia, K., Li, B., Guo, D., Zhang, E., Qin, C.: Reversible image steganography scheme based on a U-Net structure. IEEE Access **7**, 9314–9323 (2019)
8. Zhang, R., Dong, S., Liu, J.: Invisible steganography via generative adversarial networks. Multimed. Tools Appl. **78**(7), 8559–8575 (2018). https://doi.org/10.1007/s11042-018-6951-z
9. Chanu, Y.J., Singh, K.M., Tuithung, T.: Image steganography and steganalysis: a survey. Int. J. Comput. Appl. **52**(2), 1–11 (2012)
10. Kadhim, I.J., Premaratne, P., Vial, P.J., Halloran, B.: Comprehensive survey of image steganography: techniques, evaluations, and trends in future research. Neurocomputing **335**, 299–326 (2019)
11. Chan, C.-K., Cheng, L.-M.: Hiding data in images by simple LSB substitution. Pattern Recogn. **37**(3), 469–474 (2004)
12. Cogranne, R., Zitzmann, C., Fillatre, L., Retraint, F., Nikiforov, I., Cornu, P.: A cover image model for reliable steganalysis. In: International Workshop on Information Hiding, pp. 178–192. Springer (2011)
13. Fridrich, J., Goljan, M., Du, R.: Detecting LSB steganography in color, and gray-scale images. IEEE Multimedia **8**(4), 22–28 (2001)
14. Hawi, T.A., Qutayri, M., Barada, H.: Steganalysis attacks on stego-images using stego-signatures and statistical image properties. In: 2004 IEEE Region 10 Conference TENCON 2004, pp. 104–107. IEEE (2004)
15. Ruanaidh, J., Dowling, W., Boland, F.M.: Phase watermarking of digital images. In: Proceedings of 3rd IEEE International Conference on Image Processing, pp. 239–242. IEEE (1996)
16. Hsu, C.-T., Wu, J.-L.: Hidden digital watermarks in images. IEEE Trans. Image Process. **8**(1), 58–68 (1999)
17. Barni, M., Bartolini, F., Piva, A.: Improved wavelet-based watermarking through pixel-wise masking. IEEE Trans. Image Process. **10**(5), 783–791 (2001)
18. Yin, C., Zhu, Y., Fei, J., He, X.: A deep learning approach for intrusion detection using recurrent neural networks. IEEE Access **5**, 21954–21961 (2017)
19. Hayes, J., Danezis, G.: Generating steganographic images via adversarial training. Adv. Neural Inform. Process. Syst. **30** (2017)
20. Zhu, J., Kaplan, R., Johnson, J., Fei-Fei, L.: Hidden: Hiding data with deep networks. In: Proceedings of the European Conference on Computer Vision (ECCV), pp. 657–672 (2018)
21. Dinh, L., Krueger, D., Bengio, Y.: Nice: non-linear independent components estimation. arXiv preprint arXiv:1410.8516 (2014)
22. Dinh, L., Sohl-Dickstein, J., Bengio, S.: Density estimation using real nvp. arXiv preprint arXiv:1605.08803 (2016)
23. Kingma, D.P., Dhariwal, P.: Glow: generative flow with invertible 1x1 convolutions. Adv. Neural Inform. Process. Syst. **31** (2018)
24. Gilbert, A.C., Zhang, Y., Lee, K., Zhang, Y., Lee, H.: Towards understanding the invertibility of convolutional neural networks. arXiv preprint arXiv:1705.08664 (2017)
25. Song, Y., Meng, C., Ermon, S.: Mintnet: building invertible neural networks with masked convolutions. Adv. Neural Inform. Process. Syst. **32** (2019)
26. Jing, J., Deng, X., Xu, M., Wang, J., Guan, Z.: HiNet: deep image hiding by invertible network. In: Proceedings of the IEEE/CVF International Conference on Computer Vision, pp. 4733–4742 (2021)
27. Lin, T.-Y., Dollár, P., Girshick, R., He, K., Hariharan, B., Belongie, S.: Feature pyramid networks for object detection. In: Proceedings of the IEEE Conference on Computer Vision and Pattern Recognition, pp. 2117–2125 (2017)
28. Singh, B., Davis, L.S.: An analysis of scale invariance in object detection snip. In: Proceedings of the IEEE Conference on Computer Vision and Pattern Recognition, pp. 3578–3587 (2018)

29. Singh, B., Najibi, M., Davis, L.S.: Sniper: efficient multi-scale training. Adv. Neural Inform. Process. Syst. **31** (2018)
30. Vaswani, A., et al.: Attention is all you need. Adv. Neural Inform. Process. Syst. **30** (2017)
31. Dosovitskiy, A., et al: An image is worth 16x16 words: transformers for image recognition at scale. arXiv preprint arXiv:2010.11929 (2020)
32. Liu, Z., et al.: Swin transformer: hierarchical vision transformer using shifted windows. In: Proceedings of the IEEE/CVF International Conference on Computer Vision, pp. 10012–10022 (2021)
33. Weng, X., Li, Y., Chi, L., Mu, Y.: High-capacity convolutional video steganography with temporal residual modeling. In: Proceedings of the 2019 on International Conference on Multimedia Retrieval, pp. 87–95 (2019)
34. Agustsson, E., Timofte, R.: Ntire 2017 challenge on single image super-resolution: dataset and study. In: Proceedings of the IEEE Conference on Computer Vision and Pattern Recognition Workshops, pp. 126–135 (2017)
35. Wang, Z., Bovik, A.C., Sheikh, H.R., Simoncelli, E.P.: Image quality assessment: from error visibility to structural similarity. IEEE Trans. Image Process. **13**(4), 600–612 (2004)
36. Baluja, S.: Hiding images within images. IEEE Trans. Pattern Anal. Mach. Intell. **42**(7), 1685–1697 (2019)

Modeling and Analysis of Combat System Confrontation Based on Large-Scale Knowledge Graph Network

Rupeng Liang[✉], Lizhi Ying, Kebo Deng, Huawei Zhu, Wei Ma, and Shaoqiu Zheng

CETC28th Key Laboratory of Information System Requirement, Nanjing 210007, China
rupengliang@163.com

Abstract. Focusing on the confrontation analysis requirements of joint operation system of systems, this paper proposes an intelligent matching method of operational elements based on semantic features for typical large-scale combat system such as reconnaissance and fire strike, which can provide intelligent auxiliary support for rapid and dynamic reconfiguration of operational system of systems. On this basis, a general framework for system of systems confrontation modeling and combination analysis is built, which can support networked combat system mapping, flexible expansion of system of systems capabilities analysis, dynamic generation of systems knowledge graph and customization of system of systems. The framework provides quantitative evaluation of networked combat system capabilities, which can provide intelligent auxiliary support for commanders to rapidly build the combat system, dynamically analyze and accurately evaluate the confrontation effectiveness of the combat system.

Keywords: Combat system modeling · Knowledge graph · System analysis

1 Introduction

With the networked characteristics of modern warfare, its capability generation mode and the complexity of typical combat process have been further improved. Its combat process is based on the combination of geographical wide area distribution. The combat system can be characterized as a combat system composed of multiple types of operational sub networks, including sensor networks, communication networks, intelligence networks, control networks, fire networks, etc., forming a "multi network integrated" complex combat system confrontation network.

In the era of networked warfare, the combat system has developed from the traditional hierarchical structure to the networked flat command mode, and the war power generation mode has developed from the traditional linear superposition mode to the network system capability. For the representation method of the combat system, the hierarchical tree structure cannot adapt to the representation problem of the networked combat system [1]. As an efficient graph structured data representation method, knowledge graph has strong advantages in representing networked combat system of systems, which can map

© The Author(s), under exclusive license to Springer Nature Singapore Pte Ltd. 2022
Y. Tan and Y. Shi (Eds.): DMBD 2022, CCIS 1745, pp. 395–406, 2022.
https://doi.org/10.1007/978-981-19-8991-9_28

combat system elements to nodes of knowledge graph, and effectively represent the complex relationship between combat system elements through the edges of the graph [2].

At the same time, the engagement process of the networked combat system is that the warring parties acquire and perceive target data from the battlefield space based on geographically distributed sensor nodes, then transmit and distribute the acquired information through communication nodes, and then obtain state information through intelligence fusion nodes. The battlefield situation is understood, developed, researched, judged, and used by the battle commander to form operational plans, plans, and commands, Finally, command specific forces and firepower elements through the command and control network to carry out firepower attack [1, 10]. It can be seen that the system of systems combat activities are based on the cyclic process of OODA (observation judgment decision action), and only a complete command loop can produce networked combat benefits [3].

At the same time, the combat system has the characteristics of complex dynamic confrontation evolution [4]. For the construction of a multi temporal and multi-stage combat system, it is necessary to automatically and quickly reconstruct the nodes and node mapping relationships of the combat system of systems. The complexity of the combat system oriented system of systems is further enhanced. It is difficult to fully express the relationship between the combat systems under large-scale confrontation conditions. It includes two difficult problems: one is the problem of automatic mapping between combat system nodes and actual equipment/system nodes, and the other is the problem of automatic identification of association between system element nodes and other confrontation modeling representation problems.

2 General Framework for Combat System Analysis

The process of military system confrontation is characterized by huge scale, dynamic change, diversity and openness. Especially under the condition of informatization, the system confrontation process is carried out on the basis of information and network, and there are a lot of uncertain factors in the process, which are characterized by randomness and fuzziness. The modeling and characterization of the military complex system of system confrontation process and the evaluation of the comprehensive effectiveness of the system of system confrontation are the key problems which need to be solved urgently in the system of systems confrontation, and of great significance for assisting the battlefield command decision-making in large-scale combat scenarios.

The key to the modeling of the system of systems confrontation process is to find a suitable and correct model to reflect the actual combat process as closely as possible. Because it studies the confrontation process from the campaign level, its modeling needs to be different from the mathematical modeling of the tactical level. According to the linkage structure of "System of Engagement - System Effectiveness - System Key Points - Operations - Operational Resources", a general framework for system of system confrontation process modeling and comprehensive effectiveness evaluation is designed and constructed.

In view of the network system effect and dynamic confrontation evolution characteristics of modern warfare, a multi-level tool set of "combat system integration, combat network analysis, combat capability analysis, and comprehensive confrontation analysis" is designed according to the functional process of "combat system construction, general basic analysis, and combined application analysis", It supports the construction of a common system of system confrontation analysis framework of "graphical representation of combat system association, evaluation of networked combat system capability, and modeling of composable system of system confrontation application", supports the construction of combat system association, quantitative evaluation of system capability, and integrated application of system of system confrontation, achieves the design goal of "comprehensive universality of basic capabilities, and expansion of application capabilities as needed", and supports commanders to make accurate and efficient decisions. The overall framework is shown in Fig. 1.

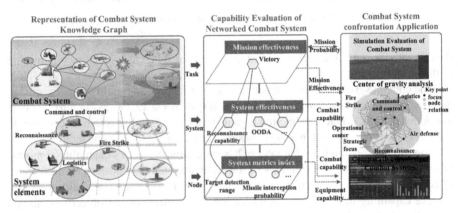

Fig. 1. General framework for system of systems confrontation analysis

3 Modeling of the Combat System Knowledge Graph

3.1 Combat System Representation Based on Knowledge Graph

The combat system consists of a set of capabilities for specific tasks; The combat system is composed of system elements, which need to describe three aspects of information, one is combat capability, that is, target image of the combat system, the other is combat elements, that is, equipment elements; The third is task information, that is, the task combination relationship of combat equipment and forces [5].

The combat system has hierarchical characteristics. The combat system is formed by element nodes, and the complex system is formed by the combat system. In order to achieve the effective representation of the multi-level combat system, knowledge mapping technology can be used to support the effective definition of the network characteristics and dynamic change attributes of the combat system. The principle is shown in Fig. 2.

The basic graph of the system is constructed based on the military knowledge graph, which can describe the force and equipment ontology. At the same time, it can support

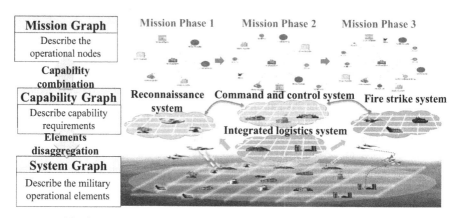

Fig. 2. Integration and construction of combat system knowledge graph

the characterization of element relationship through the inherent association relationship of the military graph.

The combat system has the characteristics of multi time and multi stage. In order to describe the dynamic combination of the combat system's tasks, the task graph is adopted to achieve the task oriented extraction organization of the combat system. According to different task types, the task graph is constructed according to the style template.

The mission oriented combat system has the characteristics of capability combination. To verify whether the elements of the combat system can meet the requirements of combat capability, a capability graph is built, to form a system capability loop, and achieve capability matching and optimization for specific combat objectives through capability aggregation.

The capability graph, system graph and mission graph can be used to describe the combat system of system in a multi perspective and multi granularity manner. The capability graph starts from the top goal and decomposes the goal into several capability sub items; The formation of operational capability should rely on the description of operational equipment and force elements through the way of element disaggregation; According to the characteristics of mission oriented dynamic combination of the combat system of systems, specific capability sub items can be oriented to form the component relationship of the mission; At the same time, the mission graph is associated with the capability graph to realize the mapping from the operational objectives to the operational tasks. Through the definition of the three graphes, the formal dynamic description of the networked dynamic combination attributes of the combat system of systems is realized.

3.2   Mapping Modeling of Large Scale Combat System of System

Based on the military knowledge graph, the combat system representation is constructed. Through the system graph, task graph, and capability graph to support the multi-level formal modeling of system confrontation, the knowledge graph is used to achieve effective representation of the multi temporal and multi-stage adversary to friend combat system confrontation situation. The technical principle is shown in Fig. 3.

(1) Basic graph construction of combat system

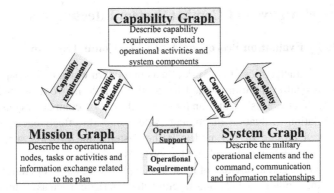

Fig. 3. Representation of combat system based on Knowledge graph

The basic graph describes all the operational elements. It is entered into the system through the system building and integration tool, and the operational relationships between the operational elements, such as command relationship, communication relationship, support relationship, etc., are built to form a full range of basic graph, including typical operational system nodes, such as fixed facilities, mobile platforms, combat forces, network electrical targets, moving targets and static targets distinguished according to the form of operations.

(2) Construction of combat system mission graph

The mission graph, from the commander's perspective, describes the commander's demand for connectivity under the current system. The mission graph is constructed through the virtual demand relationship, and the typical mission system facing different operational scenarios from the commander's perspective is constructed, such as reconnaissance and early warning, command and control, air control operations, maritime operations, ground operations, fire strikes, integrated support and other mission graphs.

(3) Construction of combat system capability graph

The capability graph aims at the task graph and is based on the basic graph. The capability graph spectrum that meets the requirements of the task graph is calculated through the background sub graph query algorithm based on map coding, Top-K related sub graph query algorithm and distance connection based sub graph pattern matching algorithm. Each task graph requirement is a connectivity sub graph in the basic graph. All connectivity links that are calculated form the capability graph, including typical capability systems such as reconnaissance and early warning, fire strike, electronic countermeasure, command and communication.

Through the construction of task oriented dynamic integration of the system of system, flexible configuration of the combat system composition and rapid adjustment of the combat relationship can be realized. Through the construction of human-computer aided system integration tools, the system of systems analysis capability of complex systems and the processing efficiency of frequently changing combat task requirements can be improved.

4 Multilevel Analysis of Combat System Effectiveness

4.1 Capability Evaluation Process of Networked Combat System

In view of the characteristics of network effects in modern warfare, this paper proposes a multi-dimensional evaluation method integrating "battle network analysis dynamic confrontation effectiveness", static analytic calculation of combat system capability, dynamic simulation evaluation of combat system mission effectiveness, support for mission oriented mining of key nodes of the system, and provide support for the comprehensive evaluation of friend and foe systems.

Focusing on the characteristics of networked operations, at the operational network level, analyze the topological network structure characteristics such as system node units and node relationships, and analyze the information flow relationships of operational networks from information flow, command and control information flow, collaborative information flow, etc. The cascading impact of the system of operations is analyzed from the system composition within the system of operations and the cross mission system of operations. At the operational task level, from the formation and grouping, analysis of the elements of the hierarchical or regional operational system, aggregation and analysis of operational capabilities from multiple levels such as the single equipment system of systems, and from the task effectiveness level, based on the impact factor of the target completion probability, analysis of the strengths and weaknesses of the operational system, target network value, and key points of the system. The specific technical approach to computing the capabilities of the networked operational system is shown in Fig. 4.

The first difficulty is to consider the networked system effect in the system capability analysis. The complex network analysis method can be used to realize the quantitative analysis of the vulnerability, cross system dependency and system cascade effect of the operational system through the characterization of typical operational node units and node relationships such as command, intelligence, fire, and the analysis of complex network structure characteristics and information flow characteristics; The second difficulty is to consider the impact of dynamic confrontation factors of networked systems at the application level, and to achieve dynamic analysis of the comprehensive effectiveness of the system in multi-phase confrontation through system simulation sample data by adopting methods such as simulation confrontation based on Lanchester equation, confrontation simulation based on intelligent game, system balance factor calculation based on system dynamic evolution, and red blue confrontation deduction.

Aiming at the key problems of computing the network effect of the operational system analysis, the dynamic analysis and evaluation index of the operational capability of the networked system is constructed. Based on the analysis of the topological correlation characteristics of the complex network system, the hierarchical network analysis index framework and the system effectiveness evaluation method oriented to the OODA operational ring are adopted to solve the problem of constructing and evaluating the network system capability index, and finally a set of analysis object clusters are formed A set of general evaluation methods and a result library of evaluation cases, which support evaluation objects such as system composition analysis, system capability analysis, system threat analysis, etc., evaluation methods such as hierarchical analysis, exponential comprehensive analysis, cascading failure analysis, system attack analysis, etc., as well as achievement products such as strength and weakness points, key point sets, etc. of the combat system.

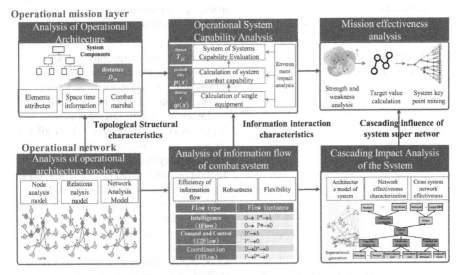

Fig. 4. Capability evaluation process of networked combat system

4.2   Modeling of Operational Effectiveness Evaluation Combat System

The weaponry system of systems constitutes a network of operations, and the network effect of confrontation interaction generates the emerging capability of the system [6–9]. Therefore, corresponding to the modeling of system combat capability evaluation indicators, on the one hand, it is necessary to fully describe and reflect the networked characteristics of the system architecture, on the other hand, it is necessary to pay attention to the indicators that can describe the performance of the network architecture. The combat effectiveness evaluation indicators of the networked system are shown in Table 1.

This paper adopts and integrates the two evaluation methods of "static hierarchical structure dynamic network association" to build a framework of "two categories and four layers" network evaluation index system. Centered on "network structure effectiveness index", the four layers of indicators are formed by linking "equipment measurement index, system integrity effectiveness index, and system mission effectiveness index" to achieve static analysis of command and control. The operational capabilities of systems such as reconnaissance and early warning, fire strike, and comprehensive support, the system effectiveness of dynamic assessment of combat results and damage, and the degree of mission completion, support the mining of key points, strengths and weaknesses of the system, and the framework of the network centric assessment index system is shown in Fig. 5.

Table 1. System effectiveness evaluation index reference list [1]

	Indicator layer	Description of information
1	System mission and task Performance indicators	Battle result, battle loss, battle loss ratio, battle speed, mission completion degree, mission completion probability, active/passive defense rate
2	System integrity Performance indicators	Sensor coordination capability, attack coordination capability, architecture vulnerability, cross domain dependency of the system, system capability multiplier effect, system invulnerability, recombination, dispersion, concealment, proximity, flexibility, efficiency, adaptability, survivability, adaptability, dynamics, robustness and flexibility, cascading failure, brittleness, center of gravity, detection capability, network communication capability Information sharing ability, perception judgment ability, judgment sharing ability, combat effectiveness, command and control ability, combat mobility ability, action coordination ability, decision-making ability, OODA loop effectiveness
3	Network architecture performance indicators	Network connectivity, network robustness, network sparsity, network vulnerability, network propagation capability, network controllability, network synchronization capability, network correlation, and network node importance
4	Equipment function performance index	Detection range, target accuracy, command transmission speed, situation processing speed, planning efficiency, strike efficiency, strike range, node capacity

4.3   Analysis and Calculation of Multi-level Typical System Combat Capability

The basic idea of system of systems combat capability evaluation is shown in Fig. 6. First of all, the comprehensive evaluation of the combat capability of the system is decomposed into several sub problems, and based on this, the evaluation index system of the combat scenario is built, that is, the evaluation index system is built from the three levels of the composition of the combat elements, the topology and information flow of the combat system, and the mission effectiveness of the combat system. Then, each sub problem is analyzed and solved, and the evaluation value of each evaluation index is obtained through simulation evaluation, expert scoring and other evaluation methods. On this basis, all index item data shall be comprehensively evaluated, including preprocessing, normalization and aggregation of index item data to obtain the evaluation value of specific

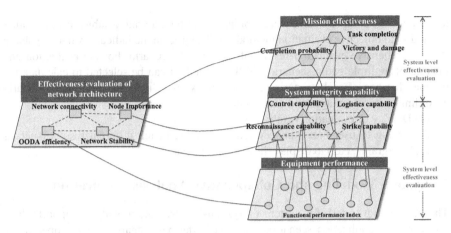

Fig. 5. Evaluation index framework of network centric system effectiveness

combat system, judge its advantages and disadvantages, support the optimization of combat system structure, and support the analysis of strengths and weaknesses of combat system.

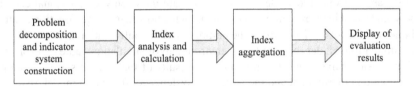

Fig. 6. Comprehensive evaluation process of combat capability

(1) Problem decomposition and indicator system construction

The "decomposition aggregation" method is adopted to decompose the operational scenario verification and evaluation into three levels: operational element level, operational architecture and process, and operational mission effectiveness evaluation, including the primary evaluation indicators such as operational system element analysis, operational system topology association analysis, and operational capability analysis.

(2) Index analysis and calculation

The evaluation method library is used to evaluate typical combat scenarios. Indicator pretreatment: indicators are divided into qualitative indicators and quantitative indicators. Qualitative indicators must be quantified first, and direct scoring method and quantitative ruler quantification method can be used; then the indexes are normalized by range transformation, linear scale transformation and other methods.

(3) Index aggregation

According to the specific conditions of the combat scenario, appropriate comprehensive evaluation methods are selected, such as analytic hierarchy process, fuzzy comprehensive evaluation method, and hierarchical method. They are used to calculate the weight of each indicator item during indicator synthesis [11–14]. They can also be used to calculate the comprehensive weight of indicators by integrating subjective evaluation methods and objective evaluation methods, and aggregate the indicator values to obtain the comprehensive evaluation results of the combat scenario. For the evaluation and ranking of multiple battle scenarios, TOPSIS method can be selected to calculate the optimal distance of each scenario and each index, and then rank each battle scenario according to its advantages and disadvantages.

(4) Display of evaluation results

According to user habits and evaluation results, match different results (such as tables, histograms, etc.) to display the evaluation results.

5   System Modeling and Collaborative Analysis Application

The general framework for system of systems confrontation analysis supports three types of core application scenarios: the first is the basic analysis of the operational system based on network topology, which is to analyze and compare the advantages and disadvantages of the topological structure of the operational system and the strengths and weaknesses of the system under the static scenario conditions, and to discover the key points and strengths and weaknesses of the friend or foe force configuration; The second is the dynamic analysis of the combat system based on the real environment, which is to load the dynamic data of the battlefield environment, analyze the target system and the enemy's and our operational deployment, calculate the enemy's operational center of gravity, and assist in the research and judgment of the hostile map, the direction of attack, and our defense focus. The third is the combat system confrontation analysis based on game simulation. Under the simulation environment of simulation game confrontation, load the basic analysis and dynamic analysis results of the combat system, configure the simulation environment and the system of systems confrontation model, realize the simulation of the system of systems confrontation process, predict the combat system confrontation results, and evaluate the advantages and disadvantages of the combat system. The organizational application mode of system confrontation analysis is shown in Fig. 7.

(1) Combat System Integration Analysis

Using the cooperative integration tool of the combat system of operations, we can uniformly organize multiple elements to carry out cooperative integration around the combat scenario, and automatically associate system node elements in the form of a knowledge graph. The combat system of operations integration tool supports multi seat and multi element cooperative integration node types and associations, and can share the results of the system of systems integration in real time. Relying on complex network computing and operational effectiveness analysis capabilities of networked systems, synchronous computing shows the operational capabilities of current systems such as reconnaissance and early warning, command and control, and fire strike, and analyzes and excavates the key points of the system. At the same time, in the process of combat system integration, provide intelligent recommendation of the node relationship of the combat system, and improve the dynamic integration capability of the combat system.

(2) Comprehensive Comparative Analysis of Combat Systems

Based on the operational rule models such as system operation and system analysis, analyze and calculate the details of the operational capabilities of the systems such

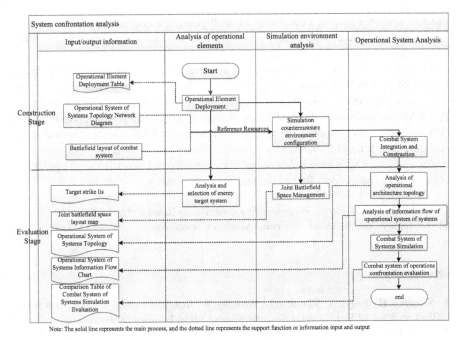

Fig. 7. System confrontation analysis organization application process

as reconnaissance and early warning, fire strike, air defense and antimissile from the aspects of comprehensive strength, operational capability, system topology, key nodes and threat value; The key points of the system are analyzed and located by using AHP, system cascading failure and other models.

(3) Comprehensive presentation of system strength changes

The elements of the operational plan focus on typical scenarios, and based on the operational system of systems assembly and arrangement tools, organize all elements to conduct system coordination analysis. The first is the dynamic analysis of system capability, which can compare and analyze the strength changes of the enemy and our combat systems in real time in combination with the battlefield; The second is to show the comparative advantages of the enemy and ourselves in regions, and show the confrontation situation of the enemy and ourselves through thematic maps; The third is to simulate and predict the confrontation results. According to the current deployment of the enemy and our forces, combined with the operational plan, we can predict the confrontation results of the enemy and our system through large sample simulation to help optimize the deployment of forces.

6 Summary and Conclusions

This paper focuses on the capability analysis requirements of multi-layer, multi domain and multi-dimensional systems. In order to meet the challenges of rapid reconfiguration of large-scale combat systems, it provides a formal description of operational knowledge based on system of systems graphs. Through the feature representation based on military knowledge graphs, it constructs an intelligent recommendation method for operational elements based on knowledge graphs, which provides a solution for the dynamic modeling of refined combat systems.

At the same time, a four tier system of systems confrontation analysis framework of "combat system integration - basic general analysis - system comprehensive analysis - combined application analysis" is designed and constructed to form two types of capability evaluation methods of "static analytical computation - dynamic simulation confrontation", which supports the rapid construction of combat system, dynamic analysis of the capabilities of friend and foe systems, mining and discovering key nodes of the system, and assisting in identifying the center of gravity and attack intent of operations, providing effective support for operational decision-making.

Acknowledgments. The paper is supported by Basic Theory Research Foundation of The Science and Technology Commission of the Central Military Commission.

References

1. Xiaofeng, H., Jingyu, Y., Zhiming, Z., Wenfeng, W.: Research on Analysis and Evaluation of the Capability of War Complex Systems. Science Press, Beijing (2019)
2. Ming, L., Sheng, L., Kun, D.: Application of knowledge graph in the scenario of naval formation confrontation. Comm. Inform. Syst. Technol. **13**(2), 67–72 (2022)
3. Mingzhi, Z., Li, M., Ming, J.: Networked system-of system combat OODA command cycle time mesuring modeling and experiment. J. Comm. Control **1**(1), 50–55 (2015)
4. Lizhi, Y., Heng, D., Shengquan, L.: A multi domain system combat modeling method based on Lanchester equation. In: Proceedings of the 8th China Command and Control Conference, pp. 543–547 (2020)
5. Jiangang, Y.: Operational Modeling. Military Science Press, Beijing (2017)
6. Xiaofeng, L., Huan, W., Ziyang, W.: UAV game countermeasure technology based on generation countermeasure network. Comm. Inform. Syst. Technol. **12**(5), 1–5 (2021)
7. Qinzhang, Y.: Research on combat effectiveness evaluation method of equipment system of system based on overall effect. Syst. Simul. Technol. **7**(3), 183–189 (2011)
8. Xiaofeng, H., Yu, Z., Renjian, L.: Network system capability evaluation. Syst. Eng. Theory Pract. **8**(5), 1317–1323 (2015)
9. Li, M., Zhiming, Z.: Research on effectiveness evaluation modeling of networked architecture. J. Syst. Simul. **27**(2), 217–225 (2015)
10. Lina, C.: Research on Network Topology Modeling and Analysis Method of Military Information System. National University of Defense Science and Technology, Changsha (2017)
11. Hu, B., Shi, C., Zhao, W.X., Yu, P.S.: Leveraging meta-path based context for top-N recommendation with a neural co-attention model. In: Proceedings of the 24th ACM SIGKDD International Conference on Knowledge Discovery & Data Mining. ACM, pp. 1531–1540 (2018).
12. Rupeng, L., Kebo, D., Zexiang, M.: A semantic matching method of combat plan based on military knowledge graph. J. Comm. Control **5**(2), 115–120 (2019)
13. Jianghao, L., Yongmei, Z., Aimin, Y.: Emotion feature vector extraction method based on semantic similarity. Comput. Sci. **44**(10), 296–301 (2017)
14. Qin, C., et al.: A survey on knowledge graph-based recommender systems (in Chinese). Sci. Sin. Inform. **50**(7), 937–956 (2020)

Generating Adversarial Examples
and Other Applications

Generating Adversarial Malware Examples for Black-Box Attacks Based on GAN

Weiwei Hu[1,2,3] and Ying Tan[1,2,3(✉)]

[1] School of Intelligence Science and Technology, Peking University,
Beijing 100871, China
{weiwei.hu,ytan}@pku.edu.cn
[2] Key Laboratory of Machine Perceptron (MOE), Peking University,
Beijing 100871, China
[3] Institute for Artificial Intelligence, Peking University, Beijing 100871, China

Abstract. Machine learning has been used to detect new malware in recent years, while malware authors have strong motivation to attack such algorithms. Malware authors usually have no access to the detailed structures and parameters of the machine learning models used by malware detection systems, and therefore they can only perform black-box attacks. This paper proposes a generative adversarial network (GAN) based algorithm named MalGAN to generate adversarial malware examples, which are able to bypass black-box machine learning based detection models. MalGAN uses a substitute detector to fit the black-box malware detection system. A generative network is trained to minimize the generated adversarial examples' malicious probabilities predicted by the substitute detector. The superiority of MalGAN over traditional gradient based adversarial example generation algorithms is that MalGAN is able to decrease the detection rate to nearly zero and make the retraining based defensive method against adversarial examples hard to work.

Keywords: Malware detection · Adversarial examples · Generative adversarial network

1 Introduction

In recent years, many machine learning based algorithms have been proposed to detect malware, which extract features from programs and use a classifier to classify programs between benign programs and malware. For example, Schultz et al. proposed to use dynamic-link libraries (DLL), application programming interfaces (API) and strings as features for classification [24], while Kolter et al. used byte level n-gram as features [10,11].

Most researchers focused their efforts on improving the detection performance (e.g. true positive rate, accuracy and AUC) of such algorithms, but ignored the

This paper is the arXiv version of https://arxiv.org/abs/1702.05983.

ⓒ The Author(s), under exclusive license to Springer Nature Singapore Pte Ltd. 2022
Y. Tan and Y. Shi (Eds.): DMBD 2022, CCIS 1745, pp. 409–423, 2022.
https://doi.org/10.1007/978-981-19-8991-9_29

robustness of these algorithms. Generally speaking, the propagation of malware will benefit malware authors. Therefore, malware authors have sufficient motivation to attack malware detection algorithms.

Many machine learning algorithms are very vulnerable to intentional attacks. Machine learning based malware detection algorithms cannot be used in real-world applications if they are easily to be bypassed by some adversarial techniques.

Recently, adversarial examples of deep learning models have attracted the attention of many researchers. Szegedy et al. added imperceptible perturbations to images to maximize a trained neural network's classification errors, making the network unable to classify the images correctly [25]. The examples after adding perturbations are called adversarial examples. Goodfellow et al. proposed a gradient based algorithm to generate adversarial examples [6]. Papernot et al. used the Jacobian matrix to determine which features to modify when generating adversarial examples [18]. The Jacobian matrix based approach is also a kind of gradient based algorithm.

Grosse et al. proposed to use the gradient based approach to generate adversarial Android malware examples [7]. The adversarial examples are used to fool a neural network based malware detection model. They assumed that attackers have full access to the parameters of the malware detection model. For different sizes of neural networks, the misclassification rates after adversarial crafting range from 35% to 84%.

In some cases, attackers have no access to the architecture and weights of the neural network to be attacked; the target model is a black box to attackers. Papernot et al. used a substitute neural network to fit the black-box neural network and then generated adversarial examples according to the substitute neural network [17]. They also used a substitute neural network to attack other machine learning algorithms such as logistic regression, support vector machines, decision trees and nearest neighbors [16]. Liu et al. performed black-box attacks without a substitute model [13], based on the principle that adversarial examples can transfer among different models [25].

Machine learning based malware detection algorithms are usually integrated into antivirus software or hosted on the cloud side, and therefore they are black-box systems to malware authors. It is hard for malware authors to know which classifier a malware detection system uses and the parameters of the classifier.

However, it is possible to figure out what features a malware detection algorithm uses by feeding some carefully designed test cases to the black-box algorithm. For example, if a malware detection algorithm uses static DLL or API features from the import directory table or the import lookup tables of PE programs [14], malware authors can manually modify some DLL or API names in the import directory table or the import lookup tables. They can modify a benign program's DLL or API names to malware's DLL or API names, and vice versa. If the detection results change after most of the modifications, they can judge that the malware detection algorithm uses DLL or API features. Therefore, in this paper we assume that malware authors are able to know what features a malware detection algorithm uses, but know nothing about the machine learning model.

Existing algorithms mainly use gradient information and hand-crafted rules to transform original samples into adversarial examples. This paper proposes a generative neural network based approach which takes original samples as inputs and outputs adversarial examples. The intrinsic non-linear structure of neural networks enables them to generate more complex and flexible adversarial examples to fool the target model.

The learning algorithm of our proposed model is inspired by generative adversarial networks (GAN) [5]. In GAN, a discriminative model is used to distinguish between generated samples and real samples, and a generative model is trained to make the discriminative model misclassify generated samples as real samples. GAN has shown good performance in generating realistic images [4,15].

The proposed model in this paper is named as MalGAN, which generates adversarial examples to attack black-box malware detection algorithms. A substitute detector is trained to fit the black-box malware detection algorithm, and a generative network is used to transform malware samples into adversarial examples. Experimental results show that most of the adversarial examples generated by MalGAN successfully bypass the detection algorithms and MalGAN is very flexible to fool further defensive methods of detection algorithms.

2   Architecture of MalGAN

2.1   Overview

The architecture of the proposed MalGAN is shown in Fig. 1.

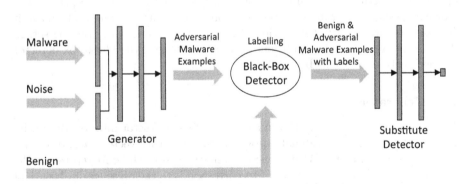

Fig. 1. The architecture of MalGAN.

The black-box detector is an external system which adopts machine learning based malware detection algorithms. We assume that the only thing malware authors know about the black-box detector is what kind of features it uses. Malware authors do not know what machine learning algorithm it uses and do not have access to the parameters of the trained model. Malware authors are able to get the detection results of their programs from the black-box detector. The whole model contains a generator and a substitute detector, which are both feed-forward neural networks. The generator and the substitute detector work together to attack a machine learning based black-box malware detector.

In this paper we only generate adversarial examples for binary features, because binary features are widely used by malware detection researchers and are able to result in high detection accuracy. Here we take API feature as an example to show how to represent a program. For malware detection on the Microsoft Windows operating systems, APIs are the most used features. If M APIs are used as features, an M-dimensional feature vector is constructed for a program. If the program calls the d-th API, the d-th feature value is set to 1, otherwise it is set to 0. For Android malware detection, additional features such as permissions from the manifest file of an APK are also used by many researchers [3,20,22]. In such case, if an Android program requires a permission, the corresponding feature value is set to 1.

The main difference between this model and existing algorithms is that the adversarial examples are dynamically generated according to the feedback of the black-box detector, while most existing algorithms use static gradient based approaches to generate adversarial examples.

The probability distribution of adversarial examples from MalGAN is determined by the weights of the generator. To make a machine learning algorithm effective, the samples in the training set and the test set should follow the same probability distribution or similar probability distributions. However, the generator can change the probability distribution of adversarial examples to make it far from the probability distribution of the black-box detector's training set. In this case the generator has sufficient opportunity to lead the black-box detector to misclassify malware as benign.

2.2   Generator

The generator is used to transform a malware feature vector into its adversarial version. It takes the concatenation of a malware feature vector m and a noise vector z as input. m is a M-dimensional binary vector, where M represents the number of features. Each element of m corresponds to the presence or absence of a feature. z is a Z-dimensional vector, where Z is a hyper-parameter. Each element of z is a random number sampled from a uniform distribution in the range $[0, 1)$. The effect of z is to allow the generator to generate diverse adversarial examples from a single malware feature vector.

The input vector is fed into a multi-layer feed-forward neural network with weights θ_g. The output layer of this network has M neurons and the activation function used by the last layer is sigmoid which restricts the output to the range

$(0, 1)$. The output of this network is denoted as o. Since malware feature values are binary, binarization transformation is applied to o according to whether an element is greater than 0.5 or not, and this process produces a binary vector o'.

When generating adversarial examples for binary malware features we only consider to add some irrelevant features to malware. Removing a feature from the original malware may crack it. For example, if the "WriteFile" API is removed from a program, the program is unable to perform normal writing function and the malware may crack. The non-zero features in the binary vector o' which have zero feature values in m act as the irrelevant features to be added to the original malware. The final generated adversarial example can be expressed as $m' = m|o'$ where "|" is element-wise binary OR operation.

To make the adversarial example executable, malware authors need to add the irrelevant features to the source code of the original malware. For example, if a malware detection algorithm uses API features, malware authors should intentionally call the irrelevant APIs in the source code. Then the modified source code should be compiled into the final adversarial malware program. The adversarial malware will have the whole malicious functions of the original malware. The source code should be modified carefully, to make sure that adding the irrelevant features does not influence the existing functions of the original malware. Malware authors can also develop some automatic tools for adding irrelevant features, in order to generate a large number of adversarial malware examples.

For Android malware features extracted from the manifest files of APKs, it is more easy to insert the irrelevant features. For example, if an Android malware detection algorithm uses permission features, the irrelevant permissions can be easily inserted into the manifest file without influencing the original function of the malware.

m' is a binary vector, and therefore the gradients are unable to back propagate from the substitute detector to the generator. A smooth function G is defined to receive gradient information from the substitute detector, as shown in Formula 1.

$$G_{\theta_g}(m, z) = \max(m, o).$$ (1)

$\max(\cdot, \cdot)$ represents element-wise max operation. If an element of m has the value 1, the corresponding result of G is also 1, which is unable to back propagate the gradients. If an element of m has the value 0, the result of G is the neural network's real number output in the corresponding dimension, and gradient information is able to go through. It can be seen that m' is actually the binarization transformed version of $G_{\theta_g}(m, z)$.

2.3   Substitute Detector

Since malware authors know nothing about the detailed structure of the black-box detector, the substitute detector is used to fit the black-box detector and provides gradient information to train the generator.

The substitute detector is a multi-layer feed-forward neural network with weights θ_d which takes a program feature vector $\boldsymbol{x}$ as input. It classifies the program between benign program and malware. We denote the predicted probability that $\boldsymbol{x}$ is malware as $D_{\theta_d}(\boldsymbol{x})$.

The training data of the substitute detector consist of adversarial malware examples from the generator, and benign programs from an additional benign dataset collected by malware authors. The ground-truth labels of the training data are not used to train the substitute detector. The goal of the substitute detector is to fit the black-box detector. The black-box detector will detect this training data first and output whether a program is benign or malware. The predicted labels from the black-box detector are used by the substitute detector.

3   Training MalGAN

To train MalGAN malware authors should collect a malware dataset and a benign dataset first.

The loss function of the substitute detector is defined in Formula 2.

$$
\begin{aligned}
L_D = & -\mathbb{E}_{\boldsymbol{x} \in BB_{Benign}} \log \left(1 - D_{\theta_d}(\boldsymbol{x})\right) \\
& -\mathbb{E}_{\boldsymbol{x} \in BB_{Malware}} \log D_{\theta_d}(\boldsymbol{x}).
\end{aligned}
\tag{2}
$$

BB_{Benign} is the set of programs that are recognized as benign by the black-box detector, and $BB_{Malware}$ is the set of programs that are detected as malware by the black-box detector.

To train the substitute detector, L_D should be minimized with respect to the weights of the substitute detector.

The loss function of the generator is defined in Formula 3.

$$
L_G = \mathbb{E}_{\boldsymbol{m} \in S_{Malware}, \boldsymbol{z} \sim p_{\text{uniform}[0,1)}} \log D_{\theta_d}\left(G_{\theta_g}(\boldsymbol{m}, \boldsymbol{z})\right).
\tag{3}
$$

$S_{Malware}$ is the actual malware dataset, not the malware set labelled by the black-box detector. L_G is minimized with respect to the weights of the generator.

Minimizing L_G will reduce the predicted malicious probability of malware and push the substitute detector to recognize malware as benign. Since the substitute detector tries to fit the black-box detector, the training of the generator will further fool the black-box detector.

The whole process of training MalGAN is shown in Algorithm 1.

In line 2 and line 4, different sizes of minibatches are used for malware and benign programs. The ratio of $\boldsymbol{M}$'s size to $\boldsymbol{B}$'s size is the same as the ratio of the malware dataset's size to the benign dataset's size.

Algorithm 1. The Training Process of MalGAN

1: **while** not converging **do**
2:    Sample a minibatch of malware M
3:    Generate adversarial examples M' from the generator for M
4:    Sample a minibatch of benign programs B
5:    Label M' and B using the black-box detector
6:    Update the substitute detector's weights θ_d by descending along the gradient $\nabla_{\theta_d} L_D$
7:     Update the generator's weights θ_g by descending along the gradient $\nabla_{\theta_g} L_G$
8: **end while**

4 Experiments

4.1 Experimental Setup

The main dataset used in this paper was crawled from a program sharing website[1]. We downloaded 180 thousand PC programs in Microsoft Windows operating systems from this website and about 70% of them are malware. API features are used for this dataset. An 160-dimensional binary feature vector is constructed for each program, based on 160 system level APIs.

We will also report the results on the Drebin Android malware dataset[2] when comparing MalGAN with the algorithm proposed by Grosse et al., since Grosse et al. used this Android dataset [7]. The Drebin dataset contains 8 kinds of features, such as hardware components, requested permissions and API calls. After removing the features which appear less than 5 times in the dataset, we got 44942 features and used these features to train MalGAN. However, the dataset only contains 5560 malware samples, which is too small for normal deep learning applications. Therefore, we only used this dataset as a supplemental dataset for comparison. Most experiments and analyses were conducted on the crawled 180 thousand programs.

In order to validate the transferability of adversarial examples generated by MalGAN, we tried several different machine learning algorithms for the black-box detector. The used classifiers include random forest (RF), logistic regression (LR), decision trees (DT), support vector machines (SVM), multi-layer perceptron (MLP), and a voting based ensemble of these classifiers (VOTE).

We adopted two ways to split the dataset. The first splitting way regards 80% of the dataset as the training set and the remaining 20% as the test set. MalGAN and the black-box detector share the same training set. MalGAN further picks out 25% of the training data as the validation set and uses the remaining training data to train the neural networks. Some black-box classifiers such as MLP also need a validation set for early stopping. The validation set of MalGAN cannot be used for the black-box detector since malware authors and antivirus vendors do

---

[1] https://malwr.com/.
[2] https://www.sec.cs.tu-bs.de/~danarp/drebin/index.html.

not communicate on how to split dataset. Splitting validation set for the black-box detector should be independent of MalGAN; MalGAN and the black-box detector should use different random seeds to pick out the validation data.

The second splitting way picks out 40% of the dataset as the training set for MalGAN, picks out another 40% of the dataset as the training set for the black-box detector, and uses the remaining 20% of the dataset as the test set.

In real-world scenes the training data collected by the malware authors and the antivirus vendors cannot be the same. However, their training data will overlap with each other if they collect data from public sources. In this case the actual performance of MalGAN will be between the performances of the two splitting ways.

Adam [9] was chosen as the optimizer. We tuned the hyper-parameters on the validation set. For the dataset with 180 thousand programs, 10 was chosen as the dimension of the noise vector z. The generator's layer size was set to 170-256-160, the substitute detector's layer size was set to 160-256-1, and the learning rate 0.001 was used for both the generator and the substitute detector. For the Drebin dataset, we used the same network structures as Grosse et al.[7]. The maximum number of epochs to train MalGAN was set to 100. The epoch with the lowest detection rate on the validation set is finally chosen to test the performance of MalGAN.

4.2   Experimental Results

We first analyze the case where MalGAN and the black-box detector use the same training set. For malware detection, the true positive rate (TPR) means the detection rate of malware. After adversarial attacks, the reduction in TPR can reflect how many malware samples successfully bypass the detection algorithm. TPR on the training set and the test set of original samples and adversarial examples is shown in Table 1. The datasets with 180 thousand programs is used here.

Table 1. True positive rate (in percentage) on original samples and adversarial examples when MalGAN and the black-box detector are trained on the same training set. "Adver." represents adversarial examples.

	Training set		Test set	
	Original	Adver.	Original	Adver.
RF	97.62	0.20	95.38	0.19
LR	92.20	0.00	92.27	0.00
DT	97.89	0.16	93.98	0.16
SVM	93.11	0.00	93.13	0.00
MLP	95.11	0.00	94.89	0.00
VOTE	97.23	0.00	95.64	0.00

For random forest and decision trees, the TPRs on adversarial examples range from 0.16% to 0.20% for both the training set and the test set, while the TPRs on the original samples are all greater than 93%. When using other classifiers as the black-box detector, MalGAN is able to decrease the TPR on generated adversarial examples to zero for both the training set and the test set. That is to say, for all of the backend classifiers, the black-box detector can hardly detect any malware generated by the generator. The proposed model has successfully learned to bypass these machine learning based malware detection algorithms.

The structures of logistic regression and support vector machines are very similar to neural networks and MLP is actually a neural network. Therefore, the substitute detector is able to fit them with a very high accuracy. This is why MalGAN can achieve zero TPR for these classifiers. While random forest and decision trees have quite different structures from neural networks so that Mal-GAN results in non-zero TPRs. The TPRs of random forest and decision trees on adversarial examples are still quite small, which means the neural network has enough capacity to represent other models with quite different structures. The voting of these algorithms also achieves zero TPR. We can conclude that the classifiers with similar structures to neural networks are in the majority during voting.

The convergence curve of TPR on the training set and the validation set during the training process of MalGAN is shown in Fig. 2. The black-box detector used here is random forest, since random forest performs very well in Table 1.

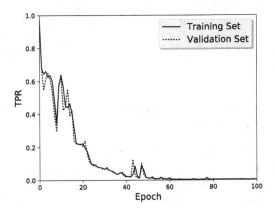

Fig. 2. The change of the true positive rate on the training set and the validation set over time.

TPR converges to about zero near the 40th epoch, but the convergence curve is a bit shaking, not a smooth one. This curve reflects the fact that the training of GAN is usually unstable. How to stabilize the training of GAN has attracted the attention of many researchers [1,21,23].

Now we will analyze the results when MalGAN and the black-box detector are trained on different training sets. Fitting the black-box detector trained on a different dataset is more difficult for the substitute detector. The experimental results are shown in Table 2.

Table 2. True positive rate (in percentage) on original samples and adversarial examples when MalGAN and the black-box detector are trained on different training sets. "Adver." represents adversarial examples.

	Training set		Test set	
	Original	Adver.	Original	Adver.
RF	95.10	0.71	94.95	0.80
LR	91.58	0.00	91.81	0.01
DT	91.92	2.18	91.97	2.11
SVM	92.50	0.00	92.78	0.00
MLP	94.32	0.00	94.40	0.00
VOTE	94.30	0.00	94.45	0.00

For SVM, MLP and VOTE, TPR reaches zero, and TPR of LR is nearly zero. These results are very similar to Table 1. TPRs of random forest and decision trees on adversarial examples become higher compared with the case where MalGAN and the black-box detector use the same training data. For decision trees the TPRs rise to 2.18% and 2.11% on the training set and the test set respectively. However, 2% is still a very small number and the black-box detector will still miss to detect most of the adversarial malware examples. It can be concluded that MalGAN is still able to fool the black-box detector even trained on a different training set.

4.3 Comparison with the Gradient Based Algorithm to Generate Adversarial Examples

Existing algorithms of generating adversarial examples are mainly for images. The difference between image and malware is that image features are continuous while malware features are binary.

Grosse et al. modified the traditional gradient based algorithm to generate binary adversarial malware examples [7]. They did not regard the malware detection algorithm as a black-box system and assumed that malware authors have full access to the architecture and the weights of the neural network based malware detection model. The misclassification rates of adversarial examples range from 35% to 84% under different hyper-parameters.

We applied MalGAN on the Drebin dataset used by Grosse et al. with a malware ratio of 0.5 to attack a black-box random forest. The TPRs on the test set are 5.63% and 6.87% respectively when MalGAN and random forest are trained on the same training set and on different training sets. MalGAN is able to make more malware undetected than the gradient based approach. This gradient based approach is under the white-box assumption, while MalGAN produces better results with a harder black-box assumption. In the following experiments we will continue to use the dataset with 180 thousand programs since it has much more malware examples than the Drebin dataset.

The algorithm proposed by Grosse et al. uses an iterative approach to generate adversarial malware examples. At each iteration the algorithm finds the feature with the maximum likelihood to change the malware's label from malware to benign. The algorithm modifies one feature at each iteration, until the malware is successfully classified as a benign program or there are no features available to be modified.

We tried to migrate this algorithm to attack a random forest based black-box detection algorithm. A substitute neural network is trained to fit the black-box random forest. Adversarial malware examples are generated based on the gradient information of the substitute neural network.

TPR on the adversarial examples over the iterative process is shown in Fig. 3. Please note that at each iteration not all of the malware samples are modified. If a malware sample has already been classified as a benign program at previous iterations or there are no modifiable features, the algorithm will do nothing on the malware sample at this iteration.

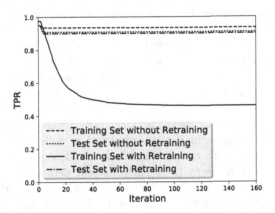

Fig. 3. True positive rate on the adversarial examples over the iterative process when using the algorithm proposed by Grosse et al..

On the training set and the test set, TPR converges to 93.52% and 90.96% respectively. In this case the black-box random forest is able to detect most of the adversarial examples. The substitute neural network is trained on the original training set, while after several iterations the probability distribution of adversarial examples will become quite different from the probability distribution of the original training set. Therefore, the substitute neural network cannot approximate the black-box random forest well on the adversarial examples. In this case the adversarial examples generated from the substitute neural network are unable to fool the black-box random forest.

In order to fit the black-box random forest more accurately on the adversarial examples, we tried to retrain the substitute neural network on the adversarial examples. At each iteration, the current generated adversarial examples from the whole training set are used to retrain the substitute neural network. As shown in Fig. 3, the retraining approach make TPR converge to 46.18% on the training set, which means the black-box random forest can still detect about half of the adversarial examples. However, the retrained model is unable to generalize to the test set, since the TPR on the test set converges to 90.12%. The odd probability distribution of these adversarial examples limits the generalization ability of the substitute neural network.

MalGAN uses a generative network to transform original samples into adversarial samples. The neural network has enough representation ability to perform complex transformations, making MalGAN able to result in very low TPRs on both the training set and the test set. While the representation ability of the gradient based approach is too limited to generate high-quality adversarial examples.

4.4   Retraining the Black-Box Detector

Several defensive algorithms have been proposed to deal with adversarial examples. Gu et al. proposed to use auto-encoders to map adversarial samples to clean input data [8]. An algorithm named defensive distillation was proposed by Papernot et al. to weaken the effectiveness of adversarial perturbations [19]. Li et al. found that adversarial retraining can boost the robustness of machine learning algorithms [12]. Chen et al. compared these defensive algorithms and concluded that retraining is a very effective way to defend against adversarial examples, and is robust even against repeated attacks [2].

In this section we will analyze the performance of MalGAN under the retraining based defensive approach. If antivirus vendors collect enough adversarial malware examples, the can retrain the black-box detector on these adversarial examples in order to learn their patterns and detect them. Here we only use random forest as the black-box detector due to its good performance. After retraining the black-box detector, it is able to detect all adversarial examples, as shown in the middle column of Table 3.

Table 3. True positive rate (in percentage) on the adversarial examples after the black-box detector is retrained.

	Before retraining MalGAN	After retraining MalGAN
Training set	100	0
Test set	100	0

However, once antivirus vendors release the updated black-box detector publicly, malware authors will be able to get a copy of it and retrain MalGAN to attack the new black-box detector. After this process the black-box detector can hardly detect any malware again, as shown in the last column of Table 3. We found that reducing TPR from 100% to 0% can be done within one epoch during retraining MalGAN. We alternated retraining the black-box detector and retraining MalGAN for ten times. The results are the same as Table 3 for the ten times.

To retrain the black-box detector antivirus vendors have to collect enough adversarial examples. It is a long process to collect a large number of malware samples and label them. Adversarial malware examples have enough time to propagate before the black-box detector is retrained and updated. Once the black-box detector is updated, malware authors will attack it immediately by retraining MalGAN and our experiments showed that retraining MalGAN takes much less time than the first-time training. After retraining MalGAN, new adversarial examples remain undetected. This dynamic adversarial process lands antivirus vendors in a passive position. Machine learning based malware detection algorithms can hardly work in this case.

5   Conclusions

This paper proposed a novel algorithm named MalGAN to generate adversarial examples from a machine learning based black-box malware detector. A neural network based substitute detector is used to fit the black-box detector. A generator is trained to generate adversarial examples which are able to fool the substitute detector. Experimental results showed that the generated adversarial examples are able to effectively bypass the black-box detector.

Adversarial examples' probability distribution is controlled by the weights of the generator. Malware authors are able to frequently change the probability distribution by retraining MalGAN, making the black-box detector cannot keep up with it, and unable to learn stable patterns from it. Once the black-box detector is updated malware authors can immediately crack it. This process making machine learning based malware detection algorithms unable to work.

Acknowledgment. This work is supported by the Science and Technology Innovation 2030 - 'New Generation Artificial Intelligence' Major Project (Grant Nos.: 2018AAA0100302), and partially supported by National Natural Science Foundation of China (Grant No. 62076010 and 62276008).

References

1. Arjovsky, M., Bottou, L.: Towards principled methods for training generative adversarial networks. In: NIPS 2016 Workshop on Adversarial Training. In review for ICLR, vol. 2016 (2017)
2. Chen, X., Li, B., Vorobeychik, Y.: Evaluation of defensive methods for DNNs against multiple adversarial evasion models (2016). https://openreview.net/forum?id=ByToKu9ll

3. Daniel, A., Michael, S., Malte, H., Hugo, G., Konrad, R.: Drebin: efficient and explainable detection of android malware in your pocket. In: Proceedings of 21th Annual Network and Distributed System Security Symposium (NDSS) (2014)
4. Denton, E.L., Chintala, S., Fergus, R., et al.: Deep generative image models using a Laplacian pyramid of adversarial networks. In: Advances in Neural Information Processing Systems, pp. 1486–1494 (2015)
5. Goodfellow, I., et al.: Generative adversarial nets. In: Advances in Neural Information Processing Systems, pp. 2672–2680 (2014)
6. Goodfellow, I.J., Shlens, J., Szegedy, C.: Explaining and harnessing adversarial examples. arXiv preprint arXiv:1412.6572 (2014)
7. Grosse, K., Papernot, N., Manoharan, P., Backes, M., McDaniel, P.: Adversarial perturbations against deep neural networks for malware classification. arXiv preprint arXiv:1606.04435 (2016)
8. Gu, S., Rigazio, L.: Towards deep neural network architectures robust to adversarial examples. arXiv preprint arXiv:1412.5068 (2014)
9. Kingma, D., Ba, J.: Adam: a method for stochastic optimization. arXiv preprint arXiv:1412.6980 (2014)
10. Kolter, J.Z., Maloof, M.A.: Learning to detect and classify malicious executables in the wild. J. Mach. Learn. Res. **7**, 2721–2744 (2006)
11. Kolter, J.Z., Maloof, M.A.: Learning to detect malicious executables in the wild. In: Proceedings of the Tenth ACM SIGKDD International Conference on Knowledge Discovery and Data Mining, pp. 470–478. ACM (2004)
12. Li, B., Vorobeychik, Y., Chen, X.: A general retraining framework for scalable adversarial classification. arXiv preprint arXiv:1604.02606 (2016)
13. Liu, Y., Chen, X., Liu, C., Song, D.: Delving into transferable adversarial examples and black-box attacks. arXiv preprint arXiv:1611.02770 (2016)
14. Microsoft: Microsoft portable executable and common object file format specification (2013). https://download.microsoft.com/download/9/c/5/9c5b2167-8017-4bae-9fde-d599bac8184a/pecoff_v83.docx
15. Mirza, M., Osindero, S.: Conditional generative adversarial nets. arXiv preprint arXiv:1411.1784 (2014)
16. Papernot, N., McDaniel, P., Goodfellow, I.: Transferability in machine learning: from phenomena to black-box attacks using adversarial samples. arXiv preprint arXiv:1605.07277 (2016)
17. Papernot, N., McDaniel, P., Goodfellow, I., Jha, S., Celik, Z.B., Swami, A.: Practical black-box attacks against deep learning systems using adversarial examples. arXiv preprint arXiv:1602.02697 (2016)
18. Papernot, N., McDaniel, P., Jha, S., Fredrikson, M., Celik, Z.B., Swami, A.: The limitations of deep learning in adversarial settings. In: 2016 IEEE European Symposium on Security and Privacy (EuroS&P), pp. 372–387. IEEE (2016)
19. Papernot, N., McDaniel, P., Wu, X., Jha, S., Swami, A.: Distillation as a defense to adversarial perturbations against deep neural networks. In: 2016 IEEE Symposium on Security and Privacy (SP), pp. 582–597. IEEE (2016)
20. Peiravian, N., Zhu, X.: Machine learning for android malware detection using permission and API calls. In: 2013 IEEE 25th International Conference on Tools with Artificial Intelligence (ICTAI), pp. 300–305. IEEE (2013)
21. Radford, A., Metz, L., Chintala, S.: Unsupervised representation learning with deep convolutional generative adversarial networks. arXiv preprint arXiv:1511.06434 (2015)

22. Sahs, J., Khan, L.: A machine learning approach to android malware detection. In: 2012 European Intelligence and Security Informatics Conference (EISIC), pp. 141–147. IEEE (2012)

23. Salimans, T., Goodfellow, I., Zaremba, W., Cheung, V., Radford, A., Chen, X.: Improved techniques for training GANs. In: Advances in Neural Information Processing Systems, pp. 2226–2234 (2016)

24. Schultz, M.G., Eskin, E., Zadok, E., Stolfo, S.J.: Data mining methods for detection of new malicious executables. In: 2001 IEEE Symposium on Security and Privacy, 2001. S&P 2001. Proceedings, pp. 38–49. IEEE (2001)

25. Szegedy, C., et al.: Intriguing properties of neural networks. arXiv preprint arXiv:1312.6199 (2013)

Defending Adversarial Examples by Negative Correlation Ensemble

Wenjian Luo[1]([✉]), Hongwei Zhang[1], Linghao Kong[1], Zhijian Chen[1],
and Ke Tang[2]

[1] School of Computer Science and Technology, Harbin Institute of Technology,
Shenzhen 518055, Guangdong, China
{luowenjian@hit.edu.cn, {20S151127,20S151073,21B951010}@stu.hit.edu.cn
[2] Guangdong Provincial Key Laboratory of Brain-inspired Intelligent Computation,
School of Computer Science and Engineering, Southern University of Science and
Technology, Shenzhen 518055, Guangdong, China
tangk3@sustech.edu.cn

Abstract. The security issues in DNNs, such as adversarial examples, have attracted much attention. Adversarial examples refer to the examples which are capable to induce the DNNs return incorrect predictions by introducing carefully designed perturbations. Obviously, adversarial examples bring great security risks to the real-world applications of deep learning. Recently, some defence approaches against adversarial examples have been proposed. However, the performance of these approaches are still limited. In this paper, we propose a new ensemble defence approach named the Negative Correlation Ensemble (NCEn), which achieves competitive results by making each member of the ensemble negatively correlated in gradient direction and gradient magnitude. NCEn can reduce the transferability of the adversarial samples among the members in ensemble. Extensive experiments have been conducted, and the results demonstrate that NCEn could improve the adversarial robustness of ensembles effectively.

Keywords: Deep learning · Adversarial examples · Ensemble · Negative correlation

1 Introduction

Deep Neural Networks (DNN) have achieved significant improvements in various domains, like image classification, face recognition and autonomous driving [11, 14,31]. However, there are serious security issues in DNNs which have attracted much attention in recent years [26]. Specifically, studies have shown that DNN are vulnerable to adversarial examples, which are generated by adding delicate

This study is supported by the Major Key Project of PCL (Grant No. PCL2022A03, PCL2021A02, PCL2021A09), and the Guangdong Provincial Key Laboratory (Grant No. 2020B121201001).

© The Author(s), under exclusive license to Springer Nature Singapore Pte Ltd. 2022
Y. Tan and Y. Shi (Eds.): DMBD 2022, CCIS 1745, pp. 424–438, 2022.
https://doi.org/10.1007/978-981-19-8991-9_30

and imperceptible perturbation to the original examples, and aims to prompt the DNNs to make incorrect predictions [9].

Many algorithms have been proposed to generate adversarial examples. These algorithms can be classified according to accessibility into white-box attacks such as Fast Gradient Sign Method (FGSM) [9], DeepFool [19] and C&W [4], and black-box attacks, such as Zero Order Optimization (ZOO) [6], Boundary Attack [3], Momentum Iterative Fast Gradient Sign Method (MI-FGSM) [8] and Skip Gradient Method (SGM) [29]. Notably, the black-box algorithms such as MI-FGSM can also be used in white-box setting scenarios, if the adversary can directly access the target model.

Effective defences against adversarial examples are usually achieved by detecting adversarial perturbations or improving the robustness of the model. The approaches of detecting adversarial perturbations, such as the key-based network in [32], the MagNet framework in [18] and the feature squeezing in [30], are implemented mainly by detecting or cleaning the input data through technical means. Differently, the approaches of improving the robustness of the model, such as the gradient regularization [24], adversarial training [13] and the defensive distillation [4], are implemented by changing some specific properties of the target model.

Recently, some studies have found that, for the same learning task, different models will learn different decision boundaries due to the differences in their model structures, initial weights, and training methods, and by which we can infer that an adversarial example which can fool one model may not be capable to fool others [2]. Intuitively, the vulnerability of a single model can be avoided through a model ensemble. Some researchers have made important advances in the defence of ensemble [7,10,21]. Although the ensemble methods can achieve adversarial robustness by increasing the diversity, the complementarity among members has not been well investigated during the training which may lead to low performance when facing various adversarial examples attack.

In this paper, in order to take advantage of the interactions between the members of ensemble and reduce the transferability of adversarial examples, we propose to train classifiers in an ensemble based on the negative correlation principle and accordingly design a new ensemble defence strategy (NCEn) to improve the adversarial robustness of ensembles. In NCEn, we make the gradient direction and the gradient magnitude of each member with respect to the input x negatively correlated, thus prompting the gradient directions to have the greatest diversity, and the gradient magnitude to be balanced. So that we can reduce the number of members that are vulnerable to the same adversarial perturbation.

The contributions of this paper can be summarized as follows.

- We propose a novel negative correlation ensemble (NCEn). Based on the principle of negative correlation, NCEn maximizes the diversity of members in the ensemble and reduces the transferability of adversarial examples by constraining the gradient direction and the gradient magnitude of each member.
- Extensive experiments have been conducted, and experimental results show that the performance of the negative correlation ensemble (NCEn) exceeds

the state-of-the-art ensemble-based defence strategies. What's more, experimental results also show that NCEn can effectively reduce the transferability of adversarial examples as well as improving the diversity and robustness of the ensemble.

The rest of this paper is organized as follows. Section 2 introduces related work. We then introduce our approach in Sect. 3. Section 4 presents our experimental results. A brief conclusion of this paper is given in Sect. 5.

2   Related Work

2.1   Adversarial Examples

In 2014, Szegedy et al. [26] proposed the concept of adversarial examples. From then on, numerous adversarial examples generation algorithms have been proposed in past years. Goodfellow et al. [9] proposed the FGSM algorithm. The advantage of FGSM is that it can generate adversarial examples quickly, and can be applied to a variety of deep neural networks. The momentum iterative FGSM (MI-FGSM) [8] is an iterative attack method based on FGSM. By adding a momentum term to the iterative attack method, the transferability of adversarial examples is improved. The project Gradient Descent (PGD) [17] is another iterative attack method based on FGSM. In each iteration process, the perturbation is clipped to the specified range to generate efficient adversarial examples. In 2017, Kurakin et al. [12] proposed the basic iterative method (BIM). By limiting each pixel of the adversarial example to be within the l_p field of the original example x, they constructed the adversarial examples in the real scenarios.

In order to defend against the adversarial examples, a lot of methods have been proposed, such as adversarial training, networks modification, feature squeezing as well as using additional networks [13,24,32]. Specifically, the method of adversarial training improves the robustness of the model by generating adversarial examples and updating model parameters accordingly [9,26]. In order to keep the effectiveness, this method needs to use high-intensity adversarial examples, and at the same time, the network should have sufficient expressive power. Therefore, such method requires a large amount of adversarial example training data, so it is also called brute force adversarial training. In addition, existing works show that adversarial training can help regularize the models and mitigate overfitting [14,23]. However, these adversarial trained models still lack robustness to unseen adversarial examples.

2.2   Adversarial Robustness of Ensembles

An efficient way to defend against adversarial examples is to use an ensemble of deep neural networks [1,2,10,21]. Strauss et al. [25] have shown that the neural network ensemble can not only improve the prediction accuracy, but also improve the robustness to adversarial examples. Tramèr et al. [27] have proposed to use the adversarial training to enhance the adversarial robustness of an ensemble.

If the gradients of the models in the ensemble share similar directions, an adversarial example which can fool one model may also be capable to fool the others in the ensemble. For this, Kariyappa et al. [10] proposed Gradient Alignment Loss (GAL) to improve the adversarial robustness of the ensemble by considering the diversity of gradient directions. Specifically, it focuses on training the ensemble whose members have irrelevant loss functions by using diversified training. However, GAL does not consider the optimal geometric boundary for the diversification of gradient directions in the ensemble, and does not balance the gradient magnitude of each member in the ensemble. Based on this, Dabouei et al. [7] have proposed gradient phase and magnitude regularization (GPMR) [7]. The basic principle of GPMR is to increase the lower bound of the adversarial perturbation that changes the score of the classifier by considering the optimal geometric boundary to diversify the gradient direction in the ensemble, and to balance the gradient magnitude of the members, thereby constructing the first-order defence interaction of the members in the ensemble. However, GPMR does not fully consider the interaction between members in the ensemble. In contrast, our work builds a good ensemble defence system by considering the interaction between members in the ensemble, thereby improving the robustness of the ensemble.

2.3 Negative Correlation Learning

Liu and Yao [15] proposed a cooperative ensemble learning system (CELS), and the purpose is to interactively and simultaneously train all individual models in the ensemble in a single learning process through negative correlation learning (NCL). Through negative correlation learning, different models in the ensemble can learn different features of the training set. Theoretical and experimental results show that NCL can promote the diversity of the models as well as keeping a high prediction accuracy.

Liu et al. [16] also have tried to solve the problem of the optimal number of neural networks in the ensemble on the premise of maintaining the good interaction of individual members in the ensemble through negative correlation learning and evolutionary learning. Chan et al. [5] proposed NCCD, which implemented negative correlation learning via correlation corrected data. NCCD can reduce the communication bandwidth between individual networks, and can be applied to the ensemble of any type of network structures. In addition, because NCCD does not modify the error function of the network for negative correlation learning, but modifies the training data for negative correlation learning, it can accelerate the learning speed through parallel computing.

Wang et al. [28] proposed a new negative correlation learning algorithm named AdaBoost.NC. The flexibility of AdaBoost is used to overcome the shortcomings of NCL, such as sensitivity to parameters setting and long training time, and the overfitting problem of AdaBoost is solved by introducing diversity [20,22]. Experimental results show that AdaBoost.NC has better generalization performance than NCCD, and the time cost is significantly less than CELS and NCCD.

In this paper, for the first time, we propose a defence approach against adversarial examples by leveraging the negative correlation method. We first make the gradient direction of each member in the ensemble negatively correlated. Secondly, we make the gradient magnitude of each member in the ensemble negatively correlated with the average gradient magnitude, such that help improve the diversity of the ensemble and balance the gradient magnitude of each member in the ensemble. The details will be given in the next section.

3   The Proposed Method

In this section, we will show how negative correlation principle can be exploited to improve the adversarial robustness.

3.1   On Gradient Directions of Members

The gradient of the loss to the input x refers to a direction where the directional derivative of the loss achieves a maximum along this direction, i.e., the loss changes fastest when a perturbation ϵ is introduced along this direction.

From Fig. 1, where ∇J_i indicates the model gradient of the ith member ($i = 0, 1, 2$), and $\nabla J_{ensemble}$ indicates averaged gradients of all members, The adversarial perturbation added along the direction of $\nabla J_{ensemble}$ can affect most members of the ensemble. Firstly, we prompt the angle between ∇J_i and $\nabla J_{ensemble}$ negatively correlated with the angle between ∇J_j ($j \neq i$) of other members and $\nabla J_{ensemble}$. After negative correlation training, the gradient direction of all members in the ensemble with respect to whole dataset will be maximally different, which means that an adversarial perturbation increasing the loss function of one member will not absolutely increase the loss of other members.

In detail, we use cosine similarity (CS) to measure the gradient angle between members, and it can be calculated as Formula (1).

$$CS(\nabla J_i, \nabla J_j) = \frac{< \nabla J_i, \nabla J_j >}{\|\nabla J_i\|_2 \cdot \|\nabla J_j\|_2} \tag{1}$$

The smaller the CS, the larger the angle between the gradients, and the greater the diversity among the members. This means that the loss of each member will not grow in a positive correlation manner for the same adversarial perturbation. Therefore, it is hard for an adversarial perturbation to fool all members simultaneously. Meanwhile, the ensemble with increased diversity is still capable to keep a high prediction accuracy. The relevant regularization term can be expressed as Formula (2).

$$\text{Loss}_{cos} = \text{CS}\left(\nabla J_i, \nabla J_{ensemble}\right) \sum_{j \neq i}^{k} \text{CS}\left(\nabla J_j, \nabla J_{ensemble}\right) \tag{2}$$

$$\nabla J_{ensemble} = \frac{1}{k} \sum_{i=1}^{k} \nabla J_i \tag{3}$$

Where k is the number of members. Minimizing the regularization term will help all members train interactively, thus facilitating the maximization of diversity in gradient directions.

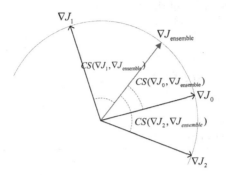

Fig. 1. Improve the ensemble diversity from the view of gradient direction; ∇J_i indicate the model gradient of the ith member ($i = 0, 1, 2$), and $\nabla J_{ensemble}$ indicate the ensemble gradient

We use CS as the regularization term for enhancing the adversarial robustness, and the loss function can be expressed as Formula (4), where CE is the mean of the cross-entropy loss and λ_{cos} is the weight coefficient. The ce_{loss} in Formula (5) is the cross-entropy loss of a single model.

$$Loss = CE + \lambda_{cos} Loss_{cos} \tag{4}$$

$$CE = \frac{1}{k} \sum_{i=1}^{k} ce_{loss} \tag{5}$$

The algorithm for calculating the regularization term of the ith member on the gradient direction using negative correlation is shown in Algorithm 1, where k is the number of members in the ensemble. Firstly, it calculates the cosine similarity $cos1$ between the gradient of the ith member and the ensemble as well as the sum of cosine similarity $cos2$ between the gradients of the other members and the ensemble. Secondly, the regularization term $Loss_{cos}$ of the ith member is calculated and will be minimized in the training process.

3.2   On the Gradient Magnitudes of Members

The gradient magnitude represents the magnitude of the change in the loss caused by the adversarial perturbation ϵ. Adding an adversarial perturbation ϵ along the gradient direction will influence the loss more if there is a larger gradient magnitude. In the white-box attack scenario, the attacker can easily attack the classifiers with the largest gradient magnitude on the original input.

Algorithm 1. Calculating $Loss_{cos}$ for the ith member

Require: Gradient of the ith member: ∇J_i; Gradient of other members in the ensemble: $\nabla J_j (j \neq i)$; Ensemble gradient: $\nabla J_{ensemble}$; Number of models in the ensemble: k

Ensure: Regularization term of the ith member: $Loss_{cos}$

    $cos1 \leftarrow CS(\nabla J_i, \nabla J_{ensemble})$

    $cos2 \leftarrow 0;$

    for $j \leftarrow 1$ **to** k **do**

      if $j \neq i$ **then**

        $cos2 \leftarrow cos2 + CS(\nabla J_j, \nabla J_{ensemble})$

      end if

    end for

    $Loss_{cos} \leftarrow cos1 * cos2$

    Return the regularization term: $Loss_{cos}$

As shown in Fig. 2, where g is the mean value of the gradient magnitudes of all members, k is the number of members in the ensemble and ∇J_i represents the gradient of the ith member. We use the L_2 norm of the gradient to calculate the gradient magnitude of each member in the ensemble. According to the negative correlation principle, we make the gradient magnitude of the ith member and the ensemble gradient magnitude negatively correlated with the gradient magnitude of other members in the ensemble. By minimizing the regularization term, the gradient magnitudes of all members in the ensemble is negatively correlated, which means different members can learn better over different features.

Therefore, we propose the second regularization term, which is shown in Formula (6).

$$\text{Loss}_{norm} = \frac{1}{g^2} \left(\|\nabla J_i\|_2 - g \right) \sum_{j \neq i}^{k} \left(\|\nabla J_j\|_2 - g \right) \tag{6}$$

$$g = \frac{1}{k} \sum_{i=1}^{k} \|\nabla J_i\|_2 \tag{7}$$

Considering all members are trained simultaneously, different members can learn different features over the training dataset and have different gradient magnitudes on the same input since it is not easy to always own very small gradient magnitudes over the whole input space. Therefore, it can be avoided that the adversaries attack the ensemble successfully by attacking only the models with larger gradient magnitude.

We use this to regularize the training for improving the ensemble diversity and the loss function can be expressed as Formula (8). Where CE is the cross-entropy loss and λ_{norm} is the weight coefficient.

$$\text{Loss} = CE + \lambda_{norm} \text{Loss}_{norm} \tag{8}$$

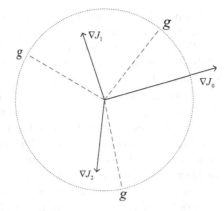

Fig. 2. Improving the ensemble diversity from the view of the gradient magnitude; ∇J_i indicates model gradients in the ensemble $(i = 0, 1, 2)$, and g indicates the mean value of the gradient magnitudes of all members in the ensemble

The algorithm for calculating $Loss_{norm}$ is shown in Algorithm 2, where k is the number of members in ensemble. Firstly, we calculate the difference $norm1$ between the gradient magnitude of the ith member and the mean value g as well as the difference $norm2$ between the gradient magnitude of other members in the ensemble and the mean value g. Secondly, according to the negative correlation method, $Loss_{norm}$ is calculated and treated as a regularization term for the training.

Algorithm 2. Calculating $Loss_{norm}$ for the ith member

Require: Gradient of the ith member: ∇J_i; Gradient of other members in the ensemble: $\nabla J_j (j \neq i)$; the mean value of the gradient magnitude: g
Ensure: Regularization term: $Loss_{norm}$
   $norm1 \leftarrow (\|\nabla J_i\|_2 - g)/g$
   $norm2 \leftarrow 0$
   for $j \leftarrow 1$ **to** k **do**
     if $j \neq i$ **then**
       $norm2 \leftarrow norm2 + (\|\nabla J_j\|_2 - g)/g$
     end if
   end for
   $Loss_{norm} \leftarrow norm1 * norm2$
   Return the regularization term: $Loss_{norm}$

3.3   The Proposed NCEn

We have proposed two methods to increase the adversarial robustness, however, we find that using each method alone is still limits in performance. Specifically, if only considering the influence of the gradient direction of each member in the ensemble, an adversary can attack a few members with large gradient magnitudes to make the ensemble predict incorrectly. While if only considering the influence of the gradient magnitude of each member in the ensemble, there could be a phenomenon that the gradient directions of all members are similar. At this time, the loss of each member in the ensemble will grow positively corrected, i.e., adversarial examples generated along the gradient direction can make most members of the ensemble predict incorrectly. So that the defence performance of the ensemble is similar to that of a single model, which is not robust enough.

Therefore, we will consider both the influence of member gradient directions and the influence of member gradient magnitudes, and use two regularization terms simultaneously to improve the adversarial robustness. The loss function is shown in Formula (9), where CE is cross-entropy loss and the combined regularization term NCE can be calculated by Formula (10).

$$\text{Loss} = CE + NCE \tag{9}$$

$$NCE = \frac{1}{k} \sum_{i=1}^{k} (\lambda_{\text{norm}} \text{Loss}_{\text{norm}} + \lambda_{\text{cos}} \text{Loss}_{\text{cos}}) \tag{10}$$

The specific implementation of the ensemble training process is shown in Algorithm 3. In each epoch, we first get the predicted value $pred$ of each member in the ensemble. Next, we use the predicted value $pred$ and the real label $label$ to calculate the cross entropy loss ce_{loss} of each member in the ensemble. Then, we calculate the mean value CE of the cross-entropy loss of all members in the ensemble. Finally, we use Formula (10) to calculate the regularization term NCE, and by which we can update the parameters of all members.

Algorithm 3. Negative Correlation Ensemble

Require: Dataset: X; Correct label for dataset X: $label$
Ensure: Trained ensemble
    Get a list of all the members in ensemble: $f_i (i = 1, 2, ..., k)$
    for $epoch \leftarrow begin\_epoch$ **to** end_epoch **do**
        for $model \leftarrow f_1$ **to** f_k **do**
            $pred \leftarrow model(X)$
            $ce_{loss} \leftarrow CE(pred, label)$
        end for
        Calculate $CE \leftarrow \frac{1}{k} \sum_{i=1}^{k} ce_{loss}$
        Get the value of the regularization term: NCE
        Back propagation using the sum of CE and NCE
        Update the model parameters of each model
    end for

Table 1. Ensemble model structures.

Name	Ensemble structures
Ensemble1	$3 * ResNet20$
Ensemble2	$3 * ResNet26$
Ensemble3	$3 * ResNet32$
Ensemble4	$1 * ResNet20 + 1 * ResNet26 + 1 * ResNet32$

4 Experiments

In this section, we conduct experiments on the FashionMNIST and CIFAR-10 datasets. We first give our experimental settings. Secondly, we compare the adversarial robustness of NCEn with different ensemble defence approaches. Furthermore, we show that NCEn is capable to reduce the transferability of adversarial examples, which proves that NCEn leverages the interactions of different members to improve the adversarial robustness. The source codes of this work are available at https://github.com/MiLabHITSZ/2022ZhangNCEn.

4.1 Experimental Setup

In our experiments, we use three ensemble defence strategies as baselines to evaluate the performance of NCEn. The first one is the ensemble being trained without any regularization term, which $\lambda_{cos} = \lambda_{norm} = 0$. The second one is to use GAL for diversified training to improve the adversarial robustness of the ensemble [10]. The third one is GPMR proposed by Dabouei et al. [7], which constructs the first-order defence interaction of the members in the ensemble to improve the adversarial robustness of the ensemble. Both GAL and GPMR are state-of-the-art ensemble defence strategies.

In our experiments, we used four different ensemble structures to evaluate the experimental performance, as shown in Table 1. We evaluate the adversarial robustness of the ensemble on the FashionMNIST and CIFAR-10 datasets. For GAL, the coefficient of the regularization term is set to 0.5. For GPMR, λ_{div} of FashionMNIST is set to 0.1, λ_{div} of CIFAR-10 is set to 0.04, and λ_{eq} is set to 10 for all datasets. As for NCEn, we set $\lambda_{cos} = 0.02$ and $\lambda_{norm} = 0.02$ for FashionMNIST, $\lambda_{cos} = 0.06$ and $\lambda_{norm} = 0.04$ for CIFAR-10.

We use test accuracy of clean examples (ACE) and test accuracy of adversarial examples (AAE) as the evaluation metrics. AAE refers to the ratio that a new example set, which is constructed by adding adversarial perturbations to the clean examples, can still be correctly classified by the ensemble. We use the averaged CE loss of all models in the ensemble as the objective function of the attack.

4.2 Defence Performance

We use several powerful white-box attack methods to test the defensive performance of ensembles, including the fast gradient sign method (FGSM) [9], the momentum iterative fast gradient sign method (MI-FGSM) [8], projected gradient descent (PGD) [17], the basic iterative method (BIM) [12]. The specific settings of attack methods are as follows. FGSM adds a perturbation with a step length of ϵ in the gradient direction. For MI-FGSM, each step size is set to 0.01, while keeping the maximum distortion always within ϵ. For PGD, the number of iterations is set to 40, and the maximum perturbation and single-step attack steps are both ϵ. For BIM, the number of iterations is set to 10, and the maximum perturbation and single-step attack steps are both ϵ. All attack methods are implemented by AdverTorch.

Table 2. the classification accuracy of four ensemble defence strategies on Fashion-MNIST and CIFAR-10, when the model number is 3. ACE means accuracy of clean examples.

Ensemble	Attack	Setting	FashionMNIST				Setting	CIFAR-10			
			BL	GAL	GPMR	NCEn		BL	GAL	GPMR	NCEn
Ensemble1	ACE		0.9337	0.8925	0.9205	0.9184	ACE	0.8639	0.8070	0.8433	0.8436
	FGSM	ϵ=0.1	0.8459	0.8168	0.8178	**0.8656**	ϵ=0.03	0.6744	0.6102	0.6118	**0.7473**
		ϵ=0.3	0.6131	**0.6885**	0.6847	0.6414	ϵ=0.09	0.5462	0.4421	0.4986	**0.6217**
	MI-FGSM	ϵ=0.1	0.6310	0.5253	0.5720	**0.6882**	ϵ=0.03	0.2067	0.0131	0.1530	**0.3000**
		ϵ=0.3	**0.4759**	0.3396	0.3867	0.4412	ϵ=0.09	0.0625	0.0004	0.0500	**0.1157**
	PGD	ϵ=0.1	0.7002	0.6406	0.5982	**0.7694**	ϵ=0.01	0.5661	0.5708	0.4963	**0.6473**
		ϵ=0.15	0.6163	0.5434	0.4983	**0.7362**	ϵ=0.02	0.4307	0.2117	0.3459	**0.5305**
	BIM	ϵ=0.1	0.7079	0.6674	0.6291	**0.7783**	ϵ=0.01	0.6119	0.5382	0.5241	**0.6740**
		ϵ=0.15	0.6292	0.5620	0.5264	**0.7383**	ϵ=0.2	0.4722	0.2469	0.3916	**0.5716**
Ensemble2	ACE		0.9326	0.6724	0.9203	0.9208	ACE	0.8688	0.7842	0.8385	0.8571
	FGSM	ϵ=0.1	0.8396	0.9284	0.7995	**0.8525**	ϵ=0.03	**0.6862**	0.6884	0.5933	0.6844
		ϵ=0.3	0.6025	0.7754	**0.6975**	0.6564	ϵ=0.09	**0.5606**	0.5673	0.4697	0.5570
	MI-FGSM	ϵ=0.1	0.6155	0.7751	0.5605	**0.6725**	ϵ=0.03	0.2107	0.0175	0.1404	**0.2405**
		ϵ=0.3	0.4461	0.4531	0.4018	**0.4549**	ϵ=0.09	0.0709	0.0051	0.0374	**0.0851**
	PGD	ϵ=0.1	0.6904	0.8334	0.6014	**0.7516**	ϵ=0.01	0.5719	0.5728	0.4819	**0.6013**
		ϵ=0.15	0.6210	0.7360	0.4883	**0.6917**	ϵ=0.02	0.4391	0.3555	0.3378	**0.4735**
	BIM	ϵ=0.1	0.7060	0.8511	0.6220	**0.7671**	ϵ=0.01	0.6109	0.5618	0.5197	**0.6472**
		ϵ=0.15	0.6107	0.7473	0.5182	**0.6933**	ϵ=0.2	0.4762	0.3816	0.3831	**0.5061**
Ensemble3	ACE		0.9316	0.5259	0.9198	0.9212	ACE	0.8665	0.7589	0.8387	0.8408
	FGSM	ϵ=0.1	0.8535	0.8836	0.8259	**0.8782**	ϵ=0.03	0.6873	0.5577	0.6076	**0.7614**
		ϵ=0.3	0.6327	0.7649	**0.6797**	0.6651	ϵ=0.09	0.5644	0.4507	0.4864	**0.6321**
	MI-FGSM	ϵ=0.1	0.6456	0.6280	0.5842	**0.7028**	ϵ=0.03	0.2148	0.0052	0.1423	**0.3159**
		ϵ=0.3	0.4913	0.4772	0.4016	**0.5593**	ϵ=0.09	0.0679	0.0006	0.0337	**0.1202**
	PGD	ϵ=0.1	0.7075	0.7837	0.6133	**0.7871**	ϵ=0.01	0.5764	0.3464	0.4914	**0.6678**
		ϵ=0.15	0.6412	0.6773	0.5310	**0.7147**	ϵ=0.02	0.4482	0.2582	0.3369	**0.5448**
	BIM	ϵ=0.1	0.7183	0.7961	0.6428	**0.7864**	ϵ=0.01	0.6168	0.3390	0.5218	**0.6912**
		ϵ=0.15	0.6384	0.7003	0.5472	**0.7206**	ϵ=0.2	0.4859	0.2205	0.3851	**0.5936**
Ensemble4	ACE		0.9309	0.7503	0.9205	0.8428	ACE	0.8695	0.6851	0.8426	0.8492
	FGSM	ϵ=0.1	0.8505	0.9338	0.8116	**0.8992**	ϵ=0.03	0.6813	0.6293	0.6011	**0.7081**
		ϵ=0.3	0.6319	0.8501	0.6793	0.7257	ϵ=0.09	0.5587	0.4936	0.4831	**0.5827**
	MI-FGSM	ϵ=0.1	0.6360	0.7722	0.6015	**0.7734**	ϵ=0.03	0.2118	0.1224	0.1482	**0.2731**
		ϵ=0.3	0.4820	0.5316	0.4285	**0.5202**	ϵ=0.09	0.0672	0.0389	0.0431	**0.0959**
	PGD	ϵ=0.1	0.6954	0.8527	0.6160	**0.8054**	ϵ=0.01	0.5738	0.5831	0.4897	**0.6295**
		ϵ=0.15	0.6235	0.7651	0.5177	**0.7469**	ϵ=0.02	0.4426	0.3595	0.3332	**0.4981**
	BIM	ϵ=0.1	0.7073	0.8571	0.6337	**0.8156**	ϵ=0.01	0.6165	0.5739	0.5185	**0.6637**
		ϵ=0.15	0.6231	0.7654	0.5434	**0.7543**	ϵ=0.2	0.4833	0.3908	0.3876	**0.5449**

The results of different approaches on datasets FashionMNIST and CIFAR-10 are shown in Table 2. Compared with BL, GAL and GPMR, the adversarial robustness of NCEn is significantly improved. When we use the ensemble model structure of Ensemble2, Ensemble3 and Ensemble4, respectively, the ACE of GAL drops below 0.8. At this time, the AAE of GAL is unworthy of consideration. Such AAE are marked with gray background as well as the corresponding ACE. Unlike GAL, NCEn can not only maintain high ACE in all ensemble model structures, but also achieve better adversarial robustness. Specifically, on FashionMNIST, except FGSM and MI-FGSM with a large attack step, NCEn has better adversarial robustness in all ensemble structures. AAE has the highest improvement of 0.14 on Ensemble4 and MI-FGSM ($\epsilon = 0.1$). On CIFAR-10, the adversarial robustness of NCEn is better or very close to the existing best baselines, and AAE can be improved by 0.11 at most.

4.3 Transferability Between Members

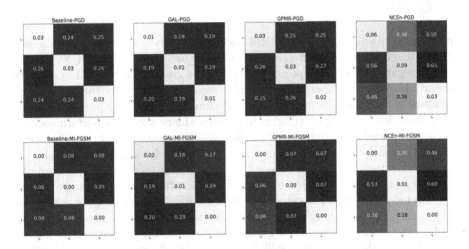

Fig. 3. The confusion matrix for adversarial transferability. Rows and columns respectively represent the model for generating adversarial examples and the model for testing the accuracy of adversarial examples.

Transferability refers to the success rate of being able to attack other models at the same time when an adversarial example is designed to attack a particular model. The less transferable the adversarial example is, the better the diversity of the models.

Therefore, we can use the transferability of adversarial examples between different models to evaluate the similarity between members in the ensemble. We perform transferability experiments using PGD [17] and MI-FGSM [8], We generate adversarial examples for each member, and then evaluate their transferability on other members by calculating AAE. The perturbation magnitude of all attacks is set to $\epsilon = 0.05$. We use Ensemble4 in Table 1 to conduct the transferability experiments, and the results are shown in Fig. 3.

As shown in Fig. 3, we use the heat map of the confusion matrix to show transferability. The ith row and jth column in the heat map represents the test accuracy of the adversarial examples on the jth member, while the adversarial examples are generated over the ith member. When the value of other positions in the confusion matrix is closer to 0, it means that the adversarial examples generated by the ith model can successfully attack other models in the ensemble. The closer the values in the confusion matrix are, the higher the transferability of the adversarial examples and the higher the similarity between members in the ensemble. On the contrary, it means that the diversity among members in the ensemble is higher, and the ensemble has better adversarial robustness. It can be seen from the confusion matrix that the transferability of adversarial examples in NCEn ensemble is poor, which indicates that NCEn has better diversity, such that it can provide better defence interactions for members.

5   Conclusion

In this paper, we propose a practical and feasible adversarial examples defence scheme based on the negative correlation ensemble, which is named NCEn. We use the negative correlation principle to make the gradient direction and gradient magnitude of each member in the ensemble negatively correlated, and to train all members in the ensemble interactively and simultaneously. The purpose of negative correlation training in NCEn is to produce the best defence performance for the whole ensemble. Experimental results demonstrate that NCEn can achieve a better adversarial robustness than other ensemble defence schemes. Finally, we demonstrate that NCEn can reduce the transferability of adversarial examples between members in the ensemble through the confusion matrix. In general, we can conclude that NCEn is capable to improve the diversity and the robustness of the ensemble by making the gradient direction and gradient magnitude negatively correlated. However, for a given task, how to find the optimal number of the models in the ensemble is still a question. Too Many models could not be better. In the future, in order to obtain the best robustness, we will study how to automatically set the optimal number of the models in the ensemble.

References

1. Abbasi, M., Gagné, C.: Robustness to adversarial examples through an ensemble of specialists. In: Proceedings of the 5th International Conference on Learning Representations (2017)
2. Bagnall, A., Bunescu, R., Stewart, G.: Training ensembles to detect adversarial examples. arXiv preprint arXiv:1712.04006 (2017)
3. Brendel, W., Rauber, J., Bethge, M.: Decision-based adversarial attacks: Reliable attacks against black-box machine learning models. In: Proceedings of the 6th International Conference on Learning Representations (2018)

4. Carlini, N., Wagner, D.A.: Towards evaluating the robustness of neural networks. In: Proceedings of the 2017 IEEE Symposium on Security and Privacy, pp. 39–57. IEEE (2017)

5. Chan, Z.S.H., Kasabov, N.K.: A preliminary study on negative correlation learning via correlation-corrected data (NCCD). Neural Process. Lett. **21**(3), 207–214 (2005)

6. Chen, P., Zhang, H., Sharma, Y., Yi, J., Hsieh, C.: ZOO: zeroth order optimization based black-box attacks to deep neural networks without training substitute models. In: Proceedings of the 10th ACM Workshop on Artificial Intelligence and Security, pp. 15–26. ACM (2017)

7. Dabouei, A., Soleymani, S., Taherkhani, F., Dawson, J.M., Nasrabadi, N.M.: Exploiting joint robustness to adversarial perturbations. In: 2020 IEEE/CVF Conference on Computer Vision and Pattern Recognition, pp. 1119–1128. IEEE (2020)

8. Dong, Y., et al.: Boosting adversarial attacks with momentum. In: Proceedings of the 2018 IEEE Conference on Computer Vision and Pattern Recognition, pp. 9185–9193. IEEE (2018)

9. Goodfellow, I.J., Shlens, J., Szegedy, C.: Explaining and harnessing adversarial examples. In: Proceedings of the 3rd International Conference on Learning Representations (2015)

10. Kariyappa, S., Qureshi, M.K.: Improving adversarial robustness of ensembles with diversity training. arXiv preprint arXiv:1901.09981 (2019)

11. Krizhevsky, A., Sutskever, I., Hinton, G.E.: ImageNet classification with deep convolutional neural networks. Adv. Neural Inf. Process. Syst. **25**, 1097–1105 (2012)

12. Kurakin, A., Goodfellow, I.J., Bengio, S.: Adversarial examples in the physical world. In: Proceedings of the 5th International Conference on Learning Representations (2017)

13. Kurakin, A., Goodfellow, I.J., Bengio, S.: Adversarial machine learning at scale. In: Proceedings of the 5th International Conference on Learning Representations (2017)

14. LeCun, Y., Bengio, Y., Hinton, G.E.: Deep learning. Nature **521**(7553), 436–444 (2015)

15. Liu, Y., Yao, X.: Simultaneous training of negatively correlated neural networks in an ensemble. IEEE Trans. Syst. Man Cybern. **29**(6), 716–725 (1999)

16. Liu, Y., Yao, X., Higuchi, T.: Evolutionary ensembles with negative correlation learning. IEEE Trans. Evol. Comput. **4**(4), 380–387 (2000)

17. Madry, A., Makelov, A., Schmidt, L., Tsipras, D., Vladu, A.: Towards deep learning models resistant to adversarial attacks. In: Proceedings of the 6th International Conference on Learning Representations (2018)

18. Meng, D., Chen, H.: MagNet: a two-pronged defense against adversarial examples. In: Proceedings of the 2017 ACM SIGSAC Conference on Computer and Communications Security, pp. 135–147. ACM (2017)

19. Moosavi-Dezfooli, S., Fawzi, A., Frossard, P.: DeepFool: a simple and accurate method to fool deep neural networks. In: Proceedings of the 2016 IEEE Conference on Computer Vision and Pattern Recognition, pp. 2574–2582. IEEE (2016)

20. Opitz, D.W., Maclin, R.: Popular ensemble methods: an empirical study. J. Artif. Intell. Res. **11**, 169–198 (1999)

21. Pang, T., Xu, K., Du, C., Chen, N., Zhu, J.: Improving adversarial robustness via promoting ensemble diversity. In: Proceedings of the 36th International Conference on Machine Learning, vol. 97, pp. 4970–4979. PMLR (2019)

22. Quinlan, J.R.: Bagging, boosting, and C4.5. In: Proceedings of the Thirteenth National Conference on Artificial Intelligence and Eighth Innovative Applications of Artificial Intelligence Conference, pp. 725–730. AAAI (1996)

23. Sankaranarayanan, S., Jain, A., Chellappa, R., Lim, S.N.: Regularizing deep networks using efficient layerwise adversarial training. In: Proceedings of the AAAI Conference on Artificial Intelligence, vol. 32, pp. 4008–4015. AAAI (2018)

24. Sinha, A., Chen, Z., Badrinarayanan, V., Rabinovich, A.: Gradient adversarial training of neural networks. arXiv preprint arXiv:1806.08028 (2018)

25. Strauss, T., Hanselmann, M., Junginger, A., Ulmer, H.: Ensemble methods as a defense to adversarial perturbations against deep neural networks. arXiv preprint arXiv:1709.03423 (2017)

26. Szegedy, C., et al.: Intriguing properties of neural networks. In: Proceedings of the 2nd International Conference on Learning Representations (2014)

27. Tramèr, F., Kurakin, A., Papernot, N., Goodfellow, I.J., Boneh, D., McDaniel, P.D.: Ensemble adversarial training: attacks and defenses. In: Proceedings of the 6th International Conference on Learning Representations (2018)

28. Wang, S., Chen, H., Yao, X.: Negative correlation learning for classification ensembles. In: Proceedings of the International Joint Conference on Neural Networks, pp. 1–8. IEEE (2010)

29. Wu, D., Wang, Y., Xia, S., Bailey, J., Ma, X.: Skip connections matter: On the transferability of adversarial examples generated with resnets. In: Proceedings of the 8th International Conference on Learning Representations (2020)

30. Xu, W., Evans, D., Qi, Y.: Feature squeezing: detecting adversarial examples in deep neural networks. In: Proceedings of the 25th Annual Network and Distributed System Security Symposium. The Internet Society (2018)

31. Yan, S., Xiong, Y., Lin, D.: Spatial temporal graph convolutional networks for skeleton-based action recognition. In: Proceedings of the Thirty-Second AAAI Conference on Artificial Intelligence, pp. 7444–7452. AAAI (2018)

32. Zhao, P., Fu, Z., Wu, O., Hu, Q., Wang, J.: Detecting adversarial examples via key-based network. arXiv preprint arXiv:1806.00580 (2018)

Accurate Decision-Making Method for Air Combat Pilots Based on Data-Driven

Yiming Mao[(⊠)], Zhijie Xia, Qingwei Li, Jiafan He, and Aiguo Fei

Science and Technology on Information Systems Engineering Laboratory,
Nanjing 210023, China
maoyiming@cetc.com.cn

Abstract. The development of science and technology has constantly changed the air combat battlefield. At present, more and more researches focus on the optimization of air combat pilot Expert System(ES). The ES can be divided into two parts: tactical state decision-making and maneuver behavior decision-making. Although a lot of work had optimized the generation method of maneuver behavior decision-making, the tactical state decision-making still follows the original human rules. Based on a large number of tactical state decision-making sample data, this paper uses data-driven method to build a deep learning network. Experiments showed that this method can learn high-level decision empirical data and replace rule models, and can be applied to pilot's accurate tactical state decision-making in the future.

Keywords: Air combat · Deep learning · Date-driven · Decision-making

1 Introduction

With the development of science and technology, the information acquisition capability, attack range and information transmission capacity of sensors, airborne weapons and airborne communication equipment on the new generation of combat aircraft have been greatly improved [1]. The environment of battlefield become more complex. While controlling the fighter to make complex tactical maneuvers, it is also necessary to consider the critical decision-making opportunities for itself against the threat from the enemy, which greatly tests the physiological and psychological limits of pilots.

In the field of air combat decision-making, the research focuses on the construction and optimization of expert systems. The pure expert system like the Adaptive Maneuver Logic(AML) of the U.S. military [2] and the BOSES(Abbreviation of "On board Execution and Advice System" in Russian) of the Russian military were made by rules constructed by IF-THEN-ELSE logic to assist pilots in quickly decision-making.

A large number of researchers attached importance to the optimization of expert systems. Ernest N et al. combined expert system and optimization methods together to create the AlphaAI [3]. It uses decision trees on expert rules

© The Author(s), under exclusive license to Springer Nature Singapore Pte Ltd. 2022
Y. Tan and Y. Shi (Eds.): DMBD 2022, CCIS 1745, pp. 439–448, 2022.
https://doi.org/10.1007/978-981-19-8991-9_31

to determine tactical states, and optimization method based on Genetic Fuzzy Tress(GFT) to judge maneuver behavior. The combination of the two can lead to better expert system. Teng T H et al. used self-organized neural network to learn from a large number of air combat maneuver [4], and generalize the of typical scenes into atypical scenes. However, in these methods, the tactical state decision-making still followed the logic rules made by human, and the impact of optimization on its process is only reflected in the ability to obtain better maneuver behavior decision-making, which cannot eliminate the level gap between expert systems and high-level pilots due to the difference in the accuracy of tactical status decision-making.

There were also some end-to-end control methods that abandon the traditional expert system concept. For example, YANG Q et al. used DQN network to train the maneuver strategy selection of UAV in short-range dog fight [6]. Pope A P et al. from Lockheed Martin trained air combat agent with hierarchical reinforcement learning method [7]. However, these methods were limited to simplified air combat scenarios, with transparent situation information, poor generalization and no interpretability.

Therefore, on the basis of these research, this paper innovatively proposes a data-driven accurate decision-making method. Through a large number of pilot sample data, this method can learn the pilot's experience and knowledge, replacing the rules of tactical state decision-making in traditional expert system. Experiments show that this method is consistent with the pilot's thinking process. With the continuous deepening of data, it can provide precise assistance for the pilot's air combat decision-making.

The main problems solved in this paper:

(1) Describe the decision-making process of the traditional pilot expert systems.
(2) Based on Transformer network, a decision-making model is built and pilot expert system experience knowledge is learned, which can replace the tactical state decision-making process based on IF-THEN-ELSE logic in traditional expert systems.
(3) Explore the influence of different data quantities on the accuracy of the decision-making model.

2   The Decision-Making Process of Pilot Expert System

In the traditional decision-making logic of expert system, it can be typically divided into two parts of processes: tactical state decision-making and maneuver behavior decision-making. The decision-making flow chart of the entire expert system is shown in Fig. 1. The expert system needs to solve the decision-making from battlefield information to tactical state, which is a typical multi classification problem. In the one-to-one air combat scenario, it can be divided into three tactical states: "Patrol", "Attack" and "Escape" (which will be more complex in the case of multi-aircraft air combat). They respectively express:

(1) Patrol: Fly steadily in a certain direction or a certain fixed point.

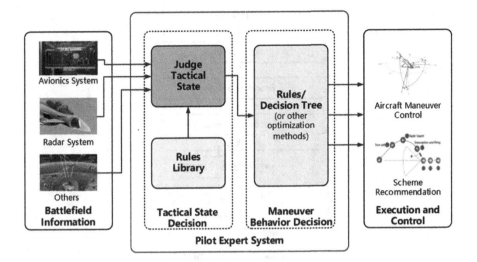

Fig. 1. The Decision-making process of pilot expert system

(2) Attack: Use all means to attack the enemy.
(3) Escape: Use all means to avoid enemy threats

Pilots can only be in one of these states. Therefore, in the traditional expert system, people will formulate rules to complete the one-to-one mapping from the battlefield information to the tactical state.

For the decision-making from tactical state to maneuver behavior, it is to solve how the system assists people at flight control or weapons control after the decision of tactical state. On this issue, different expert systems adopt different methods according to different needs, which can be generally divided into:

(1) Tips and Suggestions: According to the matching results of the maneuver database and the tactical state, prompt the appropriate tactical altitude, tactical speed, tactical orientation, tactical distance, etc., which is relatively simple.
(2) Autonomous Maneuver Control: according to the tactical state and the fighter's information, match the maneuver database, solve and execute appropriate maneuver actions, which is relatively complex.

This paper focuses on the classification of tactical state decision-making process, and carries out follow-up research.

3 Construction of Deep Network Based on Data-Driven

3.1 Network Model Selection

For the one-to-one air combat scenario, the whole problem of tactical state decision-making process is transformed into a multi classification problem from battlefield information to tactical state.

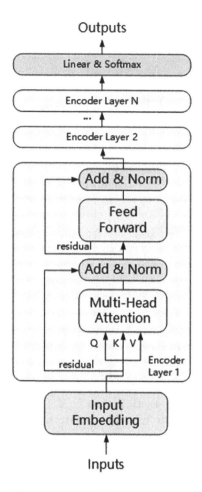

Fig. 2. The structure of the transformer encoder

Neural network model can automatically learn features and multi-level representation and abstraction from data, which solves the problem of manually designing features in traditional machine learning [8]. In particular, focusing on the typical temporal relationship of battlefield information data, this paper adopts Transformer network based on Self Attention mechanism [9].Transformer network originated from a paper published by Google in 2017, and it has made outstanding achievements in machine translation tasks at the beginning. The Transformer structure proposed in this paper cancels the RNN and CNN neural network units in the traditional Seg2Seg model and replaces them with the Self-Attention Mechanism computing unit. This computing unit has high degree of parallelism and short training time [10]. Therefore, Transformer has attracted extensive attention from academia and industry. With the deep excavation of academic circles, Transformer network has shown its excellent performance in different fields.

Transformer network uses Encoder and Decoder structure when dealing with semantic problems, which is relatively complex. In this paper, extracting its Encoder part for adjustment has been able to reasonably complete the classification from battlefield information to tactical state. The structure of the entire Transformer is adjusted as Fig. 2.

The EncoderLayer is composed of Multi Head Attention unit and Feed Forwad unit. After that, the dimension is shrunk according to the number of classes through linear layers, and finally it becomes a probability distribution through Softmax function.

3.2 Battlefield Data Sampling Dimensions

For the whole air combat, in the course of confrontation, the information data that pilots can obtain is lengthy and jumbled. As shown in the right side of Fig. 1, the pilot can obtain avionics system information, radar system information, electronic warfare(EW) information and others. The elements that affect the pilot's tactical state can be divided into four types:My fighter's information, My missile's information, Enemy fighter's information(4-dimensions) and Enemy Missile's information.

3.3 Loss Function and Accuracy Function

In the traditional classification problem, the Mean Square Error(MSE) is often used as loss function, which assumes that the data conforms to the Gaussian distribution. However, MSE has to pay attention to the difference between the prediction probability and the real probability on all classes, and its performance on multi classification problem is inferior to that of Cross-Entropy function [11]. The Cross-Entropy loss function is based on the concept of cross entropy in information theory, is an other way to reflect the difference between the predicted probability distribution and the real probability distribution.

Under the multi classification problem, the loss function based on cross entropy is:

$$L = \frac{1}{N} \sum_{i=1}^{N} \sum_{k=1}^{K} y_i^k \times \log\left(\hat{y}_i^k\right) \tag{1}$$

where, y_i and $\hat{y}_i$ are the real and predicted values of the ith sample respectively. Usually, the true probability distribution of each sample is one-hot type, that is, each sample must belong to a certain category:

$$y_i^j = \begin{cases} 0 \ j \neq k_i \\ 1 \ j = k_i \end{cases} \quad \forall i \in \{1, 2, ..., N\} \tag{2}$$

where k_i is the category of the ith sample, so the above equation is equal to:

$$L = \frac{1}{N} \sum_{i=1}^{N} \log(\hat{y}_i^k) \tag{3}$$

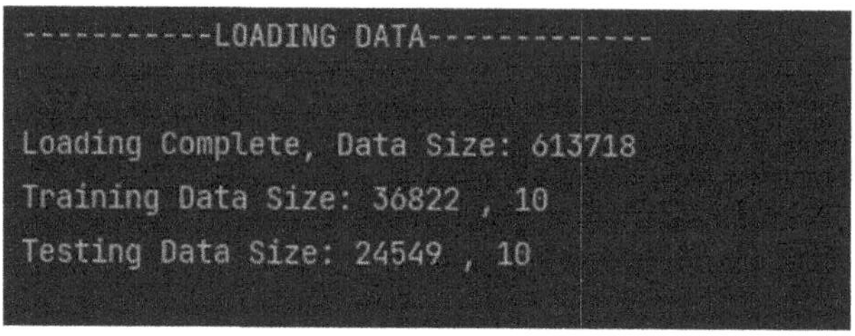

Fig. 3. The data scale

In this paper, the accuracy rate is used to replace the traditional precise rate or recall rate. It is the proportion of all correctly predicted samples. The formula is:

$$A = \frac{1}{N} \sum_{i=1}^{N} y_i^{argmax(\widehat{y}_i)} \tag{4}$$

where, $argmax(\widehat{y}_i)$ is the classification of the maximum probability in the prediction results. Therefore, when the prediction class is consistent with the real class, the value is 1, and when error the value is 0.

3.4 Construction of Deep Learning Network

For the one-to-one air combat game, this paper models the problem as a multi classification problem that divides battlefield information into three types of states. Transformer network is used, Loss function is Cross-Entropy, and the optimizer is Adaptive Moment Estimation(Adam).

4 Experiments and Results

4.1 Data Scales and Preprocessing

In this paper, we sampled 100 battles of the data of the expert system, and the sampling evaluation rate was 10 times per second. Combined with the internal data of manual and expert system itself, we labeled the samples. The overall data scales is shown in the Fig. 3. We toke the first 60% as the training set and 40% as the test set.

4.2 Training Result

The model we constructed was based on Pytorch, and used RTX3090 for training. At the same time, as a contrast, we also implemented classification networks based on Long-short Term Memory(LSTM) and Gate Recurrent Unit(GRU). For comparison, we had trained 2000 Epochs for all three networks. The training results of Loss curve and Accuracy curve are shown in the Fig. 4 and 5.

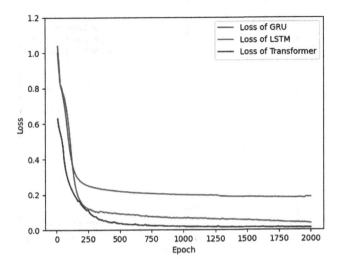

Fig. 4. The loss curve of three models

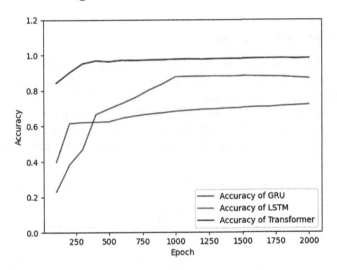

Fig. 5. The accuracy curve of three models

These two figures show that the Transformer model has played an amazing role in this problem. Its loss value on the training set decreases slightly lower than LSTM and GRU at the initial stage, but its final loss and accuracy are far better than both. In the end, Transformer's accuracy on test set reaches an amazing 98%, while GRU and LSTM are around 72% and 82%.

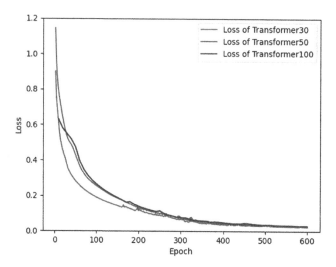

Fig. 6. The loss curve of different training set scales

4.3   Data Scales Compression

At the end of the experiment, based on Transformer network, we verified the impact of data scales on the accuracy of model. We take 30% and 50% data from training set, compared with the full training set. It can be seen in Fig. 6 that the Transformer network we built can fit the training set with almost the same performance. The fewer the training set scales, the faster the fitting speed. However, the final loss is basically the same. But there is a significant difference

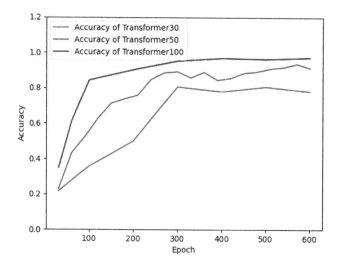

Fig. 7. The accuracy curve of different training set scales

in the accuracy on the test set. The Fig. 7 shows that the more training set scales, the higher accuracy of the final model.

5   Conclusion

This paper innovatively analyzes the decision-making process of traditional expert system, and divides it into two processes: tactical state decision-Making and maneuver behavior decision-making. At present, almost all the optimization of expert system is worked on maneuver behavior decision-making process. In this paper, using Transformer network, a modeling method is proposed for the tactical state decision-making process, which can learn knowledge form historical data. This method can replace traditional rules designed by human, and provide pilots with accurate tactical state. The results show that Transformer network is significantly better than LSTM and GRU methods in dealing with this problem, and the accuracy is affected by data scales.

Acknowledge. This work was supported by the Special Project of Academician Aiguo Fei's Workstation, No. 400119Z012.

References

1. Mao, Y., Li, Q., He, J., Xia, Z., Fei, A.: Construction method of air combat agent based on reinforcement learning. In: China Conference on Command and Control, pp. 98–110. Springer, Singapore (2022). https://doi.org/10.1007/978-981-19-6052-9_10
2. An adaptive maneuvering logic computer program for the simulation of one-on-one air-to-air combat:volume 1:general description. https://core.ac.uk/display/42887441
3. Ernest, N., Carroll, D., Schumacher, C., Clark, M., Cohen, K., Lee, G.: Genetic fuzzy based artificial intelligence for unmanned combat aerial vehicle control in simulated air combat missions. J. Defense Manag. **6**(1), 2167–0374 (2016). https://doi.org/10.4172/2167-0374.1000144
4. Teng, T.H., Tan, A.H., Tan, Y.S., Yeo, A. Self-organizing neural networks for learning air combat maneuvers. In: The 2012 International Joint Conference on Neural Networks (IJCNN), pp. 1–8. IEEE Press, New York (2012). https://doi.org/10.1109/ijcnn.2012.6252763
5. Jiafan, H., Man, W., Feng, F., Qingwei, L., Aiguo, F.: Application of deep reinforcement learning technology in intelligent air combat. Command Information System and Technology, vol. 12(5), pp. 6–13. Science and Technology on Information Systems Engineering Laboratory, Nanjing (2021). https://doi.org/10.15908/j.cnki.cist.2021.05.002
6. Yang, Q., Zhang, J., Shi, G., Hu, J., Wu, Y.: Maneuver decision of UAV in short-range air combat based on deep reinforcement learning. IEEE Access **8**, 363–378 (2019). https://doi.org/10.1109/ijcnn.2012.6252763
7. Pope, A.P., et al .: Hierarchical reinforcement learning for air-to-air combat. In: 2021 International Conference on Unmanned Aircraft Systems (ICUAS), pp. 275–284. IEEE Press, New York (2021)

8. Abiodun, O.I., Jantan, A., Omolara, A.E., Dada, K.V., Mohamed, N.A., Arshad, H.: State-of-the-art in artificial neural network applications: a survey. Heliyon **4**(11), e00938 (2018). https://doi.org/10.1016/j.heliyon.2018.e00938

9. Vaswani, A., et al.: Attention is all you need. In: Advances in Neural Information Processing Systems, **30** (2017)

10. Vaswani, A., et al.: Tensor2tensor for neural machine translation. arXiv preprint. arXiv:1803.07416 (2018)

11. Zhang, Z., Sabuncu, M.: Generalized cross entropy loss for training deep neural networks with noisy labels. In: Advances in Neural Information Processing Systems, **31** (2018)

Establishment of Empirical Expression of Atmospheric Scattering Coefficient for Line-of-Sight Ultraviolet Propagation in Coastal Area

Bifeng Li[1], Bing Xue[1], Jiafang Kang[2], Chuntao Cai[1], and Yue Liu[1](✉)

[1] College of Weaponry Engineering, Naval University of Engineering,
Wuhan, Hubei 430033, China
liuyuehjgc@163.com

[2] Department of Aeronautical Communication, Naval Aviation University,
Yantai, Shangdong 264001, China

Abstract. For the problems of hard quantification of atmospheric attenuation effect, difficult operation and time-consuming application of traditional MODerate resolution atmospheric TRANsmission (MODTRAN) software in the current ultraviolet propagation process, the atmospheric attenuation effect in the ultraviolet propagation process is studied in coastal area. Based on the applicability verification of MODTRAN in coastal area, the empirical expression of atmospheric scattering coefficient for line-of-sight (LOS) ultraviolet propagation in coastal area is built on the basis of the classical Kim model structure. In comparison with the MODTRAN computation, the small error indicates that the established empirical expression of atmospheric scattering coefficient has reasonable structure and good applicability, it can provide an important support for the channel research and the system design of ultraviolet communication.

Keywords: Los ultraviolet propagation · MODTRAN · Atmospheric scattering coefficient · Kim model

1 Introduction

Ultraviolet communication (UVC) has become a emerged wireless optical communication technology in recent years due to its outstanding characteristics, such as non-line-of sight, no need for spectrum application, strong anti-interference ability, high confidentiality, all-round work and easy deployment, which has broad application prospects in commercial and military occasions, such as aircraft cabins, hospital operating rooms, wharf and port, complex mountains and dense jungles. As the research basis of UVC, the characteristics of atmospheric

Supported by organization x.

© The Author(s), under exclusive license to Springer Nature Singapore Pte Ltd. 2022
Y. Tan and Y. Shi (Eds.): DMBD 2022, CCIS 1745, pp. 449–461, 2022.
https://doi.org/10.1007/978-981-19-8991-9_32

channel show obvious complexity, randomness and regionality due to the comprehensive influence of human activities, weather conditions, seasonal climate, geographical location, underlying surface and other factors. On account of lack of data support, there are currently few studies in this area at home and abroad, especially in coastal area where the characteristics of atmospheric environment are between inland and marine scenes.

Atmospheric attenuation effect is one of the basic characteristics of atmospheric channel in the process of ultraviolet propagation, which is also the basic form of influence leading to optical power loss. Atmospheric attenuation is usually quantified by the atmospheric absorption coefficient, scattering coefficient and extinction coefficient, which are collectively referred as the atmospheric attenuation coefficient. It is undoubtedly an effective and accurate way to measure the atmospheric attenuation coefficient with exclusive equipment directly. However, the expensive equipment cost, harsh experimental environment and repeated tests require a lot of manpower and material resources, which can not meet the needs of all researchers. Therefore, establishing the empirical expression of atmospheric attenuation coefficient has become a practical and feasible direction of endeavor. Based on a novel, lightweight and calibrated ultraviolet spectrometer, the ultraviolet sky radiation and the ozone (O_3) inclined column density were measured in Xinjiang with the help of hot-air balloon [1]. In order to measure the loss of O_3 over the Arctic sea ice, a 266 nm differential lidar was used to measure the O_3 concentration based on an aircraft platform [2]. As the ground lidar could not measure the O_3 concentration under 500 m of the atmospheric boundary layer, [3] developed a ground Lidar that could be used to measure the O_3 concentration in the atmospheric boundary layer and observed the O_3 concentration for a long time. Subsequently, [4] measured the O_3 concentration on the 540 m path based on the supercontinuum absorption spectrum technology. At present, the lidar or wireless optical communication systems at the visible and near-infrared bands are used to measure the atmospheric scattering coefficient or extinction coefficient [5]- [8]. There are few reports exclusive measuring equipment at ultraviolet band. However, the expensive equipment costs can not meet the research needs of many scientific research groups. For the absorption coefficient of O_3, [9,10] presented an empirical expression based on the O_3 absorption cross-section and the O_3 concentration. Under non-sunny weather conditions, an empirical model for estimating aerosol scattering coefficient was proposed in [11], furthermore, a modified empirical model for atmospheric visibility within 6 km was proposed in [12], both are only applicable to the visible to near-infrared bands. In addition, [13] proposed an empirical model for atmospheric extinction coefficient in the wavelength range of 0.69–1.55 um and the distance range of 50–1000 m m for the case of advection fog and radiation fog. The empirical model of atmospheric scattering coefficient or extinction coefficient suitable for ultraviolet band has not been reported yet. Hence, the authoritative atmospheric radiative propagation model software (MODerate resolution atmospheric TRANsmission, MODTRAN) is mainly used to study the attenuation of ultraviolet propagation. On the basis of MODTRAN, [14] analyzed the influence of different atmospheric models, weather conditions and O_3 concentration on the propagation attenuation of ultraviolet atmospheric transmittance. Based on the non-line-of-sight ultraviolet multi-scattering model of Monte Carlo (MC) method, the relationship between the propagation distance and the atmospheric visibility, rainfall, wind speed, emission power and detector sensitivity was studied in combination with MODTRAN in [15]. To solve the problem of unclear measurement of solar radiation attenuation loss between solar reflector and receiver, [16] studied the variation of solar radiation transmittance with oblique distance based on MODTRAN in the situations of 250–2500 nm nm solar spectrum and different rural atmospheric visibility, and established the corresponding empirical expression. However, the complex structural design and a number of input parameter settings of MODTRAN make it complex operation, time-consuming application, unable to directly see the effect of output key parameters and difficult to be directly called by other programs, as described in [17,18], which also correspondingly weakens the convenience of studying the atmospheric attenuation effect of ultraviolet propagation.

In order to further study the atmospheric attenuation effect in the process of ultraviolet propagation, on the basis of verifying the applicability of MODTRAN in combination with the observations of Mie scattering lidar (ML) of wireless optical atmospheric channel characteristic test station in Yantai, a coastal city which is located at the east of Shangdong Province, China, the empirical expression of atmospheric attenuation coefficient of line-of-sight (LOS) ultraviolet propagation is established based on the Kim model structure in this paper.

2 Applicability Verification of MODTRAN in Coastal Area Introduction

As described in [19, 20], MODTRAN is an atmospheric radiation propagation model developed by the Air Force Geophysical Laboratory, which can effectively calculate the atmospheric transmittance, direct radiation, thermal radiation, scattering radiation and band-mode gas absorption within the spectrum range 0–$50000 \, cm^{-1}$ or 0.2–∞ um. The MODTRAN includes six reference atmospheric modes, those are American standard atmosphere in 1976, tropical atmosphere, mid-latitude summer, mid-latitude winter, sub-arctic summer and sub-arctic winter. These modes are associated with temperature, pressure, density considered as a function of altitude and a large number of gases mixture ratios, such as H_2O, O_3, CH_4, CO and N_2O et al. In addition, the modes also include representative aerosol models of cloud, rain and fog and three aerosol environmental categories of rural, urban and marine, which is convenient to study the transmission characteristics under complex atmospheric conditions. In addition to the mode's own aerosol model, users can also input atmospheric visibility according to the actual situation in different aerosol environment categories, thereby establishing the connection between the actual atmospheric environment and the MODTRAN. Meanwhile, MODTRAN also considers three radiation propagation paths including horizon, verticality and gradient, which allows users to choose the propagation path based on actual needs.

In the coastal area, in order to inversely calculate the atmospheric propagation attenuation at the ultraviolet band by using MODTRAN effectively, the atmospheric visibility and horizontal atmospheric extinction coefficient measured by 532 nm ML are used to verify the atmospheric extinction coefficient calculated by MODTRAN at this wavelength. The working mechanism of ML is referred to [21,22]. The atmospheric visibility is the main input parameter and the atmospheric transmittance is the output for MODTRAN. The atmospheric extinction coefficient is calculated by atmospheric transmittance inversely.

The atmospheric extinction coefficient is generally expressed as the sum of absorption coefficient and scattering coefficient

$$\sigma = \sigma_m + k_m + \sigma_a + k_a \tag{1}$$

where σ is the atmospheric extinction coefficient, σ_m is the molecular absorption coefficient, k_m is the molecular scattering coefficient, σ_a is the aerosol absorption coefficient, k_a is the aerosol scattering coefficient. In non-sunny weather, aerosol particles are the main components in the atmosphere. The light scattering of aerosol particles which is shown as Mie scattering is much greater than the Rayleigh scattering of molecules. The Kruse model based on atmospheric visibility is an empirical model with extensive applications and convenient employments, which is given by [11]

$$k_s^{Mie} = \frac{\ln(1/\eta)}{R_v} \left(\frac{550}{\lambda}\right)^q \tag{2}$$

where R_v is the atmospheric visibility (in km), λ is the laser propagation wavelength (in nm), q is the particle size distribution coefficient, which is the relevant parameter to R_v. η is the visual threshold of brightness contrast, which is 2% in Kruse model and 5% in visual range quantization of airport runway. In Kruse model,q is expressed as [11]

$$q = \begin{cases} 1.6 & R_v > 50 \\ 1.3 & 6 < R_v < 50 \\ 0.585 R_v^{1/3} & R_v < 6 \end{cases} \tag{3}$$

For the visibility range of 0–6 km, q is further modified in Kim model as [12]

$$q = \begin{cases} 1.6 & R_v > 50 \\ 1.3 & 6 < R_v < 50 \\ 0.16 R_v + 0.34 & 1 < R_v < 6 \\ R_v - 0.5 & 0.5 < R_v < 1 \\ 0 & R_v < 0.5 \end{cases} \tag{4}$$

Assuming that the atmosphere is homogeneous and isotropic, the atmospheric transmittance on the horizontal link can be obtained by [23]

$$\tau(\lambda) = \exp[-\sigma(\lambda) L] \tag{5}$$

where λ is the wavelength, $\tau(\lambda)$ is the atmospheric transmittance associated with wavelength, $\sigma(\lambda)$ is the atmospheric extinction coefficient associated with wavelength, L is the propagation distance. Therefore, the atmospheric extinction coefficient can be inverted as

$$\sigma(\lambda) = -\frac{\ln[\tau(\lambda)]}{L} \tag{6}$$

In order to fully verify the applicability of the MODTRAN to calculate atmospheric propagation attenuation in coastal area, the verification considers the test data of the ML in different years, months and time periods of a day for mid-latitude summer and mid-latitude winter atmospheric modes of MODTRAN. It should be noted that the mid-latitude summer refers to 30°–45° in spring and summer, and the corresponding mid-latitude winter refers to 30°–45° N in autumn and winter. Yantai is located at about 37° N, so the mid-latitude summer or winter atmospheric mode is selected.

The validation data is selected from 08:00–14:00 on August 28, 2012, 20:00–00:00 on March 27, 2013 and 00:00–07:00 on September 29, 2014. Four groups of the atmospheric visibility and atmospheric extinction coefficient data are taken for each time period. The MODTRAN settings in combination with coastal area are given as follows, the atmospheric mode is mid-latitude summer or winter, the type of atmospheric path is horizontal link, the operation mode is transmittance, and the aerosol mode is marine mode. The atmospheric visibility is manually input according to the ML measurements. The altitude of the observation position is 60 m, the path length is 1 km, and the wavelength range is 400–700 nm. For the atmospheric extinction coefficient, Table 1 gives the comparison of the ML measurements and the MODTRAN calculations for 532 nm and 550 nm, respectively. Figure 1 and Fig. 2 show the comparison of them. Table 2 shows the comprehensive evaluation of MODTRAN calculations.

Table 1. Comparison of the ML measurements and the MODTRAN calculations for atmospheric extinction coefficient.

Data	Time	Atmospheric visibility (km)	ML measurements (km^{-1})	MODTRAN calculations at 532 nm (km^{-1})	MODTRAN calculations at 550 nm (km^{-1})
2012.8.28	09:30	5.043	0.7758	0.7831	0.7759
	11:00	12.575	0.3111	0.3153	0.3114
	11:30	9.089	0.4304	0.4354	0.4308
	14:00	14.005	0.2793	0.2833	0.2797
2013.3.27	20:00	6.362	0.6149	0.6205	0.6145
	20:50	4.354	0.8984	0.9058	0.8977
	22:10	7.728	0.5062	0.5108	0.5058
	23:30	5.853	0.6684	0.6743	0.6681
2014.9.29	00:30	8.392	0.4661	0.4714	0.4665
	02:45	7.034	0.5562	0.5619	0.5563
	04:45	13.303	0.2941	0.2981	0.2945
	07:00	9.630	0.4062	0.4110	0.4066

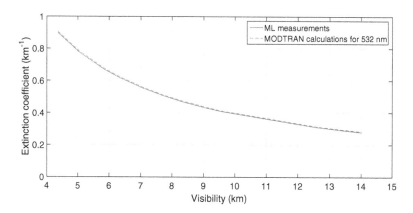

Fig. 1. Matching effect of the ML measurements and MODTRAN calculations for 532 nm.

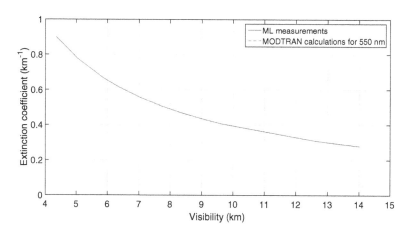

Fig. 2. Matching effect of the ML measurements and MODTRAN calculations for 550 nm.

Table 2. Comprehensive evaluation of the MODTRAN calculations.

Comparison of ML and MODTRAN calculations	SSE	RMSE
532 nm	3.548E-4	0.00544
550 nm	1.783E-6	3.855E-4

It can be seen from Table 1, Table 2, Fig. 1 and Fig. 2 that the atmospheric extinction coefficient inversely calculated by MODTRAN at 550 nm wavelength is in good agreement with the measurements of 532 nm ML. While there is a slight difference between the inverse calculations of MODTRAN at 532 nm wavelength and the measurements of 532 nm ML. This is because the 532 nm ML inversely calculating the atmospheric visibility with the measured atmospheric extinction coefficient is obtained by the empirical expression of Mie scattering coefficient in Equation (2). However, engineering approximation is carried out in the process, that is to say, the item of Equation (2) $(550/532)^q$ is approximately regarded as 1. In other words, ML directly approximates the 532 nm wavelength to the 550 nm wavelength in the inverse calculation. However, no matter how approximate it is in engineering, it can still be verified by the above tables and figures that MODTRAN has good applicability in coastal area, simultaneously, the influence of wavelength difference on atmospheric extinction coefficient is also well demonstrated. Therefore, MODTRAN can be effectively used to invert the ultraviolet atmospheric propagation attenuation under the existing parameter settings.

3   Establishment of Empirical Expression of Atmospheric Scattering Coefficient of LOS Ultraviolet Propagation in Coastal Area

3.1   Calculation of Atmospheric Scattering Coefficient

According to the development of ultraviolet emitter and the research of UVC system reported in the existing literature, it has been found that the wavelength of 254 nm, 260 nm, 266 nm, 270 nm, 274 nm and 365 nm are commonly used in light-emitting devices. Therefore, these wavelengths are mainly considered when calculating the ultraviolet atmospheric scattering coefficient. In addition, O_3 is the main absorber in the process of ultraviolet propagation. Therefore, when considering the atmospheric absorption, only the influence of O_3 molecules is considered, while the influence of other molecules is ignored. In combination with the function of MODTRAN, the calculation steps of atmospheric scattering coefficient of LOS ultraviolet propagation are as follows

Step one, according to the atmospheric visibility range demarcated by Kruse or Kim model, the typical inputs of atmospheric visibility are defined in combination with the distribution range of long-term observation data of atmospheric visibility by ML and the usual meteorological observation records.

The purpose of above processing is to establish the empirical expression of ultraviolet atmospheric scattering coefficient. In addition, considering the operation complexity of MODTRAN and the purely manual calculations of atmospheric attenuation coefficient, it can not meet the batch inputs of atmospheric visibility data.

Step two, under the condition of coastal area setting, the atmospheric transmittance and the O_3 absorption of different ultraviolet wavelengths are calculated by the inputs of typical atmospheric visibility.

It should be noted that the O_3 absorption is determined by MODTRAN atmospheric mode. The modes of mid-latitude summer and winter are selected in combination with the geographical location of Yantai.

Step three, the atmospheric extinction coefficient of LOS ultraviolet propagation is inversely calculated by the expression of atmospheric transmittance, and the atmospheric scattering coefficient is calculated in combination with O_3 absorption.

Except that the wavelength range is set to 250–366 nm and the path length is set to 200 m, other settings of LOS scenario in coastal area are the same as Sect. 2. The calculations of atmospheric scattering coefficient of LOS ultraviolet propagation in coastal area are given in Table 3 based on MODTRAN.

Table 3. Calculations of atmospheric scattering coefficient of LOS ultraviolet propagation in coastal area.

Atmospheric visibility (km)	Atmospheric scattering coefficient $\left(km^{-1}\right)$ (middle latitude summer)						Atmospheric scattering coefficient $\left(km^{-1}\right)$ (middle latitude winter)					
	Wavelength (nm)						Wavelength (nm)					
	254	260	266	270	274	365	254	260	266	270	274	365
0.10	45.19	45.25	45.33	45.45	45.60	42.59	45.19	45.25	45.33	45.45	45.61	42.59
0.20	24.32	24.15	23.95	23.86	23.76	21.99	24.17	23.94	23.75	23.67	23.57	21.83
0.35	14.11	13.93	13.80	13.73	13.66	12.58	14.03	13.85	13.70	13.63	13.56	12.51
0.50	10.02	09.86	09.74	09.68	09.62	08.82	09.98	09.80	09.68	09.61	09.54	08.77
0.60	08.43	08.27	08.16	08.10	08.05	07.36	08.40	08.23	08.11	08.05	08.01	07.32
0.80	06.44	06.29	06.19	06.13	06.09	05.53	06.43	06.27	06.16	06.10	06.06	05.50
1.00	05.24	05.10	05.01	04.95	04.91	04.43	05.25	05.09	04.99	04.93	04.89	04.41
1.50	03.65	03.51	03.42	03.38	03.34	02.97	03.67	03.52	03.42	03.37	03.33	02.96
2.00	02.86	02.72	02.63	02.59	02.56	02.24	02.88	02.73	02.64	02.59	02.55	02.23
2.50	02.38	02.25	02.16	02.12	02.08	01.81	02.41	02.26	02.17	02.12	02.09	01.80
3.00	02.06	01.93	01.84	01.80	01.77	01.51	02.10	01.95	01.86	01.81	01.78	01.51
3.50	01.83	01.70	01.62	01.58	01.55	01.30	01.87	01.73	01.63	01.59	01.55	01.30
4.00	01.66	01.53	01.45	01.41	01.38	01.15	01.70	01.56	01.46	01.42	01.39	01.14
5.00	01.42	01.29	01.21	01.17	01.14	00.93	01.47	01.32	01.23	01.19	01.15	00.93
6.00	01.27	01.14	01.05	01.02	00.98	00.78	01.31	01.16	01.07	01.03	01.00	00.78
7.00	01.15	01.02	00.94	00.90	00.87	00.68	01.19	01.05	00.96	00.92	00.88	00.68
8.00	01.07	00.94	00.86	00.82	00.79	00.60	01.11	00.97	00.88	00.83	00.80	00.56
10.0	00.95	00.82	00.74	00.70	00.67	00.49	00.99	00.85	00.76	00.72	00.68	00.49
15.0	00.79	00.66	00.58	00.54	00.51	00.34	00.83	00.69	00.60	00.56	00.53	00.34
20.0	00.71	00.58	00.50	00.46	00.43	00.27	00.75	00.61	00.52	00.48	00.45	00.27
35.0	00.61	00.48	00.40	00.36	00.33	00.17	00.65	00.51	00.42	00.38	00.35	00.18
50.0	00.56	00.44	00.36	00.32	00.29	00.14	00.61	00.47	00.38	00.34	00.31	00.14
70.0	00.54	00.41	00.33	00.29	00.27	00.11	00.59	00.44	00.36	00.31	00.28	00.12

4 Establishment of Empirical Expression of Atmospheric Scattering Coefficient in Coastal Area

In Sect. 1, it has been stated that the Kruse or Kim model of Mie scattering is only applicable to the visible to near-infrared bands. However, the Mie scattering empirical model that is applicable to ultraviolet band has not been reported so far. Therefore, the Mie scattering coefficient of ultraviolet propagation is often approximately calculated by Kruse model or Kim model. Based on the ultraviolet atmospheric scattering coefficient calculated by MODTRAN in Table 3, the applicable effect of Kim model at different ultraviolet bands are presented in Fig. 3. There is little difference between mid-latitude summer and mid-latitude winter, which is only shown in Fig. 3(a) for the wavelength of 254 nm, and Fig. 3(b)–Fig. 3(f) show the mean of the two for other wavelengths respectively.

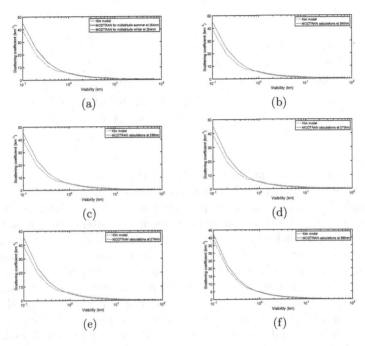

Fig. 3. Applicable effect of Kim model for different wavelength with (a) 254 nm, (b) 260 nm, (c) 266 nm, (d) 270 nm, (e) 274 nm, (f) 365 nm.

It can be seen from Fig. 3(a)–Fig. 3(f) that Kim model is not fully applicable to common ultraviolet wavelengths. Especially in the visibility range of 0–900 m, the application effect is unsatisfied. The applicable effect is greatly improved with the visibility in the range of 900 m–20 km, however, there is still a certain difference compared with the MODTRAN calculations. The applicability of Kim model is obvious when the visibility is larger than 20 km, even though there still exist little differences at 254 nm, 260 nm and 266 nm wavelengths. For the commonly used solar-blind ultraviolet band of 200–280 nm, the calculation difference between the Kim model and the MODTRAN is large and obvious. However, this difference becomes smaller at 365 nm wavelength. Even so, the calculations of Kim model and MODTRAN have the same variation trend and difference trend at all the given ultraviolet wavelengths. This better shows the strong applicability of Kim model, and also lays the construction direction of empirical expression of ultraviolet atmospheric scattering coefficient. Table 4 shows the evaluation index of the Kim model applicability. The closer the sum of squared error (SSE) and the root mean squared error (RMSE) are to 0, the better applicability of Kim model is. The closer the coefficient of determination (R-Square) is to 1, the stronger explanatory ability of atmospheric visibility to Kim model is.

Table 4. Evaluation index of the Kim model applicability.

Evaluation index	Wavelength (nm)					
	254	260	266	270	274	365
SSE	77.351	73.468	71.793	72.000	72.528	21.805
RMSE	01.834	01.787	01.767	01.769	01.776	00.974
R-square	00.710	00.708	00.707	00.704	00.702	00.818

It can be seen from Equations (2)–(4) that the Kruse model structure is similar to that of Kim model, both of which consider the two important parameters of atmospheric visibility and laser propagation wavelength. Kim model is just more refined about the classification of atmospheric visibility than Kruse model. Therefore, the establishment of empirical expression of ultraviolet atmospheric scattering coefficient is still on the basis of the modification of Kim model. It just needs to refine the range of atmospheric visibility and adjust the corresponding value of q in combination with different wavelengths and the difference trend of calculations between Kim model and MODTRAN. Based on the structure of Kim model, the empirical expression of atmospheric scattering coefficient wihich is suitable for different ultraviolet wavelengths mentioned above is finally determined after several fitting attempts, where the expression of q is obtained by

$$q = \begin{cases} 2.2 & 20 < R_v \\ 0.1R_v & 6 < R_v < 20 \\ 0.16R_v & 3 < R_v < 6 \\ 0.16R_v + 0.18 & 0.9 < R_v < 3 \\ 0.2R_v + 0.2 & 0.2 < R_v < 0.9 \\ R_v + 0.09 & 0.1 < R_v < 0.2 \end{cases} \tag{7}$$

Figure 4 shows the matching effect of empirical expression of atmospheric scattering coefficient for LOS ultraviolet propagation. Table 5 shows the evaluation index of empirical expression of atmospheric scattering coefficient for LOS ultraviolet propagation. As shown in Fig. 4(a)–Fig. 4(f), the calculations of the empirical expression of atmospheric scattering coefficient for LOS ultraviolet propagation have good matching effect with that of MODTRAN at different ultraviolet wavelengths after the modification of . This can also be seen from the evaluation index of SSE and RMSE in Table 5. Compared with Table 4, the indexes have been greatly improved. In addition, the R-square is very close to 1, which indicates that the established empirical expression of atmospheric scattering coefficient can well interpret the MODTRAN calculations.

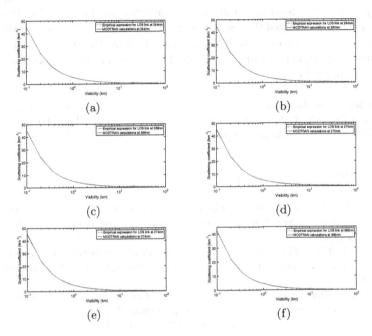

Fig. 4. Matching effect of empirical expression of atmospheric scattering coefficient for LOS ultraviolet propagation with (a) 254 nm, (b) 260 nm, (c) 266 nm, (d) 270 nm, (e) 274 nm, (f) 365 nm.

Table 5. Evaluation index of empirical expression of atmospheric scattering coefficient for LOS ultraviolet propagation.

Evaluation index	Wavelength (nm)					
	254	260	266	270	274	365
SSE	0.444	0.421	0.762	1.127	1.654	0.432
RMSE	0.139	0.135	0.182	0.221	0.268	0.137
R-square	0.995	0.994	0.982	0.972	0.962	0.983

5   Conclusion

For the problem that atmospheric attenuation coefficient is difficult to calculate conveniently in the process of ultraviolet light propagation, on the basis of the applicability verification of MODTRAN in coastal area, this paper establishes the empirical expression of atmospheric scattering coefficient of LOS ultraviolet propagation in coastal area based on the classical Kim model structure. Compared with the error of MODTRAN calculations, the structural rationality and convenient application of the empirical expression of atmospheric scattering coefficient are explained.

Acknowledgements. This work was supported by the National Natural Science Foundation Project of China (No.: 62073334) and the Special Foundation Project of Taishan Scholar of Shandong Province, China.

References

1. Si, F., Xie, P., Liu, C., et al.: Retrieval of ultraviolet skylight radiances and O_3 slant column densities from balloon-borne limb spectrometer. Chin. Opt. Lett. **6**, 541–543 (2008)
2. Seabrook, J.A., Whiteway, J.A., Gray, L.H., et al.: Airborne lidar measurements of surface ozone depletion over arctic sea ice. Atmos. Chem. Phys. **13**, 6023–6029 (2013)
3. Kuang, S., Newchurch, M.J., Burris, J., et al.: Ground-based lidar for atmospheric boundary layer ozone measurements. Appl. Optics **52**, 3557–3566 (2013)
4. Brown, D.M., Brown, A.M., Edwards, P.S., et al.: Measurement of atmospheric oxygen using long-path supercontinuum absorption spectroscopy. J. Appl. Remote Sens. **8**, 083557 (2014)
5. Fernald, F.G.: Analysis of atmospheric lidar observations: some comments. Appl. Optics **8**, 652–653 (1984)
6. Dho, S.W., Park, Y.J., Kong, H.J.: Experimental determination of ageometric form factor in the lidar equation for an inhomogeneous atmosphere. Appl. Optics **36**, 6009–6010 (1997)
7. Rodionov, I.D., et al.: Passage of UV-C, visible, and near-infrared radiation through the atmosphere. Russ. J. Phys. Chem. B **13**(4), 667–673 (2019). https://doi.org/10.1134/S1990793119040134
8. Chen, C., Song, X.Q., Wang, Z.J., et al.: Observations of Atmospheric Aerosol and Cloud Using a Polarized Micropulse Lidar in Xian, China. Atmosphere **796**, 1–17 (2021)
9. Tanaka, Y., Inn, E.C.Y., Watanabe, K.: Absorption coefficients of gases in the vacuum ultraviolet. J. Chem. Phys. **21**, 1951–1953 (1953)
10. Reilly, D.M., Moriarty, D.T., Maynard, J.A.: Unique properties of solar blind ultraviolet communication systems for unattended ground sensor networks. Proc. SPIE **5611**, 244–254 (2004)
11. Kruse, P.W., McGlauchlin, L.D., McQuistan, R.B.: Elements of Infrared Technology: Generation Transmission and Detection. John Wiley & Sons, New York (1962)

12. Kim, I.I., McArthur, B., Korevaar, E.: Comparison of laser beam propagation at 785 nm and 850 nm in Fog and Haze for optical wireless communications. Proc. SPIE **4214**, 26–37 (2001)
13. Al Naboulsi, M.C., Sizun, H., de Fornel, F.: Fog attenuation prediction for optical and infrared waves. Opt Eng. **43**, 319–329 (2004)
14. Tang, Y., Ni, G.Q., Lan, T., et al.: Simulation and evaluation of transmission distance in solar-blind UV communication systems. Opt. Tech. **33**, 27–30 (2007)
15. Yin, H.W., Chang, S.L., Jia, H.H., et al.: Several factors influencing range of non-line-of-sight UV transmission. Opt. Optoelectron. Technol. **5**, 18–20 (2007)
16. Ballestrin, J., Marzo, A.: Solar radiation attenuation in solar tower plants. Sol. Energy **86**, 388–392 (2012)
17. Zhang, F., Wu, Z., Ye, S.: Simulation system of atmospheric transmission attenuation effect for mid-wave infrared radiation. Adv. Mat. Res. **760**, 60–64 (2013)
18. Avishai, B.D., Sagripanti, J.L.: Regression model for estimating inactivation of microbial aerosols by solar radiation. Photochem. Photobiol. **89**, 995–999 (2013)
19. Wang, J.P., Kou, Y.W., Shen, C., et al.: Correlation analysis of the MODIS water vapour channel spectral feature and the sea visibility based on the MODTRAN mode. Mar. Forecasts **28**, 55–59 (2011)
20. Liu, W.C., Qi, L.L., He, H.R., et al.: Numerical study on atmospheric transmission of 1.06 pm laser. Laser Infrared **41**, 520–524 (2011)
21. Wu, X.J., Liu, M., Li, B.F., et al.: Research on the performance for free space optical communication system with the observation data from ladar. J. Optoelectron. Laser **25**, 2146–2151 (2014)
22. Wu, X.J., Wang, H.X., Song, B.: Measurement of fog and haze extinction characteristics and availability evaluation of free space optical link under the sea surface environment. Appl. Optics **54**, 1015–1026 (2015)
23. Ke, X.Z., Xi, X.L.: Probability of Wireless Laser Communication. BUPT Press, Beijing (2004)

Author Index

Printed in the United States
by Baker & Taylor Publisher Services

Printed in the United States
by Baker & Taylor Publisher Services